HUMAN RESOURCE INFORMATION SYSTEMS

To my wife Barbara and my sons Sean, Colin, and Timothy—M. J. K.

To my wife Anjana, daughter Pallavi, and son Parag—M. T.

HUMAN RESOURCE INFORMATION SYSTEMS

Basics, Applications, and Future Directions

Michael J. Kavanagh
The University at Albany

Mohan Thite
Griffith University, Australia

Los Angeles • London • New Delhi • Singapore • Washington DC

For information:

SAGE Publications, Inc.
2455 Teller Road
Thousand Oaks, California 91320
E-mail: order@sagepub.com

SAGE Publications Ltd.
1 Oliver's Yard
55 City Road
London, EC1Y 1SP
United Kingdom

SAGE Publications India Pvt. Ltd.
B 1/I 1 Mohan Cooperative Industrial Area
Mathura Road, New Delhi 110 044
India

SAGE Publications Asia-Pacific Pte. Ltd.
33 Pekin Street #02-01
Far East Square
Singapore 048 763

Printed in the United States of America

Library of Congress Cataloging-in-Publication Data

Human resource information systems: Basics, applications, and future directions/[edited by] Michael J. Kavanagh, Mohan Thite.
  p. cm.
Includes bibliographical references and index.
ISBN 978-1-4129-4455-7 (cloth)
ISBN 978-1-4129-4456-4 (pbk.)
  1. Personnel management—Information technology. 2. Personnel management—Data processing.
I. Kavanagh, Michael J. II. Thite, Mohan.

HF5549.5.D37H86 2009
658.300285—dc22   2008023612

Printed on acid-free paper

09 10 11 12 10 9 8 7 6 5 4 3 2

Acquiring Editor:	Lisa Cuevas Shaw
Editorial Assistant:	MaryAnn Vail
Production Editor:	Sarah K. Quesenberry
Copy Editor:	QuADS Prepress (P) Ltd
Proofreader:	Sally Jaskold
Indexer:	Will Ragsdale
Typesetter:	C&M Digitals (P) Ltd.
Cover Designer:	Edgar Abarca
Marketing Manager:	Jennifer Reed Banando

Contents

Chapter 5. System Design and Acquisition — 99

RICHARD D. JOHNSON AND JAMES H. DULEBOHN

Chapter 6. Cost Justifying HRIS Investments — 121

KEVIN D. CARLSON AND MICHAEL J. KAVANAGH

PART III: HRIS IMPLEMENTATION

Chapter 7. Project Management Development and HRIS Acceptance 155

SALVATORE BELARDO, PETER OTTO, AND MICHAEL J. KAVANAGH

Chapter 8. Change Management: Implementation, Integration, and Maintenance of the HRIS   173

ROMUALD A. STONE AND JOYCE MASON DAVIS

PART IV: HRIS APPLICATIONS

Chapter 9. HR Administration and HRIS

211

Linda C. Isenhour

Chapter 14. International Human Resource Management 361

MICHAEL J. KAVANAGH AND JOHN W. MICHEL

PART V: SPECIAL TOPICS IN HRIS

Chapter 15. Information Security and Privacy in HRIS 395

Yuk Kuen Wong and Mohan Thite

Chapter 16. The Future of HRIS: Emerging Trends in HRM and IT 409

Michael J. Kavanagh and Mohan Thite

Preface

In the preface to their 1990 book, *Human Resource Information Systems*, M. J. Kavanagh, H. G. Gueutal, and S. I. Tannenbaum began by stating, "Among the most significant changes in the field of human resources management in the past decade has been the use of computers to develop what have become known as human resource information systems (HRIS)" (p. v). One might infer from this statement that the introduction of computers and Information Systems/Information Technology (IS/IT) concepts to the field of human resource management (HRM) through the early 1990s was either a *revolutionary change* or an *evolutionary change*. The dictionary defines *revolutionary* as "constituting or bringing about a major or fundamental change" and *evolution* as "a process of continuous change from a lower, simpler, or worse to a higher, more complex, or better state" (Merriam-Webster Online, www.merriam-webster.com, accessed April 21, 2008).

If one considers that the purpose of the HRM function during its pre–World War II era was primarily to be a record keeper, as described in Chapter 1, then the change in its role to that of an emerging strategic partner in the early 1990s must be considered revolutionary. This dramatic change in the role of the HRM function, as noted by Kavanagh et al. (1990), was due to the increased use of computer technology in HRM; that is, the creation of the HRIS was due to a "fundamental change" in thinking about the HRM function.

Now the question remains, Do the developments in HRIS since 1990 represent another revolutionary change in the field or rather one of evolution? We would argue that the changes from 1990 on, although very important and requiring more complex technology, represent an evolutionary change. Our judgment is based on the fact that the *conception* of the role of HRM has not undergone another fundamental change since 1990 but rather an evolutionary one that involved a "a process of continuous change from a lower, simpler, or worse to a higher, more complex, or better state." The role of HRM as a strategic partner continues; however, sophistication in the use of computer technology to improve the delivery of HR programs and activities to management has grown immensely. The most important aspect of this growth has been the advance in the use of people knowledge in managerial decisions. This people knowledge can be acquired much more quickly than in 1990, and with a higher degree of accuracy. This marriage of HR with IT/IS in the development and improvement of an HRIS has increased the ability of management to use people knowledge to gain a competitive advantage in the marketplace.

What does this mean to the student or professional working in HR or IT fields? First, it is not sufficient to begin one's study with the improved products and processes that have occurred due to evolutionary changes. For example, it would not be wise or fruitful to begin one's study of the HRIS field with a focus on Service Oriented Architecture (SOA), N-tier architectures, or the use of Web 2.0 in HRM. This would be like starting with Chapter 16 of this book and then proceeding backward through the book. Unfortunately, many people do, in fact, focus on learning the technological advances in HRIS without understanding the basics first. Since the changes in HRM up though the early 1990s represent a revolutionary way of thinking about the field, one must understand what this revolution represented. Only then can the learner move on to the improved products developed through the evolutionary process.

In this book, we have attempted to describe these major advances in the field of HRIS and the relation of HRIS to managerial decision making and, at the same time, to explore the basic concept of an HRIS; the book represents the intersection of the best thinking and concepts from the two fields of HRM and IS/IT. It was the early intersection of these two fields that changed the role of HR in organizations from record keeper to strategic partner. After introducing the use of this basic, and revolutionary, new approach to the field of HRM in the organization, we can then proceed to the more advanced, and evolutionary, changes. The basic philosophy of this book is that the integration or harmonization of technology with people management in an HRIS will create a distinct competitive advantage. We hope that you, the reader, gain this understanding and that you enjoy this book.

Many individuals contributed in a variety of ways to provide assistance in the completion of this book, and we would like to thank them. First of all, we would like to thank all the authors who contributed chapters. We know how difficult it is to write a chapter for an edited book, particularly when the editors have defined the philosophy and approach to be used. In addition, special thanks go to those individuals who provided invaluable insights during informal discussions and in e-mails. Our thanks to Hal Gueutal and Janet Marler at the University of Albany, to Scott Behson of Farleigh Dickinson University for the use of his office for a meeting, and especially to Dianna Stone of the University of Texas at San Antonio for her great assistance in finding (and probably recruiting) authors to write chapters. We would also like to thank the folks who responded with great comments to our announcement in HR_Net (in early 2005) that we were beginning to think about a new book on HRIS. Our thanks also go to the numerous professionals in the International Association for Human Resource Information Management (IHRIM) and the Society for Human Resource Management (SHRM) who patiently listened and responded to our ideas regarding this book. Finally, we would like to thank Al Bruckner of Sage for his understanding interactions with us, and a big thanks to MaryAnn Vail for her patience during this long process. Finally, we would like to thank Sarah Quesenberry and her staff for correcting our grammar as needed and finding those mistyped words done by gremlins.

Finally, we would like to thank our families, who provided the warmth and support we needed when frustration and writer's block crept in!

—Michael J. Kavanagh and Mohan Thite

PART I

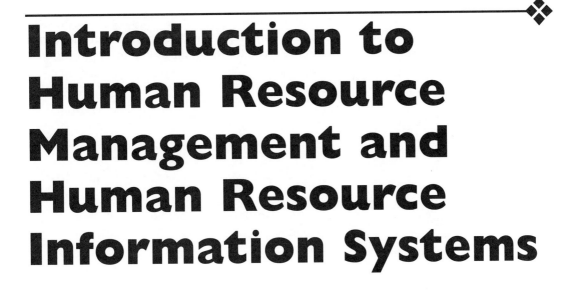

Introduction to Human Resource Management and Human Resource Information Systems

Evolution of Human Resource Management and Human Resource Information Systems

The Role of Information Technology

Mohan Thite

Michael J. Kavanagh

EDITORS' NOTE

The purpose of this chapter is to provide an introduction to the fields of **human resource management (HRM)** and information technology (IT), and the combination of these two fields into **human resource information systems (HRIS)**. The first chapter will lay the groundwork for the remainder of this book, and as such, it is important to thoroughly understand the concepts and ideas in this chapter. This chapter contains definitions for a number of terms in common use in the HRM, IT, and HRIS fields and will emphasize the major underlying themes of this book. Finally, an overview of the entire book will be covered, showing how each chapter is an integral part of the entire field of HRIS.

CHAPTER OBJECTIVES

After completing this chapter, you should be able to

♦ Describe the historical evolution of HRM, including the changing role of the human resources (HR) professional

♦ Discuss the impact of computer technology on the evolution of HRM

♦ Describe the three types of HR activities

♦ Explain the relationship between strategic HRM and HRIS

♦ Explain the purpose and nature of HRIS as well as the differences between the types of HRIS

♦ Discuss the use of information from an HRIS in decision making

♦ Describe the central themes of the book and how they relate to managerial decision making

♦ Understand how HRM and HRIS fit into a comprehensive model of organizational functioning

VIGNETTE

There are numerous federal and state laws and regulations regarding the treatment of employees, as will be discussed throughout this book. For example, some of these laws regulate the number of working hours in a week and overtime requirements, union-management relations, and unfair discrimination in the personnel practices of a firm. One such law, Title VII of the Civil Rights Law of 1964 as amended by the Equal Opportunity Act of 1972, protects individuals against unfair discrimination based on race, national origin, and gender in any personnel decision—for example, hiring. This law protecting the rights of individuals is generally referred to as **Equal Employment Opportunity (EEO)** legislation. To determine if organizations are complying with this law, all U.S. companies must complete an annual report for the federal government, called the EEO-1 report. This report describes the composition of the work force by job in terms of gender, race, and national origin (see Chapter 9). This report is often referred to as an EEO or Affirmative Action Audit. The important point is that the employees must be categorized into jobs, and then the number and percentage distributions of racial, gender, and national origin of employees must be determined.

A regional distributor and service center for a national appliance company with 300 employees had to complete all annual government reports on employees for the previous year by January 31. All the employee records were in paper files. The Director of Human Resources indicated that the compliance with the EEO laws in terms of completing the EEO-1 report took one full-time HR employee working for 1 month to complete the report. The lengthy time taken to complete the report was due to the fact that the employee records had to be searched each year since there were new hiring, promotions, terminations, and other turnover during the year. After this company acquired HRIS software for all government reports, it only took about 4 hours to complete the EEO-1 report.

This company example illustrates one important advantage of conversion to an HRIS from a paper-based system—reduction of staff time on reports. It should be noted, however, that accuracy of reports is still a concern, and accuracy of employee records is determined mainly from the correct inputting of employee data for the software programs. It is also important to note that the cost savings of reducing staff time to generate the report is not the only benefit from adoption of computer-based HR software. As will be discussed later in this chapter, the time saving means that the HR professional can be assigned to other, more important tasks for the company. These characteristics of an HRIS—speed and accuracy—will be emphasized throughout this book as the major advantage of an HRIS.

Introduction

Leading management thinkers suggest that "it is not technology, but the art of human- and humane-management" that is the continuing challenge for executives in the 21st century (Drucker, Dyson, Handy, Saffo, & Senge, 1997). Similarly, Smith and Kelly (1997) believe that "future economic and strategic advantage will rest with the organizations that can most effectively attract, develop and retain a diverse group of the best and the brightest human talent in the market place" (p. 200).

In general, to maintain a competitive advantage in the marketplace, firms need to balance the resources available to the firm to achieve the desired results of profitability and survival. The resources that are available to the firm fall into three general categories: physical, organizational, and human. In discussing how to gain a competitive advantage in the global market, Porter (1990) noted that management of the human resources is the most critical of the three. The idea of treating human resources as a means of gaining a competitive advantage in both the domestic and the global marketplace has been echoed by other authors. As Greer (1995) states,

> In a growing number of organizations human resources are now viewed as a source of competitive advantage. There is greater recognition that distinctive competencies are obtained through highly developed employee skills, distinctive organizational cultures,

management processes, and systems. This is in contrast to the traditional emphasis on transferable resources such as equipment. . . . Increasingly, it is being recognized that competitive advantage can be obtained with a high quality work force that enables organizations to compete on the basis of market responsiveness, product and service quality, differentiated products, and technological innovation. (p. 105)

The effective management of human resources in a firm to gain a competitive advantage in the marketplace requires timely and accurate **information** on current employees and potential employees in the labor market. With the evolution of computer technology, meeting this information requirement has been greatly enhanced through the creation of HRIS. A basic assumption behind this book is that the management of employee information will be the critical process that helps a firm maximize the use of its human resources and maintain competitiveness in its market.

The first purpose of this book is to provide information on the development, implementation, and **maintenance** of an HRIS. The second purpose is to demonstrate how an HRIS can be used in HRM programs, such as selecting and training employees, to make them more efficient and effective. The final purpose is to provide an opportunity for you to apply your knowledge through the analysis of the cases at the end of each chapter.

Historical Evolution of HRM and HRIS

One can analyze the historical trends of the HR function from different viewpoints: the evolution of HRM as a professional and scientific discipline, as an aid to management, as a political and economic conflict between management and employees, and as a growing movement of employee involvement influenced by developments in industrial/organizational and social psychology. This historical analysis will demonstrate the growing importance of employees from being just one of the means of production in the 20th-century industrial economy to being a key source of sustainable competitive advantage in the 21st-century knowledge economy.

Since this is a book on HRIS, we will examine the development of the fields of both HR and IT in terms of their evolution since the early 20th century. This means examining the evolution of HRM intertwined with developments in IT and describing how IT has played an increasing role in the HRM function. In addition, this historical analysis will show how the role of HRM in the firm has changed over time from primarily being concerned with routine **transactional HR** activities to dealing with complex transformational ones. Transactional activities are the routine bookkeeping tasks—for example, changing an employee's home address or health care provider—whereas transformational activities are those actions of an organization that "add value" to the consumption of the firm's product or service. An example of a **transformational HR** activity would be a training program for retail clerks to improve customer service behavior. Thus, transformational activities increase the strategic importance and visibility of the HR function in the firm. This general change over time is illustrated in Figure 1.1 and will become evident as we trace the historical evolution of HRM in terms of five broad phases of the historical development of industry in the United States. For more information on this historical development, you should consult Kavanagh, Gueutal, and Tannenbaum (1990) or Walker (1982).

❖ **Figure 1.1**   Historical Evolution of HRM

Role of HRM	
Early 20th Century	*21st Century*
Caretaker	Strategic partner
Employee focus Records	Cost effectiveness Employee development

Pre–World War II

In the early 20th century and prior to World War II, the personnel function (the precursor of the term *human resource management*) was primarily involved in record keeping of employee information; in other words, it fulfilled a "caretaker" function. During this period of time, the prevailing management philosophy was called "scientific management." The central thrust of scientific management was to maximize employee productivity. It was thought that there was one best way to do any work, and this best way was determined through time and motion studies that determined the most efficient use of human capabilities in the production process. Then, the work could be divided into pieces, and the number of tasks to be completed by a worker during an average workday could be computed. These findings formed the basis of piece-rate pay systems, which were seen as the most efficient way to motivate employees.

At this point in history, there were very few government influences in employment relations, and thus, employment terms, practices, and conditions were left to the owners of the firm. As a result, employee abuses such as child labor and unsafe working conditions were common. Some employers set up labor welfare and administration departments to look after the interests of workers by maintaining records on health and safety as well as recording hours worked and payroll. It is interesting to note that record keeping is one of the major functions built into the design of an HRIS today; however, there was simply no computer technology to automate the records at this time in history. Of course, paper records were kept, and we can still see paper record HR systems in many smaller firms today.

Post–World War II (1945–1960)

The mobilization and utilization of labor during the War had a great impact on the development of the personnel function. Managers realized that employee productivity and motivation had a significant impact on the profitability of the firm. The human relations movement after the War emphasized that employees were motivated not just by money but also by social and psychological factors, such as recognition of work achievements and work norms.

Due to the need for classification of large numbers of individuals in military service during the war, systematic efforts began to classify workers around occupational categories in order to improve recruitment and selection procedures. The central aspect of these classification systems was the **job description**, which listed the tasks, duties, and responsibilities of any individual who held the job in question. These job description classification systems could also be used to design appropriate compensation programs, evaluate individual employee performance, and provide a basis for termination.

Because of the abusive worker practices prior to the War, employees started forming trade unions, which played an important role in bargaining for better employment terms and conditions. There were a significant number of employment laws enacted that allowed the establishment of labor unions and defined their scope in relationship with management. Thus, personnel departments had to assume considerably more record keeping and reporting to governmental agencies. Because of these trends, the personnel department had to establish specialist divisions, such as recruitment, labor relations, training and benefits, and government relations.

With its changing and expanding role, personnel departments started keeping increasing numbers and types of employee records, and computer technology began to emerge as a possible way to store and retrieve employee information. In some cases in the defense industry, **job analysis** and classification data were inputted into computers to better understand, plan, and use employee skills against needs. For example, the U.S. Air Force conducted a thorough and systematic job analysis and classification through its Air Force Human Resources Laboratory (AFHRL), which resulted in a comprehensive occupational structure. The AFHRL collected data from thousands of airmen in jobs within the Air Force, and through the use of a computer software program called the Comprehensive Occupational Data Analysis Program (CODAP), it was able to more accurately establish a job description classification system for Air Force jobs.

Personnel departments outside the defense industry were not using computers at this time. Computers were being used for billing and inventory control, and there was very little use in the personnel function except for payroll. The payroll function was the first to be automated. Large firms began harvesting the benefits of new computer technology to keep track of employee compensation, but this function was usually outsourced to vendors since it was still extremely expensive for a firm to acquire or develop the software for payroll. It is important to realize that computer technology was just beginning to be used at this time, and it was complex and costly. With increasing legislation on employment relations and employee unionization, industrial relations became one of the main foci of the department. Union-management bargaining over employment contracts dominated the activity of the personnel department, and these negotiations were not computer based. Record keeping was still done manually despite the growing use of computerized data processing in other departments, such as accounts and materials management. What resulted was an initial reluctance among personnel departments to acquire and use computer technology for their programs. This had a long-term effect in many firms when it came to adopting advancements in computer technology even though it got cheaper and easier to use.

Social Issues Era (1963–1980)

This period witnessed an unprecedented increase in the amount of labor legislation that governed various parts of the employment relationship, such as prohibition of discriminatory practices, occupational health and safety, retirement benefits, and tax regulation. As a result, the personnel department was burdened with the additional responsibility of legislative compliance that required collection, analysis, and reporting of voluminous data to statutory authorities. For example, to demonstrate that there was no unfair discrimination in employment practices, data pertaining to *all* employment functions, such as recruitment, training, compensation, and benefits, had to be diligently collected, analyzed, and stored. To avoid the threat of punitive damages for noncompliance, it was necessary to ensure that the data were comprehensive, accurate, and up-to-date, which made it essential to automate the data collection, analysis, and report generation process. As you go through the chapters of this book, these varying laws and government guidelines will be covered within the specific HR topics.

It was about this time that personnel departments were beginning to be called Human Resources Departments and the field of human resource management was born. The increasing need to be in compliance with numerous employee protection legislations or suffer significant monetary penalties made senior managers aware of the importance of the HRM function. In other words, effective and correct practices in HRM were starting to affect the "bottom line" of the firms, so there was a significant growth of HR departments, and computer technology had advanced to the point where it was beginning to be used. As a result, there was an increasing demand for HR departments to adopt computer technology to process employee information more effectively and efficiently. This trend resulted in an explosion in the number of vendors who could assist HR departments in automating their programs in terms of both hardware and software.

Simultaneously, computer technology was evolving, and delivering better productivity at lower costs. These technology developments and increased vendor activity led to the development of a comprehensive management information system (MIS) for HRM. The decreasing costs of computer technology versus the increasing costs of employee compensation and benefits made acquisition of computer-based HR systems (HRIS) a necessary business decision. However, the personnel departments were still slow in adopting computer technology, even though it was inexpensive relative to the power it could deliver for the storage and retrieval of employee information in MIS reports. So, the major issue at this time in the historical development of HRIS was not the need or capabilities of technology but how to best implement it.

Another factor was the booming economy in most industrialized countries. As a result, employee trade unions successfully bargained for better employment terms, such as health care and retirement benefits. As a result, labor costs increased, which put pressure on personnel managers to justify cost increases against productivity improvements. With the increased emphasis on employee participation and empowerment, the personnel function transformed into a "protector" rather than a "caretaker" function, shifting the focus away from maintenance to development of employees. Thus, the breadth and depth of HRM functions expanded, necessitating the need for strategic thinking and better delivery of HR services.

Cost-Effectiveness Era (1980 to the Early 1990s)

With increasing competition from emerging European and Asian economies, U.S. and other multinational firms increased their focus on cost reduction through automation and other productivity improvement measures. As regards HRM, the increased administrative burden intensified the need to fulfill a growing number of legislative requirements, while the overall functional focus shifted from employee administration to employee development and involvement. To improve effectiveness and efficiency in service delivery, through cost reduction and value-added services, the HR departments came under pressure to harness technology that was becoming cheaper and more powerful.

In addition, there was a growing realization within management that people costs were a very significant part of their budgets. Some companies estimated that personnel costs were as high as 80% of their operating costs. As a result, there was a growing demand on the HRM function to cost justify their employee programs and services. In one of the first books to address this growing need to cost justify the HRM function, Cascio (1984) indicated that the language of business is dollars and cents and HR managers need to realize this fact. In a later edition of his book, Cascio (1991) quotes Jacques Fitz-Enz (1980), who more accurately states the need for HRM to cost justify their function:

> Few human resources managers—even the most energetic—take the time to analyse the return on the corporation's personnel dollar. We feel we aren't valued in our own organizations, that we can't get the resources we need. We complain that management won't buy our proposals and wonder why our advice is so often ignored until the crisis stage. But the human resources manager seldom stands back to look at the total business and ask: Why am I at the bottom looking up? The answer is painfully apparent. We don't act like business managers—like entrepreneurs whose business happens to be people. (p. 41)

Even small and medium firms could afford computer-based HR systems that were run by increasingly user friendly microcomputers, and could be shown to be cost-effective. The prevailing management thinking regarding the use of computers in HR was not a reduction in the number of employees needed in HR departments but that their activities and time could be shifted from the transactional record keeping to more transformational activities that would add value to the organization. This change in the function of HRM could then be clearly measured in terms of cost-benefit ratios to the "bottom line" of the company.

Technological Advancement Era and Emergence of Strategic HRM (1990 to Present)

The economic landscape underwent radical changes throughout the 1990s with increasing globalization, technological breakthroughs (particularly Internet-enabled Web services), and hypercompetition. Business process reengineering exercises became more common and frequent, with several initiatives, such as right sizing of employee numbers, reducing the layers of management, reducing the bureaucracy of organizational structures, autonomous work teams, and **outsourcing**.

Firms today realize that innovative and creative employees who hold the key to organizational knowledge provide a sustainable competitive advantage because unlike other resources, intellectual capital is difficult to imitate by competitors. Accordingly, the people management function has become strategic in its importance and outlook and is geared to attract, retain, and engage talent. These developments have led to the creation of the HR or workforce scorecard (Becker, Huselid, & Ulrich, 2001; Huselid, Becker, & Beatty, 2005) as well as added emphasis on the return on investment (ROI) of the HR function and its programs (Cascio, 2000; Fitz-Enz, 2000, 2002).

The increased use of technology and the changed focus of the HRM function as adding value to the organization's product or service led to the emergence of the HR department as a strategic partner. With the growing importance and recognition of people and people management in contemporary organizations, **strategic HRM (SHRM)** has become critically important in management thinking and practice. SHRM derives its theoretical significance from the resource-based view of the firm that treats **human capital** as a strategic asset and a competitive advantage in improving organizational performance (Becker & Huselid, 2006).

Reflecting the systems view, Becker and Huselid (2006, p. 899) stress the importance of HR structure—that is, the "systems, practices, competencies, and employee performance behaviors that reflect the development and management of the firm's strategic human capital"—for organizational performance. Context is a crucial element in SHRM, and therefore, researchers increasingly emphasize the "best-fit" approach to SHRM as opposed to the "best-practice" approach. The success of SHRM is contingent on several factors, such as national and organizational culture, size, industry type, occupational category, and business strategy. Accordingly, Becker and Huselid (2006) argued that "it is the fit between the HR architecture and the strategic capabilities and business processes that implement strategy that is the basis of HR's contribution to competitive advantage" (p. 899).

A good example of the importance of HR and the information provided by an HRIS can be found in the human resources planning (HRP) function. HRP is primarily concerned with forecasting the need for additional employees in the future and the availability of those employees either inside or external to the company. A good example is when a company is considering a strategic decision to expand by establishing a production facility in a new location. Using the information recorded and analyzed in the HRIS, HRP can provide estimates of whether or not there are enough people available in the external labor market of the new location to staff the new facility. Thus, the availability of potential employees in the labor market may be critical to the strategic decision to build the new facility, and this, of course, could involve millions or billons of dollars.

Therefore, in determining the strategic fit between technology and HR, it is not the strategy per se that leads to competitive advantage but rather how well it is "implemented," taking into account the environmental realities that can be unique to each organization and, indeed, between units and functions of the organization.

HR Activities

Typical HR programs involve things such as record keeping, recruiting, selection, training, employee relations, and compensation. However, all these programs involve multiple activities, and these HR activities can be classified into three broad categories: transactional, traditional, and transformational (Wright, McMahan, Snell, & Gerhart, 1998). Transactional activities involve day-to-day transactions that have to deal mostly with record keeping—for example, entering payroll information, employee status changes, and the administration of employee benefits. Traditional activities involve HR programs such as planning, recruiting, selection, training, compensation, and performance management. These activities can have strategic value for the organization if their results or outcomes are consistent with the strategic goals of the organization. Transformational activities are those activities that add value to the organization—for example, cultural or organizational change, structural realignment, strategic redirection, and increasing innovation.

Wright et al. (1998) estimate that most HR departments spend approximately 65% to 75% on transactional activities, 15% to 30% on traditional activities, and 5% to 15% on transformational activities. One of the major advantages of the design, development, and implementation of an HRIS is to reduce the amount of time the HR staff have to spend on transactional activities, allowing the staff to spend more time on traditional and transformational activities. This notion of using technology to process transactional activities more efficiently is the central theme of this book and provides one of the primary justifications for a computer-based system. In later chapters that discuss various HR programs such as selection and training, we will see how a computer-based system can aid in both traditional and transformational activities to make them consistent with the strategic goals of the organization.

Interface Between HR and Technology

The IT-driven automation and redesign of work processes certainly help reduce costs and cycle times as well as improve quality. **Management information systems (MIS)** can further help decision makers to make and implement strategic decisions. However, IT is only a tool and can only complement, not substitute, the people who drive it. Often, organizations mistake IT as a message and not the messenger and divert time, effort, and money away from long-term investment in people to developing and deploying information technologies (Thite, 2004). In fact, the critical success factors in information systems project implementation are nontechnical and are due more to social and managerial issues (Martinsons & Chong, 1999).

With the increasing use of information technologies in HR planning and delivery, the way people in organizations look at the nature and role of HR itself may change (Roehling et al., 2005). With HR data and reports now being readily available on their desktop, would managers interact less with the HR department and see it as being less important? If that is so, how would it affect the attitude of HR professionals toward their jobs and profession? Would they resist adoption of technology if they perceive that technology lessens their status?

In traditional organizations with silo mentalities, turf wars between departments and functions acting as independent entities are common. Therefore, top management needs to be mindful of organizational politics in managing change. Through most of its evolution, HRM has had an administrative and caretaker focus in its delivery. With technology significantly decreasing the time required for administrative tasks, many HR professionals may find it difficult to redefine their jobs and may thus resist the change to an HRIS. This calls for redefining and transforming the role of HRM through value-added, strategic initiatives and interventions. This also involves learning new skills for HR professionals and rethinking the way the HR department is organized and delivers its services. With the improved job skills of HR professionals, technology will be seen as HR's "partner in progress." While having an advanced, full-fledged system will not automatically make HR a strategic business partner, it acts as a building block and an effective aid in the process (Lawler & Mohrman, 2003).

A Primer on HRIS

What Is an HRIS?

After reviewing the many definitions of an HRIS, Kavanagh et al. (1990) defined it as a

> system used to acquire, store, manipulate, analyze, retrieve, and distribute information regarding an organization's human resources. An HRIS is not simply computer hardware and associated HR-related software. Although an HRIS includes hardware and software, it also includes people, forms, policies and procedures, and data. (p. 29)

It is important to note that a company that does not have a computerized system still has an HRM system; that is, the paper systems that most companies used before the development of computer technology were still comparable with an HRIS, but the management of employee information was not done as quickly as in a computerized system. If a company did not have a paper system, the development and implementation of a computerized system would be extremely difficult. For the purpose of this book, however, we will use the term *HRIS* to refer to a computerized system designed to manage the company's HR.

The purpose of the HRIS is to provide service, in the form of accurate and timely information, to the "clients" of the system. As there are a variety of potential users of HR information, it may be used for strategic, tactical, and operational decision making (e.g., to plan for needed employees in a merger); to avoid litigation (e.g., to identify discrimination problems in hiring); to evaluate programs, policies, or practices (e.g., to evaluate the effectiveness of a training program); and/or to support daily operations (e.g., to help managers monitor time and attendance of their employees). All these uses mean that there is a mandatory requirement that data and reports be accurate and timely and that the "client" can understand how to use the information.

Because of the complexity and data intensiveness of the HRM function, it is one of the last management functions to be targeted for automation (Bussler & Davis, 2001/2002). This fact does not mean that an HRIS is not important; it just indicates the difficulty of developing and implementing it compared with other business functions—for example, billing and accounting systems. Powered by information systems and the Internet, today almost every process in every function of HRM is being computerized.

The systems and process focus helps organizations keep the customer perspective in mind, since quality is primarily defined and operationalized in terms of total customer satisfaction (Evans, 2005). Today's competitive environment requires organizations to integrate the activities of each functional department while keeping the customer in mind. An effective HRIS helps by providing the technology to generate accurate and timely employee information to fulfill this objective.

Why Do We Need HRIS?

There are several advantages to firms in using HRIS (Beckers & Bsat, 2002). They include the following:

- Providing a comprehensive information picture as a single, comprehensive database; this enables organizations to provide structural connectivity across units and activities and increase the speed of information transactions (Lengnick-Hall & Lengnick-Hall, 2006)
- Increasing competitiveness by improving HR operations and improving management processes
- Collecting appropriate data and converting them to information and knowledge for improved timeliness and quality of decision making
- Producing a greater number and variety of accurate and real-time HR-related reports
- Streamlining and enhancing the efficiency and effectiveness of HR administrative functions
- Shifting the focus of HR from the processing of transactions to strategic HRM
- Reengineering HR processes and functions
- Improving employee satisfaction by delivering HR services more quickly and accurately to them

The ability of firms to harness the potential of HRIS depends on a variety of factors, such as

- the size of the organization, with large firms generally reaping greater benefits;
- the amount of top management support and commitment;
- the availability of resources (time, money, and personnel);
- the HR philosophy of the company as well as its vision, organizational culture, structure, and systems;
- managerial competence in cross-functional decision making, employee involvement, and coaching; and
- the ability and motivation of employees in adopting change, such as increased automation across and between functions (Ngai & Wat, 2004).

In assessing the benefits and impact of an HRIS to an organization, typical accounting methods do not work with the HRM function (Becker et al., 2001; Cascio, 2000; Fitz-Enz, 2000, 2002; Huselid et al., 2005; Thite, 2004; Ulrich & Smallwood, 2005). While there are several tangible benefits in implementing an HRIS, such as payroll efficiencies and reduction in labor costs due to automation, there are several intangible or hidden benefits as well (Roberts, 1999). They include employee satisfaction with streamlined and efficient HR processes and freeing up HR from routine, administrative matters to focus on strategic goals.

Furthermore, HR practices can help organizations untangle the rigidity and inertia associated with the mechanistic, routine nature of **enterprise resource planning (ERP)**. ERP software applications are a set of integrated database applications or modules that carry out the most common business functions, including HR, general ledger, accounts payable, accounts receivable, order management, inventory control, and customer relationship management. Obviously, HRM's emphasis on knowledge management, human capital stewardship, and relationship building can provide considerable assistance in the implementation and use of ERPs (Lengnick-Hall & Lengnick-Hall, 2006). Therefore, active engagement of HR professionals in the introduction and ongoing functioning of an ERP is important so that organizations can realize the strategic benefits associated with these systems (Dery & Wailes, 2005).

Different Types of HRIS

There are multiple typologies for the classification of computer-based systems; however, we are going to define the most basic types of systems and then apply them to their development and use within an HRIS. One of the earliest books in the field of computer-based systems (Sprague & Carlson, 1982) placed systems under three basic categories: **Electronic Data Processing (EDP)**, Management Information Systems (MIS), and Decision Support Systems (DSS). EDP is primarily electronic storage of information and was first applied to automate paperwork. As Sprague and Carlson (1982) note,

> Its basic characteristics include:
>
> - A focus on data, storage, processing, and flows at the operational level
> - Efficient transaction processing
> - Scheduled and optimised computer runs
> - Integrated files for related jobs
> - Summary reports for management (p. 6)

As discussed earlier in this chapter, this category of HRIS was the earliest form introduced in the HR field and fits in with the transactional level of HR activities.

In the MIS category, Sprague and Carlson (1982) state that

> the characteristics of MIS include:
>
> - An information focus, aimed at middle managers
> - Structured information flows
> - Integration of EDP jobs by business function (production MIS, marketing MIS . . .)
> - Inquiry and report generation (usually with a data base) (p. 7)

This type of HRIS emerged as technology improved over time, and it fits the traditional level of HR activities, such as recruitment, selection, and compensation.

Sprague and Carlson (1982) note that

> DSS are focused still higher in the organization, with an emphasis on the following characteristics:
>
> - Decision focused, aimed at top managers and executive decision makers
> - Emphasis on flexibility, adaptability, and quick response
> - User initiated and controlled
> - Support for the personal decision-making styles of individual managers (p. 7)

HRIS at this level began to emerge in the cost-effectiveness era of HRM development, and it fits the transformational level of HR activities—adding value to organizational processes.

There is another type of HRIS, identified by Kavanagh et al. (1990), which should be used in organizations to maximize the effect of computer-generated knowledge on managerial decision making. There are numerous reports generated on a regular basis from both the EDP and the MIS types of HRIS—for example, overtime and benefits usage. The critical question is, How many of these reports are used by either line managers or HR professionals in their daily work, *particularly in their decision-making capacity?* All HRIS software is designed to generate a standard set of reports, but surveys and reports from both managers and HR professionals indicate that many of these reports are typically discarded. Thus, it is apparent that another type of HRIS exists—the human resources management decision system (HRMDS). This type has the following characteristics:

- Report formation and generation based on identified managerial needs for decision making
- Categorization of reports by management level
- Timing of report generation based on frequency of managerial use: daily, weekly, monthly
- Historical information retained and reported in a timely manner so that managers and HR professionals can see the results of their use of the information in their previous decisions

This type of system could be described as the ideal system since it provides critical information for decisions involving the human resources of the company, and thus, should be used as a standard for the development and application of any HRIS.

System Development Process for an HRIS

From the engineering and information processing literature, the formal design of any information processing system is supposed to follow a set of steps labeled the System Development Life Cycle (SDLC). However, as Sprague and Carlson (1982) and other writers (Aktas, 1987; Davis, 1983) have noted, the traditional SDLC is somewhat difficult to use as originally specified. But there is agreement that the SDLC has five general phases: (1) planning, (2) analysis, (3) design, (4) implementation, and (5) maintenance. As will be seen, particularly in Parts I and II of this book, there are multiple references to the SDLC and its phases.

Kavanagh et al. (1990), applying the main concepts and phases of the traditional SDLC to the HRM function, recommended the following system development process for an HRIS: "The HRIS development process refers to the steps taken from the time a company considers computerizing its human resources functions through the analysis, design, development, implementation, maintenance, evaluations, and improvement of the system" (pp. 92–93). This system development process is quite similar to the one proposed by Walker (1982). He indicated that development of an effective HRIS should follow seven stages: "Proposal to Management, Needs Analysis, System Specifications, System Design, System Development, Installation and Conversion, and Evaluation" (p. 38).

Although this book will cover all the phases in the development and implementation of an HRIS, there are two *critical* points to be emphasized from these descriptions of the phases or stages of system development. One, the system development process *begins* when the company first begins to consider computerizing its HR functions. It is important to *document* this beginning of the process so that it can be considered when the system is being evaluated and maintained. The second critical point is the *importance of the evaluation* and, as needed, improvements to the system. This evaluation must be continuous and occur not only after the system has been implemented but also at every stage of the development. The quality of these evaluations of the system will depend heavily on the documentation of the stages of the entire system development process. The documentation of the planning and development of a system is one of the most important determinants of successful system implementation, and continued improvement.

A Model of Organizational Functioning

Figure 1.2 depicts a model of an organizational system centered on HRIS. This model depicts the interrelatedness of the parts of an organization that can affect the functioning of the organization. It shows the interrelatedness between the strategic management system, the strategic HRM system, and the performance goals, business and HR, that are generated during the strategic planning process. Note particularly how the business goals directly affect the HR goals, and this relationship should be an ongoing process in an organization to make adjustments to either set of goals as needed. The HR goals drive the HR programs that provide management the tools for the efficient and effective use of employees. As will be emphasized throughout this book, the *alignment* between the strategic management system, the strategic HR management system, the business goals, the HR goals, and the HR programs is critical to the organization to maintain its competitiveness in its market (Evans & Davis, 2005; Huselid, Jackson, & Schuler, 1997).

There are several aspects of this model that are critical for its use in this book. First, this model is a framework to use in reading, organizing, and understanding the information given in this book. Second, this is a systems model; that is, it is organic and can change over time as represented by the feedback loops from goal achievement to other parts of the model. Third, the model is centered on the use of an HRIS as critical to the efficient operation of an organization. Note that if the HRIS were removed, it would still be a model of organizational functioning. However, it is our contention that it would run more slowly and less efficiently, and this could hurt the competitiveness of an organization in its marketplace. Fourth, the HRIS and the HR program evaluation results in terms of HR metrics, and cost-benefit results (value added and ROI) are in continual interaction. This emphasis is consistent with current thinking in the HRM field (Cascio, 2000; Fitz-Enz, 2000, 2002) and has generated the HR or workforce scorecard (Becker et al., 2001; Huselid et al., 2005). Finally, it is important to note that the *successful* design, development, and implementation of an HRIS *depend equally on IT and on HR knowledge,* which is the basic philosophy of this entire book.

There are other aspects of this model that are important. First, all the factors in the external environment will influence the internal functioning of the organization. The most important of these factors is national culture. National culture will affect all the factors in the external environment: government regulations, labor market, societal concerns, technology, HRM research, and competition. These factors in turn will have an impact on the

❖ **Figure 1.2**   Model of an Organizational System Centered on HRIS

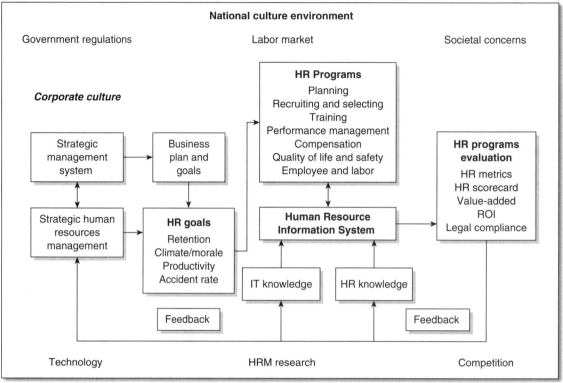

organization. Simple comparisons across various countries—for example, the United States, Australia, Europe, and China—on most of these six factors would provide significant differences on each of these external factors. We feel that these differences are important and have devoted a chapter to them. Second, the two-way arrow between the strategic management system and strategic HR indicates our understanding that this interaction will improve the functioning of the organization. Finally, note that corporate culture influences the entire internal operation of the organization. In the next section, the major themes of this book that are central to the operation of this model are discussed.

Central Themes of the Book

There are some central themes that are emphasized in this book, which can also be seen in the model of organizational functioning. These are the major factors that influence the effective operation of the organization through their effects on managerial decisions. In addition, they directly affect the success of both the HRM programs and the use of the HRIS. These factors are as follows:

1. The effective alignment between the strategy of the firm, the HR strategy, and HR programs

2. The importance of legal considerations in all HR programs and functions

3. The need for a cooperative relationship between HR and IT professionals

4. The critical need for the creation and use of HR metrics to both guide decision making and evaluate the cost effectiveness of the HR strategy and programs

All the chapters of this book will contain some reference to some or all of these factors, and their effects will be discussed in detail in the chapters.

Overview and Structure of the Book

This book is divided into five main parts. Part I, "Introduction to Human Resource Management and Human Resource Information Systems," includes three chapters. In this first chapter, the evolution of HRM and its interface with IT was covered to show how the field of HRIS emerged. In addition, a general introduction to the types of activities in which HRM engages was provided, as well as a brief introduction to the current interface between HR and technology. Finally, a detailed description of an HRIS was provided, and the model of organizational functioning was discussed. At the beginning of each chapter, the place of the chapter topics in the model will be identified so that there is a unifying theme in the book.

The second chapter, "Database Concepts and Applications in HRIS" by Janet Marler and Barry Floyd, is focused on understanding databases and the applications of IT on the HRIS. This is an introductory chapter, which provides a solid basis for later chapters in the book. The third chapter, "Systems Considerations in the Design of an HRIS: Planning for Implementation," by Michael Bedell, Michael Canniff, and Cheryl Wyrick, is focused on foundation knowledge that is critical for the design and subsequent implementation of an HRIS. The different types of information about users/customers of the HRIS, categorization of HRIS data into categories of human capital, and the main concepts of hardware and database security are covered. This chapter is also a good lead-in for the next part of the book—"Determining HRIS Needs."

Chapter 4, "HRIS Needs Analysis" by Bradley Alge and Karen Upright, covers the first formal analysis of the need for an HRIS in an organization. It should be noted that a needs analysis can be done for an organization that only has a paper system or for an organization that is planning to improve or update its current HRIS. In this chapter, the steps in an HRIS needs assessment are covered—namely, who is involved in the assessment and the deliverables from a comprehensive needs assessment. In Chapter 5, "System Design and Acquisition" by Richard Johnson and Jim Dulebohn, the fundamentals of system design based on the needs assessment are covered. Chapter 5 also covers the process of acquiring a system once the design has been completed. It should be noted that the activities described in Chapters 4 and 5 always remain focused on implementation of the HRIS since this is an important element in the success of the HRIS. Chapter 6, "Cost Justifying HRIS Investments" by Kevin Carlson and Michael Kavanagh, describes one of the most important aspects of the needs analysis, design, and development of the HRIS—cost justification of the HRIS. Without a careful analysis of the costs and benefits of an HRIS, there should not be any attempt to implement the system. There are numerous stories and examples of failed systems that were implemented without a comprehensive needs assessment. In addition, a comprehensive needs assessment will be very useful during the evaluation phase after the system has been fully implemented. The needs assessment will define many of the evaluative criteria by which to judge the success of the HRIS. Thus, this chapter is a convenient introduction to Part III of the book—"HRIS Implementation."

Chapter 7, "Project Management Development and HRIS Acceptance" by Sal Belardo, Peter Otto, and Michael Kavanagh, provides a comprehensive discussion of project management techniques and their importance to the implementation and acceptance of an HRIS. Project management provides excellent tools for ensuring that the implementation of the HRIS proceeds in an orderly fashion by establishing goals and timetables for the tasks and activities during implementation. Chapter 8, "Change Management: Implementation, Integration, and Maintenance of the HRIS" by Romuald Stone and Joyce Davis, emphasizes the people processes necessary for successful implementation of an HRIS—a major organizational change. Although there typically will be some technical difficulties during the HRIS implementation, the major issues will be with the lack of employee and user involvement in the implementation. Chapter 8 offers a variety of approaches to organizational change, both theoretical and practical, that can be used to focus on the behavioral aspects of the HRIS implementation.

Part IV of the book, "HRIS Applications," provides information and guidelines for the use of an HRIS in the programs involved in the operation of the HRM function. In Chapter 9, "HR Administration and HRIS," Linda Isenhour covers the administrative, transactional aspects of HRM. This chapter illustrates the fact that HRM is still a caretaker of employee records; however, the existence of an HRIS makes this information readily available and useful for managerial decision making. Most important, Linda discusses how the HRIS can cover legal compliance with government mandates much more easily than a paper system. In Chapter 10, "Job Analysis and HR Planning," Hazel Williams discusses the use of an HRIS in completing job analysis and job description in an orderly and accurate fashion. HRP is discussed in Chapter 10 with a focus on the speed of obtaining employee information when discussing potential strategic plans for the company. In Chapter 11, "Recruitment and Selection in an Internet Context," by Kimberly Lukaszewski, David Dickter, Brian Lyons, and Jerard Kehoe cover both HRIS and Internet applications within the context of a computer-based HRM function. Chapter 12, "Training and Development: Issues and HRIS Applications" by Ralf Burbach, provides information and ideas for how to use the power of an HRIS to address important issues in training and development programs. In Chapter 13, "Performance Management, Compensation, Benefits, Payroll, and the HRIS," Charles Fay and Ren Nardoni focus on one of the major motivational aspects of the HRM system and how the existence of an HRIS can improve the operation of many aspects of the management and motivation of employees. Finally, Chapter 14, "International Human Resource Management" by Michael Kavanagh and John Michel, covers the complexities that are created when a company enters the international marketplace.

The last part of this book, "Special Topics in HRIS," covers two additional topics of importance to the effective operation of an HRIS. In Chapter 15, "Information Security and Privacy in HRIS," Yuk Kuen Wong and Mohan Thite discuss the many legal, ethical, and moral issues that surround the use of an HRIS, with a focus on e-HR. In the final chapter, "The Future of HRIS: Emerging Trends in HRM and IT," Michael Kavanagh and Mohan Thite take a look at what new developments to expect in the continuing use of an HRIS in the operation of the HRM function in an organization.

DISCUSSION QUESTIONS

1. What are the factors that changed the primary role of HRM from a caretaker of records to a strategic partner?

2. How does technology help deliver transactional, traditional, and transformational HR activities more efficiently and effectively?

3. Justify the need for an HRIS.

4. Explain how an organization that is yet to use technology to automate its HR function can graduate from EDP to MIS and finally to DSS.

5. Using the organizational model presented in this chapter, explain why and how national culture and organizational culture influence the nature and importance of the HRIS function.

CASE STUDY: POSITION DESCRIPTION AND SPECIFICATION FOR AN HRIS MANAGER

One great way to assess the nature and importance of a particular function or position is to examine the job description and job specification as they tell us what is involved in the job and what is required to perform the job. The following real job advertisement for an HRIS manager for a community college was placed in the Job Central section of the Internet site for **the International Association for Human Resource Information Management** (www.ihrim.org, accessed September 7, 2007).

Manager—HRIS

In this position the Manager will manage all operational aspects of the Human Resources information process, including the timely and accurate processing, reporting, analysis, and documentation of HR data, HRIM security and the implementation and coordination of associated processes, procedures and technologies.

Additional responsibilities are as follows:

- Supervises the Human Resources information management team
- Ensures data integrity in both personnel files and the online Human Resource Information System
- Organizes and manages personnel file audits to ensure compliance with all regulations, policies, procedures, and guidelines for records management
- Updates and administers enhancements to the Human Resource Information System
- Updates and maintains system tables
- Ensures security of the HRIS and time and attendance system
- Works in collaboration with Payroll and Finance to maintain the online interactive Position Control, Personnel, and Payroll database systems
- Works with end-users and business managers to understand business processes and determine how to use the system to meet those needs

- Partners with Technology Systems Resources to support upgrades, testing, and other technical projects
- Develops HR dashboards and develops and runs reports, both scheduled and ad-hoc
- Provides detail and aggregate information for salary surveys and regulatory reporting (i.e., CUPA, EEO, OSHA, IPEDS)
- Collaborates with the Human Resource Technical Consultant and other Human Resource staff on operational issues and special projects
- Maintains current knowledge of best practices, vendor offerings, and market trends
- Other related duties as assigned

Required qualifications:

- Bachelor's degree
- Minimum four years of Human Resources Information Systems (HRIS) experience
- Proven leadership and team building skills
- Working knowledge of ERP technology, with specific focus on HR modules
- Proficiency with Microsoft Office software applications, reporting writing tools, and SQL query language
- Strong written, verbal, and interpersonal communication skills
- Strong analytical thinking and decision making skills
- Excellent project management skills
- Demonstrated experience in maintaining confidentiality and data integrity
- Demonstrated ability to interact and collaborate with individuals at all levels

Case Study Questions

1. How does this position help the HR function become a strategic partner of the organization?

2. From the position description, identify the traditional, transactional, and transformational HR activities that this position is involved with.

3. Using the key responsibilities identified for this position, explain why and how the HRIS function plays a pivotal role in the organizational model as described in this chapter.

REFERENCES

Aktas, A. Z. (1987). *Structured analysis and design of information systems.* Englewood Cliffs, NJ: Prentice Hall.

Becker, B. E., & Huselid, M. A. (2006). Strategic human resource management: Where do we go from here? *Journal of Management, 32*(6), 898–925.

Becker, B. E., Huselid, M. A., & Ulrich, D. (2001). *The HR scorecard: Linking people, strategy, and performance.* Boston: Harvard Business School Press.

Beckers, A. M., & Bsat, M. Z. (2002). A DSS classification model for research in human resource information systems. *Information Systems Management, 19*(3), 41–50.

Bussler, L., & Davis, E. (2001/2002). Information systems: The quiet revolution in human resource management. *Journal of Computer Information Systems, 42*(2), 17–20.

Cascio, W. F. (1984). *Costing human resources: The financial impact of behavior in organizations.* Boston: PWS-Kent.

Cascio, W. F. (1991). *Costing human resources: The financial impact of behavior in organizations* (3rd ed.). Boston: PWS-Kent.

Cascio, W. F. (2000). *Costing human resources: The financial impact of behavior in organizations* (4th ed.). Cincinnati, OH: South-Western College.

Davis, W. S. (1983). *Systems analysis and design: A structured approach.* Reading, MA: Addison-Wesley.

Dery, K., & Wailes, N. (2005). Necessary but not sufficient: ERPs and strategic HRM. *Strategic Change, 14,* 265–272.

Drucker, P. F., Dyson, E., Handy, C., Saffo, P., & Senge, P. M. (1997). Looking ahead: Implications of the present. *Harvard Business Review, 75*(5), 18–24.

Evans, J. R. (2005). *Total quality.* Toronto, Ontario, Canada: Thomson.

Evans, W. R., & Davis, W. D. (2005). High-performance work systems and organizational performance: The mediating role of internal social structure. *Journal of Management, 31,* 758–775.

Fitz-Enz, J. (1980). Quantifying the human resources function. *Personnel, 57*(3), 41–52.

Fitz-Enz, J. (2000). *The ROI of human capital: Measuring the economic value of employee performance.* New York: AMACOM/American Management Association.

Fitz-Enz, J. (2002). *How to measure human resource management* (3rd ed.). New York: McGraw-Hill.

Greer, C. (1995). *Strategy and human resources: A general managerial perspective.* Englewood Cliffs, NJ: Prentice Hall.

Huselid, M. A., Becker, B. E., & Beatty, R. W. (2005). *The workforce scorecard: Managing human capital to execute strategy.* Boston: Harvard Business School Press.

Huselid, M. A., Jackson, S. E., & Schuler, R. S. (1997). Technical and strategic human resource management effectiveness as determinants of firm performance. *Academy of Management Journal, 40,* 171–188.

Kavanagh, M. J., Gueutal, H. G., & Tannenbaum, S. I. (1990). *Human resource information systems.* Boston: PWS-Kent.

Lawler, E. E., & Mohrman, S. A. (2003). HR as a strategic business partner: What does it take to make it happen? *Human Resource Planning, 26*(3), 15–29.

Lengnick-Hall, C. A., & Lengnick-Hall, M. L. (2006). HR, ERP, and knowledge for competitive advantage. *Human Resource Management, 45*(2), 179–194.

Martinsons, M. G., & Chong, P. K. C. (1999). The influence of human factors and specialist involvement on information systems success. *Human Relations, 52*(1), 123–152.

Ngai, E. W. T., & Wat, F. K. T. (2004). Human resource information systems: A review and empirical analysis. *Personnel Review, 35*(3), 297–314.

Porter, M. E. (1990). *The competitive advantage of nations.* Boston: Free Press.

Roberts, B. (1999). Calculating return on investment for HRIS. *HR Magazine, 44*(13), 122–127.

Roehling, M. V., Boswell, W. R., Caligiuri, P., Feldman, D., Graham, M. E., Guthrie, J. P., et al. (2005). The future of HR management: Research needs and directions. *Human Resource Management, 44*(2), 207–216.

Smith, A. F., & Kelly, T. (1997). Human capital in the digital economy. In F. Hesselbein, M. Goldsmith, & R. Beckhard (Eds.), *The organization of the future* (pp. 199–212). San Francisco: Jossey-Bass.

Sprague, R. H., & Carlson, E. D. (1982). *Building effective decision support systems.* Englewood Cliffs, NJ: Prentice Hall.

Thite, M. (2004). *Managing people in the new economy.* New Delhi, India: Sage.

Ulrich, D., & Smallwood, N. (2005). HR's new ROI: Return on intangibles. *Human Resource Management, 44*(2), 137–142.

Walker, A. J. (1982). *HRIS development: A project team guide to building an effective personnel information system.* New York: Van Nostrand Reinhold.

Wright, P., McMahan, G., Snell, S., & Gerhart, B. (1998). *Strategic human resource management: Building human capital and organizational capacity* (Technical report). Ithaca, NY: Cornell University.

2

Database Concepts and Applications in HRIS

Janet H. Marler

Barry D. Floyd

EDITORS' NOTE

As mentioned in the book overview in Chapter 1, this chapter is focused on understanding databases and the applications of IT to the development and use of an HRIS. Although this chapter may be a review for some students, the material in it is critical to understanding the remaining chapters of the book. As such, students may want to refer back to this chapter as they are studying subsequent chapters. This introductory chapter is also an excellent example of the contribution of IT to the field of HRM in building an HRIS.

CHAPTER OBJECTIVES

After completing this chapter, you should be able to

♦ Discuss the difference between data, information, and knowledge

♦ Identify problems with early database structures

- ◆ Understand what a relational database is and why it is better than older database structures
- ◆ Discuss three types of data sharing and why they are important
- ◆ Know where data in a database are stored
- ◆ Know the different ways in which data can be delivered to the end user
- ◆ Know what a query is and discuss three different types of queries
- ◆ Discuss how queries are used to support decision making
- ◆ Discuss the key steps involved in designing a simple database in Microsoft (MS) Access
- ◆ Know what the top HR databases are
- ◆ Identify key data fields in an HR database
- ◆ Understand the difference between operational databases and a data warehouse
- ◆ Discuss how business intelligence software can support HR decision making

Introduction

Data are produced, stored, updated, and used by HR employees and managers on a daily basis. In fact, this process is so pervasive that it often goes unnoticed. For example, an HR recruiter who reviews a job applicant's resume and then files it for later action is collecting, using, and storing business data about a potential hire. Indeed, effective collection, storage, and use of data are essential for any business, and the most successful organizations are masters of this process! Many believe that managing data and turning data into information is a competency necessary to succeed in today's marketplace.

Today's HRIS consist of **business applications** that work in conjunction with an electronic database. Together these software programs transform data into information that is essential for business operations and for decision making. In this chapter, we will discuss how **database management systems (DBMS)** and business applications work together to process and share data that are the foundation of business information for managers and executives. We define key **relational database** terminology, describe how a database is structured, and show how to develop a basic database using MS Access, a basic DBMS, as an example. We close by providing examples of HRIS built on MS Access and other larger commercial databases.

Data, Information, and Knowledge

Data are the lifeblood of an organization. Its production and maintenance are critical to the smooth operation of every part of the organization. Data represent the "facts" of transactions that occur on a daily basis. A transaction can be thought of as an event of consequence, such as hiring a new employee for a particular position for a specified salary. The organization attempts to capture the data (facts) associated with each of these transactions, such as the date hired, the name of the person hired, the title of the position, the location where the new hire will be located, and so on, and then store these data for future use.

Information on the other hand is the interpretation of these data. An interpretation of data always has some goal and context such as making a hiring decision for a particular department or understanding of the performance of the company to make an improvement. Note that sometimes the data themselves can be informative without any additional transformation (e.g., the salary range of the job is also stored in the database and is used to help make the transaction occur quickly). But other times, we must do additional work to turn the data into information to answer important questions such as "What is our fulltime employee headcount in Corporate Sales?" or "How does our total salary expense for managers compare with industry norms?"

Knowledge is different from data and information. While information refers to data that have been given structure, knowledge is information that has been given meaning (Whitehill, 1997). For example, in HRIS, facts about age, gender, and education are the data. When these data are transformed into average age, gender ratio, and number and types of graduates at the unit level, they become information. Such information helps plan recruitment, launch affirmative action programs, and schedule training programs to bridge skill gaps, but "how" one can do that is what constitutes knowledge. More than what and why, knowledge is about how. It is procedural and mostly hidden in the minds of individuals and groups in the organization.

In the HR function, data about employees and jobs are the foundation of most of the information that is critical to analyzing and making HR decisions. Knowledge constitutes knowing what information is needed from a database and how to use it to achieve HR objectives.

Database Management Systems

DBMS and their associated databases electronically allow organizations to effectively manage data. This involves defining the data needed to make decisions, storing those data in a manner that promotes data quality, retrieving data at the right level of detail and in the right format, and finally managing who has access to it. By performing these functions effectively, DBMS turn data into an organizational resource.

A database management system is a set of software applications (i.e., programs) combined with a database. The main functions of a DBMS are to create the database, insert, read, update, and delete database data, maintain data integrity (i.e., making sure that the data are correct) and security (i.e., making sure that only the right people have access to the data), and prevent data from being lost by providing backup and recovery capabilities.

A database is a set of data. Importantly, it is a permanent, self-descriptive store of interrelated data items that can be processed by one or more business applications. *Interrelated* means that there are "links" between different sets of data in the database. For example, there can be a link between the data about employees and the jobs that they have. As a central repository of data, a database is a valuable organizational asset and, therefore, needs to be managed appropriately.

❖ **Figure 2.1** Database, Database Management System, and Business Applications

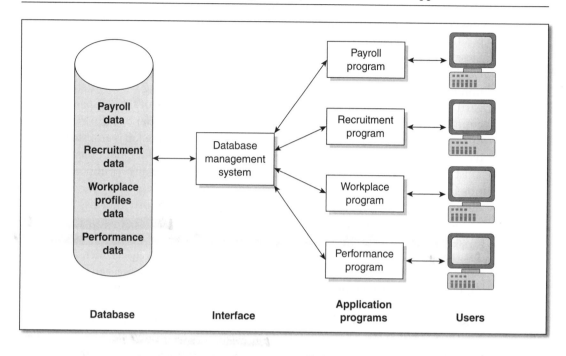

DBMS and databases work in conjunction with business applications, such as **transaction processing systems,** to make organizations run smoothly. As shown in Figure 2.1, these business applications consist of a set of one or more computer programs that serve as an intermediary between the user and the DBMS while providing the "functions" or "tasks" that the user wants performed (e.g., store data about the new hire) (Kroenke, 2003). The business application must talk both to the user sitting at a computer terminal in an easy-to-use manner and to the database in a way that is very efficient. For example, a payroll business application involves collecting data from an employee's time card, storing these data in a database, and then retrieving and manipulating these data to produce a paycheck. Data from this transaction processing system can also be used to generate **reports** on monthly personnel expenses. These reports are the basis of **management reporting systems.** We'll talk more about these later in the chapter.

There are thousands of commercially available business applications that work in conjunction with a DBMS to process business transactions. In a 2000 census of comprehensive HR software for the HR function, Richard Frantzreb cataloged more than 150 HR applications (Meade, 2003). In another census of specialized HR products under headings such as employment management, Equal Employment Opportunity (EEO), training management, career development, HR planning, performance management, personnel policy, survey processing, employee scheduling, attendance/timekeeping, payroll, and so on, Frantzreb counted 2,500 HR software products from about 1,700 vendors (Meade, 2003).

❖ **Figure 2.2**   Hierarchical and Network Database Structures

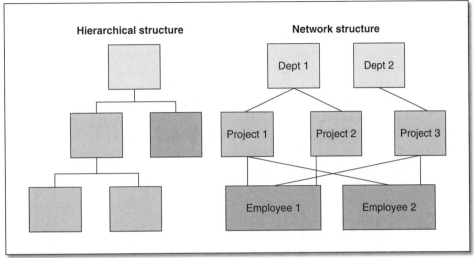

Early DBMS[1]

Early DBMS were simply data-processing systems that performed record-keeping functions that mimicked existing manual procedures. Thus, electronic data were stored in computers in much the same way that they were stored in paper filing systems. Paper filing systems typically consisted of a filing cabinet and a drawer for each type of business document (e.g., an employee personnel form). These documents were also called "records." Inside would be paper documents with each document being a "record" of a transaction (e.g., promoting Susan to Senior Manager). Computer systems mimicked this, creating individual computer files, typically one for each type of document. For example, there would be an Employee File with employee records, a Time Card File with time card records, and multiple Employee Benefit Files with their associated documents, and so on. The main objective of these file-processing systems was to process transactions such as update payroll records and produce payroll checks as efficiently as possible.

These traditional **file-oriented data structures** had a number of shortcomings, however, including (a) data redundancy—an employee's name and address could be stored in many different files; (b) poor data control—if you had access to the file you had access to *all* the data in the file, which may not be desirable because you may want to restrict the data viewed by a particular user; (c) inadequate data manipulation capabilities—it was very difficult to combine the data across files and to easily update and to add new data; and (d) excessive programming effort—any change in the data required extensive changes in the programming that accessed the data.

In general, early file systems were good at specialized transaction processing. They were not designed to easily and quickly provide information to answer questions such as "What were the average hours worked by female programmers last year compared with this year?" because the data to answer the more complicated questions came from different files; for example, employee gender would be in the master file on employees, and hours worked would be in the time-card transaction file. Difficulties arose when managers in the organization wanted to share data across applications: Fundamentally, there was no easy way to "link" information. For example, managers could not connect information about employee salaries and sales projections.

To overcome the shortcoming of file-oriented structures, *hierarchical and network database systems* evolved in the mid-1960s and early 1970s. The key to these systems was that **relationships** between different records were explicitly maintained. Although relationships among the data were created between sets of data, as illustrated in Figure 2.2, the relationships were created based on where the data were stored (e.g., the job records for Employee X are located in Sector 3 of Disk 4). Thus, only the very knowledgeable technical staff were able to effectively interact with the database. These database systems also required excessive programming effort and suffered from inadequate data manipulation capabilities if the program was poorly designed.

The advent of *relational database management systems* addressed the many problems associated with these older DBMS and database structures.

Relational DBMS

In 1970, E. F. Codd introduced the notion that rather than programming relationships between data based on physical location, the information needed to integrate data should reside within the data (Hansen & Hansen, 1996). Included in Codd's proposal was that data be stored in **tables** where each table represented one "**entity**" in the real world and the information associated with that "entity'" be stored only in that table. For example, a company could have an employee table (i.e., employee is an "entity"), and so information about the employee, such as name, address, date of hire, would only be stored in that table and nowhere else. Such an idea removed problems with redundancies such as storing the employee's address in many locations and then not knowing which one is the correct one, if one is changed and the other one is not changed. These tables were called relations, and from this model came the name *relational database.*

In relational database systems, retrieval of data was based on logical relationships built into the data structure, which made feasible the creation of a query capability that was much more accessible to end users who generally had limited programming experience. We'll talk more about this a bit later in the chapter.

Perhaps, the most significant difference between a file-based system and a relational database system is that data are easily shared. There are three types of *data sharing:* (1) data sharing between functional units, (2) data sharing between management levels, and (3) data sharing across geographically dispersed locations. Data sharing requires a major change in end-user thinking, particularly in those who are accustomed to owning their own data on their PCs. Fundamentally, sharing data means sharing power because both data and information are power. Sharing data also means being a good citizen and making certain that the data you enter is correct.

Data Sharing Between Different Functions

Relational DBMS facilitate data integration across different functions such that each function might have access not only to its own data but also to other data as well. Thus, the HR department is able to maintain its employee database but also access cost information from the accounting department's database. As a result, relational database technology increased the feasibility and popularity of integrated business applications. These integrated applications used in large organizations are referred to as enterprise resource planning (ERP) business applications.

ERP software applications are a set of integrated database applications, or modules, that carry out the most common business functions, including HR, general ledger, accounts payable, accounts receivable, order management, inventory control, and customer relationship management. ERP modules are integrated, primarily through a common set of definitions and a common database (Martin, Brown, DeHayes, Hoffer, & Perkins, 1999).

Data Sharing Between Different Levels

Operational employees, managers, and executives also share data but have different objectives and, thus, different information needs. Operational employees focus on data-processing transactions to ensure smooth operation of critical business transactions. At this level, transaction-processing information systems help conduct business on a day-to-day basis to provide timely and accurate information to managers and executives. For example, transaction-processing systems update employee work history, attendance, and work hours. Operational employees are concerned with the accuracy and efficiency with which these data are processed.

Managers, on the other hand, are more interested in summary data, such as reports generated from daily operational data that can be summarized into daily, weekly or monthly reports on hours worked by employee or absences by employee.

Executives rely on information produced at an even more aggregated level to evaluate trends and develop business strategies. For example, executives might ask for reports that compare turnover statistics across business groups and over time.

These three different levels of use correspond to three different types of software systems that have evolved over the past three decades: transaction processing systems (TPS), management reporting systems (MRS), and decision support systems (DSS) (Hansen & Hansen, 1996). TPS were first applied to lower operational levels of the organization to automate manual processes such as payroll. Their basic characteristics include (a) a focus on data storage, processing, and flows at the daily operational level; (b) efficient transaction processing; and (c) summary reports for management (Sprague & Watson, 1989). Early ERP applications were used primarily for their transaction processing functionality.

Note the similarity between the categorization of information systems into electronic data processing (EDP), management information systems (MIS), and decision support systems (DSS) discussed in Chapter 1 (Sprague & Carlson, 1982). These terms correspond to TPS, MRS, and DSS in this chapter. As you may recall from Chapter 1, an additional information system was identified—the human resources management decision system (HRMDS). The HRMDS was described as consisting of the reports managers and HR professionals receive on a regular basis but that are actually used in their daily work, *particularly in their decision-making capacity.* The HRMDS could be classified as a special instance of an MRS or MIS system but focused specifically on information used in decision making—a central theme of this book.

In addition to TPS capabilities, relational databases can also provide MRS capability. Characteristics of an MRS include (1) information aimed at middle managers; (2) integration of TPS data by business functions such as manufacturing, marketing, and HR; and (3) inquiry and report generation from the database (Sprague & Watson, 1989). Management reporting systems can be designed to provide daily, monthly, quarterly, or annual summary reports of key transactions such as employee headcounts by department or EEO reports for compliance purposes.

Decision support systems assist senior managers and business professionals in making business decisions. Data mining, data analytics, and **business intelligence** (**BI**) are examples of information derived from a DSS, which relies on data warehouses. Data warehouses represent aggregated data collected from various databases available to a business.

Data Sharing Across Locations

In today's global environment, access to data from any physical location in the world is increasingly important. Teams of employees may be stationed in Thailand, India, and the United States. Two issues arise when data are shared across wide geographic locations. These are (1) managing the day/time of a transaction and (2) determining where to store the various components of the business application, DBMS, and database.

To deal with day/time, developers of DBMS such as Oracle, MS SQL Server, and IBM DB2 are building the capability to deal with recording dates and times according to the time zone in which the data originated. So, for example, if a database is stored in London and an employee records a transaction while sitting at a terminal in Los Angeles, in addition to the time (say 1 P.M. in Los Angeles), the time zone (−08:00 from Greenwich Mean Time) is also stored with the transaction.

As part of a global information system design, organizations have chosen to break their business application and DBMS into components, often called "tiers." More detail on tiers will also be covered in Chapter 3. Traditional client-server architectures broke an application into two tiers, typically with the **user interface** and some business logic on the user's computer, such as a PC (the client) and the database and mainstream parts of the application stored on a server. In today's global environment with high-speed data networks, **N-tier architectures** exist with databases and applications being distributed among many different computers around the world. So if, for example, you are in an Internet café in Bangkok trying to get information about your benefit election, the hosting computer may be in London and the data may be located on a computer in Chicago. In sum, computer networks are created that provide instant access to these operational data, allowing real-time managerial decision capability regardless of physical location.

A centralized database allows a company to confine its data to a single location and, therefore, more easily control data integrity, updating, backup, query, and control access to the database. A company with many locations and telecommuters, however, must develop a communications infrastructure to facilitate data sharing over a wide geographical area. The advent of the Internet and a standardized communication protocol made the centralized database structures and geographically dispersed data sharing feasible.

Key Relational Database Terminology

As discussed earlier, relational DBMS are used to store data important to the organization. Key terms in relational database management include entities, attributes, tables, **primary keys,** foreign keys and relationships, queries, **forms,** and reports. Below we define each term and describe its function in a database.

Entities and Attributes

Entities are things such as employees, jobs, promotion transactions, positions in company, and so on. They include both physical things such as desks and conceptual things such as bank accounts. A company must analyze its business operations and identify all the entities that it believes are important.

Each of these entities is made up of "attributes." An attribute is a characteristic of the entity. For example, an employee has a name, address, phone number, education, and so on.

In addition to identifying the entities and attributes, the relationships among the entities must be defined. For example, a company may have an employee entity and a department entity. Then the company must define the relationship between the employee entity and the department entity (e.g., Does an employee have to be assigned to a department? Can an employee be assigned to more than one department?).

Tables

How does this information fit into a relational DBMS? Tables are used to store information about entities. As illustrated in Figure 2.3, one table is created for each entity—in this example, driver table, car table, moving violation table, and parking violation table. Attributes are stored as the columns (also called fields) in the table. As noted earlier, attributes represent a single data element or characteristic of the data table. For example, a table of driver data would have the following columns or characteristics: first name, last name, street address, city, state, driver license number, expiration, and so on. Each of these characteristics represents an attribute or field of the table.

Each table in a database contains rows. Rows are also referred to as records and represent an "instance" of the entity. For example, in the driver table, each row contains data about a particular driver, and each column contains data that represent an attribute of that driver, such as name, phone number, and license number.

Relationships, Primary Keys, and Foreign Keys

To represent the relationships among the tables, we have to do a bit more work. In a relational DBMS, relationships are created by having the same attribute in each table with the value of the attribute being the same in each table. Most often this is done by taking the "primary key" of one table and including it in the related table. What is a "primary key"?

❖ **Figure 2.3** Relational Database Structure

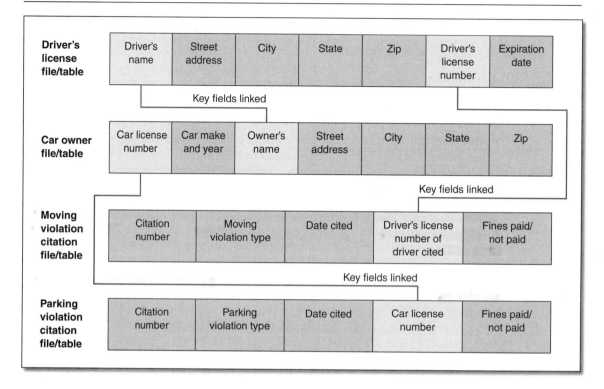

Typically, each entity has an attribute that has unique values for each instance of the entity. For example, each employee has a social security number that is unique (i.e., only one person has a particular number). Other entities, such as jobs, locations, and positions can be assigned a unique number if one doesn't exist. These unique attributes can be used as a table's "primary key." Given that we have a unique attribute, to create a relationship, we simply store that attribute in the related table. So if an employee is associated with a position, we have two tables, an employee table and a positions table. We then take the primary key of the employee table and store it in the position table. In the example in Figure 2.3, the driver's license number is the primary key in the driver table and it is also stored in the moving violation table. When a primary key from one table is stored as an attribute of another table, that attribute is called a "foreign key." Thus, in Figure 2.3, driver's license is the primary key in the driver table and is the foreign key in the moving violations table.

Storing data in tables allows the database application to create queries, forms, and reports that permit users to retrieve, update, or analyze these data.

Queries[2]

A **query** is a question that you ask about the data stored in a database. For example, you may want to know which employees live within a specific zip code. You could generate these results by scrolling through the relevant table or by sorting the table by zip code but this is both time-consuming and temporary. If you use a query to answer this question, you can save the query in the database and use it again and again. When creating a query, only the definition is stored (e.g., show all employees with zip code 93407), and when the query is executed, it searches through the current table records and lists the results in a new table. Queries retrieve specific data in a particular order, but it is important to note that queries do not store data! All data are stored in tables. Queries only report on data currently in the table.

There are three different kinds of queries: select queries, action queries, and cross-tab queries. A **select query** allows you to ask a question based on one or more tables in a database. This is the most commonly used query. These queries can be quite general or quite specific. For example, a general query might extract all employees from the database that have reached retirement age. A more specific query might retrieve employees who have reached retirement age and who live in New York and are engineers.

An **action query** performs an action on the table on which it is based. Actions include updating data in the table (e.g., increasing the base salary of all employees who were rated above average in the latest performance rating), deleting records from the table (e.g., removing employees from the employees table if they no longer work at the company), or inserting records (e.g., the query may add a new set of benefits to the benefits table). You can also use this type of query to create new tables.

A **cross-tab query** performs calculations on the values in a field and displays the results in a datasheet. The reason it is called "cross-tab" is that it tabulates the data for a set of descriptor attributes, contrasting them or crossing them in a table format. For example, we might want to see the total personnel count by gender by region. So we would see the gender on the left-hand side and the different regions listed across the top of a table. A cross-tab query could display different aspects of the data, including sums or averages or minimum or maximum values. As another example, a cross-tab query could determine headcount by department or determine pay range maximums and minimums in pay grades by department.

Select queries and cross-tab queries provide the information that managers and executives expect from IT. These queries can serve as the foundation for MRS and DSS information and decision making. Action queries, on the other hand, improve the operational efficiency of managing and maintaining a database. These tasks are important to the operational staff but of less interest to HR managers and executives.

Queries are also used as the basis for forms and reports. In addition to retrieving data, they can add, update, and delete records in tables. You can define fields in a query that perform calculations, such as sums and averages. The following list summarizes the typical capabilities of queries (Bast, Cygman, Flynn, & Tidwell, 2006):

- Display selected fields and records from a table
- Sort records on one or multiple fields
- Perform calculations
- Generate data for forms, reports, and other queries
- Update data in the tables of a database
- Find and display data from two or more tables
- Create new tables
- Delete records in a table based on one or more criteria

Forms[3]

A form is an object in a database that you can use to maintain, view, and print records in a database in a more "structured" manner. Although you can perform these same functions with tables and queries, forms can present data in many customized and useful ways. For example, you can design a form to look like the time sheet submitted by an employee. Well-designed forms can improve data input efficiency and accuracy. Consequently, forms represent the main mechanism for creating end-user interfaces.

A form can be based on a table, multiple tables, or queries. A form can display one record at a time or many records. Often, we select only one record and then create a nice-looking, easy-to-use layout to work with the data in that one record. To view and maintain or add data using a form, you must know how to move from field to field and from record to record. Forms provide navigation buttons that facilitate moving from field to field and from record to record. Data that entered or changed in a form automatically change the values in the underlying table once you save the changes.

Reports

A report is a formatted presentation of data from a table, multiple tables, or queries that is created as a printout or to be viewed on screen. Data displayed in a report are dynamic, reflecting the latest data from the tables on which the report is based. Unlike forms, however, you cannot change the data or add a new record in a report. You can only view the data in a report.

Although you can print data appearing in tables, queries, and forms, reports provide you with the greatest flexibility for formatting printed output. As with forms, you can design your own reports or use a Report Wizard to create reports automatically.[4]

Introduction to MS Access

MS Access differs from other commercial database management software such as Oracle, DB2, or MYSQL in that it integrates both database application and DBMS software into one. MS Access is a relational DBMS in which data are organized as a collection of tables. Like any relational database, the data in tables can be queried. MS Access also makes it easy to create forms and reports through the use of form or report wizards. A form or report wizard is a computer program or tool that guides you through the creation of a form by asking you a series of questions. For example, which table is the form to be created from, and which attributes do you want to be displayed on the form? The form or report is created based on your answers.

MS Access is designed for relatively small databases and assumes limited knowledge of database programming. MS Access provides the following functions (Adamski & Finnegan, 2005):

- It allows you to create databases containing tables and table relationships.
- It lets you easily add new records, change table values in existing records, and delete records.
- It contains a built-in query language, which lets you obtain immediate answers to questions you ask about your data.

- It contains a built-in report generator and Report Wizard, which lets you produce professional-looking, formatted reports from your data.
- It provides protection of databases through security, control, and recovery facilities.

Data in an MS Access table or query can be exported to other database applications or to spreadsheet programs such as Excel or Lotus 123. Once these records are in a spreadsheet program, then further analyses may be conducted and graphs and charts constructed to enhance analytical HR metric reports. Data can be exported by simply opening the database that has the object—for example, table or query—that you want to export. Then select File, Export from the database menu. Select the type of file—for example, .xls—you want the object to be saved to and specify a name. Click Save. Now you can open the file in Excel. You may also "link" the data in the database to the spreadsheet. When the spreadsheet is opened, the most recent data from the database are retrieved and presented in the spreadsheet.

Unlike spreadsheet software programs, MS Access handles substantially more data and contains the ability to model relationships. Each MS Access database, for example, can be up to 2 GB in size and can contain up to 32,768 objects, including tables, queries, forms, reports, and so on.

Designing an MS Access Database

The design process begins with an analysis of the data and information that the users of the database will need to have stored and retrieved in order to accomplish their work. Typically, we think of work as consisting of tasks within a business process, and so we can think of the data that will be required to be stored in a database and of the information that will need to be extracted. We find out the data to be stored by interviewing the intended end users of the database. We ask about entities that they need to keep information on, the attributes of those entities and also how the entities are related. In addition, we may watch users at work and look at the forms, reports, and other business documents that they use to be successful. Gathering copies of all existing forms and reports currently used may also act as guidelines for creating forms and reports, though sometimes our intention is to change how they are doing business, and so some of these documents may be significantly changed or even discarded.

In general, the database design process can be broken down into several steps that are somewhat sequential but oftentimes have to be repeated until the database meets the users' needs:

- Determine what the users want from the database: what questions need to be answered, what information needs to be tracked, what reports are produced, and what data are needed to provide the basis for those results.
- Identify the data fields needed to produce the required information; in doing so, we also identify rules that define the integrity of the data, including data type (number, character) and data limits (e.g., if we are storing days, we might only allow the numbers 1 to 31).
- Group related fields into tables (entities).
- Determine each table's primary key.
- Normalize the data: Make sure the data for an entity are really associated with only that entity.

- Determine how the tables are related to one another and include common keys.
- Create the relationships among the different entities.
- Create queries to define data needs that are not handled by only looking at individual tables.
- Create reports to provide a structured view of the data.
- Create forms, and in doing so, identify a common design for the forms: Typically, we create a form for each table along with a "main menu" form that allows the user to navigate to each form associated with a table and to view queries and reports.
- Enter test data to verify the quality/accuracy of the system design.
- Test the system: Do all the queries work correctly? Are the forms easy to use? Are the end users happy?
- Enter or populate the database.

HR Database Application Using MS Access

For small companies, generally with less than 1,000 employees, there are commercially available HR database applications based on MS Access. Two such systems are HRSource from Auxillium West (www.auxillium.com) and HRVantage for Spectrum Human Resources Systems Corporation (www.spectrumhr.com). Both software products offer wide breadth of functionality and flexibility to import and export data from and to Excel and to integrate with other database applications, particularly payroll. Both provide a centralized relational database with basic transaction processing and management reporting systems.

Both HRSource and HRVantage have familiar MS Access forms as user interfaces. They both allow users to create custom queries and reports. However, the database applications also come with preconfigured reports and queries. For example, HRVantage provides more than 150 standard reports, which include Absence reports, EEO reports and graphs, termination analyses, employee skill searches, employee profiles, OSHA reports, employee performance reports, and many others. HRSource offers users 70 built-in reports. Customers also claim that with a little expertise in MS Access, they are able to mine their HR information in a way that they never could before they centralized on one HRIS database (Meade, 2003).

Other HR Databases

A few decades ago, database application programs were often written by companies for their particular use; in today's business environment, customized application programs termed *legacy systems* are being replaced by commercially developed database application programs (e.g., PeopleSoft Enterprise HCM, MySAP ERP HCM, Lawson HCM, HR Spectrum, UltiPro HR). As a result, over the past 10 years, the number of HR business application programs has mushroomed. According to a Web site published by TechTarget (www.techtarget.com), an integrated media publishing company targeting IT professionals, the top 10 HR database software applications are as listed in Table 2.1.

Most of these top selling HR database applications use Microsoft SQL Server as their DBMS.[5] The most well-known HR database applications, such as MySAP ERP HCM licensed by SAP America, Inc. and PeopleSoft Enterprise Human Capital Management licensed by Oracle, operate on multiple DBMS platforms (e.g., Oracle, SQL Server, DBS2).

❖ **Table 2.1**   HR Database Software Applications

Product Name	Modules	Technology	Comments
MySAP ERP HCM (SAP America, Inc.)	Talent Management, Workforce Process Management, Workforce Deployment	Built on the components of mySAP Business Suite that runs on various DBMS platforms	A module of ERP software
PeopleSoft Enterprise Human Capital Management (Oracle)	Human Resources, HCM Warehouse, HRMS Portal Pack, Employee Benefits and Compensation Modules, Recruiting Modules, Payroll Modules, eDevelopment, Learning Management, ePerformance, Workforce Planning, Absence Management, Directory Interface, eProfile, Time and Labor	Leveraging a pure Internet architecture, PeopleSoft Enterprise Human Capital Management gives you access to real-time information. It runs on various DBMS platforms	A module of ERP software
Microsoft Dynamics GP Enterprise–Human Resource Management	Analytics, Business Portal, Customization Tools, Human Resources Management, Financial Management, Field Service Management, Manufacturing, Project Management	MS SQL Server is the back-end RDBMS	An ERP software
Lawson Human Capital Management (Lawson)	Payroll, Absence Management, Benefits Administration, Employee and Manager Self-Service, e-Recruiting, Lawson Performance Management, Personnel Administration, Workforce Analytics		

(Continued)

❖ **Table 2.1** (Continued)

Product Name	Modules	Technology	Comments
e-Synergy HR Management (Exact Software)	Web Shop, Event Manager, Sarbanes Oxley, Software Development Kit, Customer Relationship Management, HR Management, Document/Knowledge Management	MS SQL Server RDBMS	Is part of a customer relationship management software
Microsoft Dynamics AX Human Resources Management	Supply Chain Management, Manufacturing, Financial Management and Accounting Analytics, Human Resources Management, Sales and Marketing, E-Commerce	Uses the Microsoft Windows environments and ASP interface to access data in MS SQL and Oracle DBMS	An ERP software
UltiPro HR (Ultimate Software)	UltiPro Workforce Portal, eEmployee Self-Service, eManager Self-Service, eAdministration, eHuman Resources, ePayroll Processing, eRecruitment, eBenefits Enrollment, eTraining Enrollment, eReporting and UltiPro Business Intelligence, Position Management	Uses a Web interface to access a proprietary database system	Application service provider that provides proprietary application and DBMS bundled
Sage Abra HRMS (Sage Abra)	Abra HR, Abra Payroll, Abra Recruiting Solution, Abra Attendance, Abra Train, Abra OrgPlus, Abra alers, Abra Workforce Connections, Abra ESS, Abra Benefits Enrollment	Uses a proprietary DBMS and works within the MS Windows environments	

Product Name	Modules	Technology	Comments
Sage MAS 500 Human Resources-Abra HR, Alerts, Attendance & Payroll (Sage Software)	Accounts Payable, Accounts Receivable, Cash Management, Fixed Asset Accounting and Inventory, General Ledger, Business Insights Analyzer, Sage MAS 500 Office, eExecutive,	MS SQL Server	An ERP software
ESP 21 Human Resources (Enterprise Software)	Supply Chain Management, Purchasing Burdens, Cash Management, Contract Documents, General Ledger, Human Resources, Job Cost, Order Entry, Organizations, Time Cards, Communications, Collaboration and Resources Management	MS SQL Server	

NOTE: DBMS, database management systems; ERP, enterprise resource planning; HRMS, human resources management systems; RDBMS, relational database management systems.

To know what information can be derived from any database, one must have an idea of what tables and attributes (fields) are in the database. Software vendors should be able to provide this information to end users; however, for the large complex HR applications, this may run into thousands of tables and fields! Auxillim West, makers of a low-priced HRIS, offer a document to prospective customers that lists the data items commonly tracked. Their most commonly tracked HR fields are listed in Table 2.2 (Meade, 2003).

Although the list in Table 2.2 appears to be comprehensive, in fact, it is quite sparse when compared with more complex database applications. More complex database applications will also have fields that relate to business processes other than HR, such as accounting. Integrated databases allow sophisticated queries and analytical reports, such as hours spent on recruiting, recruiters' hourly pay, job board posting costs, number of positions filled, number of declined offers, number of open positions, number of voluntary terminations, and number of involuntary terminations.

Data Warehouses, Business Intelligence, and Data Mining

An organization's ability to generate meaningful information to make good decisions is only as good as its underlying database. As Dr. John Sullivan notes, "I have found

❖ Table 2.2   Examples of Common Fields in an HR Database

Employee ID	Job Code/Title
First Name	Pay Rate Type
Last Name	Rate Effective Date
Address	Salary
City	Bonuses
State	Status
Zip Code	Category (full-time/part-time)
Home Phone Number	Contract Employee Status
Gender	Department
Ethnic Code	Office information
Birth Date	Manager
Veteran Status	Division/Location
Visa Expiration Date	Company Property
Education	Emergency contact
Past Employment	Time-Off Accruals
Skill Code	Benefits
Training/Certification	Work-Related Injuries
Performance rating	Disability
Next Review Date	
Hire Date	
Termination Date	
Termination Reason	
Rehire Date as Applicable	

that the largest single difference between a great HR department and an average one is the use of metrics" (Gur, 2006). Metrics are various measures of organizational performance that are derived from organizational data. A current goal and emphasis in HRM is functioning as a strategic business partner. A requisite to this is the use of methodologies or metrics to assess and monitor quantitative HRM data. The overarching objective of HR metrics is to improve organizational efficiency and effectiveness. The use of metrics in HRM will be discussed in greater detail in Chapter 6.

Much of the data now available to create HR metrics come from an organization's data warehouse. A data warehouse is a special type of database that is optimized for reporting and analysis and is the raw material for management's decision support system. Business intelligence is a broad category of business applications and technologies for creating data warehouses and for analyzing and providing access to these specialized data to help enterprise users make better business decisions. BI applications include the activities of decision support systems, query and reporting, statistical analysis, forecasting, and data mining.

BI systems allow organizations to improve business performance by leveraging information about customers, suppliers, and internal business operations from databases across functions and organizational boundaries. Essentially, BI systems retrieve specified data from multiple databases, including old legacy file database systems, and store these data into a new database, which becomes that data warehouse. The data in the data warehouse can then be accessed via queries and used to uncover patterns and diagnose problems.

Patterns in large data sets are identified through data mining, which involves statistically analyzing large data sets to identify recurring relationships. For example, data mining an employee database might reveal that most employees reside within a group of particular zip codes. This may help if the organization wants to supply transportation or encourage car pooling. Data mining is relatively new to business analytics and has not yet been widely used for HRM decisions.

BI systems also provide reporting tools and interfaces (e.g., forms) that distribute the information to Excel spreadsheets, Internet-based portals, pdf files, or hard copies. These results can also be distributed to key executives in specialized formats known as executive dashboards, which are becoming a popular executive decision support tool.

A major reason for a DBMS is to provide information from various parts of the organization in an "ad hoc" manner. Ad hoc means that a user can ask a question of the data that no one has thought about yet. The user can sign into the data and pose his or her question in the form of a query. This is a very powerful concept that enables all levels of the organization. Data warehouses and BI software enable managers to create information from an even greater store of data.

Summary

In this chapter, we have described the key aspects of current DBMS technologies and how they work to create, store, and manage critical data about an organization. Data are transformed into information by relational DBMS and business applications that work together. The underlying data in a database are collected from business transactions and stored in tables that are related to each other through shared fields called primary and foreign keys. Queries represent questions asked of the data and are used to access specific data stored in tables. The results of queries can be viewed in forms or reports that are customized so that the end user can better interpret the data that are retrieved from the database. More sophisticated data analyses and reports such as executive dashboards are produced from specialized databases called data warehouses and business application software called BI software.

Most HRIS rely on an underlying database. Understanding how database systems work, therefore, is relevant to HR decision makers because knowledge about how to create, store, and access data can be a key differentiator in a competitive environment. Small HR databases can be created using MS Access, or more sophisticated ones can be purchased from software vendors. There are literally hundreds of HR database business applications that create, process, and analyze HR data. The challenge is to find one that can most cost-effectively collect and share data from which meaningful information can be extracted to support making good decisions.

DISCUSSION QUESTIONS

1. Explain the differences between data, information, and knowledge.

2. What are the main functions of a database management system and how is it different from a database?

3. What were the shortcomings of early file-oriented database structures?

4. What are the three types of data sharing?

5. Define the key terms in a relational database.

6. What is the difference between a primary key and a foreign key?

7. What are the three types of queries?

8. How are forms and reports similar and how are they different?

9. Take the list of HR database common fields and group them into tables.

10. What are the differences between data warehouses, BI, and data mining?

11. Can knowledge be turned into a database?

CASE STUDY

You have been asked to create an applicant database for a small recruiting firm that specializes in recruiting HR professionals for small to medium firms. Describe the process that you would use to design this database. Use MS Access to develop a prototype of the database that you could show your manager.

NOTES

1. For a more detailed discussion, see Hansen and Hansen (1996, pp. 52–56).

2. For a more detailed discussion, see Bast et al. (2006, chap. 3).

3. For a more detailed treatment see Tutorials 4 and 5 in Adamski and Finnegan (2005).

4. For a more detailed treatment see Tutorials 4 and 6 in Adamski and Finnegan (2005).

5. Go to www.2020software.com/software/display.asp for a comparison and description of the top 10 HR software solutions.

REFERENCES

Adamski, J., & Finnegan, K. (2005). *New perspectives on Microsoft Access 2003.* Boston: Course Technology Thomson Learning.

Bast, K., Cygman, L., Flynn, G., & Tidwell, R. (2006). *Succeeding in business with Microsoft Office Access 2003.* Boston: Course Technology Thomson Learning.

Gur, Z. (2006, June/July). Up.link. *IHRIM.link,* 5.

Hansen, G. W., & Hansen, J. V. (1996). *Database management and design.* Upper Saddle River, NJ: Prentice Hall.

Kroenke, D. M. (2003). *Database concepts.* Upper Saddle River, NJ: Prentice Hall.

Martin, E., Brown, C., DeHayes, D., Hoffer, J., & Perkins, W. (1999). *Managing information technology.* Upper Saddle River, NJ: Prentice Hall.

Meade, J. (2003). *The human resources software handbook.* San Francisco: Jossey-Bass.

Sprague, R. H., & Carlson, E. D. (1982). *Building effective decision support systems.* Englewood Cliffs, NJ: Prentice Hall.

Sprague, R., & Watson, H. (1989). *Decision support systems* (2nd ed.). Englewood Cliffs, NJ: Prentice Hall.

Whitehill, M. (1997). Knowledge-based strategy to deliver sustained competitive advantage. *Long Range Planning, 30*(4), 621–627.

Systems Considerations in the Design of an HRIS

Planning for Implementation

Michael D. Bedell

Michael Canniff

Cheryl Wyrick

EDITORS' NOTE

This chapter covers the information necessary to understand the system development process for HRIS. As mentioned in Chapter 1, the system development process involves multiple stages from initial design to implementation and evaluation. Failure to follow these steps or rushing through them will result in a poorly designed system that will ultimately fail when it is implemented. Thus, this chapter begins to identify some of the information that is critical for the eventual implementation of an HRIS. The authors start with a focus on the users of the system to help the system development process in its beginning steps. The types of information about users/customers of the HRIS, the sorting of HRIS data into categories of human capital, and the main concepts of hardware and database security are covered.

CHAPTER OBJECTIVES

After completing this chapter, you should be able to

- ♦ Understand the system design process and its importance to HRIS implementation
- ♦ Discover that there are multiple users/customers of the implemented HRIS and be able to identify that they each have very different data needs
- ♦ Be able to categorize HRIS data into appropriate categories related to human capital, the organization, or the interaction of human capital and the organization
- ♦ Be able to discuss the differences between the six general hardware architectures that are presented, from "dinosaur" to "best of breed"
- ♦ Be able to discuss, very generally, the main concepts of hardware and database security
- ♦ Develop an understanding of the general steps in a system implementation
- ♦ Understand the pros/cons of implementing a changeover from one software system to another

VIGNETTE

A billion dollar retailer with 4,000+ stores finds that it cannot move fast enough to beat out the competition. The organization's senior management arrives at the conclusion that it would be easier to achieve the strategic goals enumerated by the board of directors if the various organizational functions would share information. Shared information would enable them to develop and deploy new actions and tactics more quickly. The CEO and President have therefore ordered the major functions to update their information systems immediately so that data sharing is possible. The senior vice presidents (SVPs) of Accounting and Human Resources immediately decide that the only solution is to jointly decide on an enterprise resource planning (ERP) product. ERP software applications are a set of integrated database applications, or modules, that carry out the most common business functions, including human resources, general ledger, accounts payable, accounts receivable, order management, inventory control, and customer relationship management (see www.erpsupersite.com). To speed the installation along, they will install it using a rapid-implementation methodology that a company down the street used. The goal is to have the new systems operational in 9 months.

Shortly after this decision has been made, the SVP of HR calls you into his office and tells you that you will be **management sponsor** for this project. You have to decide on everything. You sit back in your nice office and think,

What's the problem with this scenario? It shouldn't be difficult to select a vendor and then bor-row the methodology from down the street. It worked for them, it should work for us! We'll call a few vendors in the morning and find out about cost, time frame, and implementation meth-ods. In the meantime, I should find out a little more about how to do this and who will be using it. I remember from my information systems class in college that this is a reasonable first step when it comes to buying software.

What do you think your response would be to this inquiry? As you go through this chapter's material, keep this vignette in mind, and see if your answer changes.

Introduction

Successful implementation is the central goal of every HRIS project, and it begins with a comprehensive design for the system. As the steps in the system development process are covered in this chapter, the foundation knowledge that is critical to the **implementation** process will be emphasized. Only by understanding the users/customers of the HRIS, the technical possibilities, the software solution parameters, and the systems implementation process can we increase the probability that the completed software installation will adequately meet the needs of the HRM function and the organization. The chapter will begin by identifying the potential users and the kind of information that the (HRIS) will be managing/storing to facilitate decision making. The chapter will next discuss the technical infrastructure, how the technical infrastructure has evolved, and the many choices that the organization must make. After the technology is discussed, the systems implementation process will be presented.

Those who have participated in a system implementation will tell you that success is the result of careful planning, a dedicated team, top-management support, and an awareness of potential pitfalls. These same people will also tell you that the implementation process provides a host of opportunities to reengineer and systematically improve nonsoftware processes to reflect best practices in HRM. These opportunities should not be ignored, as they can benefit the organization as much as implementing the software will. Finally, the **implementation team** members will tell you that it was the most intense 6 months, year, or 2 years of their work life but that they learned a lot and every moment of the experience was worth the time.

There are four things that should be remembered throughout the chapter:

1. Who is the customer of the data, the process, and the decisions that will be made?

2. Everything about HRM is a process designed to support the achievement of strategic organizational goals. The HRIS in turn supports and helps manage these HR processes.

3. An HRIS implementation done poorly may result in an HRIS that fails to meet the needs of the organization or worse.

4. Successful implementation requires careful attention to every step in the system design process. However, done well, the implementation process is full of opportunities to improve the organization and processes. More consistent processes will contribute to enhanced organizational performance.

HRIS Customers/Users: Data Importance

Individuals who will be using the HRIS can be split into two general groups: employees and nonemployees. The employee category includes

- managers who rely on the HRIS and the data analyzed by the analyst/power user to make decisions;
- analyst/power users who use the HRIS to evaluate potential decision choices and opportunities;
- technical staff who are responsible for providing a system that is usable and up-to-date for each user and clerical employees who largely engage in data entry; and
- employees who use the HRIS on a self-service basis to obtain personal information, for example, to look up paycheck information, to make choices about benefits during open enrollment, or to see how much vacation time they have available.

The nonemployee group includes potential employees, suppliers, and partners. Potential employees are those who might log in via a Web portal to search for and apply for a position. Suppliers and partners are organizations that interface with the HR function for a variety of purposes, from recruiting to benefits administration and payroll.

Employees

Managers

The managers referred to within this section may have a variety of titles: manager, director, vice president, and even CEO. What they all have in common is that their primary HRIS need is to have real-time access to accurate data that facilitate decision making with regard to their people (Miller, 1998). The HRIS provides the manager with data for performance management, recruiting and retention, team management, project management, and employee development (Fein, 2001). The HRIS must also provide the information necessary to help the functional manager make decisions that will contribute to the achievement of the unit's strategic goals and objectives (Hendrickson, 2003). Easy access to accurate employee data enables the manager for each employee to view and engage in employee life cycle changes such as salary decisions, job requisitions, hiring, disciplinary action, promotions, and training program enrollment (Walker, 2001; Zampetti & Adamson, 2001).

Many HRIS products provide real-time reporting and even screen-based historical information about the employees and/or the functional unit that can provide the manager with the information they need. There are also several third-party software products available that provide managers with almost continuous data about the status of their unit and the organization—much as a dashboard on a car provides immediate information. The analysis of more complex situations is beyond the capabilities of many of these reporting and query tools. To facilitate decision making on complex issues, the manager usually relies on the analyst/power user to complete some type of analysis before making a decision.

Analyst (Power User)

The analyst/power user is perhaps the most demanding user of the HRIS. The primary role of the analyst is to acquire as much relevant data as possible, examine it, and provide reasonable alternatives with appropriate supporting information to facilitate the decision process of the manager. The analyst is referred to as a power user because this person accesses more areas of the HRIS than almost any other user. Analysts must be proficient with reporting and query tools. Analysts must also understand the process used to collect the data, how new data are verified, and how the HRIS and the employee life cycle interact. They also need to understand the data definitions in terms of what data exist, the structure of the data, and what data fields are up-to-date and complete. Some HRIS also provide tools that the analyst can use to model scenarios or perform "what-if" analyses on questions of interest.

As an example, a recruiting analyst might be asked to provide a short-list of potential internal candidates for a position that opened in the marketing function of a large retailer. Characteristics of interest of the potential candidate are queried and may include (1) when they were last promoted, (2) whether they have engaged in continuous personal-skills development, (3) what their undergraduate degree was, and (4) whether they have ever expressed any interest in marketing. The analyst would query appropriate tables and develop a list of internal candidates.

Another example might have the HR analyst completing an analysis of corporate headquarters turnover to determine if a particular function or salary issue is the cause of the problem. This information would be drawn from existing reports, ad hoc queries, and available salary information. This information could be compiled into categories by salary, function, gender, or organizational level and examined to determine if the cause of the turnover can be pinpointed and then countered.

Technician (HRIS Expert)

HRIS experts straddle the boundary of two functions. Their role is to ensure that appropriate HR staff have all the access, information, and tools necessary to do their jobs. HRIS experts do this by understanding what is needed from an HR-process standpoint and then interpreting that into technical language so that the technical staff—programmers, database administrators, and application administrators—know exactly what to do. When the technical staff is planning to install the latest update and one of the results will be a change in functionality, the HRIS expert must take what the technical staff provides and interpret that into language HR users understand so as to indicate how processes and activities might change. For example, if an HR professional required that a new report be generated every other Tuesday, the HRIS expert would learn what data the report requires—perhaps mock the report up with the user—and then explain to the technical people how to make sure that this report is automatically generated on the time schedule.

Clerical Employee

Much like power users, these employees also spend a significant portion of their day interacting with the HRIS. The difference is that of depth. The clerical employee must understand the process required to enter information into the HRIS and may also need to start the process or generate periodic reports. While clerical staff in the HR employment department do not generally provide input about whether to hire an individual to a particular position, they bear considerable responsibility for seeing that the new employee gets paid properly. Hiring a new employee requires that someone, for example, a clerical employee, enter the appropriate information into the HRIS—such as the reporting relationship of the new employee as well as his or her benefits, salary, and direct deposit information.

Employee Self-Service

All the employees in the organization may interface with the HRIS through a self-service Web portal or secure employee kiosk, removing the necessity of an HR clerk or staff member assisting with many routine HR record modifications (Walker, 2001). Self-service capabilities encourage employees to manage their personal HR profiles with respect to a variety of functions, such as benefit and retirement plan monitoring or computerized training, in addition to using HRIS-based systems to complete numerous personnel forms (Adamson & Zampetti, 2001; Zampetti & Adamson, 2001). Typical self-service applications are accessible most of the day throughout the week. Employees log on to the system, where their identity is authenticated and verified. Then appropriate change options are offered to the employee based on certain parameters that control the areas where the employee is allowed to make valid alterations to the HRIS—such as personnel data updates, job postings, or desired training enrollments (Adamson & Zampetti, 2001; Zampetti & Adamson, 2001). One fairly large financial-services organization noted that self-service options significantly enabled them to reduce the annual benefits open-enrollment process by reducing the paper generated, reducing necessary mailings, and reducing the data that had to be read and entered into the HRIS. Data entry time alone was reduced from 6 to 2 weeks (Bedell, 2003a).

Nonemployees

Job Seekers

It is estimated that 70% to 90% of large organizations use online recruitment, and that number continues to increase (Stone, Lukaszewski, & Isenhour, 2005). Online recruiting tends to attract individuals who are well educated, Internet savvy, and searching for higher-level positions (McManus & Ferguson, 2003). Online recruitment also attracts people born since 1980, who have grown up with computers and are therefore comfortable with obtaining information on the Internet (Zusman & Landis, 2002). A successful recruitment Web site needs to be user-friendly and easy to navigate, while attracting candidates to apply to an organization by clearly communicating the benefits of joining it.

The job seeker has little or no prior information about how to interface with the HRIS and has had nearly zero training opportunity with the HRIS. Therefore, the recruiting portal needs to provide ease of use and ease of access to up-to-date job information. The Web form that is used to collect applicant data must also be reliably entered into the appropriate fields within the company's HRIS database. This online recruiting activity will facilitate searches for new employees to fill existing and future positions.

Partner Organizations

The partner organizations to HR functions require certain information to complete their tasks. **Sourcing partners** such as Monster.com, Adecco, and most executive recruiting firms require information about vacant positions including a position description, job specifications, desired candidate competencies, potential salary range, and contact information. The information provided is limited to specific searches for open jobs and is updated as needed.

Business partners that are the recipients of decisions to outsource portions of the HR function (e.g., benefit management firms) or that facilitate process completion on behalf of the employee (e.g., banks) require information that is related to current employees. This requirement increases the need for accurate data, training, and specialized security assurances, as employee information is leaving the organization.

Important Data

As is evident in the above sections, each customer/user of the HRIS has slightly different needs with regard to what information he or she will be using. Some users simply input data and information, a few simply look at data and information provided in the form of reports, while a few others analyze the data and information to make decisions. What these users all have in common is that all the information is about potential and current employees with a focus on managing the organization's human capital to achieve strategic organizational goals. Specific data from the HRIS database fit into three categories:

1. Information about people, such as biographical information and competencies (knowledge, skills, abilities, and other factors)

2. Information about the organization, such as jobs, positions, job specifications, organizational structure, compensation, employee/labor relations, and legally required data

3. Data that are created as a result of the interaction of the first two categories, for example, individual job history, performance appraisals, and compensation information

HRIS Architecture

The HRIS "Dinosaur"

In the early days of HR applications (in the 1970s), large "dinosaurs" roamed the IT landscape. These were called mainframe computers and were primarily built by International Business Machines (IBM). These large systems hosted payroll applications for most enterprises. Users of the system, which mainly consisted of IT personnel and HRMS (human resource management system) administrators, executed large batch processes while directly logged onto the mainframe computer. Although access to the mainframe could be done via a desktop monitor, no processing was done locally. This architecture is commonly called a single-tier computing system—user interface, application processing, and data storage resided on the mainframe.

❖ **Figure 3.1** Two-Tier Architecture (Client-Server)

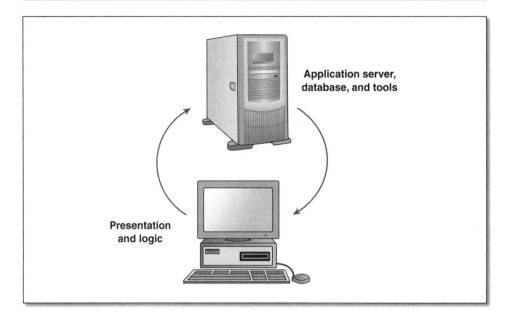

Application server,
database, and tools

Presentation
and logic

Two-Tier Architecture (Client-Server)

During the 1980s, it was discovered that many typical HR functions (such as employee benefits and recruiting) did not require the high-powered and expensive processing available on the mainframe computers. With the advent of the personal computer (PC), many of these functions could be reallocated to the local processing-power of the PC. By the end of the decade, HRIS software **vendors** such as PeopleSoft began using this power of PCs and created the client-server architecture (see Figure 3.1).

The purpose of client-server architecture was to spread out low-powered processing capability to the dozens of PCs now being used across an organization. High-performance applications such as Payroll would still be run in a batch process on the mainframe computer or outsourced to vendors such as Automated Data Processing (ADP). But day-to-day processing could be implemented on the PC. In this case, an HR application's logic or set of business rules would run on the local machine. Issues such as having valid data entries for hiring dates, home addresses, and name formats would be checked instantly by the PC, that is, without looking up the business rule at the server on the mainframe. Even more complex checks such as term of employment and salary deduction calculations could be done on the local PC. In addition, software applications could apply the more graphics-oriented user interface of the Windows environment. Ease of computer usage was a major factor that enabled individuals with a relatively low level of technology experience to use the applications.

This meant that the HR software application technology could be divorced from the database technology. This separation simplified the HR application and allowed enterprises to select the most appropriate database management system (DBMS) for their needs. (See Chapter 2 for an extended discussion of DBMS.) The most common database design is the relational model. This model standardizes how data are physically stored on the computer and provides standard data access via the **Structured Query Language (SQL)**. In fact, most software products are able to communicate to a variety of DBMS servers. This **2-tier architecture** was a huge leap forward in allowing HR professionals to serve many more employees—data were still located in a centralized database, but logic could be distributed to the PC that needed to run the specific application, and thus usability of the HRIS increased!

Three-Tier Architecture

Throughout the 1990s and into the current decade, this division of processing activity expanded from 2-tier to 3-tier and, finally, N-tier architectures. With a **3-tier architecture**, the servers have two roles—as database (DBMS) server and as **application server**(s) (see Figure 3.2).

With the development of the 2-tier and 3-tier systems, the HRIS professional still managed the user interface, but more demanding processing occurred in the middle, application server, tier. Products such as BEA's Tuxedo[1] transaction processor implemented transaction logic to maintain data reliability. For example, if two recruiters updated the same job position at the same time, a transaction processor would ensure that both updates were entered into the database. This allowed several users to access the central database simultaneously. This type of software, which performed tasks between the client and the database server, became known as **middleware**—software that managed data and transactions before they were saved to the database. There are a couple of drawbacks with both 2-tier and 3-tier systems. First, a large amount of information has to move from the client computer across the network to the server to execute database transactions quickly, which necessitates the use of significant **bandwidth**, or the ability to move lots of data quickly between computers. Second, the user

❖ **Figure 3.2** Three-Tier Architecture

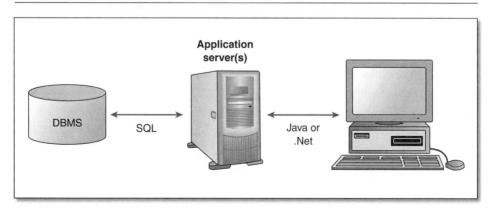

❖ **Figure 3.3** N-Tier Architecture

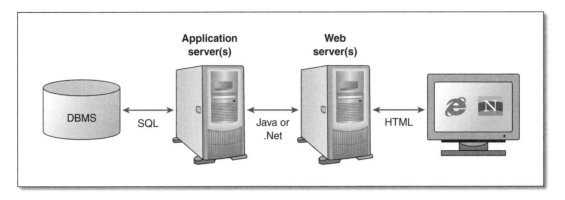

interface client needs to be installed (along with database drivers) on every PC needed to access the HRIS. The corollary issue of this requirement is that employees need to be trained on this application. Therefore, HRIS access tended to be limited to employees within the "four walls" of the enterprise, that is, only those residing within the local area network of the organization. Low-bandwidth access, such as Internet dial up, was impractical.

To provide for employee self-service, the Web browser was adopted to solve the above issues. The browser provides a "thin client" and is a relatively small piece of software requiring fairly small client computing resources, made possible by the 3-tier computing model. A "thick client" would require a significant-sized software product and computing power at the client location (as necessitated by the 2-tier model). An Internet Web browser comes installed on all major operating systems (Windows, Mac OS, Linux, and even Palm OS). The browser's user interface has become ubiquitous. Therefore, very little employee training is required to use a browser-based application. Finally, a browser works well in a low-bandwidth network environment. So now the typical HRIS application architecture looks like Figure 3.3.

A standard Web server, such as Microsoft's Internet Information Server (IIS) or Apache's Web server, manages communication between the browser and the application server using the **Hypertext Markup Language (HTML)**. The application server manages multiple user sessions logged onto the system at the same time as well as more complex business rule execution. And the application server also issues transactions to the centralized database server. Instead of just limiting ourselves to a 4-tier label, this architecture has been labeled N-tier for the following reasons:

- It is expandable to multiple Web servers and application servers to handle **load balancing**.
- Web servers can be geographically dispersed to provide worldwide access.
- Additional file servers can be added to save documents, reports, error logs, and so on, that are generated on a daily basis.

- Multiple print servers or specialized printers can be added as needed. For example, Payroll check printing requires a security-enabled toner called **MICR** (**Magnetic Ink Character Recognition**) to print encoded checks for bank cashing. These check printers can be physically located in a secure environment but connected to the HRIS N-tier architecture like any other printer.
- Additional "process schedulers" can be added to handle large batch jobs such as payroll cycles. These servers offload "heavy" processing from the main application server so that user interaction is not affected.

N-Tier Architecture With Enterprise Resource Planning

The architecture diagram becomes even more complicated when other ERP components are added. HRIS do not exist in a vacuum. They interact with other business operations within the company. For example, when Payroll is run, these financial-related transactions need to be registered in the company's General Ledger (GL) application. Typically, GL exists within the Financial/Accounting component of large ERP systems from SAP, Oracle, and Microsoft. Therefore, GL transactions must be interfaced between Payroll and these systems. So additional application servers and databases enter the picture, as depicted in Figure 3.3. In this figure, the Internet browser communicates (using HTML) to one or more Web servers. The Web server manages various client sessions to accommodate many users at the same time. The Web server passes requests to the application server, where the business logic for the application is executed. Finally, information is stored in the DBMS as in the 2- and 3-tier models. There exist many variations of this diagram: In some cases, databases can be shared (in this situation, HRIS is subsumed within the ERP system); in other cases, Internet technologies such as the **eXtensible Markup Language** (**XML**, which is similar to HTML) and Web services are used to integrate HRIS and ERP. The ultimate goal is to provide a **single data truth** so that all enterprise data can be accessed by all users wherever and whenever needed. Data should not be duplicated, reentered, or copied to multiple systems. ERP applications provide the infrastructure to avoid this problem. So even though the architecture may be more complicated, this complexity is hidden from the end user, and the logical view of the system remains relatively simple. For example, a consultant for a large IT services company can travel throughout the world, work with multiple clients, but still be able to record his or her time and prepare expense reports using a single browser application from any hotel room.

Security

Security ranks as a top priority for any HRIS. Security needs to be addressed to handle the following situations:

- Exposure of sensitive Payroll and Benefits data among employees
- Loss of sensitive personnel data outside the enterprise (such as the Social Security Number)
- Unauthorized updates of key data such as salary amounts, stock options (both quantity and dates), and so on

- Sharing of personnel or applicant review—comments to unauthorized employees
- Sharing data with external organizations and service providers, such as those described in the Recruitment, Payroll, and Benefits sections (below)

Security needs to be maintained at a variety of levels. First, physical access to the DBMS and application server needs to be limited so that machines cannot be destroyed or logged into directly. Network, operating system, and DBMS access must be limited so that tools outside the HR application cannot be used to query sensitive data. This includes hackers directing probes at the systems or using a variety of techniques to gain access. In the case of external users, special network access may need to be set up. A **virtual private network (VPN)** can be implemented so that users outside the company can log into the computing resources as if they were within the firewall. Alternatively, many HRIS applications provide specially built "portals" that enable Internet browser access to specific components of the system. This leads to segregation of users into different security categories.

All enterprise-level HRIS implement their own level of security on top of the operating system and DBMS. Typically, this security is administered via users and user roles. A user of the system is assigned a security role (such as Recruiter, Benefits Administrator, Manager, Payroll Administrator, or basic Employee). Then each role can be assigned to access certain parts of the system. Security can thus be limited or allowed along three dimensions—the role, the column, and the row of the HRIS database:

1. What menu items, links, pages, or screens can the user role access? For example, only the Payroll Administrator should be able to see links to the Payroll setup and execution processes. The average employee would not know that these pages exist.

2. Once on a particular page or screen, a specific user role may be able to edit or change certain fields. This is called **column-level security**. An ordinary employee, on the other hand, would be able to view only his or her own Job Title and Salary information and would not be able to change these values.

3. Also, within a particular page or screen, a specific user role retrieves only the data belonging to that user. This is called **row-level security**. For example, employees can view their own check stub history for prior weeks' payment. But they cannot access other employees' history. Row-level security supports **hierarchical access**—the greater the number of persons who report to an employee such as a manager or a supervisor, the more the quantity of data that becomes viewable. In some cases, managers may need to allocate bonuses across several departments. Employees can see only their bonuses, while managers can edit the bonus data of all employees reporting to them.

Within the typical corporation, the HR function exists primarily as support for the operational components of the corporation (Sales, Marketing, Procurement, and Manufacturing). In the same way, HRIS support the general ERP system operations. Employee information must be shared between Procurement and HR so that approval processes can be maintained. Employee data are also shared between Sales Force Automation and Payroll to determine commissions. There exist many other examples that demonstrate the need for HRIS to be integrated within the ERP. This heightens the need for security in the HRIS database because it is important to enable business processes that span information silos and eliminate data redundancy.

Best of Breed

An HRIS, as discussed in the previous section, exists as one of the main parts of an overall ERP software solution for the company. Yet the HRIS is not a monolithic solution even within HR business processes. There exist alternative software applications that solve specific HR business issues. This section addresses these types of solutions, the pros and cons of using multiple applications, and technical infrastructure. In general, an architecture that combines products from multiple vendors is called **"best of breed"** (**BOB**).

The most well-known example of this comes from the audio industry— surround-sound receivers combined with CD players, DVD players, high-end speakers, and even the occasional retro turntable. All these components "plug and play" with each other to provide the best possible sound experience. This architecture works because of the standards that have been established for decades that enable different devices to work together. We will see below that BOB software components for an HRIS still need to mature somewhat to reach the capability of the analog audio components. Yet the goal remains the same—deliver the best possible point solution to meet the business need.

For this synergy to work properly, three conditions need to be present for each software solution.

- First, there should be a perceived need for a specialized solution. For example, an **Optical Character Recognition** (**OCR**) program for paper resume scanning would not be needed if a company expects to receive electronic job applications, over the Internet, 90%+ of the time.

- Second, a universally agreed-on set of guidelines for interoperability must exist between applications. This exists at both the syntactical and the semantic levels. *Syntactical* refers to the base "alphabet" used to describe an interface. For any two applications to communicate, they will need to share data. This data exchange can be done with databases, simple text files (such as Excel), or, increasingly, XML. Basically, XML is similar to HTML, which is used in all Internet browsers. XML files can be shared or transmitted between most software applications today. XML presents a structured syntax—an alphabet—to describe any data elements within an HRIS. See the Technical Section at the end of the chapter for more on BOB architecture.

An HR example would consist of selecting the most robust HR software applications— regardless of vendor—for each need and then using the XML language to efficiently move data among those applications. This might consist of selecting the Resumix software for resume tracking, Oracle/PeopleSoft for the majority of HR applications and data management, Chronos software for time and labor tracking, ADP software for payroll purposes, and a proprietary vendor product for outsourced HR benefits administration.

• Third, applications need to "speak the same language." Just as the Roman alphabet allows the spelling of words in multiple different languages and formats, XML enables data to be described with many different tags. The semantics of the language need to map between software applications. An employee's data description may consist of Name, Address, Birth Date, Phone, Title, Location, and so on. If one of the applications does not have most of the same set of XML tags, it will not be able to exchange employee data. As important as the data semantics between applications is the business process semantics. For example, a time-keeping system may have a different definition of a pay period from the payroll application that actually prints employee checks.

If the above conditions are met, HRIS applications should be able to interoperate with many point solutions. What are the typical solutions found in an HRIS implementation? The following sections will detail examples of solutions for some of the HR programs in an organization.

Recruitment

The business process to recruit new employees for a company has many BOB opportunities. Large HRIS applications tend to focus on the internal hiring processes of the company—creating and approving job requisitions, saving applicant data, scheduling interviews, capturing interview results, and finally hiring the new employee. Yet there exist other software applications to "fine tune" the hiring process. OCR scanning applications can eliminate rekeying of applicant data from paper-based resumes, performing applicant database searches, posting job requisitions directly to Internet job sites, and running background applicant checks. These examples of specific functionality are typically not provided in an HRIS. See the Technical Section at the end of the chapter for details on how Oracle's alliance program provides value to enterprises using their recruiting solution.

Time Collection

Most companies require employees to submit time-keeping data each pay period. For hourly employees, this typically means using a punch card and time clock to track hours. Some solutions use employee badges with magnetic stripes to clock in and out. Again, most HRIS vendors do not provide the hardware needed to track time. Time-keeping systems will capture the hourly data from various readers throughout a site. Employee scheduling for various shift coverages can be implemented with time collection/planning software. For example, transit districts schedule bus operators to cover a very complex route system throughout the week. Unionized rules force certain break periods and preferences for senior operators. Driver schedules are posted for future pay periods; and actual hours worked, reported sick, taken as vacation time, and so on, are collected for prior pay periods. Such data will be reviewed each pay period prior to transmitting to the HRIS payroll application.

Payroll

In some cases, the entire Payroll process may be outsourced to another vendor, such as ADP. ADP specializes in providing payroll services for companies of all sizes. For some enterprises, the cost of maintaining a payroll application and staff in-house may outweigh the benefits of controlling the process. In this case, employee time data, pay rate, and benefit information would be transmitted to ADP for processing. This choice of using an outside provider is conceptually the reverse of the typical BOB motivation. The enterprise is not looking for the best technical or functional solution but for the lowest-cost provider of a commodity service. In the case of a large multinational corporation with lots of employee levels, it would probably be prudent to purchase the HRIS payroll application.

Benefits

Each year, most employers present their employees with what is called the Benefits Open Enrollment period. This is similar to course enrollment for students each semester. Instead of enrolling in courses, employees enroll for Major Medical, Dental, and Insurance benefits. For example, employees choose between health care providers such as Kaiser or Blue Cross for their medical insurance. These providers support interfaces with the major HRIS applications so that as employees log into the enrollment software, they can review offerings tailored to their company's plan. On selecting a particular insurance program, enrollment data can be transmitted to the provider.

As one can see in Figure 3.4, BOB solutions introduce additional complexity into the software architecture. This complexity adds IT expense in the form of new software licensing and/or programming charges. The justification for the added functionality needs to compensate for these additional costs. So a cost-benefit analysis should be performed by the HR function to determine whether the BOB alternative is to be used. Detailed procedures to compute a cost-benefit analysis are covered in Chapter 6.

In summary, BOB options can create a much more powerful solution than a stand-alone HRIS. The BOB alternative also creates system flexibility, as each application can be managed and upgraded independently. Yet this power and flexibility may end up costing the IT department, by giving rise to more complex systems administration issues.

System Implementation Process

A variety of authors, consultants, and others have discussed implementation methods for information systems. Rampton, Turnbull, and Doran (1999) discuss 13 steps in the implementation process. Jessup and Valacich (1999) divide the implementation of a system into 5 steps, with a focus on the systems side of the process. Regan and

❖ **Figure 3.4** Best-of-Breed Solutions Architecture

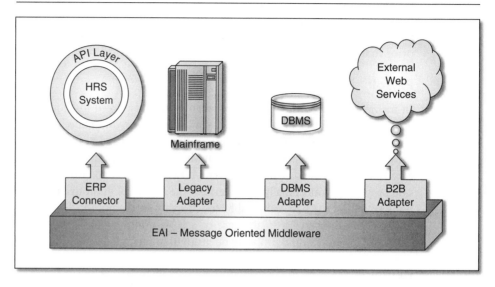

O'Conner (2002) provide 8 steps for implementing information systems. Some organizations have proprietary processes that they use for all implementations. Points to remember as this section is examined are as follows: (1) this is a process that will take a team of individuals anywhere from 6 weeks to 3 years to complete; (2) a variety of ways to manage this process may be attempted, so long as the key issues are examined and organizational goals for the implementation are achieved; and (3) there is no single definitive approach to be used in all situations.

Planning

The first key step is planning. This is an absolutely critical step in any business process and especially in the design of any large-scale software implementation involving multiple-process interfaces. Note that the planning process doesn't guarantee success—rather, it increases the probability that the implementation will be successful. The systematic examination of the following topics provides the organization with the opportunity to see how the implementation will work—to peer into the crystal ball—and identify some contingencies for implementation steps that might not go perfectly. In other words, a robust planning process provides a framework within which the implementation team can proceed, and it provides some decision-making parameters for any unforeseen difficulties that might appear (Bedell, 2003b).

The topics that need to be discussed during the various steps of the planning process include, but are not limited to, the following:

- Project Manager or Project Leader
- **Steering Committee**/Project Charter
- Implementation Team
- Project Scope
- Management Sponsorship
- **Process Mapping**

- Software Implementation
- Customization (Vanilla vs. Custom)
- Change Management
- "Go Live"
- Evaluation of Project
- Potential Pitfalls

Project Manager

The choice of project manager deserves some serious thought. There are really three good options for project manager. The first choice is to hire a consultant to be the project manager. This is the most expensive option and provides the best project management expertise but brings the least knowledge of your organization's mission, processes, and needs.

The second option is to hire a full-time project manager who has presumably been certified by the project management institute. This option is more affordable, although you must have plenty of projects to justify this position. A full-time position requires project management knowledge/certification and the project manager to have personal knowledge of your organization's mission, goals, and, to a lesser extent, HR processes.

The third option is to select someone who is involved in the project and temporarily move him or her into a project management role. This person should bring excellent knowledge of the organization's mission, processes, and needs. However, unless the candidate has a project management certification, he or she may not be the strongest choice to keep a project on time. This decision is largely about the trade-off between cost and existing organizational knowledge.

Steering Committee/Project Charter

While project managers are responsible for the project, they are often assisted with the planning and implementation process by a team of individuals known as the steering committee. The steering committee is usually composed of the project manager, the senior-management member who is the project sponsor, and the lead employee from each involved area (e.g., lead systems analyst, lead database administrator). Also on the steering committee are **HR functional experts**, whose role is to provide expertise about what HR data are needed, how the HR process maps should be interpreted, and what data are required for decision making.

The steering committee has three key purposes. First, this group works under the direction of the project manager to establish the project scope, which is then often codified through the development of a project charter document. A second role of the steering committee is to develop a change management plan. The third major role of the steering committee is to assist the project manager in decision making.

Once a set of preliminary planning decisions are completed, the steering committee may develop a document known as the project charter, which will help maintain the guidelines on how the project should function. The charter is an all-encompassing document that

- makes the case for the implementation,
- shows the project's connection to organizational goals and strategies,

- provides identification of project scope,
- identifies implementation team members,
- identifies additional expertise that might be available,
- provides a training plan,
- explains the agreed on decision-making process,
- discusses the process by which customization requests will be reviewed and acted on,
- covers the project management methods used,
- defines reporting,
- identifies deliverables, and
- defines political reporting relationships.

The project charter helps keep the entire team focused on the goals for the project by forcing the team to agree on what is critical. The project charter can also serve as a valuable political document within the organization, as some members of top management are usually asked to participate in developing the charter through an approval process or by helping draft the document. This approval process signifies to other, less involved management individuals that the implementation of this software is an expected organizational goal. Finally, the charter provides all the team members with key "talking points" about the project so that the scope, process, and goals can be clearly and consistently shared with those who might have questions. An example of a real steering committee's list of responsibilities is presented in Figure 3.5.

❖ **Figure 3.5**   Example of a Steering Committee's List of Responsibilities

- Decides issues that involve policies and dollar amounts under the charge of the Executive Sponsor Committee
- Resolves issues where there is no consensus within the functional implementation team
- Reviews and approves plan, approach, and key decisions
- Reviews project budget, agreeing on necessary funds, and champions availability
- Manages expectations and guides communications
- Ensures that appropriate resources are available to the project
- Recommends policy and advocates needed change; ensures that policies are carried out
- Reviews progress as it relates to implementation timetable
- Provides periodic reports and advice to the executive management team

SOURCE: This is from an HRIS implementation that was early and under budget—a rarity (M. D. Bedell, personal communication, 2002).

Implementation Team

The implementation team works with the project manager to complete the actual software implementation. A good **configuration** for the implementation team includes both functional and technical personnel. Functional personnel are usually drawn from the ranks of the HR department in the form of HR professionals with some technological proficiency. These functional experts are most often the power users, and they bring to the implementation team their extensive knowledge about HR processes as well as some technological skills. Technical personnel include HRIS specialists, systems analysts, database administrators, and hardware experts.

Ideally, the technical personnel will have more than just a passing familiarity with HR processes; however, it is most likely that the HRIS specialist will be interpreting the functional references of the HR functional experts into the technical language of the technical personnel. The implementation team reports to the project manager while working on project-related activities; however, it is very likely that a matrix organizational structure will develop for the duration of the project. In this matrix structure, the implementation team members continue to be evaluated by the regular supervisors, yet they also report to the project manager for project-related issues.

The lead implementation team members—both functional and technical—are usually also included on the steering committee, as described in the previous section.

As soon as the implementation team is chosen, two steps need to be taken quickly. First, the functional team experts should begin process mapping (see below). Second, implementation team training provided by the software vendor should be identified and scheduled by the project manager for the implementation team to attend.

Project Scope

Project scope is defined as those portions of the information system that need to be completely operational to satisfy the needs of the various customers, employees, and senior management. This definition of the scope of the project is absolutely critical to success. One difficulty that all steering committees face is project creep. Project creep occurs when decisions are made to implement additional functionality beyond what was defined in the project scope. The problem with project creep is that it may lead to huge cost overruns, a failure to complete the project on schedule, and then, in the rush to meet final deadlines, the delivery of a project that fails to meet the needs of the customers (see Sidebar 1).

Sidebar 1

One of the authors participated in an implementation where a midsized oil company changed their HR system from PeopleSoft to SAP to match the financial product they were using. They used a methodology to define the project scope (and avoid project creep) by asking all the HR professionals to spend a few days with them over a couple of weeks discussing what HRIS capabilities would be implemented. Capabilities were divided into categories of "mission critical," would "make our lives easier," and "in our wildest dreams." The "mission critical" items were of course implemented. The "make our lives easier" items were prioritized into three categories: (1) those that were added, (2) those that would be implemented if the project were ahead of schedule, and (3) those that could be implemented during the second phase. The "wildest dreams" category items were given to the IT folks to work on in the future as time allowed (Bedell, 2002).

Management Sponsorship

Management sponsorship of the implementation project is crucial. Senior management has the ability to add or remove budget dollars/resources as needed, move political hurdles out of the way, and facilitate the change management process through publicly demonstrated support for the project. Needless to say, the project manager and steering committee would be politically astute enough to develop and maintain an open, honest relationship with the management sponsor. A strong relationship with the senior management sponsor also reassures other senior managers that their employees are working. Remember, the implementation team usually consists of individuals from HR, Systems, Accounting, and potentially other functions. Their supervisors are not necessarily involved.

The senior management sponsor usually has a vested interest in the project. However, his or her formal acceptance as a project sponsor probably will not happen until the project charter is completed and the business case has also been made as to why the implementation should take place.

Process Mapping

The implementation of any new information system represents an immense change from the way processes and decisions were previously made. To facilitate that end, it is important to understand an existing process before starting any implementation. On the surface, this appears to be a rather straightforward task—simply flowchart the process and identify (1) the data elements that go into the process at each step, (2) how those data elements are stored and modified, and (3) what output exists. In reality, additional information and structure are required to ensure that the essence of the entire organizational process is captured.

The first step is to generate a list of all the processes performed by each area of the HR function and a second list of processes that are touched by more than one area of the HR function. For example, three processes of interest in the recruiting department are (1) bringing candidates in for interviews, (2) checking references, and (3) extending offers. The functional team experts would ask questions such as the following: Are these three processes or steps of one larger process? What data are required? Are there processes (or steps) that are completed by other departments that are critical? Does the compensation area do anything to help determine what an appropriate salary is? If it's a new position, does the organizational development group have to make a decision about how to place this position with regard to formal reporting and budgeting relationships?

The second step is to start generating a model of each process within the entire HR function. A successful model will incorporate both a flowchart picture and a dataflow model (i.e., what data elements, processes, and outputs go with each step of the process). One of the authors helped develop a template for an implementation he was previously involved with. This template is presented in Figure 3.6 and is designed to be used by any subject matter expert as a guide to mapping processes. The example in question requires the subject matter expert or functional implementation team member to provide the name of the business process, a description of the process, as well as the procedure. In addition, the person mapping this process is asked to provide

❖ Figure 3.6   Process-Mapping Template

Business Process/Function Description	Procedure Description

A. General description
    – Describe the business purpose
    – Provide a flowchart of the process
B. Customers
    – Who are the customers of the process (who needs the process completed)?
C. Group differences
    1. Does this process apply to different subgroups?
    2. Is the purpose different for different subgroups?
    3. Is the timing different for different subgroups?
D. Workload
    1. Frequency of the process (daily/weekly/monthly/ad hoc)
    2. Approximate elapsed time from start to finish of process
    3. Estimated total work hours of process
	A. Inputs
	    1. What kicks off the process? How do you know when to start?
	    2. What information do you need for the process?
	    3. What are the inputs to the process? What tools are used? (forms, worksheets, electronic information, etc.)
	    4. Are there any difficulties or complications getting the information?
	    5. Are the inputs different for different subgroups?
	B. Steps
	    1. How is the process performed (step-by-step)?
	    2. Are the steps different for different subgroups?
	C. Outputs

Input Inventory

What?			How?	Who?	When?
Form/input name	Form ID	Description	Paper/electronic?	Who supplies the input?	How much and how often?

Output Inventory

What?			How?	Who?	When?
Report/output name	Report ID	Description	Paper or electronic?	Who supplies the input?	How much and how often?

SOURCE: From Darter and Bedell (1997).

an inventory of the inputs needed as well as the outputs created by the process. In all cases, it is useful for the person completing the process to provide an example of each input and output.

The steering committee and implementation team that are interested in receiving the maximum benefit from this process will note that the process identification and mapping process provides information that is comparable with that which is used in many reengineering processes (Hammer & Champy, 1993). Much of the value of reengineering—as well as this implementation process—comes from taking a systematic look at processes and removing duplication of effort and processes that are no longer necessary. Of the implementations in which one author was involved, one implementation "accidentally" found cost savings as a result of this mapping process; another intentionally set time aside to ask these questions and found considerable duplication and potential processes cost savings; and a third implementation did not care to take the time (M. D. Bedell, personal communication, 2002, 2004; Darter & Bedell, 1997).

The completed process maps are ideally compiled into a large chart that provides an overall view of the organization's processes. The details of the processes can be stored electronically in an easy-to-access central storage location, and it is useful to have copies in binders that can be distributed during the software implementation and configuration process.

Software Implementation

Once the planning process is reasonably complete, the process-mapping process is nearly completed, and the implementation team has received most of their training, the actual software implementation can begin. This software implementation involves eight steps. Some of the steps go on concurrently, while some work in sequence. For example, the first step—hardware verification—must precede any software installation. Hardware verification consists of examining the specifications of the various software components (e.g., database, file server, compiler) and ensuring that the hardware can meet the needs of the organization now and in the near future. After the hardware is verified, the software installation process begins. Usually, an installer from the vendor works with the organization's technical professionals to install the ERP software and any related software tools. Note that this is also a training situation for the technical professionals as they work with the installer.

Data migration and configuration/**fit-gap** processes should also be ongoing. Data migration involves identifying which data should be migrated and how much historical data should be included, as well as the actual process of moving the data. The configuration or "fit-gap" process consists of systematically working through every HR process and matching each of those to each of the integral HRIS processes. The result is an understanding of where organizational processes and the software processes mesh (fit) and where they do not (gap). Any gaps that are identified need to be closed either through modification of organizational processes or by software **customization**.

The last step of the software implementation is system testing. In most cases, extensive testing is done while data are migrated, to verify data integrity. Data integrity means that the information is stored where it should be, that it can be queried, and that it is available to individuals with appropriate security clearance. The technical software team members test each module for proper functionality, and the functional HR team members verify that the module functions and maintains data integrity. For example, payroll modules have to be tested thoroughly to avoid double payments or missing payments and to make sure that checks print.

Throughout the entire implementation process, documentation of each action and decision must be recorded. This will provide the ongoing maintenance team with the roadmap to follow while they work on each new update, patch, security adjustment, or biannual legal change.

Customization

One of the most difficult decisions that many steering committees face is the desire to customize—especially since modern HR software comes with ample opportunity and excellent tools for customization. This decision appears to be simple. Customization will enable the software to match the organization's process more closely. The organization will have to do less change management training since all the screens and reports will look just like the old ones. The main downside to customization is that there will be significant maintenance costs, as every tiny change has to be customized all over again with each software upgrade.

With no customization, the version of the software to be implemented is referred to as the "vanilla" version. The advantage of a vanilla implementation is that it provides a catalyst for the organization to engage in **process reengineering** in order to develop best practices that will match the industry best practices that the software is developed around. The downside is that the cost of change management efforts will increase. Most steering committees will decide that truly unique processes that are related to organizational competitive advantage are worth customizing. To simply customize so as to replicate old reports or screens is usually determined to be not worth the cost. A good method to determine which modifications need to be done is to have the steering committee request a complete business case, including a cost-benefit analysis, from the person requesting the customization. The goal of the business case is to determine whether the modification will help the software manage mission-critical decisions well enough to justify the cost.

Change Management

Change management focuses on the most difficult part of the implementation process—the interaction between the user and the software. The major obstacle is to get user acceptance of the new HRIS. The introduction of this new system will typically encounter strong resistance from the employees. Thus, it is important that the implementation team develop a change management plan consisting of communication, education, and training to prevent and solve these issues. Failure to develop a change management plan may lead to morale issues, fear, and potential turnover among the workforce. Chapter 8 covers the issues of and solutions to the change management problem.

"Go Live!"

This is the moment of truth. It is time for the implementation to be put in place. There are two possible ways that the new software can be put to use. Option 1 is to do an immediate change, where the old software is turned off and the new software is turned on. As issues with the new software are identified, they are reported, and adjustments are made. The positive of an immediate change is that it is done! The potential negative of deciding to do an immediate change is that, regardless of training and the change management process, there is an organization-wide learning curve while the users adjust to the new software. There may be a period when customers may be served at a level that is less than expected. And—as illustrated by Hershey's choice to use this "go-live" option in 1999 on their distribution system—if there are significant problems, significant profits may be destroyed as well. In Hershey's case, they could not deliver $100 million of inventory to stores during the Halloween sales season (Koch, 2002).

The second option is a parallel change. This option turns the new software on some period of time before the old software is to be turned off, and it incorporates final system testing into the changeover process. The time period in question is usually a meaningful business cycle to the organization (e.g., a month or a quarter). During this time, both software systems are functioning, receiving input, running reports, being queried. The positive of a parallel change is that there is enormous testing that goes on before the old software disappears. The negatives are that the users will hang on to the old software because it is comfortable and that there will have to be dual data entry performed for every task.

Regardless of which option is chosen, it is absolutely critical that appropriate support for training and software be in place. Many of the larger HRIS products employ context-sensitive help modules that rely on the end-user training materials to remind users of what they previously had learned. The user should also have access to helpdesk staff, who are aware of the change and able to help the user get through a variety of tasks.

Evaluation of Project

Every project provides an opportunity to learn something about what might have been done better. Any organization that plans to maintain a large information system should begin to collect regular data about what worked, what did not work, and where potential areas for improvement exist. A specific schedule of measurement or identification of milestones and related reporting should be created during the planning process and adhered to rigorously. Measurement milestones could be weekly, quarterly, or attached to each major step in the implementation process. In addition, a dollar value should be assigned to each critical step so that budgets can be assessed and evaluated. The emphasis here should be on measurement of important business metrics; this topic is covered in Chapter 6.

Potential Pitfalls

A comprehensive list of what might go wrong during an HRIS implementation would be woefully incomplete. Instead, some of the most common pitfalls are reiterated here:

- Poor planning
- Incomplete steering committee or steering committee without top management support
- Implementation team problems or incomplete implementation team
- Failure to adequately assess the politics of the organization
- Insufficient process mapping
- Scope creep
- Poor implementation of or insufficient change management

Summary

This chapter attempts to provide a snapshot of all that must be understood to successfully manage an HRIS implementation. The first discussion focuses on knowing the users/customers of the HRIS and organizational goals. Next, the three main categories of HRIS data are enumerated. A comprehensive list would be ideal but was omitted here as the list would stretch for pages and would undoubtedly still be incomplete. From these three components, parameters can be identified so that implementation planning may begin.

The next major section of the chapter discusses various hardware configurations, from the legacy "dinosaur" system to the contemporary N-tier architecture with BOB opportunities. In addition, the XML language is described to demonstrate that it is possible to assemble an outstanding HRIS and even an ERP system without relying on a single vendor.

The chapter concludes with a general discussion of the steps that one might take to plan and implement an HRIS. A brief discussion of the need to document and learn from the implementation for organizational learning purposes was included. In addition, some mention of metrics is provided, as the HRIS implementation team should be able to prove that they met their goals in terms of budget, functionality, and usability.

DISCUSSION QUESTIONS

1. Identify the various types of users/customers of an HRIS.

2. What are the three broad categories of data that an HRIS manages?

3. How does network bandwidth affect a 2-tier client server architecture?

4. How does an N-tier architecture simplify IT departments' task of maintaining client software?

5. Discuss row-level security. How does this work? Why may this be more valuable to an HRIS than a manufacturing software solution?

6. Research various middleware products from IBM, BEA, or Oracle, and discuss how these products can be leveraged in an HRIS.

7. Given the role of **enterprise application integration (EAI)** products in supporting BOB solutions, how could these products be used to integrate with other ERP components (Financials, CRM, etc.)? (See the Technical Section of this chapter for an explanation of EAI products.)

8. Research hr-xml.org. How many transactions or interfaces do the standards support? How many software vendors are involved with the organization?

9. Take a specific industry, say the K-12 education industry. How might HireRight's integration with PeopleSoft/Oracle assist the process of hiring employees such as bus drivers, janitors, campus security?

10. When might BOB not be "best"?

11. The systems development process has been discussed by many. Name five discussion topics that need to be completed during the planning process.

12. Discuss the different project manager options and explain the pros and cons of each.

13. What is a project charter? Why is it important?

14. Why is it absolutely critical to have the scope of the project identified?

15. Why is project creep not a good thing?

16. Complete a flowchart of the process you follow to enroll in classes and pay your tuition. Then apply the process template in the section System Implementation Process.

17. Why do employees fear change? Give some examples as to how you might eliminate the fear of change.

CASE STUDY: VIGNETTE REVISITED

This case is revisited with some additional information that involves the understanding of the material in this chapter. The additional information will be added to the situation described in the vignette at the beginning of this chapter.

A billion dollar retailer with 4,000+ stores finds that it cannot move fast enough to beat the competition. The organization's senior management arrives at the conclusion that it would be easier to achieve the strategic goals enumerated by the board of directors if the various organizational functions would share information. Shared information would enable them to develop and deploy new actions and tactics more quickly. The CEO and the President have therefore ordered the major functions to immediately update their information systems so that data sharing is possible. The senior vice presidents (SVP) of accounting and human resources immediately decide that the only solution is to jointly decide on an ERP product. ERP software applications are a set of integrated database applications, or modules, that carry out the most common business functions, including human resources, general ledger, accounts payable, accounts receivable, order management, inventory control, and customer relationship management. To speed the installation along, they will install it using a rapid implementation methodology that a company down the street used. The goal is to have the new systems operational in 9 months.

Shortly after this decision has been made, the SVP of HR calls you into his office and tells you that you will be management sponsor for this project. You have to decide on everything. You sit back in your nice office and think,

> *What's the problem with this scenario? It shouldn't be difficult to select a vendor and then borrow the methodology from down the street. It worked for them, it should work for us! We'll call a few vendors in the morning and find out about cost, time frame, and implementation methods. In the meantime, I should find out a little more about how to do this and who will be using it. I remember from my information systems class in college that this is a reasonable first step when it comes to buying software.*

What do you think your response would be to this inquiry? As you go through this chapter's material, keep this vignette in mind and see if your answer changes.

New Information for the Case: Part 1

After some discussions with department heads from all the departments in the organization, you realize that there are a large number of people (stakeholders) who will be affected by the new systems. Furthermore, you come to realize how important HR data really are to these stakeholders. Based on this information, you think, *Wow, there are far more people who could be potentially using this information system than I expected. The old textbook and the vendor information should provide a lot to think about!*

Using the information from the section of this chapter titled HRIS Customers/ Users: Data Importance, please answer the following questions:

1. Identify some of the customers who would be logical members of the implementation team and explain why.

2. Think through an HR process and sketch out what data are necessary to complete your sample process well. How much history does the organization need to convert to continue functioning?

3. Pick one area of the HR function (e.g., recruiting), and make a list of processes that will need to be mapped and possibly reengineered during this implementation.

New Information for the Case: Part 2

Over the next month as you continue to obtain information about the design and implementation of the new system, you are still somewhat confused about what to do. Once again, we find you in your office thinking,

> *There are so many potential decisions to make with regard to hardware! I wonder what we need to schedule, if we need to buy hardware, and how we should configure the servers to ensure maximum security. It's time to make another list of questions!*

Based on the information in the section of the chapter titled HRIS Architecture, please respond to the following:

1. Make a list of questions for each of the following individuals: lead hardware technical expert, network manager, and chief software manager.

2. What configuration should the company use? Make a suggestion and support it!

New Information for the Case: Part 3

As part of your investigation, you have uncovered a system concept called "best of breed." You are in your office again trying to decide what to do, and you think, *Perhaps best of breed might be the easiest and best way to go.*

1. Make a recommendation as to whether a BOB option should be chosen or a more standardized option with simpler interfaces between hardware and software should be elected.

2. Think about what the best answer should be when you have to connect your system with accounting and finance. Make a recommendation and support it!

New Information for the Case: Part 4

You have just sat down in your office feeling as if there is way too much to do! Your IS software professional has given you the information from one of the potential vendors about the various steps that need to be taken in implementation of the HRIS. Your immediate reaction is *Man am I going to be at work late for the next many months!*

Based on the information in this chapter, answer the following questions:

1. Develop the first few steps of the project plan.

2. Discuss the potential political necessities outlined in this section as they relate to this type of implementation.

3. Think about and create a list of steps that make sense for your organization.

4. Is the 9-month rapid-implementation time frame feasible? Or will it just lead to failure?

TECHNICAL SECTION

Best-of-Breed Architecture

The software "Plug and Play" standard is called eXtensible Markup Language (XML). XML is a tagged language very similar to HTML. Whereas HTML has a very well-defined (and somewhat limited) set of tags, XML can be extended to include any tag set. Note the tags in the following Recruitment Open position (used to hire a DBMS administrator).

Data can be shared between software applications by passing XML (either over the Internet or via files) to each other. Some service providers, such as job services, have further refined the XML standard so that common tag and document structures are used between applications (even from different vendors). The XML tags can be thought of as the alphabet, and various industry or process standards as the language. Once a group of people agree on an alphabet and a dictionary, one can spell as many sentences as needed! A specific example of a language is HR-XML (www.hr-xml.org). The HR-XML Consortium provides a standard set of XML tags so that multiple HR applications can exchange data sets more easily. A full description of XML is beyond the scope of this text.

In natural-language conversations there occasionally exists a need for a translator. This person acts as a bridge between the two individuals communicating. This same situation exists between software applications, because even if the two applications adhere to the same standard (language), there is typically only an 80% to 90% actual match (think of natural-language dialects of the English language). In the computer world, the role of the interpreter is played by specialized software called middleware. More specifically, enterprise application integration (EAI) software will act as a communication hub between multiple application spokes. Think of EAI as a traffic controller that not only routes XML data but also translates the XML tags between HR applications. (See Figure 3.7.)

❖ **Figure 3.7**   eXtensible Markup Language (XML)

```
<?xml version="1.0" encoding="UTF-8" ?>
- <PositionOpening xmlns="http://ns.hr-xml.org/2006-
02-28" xmlns:xsi="http://www.w3.0rg/2001/XMLSchema-
instance"
xsi:schemaLocation="http://ns.hr-xml.org/2006-02-28
PositionOpening.xsd">
-    <PositionRecordInfo>
-    <Id validFrom="2003-12-01" validTo="2003-12-31"
idOwner="ABC Company">
    <IdValue>Order#123456</IdValue>
     </Id>
    <Status validFrom="2003-11-10" validTo="2003-11-
30">Active</Status>
</PositionRecordInfo>
-    <PositionPosting>
-    <Id validFrom="2003-11-10" validTo="2003-11-20"
idOwner="XYZ Job Board">
    <IdValue>Posting-EN345678</IdValue>
    </Id>
    <Title>Database Administrator-English</Title>
</PositionPosting>
-          <NumberToFill>1</NumberToFill>
</PositionOpening>
```

Alliance Programs

Most of the major HRIS software companies (Oracle, SAP, Microsoft) invest in alliances with other independent software vendors (ISVs). The primary goal is to provide a total solution to make both vendors' products more attractive and effective for their customer base. A secondary goal for the HRIS vendors is to create an "ecosystem" of solutions that can compete more effectively with other HRIS applications. The larger the ecosystem or number of partners in a program, the bigger the footprint the HRIS application will have. A side effect is that the HRIS provider appears to be more "open" from a technical perspective. In fact, Oracle, SAP, and Microsoft are actively selling their technical integration capabilities (middleware) alongside the HR applications.

Oracle has more than 100 partners focused on just HR alone within their alliance program (Refer to www.oracle.com for details.) In many cases, these partners have pre-built integrations that are delivered to joint customers. Oracle offers a validation program that verifies whether the interfaces work as promised. Tom Herrmann, Vice

President, ISV Management and Programs at Oracle, states, "Oracle recognizes the need to provide key services that have been validated to work with our HR applications. This provides a higher level of quality and faster implementation times to our customers" (personal communication, 2007). Let's examine the "Attract to Onboard" recruitment process. One specific Oracle partner provides a unique service for recruiters. Most companies employ background checks for potential employees during the recruitment process. HireRight (www.hireright.com) provides this service for employers—including criminal record checks, employment/education verification, motor vehicle records, drug screening, and so on. Hiring managers and recruiters may select a background

❖ **Figure 3.8**   Oracle Alliance Program Illustration

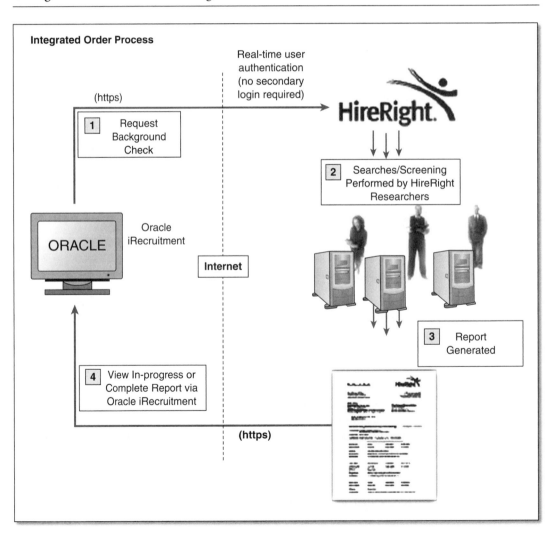

check for applicants directly from within the PeopleSoft eRecruit and Talent Acquisition Manager or Oracle iRecruitment products. According to John Reese, Marketing Director at HireRight,

> This combined solution has helped organizations to get more return on investment from their recruitment application and take advantage of today's most streamlined process for safe hiring. The pre-integrated screening solution from HireRight creates a seamless Recruiting → Screening → Hiring process for users of the recruitment application. (personal communication, 2007)

Once the check is complete, the user is notified and can view the screening results from within the recruitment application. Since this is all done from within the HRIS application, users benefit in that they do not need to learn additional software applications to complete tasks related to the hiring process. At a technical level, Oracle and HireRight leverage the HR-XML standard to exchange information. Executed in "real time," this solution improves the efficiency of the candidate selection process. This program flow is depicted in Figure 3.8.

NOTE

1. BEA is a large software company located in Silicon Valley. Tuxedo is their flagship product to manage high-volume data. See www.bea.com/framework.jsp?CNT=index .htm&FP=/content/products/tux&WT.ac=topnav_products_tux

REFERENCES

Adamson, L., & Zampetti, R. (2001). Web-based manager self-service. In A. J. Walker (Ed.), *Web-based human resources* (pp. 24–35). New York: McGraw-Hill.

Bedell, M. (2002). *A PeopleSoft to SAP conversion/implementation.* Unpublished research notes.

Bedell, M. (2003a). *An identification of the cost savings resulting from an HR information system implementation.* Paper presented at the meeting of the American Society of Business and Behavioral Sciences, Las Vegas, NV.

Bedell, M. (2003b). Human resources information systems. In H. Bidgoli (Ed.), *The encyclopedia of information systems* (Vol. 2, pp. 537–549). Burlington, MA: Academic Press.

Darter, K., & Bedell, M. (1997). *Process mapping template.* Unpublished research notes on a PeopleSoft ver. 7.0 implementation.

Fein, S. (2001). Preface. In A. J. Walker (Ed.), *Web-based human resources* (pp. vii–x). New York: McGraw-Hill.

Hammer, M., & Champy, J. (1993). *Reengineering the corporation: A manifesto for business revolution.* New York: HarperCollins.

Hendrickson, A. R. (2003). Human resource information systems: Backbone technology of contemporary human resources. *Journal of Labor Research, 24*(3), 381–394.

Jessup, L., & Valacich, J. (1999). Information systems foundations. In L. Jessup & J. Valacich (Eds.), *Que Education & Training* (pp. 4–10). Indianapolis, IN: Macmillan.

Koch, C. (2002). Hershey's bittersweet lesson [Electronic version]. *CIO Magazine.* Retrieved June 18, 2008, from www.cio.com/article/31518

McManus, M. A., & Ferguson, M. W. (2003). Biodata, personality, and demographic differences of recruits from three sources. *International Journal of Selection and Assessment, 11,* 175–183.

Miller, M. S. (1998). Great expectations: Is your HRIS meeting them? *HR Focus, 75,* 1–2.

Rampton, G. M., Turnbull, J., & Doran, J. A. (1999). *Human resources management systems: A practical approach* (p. 142). Toronto, Ontario, Canada: Carswell.

Regan, E., & O'Conner, B. (2002). *End-user information systems: Implementing individual and work group technologies* (pp. 26–28, 368–369). Upper Saddle River, NJ: Prentice Hall.

Stone, D. L., Lukaszewski, K. M, & Isenhour, L. C. (2005). e-Recruiting: Online strategies for attracting talent. In H. B. Gueutal & D. L. Stone (Eds.), *The brave new world of eHR.* San Francisco: Jossey-Bass.

Walker, A. J. (2001) Best practices in HR technology. In A. J. Walker (Ed.). *Web-based human resources* (pp. 3–12). New York: McGraw-Hill.

Zampetti, R., & Adamson, L. (2001). Web-based employee self-service. In A. J. Walker (Ed.), *Web-based Human Resources.* New York: McGraw-Hill.

Zusman, R. R., & Landis, R. S. (2002). Applicant preferences for Web-based versus traditional job postings. *Computers in Human Behavior, 18,* 285–296.

PART II

Determining HRIS Needs

4

HRIS Needs Analysis

Bradley J. Alge

Karen Bruner Upright

EDITORS' NOTE

This chapter begins the section of the book focused on how to determine the needs for an HRIS and how that determination affects the design of the HRIS. The idea that there will be different users of the HRIS with differing data and information needs was introduced briefly in Chapter 3. In this chapter, you will see the importance of the initial **needs analysis** and how it is done. The authors emphasize that the needs analysis begins the process of HRIS design but that it is also done continuously throughout the system design process. This notion of continuous updating of the needs analysis recognizes the possibility of both potential organizational and technology changes during the development and implementation of the HRIS. In addition, it is important to complete an accurate and comprehensive needs analysis because this will provide the blueprint for the evaluation of the HRIS after it is implemented.

CHAPTER OBJECTIVES

The learning goals for this chapter are listed below. At the end of this chapter, you should be able to address the following questions:

- ♦ What is a needs analysis, and why is it important?
- ♦ What is phase containment, and how does it relate to a needs analysis?

- ◆ Where does a needs analysis fit within the broader scope of an HRIS project?
- ◆ What are the "Big 3" questions?
- ◆ What's involved in an HRIS needs analysis? What types of activities are performed?
- ◆ Who is typically involved in an HRIS needs analysis?
- ◆ What are the key deliverables of an HRIS needs analysis? Related to this question, what is a gap analysis, and what might a gap analysis report look like?
- ◆ How would a gap analysis be used in the needs analysis?

VIGNETTE

Failing to plan is planning to fail.

A multimedia company planned to offer a special benefits package to a select group of employees. The purpose of the package was to encourage some employees to retire early, which would provide cost savings to the company as well as meet some of its other needs, such as providing promotional opportunities to help attract and retain younger employees. The special package included granting additional years of service for purposes of calculating retirement and retiree medical benefits, granting additional age to employees to be used in the calculation of eligibility for early retirement incentives from the pension plan, and eliminating some portion of the normal reductions for early retirement in pension plan benefits. The cost of implementing these changes in the existing system for the estimated eligible group of just over 500 employees was prohibitive due to the complex nature of the calculations involved.

The project was in danger of being canceled until a careful needs analysis was done. For 500 employees, did the solution need to be fully automated? Did employees need to be able to model their retirement benefits on the Internet? How much manual work could be relied on to handle the work load? Did the project need to be repeatable?

The answer for the multimedia company was to build a simple solution outside its HRIS using spreadsheet and word merge applications and to couple that simple solution with a high-touch customer service group who were able to respond to the needs of program participants, manage the increased manual paperwork requirements, and perform the interventions into the system to make the components that had to be automated, such as the payment of benefits, function properly. The program that had nearly been canceled was a success, so much so that it was repeated just the next year in another company division.

Implementing the changes in the existing HRIS would have been the obvious solution, but creating a one-time solution where it appeared there would be little future need for a complicated implementation was the right choice in this case. Careful, honest, and practical needs analysis made possible what had been impractical due to cost concerns. It should be noted, however, that the HRIS provider recognized the need the multimedia company had expressed and later made a decision to augment its software to include features that would provide greater flexibility for future offerings, meeting a need the provider hadn't recognized during its own original planning and needs analysis phases.

Introduction: HRIS Needs—Planning and Analysis

In this chapter, the focus is on a critical set of activities that takes place early in the life cycle of an HRIS—namely, the planning and analysis of an organization's *HRIS needs.* An HRIS needs analysis usually takes on a particularly prominent role in the planning and analysis stages of an HRIS development project, prior to significant design and implementation activities. It is important to note, however, that the needs analysis for the HRIS continues through the entire system development process since each stage in the process could lead to the identification of new needs for the HRIS.

Successful HRIS implementations are critically dependent on planning. In turn, successful planning is critically dependent on a comprehensive needs analysis. Consider some of the potential costs of not planning and conducting a thorough needs analysis:

- Users reject an HRIS that fails to provide the functionality they need.
- Vendor software packages are selected based on incomplete, inaccurate, or irrelevant criteria.
- Costly custom systems are developed and built based on arbitrary data.
- Custom additions to the HRIS are required to fill needs after implementation that were not properly identified during the needs analysis.
- Scope creep: New, but unneeded, functionality is erroneously added to the system increasing the time and cost of implementation.

Consequently, planning and needs analysis are not something that HRIS project personnel choose to do; it is something they must do. *Needs analysis* refers to the process of thoroughly gathering, prioritizing, and documenting an organization's HR information requirements and serves as a necessary input for the subsequent design and implementation of an HRIS. The following sections in this chapter provide a road map for conducting a needs analysis. As a beginning, planning and needs analysis will be described as phases within the **system development life cycle.**

System Development Life Cycle (SDLC)

This description of the SDLC is similar to the description of the system implementation process in Chapter 3. However, the focus in Chapter 3 was on the implementation phase of an HRIS project, whereas the focus here is on the completion of an accurate HRIS needs analysis within the SDLC. The overlap between these chapters is deliberate since the specific details on both needs analysis and implementation are complementary and represent two important parts of the development and design of an HRIS.

Scholars and practitioners may disagree on the number of steps and terminology used in describing the SDLC, but most would agree that the following activities take place at

❖ **Figure 4.1**   An Example of the Phases in a Typical System Development Life
Cycle (SDLC)

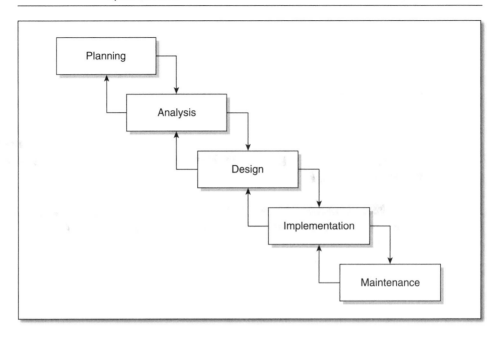

various stages throughout the conceptualization and ultimate implementation of any
technological system: planning, analysis, design, implementation, and maintenance. These
activities are formally codified as a set of five distinct, yet related, phases (see Figure 4.1).

1. *Planning:* The planning phase of the SDLC includes both long-range or strategic planning and short-range operational planning. Because of the integral nature of needs
   analysis to planning, we devote an entire section to planning below.

2. *Analysis:* It is in the analysis phase that an organization's current capabilities are documented,
   new needs are identified, and the scope of an HRIS is determined. Again, because needs analysis is such an integral part of the analysis phase, we devote an entire section to analysis below.

3. *Design:* In the design phase, the "blueprint" for the system is finalized. Whereas the
   analysis phase finalized the needs or requirements for the HRIS, here the detailed specifications for the final system are laid out. It is often here that the final vendor evaluation and selection occurs. (This topic is covered in detail in the next chapter.) It is also
   here that business process reengineering, or the redesign of HR work processes, occurs
   and the final specifications of the system and its HR functionality are defined. Design
   is covered more extensively in the next chapter.

4. *Implementation:* Implementation is where the HRIS system is built, tested, and readied
   for actual rollout or "go live"—the point in the SDLC where the old system is turned off
   and the new system is put into operation. Key steps in this process include coding or
   configuring modules, system testing, finalizing procedures, converting old data for use
   in the new system, and training end users.

5. *Maintenance:* The SDLC does not end once the "go live" date arrives. The maintenance phase, sometimes referred to as the "forgotten phase" (Smith, 2001), is that phase in the life of an HRIS where the primary objective is to prolong the useful life of the HRIS, and it begins once the new system is put into operation. As such, a crucial part of maintenance is the evaluation of the HRIS. Does it meet the needs of all users as determined during the earlier phase of the SDLC? Has it been accepted by the users? Is the HRIS being used properly?

In addition, maintenance has four other important functions:

1. Maintenance is also corrective—to fix something that is broken or not functioning properly (e.g., computer bugs, misinterpreted designs, misspecified designs, or identified needs ignored).

2. Maintenance can also be adaptive; that is, changes are implemented such that the HRIS changes to meet the changing demands of the environment within which it operates. For example, new government regulations affecting HR practices such as racial and gender discrimination can prompt new requirements or alter old requirements of the system.

3. Maintenance can be perfective; that is, some maintenance is designed to tweak or improve on the existing system. For example, a more efficient routine that speeds up processing times could be developed in the maintenance phase.

4. Finally, some maintenance is preventative. For example, a growing company may need to expand its hardware storage capacity to accommodate the growth in new employees and employee record-keeping requirements. Such a maintenance action will prevent future system crashes due to inadequate hardware. Regardless of the type of maintenance, a careful assessment of need is required to ensure an efficiently run maintenance function.

Having briefly reviewed the SDLC, the remaining discussion of this chapter focuses on needs analysis. Although needs analysis is important throughout the life of a project, it is particularly important early in the project—in the planning and analysis phases. Although the focus here is on planning and needs analysis in these two early phases of the SDLC, the feedback loops in Figure 4.1 are meant to depict the continuous and iterative nature of planning and needs reanalysis. Thus, the concepts discussed in the planning and analysis phases can be applied or revisited at any point in the SDLC.

Planning

As mentioned above, planning can be divided into long-range or strategic planning and short-range, operational planning.

Needs: Long-Range Planning

Long-range planning for an HRIS examines the "big picture" of an organization's HR function and its information needs in light of its overall business strategy. Consider Sony Corporation's strategic vision in the 1950s (from Collins & Porras, 1996):

> Fifty years from now, our brand name will be as well known as any in the world . . . and will signify innovation and quality that rival the most innovative companies anywhere . . . . "Made in Japan" will mean something fine, not something shoddy. (p. 76)

If this is a company's guiding vision, how does this translate into a directive for the HR function? That is, to achieve the above vision, HR plays a pivotal role and the HRIS should be supportive in every way possible of HR's role.

A hypothetical extension of Sony's vision to HR might entail wording similar to the following: "We aspire to attract, develop, and retain the best and brightest human capital in the world by becoming an employer of choice." This statement of purpose provides a foundation on which all future HR decisions are based. When questions of need arise, the vision provides the barometer against which these needs can be assessed. For each "need" one can ask, will this particular functionality better enable our organization to attract, develop, or retain the best and brightest? Will it help us in our effort to be an employer of choice? If the answer is not a resounding yes, then that particular "need" becomes less of a priority. If the answer is yes, the need for that functionality carries strategic importance.

When considering long-range planning for HRIS needs, what time frame are we talking about? Typically, long-range planning looks beyond the present usually focusing on needs in the future 1, 5, and 10 years from now. Rapid change in technology or market competition can make planning that far in advance difficult. Consequently, long-range planning is something that is revisited annually. That is, each year, the HRIS planning team meets to assess changes and new developments in the HRIS landscape (e.g., what new technologies have entered the market), as well as the strategic environment (e.g., changes in industry, government regulations, competition), that might necessitate a change in course. Planners ask, has anything changed that would alter our long-term direction?

Planners gather information on the environment and weigh that information against their organization's strategy. Based on this assessment, they may develop a comprehensive case for change in which they lay out the reasons why the organization must take action regarding its HRIS. In particular, planners will examine the immediate future needs of the organization by identifying projects that should be examined for possible execution in the upcoming year. At the same time, these planners will also examine the status of existing projects to determine whether such projects should continue. In essence, this planning team not only sets the future direction of a firm's HRIS but also serves as a quality control group for existing and future HRIS projects. That is, they ensure that the projects are on time, on budget, within scope, and, importantly, fulfilling their intended goal in support of the organization's strategy.

One of the critical quality control functions the planning team must enforce is the concept of **phase containment**. That is, organizations should identify problems as early as possible in the life cycle of a system and, importantly, deal with those problems at that time rather than allowing the problems to continue, possibly leading to greater, more costly rework and modification later. Phase containment is a quality control principle that should guide all HRIS projects.

Y2K: A Colossal Failure of Phase Containment

The phase containment concept can be summed up with the phrase, "Pay a little now, or a lot later." Back in the early days of computing, applications were coded in such a way that only a portion of the date was stored (the last two digits; e.g., 1967 was coded as 67). The purpose of this coding procedure, at the time, was twofold: convenience (it was easier) and efficiency (it took up less valuable storage space). However, designers of the systems in the 1960s and 1970s knew that eventually systems using the truncated date function would have to be modified to reflect the year 2000 and beyond. If no changes were made to legacy systems built on the old date algorithms, it was predicted that there would be serious errors to any function that relied on a date calculation. In HR systems, for example, every existing employee hired prior to the year 2000 would have a negative tenure with their companies. A report on years working with the firm of an employee hired in 1990 would show -90 years (00-90 = -90)—a nonsensical output.

This and the countless other applications relying on date functions cumulatively became known as the *Y2K bug*—a bug that the experts insisted needed a fix, and futurists and alarmist media were predicting doom and gloom if not fixed properly (see, e.g., Peterson, Wheatley, & Kellner-Rogers, 1998). In response, organizations invested billions of dollars in the 1990s in an effort to assess the scope of their Y2K problem and develop a strategy for fixing it. In some cases, organizations saw the fixes as so expansive and so costly that they opted instead to implement an entire new Y2K-compliant system altogether—a multimillion dollar proposition for large firms. Others opted to fix their legacy systems or pay others (i.e., consultants) to do it for them. Many consulting firms became richer by specializing in Y2K audits and consultation.

How could this costly problem have been avoided? The answer lies in the discipline of phase containment. The problem was not only a result of initial legacy systems; many replacement custom systems simply replicated or converted the old programming logic without fixing it.

The key to phase containment is to create a culture wherein "mistakes are okay." Importantly, however, mistakes need to be detected and dealt with immediately.

Discussion Questions

In light of the Y2K example above, answer the following:

1. Why is adherence to the principle of phase containment so difficult? Why is adherence so important?
2. Why do you suppose so many organizations were vulnerable to the Y2K bug?
3. What processes, procedures, and safeguards can you implement in your organization to ensure phase containment?

Needs: Short-Range Planning

Short-range planning typically involves a needs analysis of the organization, but with a much more immediate focus—for example, over the next 1 to 2 years. Here, specific projects are evaluated and selected for commencement, continuation, or possible termination.

Typically, the long-range plan will identify a list of priorities or priority systems and projects for the future. The long-range plan sets budgets and allocates resources to those priorities by officially sanctioning projects. Short-term planning, therefore, refers to the planning of specific projects to be implemented in the near future following the guidelines established by the priorities in the long-range plan. In many instances, functional departments within an organization may compete for a limited pool of resources. For example, Finance may wish to implement a new financial planning system, Marketing may wish to implement a customer relationship management system, Manufacturing may wish to implement an inventory, scheduling, and material requirements system, and HR may wish to implement an HRIS. In addition, there may be competing projects and priorities for the HRIS within the HR department. For example, there might be competition for limited dollars to implement employee self-service functionality versus a need for a computer-based state-of-the-art performance management system.

What should guide such decisions? The answer lies in building a strong case for change by developing a compelling need for change and a solution that provides a strong return on investment (see Chapter 6 for a detailed discussion of this topic). When needs are identified to a point that a new or modified system is necessary, a systems investigation planning process needs to begin. To accomplish this planning, a systems investigation team will need to be formed and develop a plan. This team is typically small, headed by a functional leader or owner (e.g., HR manager), and supplemented with other expertise in the organization (e.g., HRIS and IT professionals). The **system investigation** involving short-term planning culminates with a business case report or system investigation report.

Systems investigation planning focuses on a specific system to be implemented in the short term. The steps involved in systems investigation planning include the following:

- Form a team—who specifically should be on the project.
- Identify at a high level the critical business needs that a system would need to satisfy.
- Complete scenario analysis: Identify potential solutions—the team is not selecting a system yet, but rather, gaining knowledge of the solutions that exist.
- Complete a feasibility analysis in terms of a cost-benefit analysis.
- Develop a tentative scope and schedule for viable scenarios.
- Estimate the return on investment (ROI) for viable scenarios.
- Complete a system investigation report with specific recommendations for action.

Eventually, the project steering committee that typically includes top management or those individuals controlling the resources will approve one or more projects. They will also have to make difficult decisions on whether current projects should continue (see phase containment above). For each project that is approved, a project team is formalized for the management of the project. Usually this core team is the same team that was involved in the system investigation and building the case for change. Some members may leave and new members will join a project team, but this core team will ideally form the basis for the execution of the project through the remaining phases of the System Development Life Cycle.

The Big 3: The Global Positioning System of HRIS

A simplification of the complexity of the planning and needs analysis can be accomplished by reducing the entire process to three general questions that must be answered. The questions, referred to here as "The Big 3," are as follows:

1. Where are we now?
2. Where are we going?
3. How are we going to get there?

Like a global positioning system (GPS) in your automobile, these questions provide the navigational direction for an HRIS project. Throughout an HRIS development process, these questions will be asked at varying levels of breadth and depth. First, to understand where you are going, you must know where you are now. That is, you must know the details of your current situation. For example, asking the question "Where are we at?" should spawn additional questions and answers regarding an organization's capabilities. Of course, simply knowing where "you are now" is not enough. Knowing where you are at will provide information to determine how far you need to go. In other words, you need to know where you wish to be—what future state you envision for your HR function and how an HRIS will fit into that planned destination. Finally, the question of "How are we going to get there?" bridges the "gap" between where your organization currently is and where it desires to be.

As noted, each organization might have a different way of describing their SDLC, but regardless, each specific SDLC will include planning, analysis, design, implementation, and maintenance. Answering the "Big 3" questions provides a road map throughout the life cycle of your HRIS—a mental map and physical description in a report that can be used to assess whether or not your system is on track.

Consider the recent implementation of Systems Applications and Products in data processing (SAP) HR at Purdue University—an institution with more than 19,000 employees spread across a main campus and several regional campuses. Coined as "OnePurdue," this project began with in-depth planning and analysis phases to document the existing systems and their limitations, and importantly, identify the critical functional and technical needs of the organization moving forward. The question of "Where are we going?" was guided by the OnePurdue project's guiding vision: *To transform the University's way of doing business into a flexible and user-centric portfolio of applications that integrates all Purdue enterprise data, information, and processes.*

A number of guiding principles can be drawn from this vision. First, the status quo is problematic as evident by the felt need to "transform." The existing systems were a hodgepodge of disparate systems, often developed within Purdue University using outdated hardware and software. Even getting access to data and information proved problematic. Second, future systems were required to be focused on users. This heavy emphasis on involving users, understanding their needs, and building usable technologies was paramount. Third, the future state of a new technology needed systems that were integrated. All information was to be unified into a central repository with real-time updates—that is, regardless of point of entry, information will be immediately updated and stored in a central repository and, thus, would be immediately available to all users. Users, in this future state, would be able to quickly and easily access information. Moreover, confusion over how to get the data or even where to go to get the data would be eliminated.

The above analysis of strategic vision ("Where are we going?") helped Purdue identify its needs in greater detail and select a system that best met its needs. This information served as critical input for the selection of an enterprise-wide resource planning system (ERP). Purdue chose SAP(www.sap.com/company/index.epx) as its primary software vendor for HR applications. The SDLC continued once SAP was selected following SAP's ASAP (Accelerated SAP) methodology—a road map that documents the "who, what, where, and when" for an ERP implementation (see the SAP Web site for details on ASAP). Figure 4.2 shows the ASAP process at OnePurdue and the steps that occurred.

❖ **Figure 4.2**   ASAP Process at OnePurdue

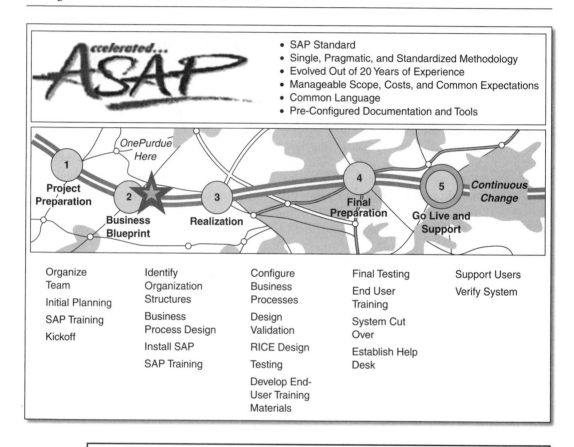

Student Challenge

Compare and contrast the generic SDLC in Figure 4.1 with the ASAP process used in the OnePurdue project in Figure 4.2. What is similar? What is different?

The Big 3 questions are not asked only one time and then ignored. Rather, the Big 3 should be revisited on a regular basis. Moreover, the Big 3 can be applied at any level of analysis—be it long-range planning and needs analysis or short-range planning and systems investigation planning. The culmination of a systems investigation process is the approval or rejection of a system proposal. If approved, the project launches into the analysis, design, and implementation phases (see Figures 4.1 and 4.2). Like the planning phase, the analysis phase is a critical step in flushing out the capabilities and needs of the organization going forward.

Analysis

The purpose of the analysis phase is to take a project that has been approved in the planning phase and

- meticulously dissect and document the organization's current capabilities, including existing data, information, systems, and work flows so as to gain a thorough and accurate understanding of an organization's current capabilities;
- thoroughly identify and prioritize needs—both current and future needs;
- conduct a gap analysis to identify critical functional and/or technical gaps between what the organization needs to do versus what it can currently do;
- revisit the feasibility analysis based on what is known about existing and desired systems and potential solutions; and
- determine the potential usefulness of the results of the gap analysis in developing a **request for proposal (RFP)** for vendors.

Detailing Where We Are

Part of analysis involves a thorough **current analysis**—developing a detailed understanding of the organization's current capabilities and limitations and, thus, answering in precise detail the question "Where are we now?" This is difficult for a single person or a small team to do alone. Indeed, a great deal of effort must be put forth in this part of the analysis phase. To accomplish the current analysis, the project team will likely increase in size. Recall that in the planning phase, a small core team is formed to conduct a systems investigation and develop a case for change. Once the project is approved and moves to the analysis phase, more personnel and resources will be needed. New people will be added to the core project team and may remain a part of the team beyond implementation. Other personnel may be brought onto the project on an as-needed basis. Figure 4.3 shows a reverse hourglass in terms of the amount of effort, and thus people, needed relative to the point in the HRIS project.

As can be seen, planning typically involves fewer resources as the project is in its infancy and may not yet have been officially sanctioned by the top management. As the project moves into analysis, design, and implementation, the amount of resources needed (e.g., employees, consultants) increases.

To conduct a proper analysis, an organization needs to identify methods of data collection and sources from which the data will be collected.

Common methods of data collection include the following:

- Interviews
- Focus groups
- Surveys and online tools
- Organizational archives

Interviews are particularly useful for getting at rich sources of information. That is, consistent with information richness theory (Daft & Lengel, 1984), when one wishes to

❖ **Figure 4.3** Reverse Hourglass: Effort/Resources Required for HRIS Project

develop a deep understanding of a situation, rich, two-way communication serves that purpose. Project leaders will need to develop a list of interviewees—people with expertise in functional or technical areas—and develop an interview schedule. A drawback of interviews is that they are time-consuming. For this reason, careful thought should be devoted to selection of interviewees, such that a large amount of valuable information can be obtained from a relatively small pool of experts. Interviews also enable project team members to develop relationships with key users and identify potential change agents or change champions—line-level employees who will serve as project liaisons to the wider organization.

In addition to interviews, focus groups provide another rich way to gather detailed information on current systems. An advantage of focus groups is that you can involve many more people in the data-gathering effort, increasing the likelihood of a more thorough analysis. Also, research shows that the more involved people are in a project, the more they are willing to feel as though they own the system and, thus, the more willing they are to accept the system when implemented. Focus groups, therefore, increase the odds of acceptance by involving more people in the analysis process. Of course, focus groups can be problematic as well. Focus groups require more time just for scheduling meetings and, thus, more coordination than individual interviews.

Surveys and online tools are an excellent way to assess the needs of an organization in a timely and efficient manner. Moreover, such methods can be applied to as many individuals in the organization as you want, with little additional cost. That is, surveys and online tools are cheap to administer and can reach many people quickly, thus enabling the project to receive input from a large percentage of the affected population. The downside of surveys is that they do not offer the opportunities of rich two-way exchanges that interviews and focus groups can provide. Moreover, surveys can be vulnerable to social desirability and other biases. Ensuring anonymity of responses can help alleviate some of these concerns.

A number of groupware systems are available that support online surveys as well as other decision-support diagnostics. For example, both *ExpertChoice* and *Advantiv* are software vendors and application service providers that provide software and services to firms looking to evaluate their system needs (see www.expertchoice.com, www.advantiv.com). Users can input needs, which can then be organized, prioritized, and voted on; that is, the user community can rank the importance of particular needs. Likewise, users can rate various vendor packages for their ability to meet particular needs. Such a tool provides a centralized system for gathering user input.

Finally, analysts can use archival methods by examining existing documentation and records. Examples of documentation include current system screens, reports, and forms. Organization charts, policy manuals, exit interviews, and performance data can also be useful in this analysis. By analyzing this information, the HRIS project team will have a better grasp on the overall business and the types of information it collects.

In addition to data-gathering methods, it is important to identify and enlist critical sources or targets of the data-gathering initiatives. These sources can both provide information on the current system as well as participate in identifying current and future needs. Sources include the following:

- HR functional experts—manager of employment recruiting and selection
- Job experts—job analysts and compensation specialists
- Technical experts—HRIS and IT professionals
- End users—including employees and nonemployees, such as customers
- Top management—individuals and teams involved in business decisions
- Consultants and other business partners

In selecting sources for input, there are certain important things to keep in mind. First, what is the level of expertise of the source? You would certainly want to have people with functional or technical expertise. People with specific knowledge of the firm who have been with it for a long period of time can contribute useful insights. However, employees with longer organizational tenure can be some of the more difficult people to accept the change to a new HRIS. Thus, involving them in the analysis can go a long way toward getting their buy-in for the project. There may also be benefits in having a few new or inexperienced users involved in the process. Such sources often do not have any strong interest or bias in a particular system and, thus, are not protective of the current system. Moreover, having people from different jobs with a diversity of job knowledge and experience participate helps ensure that the system that is developed and implemented will serve everyone's needs. Finally, hiring consultants is often worthwhile as they can bring an objective, independent perspective on a firm's needs. In particular, consultants—because they work with many clients—have a good grasp of the HRIS market, including emerging trends and best practices.

The information that is gathered and documented includes, but is not limited to, an inventory of current HR modules comprising computer programs and applications (e.g., software used in recruiting new employees), current outputs (e.g., reports and screens), **data flows** (e.g., where data are generated, where they are processed, where they are stored), data structures and definitions (e.g., what data fields are stored, how they are organized and linked), technical architecture (e.g., hardware, systems software, application software), and work processes or work flows (e.g., business process maps of how work currently gets done).

Figure 4.4 provides an example of an inventory of modules in a hypothetical system. A detailed understanding of current work flows provides a mechanism through which one can assess the efficiency and effectiveness of how work is currently being performed. During the design phase, organizations will attempt to redesign inefficient work flows. Obsolete work flows or those that no longer add value to the organization can be eliminated. In Figure 4.5, for example, a current work flow for processing a payroll is illustrated. Although this is useful information in its own right (e.g., communicating to a new payroll clerk how things work), it provides an opportunity to reanalyze the process and look for inefficiencies. For example, in the current process in Figure 4.5, there are multiple manual processes that are HR intensive and, consequently, prone to human error (e.g., data entry error). Indeed, the Hackett Best Practices Benchmark Study of Human Resources estimates that every HR transaction that occurs costs an organization $17 (as reported in Howes, 2002). Thus, data entry errors or unnecessary transaction steps that occur can greatly increase the cost of the HR module for processing payroll.

In sum, documenting the current system provides a baseline against which needs, to include opportunities for savings, can be identified and assessed.

Student Exercise

Suppose an organization has 10,000 employees that must be paid every other week. Also, suppose that the process for paying employees currently follows the process detailed in Figure 4.5.

1. What steps can be streamlined or eliminated? How (i.e., what might a new and improved process look like)?

2. Using the $17 per transaction estimated by the Hackett Survey, how much can you expect to save your organization every payroll run, based on the improvements you've made to the payroll process? How much can you expect to save annually? (Assume that every step in the process equals a transaction; thus, every person paid entails multiple steps or transactions.)

3. Based on your analysis, would you recommend a new process?

❖ **Figure 4.4** Hypothetical Example: Inventory of Current HR Applications/Modules

Inventory of Modules for Current HR Applications

Functional Area	Module ID	Module Descriptions	Manual/ Computerized	Entry/ Interface	Sourcing	Platform	Vendor (if purchased)	Owner
Staffing – Applicant Management	ST000110	Applicant Resume Scan	Computerized	Auto-generated	Vendor Purchased	Sun Solaris Server	Appli-trac ®	Staffing Manager
	ST000120	Applicant Batch Entry	Computerized	Auto-generated	Vendor Purchased	Sun Solaris Server	Appli-trac ®	Staffing Manager
	ST000120	Applicant Tracking/Update	Computerized	Ad hoc/User	Vendor Purchased	Sun Solaris Server	Appli-trac ®	Staffing Manager
	ST000130	Person-Job Matching	Computerized	Ad hoc/User	Vendor Purchased	Sun Solaris Server	Appli-trac ®	Staffing Manager
	ST000140	Applicant Reporting Menu	Computerized	Ad hoc/User	Vendor Purchased	Sun Solaris Server	Appli-trac ®	Staffing Manager
	ST000150	Requisitioning/ Job Analysis	Computerized	Ad hoc/User	Vendor Purchased	Sun Solaris Server	Appli-trac ®	Staffing Manager
	ST000210	Selection Assessment Module	Computerized	Ad hoc/User	Vendor Purchased	Sun Solaris Server	Appli-trac ®	Staffing Manager
	ST000220	EEO/AA Compliance	Computerized	Ad hoc/User	Vendor Purchased	Sun Solaris Server	Appli-trac ®	Staffing Manager
	ST000310	On-boarding Management	Computerized	Ad hoc/User	Vendor Purchased	Sun Solaris Server	Appli-trac ®	Staffing Manager
Employee Tracking	ET000110	Add New Employee	Computerized	Ad hoc/User	Made In-House	Sun Solaris Server/C#		HR Manager
	ET000120	Update/Change Employee Info	Computerized	Ad hoc/User	Made In-House	Sun Solaris Server/C#		HR Manager
Performance Management	PM000110	Employee Performance/ History Sun	Computerized	Ad hoc/User	Made In-House	PC/IBM (Excel Spreadsheet)		Line Manager
	PM000120	Employee Evaluation	Computerized (Word Processor)	Ad hoc/User	Made In-House	PC/IBM (MS Word)		Line Manager
Training & Development	TD000110	Course Management Maintenance	Computerized	Ad hoc/User	Made In-House	Sun Solaris Server/C#		Training Manager
	TD000120	Class Management Maintenance	Computerized	Ad hoc/User	Made In-House	Sun Solaris Server/C#		Training Manager
	TD000130	Training Program Maintenance	Computerized	Ad hoc/User	Made In-House	Sun Solaris Server/C#		Training Manager
Payroll	PY000100	Bi-Weekly Payroll API	Computerized ASCII File to Vendor	Auto-generated	Made In-House	Sun Solaris Server/C#		HRIS Manager
	PY000200	Bi-Weekly Payroll Batch Run	Computerized	Auto-generated	Outsourced	n/a	EasyPeople Pay ®	HRIS Manager

❖ **Figure 4.5**   Sample Work Flow for a Legacy Payroll Process

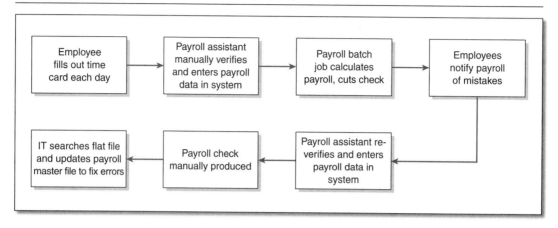

Detailing Where We Need to Go

Knowing how your organization currently operates and its capabilities and limitations is a good starting point for a needs analysis. However, developing the needs for the future—that is, answering the question "where do we want to be" in detail—is the heart of a needs analysis. Some HRIS scholars draw a distinction between a needs analysis and a **business requirements definition**. Ceriello and Freeman (1991), for example, argue that needs analysis focuses on an organization's current needs, whereas a business requirements definition focuses not only on current needs but also on future needs. Here, we use needs analysis and business requirements definitions interchangeably. They both refer to that point in analysis where an organization determines and documents its current and future needs. These needs become the targets or goals that the new system will attempt to satisfy.

One point of caution: Both *needs* and *requirements* are strong words in the sense that they imply something that the organization, and therefore the HRIS, *must have*. It is important to recognize that as needs are being identified, a process should be put into place to prioritize needs. This will result in a list of needs that fall along a continuum from high-priority or critical needs, those that definitely will be built into the system, to medium-priority needs, which are likely to be included, to low-priority needs, which may be incorporated if time and resources dictate.

Many of the same people who were involved in identifying the current system can also be used to identify future needs. However, it is always wise to bring in additional people who can bring a fresh, unencumbered perspective. In decision making, for example, using a stepladder technique that adds new people to provide fresh new insights at different phases in the project can prove useful for reaching better decisions (Rogelberg, Barnes-Farrell, & Lowe, 1992).

Gap Analysis

The culmination of a needs analysis is the gap analysis, the process of documenting and comparing the current state of the HRIS with the desired future state based on needs

❖ **Figure 4.6**   Hypothetical Gap Analysis Report for a Training Function

Function	Currently Have	Requirement	Priority	Gap
1. Manager access and enrollment online to courses, dates, and location		✓	3	Mod
2. Tracking of courses taken and production of training profile	✓	✓	4	
3. Fully online		✓	4	High
4. Ability to link with development module and core module to permit cross-comparisons with developmental plans and current job location, department, and EEO data		✓	3	Mod
5. Course content available (not just title)	✓	✓	3	
6. Ability to link participant evaluation data to internal course and external seminar tables		✓	3	Mod
7. Online registration facility with ability to maintain employee status		✓	4	High
8. Automatic linkage to facilities/classroom records for scheduling, allocating equipment, etc.		✓	4	High

that are not being met with the current system. In essence, gap analysis brings the two previous activities together (where we are now and where we are going) and provides a communication tool by which to see where the current system falls short in meeting future needs. Figure 4.6 provides an example of a hypothetical gap analysis for several capabilities within an HR training function. As can be seen, a list of functional requirements appears down the left-hand column. For each requirement, the gap analysis identifies if the organization currently performs that function. Also, priorities are assigned to each requirement. Gaps are where there is a requirement not currently being met, and the gap is classified (high, moderate, low) based on the priority of the requirement.

A gap analysis tells us what important needs are not being met with the existing system as well as those that are being met. A gap analysis is an important decision tool for HRIS project leaders. For one, it helps answer the question, does our current system enable us to meet our critical needs? Or, are there sufficient gaps in our ability to meet our current needs? Assuming that there are significant gaps, the gap analysis becomes a critical document for selecting a new solution going forward. If an outside vendor will be used to help develop and implement the HRIS, a gap analysis will be included in an organizations'

❖ **Figure 4.7**   The Big 3 Needs Triangle Relating Analysis and Design

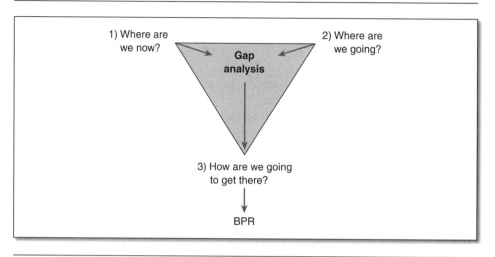

NOTE: BPR, business process reengineering.

RFP,[1] sent to competing vendors. In this regard, the gap analysis serves as a communication device—informing potential vendors of your firm's critical needs—needs that their vendor system will need to fill in order to be in contention for ultimate selection.

Importantly, the gap analysis may reveal needs that the current system does meet. However, just because the current system can meet the current needs, it does not imply that it is the best system for meeting current needs. As organizations move forward in their designs (see Chapters 3 and 5), they will ascertain the best way to meet future needs and design their systems accordingly. Figure 4.7 depicts the Big 3 triangle generated by the Big 3 questions and it summarizes the analysis process and links it to the design process. Specifically, in analysis we compare the current system (where we are at) with the envisioned future (where we are going) and create a gap analysis that identifies gaps and prioritizes needs. This information becomes critical input into the design of the new system—that phase in the HRIS project that answers the question "How are we going to get there?"

As we conclude the needs analysis and move toward designing and implementing an HRIS, let's summarize some of the critical questions or challenges in the analysis phase that the HRIS project team will need to address:

- Who should determine what our needs are going forward? That is, who should be involved in the needs analysis, and what processes are in place for prioritization?
- How can we ensure that all of our needs are identified?
- How can we be sure to exclude "needs" that might unnecessarily expand our scope, thereby threatening the schedule and cost of the project? That is, how do we limit the scope to the things we truly need?
- Is it feasible at this point to implement a system that can meet our critical needs?

DISCUSSION QUESTIONS

1. What are some critical success factors for effectively conducting an analysis of HRIS needs?
2. What is the difference between long-term and short-term planning in terms of an HRIS?
3. What is phase containment? Why is it so important? How can you ensure its adherence in an HRIS project?
4. How does analysis (including needs analysis and gap analysis) relate to later phases in an HRIS project (i.e., designing and implementation of an actual system)?

CASE STUDY: "PLANNING THE NEEDS OF OTHER ORGANIZATIONS"

If you think a thorough, high-quality needs analysis is daunting on an internal project, imagine if you are an HRIS vendor, and your job is to provide a "best of breed" system (see Chapter 3) that meets most of your many different clients' needs. Such an approach makes planning and needs analysis more challenging because difficult choices must be made as to the functionality that is sufficiently broad to go into a general market package. It is costly to vendors, and indeed may be infeasible, to include functionality that is so specific that only a small portion of its client base benefits from the function.

On the other side of the coin is the difficulty firms face when shopping for a vendor, or the critical question they must ask, "Will this system meet my needs?" As a general rule of thumb, it is wise to adhere to the 75% rule—that is, if a package can meet approximately 75% of your needs, that is pretty good. In this case, the advantages of a package begin to outweigh the disadvantages. When a package falls below the 75% rule, an organization is left with a system with significant functional gaps that will require costly custom patches or manual work-arounds, defeating the purpose of a vendor system in the first place. A needs analysis, therefore, is critical to addressing the question: Is there a vendor-packaged system available that can meet at least 75% of my business needs?

Consider the following hypothetical company, Benefast Partners, that provides a specific market niche HRIS product, benefits administration software. Their challenge: Provide comprehensive benefits administration software that meets the needs of a growing and complex benefits marketplace. According to Davis Hunter, a former employee of Benefast,

> Benefast Partners (name changed to protect confidentiality) was only doing defined benefit pension plans for large employers (20,000+ employees). When you focus your business opportunities on *Fortune* 100 companies, it limits your potential for growth to small and mid-size markets. Given that there is competition in the market for small, medium, and large clients, there was no real way to expand. We were, however, doing 401(k) retirement plan administration both on our proprietary system, designed and marketed for large employers, and on a purchased platform for smaller companies. We had interest from existing 401(k) clients to take on administration of their defined benefit plans and we felt we had lost 401(k) business in the past because we didn't offer total retirement outsourcing, just 401(k).
>
> It wasn't possible to charge small employers the kinds of fees necessary to implement their plans on our proprietary system, so our efforts centered on what could be done with the purchased system used for small to mid-size 401(k) plans. We quickly determined that the purchased system's defined benefits platform wasn't sophisticated enough from a calculation standpoint to handle most of the complexity of defined benefit plans, so we

decided to use a combination of the purchased system with the calculation engine component for the proprietary system.

We had a lot of needs analysis conversations with our colleagues in another office who were running the project. Given the multiple platforms involved, processing time was a huge concern. We decided to segment the market and only serve those customers who met a fairly stringent set of requirements. Basically, we built a system based on clients whose plans are easy to administer. In other words:

1. No multiplan clients
2. No retirement modeling
3. No coordination of benefits (no combination 401(k)/db plans)
4. Limited Web interface

So based on this segmentation, we launched our new product with one of our parent companies (a bank). By the time we had signed our third client, we had already begun to move towards a fairly complex multiplan environment. Our fourth and fifth clients were even more complex. We were over budget and off schedule on everything and then we started trying to figure out how to do coordination of benefits. We built a system for plans that were easy to administer—but plans that are easy to administer are few and far between in the marketplace and those that exist aren't typically shopping benefits vendors.

Case Study Questions

1. How would you evaluate Benefast Partners' strategy?
2. What changes (if any) would you make going forward?
3. What methods would you employ to ensure that an HRIS package meets the majority of your clients' needs?

NOTE

1. The RFP process is described in detail in Chapter 6.

REFERENCES

Ceriello, V. R., & Freeman, C. (1991). *Human resource management systems: Strategies, tactics, and techniques.* New York: Lexington Books.

Collins, J. C., & Porras, J. I. (1996, September/October). Building your company's vision. *Harvard Business Review,* 65–77.

Daft, R. L., & Lengel, R. H. (1984). Information richness: A new approach to managerial behavior and organization design. In B. Staw & L. L. Cummings (Eds.), *Research in organizational behavior* (pp. 191–234). Greenwich, CT: JAI Press.

Howes, P. (2002, February/March). ROI for an HRIS business plan. *IHRIM.link,* 12–15.

Peterson, J. L., Wheatley, M., & Kellner-Rogers, M. (1998). The Y2K problem: Social chaos or social transformation? *The Futurist, 32*(7), 21–28.

Rogelberg, S. G., Barnes-Farrell, J. L., & Lowe, C. A. (1992). The stepladder technique: An alternative group structure facilitating effective group decision making. *Journal of Applied Psychology, 77,* 730–737.

Smith, J. (2001, February/March). Knowledge transfer: The forgotten phase. *IHRIM.link,* 49, 53.

5

System Design and Acquisition

Richard D. Johnson

James H. Dulebohn

EDITORS' NOTE

Building on Chapters 3 and 4, this chapter focuses on the design and acquisition of an HRIS. Thus, the focus of this chapter is on the "design" phase of the systems development life cycle (SDLC), as illustrated in Figure 4.1. The authors differentiate between the logical and the **physical design** of an HRIS, as well as emphasizing the differences between the data and process views of a computer system. As will be discussed in this chapter, these differences are critical for the effective design of an HRIS that will meet the needs of the various stakeholders of the system, that is, HR and IT professionals, managers, and employees. Data flow diagramming is discussed as a tool used to analyze the process design characteristics prior to the actual physical design of the HRIS. In addition, the three choices or options that organizations face when moving into physical design are examined. All the effort involved in completing an accurate and comprehensive logical and physical design of the HRIS helps ensure that the acquisition of the system will be done properly. The chapter concludes with a discussion of the development of a Request for Proposal (RFP) and how to evaluate proposals received from outside vendors.

CHAPTER OBJECTIVES

After completing this chapter, the reader should be able to

◆ Understand the difference between the data and process views of a system

◆ Understand the purpose and components of the data flow diagram (DFD)

◆ Understand the hierarchy of DFDs and the concept of DFD balancing

◆ Understand the three choices or options that organizations have when moving into physical design

◆ Understand the purpose of an RFP and what information should be included in it

◆ Understand the various criteria used to evaluate vendor proposals

◆ Describe the various types of feasibility and their purpose in evaluating potential solutions

VIGNETTE

Larson Property Management Company is one of the largest property-management companies in California, with over 1,000 employees. The company provides a full array of commercial management and development services. These activities include complete management services for commercial office and retail buildings and apartment complexes; the construction, repair, and maintenance of commercial properties; and financial management and billing services for commercial real-estate clients. The company has experienced significant expansion over the past 5 years in response to the growth in apartment and commercial construction in southern California, and this has resulted in the need to hire a large number of employees on an on-going basis to staff its operations.

Larson Property Management has depended on a legacy HRIS to manage its applicant and employee databases. The system runs on a client-server computer system. The system was implemented approximately 10 years ago prior to the rapid growth of the company and when the organization had less than 100 employees. The system functionality is limited to the storage and retrieval of employee and applicant data. For recruiting purposes, the system requires a clerk to manually enter basic applicant data and whether or not an offer has been made for employment. Prior to this, applicants' files were passed around to those who reviewed the materials and were sometimes misplaced, and trying to locate a particular applicant was often a problem. The current HRIS has limited file storage capability for applicant and employee records and currently has reached the storage capacity.

Larson Property Management has decided to replace its legacy HRIS. One application module in the new HRIS that the company wants is a sophisticated applicant-tracking system (ATS). The primary objective of the ATS will be to provide a paperless hiring process. The basic functionality of the new system will be managing the requisition and approval of job openings; the ability to store resumes and job applications and retrieve the names of applicants who match job requirements through query functions; the ability to track a candidate's progress through the recruiting and selection process; and automated reporting functions. The company's managers also want an e-HR functionality that includes Internet posting of job openings through the company's Web page and external job-posting services, application and resume submission through the Web and through kiosks at their office locations, staff ability to access and use the system remotely through a Web browser, and online resume-and application-scanning capabilities.

Part of the design phase is modeling the processes that will be used in the system for applicant tracking. For Larson Property Management, this will allow the system analysts to design an efficient paperless hiring process.

Case note: As you read this chapter, keep this situation at Larson Property Management in mind. It will be the basis of the case analysis at the end of the chapter.

Introduction

> *Never tell people how to do things.*
> *Tell them what to do and they will surprise you with their ingenuity.*
>
> —General George S. Patton

The goal of this chapter is to provide a deeper understanding of the process through which an HRIS is designed and acquired. This design and acquisition of an HRIS is but one phase in a larger system development process. As noted in previous chapters, the larger development process is called the Systems Development Life Cycle. As seen in Chapter 4 (Figure 4.1), the five generic phases of the SDLC are planning, analysis, design, implementation, and maintenance. This chapter focuses on the design phase by briefly discussing the role and features of structuring of a system's requirements through process system modeling, where analysts use **data flow diagrams (DFDs)** to model the business processes that the system will use to capture, store, manipulate, and distribute data, and the options facing the HR department as they move into design. Next, the vendor-management relationship is covered, including the creation and use of a Request for a Proposal (RFP), evaluation of vendor responses, and choice of a vendor or vendors. Finally, the chapter ends with a discussion of the HRIS feasibility criteria.

Design Considerations During the Systems Development Life Cycle

As discussed in previous chapters, the SDLC is a structured set of phases focused on the analysis and design of information systems. The goal of the SDLC is to provide those organizations updating existing systems or designing new ones with a stronger, more structured process to follow. A 2004 report by the Standish Group (2004) provides evidence that as the use of structured development techniques is increasingly practiced, system quality improves. At the same time, this report also found that less than 30% of systems projects are successful and more than 50% deliver late and are over budget. Given the wide variety of program needs in the HR department, such as recruiting, selection, training, performance management, and compensation, and the complexity of these needs, the importance of following a structured approach to the development of an HRIS cannot be understated.

Although each phase in the life cycle is important, the goal of this chapter is to specifically focus on the activities associated with design of the HRIS, which can be separated into a logical and a physical design. The design phase is separated into two components because the **logical design** of a system focuses on the translation of business requirements into improved business processes, irrespective of any technological implementation. For example, a business requirement for organizations such as Larson Property Management is the acquisition of new employees. HR business processes typically include (1) identifying jobs where new employees are needed and approving those jobs, (2) analyzing the requirements of those jobs, (3) posting those positions and recruiting applicants from the labor market, (4) tracking applicants through the recruiting process, (5) selecting applicants from the recruiting pool that best fit the job requirements through the use of selection tools such as interviews, and (6) bringing new hires on board and placing them in their jobs. The HR programs associated with these processes are (1) HR planning, (2) job analysis, (3) recruiting, (4) applicant tracking, (5) selection, and (6) placement.

Conversely, the focus and goal of *physical design* is the determination of the most effective means of translating the business processes into a physical system including hardware and software. To merge the phases together can invite the temptation to focus heavily on the physical aspects of the new system (hardware/software) at the expense of improved business processes. In addition, focusing on the physical aspects of a system can invite premature decisions on a physical solution that may not be the most effective solution for the business processes identified.

For example, a new and improved version of software may appear on the market that is designed to automate and help manage compensation systems based on a combination of salary and bonus. However, a company purchasing this software because of its elegance may have made a serious error if the company's top management is planning to drop the bonus program in 2 years as part of their new strategic plan. Another example would be failure to acquire needed software features due to lack of attention on processes. Related to staffing and the acquisition of new employees, through a careful analysis of the staffing process, companies such as Larson Property Management may determine that the organization needs a particular level of workflow processing and Web enablement to track applicants and allow posting of jobs and online application of jobs.

Logical Design

As discussed in Chapter 4, the organization has completed the analysis phase of the SDLC, which resulted in a comprehensive process analysis for the new HRIS. Now, one of the key tasks facing the HR staff and development teams is to model the needs for the new system. There are two ways in which the system can be modeled: the physical model and the logical model. The physical model focuses on the computer technology for the HRIS, that is, the hardware, software, networking plans, and technical manuals. The strength of this type of model is that it focuses on how the system will actually operate. In turn, this strength also becomes its weakness because by focusing on the actual way the system will be implemented in terms of technology, analysts and HR staff may be constrained by the current, operational physical model. That is, the HR staff is familiar with the functioning of the HRIS in use and, typically, is not familiar with the technology aspects of the system or current technology available.

Therefore, system developers like to focus on the essence of the business processes independent of any technological implementation. To do this, logical models of the system are created. Logical models are HRIS models that could be operationalized in multiple ways in terms of the technology. For example, in the logical model, an organization might focus on receiving and processing applicant files. There are several physical ways in which an organization could implement this process. They could use a Web-portal in an HRIS, a kiosk at a retail outlet, direct e-mail, or physical mail. The strength of using logical models is that the HR staff and developers can focus specifically on the business processes, policies, and procedures instead of on technology. Marakas (2006) refers to this as "separating the 'what' from the 'how'" (p. 116). By focusing on what the system does or needs to be able to do, the analyst and HR staff will be less likely to be distracted by or to focus on a single technology platform. In turn, they will be more likely to design a stronger solution.

Essentially, a **logical model** is similar to the blueprints for a home or an airplane. It provides the organization with an outline of the key business processes and goals for the system. Then, as the physical system is designed, these are translated into the hardware and software platforms that best fit the business's needs. For an HRIS, there are two types of models created for the system: those focused on the system processes and those focused on the data the system captures.

Two Ways to View an HRIS: Data Versus Process

For any HRIS, the organization must look at the total HR system from two different perspectives: the data perspective and the process perspective.

The data perspective focuses on an analysis of what data the organization captures and uses, the definitions and relationships of the data, while ignoring how or where the data are used by the organization. For example, a system focusing on employee recruiting would need data about the applicants and their knowledge, skills, and abilities (e.g., name, address, degrees received, work experience). This perspective would focus on the important data but would not be concerned with the data that are to be used within the organization. In addition, the data perspective focuses on the most efficient and effective way to capture the data to ensure accuracy.

The process perspective, conversely, focuses on the business processes and activities in which the organization engages and on how data flow through the HRIS. For example, a recruiting module would have business activities such as receiving applications, sorting and scanning resumes to determine the interview pool, scheduling interviews, reporting candidate information for legal purposes, and so on, but it is not focused on the data definitions and relationships. The designer would focus on the specific business processes, including the input of the data into the system, the flow of data through the system, and the storage of the data, and not on precisely what data are captured and how they are best organized or stored. Essentially, process modeling uses tools to describe the processes that are carried out by a system.

A key question that the reader might be asking is "Why should I care about these distinctions?" The reason why the distinction between process and data perspectives is important is that each represents a portion of the total HRIS but neither provides the complete picture. By modeling each separately, the organization is better able to understand and communicate its needs to the technical staff (e.g., the project management team responsible for designing and implementing the HRIS and any external consultants, vendors, or software developers). In addition, while processes may change in the future, data generally represent the most permanent and stable part of a system. For example, employee data from prior systems is often transferred to new systems. This permanency of data and the more dynamic aspect of processes suggest the importance of dealing with each separately.

Over the past three decades, a well-established procedure for modeling information systems has been developed. The procedure is based on a process perspective that uses data flow diagramming. A common aspect of all design methodologies is the use of diagrammatic modeling techniques. While the style of the charting symbols varies, the fundamentals are well established. Our focus in this chapter is on the creation and use of process models.

Logical Process Modeling With Data Flow Diagrams

A process model describes and represents the key business processes or activities conducted by the organization, such as applicant tracking. The specific type of process model typically used by organizations is a DFD. A DFD is a graphical representation of the key business activities and processes in the HR system and the boundaries of the system, the data that flow through the system, and any external individuals or departments that interact with the system.

The focus of a DFD is on the movement of data between external entities (such as a job applicant) and processes (the applicant-tracking process) and between processes and data stores. Kendall and Kendall (2008) argue that DFDs have four distinct advantages over narrative (e.g., written) descriptions:

1. There is freedom from committing to the technical implementation of the system too early.

2. They provide a deeper understanding of the interrelatedness of systems and subsystems.

3. They allow for stronger communication of system knowledge to the employees, since the diagrams are in pictorial form.

4. They ensure a deeper analysis of the proposed system to determine if all business processes have been identified.

A DFD consists of four symbols (see Figure 5.1). These include the entity, the data flow, the process, and the data store. The entity represents any external agent (e.g., an individual, department, business, system) that either receives or supplies data to the HR system. For example, in an ATS, a manager could request that a job opening be posted, or an applicant could submit her resume online. Other examples of an entity are a manager inputting **merit pay** raise information on an employee into the payroll system or the production/manufacturing system inputting piece-rate production data about the number of products produced by an employee into the payroll system. Similarly, the time-and-labor module, which provides time-card information on employees, their start and end times on workdays, represents an entity for payroll systems. Because entities represent a specific person, place, system, or department, they are labeled with a noun in the DFD.

❖ **Figure 5.1**   Symbols of the DFD

Symbol	Meaning	Example
	Entity	Employee
→	Data flow	Employee Pay →
	Process	Print Employee Paycheck
	Data store	DI Time Card

The data flow represents the movement of a single piece of data from point to point (e.g., process to process, entity to process, or process to data store) through the system. As a data flow represents data about a person, place, or thing, it should also be labeled with a noun. The label of a data flow should describe exactly what data are contained in the flow. For example, a data flow labeled "Time Sheet" would represent an employee's time sheet, and the exact data contained in the flow would be precisely defined as part of the diagramming process. Because DFDs describe the key business processes and the flow of data between them, *an important rule to remember is that all data flows must begin and end at a process.*

The third component of a DFD is the process. A process represents a business activity. The goal of each process is to change or transform inputted data into a useful output (e.g., creating an applicant record, updating an employee record, creating a recruiting yield ratio report, reporting Equal Employment Opportunity Commission data on applicants). Since data are transformed as part of the process, processes should be labeled with an action verb, for example, *calculate, send, print,* or *verify.*

The final symbol is the data store. The data store represents data at rest in the system, or a repository of data. This could be a filing cabinet, a file on a desk, a computer file, or a **database** table. A data store contains data about a person, place, or department and should be labeled with a noun. Examples of data contained in a data store could be employee file, applicant file, employee record, customer record, or current benefits. Data stores are typically identified with a "D*n*," where D identifies it as a data store and *n* is a number reflecting its unique identifier (D1, D2, etc.). The symbols and use are illustrated in Figure 5.1.

Creating and Using the DFD

Most DFDs for integrated business systems are very complex, consisting of hundreds to thousands of processes, data flows, and data stores. If all of these were included on a single diagram, it would make the task of developing and using them too complex. Therefore, DFDs are organized by modeling the individual processes (such as the applicant-tracking process) and components (such as the recruiting module) of an information system. Furthermore, a series of DFDs are created to visually depict increasingly detailed views. The value of this is that all individuals involved in the logical design of the system can view the model at their own level of understanding and complexity. Viewing the model provides much better understanding than creating written documents to describe the model and all the processes.

The highest-level DFD developed is called the **context level diagram**. The context level diagram describes the full system, its boundaries, external entities that interact with the system, and the primary data flows between the entities outside the system and the system itself. The context level diagram contains only one HR process, representing the system, data flows, and entities. This process is labeled with the system name and is identified as the Context Level Diagram. A sample context level diagram for an ATS is shown in Figure 5.2.

The single HR process in the context level diagram is then broken into greater detail on the **Level 0 diagram** to provide a clearer picture of the HR business process. The level 0 diagram contains the major system processes and the data that flow between them. Each process should be labeled with a verb that reflects the action that the process conducts. In addition, each process is numbered consecutively starting with 1.0 (1.0, 2.0, 3.0, 4.0, etc.). It is important to note at this point that the context level diagram and the Level 0 diagrams should reflect and communicate the same information (see Figure 5.3 on p. 108).

This concept is called the *balancing* of DFDs. Notice that although the Level 0 diagram shown in Figure 5.3 has more detail than the context level diagram, it contains the same inflows and outflows from management, applicants, and human resources. For example, on both levels, the three flows, "Application," "Application Confirmation," and "Application Decision," flow between the Applicant entity and the system in the same way. Balancing DFDs is important because we want to ensure that all individuals are viewing and using the same model of the system. Otherwise, there is the risk that the system will not be designed appropriately.

❖ **Figure 5.2**   Context Level Diagram

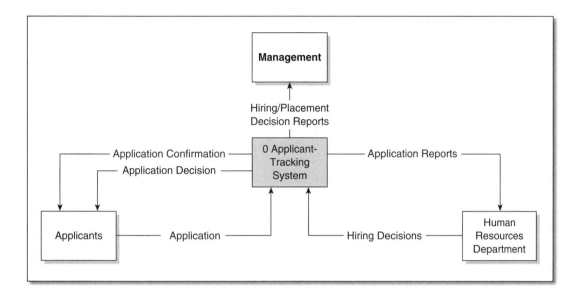

In the same manner that the context level can be decomposed into a Level 0 diagram, the Level 0 diagram can be decomposed into *additional-level diagrams*. As with the context level diagram, the Level 0 diagram in Figure 5.3 also hides specific details about all the processing tasks within the HR system. Thus, the next-level diagram (Level 1 diagram) would break down the processes within the Level 0 diagram to better portray and help understand the HR processes in the system. This level of detail will in turn improve the accuracy of the logical design of the system. The same process of decomposition could occur at successive levels (Level 2, Level 3, etc.); however, this becomes a very complex task and is beyond the scope of this book.[1] The DFD is considered complete when it includes all the components necessary for the system being modeled.

The DFD can also be used as a tool for analyzing the current system versus the desired system. In addition, DFDs are often used for business process reengineering, in an effort to improve the system. For example, through the DFD, the analysts designing the ATS for Larson Property Management might discover that data (e.g., rating) from a lower-level manager's interview of job candidates currently flow back to the HR department for approval prior to allowing the applicant file to proceed to the next-level manager's interview. Through this analysis, they could find that this step is unnecessary in the new system because the system would use a decision rule, based on minimum score needed to proceed, to forward the applicant data to the next manager automatically based on a passing score.

Physical Design

As was discussed in earlier chapters of this book, the acquisition of a system is the culmination of a series of important steps. By this point, the organization should have a strong understanding of its current operations, have developed a set of requirements

❖ **Figure 5.3**   Level 0 DFD

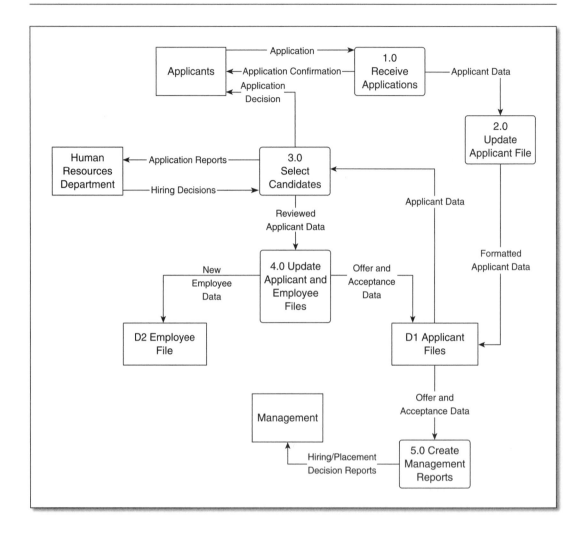

for the new system, and have developed a new logical model for how they wish the system to operate. Once the new system has been designed, and logical models of the new system have been tested against the business requirements, the organization will move to the physical design phase. The major goal of this phase of the SDLC is to translate the logical model and requirements into a physical system, including all hardware, software, and networking.

Major activities in this phase include (1) determining whether or not there is value in continuing the system design and actual implementation processes, (2) determining hardware and software options and requirements, (3) determining where to obtain the hardware and software (e.g., by in-house development, commercial software purchase), (4) developing an implementation schedule, and (5) working with potential vendors to assess and select software if system software is to be obtained externally. For most organizations, this will typically mean that the HR staff specialists (e.g., the recruiting manager) will work closely with HRIS specialists and the internal IT staff, software vendors, and any external consultants brought in to help with the physical design of the system. The extent of involvement of these various stakeholders depends on the size, scope, and type of HRIS developed.

During the physical design phase, the HRIS and IT staff will focus heavily on how any new software and hardware will fit within the current **IT architecture**. In addition, IT and HRIS staff will provide technical recommendations on the relative value and cost of building the system internally or purchasing an off-the-shelf package from a commercial vendor. The HR staff will also work with the external vendors to ensure that the focus of the system is on the business requirements and not the technology itself. It is also important at this point to remind the HR staff to be very careful of scope creep (which was discussed in detail in Chapter 4).

Three Choices in Physical Design

The first step in this design phase is to determine how to proceed with physical design. First, the organization has the option of *doing nothing*. Although this may seem to be counterintuitive because much time and money typically have been spent on the analysis and design process to date, there may be important organizational or environmental reasons for not proceeding. For example, on completion of a thorough analysis and logical redesign of the HR processes, a small organization in the southern United States was faced with a public lawsuit, and they were forced to delay the final design and implementation of the project until this was settled. In other instances, companies have postponed proceeding after learning that a target software vendor is in the process of a major revision of the software product.

The second option is to *make changes to only the HR business processes without new or upgraded technology*. Before any time or money is spent on new technology, it is important that the organization address all proposed business process changes and determine if they can be handled using the current HRIS technology. In the book *Good to Great*, Collins (2001) suggests that one important difference between good companies and great companies is that good companies view technology as a solution, whereas great companies see technology as a tool to be used to support great business processes. Furthermore, Brynjolfsson and Hitt (1998) found that organizations were much more likely to increase productivity and performance when they coupled any technology changes with business process changes.

At this point in the process, it can be easy to forget that the goal for the development of the new system should be to use technology to support HR practices, making them more efficient and adding value to the organization, and not to get caught up in the promise of a new technology with industry "best practices." In HR or IT, although using best practices is desirable, if these practices are not compatible with the specific needs of your organization as identified in the needs analysis, any business process and technical changes are likely to be less effective.

The final option that an organization can choose is to *implement the business process changes along with new or upgraded technology*. There are three basic ways that this can be done: build it, buy it, or outsource the development. Organizations that choose the first approach—to build the technology internally—will take responsibility for the development of the software and hardware. The advantage of this approach is that the organization will control all aspects of the development, including the look and feel and functionality. Using this approach, the organization will be able to write software to meet 100% of the business's requirements. Finally, internally building the software can also provide increased flexibility and creative solutions for the issues within the HR business processes.

There are several shortcomings in building the HR system internally from scratch. First, it can be much more expensive to implement than an off-the-shelf solution. In addition, since it is a unique application, the amount of software testing and the developmental risk are much higher with this approach than for an off-the-shelf system. Finally, for this approach to work, the organization must already have or readily be able to obtain the technical, functional, and project management skills necessary to effectively build the system. For most organizations, this is a daunting task because software development is generally not part of their core **competency** and they likely do not have the staff and resources available to complete such an undertaking.

For most organizations, the second approach of buying prepackaged, **commercial off-the-shelf (COTS) software** can fit many of their needs. These systems can range from small single-function applications costing a few thousand dollars to large-scale, enterprise resource planning (ERP) software packages costing millions of dollars. The advantage of using this approach to acquiring software is that the systems are well tested and proven and can be purchased and implemented in a short period. For this reason, most of the HR software adopted and used today is COTS. The good news for organizations considering the adoption of a COTS solution is that most business operations are fairly generic and there are applications available that should meet the majority of the needs of most organizations. The bad news is that even the best system will rarely meet all the specific needs of the organization, with most meeting about 70% of the organization's needs. Thus, organizations choosing to purchase a COTS solution should be prepared to either work with the vendor to customize the system to meet their unique needs or change their processes to fit with the software (and thereby opt for what is referred to as the "vanilla" approach). As mentioned briefly before, the risk of adapting your business processes to the software is that these processes may be incompatible with your organization's business processes, resulting in increased costs or reduced competitive advantage. In addition, when implementing a vendor's upgrade in the future, it will likely be necessary to redo whatever customization was done during the initial implementation.

The final approach to developing the software is to outsource the development to an external company or to obtain access to existing software through an **application service provider (ASP)**. The greatest advantage of outsourcing is that an external software development can bring vast resources, experiences, and technical skills to design a much more effective solution than would otherwise be possible. However, outsourcing the development can be risky. For example, by outsourcing, the firm may expose confidential internal information and business processes to an external organization. Second, outsourcing may not lead to reduced time and expense for the organization, because many of the tasks that would need to be completed if the software was in-house would still need to be completed *with* the external software developer.

❖ **Table 5.1**   Software Acquisition Strategies

	Development Strategy		
	In-House	**COTS**	**Outsource**
Business need	Unique	Standard	Non-core function
In-house skills	Functional and technical expertise exists	Functional expertise exists	Functional and technical expertise not in-house
Project management skills	Project has skilled and experienced project manager	Project has a manager with experience to coordinate and manage vendor relationship	Project has manager with experience to manage an outsourcing relationship
Timeframe	Flexible	Short	Flexible or short

SOURCE: Adapted from Dennis, Wixom, and Roth (2006).

As can be seen in the previous discussion, there are advantages and disadvantages in each approach for software development. Thus, the decision as to which approach to use will be based on multiple factors and may differ from organization to organization and project to project. In addition, an organization need not rely on a single approach. For most organizations, the solution chosen is often a combination of in-house and external development. The decision regarding which approach to choose is based on a series of factors, including the nature of the business process; the size, technical skills, and project management skills of the software staff; and the development time frame. Table 5.1 contains a matrix of how these different factors may influence the approach chosen.

If the decision is made to purchase and customize COTS or to outsource development, the organization will need to work closely with external software vendors. Thus, vendor selection becomes a very important decision.

Working With Vendors

Although building a new HRIS from scratch with internal resources may be a viable option for some organizations, by far the most common decision that the HR department will make is to work with an external vendor to develop or acquire the system. To do this, the HR staff will need to work closely with both the internal IT department and external vendors to ensure that the business process requirements and any or all technical requirements are presented to the vendor. The first step in this process is to develop an RFP.

An RFP is a document that solicits proposals and bids for proposed work from potential consultants or vendors. An RFP defines the organization's goals and requirements for the new information system. It provides the details that define hardware, software, and services requirements. For the organization, it provides a structured approach that minimizes the chance of omitting important criteria. On return from

❖ **Table 5.2**   Recommended Components of a Request for a Proposal

---

Data about you

- Who you are as a business
  - Company size, scope, industry, annual sales, locations, etc.
- Business requirements
  - Required business processes, functionality, and project scope
- Technical requirements
  - Does it need to work with a particular operating system, existing organization systems, etc.?
- Delivery timeframe needed
  - Is there a desired target implementation date?

Requested data from vendor

- Vendor details
  - Company, size, scope, annual sales, experience, etc.
  - Number of implemented applications
- System pricing
  - May include license fees, maintenance charges, training costs, implementation costs, and support costs
- System details
  - Functionality included in the system
  - If customization is necessary, how will this be addressed? (timing, delivery, cost, support, etc.)
  - Supported technology now and in the near future
  - Customer support options
  - Training options
- Customer references
  - Find out user and organizational experiences with the system.
  - Ask these references for other companies they know using the system to broaden your knowledge (after all, the vendor is likely to provide you with clients who have had positive experiences).
- Sample contract terms

---

vendors or consultants, it simplifies the vendor comparison process by providing a format to elicit consistent and complete responses.

The RFP provides an opportunity for the HR department to systematically record what they will need the system to do. As part of this process, any remaining implicit assumptions should be made explicit. Basically, the RFP will define what is needed and what is not needed in the system. In addition, the RFP begins the communication process and relationship building with vendors.

Although there are many different factors that will determine precisely what should be included in the RFP, experts in the field have argued for the inclusion of a key set of components. For example, Table 5.2 presents a set of key factors adapted from recommendations made by the Society for Human Resource Management and the work of Hinojos and Miller (1998).

The above table is an excellent starting point for developing an RFP, but it should not be taken to include all items that may be required. Those developing an RFP for an organization should keep in mind their unique situation and add or subtract what is included as appropriate for their needs. The information in the above table is also very general in nature, and how it is developed will be different for each organization.

When developing the RFP, organizations should keep several things in mind. The first recommendation is to *focus on the business requirements.* Given that the system is being considered in association with business process changes, an excellent place to begin the development for the vendor is to review the requirements and logical redesign of the business processes. These should then be communicated to each vendor.

Associated with this requirement, the second recommendation is to *be specific.* With all the effort placed into the needs analysis and the redesign of business processes, very specific requirements will be available and should be included in the RFP. It is important to be specific as to your organization's needs because if you are not specific, you risk allowing the vendors to determine what is included in the final system. Although it is desirable to work with a vendor to develop the final system, it is important that the system be developed to meet your specific business needs, not just match the system a vendor has available. Furthermore, an RFP that is too general may not be screened in sufficient detail by the vendor, leading to a product with too much detail and that is too complex and too expensive for the business's needs. The overall objective of the RFP is to have the vendors propose system hardware and software to meet the specific requirements you have identified for your new system.

The third recommendation is to *keep it simple.* One of the temptations in developing an RFP is to include all possible business and technical requirements in the RFP. The problem with including many technical details in the plan is that vendors may review the RFP and screen themselves out because they may feel that they cannot fill the needs outlined in the RFP. For example, it would be important to ask whether a benefits system allows for benefits reports, benefits administration, and so on. Conversely, the RFP would want to stay away from including requirements as to length of fields, types of passwords used, and so on, which do not focus on business needs but instead are focused on technical and physical design issues. Essentially, this would mean that if it's not something that is important to the HR department and reflective of the business processes modeled in the DFDs, it is best not to include it.

This leads to the fourth recommendation, which is to *work closely with the HRIS and IT staff* as the RFP is developed. The professional staff will be responsible for working with the vendor to ensure the smooth installation and maintenance of the HRIS. Therefore, it is important for the HR staff to work closely with the information systems professional staff to make sure that any essential technical considerations are included. For example, if there are existing systems that need to provide information to or receive information from the system, then this should be included. In addition, if there is a certain platform (e.g., UNIX, Windows) that the organization has experience with and with which they would like the system to integrate, this too should be included.

Vendor Selection

After the RFPs are sent, the vendors will then evaluate them to determine if they have a product that would fit the company's needs. If the HR and IT staff have put together a strong RFP, then they should get a set of vendors who have a better understanding of your company's specific needs and who can provide a better-tailored response and proposal for the HRIS. After receiving the vendor responses, you will have the opportunity to evaluate the relative strengths and weaknesses of each vendor. To do this, there are several considerations to be made and criteria you will use in assessing the software options. These are described below.

Functionality

As you evaluate the different vendor responses, it is important to evaluate how fully the functionality of the HRIS meets the HR needs. For example, a software product that meets 70% of the organization's needs will be less desirable than one that meets 98% of the requirements. On the other hand, a software that meets 98% of the organization's needs but has no additional functionality may not provide the organization with the opportunity to grow and expand its options in the future, so it may be less attractive than one that meets 90% of your HR needs but allows for growth over time. It is important that the HRIS implemented today be able to change as the organization grows. Otherwise, within a few years, the organization will have to go through the entire systems development process and purchase/develop an entirely new solution. Finally, an HRIS that will meet your organization's needs with minimal customization for actual use would be more attractive than one that will require significant customization.

IT Architecture and IT Integration

The next issue focuses on the IT architecture for the HRIS. The organization will need to know whether the HRIS will be a stand-alone system or a networked system or a Web-based one, and so on. In addition, the organization will want to know with what technology or platform the HRIS has been developed (e.g., UNIX, Linux, Windows). Finally, as important as knowing the answers to the above questions, it is also important to understand the extent to which the HRIS will integrate within the broader corporate IT architecture. An HRIS that can more readily interact and communicate with operations, manufacturing, and sales can provide a much stronger return for the company than one that stands as an isolated entity. The easier the integration with the broader IT architecture, the easier it will be to implement and use the system. In today's environment of employee self-service and Web portals, the ability to provide remote access to employees can also be a plus as different systems are considered. Finally, if functional HR systems are being considered from multiple vendors, the extent to which they can be integrated and communicate with each other also becomes important.

Price

Although price will ultimately play a very large role in the selection of an HRIS, price should be secondary to the goal of finding a system that meets your process needs. At the same time, price will ultimately determine which system is selected. The ultimate cost of the system will include the visible costs, such as cost of hardware and software, as well as the less visible costs, such as customization costs, employee training costs, licensing fees (e.g., site licenses, per seat licenses), upgrade costs, and the cost of system operation and maintenance over time. HRIS costs and cost-benefit analyses are covered in more detail in Chapter 6.

Vendor Longevity and Viability

As with any purchase decision, it is important to evaluate the quality of the vendor itself. The good news is that many vendors have been in business for 10 to 20 years, so vendor longevity is usually not an issue. In today's environment, the viability of vendors can often be assessed through their responsiveness to existing companies, their history of providing timely upgrades, and increased flexibility. Furthermore, the HRIS vendor marketplace has been undergoing some consolidation as companies seek to better position themselves to provide value-added services across the HR functional spectrum, so the vendor you sign with today may end up merging with another company.

Assessing System Feasibility

At this point in the design process, it is very important that you stop and consider whether or not the system will work for you. Although the system may meet all the requirements as defined in the requirements document, it still may not be feasible to implement for several reasons. Therefore, it is important to conduct a thorough feasibility assessment of the project. A feasibility assessment should go beyond the traditional economic metrics and should include multiple dimensions, such as technical, operational, human factors, legal, political, and economic.

Technical Feasibility

Technical feasibility focuses on the current technological capabilities of the organization and the technological capabilities required for the implementation of the proposed system. As part of any assessment of technical feasibility, the HR staff must work closely with systems analysts and technical staff to determine whether or not the current technology can be upgraded to meet the needs of the organization or whether an entirely new technological architecture will be needed to implement the proposed system changes.

Typical questions an organization might ask as part of a technical feasibility assessment are as follows:

1. Do the hardware and software exist to implement this system? Are they practical to obtain?

2. Do we add on or patch the current software or start from scratch?

3. Does our organization have the ability to construct this system?

4. Can we integrate the new system with our current systems?

Operational Feasibility

Operational feasibility focuses on how well the proposed system fits in with the current and future organizational environment. For example, a technically feasible system may make such a drastic change in how the organization operates as defined and designed that it may not have a strong chance of being successfully implemented. For example, a series of research studies in information systems has found that the more compatible a system is with an employee's current ways of working the more likely the employee will be to use the system (Agarwal, 2000). Therefore, when a system is highly incompatible, HR staff or designers might seek to change or decrease its scope to make it more manageable.

In addition, operational feasibility assesses the extent to which the project fits within the overall strategic plans of the HR and IT departments as well as the organization's overall strategy. Other areas addressed as part of the assessment of operational feasibility include the likelihood of meeting the proposed implementation schedule and delivery date. The HR staff and developers must work together to ensure that the schedule will meet any critical operational deadlines, that resources are sufficient to meet the schedule, and that the schedule takes into account key organization dates (e.g., annual budgeting). The techniques used in project management are very important and will be discussed in detail in Chapter 7.

A second area of operational feasibility focuses on human factors. An assessment of the human factors feasibility of the system focuses on how the employee uses and works with the system, the system's usability, and the training the employees receive. The usability of the system reflects the effectiveness and efficiency of the system to the user. It is often reflected in characteristics such as the usefulness of the system to users/employees and the ease of using the system. It can reflect how intuitive the interface is to navigate, the effort an employee must put into learning to use the system, and how effective the system is in supporting the employees' work.

Do not underestimate the importance of this human feasibility issue to the ultimate success of the system. Over the past 20 years, hundreds of studies have found that the usefulness and ease of use of the system play a large role in system use and adoption.[2] In addition, recent research has found that usefulness estimations can be accurately assessed by employees early in the development process but that perceptions of ease of use may evolve as employees gain direct experience with the software (Davis & Venkatesh, 2004). These human factor considerations will be covered in Chapter 8 in more detail, along with suggestions as to how to solve the acceptability issue.

Typical questions asked as part of the assessment of operational feasibility would include the following:

1. How well does the system fit within our organizational context? Will this make us better?

2. How much will our organization change because of the new business and technical changes?

3. How long will this take to do, and does the schedule fit our business's needs?

4. If we have to squeeze, then what might we be able to eliminate?

5. Do we have or can we get the personnel to do this?

6. Can people use the system?

7. What kind of training do we need?

Legal and Political Feasibility

Legal and political issues also play a very important role in assessing the feasibility of an HRIS. The best-designed and -implemented system can end up causing major headaches for the organization if it violates existing laws and regulations. This is even truer for an

HRIS than for many other types of information systems. The reason for this is that existing laws and regulations play a larger role in HR than in other core business functions (as will be discussed in Chapter 9). For example, if the HRIS fails to maintain specific employee performance records correctly, legal challenges of wrongful discharges will be more difficult for the company to defend itself against.

Political feasibility focuses on the organizational political environment in which the HRIS is being implemented. Issues such as power redistribution involving loss of individual or department control can have major political implications that can affect the effectiveness of the implementation. What is interesting is that political issues can undermine the implementation of a new HRIS more quickly and completely than any technical shortcomings. The challenge here is that while political feasibility may be fairly easy to identify, it can be challenging to effectively address. Individuals who are negatively affected by the implementation (or who perceive themselves to be negatively affected) of the system are likely to either overtly or covertly undermine, resist, or disrupt its implementation. Thus, it is important to understand and anticipate the political consequences of a system implementation at this point, before implementation is started. Again, these issues are discussed more fully in Chapter 8.

Typical questions asked as part of a **legal and political feasibility** analysis include the following:

1. Does the implementation of this system infringe on existing copyrights?

2. Are we violating any antitrust issues by implementing the system?

3. Do we have contracts with other companies that don't allow use of the new software?

4. Does the system violate any governmental policies?

5. For global companies: Does the system violate any foreign laws?

6. Who is likely to resist the implementation of the system?

7. Who may "win" or "lose" as a result of this implementation?

8. What is the risk of system sabotage?

Economic Feasibility

The final aspect of a feasibility assessment is **economic feasibility**. The goal of an economic feasibility analysis is to determine whether the costs of developing, implementing, and running the system are worth the benefits derived from its use. To do this, the appropriate costs and benefits of the HRIS should be identified, and precise values should be assigned to each. Then, these costs and benefits should be subjected to a thorough cost-benefit analysis. As mentioned earlier, Chapter 6 provides a comprehensive coverage of costs and benefits of an HRIS.

Summary

The goal of this chapter was to discuss the factors that contribute to a more effective system design strategy. First, we discussed how the HR staff and consultants will translate the requirements from previous phases of the SDLC into improved logical business processes. We then discussed how these new processes are then modeled through logical modeling tools such as the DFDs. DFDs are important because they allow the HR staff, consultants, and programmers to have a common model of the system from which to work and because they can be used to identify potential shortcomings not yet identified in the new system. Given that the cost of making changes becomes significantly more expensive once the physical design of the system has been undertaken, it is important that these models be as effective and accurate as possible to avoid system rework.

Third, we discussed the options available for the firm when developing the final physical design for the new system. One option available to firms is not to change their existing practices. Other options include building the software internally or sourcing the software through external vendors. The chapter also briefly outlined the steps of working with a vendor, from the RFP through the selection of the vendor, providing several suggestions for getting the most out of the RFP and the vendor selection process. Finally, whatever approach is chosen for the final design, any selected physical system must be assessed as to its feasibility. Although budgeting committees will pay especially close attention to the profitability of the system, we also explained the importance of considering different types of system feasibility. Although this phase of the SDLC can be complex and challenging to manage, we believe that following a structured and disciplined approach as outlined will result in the development or acquisition of a system that is a stronger fit for the organization.

DISCUSSION QUESTIONS

1. What is the difference between the data view of a system and the process view of a system? Why is this distinction important when designing a new system?

2. Discuss four reasons why a DFD is a stronger tool than a written narrative of the business processes.

3. How do companies use an RFP when sourcing software? What are the key items that should be included in the RFP?

4. If you were advising a firm on developing an RFP, what would be some key suggestions you would make to them for improving the effectiveness of the RFP?

5. When evaluating vendor offerings, what are the key factors that will help your firm determine the best software product to acquire?

6. Even if a system pays for itself financially, an organization must conduct a thorough feasibility study. What types of feasibility should be assessed, and what information does each type of feasibility provide the organization?

CASE STUDY[3]

Larson Property Management Company is one of the largest property management companies in California, with over 1,000 employees. The company provides a full array of commercial management and development services. These activities include complete management services for commercial office and retail buildings and apartment complexes; construction, repair, and maintenance of commercial properties; and financial management and billing services for commercial real-estate clients. The company has experienced significant expansion over the past 5 years in response to the growth in apartment and commercial construction in southern California, and this has resulted in the need to hire a large number of employees on an ongoing basis to staff its operations.

Larson Property Management has depended on a legacy HRIS to manage its applicant and employee databases. The system runs on a client-server computer system. The system was implemented approximately 10 years ago prior to the company's rapid growth and when it employed fewer than 100 employees. The system functionality is limited to the storage and retrieval of employee and applicant data. For recruiting purposes, the system requires a clerk to manually enter basic applicant data and the results of the application test, whether the applicant was offered employment. Prior to this, applicants' files used to be passed around to those who were reviewing the materials and were sometimes misplaced, and trying to locate a particular applicant was often a problem. The HRIS has limited file storage capability for applicant and employee records, and currently has reached the storage capacity.

Larson Property Management has decided to replace its legacy HRIS. One module in the new HRIS that the company wants is a sophisticated ATS. The primary objective of the ATS will be to provide a paperless hiring process. Basic functionality of the new system will be to manage the requisition and approval of job openings, store resumes and job applications, retrieve the names of applicants who match job requirements through query functions, track a candidate's progress through the recruiting and selection process, and automate reporting functions. The company's managers also want e-HR functionality that includes Internet posting of job openings through the company's Web page and external job-posting services, application and resume submission through the Web and through kiosks at their office locations, staff ability to access and use the system remotely through a Web browser, and online resume and application-scanning capabilities.

Part of the design phase is modeling the processes that will be used in the system for applicant tracking. For Larson Property Management, this will allow the system analysts to design an efficient paperless hiring process.

Larson Property management is well aware that the *design stage* of the SDLC is critical for the successful implementation of the new ATS. However, there is considerable confusion about how to proceed with this phase. The HR and IT professionals assigned on the ATS committee have been meeting to plan the new system. From their planning and needs analysis, it is clear that a new HRIS application is needed, can save considerable time, and can result in more accurate storage and retrieval of applicant data for cost-benefit and other management reports.

The company has had several vendors provide presentations on their approach to the design of an ATS, but these presentations were primarily focused on the physical design of the new ATS. The HR and IT committees must now begin the design process, which must be completed in 3 months.

1. Based on the material in this chapter, design a 3-month operational plan for the ATS.

   a. In your plan, make certain you differentiate between the logical and physical design of the ATS. Which one should be done first? Which one is more important?

    b. Describe the importance of the data view versus the process view for the design of the new ATS.

    c. Who are the important stakeholders to be considered in the design of the ATS?

    d. How will you determine whether these stakeholders need the information that the new ATS will deliver?

    e. Based on your personal knowledge of recruiting by companies, develop a DFD with at least two levels.

2. Based on the work you have completed for Question 1, provide a brief outline of the RFP that is to be sent to the HRIS vendors.

NOTES

1. The interested reader seeking more information on developing DFDs, including the rules for their completion as well as the decomposition process, can check out the following resources: *The Structured Analysis Wiki,* written by Ed Yourdon (http://yourdon.com/struc-analysis/wiki/index.php?title=Introduction) or any of the systems analysis and design textbooks listed in the references section.

2. Interested readers are encouraged to read Ma and Liu (2004) for a thorough review of this research.

3. Note that this is the case from the vignette, plus added material.

REFERENCES

Agarwal, R. (2000). Individual acceptance of information technologies. In R. W. Zmud (Ed.), *Framing the domains of IT management* (pp. 85–104). Cincinnati, OH: Pinnaflex Educational Resources.

Brynjolfsson, E., & Hitt, L. M. (1998). Beyond the productivity paradox. *Communications of the ACM, 41*(8), 49–55.

Collins, J. (2001). *Good to great: Why some companies make the leap . . . and others don't.* New York: HarperCollins.

Davis, F. D., & Venkatesh, V. (2004). Toward preprototype user acceptance testing of new information systems: Implications for software project management. *IEEE Transactions on Engineering Management, 51*(1), 31–46.

Dennis, A. R., Wixom, B. H., & Roth, R. M. (2006). *Systems analysis & design* (3rd ed.). Hoboken, NJ: John Wiley & Sons.

Hinojos, J. A., & Miller, M. (1998, July/August). Methodologies for selecting the right vendor. *Benefits & Compensation Solutions,* 38–42.

Kendall, K. E., & Kendall, J. E. (2008). *Systems analysis and design* (7th ed.). Upper Saddle River, NJ: Pearson.

Ma, Q., & Liu, L. (2004). The technology acceptance model: A meta-analysis of empirical findings. *Journal of End User Computing, 16*(1), 59–72.

Marakas, G. M. (2006). *Systems analysis & design: An active approach* (2nd ed.). New York: McGraw-Hill.

Standish Group. (2004). *The chaos report.* Boston: Author.

6

Cost Justifying HRIS Investments[1]

Kevin D. Carlson

Michael J. Kavanagh

EDITORS' NOTE

Central to the decision to develop and implement a new or improved HRIS will be the costs and benefits of the investment. Like most consumers, HR professionals and managers are frequently awed by the new computer-based HR applications or the entire HRIS and make a purchase decision on this basis. However, as discussed in this chapter, without a comprehensive cost-benefit analysis (CBA), this purchase could be disastrous. As emphasized by several authors (Cascio, 1987, 2000; Fitz-Enz, 2001; Kavanagh, Gueutal, & Tannenbaum, 1990), the language of business is dollars,[2] not just good feelings about an HRIS investment. The CBA for an HRIS investment needs to be made prior to purchase as well as early in the systems development life cycle. In fact, a preliminary estimate of the CBA of an HRIS investment should be presented to senior management before beginning any detailed work on the project. A more detailed analysis can then be made as part of the needs analysis. The information in this chapter provides both guidance for making CBA estimates as well as practical advice on how to make the CBA palatable to managerial decision makers. Finally, there is an emphasis on the value of the CBA and its documentation for the management of the project and its implementation, which will be covered in Chapters 7 and 8.

CHAPTER OBJECTIVES

After completing this chapter, you should be able to

♦ Understand HR metrics and explain the two ways they can be used for benchmarking HR activities and programs

♦ Explain why a CBA is critical for a successful HRIS project

♦ Explain the differences between cost reduction and organizational enhancement as strategies for HRIS investments

♦ Explain how using guidelines for approaches for investment analysis will lead to a better HRIS project

♦ Explain what the various costs and benefits are in a CBA for an HRIS investment

♦ Explain the differences between direct and indirect benefits and costs

♦ Explain how to estimate costs and benefits, both direct and indirect

♦ Explain the difference between average employee contribution (AEC) and utility analysis for estimating the value of indirect benefits

♦ Explain how the standard deviation of performance in dollars (SD_y) is used in utility analysis

♦ Discuss three common problems that can occur in an HRIS CBA

♦ Explain why variance estimates are useful in a CBA

VIGNETTE

There have been numerous examples in the HR and IT/IS literature of the failures of HRIS and other computer-based systems due to inadequate calculation of the costs and benefits of a new system. Rather than describing a specific company example in this vignette, the reader is referred to the chapters and references cited in the following chapters.

As discussed in Chapter 7, Browne and Rogich (2001) have found that "despite good faith efforts by organizations, analysts, and users, a majority of systems are either abandoned before completion or fail to meet user requirements" (p. 224). This problem has been estimated to cost organizations in the United States at least $100 billion a year (Ewusi-Mensah, 1997). Lemon, Bowitz, Burn, and Hackney (2002) have indicated that of the systems completed, over 55% will exceed cost and time estimates by a factor of 2. Furthermore, the vignettes in both Chapters 4 and 5 describe situations in which accurate cost and benefit analyses were critically needed prior to beginning an HRIS project.

Introduction

In most organizations today, an HRIS provides the primary infrastructure used to deliver HR programs, ensure HR regulatory compliance, and produce the metrics that are used to evaluate not only the HR function but also the contribution of the organizations' human resources to the accomplishment of firm-level strategic objectives. *HRIS functionality* continues to evolve and to expand—no longer simply shifting paper-and-pencil processes to their electronic equivalents but seeing new capabilities that leverage the advantages of *integrated information systems* and faster and more capable computing technologies. As a result, organizations are faced with new opportunities to extend their investments in HRIS functionality. HRIS functionality refers to the number of programs or functions—such as recruiting, compensation, job analysis—that are operational using the specific HRIS configuration as well as the features of these programs that enhance their usability and capacity to affect outcomes. Thus, HRIS functionality could include all HR programs in a fully integrated system or only a number of the more important programs, for example, compensation and benefits. HRIS functionality typically varies with organizational size, with larger companies having a greater number of programs or functions in their HRIS configurations than smaller companies.

It is important to recognize that organizations use metrics to measure or audit their HR programs and activities. Historically, the use of such audit metrics to measure the effectiveness of HR was identified by Cascio (1987) and Fitz-Enz (2001). Table 6.1 (SHRM, 2008) identifies a number of metrics that organizations can use to measure their HR effectiveness. Through *benchmarking*, described at the bottom of Table 6.1, these metrics can be used to compare your metrics against other organizations' metrics, survey data, etc. to evaluate your performance. They can also be used as benchmark data and to designate time frame (plan year, fiscal year, etc.).

There are also more detailed approaches for the measuring and benchmarking of employees' behaviors such as absenteeism (Hollmann, 2002) and turnover (Cascio, 2000), as well as for creating HR metrics for programs such as Employee Assistance and Work-Life programs (Cascio, 2000). Finally, note that there are only two return-on-investment (ROI) metrics, human capital and training, contained in Table 6.1. As will be seen later in this chapter, ROI may be used as one possible outcome for an HRIS when completing a CBA. A discussion of benchmarking for a CBA is covered later in this chapter.

In the 1990s, CBA played only a limited role in HRIS investment decisions. The pending obsolescence of noncompliant systems in Y2K (Year 2000) fueled widespread implementation of new HRIS technology. The result was one of the most concentrated and dramatic shifts in HR practice ever. During this period, purchase decisions were driven by two primary criteria: Did new systems offer the *baseline functionality* required by the organization in a *Y2K-compliant* form, and could the systems be delivered and implemented on time? It was apparent that something had to be done to meet the potential problems of Y2K, and more fine-grained investment analyses would not have affected purchase decisions. Thus, many organizations chose not to invest the time and effort to complete a CBA. However, the business landscape has changed today. Many decision makers, some of whom are still waiting to see returns from past

❖ **Table 6.1** The HR Metrics Toolkit (2008)

HR Metrics		
Absence rate	[(No. of days absent in mo.)/((Ave. no. of employees during mo.) × (No. of workdays))] × 100	Measures absenteeism. Determines if your company has an absenteeism problem. Analyzes why and how to address the issue. Analyzes further for effectiveness of attendance policy and effectiveness of management in applying policy. See Hollmann (2002).
Cost per hire	(Advertising + Agency fees + Employee referrals + Travel cost of applicants and staff + Relocation costs + Recruiter pay and benefits)/No. of hires	Costs involved with a new hire. Use *EMA/Cost per Hire Staffing Metrics Survey* as a benchmark for your organization (Kluttz, 2003). Can be used as a measurement to show any substantial improvements to savings in recruitment/retention costs. Determines what your recruiting function can do to increase savings/reduce costs, etc.
Health care costs per employee	Total cost of health care/Total employees	Per capita cost of employee benefits. Indicates cost of health care per employee. For benefit data from the Bureau of Labor Statistics (BLS). See BLS's publications titled *Employer Costs for Employee Compensation and Measuring Trends In The Structure And Levels Of Employer Costs For Employee Compensation* (BLS, 2008) for additional information on this topic.
HR expense factor	HR expense/Total operating expense	HR expenses in relation to the total operating expenses of the organization. In addition, determines if expenditures exceeded, met, or fell below budget. Analyzes HR practices that contributed to savings, if any.
Human capital ROI	(Revenue − (Operating expense − [Compensation cost + Benefit cost]))/(Compensation cost + Benefit cost)	ROI ratio for employees. Did organization get a return on their investment? Analyzes causes of positive/negative ROI metric. Uses analysis as an opportunity to optimize investment with HR practices such as recruitment, motivation, training, and development. Evaluates if HR practices have a causal relationship in positive changes to improving metric.

HR Metrics		
Human capital value added	(Revenue – (Operating Expense – [Compensation cost + Benefit Cost]))/Total no. of FTE	Value of workforce's knowledge, skill, and performance. This measurement illustrates how employees add value to an organization.
Prorating merit increases	(No. of mos. actually worked/No. of mos. under the current increase policy) × Increase in percentage the person would otherwise be entitled to	The basic steps to calculate an employees' pay increase appropriate to the period of time worked.
Revenue factor	Revenue/Total no. of FTE	Benchmark to indicate effectiveness of company and to show employees as capital rather than as an expense. Human capital can be viewed as an investment.
Time to fill	Total days elapsed to fill requisitions/No. hired	Number of days from which job requisition was approved to new hire start date. How efficient/productive is recruiting function? This is also a process measurement. See *EMA/Cost per Hire Staffing Metrics Survey* for more information.
Training investment factor	Total training cost/Headcount	Training cost per employee. Analyzes training function further for effectiveness of training (e.g., Has productivity increased as a result of acquiring new skills and knowledge? Have accidents decreased?). If not, evaluate the causes.
Training (ROI)	(Total benefit – Total costs) × 100	The total financial gain/benefit an organization realizes from a particular training program less the total direct and indirect costs incurred to develop, produce, and deliver the training program (see white paper Four Steps to Computing *Training ROI* [Lilly, 2001] for more information on this topic).
Turnover costs	Total of the costs of separation + vacancy + replacement + training	The separation, vacancy, replacement, and training costs resulting from employee turnover. This formula can be used to calculate the turnover cost for one position, a class code, a division, or the entire organization. *Exit interviews* (Drake &

❖ **Table 6.1** (Continued)

HR Metrics		
		Robb, 2002) are a useful tool in determining why employees are leaving your organization (see white paper *Employee Turnover Hurts Small And Large Company Profitability* [Galbreath, 2002] for more information on this topic). Implements retention efforts. Evaluates if HR practices are having a causal relationship in positive changes to improving cost of turnover.
Turnover rate (monthly)	(No. of separations during mo./Avg. no. of employees during mo.) × 100	Calculates and compares metric with national average, using business and legal reports at www.bls.gov/jlt/home.htm. This measures the rate at which employees leave a company. Is there a trend? Has metric increased/decreased? Analyzes what has caused increase/decrease to metric. Determines what an organization can do to improve retention efforts. Evaluates if HR practices have a causal relationship in positive changes to improving metric. (See white paper titled *Employee Turnover: Analyzing Employee Movement Out of the Organization* [Ofsanko & Napier, 1990].)
Turnover rate (annual)	((No. of employees exiting the job/Avg. actual no. of employees during the period) × 12)/No. of mos. in period	Calculates and compares metric with national average, using business and legal reports at www.bls.gov/jlt/home.htm. This measures the rate at which employees leave a company. Is there a trend? Has metric increased/decreased? Analyze what has caused increase/decrease to metric. Determines what organization can do to improve retention efforts. Evaluates if HR practices have a causal relationship in positive changes to improving metric. (See white paper titled *Employee Turnover: Analyzing Employee Movement Out of the Organization* [Ofsanko & Napier, 1990].)
Vacancy costs	Total of the costs of temporary workers + independent contractors + other outsourcing	The cost of having work completed that would have been performed by the former employee or employees less the wages and

	HR Metrics	
	+ overtime – Wages and benefits not paid for vacant position(s)	benefits that would have been paid to the vacant position(s). This formula may be used to calculate the vacancy cost for one position, a group, a division, or the entire organization.
Vacancy rate	(Total no. of vacant positions as of today/Total no. of positions as of today) × 100	Measures the organization's vacancy rates resulting from employee turnover. This formula can be used to calculate the vacancy rate for one position, a class code, a division, or the entire organization.
Workers' compensation cost per employee	Total WC cost for year/Average no. of employees	Analyzes and compares (e.g., Year 1 to Year 2, etc.) on a regular basis. You can also analyze workers' compensation further to determine trends in types of injuries, injuries by department, jobs, and so forth. HR practices such as safety training, *disability management*, and incentives can reduce costs. Use metric as benchmark to show causal relationship between HR practices and reduced workers' compensation costs.
Workers' compensation incident rate	(No. of injuries and/or illnesses per 100 FTE/Total hours worked by all employees during the calendar year) × 200,000	The "incident rate" is the *number of injuries and/or illnesses* per 100 full-time workers. 200,000 is the base for 100 FTE workers (working 40 hours/week, 50 weeks/year.) The calculated rate can be modified depending on the *nature* of the injuries and/or illnesses. For example, if you wished to determine the lost workday case rate, you would include only the cases that involved *days away from work*.
Workers' compensation severity rate	(No. of days away from work per 100 FTE/Total hours worked by all employees during the calendar year) × 200,000	The "severity rate" is the number of days away from work per 100 FTE. To calculate the severity rate, replace the number of injuries and/or illnesses per 100 FTE from the incident rate calculation with the number of days away from work per 100 FTE. More information is available regarding the types of injuries, incident

(Continued)

❖ **Table 6.1** (Continued)

HR Metrics		
		rates, and comparison with other SIC codes at www.bls.gov/iif/oshdef.htm#incidence.
Yield ratio	Percentage of applicants from a recruitment source that make it to the next stage of the selection process (e.g., 100 resumes received, 50 found acceptable = 50% yield)	A comparison of the number of applicants at one stage of the recruiting process with the number at the next stage. (*Note: Success ratio* is the proportion of selected applicants who are later judged as being successful on the job.)

SOURCE: SHRM (2008).

NOTES:

1. The HR Metrics Toolkit provides a number of factors that can be measured to show how HR contributes to the business. Measures such as absence rate, health cost per employee, and HR expense factor show that HR has a sense of the importance of human capital measurement in supporting business objectives.

   - Compare your metrics against other organizations' metrics, survey data, and so forth to evaluate your performance. Metrics can show the benefit of your HR practices and their contribution to your organization's profit.
   - Benchmark data and designate the time frame (plan year, fiscal year, etc.). Compare data going forward using the same time frame (Year 1, Year 2, Year 3, etc.) to show improvement or decline.

2. FTE, full-time equivalents; ROI, return on investment; WC, workers' compensation.

IT investments, are wary of new HRIS investments. Without an event like Y2K driving change, justifying new investments in HRIS will require strong business cases, that is, cost-benefit analyses.

Justification Strategies for HRIS Investments

Strategies for justifying HRIS investments fall into two categories—risk avoidance and organization enhancement. Risk avoidance strategies are used when investments are believed to eliminate or mitigate significant future risks faced by the organization. The potential obsolescence of *legacy computing systems* was a prototypical risk avoidance scenario. The old system simply needed to be changed to avoid Y2K problems and also simply because it was out-of-date. The need to comply with laws and regulations, for example, Equal Employment Opportunity, as well as changes to these laws, is another circumstance in which justification based on risk avoidance is popular. Risk avoidance justifications focus on the magnitude and timing of risks and often are not supported by the extensive investment analyses required by a CBA.

Organization enhancement strategies, on the other hand, highlight how effectiveness of the firm will be improved by the addition of a new or improved HRIS—as measured by increases in revenues or reductions in costs. Organization enhancement justifications are often more challenging to "sell" to decision makers than risk avoidance because enhancements do not carry the threat of real loss if no action is taken. Hence, there is often a reduced sense of urgency. This situation is supported by research on decision making under risk that consistently demonstrates that when faced with potential losses, decision makers are willing to accept much greater risk (i.e., they become more risk seeking to avoid the loss) than when alternatives are framed as gains (Kahneman & Tversky, 1979). Investments justified by organization enhancements typically require more rigorous support and are subjected to more intense scrutiny by decision makers.

Evolution of HRIS Justification

Several factors suggest that the next generation of HRIS functionality will be more difficult to justify. Much of the "low-hanging cost reduction fruit" has already been picked due to the Y2K implementation "scare." HRIS implementations in the past decade have shifted many organizations from administratively intense paper-and-pencil HR processes to electronic transaction processing supported by integrated computer systems. Employee and applicant self-service, online recruitment, electronic payroll processing, and workflow have dramatically reduced transaction costs. Employee self-service alone is reported to reduce the cost of many HR transactions by 50% or more. The next wave of HRIS functionality is unlikely to generate comparable reductions in costs, making investment decisions based on further cost reductions more difficult to justify.

Of course, there will be small and medium-size organizations that still have paper and pencil systems or HRIS legacy systems that need to be updated. For many of these organizations, the value of reducing costs, such as transactions costs, will still serve as legitimate justification for adopting or upgrading an HRIS. In addition, these firms may also use a risk avoidance approach to justify the new HRIS—for example, the need for accurate and timely employee records in litigation. However, as will be argued in this chapter, the use of an organizational enhancement approach may provide a more powerful strategy in determining the CBA for investment in a new HRIS.

It is therefore less certain that organizations with an operational HRIS will continue to pursue investments in new HRIS functionality aggressively. In fact, underinvestment in HRIS—that is, failing to approve many worthwhile investments—is likely. This is not because the benefits of new investments in HRIS functionality are too small—in absolute terms, they are still substantial. Rather, underinvestment is more likely to result from the use of outdated CBA methodologies that emphasize cost reduction and do not adequately recognize the value of organization enhancements attributable to new HRIS functionality. HRIS managers will need tools that will allow them to identify sources of value to the organization that result from HRIS investments. The field is maturing, and investment analysis tools must mature with it. This chapter examines HRIS cost-benefit dynamics and provides tools and techniques that can be used to conduct and evaluate HRIS CBAs that incorporate organizational enhancement.

Approaches to Investment Analyses
Makes a Difference: Some Guidelines

As indicated above, one *must* conduct an investment analysis for the acquisition of a new or improved HRIS. Usually, there is an HR or HRIS professional with selected team members who form the HRIS project team as described in Chapter 3. This project team, or usually a subset of it, conducts the analyses and can be referred to as the CBA team. The members of this team include senior professionals from the HR and IS departments as well as representatives from other departments who will be affected by the HRIS project. The CBA is one of the first steps in seeking approval for an HRIS project. It is important to recognize that a proper mindset has as much to do with conducting an effective HRIS investment analysis as do the tools and techniques used. Understanding why the analysis is being conducted and understanding the expectations of what is going to be done with the results will influence the judgments made by the CBA team during the analysis as well as increase the value of the results produced. Here are several considerations or guidelines that can help the CBA team approach the analysis with an improved likelihood of making the best decision for the organization. These guidelines are contained in Table 6.2.

The reason for conducting a CBA is to improve organizational effectiveness. The objective of each analysis is to make the best decision for the organization. In some instances, the best decision may be not to proceed with an investment. Making an investment should never be the ultimate objective—investments are a means to achieving some other organizationally meaningful outcome. The desired outcome is to become a more effective organization, not simply *to justify a purchase.*

Be honest with yourselves. The CBA team should enter each analysis with an open mind—not with a solution to justify. It is best to think of the analysis as an investigation devoid of any personal biases. The team needs to come into the decision process without preconceived notions, willing to approach the analysis objectively and willing to accept whatever results the analysis produces. If members of the team have a vested interest in a particular solution, it will cause difficulties in the analysis. CBA techniques can be used to identify investment opportunities and important contingencies that can influence the success of eventual implementations. Developing a reputation as an impartial evaluator will increase management decision makers' confidence in analyses done by the CBA team.

Focus on key functionality rather than on specific hardware or software solutions. Many proposals for a new HRIS have erroneously started by identifying a new software application and then trying to justify how its features and capabilities could benefit the organization. However, it is whether your organization performs more effectively after an HRIS implementation that will determine the success of any investment. The CBA team must focus on organization and its process and outcomes (i.e., reduce costs or increase revenues), identify opportunities in order to improve effectiveness, and only then look to identify software solutions that provide the desired capabilities. Centering the analysis on a specific software solution shifts the focus of the analysis to the capabilities that solution offers, not necessarily the capabilities that are most needed by the organization.

Examine benefits before you examine costs. This is often difficult to do, but training the CBA team to examine the benefits of a change in HRIS functionality before estimating costs will produce better analyses. Knowing how much would need to be spent to acquire new functionality before conducting the analysis of benefits can easily lead to an inaccurate CBA. This "backward" approach makes it almost impossible not to consider what

❖ **Table 6.2**   Keys to Successful HRIS Cost-Benefit Analysis (CBA)

Key	Description
The objective is improving organizational effectiveness	The objective of any HRIS CBA is not to purchase specific hardware or software. The objective is to improve organizational performance.
Be honest with yourself	Start each analysis with an open mind, not an investment to justify.
Focus on functionality, not products	The analysis should focus on the improvement in organization functionality that is to be achieved. Start with that functionality and let it lead to the product. Don't start with the product and attempt to identify ways to justify its purchase.
Estimate benefits first	Examine costs only after you have completed the analysis of benefits.
Know your business	This means really understanding what your business is and how your current processes allow your organization to accomplish its objectives. Understand the dynamics of your current processes and where potential for improvement can be found.
Develop the best estimate possible	Don't be overly optimistic or conservative. Develop the best estimate you can with the data available to you.
Separate the CBA from questions of how best to justify a final decision	The questions involved in developing an accurate CBA and attempting to determine how best to justify a choice are two separate processes. The latter involves choices about which sources of value should be included in the business case to be presented to decision makers. These are determined by the relative comparisons of costs with the magnitudes and types of revenue sources. The latter should be pursued only after a complete analysis has been accomplished.

level of benefits will be necessary to justify the investment. This can cause the team to abort the process of identifying and analyzing benefits prematurely if a single source of benefits appears to be sufficient to guarantee adoption of the HRIS project. It can also encourage "fishing" for questionable benefits when the initially identified benefits may not be enough to justify the HRIS investment.

Know your business. As stated in Table 6.2, this means really understanding the organization's business and how the current processes in all departments allow the organization to accomplish its objectives. Furthermore, it means that the CBA team must understand the dynamics of the current business processes and where potential for improvement exists.

Since the CBA team consists of senior representatives from all staff departments affected by the HRIS project, this business knowledge should exist within the team. Obviously, this means that the CBA team must have cooperative relationships among its members.

Develop the best estimate possible. Various methods to achieve this goal are discussed in this chapter. It is also critically important, as mentioned in the previous paragraph, that cooperative relationships exist among members of the CBA team. The project team leader must try to reduce and/or eliminate interdepartmental politics, particularly between the HR and IS departments. Chapters 7 and 8 provide more details on this topic. Finally, note the advice in Table 6.2 not to be overly optimistic or conservative but develop the best estimate possible with the available data.

Distinguish between the analysis and the packaging of that analysis for decision makers. The primary purpose of analyzing an HRIS investment is to determine whether and to what extent it will improve your organization. The objective of the analysis should be to provide the "best" estimate of the impact of an HRIS investment as is possible. Developing the estimate should be seen as separate and distinct from the process of presenting and "selling" the investment opportunity to management decision makers. Decision makers may choose to rely on specific forms of benefit evidence or to adopt conservative assumptions in order to gain approval for the investment. Inappropriate investment decisions may result if overly conservative assumptions in the HRIS investment analysis by the CBA team are compounded by the conservative bias common among decision makers.

HRIS Cost-Benefit Analysis

A CBA is simply what its name indicates—a comparison of the projected costs and benefits associated with an HRIS investment. A cost is any new outlay of cash required for the initial purchase, implementation, or ongoing maintenance of the investment. A benefit is any financial gain resulting from the investment that occurs at any time during the investment's useful life. Benefits include both revenue enhancements and cost reductions. At its core, CBA is an analysis of change in the cost-benefit ratio—a comparison of current existing circumstances with new conditions that are projected to exist after the HRIS investment.

A common misconception is that conducting meaningful CBA requires financial expertise. Knowing some financial basics, such as discounting, cost of capital, cash flow, ROI, **payback period**, net present value, and **internal rate of return**, is useful but not required. Organizations differ in the specific financial measures they use to evaluate investments. Organizations may use *ROI, internal rate of return (IRR), payback period,* or other measures alone or in combination. Therefore, it can be useful to seek out an internal advisor to help you package your analysis for the managerial decision-making process used in the organization. Typically, this internal advisor will be someone in the Finance or Accounting departments. However, regardless of the specific financial measures used in the organization, investment analyses are based on three basic pieces of information: (1) sources of costs and benefits, (2) an estimated dollar value for each cost and benefit item, and (3) the time when the organization will incur each cost and receive each benefit. These are the core data on which any investment analysis is based, including for a new HRIS. Developing these data requires a thorough understanding of your business—which includes finance and other business considerations. The remainder of this chapter will cover how these three basic pieces of information are obtained and used in a CBA.

Identifying Sources of Value for Benefits and Costs

Investments in HRIS functionality differ from more traditional investments because HR is commonly perceived as a source of costs rather than a direct source of revenue (Cascio, 2000). Any impact that HR department activities have on revenues occurs *indirectly* through the effect of HR programs and practices on other units of the organization. For example, a program focused on training retail employees to provide quality customer service is typically a cost ascribed to the HR department; however, its indirect effect of increased sales is classified as revenue for the Operations department. Thus, the effects of many HR programs or practices are often described as "soft" or, more appropriately, indirect. As a result, managerial decision makers are justifiably concerned about using "soft" benefits to justify "hard" dollars. This is particularly true for large investments such as a new HRIS. Approving an investment only to find that the expected benefits never materialize is something all decision makers fear. In the absence of obvious risk avoidance justifications and significant reductions in costs from previous HRIS investments, developing expertise in identifying and valuing the direct and indirect benefits derived from HRIS investments is one of the critical challenges that HRIS managers face.

Failing to recognize important sources of costs or benefits is a common problem in HRIS CBA. The HRIS CBA matrix shown in Figure 6.1 can be used to help uncover all reasonable benefit and cost components in HRIS investment analyses. The HRIS CBA matrix consists of six cells.

❖ **Figure 6.1**   HRIS Cost Benefit Analysis Matrix

		Direct (Hard)	*Indirect (Soft)*
Benefits	Revenue enhancement	**1** New revenue (new sales)	**2** Improvement potential (better decision making)
	Cost reduction	**3** Direct costs (cancelled vendor contracts)	**4** Potential costs (saved staff time)
Costs	New implementation costs	**5** Out-of-pocket costs (software, service agreements)	**6** Indirect costs (increased technical support needs)

The four upper cells represent sources of benefits (i.e., direct revenue enhancements, indirect revenue enhancements, direct cost reductions, and indirect cost reductions). The two cells of the bottom row capture costs of implementation (i.e., direct and indirect). A simple evaluation of each cell of the HRIS CBA matrix can ensure that important sources of benefits or costs are not overlooked.

Direct Benefits

The four "benefit" cells of the HRIS CBA matrix (Figure 6.1) represent the crossing of two dimensions. The first dimension is the type of benefit—revenue enhancements versus cost reductions. Organizations can enhance revenues by reengineering processes. These changes could result in new revenue in terms of new sales due to a more efficient procedure (i.e., training programs for new employees). Organizations can also reduce costs by reengineering processes to make them more effective. For example, an organization with a new HRIS could decide to *insource programs* (such as training) that had been outsourced to vendors. HRIS investments often involve both types of effects. HRIS investments can also permit the offering of new products and services that can increase revenues and/or enhance profit margins. Thinking about opportunities for cost reductions and revenue enhancements separately allows each to be explored more fully.

The terms *direct* and *indirect* are used here to refer to benefits and costs that might be described elsewhere as "hard" and "soft," respectively. Hard, or direct, outcomes generally refer to benefits (and costs) (a) that are very likely to occur and (b) whose values are easily estimated. Table 6.3 shows an example of a CBA analysis for an e-learning investment. As can be seen, the organization is considering having e-learning modules created by an external vendor to replace in-house training programs. The direct revenue enhancements include additional revenue the organization can earn by selling the e-learning modules as well as outsourcing the e-learning. The direct cost reductions include all the typical costs involved in training programs, as seen in Table 6.3.

Indirect Benefits

Soft, or indirect, benefits, on the other hand, are often less easily quantified because their occurrence may be less certain or because their value is more difficult to establish. Indirect revenue enhancements result from improvements in intermediate outcomes that could position the organization to be able to increase revenues. These may include outcomes such as an improved capacity to attract and retain higher-quality employees, improving employees' capacity to make decisions, or freeing up time for employees to engage in activities that more directly support the strategic objectives of the organization (see Figure 6.1). Often, indirect revenue enhancements represent intermediate outcomes that require that some additional activity or condition exist before an increase in revenues is realized. For example, to allow some HR professionals to work on activities directly related to strategic company goals, it may be necessary to restructure the HR department and provide some in-service training.

Since these benefits are not reported in a dollar metric, current CBAs typically do not include these items in the numeric analysis but will often address them in the narrative discussion supporting the investment. In the e-learning example, better customer service (i.e., that can lead to increased customer retention and repeat sales) and a more agile organization (i.e., one that can retrain or retool its employees more quickly) to respond to rapidly changing markets are examples of indirect or contingent sources of revenues.

Indirect cost reductions involve those changes that are expected to lead to reduced costs. Benefits that would fall in this category for a new HRIS include (a) reductions in time required to perform activities that do not lead to direct reductions in payroll (i.e., are not directly tied to reductions of overtime or *employee headcount*), (b) expected

❖ **Table 6.3** Example of an e-Learning CBA Matrix

	Direct (Hard)	Indirect/Contingent (Soft)
Revenue enhancements	Outsourcing e-learning Sales of locally developed learning modules or programs	Better customer service leading to increase in repeat sales A more agile organization able to respond rapidly to market changes
Cost reductions	Reduced travel expenses Reduced facilities costs/room and equipment rentals/refreshments Reduced requirements for paper-based training materials; teaching aids Reduced expenses for instructor fees or salary and benefits cost (if internal) Reduced costs for replacement workers if trainees are required to be away from their work	Improved training effectiveness through customization and just-in-time delivery = faster learning curve, less lost productivity while waiting for training, and right amount/type of content More agility, able to disseminate new cost-reducing best practices more quickly Reduction in turnover (41% of employees will look for another job within 12 months due to poor training and education; with good training and education, this percentage drops to 12%) and/or absenteeism Improved safety (fewer injuries, less lost time, fewer insurance claims, lower workers' compensation costs)
Costs of implementation	Installation support Software fee/license Software support Analyst/administrator Training administrator Courseware development Courseware purchase Bandwidth fees	Increased use of end-user help desk Courseware redevelopment Lost productivity during conversion to new system

reductions in the amount of or requirements for technical support, (c) expected reductions in absenteeism and turnover, and (d) time required to bring trainees up to the status of fully functioning employees. In many instances, time-saving applications are incorrectly projected to result in reductions of employee headcount—a direct savings in payroll expenses. More often, though, the deployment of new HRIS functionality results in a new structuring of work that saves parts of jobs, rather than whole jobs. As a result, the benefit is indirect—a saving of time that can be deployed in other activities. In the e-learning example, enhancements in training effectiveness are expected to lead to steeper learning curves and less time to proficiency. This is expected to result in fewer errors and less rework. Reductions in turnover costs are also expected because better-trained employees are expected to have higher satisfaction and remain in their jobs longer. Furthermore, improved access to safety training is also expected to result in less time lost as a result of injuries and reduced insurance claims and workers' compensation costs.

Consequently, analyses of indirect benefits can be challenging, but in many instances, these indirect effects are the real source of benefits for new HRIS functionality. Being able to identify the indirect effects and understand how they are expected to affect costs and revenues is critical to understanding how to justify HRIS investments. An important advantage of understanding how and where indirect benefits are expected to occur is that it allows the organization to specifically plan and manage HRIS implementations in ways that make it more likely for indirect benefits to actually occur. Because these benefits are often contingent on other events, knowing what those events are and managing them as a part of the implementation are likely to result in greater organizational impact.

Implementation Costs

Once benefits have been estimated, the analysis can proceed to estimating the costs of implementation. In contrast to estimating benefits, cost estimation is often easier to complete because cost information is readily available and already offered in a dollar metric. In most cases, many sources of costs will be direct costs. Direct costs will include, but are not limited to (a) costs for initial purchase and updates of software and any additional hardware and (b) ongoing costs for internal or external systems support. In the e-learning example (Table 6.3), direct costs include the purchase of any new software, hardware, and licenses required to implement the system as well as the cost of the expertise necessary to develop and manage training on this new platform.

Indirect costs refer to those areas of cost that cannot be specifically known up front but may arise in the process of implementing the system. These include the impact of the implementation on the organization, such as lost productivity in other areas while the organization completes implementation. This impact includes lost productivity for rank-and-file employees as well as the HR staff involved in implementation. The e-learning example includes increased use of end-user help desks or other support functions, costs necessary to revamp existing courseware while the organization learns how to use the new system most effectively, and the lost productivity that will occur for any current employees who will be required to take on additional responsibilities associated with the adoption of the new system.

It is important to be thorough in attempting to identify all the sources of costs. If your analysis recognizes some benefit without incorporating an offsetting change in costs, you likely have missed a source of costs in your analysis. For example, organizations that projected significant reductions in employee headcounts due to converting paper-and-pencil transactions to electronic systems often failed to recognize the full additional costs that will be required in technical support, training on the new system, or transitioning large numbers of employees out of the organization.

Also, the total costs of implementation will depend on the current state of information system development in the organization. The components of organizational information systems evolve at different speeds across organizations. Knowing the current level of evolution of the components of the total organization's information systems is quite important, and this would include systems; the staff departments concerned with finance, operations, marketing, and information systems; as well as HR. This includes evaluations of (a) the current state of their computer hardware, software, data, and processes; (b) user sophistication and networking; and (c) telecommunications technology. New HRIS investments may affect all these IS components. The greater the change in any one of these areas required to support the implementation of the new HR functionality, the more expensive the implementation will be. Total cost will be driven by (a) the scope or size of the HRIS implementation; (b) the amount of customization required; (c) the maturity of the HRIS functionality being considered—the less mature the functionality, the greater the costs of implementation and upgrades are likely to be; and (d) the experience levels of the implementers.

Where early attempts at CBA often grossly underestimated or ignored significant sources of costs, the experience of organizations over the past decade have provided insights that can be used to do a much better job of recognizing what cost items need to be included in cost analyses. Several sources for determining cost of implementation are available, including organizations that have previously implemented specific packages or functionality, vendors in the HRIS field, or implementation consultants.

Estimating the Timing of Benefits and Costs

Once you have identified and valued the benefits and costs associated with an investment in HRIS functionality, the next step of the analysis is to determine when in time each benefit and cost will be incurred during the entire HRIS project. Organizations use this information to estimate the cash outflows and inflows associated with investments. The timing of cash flows is particularly important when costs and revenues occur in different time periods and when the organizations' cost of capital is relatively high. This information will also be important in the management of the entire HRIS project, which will be discussed in Chapter 7.

The task of assigning the benefits and costs to time periods can be accomplished by constructing a simple grid that lists benefit or cost items along one axis and future time periods on the other axis. The number of time periods required will depend on the expected useful life of the investment and the relevant length of time periods (usually years, but months or quarters may be used in some instances). The critical period for most HRIS investments is the first 5 years. Few organizations are likely to approve HRIS investments with longer payback periods. Furthermore, current rates of development of HRIS functionality and computing systems suggest that most HRIS investments may be functionally obsolete after 5 years.

Estimating the Value of Indirect Benefits

Most HRIS CBAs will include some indirect benefits. One of the more difficult tasks in HRIS CBA is estimating the value of the indirect benefits. The difficulty of converting indirect benefit estimates to a dollar metric has limited their role in HR technology investment decisions. To this point, it has not been uncommon for soft benefits to be relegated to the narrative supporting an investment analysis that is otherwise based solely on estimates of direct cost reductions. For good reason, many managers consider these savings cautiously. That does not mean, though, that these benefits are any less important than direct benefits to the organization. In fact, as noted earlier, ignoring them in HRIS investment analyses could result in incorrect or misleading analyses. As a result, we need to adapt the general techniques used to analyze HR technology investments to meet these new requirements. The challenge is to provide an estimate of the value of soft, or indirect, benefits and to do so in a way that can be justified to skeptical decision makers.

Estimating Indirect Benefit Magnitude

Constructing dollar estimates of indirect benefits is challenging, but it can be done. To simplify estimation of the dollar value of indirect benefits and provide a basis for justification, one should break this task into the following three steps: (1) estimating benefit magnitude, (2) mapping benefits to cost or revenue changes, and (3) converting magnitude estimates to dollar values. By separating these steps, we can begin to understand better the factors that influence the value of indirect benefits and, perhaps more important, when they are likely to occur during the HRIS project. Also, since magnitude and value are often driven by different factors, separating these decisions provides a better framework for postimplementation evaluations. Both benefit and value estimates are then open to objective review.

An objective of HRIS CBA is to develop the best possible estimates of the likely effect of the new HRIS functionality. Therefore, using a metric to estimate the impact that is familiar or comfortable to those developing the estimate is likely to improve accuracy and, ultimately, make the project easier to manage. For instance, if the new functionality is predicted to reduce turnover, the magnitude of the expected change using "turnover rates" would be estimated first. Then the determination of the dollar value of the differences between the current rate and the expected change rate is likely to produce better estimates than if decision makers attempted to estimate the dollar impact of the expected reductions in turnover in a single step. The objective is to choose the metric and measurement procedure that will result in the most accurate estimate possible of the size of the benefit.

Once that metric has been chosen, there are three approaches for estimating benefit magnitude: (1) direct estimation, (2) benchmarking, and (3) internal assessment. Which method is the most appropriate depends on the amount of specific information that is available to the organization and the CBA team.

Direct Estimation

Direct estimation is the simplest of the three methods. It is quick and easy to perform. It relies solely on the expertise of analysts or subject matter experts in the CBA team to "estimate" the expected magnitude of the benefit. Direct estimation is *most appropriate* when the scope of the project is small, compliance or risk avoidance is a primary investment justification, other substantial sources of direct cost reduction or direct revenue enhancement exist, or no other method for estimating benefit magnitude is available. The primary limitation of direct estimation is that the accuracy of the analysis depends on the expertise of the estimator.

When several equally **qualified** subject matter experts are available, collecting independent estimates from each expert and using the average of these estimates is recommended. In addition, it can be useful to require that experts articulate the rationale for their estimates. This not only ensures that experts are thoughtful in the preparation of their estimates, but an analysis of the assumptions or expectations contained in these rationales can also be used to help improve the accuracy of future estimates.

Benchmarking

Benchmark data on the magnitude of indirect benefits achieved in other firms can be used. The advantage of benchmarking is that it allows an organization to build on the experiences of others. These data can provide evidence that a specific outcome can occur as well as evidence of its potential magnitude. Howes (2002) offers an insightful example of how benchmarking data can be used to estimate how much reduction in turnover an organization might expect. In this example, benchmark data about industry-wide levels of turnover are used to construct estimates of the potential for improvement in turnover that might be possible for a given organization. If an organization has high turnover relative to industry standards, it has the potential for greater improvement than might be expected for other firms in that industry.

Benchmarking information of various types is becoming more widely available from a number of sources (e.g., Gartner Group, Hackett Benchmarking, Saratoga Institute, the Society of Human Resource Management, Harris Associates—see Web sites provided in the Appendix). Table 6.1 contains HR metrics that can be used in benchmarking. Organizations can conduct their own benchmarking studies to gather specific data from targeted firms that may not be readily available from third-party sources. Benchmarking is preferred over direct estimation for larger, more costly projects where investment risks are greater. Benchmarking is also useful when organizations have limited experience with the targeted functionality of the HRIS project or when there is no access to local data. The primary disadvantage of benchmark data is that the experiences of other organizations may not completely generalize to your firm or business unit. A good recent source of information on benchmarking is the *SHRM Human Capital Benchmarking Study: 2006 Executive Summary* (Dooney & Smith, 2006).

Internal Assessment

Internal assessment involves the use of a firm's own internal metrics (see Table 6.1) or other forms of the firm's specific data as the basis for estimates. Use of this method requires that the organization has maintained historic records on previous information system projects. Internal assessment is best done when investment scopes are large and direct estimation and/or benchmarking suggests that benefits may not be dramatically higher or lower than costs (e.g., less than ± 30%). Internal assessment requires that the organization possess the capabilities to gather the data about their own processes necessary to support these analyses. An advantage of *integrated information systems*— systems built on common platforms that permit single instances of data to be used in several applications and the seamless transfer of data between applications—is that the marginal costs of assessments are greatly reduced, permitting cost-effective assessments of a wide range of organizational outcomes. Internal assessments offer the most precise estimates of the costs and performance of existing or newly implemented processes. Internal assessments, though, may only be able to provide a portion of needed data. That is, an organization may be able to gather accurate data about the outcomes of current processes but may need to rely on benchmark data from other organizations or obtain direct estimates of the outcomes for new processes in order to complete the analysis.

Even though possessing integrated information systems can reduce the marginal costs of assessments, conducting internal assessments and evaluating the data they produce are not costless activities. As described in Table 6.4, internal assessment provides the most precise estimates of the baseline costs and current performance of existing processes against which to compare potential improvements. However, internal assessments will result in higher costs than direct estimation and, depending on the nature of the assessment, could result in higher decision support costs than benchmarking. As noted above, internal assessment is only possible when the organization has experience with a given form of functionality. It is not possible to assess the effects of new functionality that has not previously been implemented anywhere in an organization.

Each of these three approaches is recapped in Table 6.4. The ideal method for estimating the magnitudes of indirect benefits in most HRIS analyses is to use a combination of these three approaches. This permits each benefit to be estimated using the method that is most appropriate given the availability of data and the investment's cost, risk, and opportunity characteristics. For high-stakes investment decisions, using multiple methods to develop estimates can provide additional insight and increased confidence in the final decision.

Mapping Indirect Benefits to Revenues and Costs

In some instances, the metric of choice may not be one that is easily or unambiguously tied to reductions in costs or increases in revenues. That is, estimating the value of indirect benefits requires that the analyst first be able to articulate how the indirect benefit is linked to an actual reduction in costs or an increase in revenues. For example, let's assume that an indirect benefit of a proposed investment is reduced turnover; and we predict that implementing a new HRIS functionality will result in a reduction in voluntary turnover from 10% to 5% for a targeted group of jobs. Since the effect of turnover on costs and benefits is indirect, we need to understand how reducing turnover is expected to affect an organization's revenues or costs in order to translate our 5% reduction in turnover to other metrics that are more closely associated with changes in costs and revenues.

Employee turnover is a good example because it affects costs and revenues in several ways, some of which are depicted graphically in Figure 6.2. The departure of an employee can increase costs because it may require the organization to engage in a new recruitment and hiring cycle and the new employee is likely to require training. But there are other effects as well. For instance, the loss of an employee in a position critical to the day-to-day functioning of the organization will require that efforts be made to cover the work responsibilities in that employee's absence. How an organization chooses to cover those responsibilities will influence the magnitude of the net loss of contribution that results from the vacancy. There will be salary savings for the vacant position, but the cost

❖ **Table 6.4**   Different Approaches to Estimating Benefit Magnitude

Approach	Description	When to Use It	Advantages/Limitations
Direct estimation	Direct ("gut level") estimates of the relationship of the potential benefits to the estimated costs of engaging in an investment	Best when costs are not large. Appropriate when attempting to gain compliance or mitigating extreme risks When substantial direct cost reduction or revenue enhancements exist	Quick and low cost to perform May not provide data that contain sufficient detail for use in monitoring implementation effectiveness or to perform follow-up analyses Highly dependent on the expertise of the decision maker
Benchmarking	Using benchmark data from other firms to estimate the potential benefits and costs that are likely to result from the purchase of HRIS functionality	Superior to direct estimation when costs are large When the organization either has limited experience or no data concerning the area of functionality	Allows the organization to develop more precise estimates than direct estimation based on the collective experience of other organizations Average estimates of outcomes may not generalize to the target organization
Internal assessment	Analysis based on specific internal assessments of actual costs and likely benefits (e.g., activity-based costing)	When costs are high and benefits are not obviously dramatically larger than costs When the organization has the assessment capabilities in place to gather the appropriate data	Provides the most precise estimates of the baseline costs and current performance of existing processes against which to compare potential improvements May increase both costs and time required to make decisions
Mix and match	Using combinations of these approaches	When different amounts or sources of information are available for different types of costs and benefits (e.g., most likely scenario)	Permits the organization to use the best methods available

of temporaries, shifting other employees off their primary assignments, and the opportunity costs that result from using less than fully effective temporary or overextended employees also must be considered. The total loss of this contribution is represented in Figure 6.2 by the region $A * B$—the value of the daily loss of contribution multiplied by

❖ **Figure 6.2** Conceptualizing the Effects of Turnover

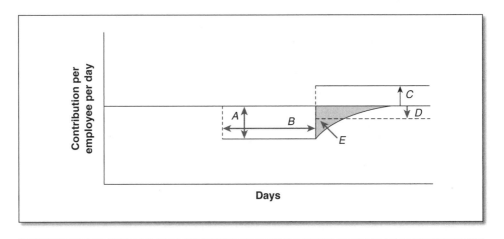

NOTE: *A* is the average value (contribution) that is lost per day that a given position is left unfilled. *B* is the number of days that a position remains unfilled. *C* and *D* represent the increase or decrease in contribution that occurs if a new hire is more or less effective, respectively, than the employee who left. The grey area noted as *E* represents the loss of contribution that occurs during the time when a new employee is learning the job.

the number of days the position remains vacant. Also, as noted in Table 6.3, turnover affects the contribution the organization derives from a position. Perhaps the departing employee was a poor performer and replacing him or her will actually result in a net gain in average long-term effectiveness for that position (i.e., *C* in Figure 6.2). Even with training, new hires will most likely require some time on the job before they can become fully effective; their effectiveness will increase as they gain expertise. But during this time, contribution will be less than would have been experienced had there been no turnover in the position (i.e., *E* in Figure 6.2). Each of these intermediate outcomes can be tied to a specific cost or revenue effect through one or more links.

In this example, a comprehensive estimate of the impact of the expected reduction in turnover is represented by the sum of the estimates of each of these components in Figure 6.2. In some cases, and for specific types of benefits, these relationships may seem quite complex. Do not be discouraged, or dissuaded from being thorough. Understanding exactly how these changes are projected to affect the organization may yield important new insights about these intermediate outcomes and contingent factors that put managers in a position to ensure the success of HRIS investments. Understanding which factors are affected by the investment can also aid in further refining magnitude estimates and is essential for estimating value. Cascio (2000) provides a complete list of the costs of voluntary turnover. In addition, Table 6.1 provides several metrics important for measuring the effects of turnover, such as "time to fill," "turnover costs," "vacancy costs," and "vacancy rate."

Methods for Estimating the Value of Indirect Benefits

Direct revenue enhancements or direct cost reductions are typically estimated in dollars, so their value is provided by the total estimate. Estimates that are developed in other metrics, such as total absenteeism in days lost, must also be converted to dollars. For indirect benefits that can be tied more directly to cost reductions or revenue enhancements (i.e., new products developed or market share increased), the task is somewhat more difficult, but it can be done. It requires estimating the strength of the relationship between the change in intermediate outcomes and changes in revenue or cost (e.g., each new account will generate $50,000 in gross profit annually; reducing scrap by 5% will save $10,000 per month). For other outcomes, such as employee time saved, these conversions are somewhat more difficult to conduct.

For this last category, employee time saved, there are two methods for estimating the value of employee time that have slightly different purposes—average employee contribution (AEC) and utility analysis. These methods are alternatives to a third practice that is *not recommended*—estimating an employee's value as equal to his or her cost to the organization. In nearly all cases, employee cost dramatically underestimates the average employee's contribution. We know that this is true because most organizations are profit-making concerns. For an organization to be profitable, each individual in that organization, on average, should contribute enough value to compensate for the cost of his or her wages and benefits and the equipment and facilities employed on the job, in addition to covering taxes and accounting for profit. This helps explain why downsizing does not always improve financial results. Downsizing only makes sense when the contribution of the employees eliminated is less than their cost in salary and benefits to the organization.

Average Employee Contribution

In the turnover example discussed earlier, estimating the value lost while a position remains open (i.e., the region represented by the area A * B in Figure 6.2) requires an estimate of the value of the average daily contribution made by an employee. The average contribution approach argues that the AEC in an organization is equal to total gross profit divided by the number of employees or *full-time equivalents* (FTE). AEC is not a metric that most organizations track, although a measure of average daily gross margin (i.e., Revenue – Cost of goods sold) generated per sales person would be an example of this type of measure. There are other metrics in Table 6.1, but this is one of the simplest that captures AEC as accurately as is needed for estimating the value of indirect benefits.

AEC = (Net revenues—Cost of goods sold)/No. of employees

By definition, in a profitable organization this number will be substantially higher than Labor costs—Total employee pay and benefits. Dividing this number by the number of workdays in a year (i.e., 252) produces an estimate of average daily contribution. As noted in the equation above, this method does not reduce contributions attributable to employees by the amount of capital expenditures and other non-employee-related expenses—the equipment and tools that aid employees in doing their jobs. The reason is that these tools are used to enhance employee contribution. The tools enhance what employees can do, but they do not generate contribution on their own. That is, if you take away the employees who use the tools and equipment, the contribution goes with them. The tools provide no independent and unique contribution to the organization in the absence of the employee.

AEC can be used to estimate the average annual contribution of an organization's employees. Obviously, average contribution can and does differ across jobs. Thus, organizations may want to adjust this number up or down for specific jobs to recognize differences in contribution potential. Jobs that more closely support the organization's mission and offer jobholders broader authority to influence the work of others and greater autonomy for choosing how and when work will be accomplished are likely to offer above-average levels of contribution. The advantage of this method is that it establishes a baseline contribution value by jobs that is consistent with the actual financial performance of the organization.

Average contribution estimates, though, provide little guidance in estimating differences in contribution between employees holding the same or similar jobs. This is represented in the turnover example in Figure 6.2 by the difference between the values C and D—the differences in contribution for two different employees who might hold the same position. Differences in contribution can be developed using internal assessment by directly examining the individual employee differences (variance) in the work outcomes produced by a large number of individuals holding equivalent positions. This can be accomplished more readily for jobs where individual production rates can be monitored (i.e., sales, transaction processing, and some manufacturing settings).

Utility Analysis

However, not all settings allow for the development of these data. There may not be a large number of people doing similar work, or a job's content may change frequently. In these instances, utility analysis techniques can be useful. Utility analysis (Boudreau, 1991; Cascio, 1987, 2000) is a set of decision-making tools and techniques used to estimate the value of HRM programs. It is based on the assumption that employees are not perfectly interchangeable; thus, selection, placement, and training are important, because they are able to affect the contribution possible from an employee holding a given position.

Utility analysis is most useful because it provides a mechanism for converting differences in estimated job performance to dollars. In utility analysis, the value of differences in job performance (i.e., contribution) among individuals is captured in a metric called the standard deviation of performance in dollars (SD_y). SD_y represents the value of a 1 standard deviation difference in average job performance. If you can estimate the magnitude of differences in expected or actual job performance and combine this with a dollar-valued estimate of the value of differences in job performance (i.e., SD_y), then it is possible to produce a dollar value estimate for the effects of the HR functionality or program designed to influence individual job performance.

The most challenging component of utility analysis is estimating SD_y. However, research suggests that, in the absence of more specific information, a baseline estimate of SD_y can be developed by multiplying annual salary by .40 (Judiesch, Schmidt, & Mount, 1992; Schmidt & Hunter, 1983; Schmidt, Hunter, McKenzie, & Muldrow, 1979). So, for example, a position with an average salary of $30,000 per year might be expected to be associated with SD_y of $12,000. Thus, employees with job performance at the 85th percentile for that job would be expected to contribute $12,000 *more* per year than employees at the 50th percentile. Similarly, employees with job performance at the 15th percentile for that job would be expected to contribute $12,000 *less* per year than employees at the 50th percentile. There are several versions of utility analysis. Readers with additional interest in these methods are encouraged to read more about the "Brodgen-Cronbach-Gleser" model described by Boudreau (1991) and the discussions and examples provided by Cascio (1987, 2000).

Obviously, the two methods described here offer relatively coarse tools for estimating the value of individual contributions in organizations. However, both are theoretically sound, and perhaps more important, they are transparent. Analysts and decision makers are likely to disagree on the inputs used in AEC calculations or utility analysis. If so, the transparency of the method permits these values to be changed, and the effects of the different inputs can be easily examined. The *critical point* is that these values can and should be estimated. These estimates will improve over time and with experience. But not using these or other methods to estimate the value of changes in employee contributions is not appropriate. These changes and differences in employee contributions do exist and are a critical component of HRIS investment analyses.

Avoiding Common Problems

It is not uncommon for HRIS CBA to include an extensive analysis of costs matched with a single source of benefits—typically, an estimate of direct cost reductions. Recognizing only direct cost reductions is problematic for two reasons. First, it ignores HR's more strategic role in improving organizational effectiveness. Online recruitment that results in hiring higher-potential employees and developing and administering training programs through online tools, for example, is designed to enhance employee job performance and organizational effectiveness—not necessarily to reduce employee head count. Ignoring these benefits can dramatically understate the actual value of HRIS investments.

A second problem is that in many instances items listed as direct cost reductions are actually indirect cost reductions. Time saved is a prime example. Many HRIS reduce the amount of time required to complete typical HR transactions, but these time savings do not result in actual reductions in overtime or head count. In these instances, time saved is actually an indirect benefit. Its value depends on how individuals spend the extra time made available to them. As noted in Chapter 1, transactional activities deal mostly with day-to-day record keeping—for example, entering payroll information, employee status changes—and the administration of employee benefits. An HRIS that reduces the time on transactional activities would allow the HR employee to spend more time on traditional or transformational activities (see Chapter 1), both of which can assist the organization in meeting its strategic goals.

Incorrectly recognizing time saved as a direct cost reduction creates the wrong expectation among decision makers. This can lead to the incorrect perception that an investment did not succeed—no reduction in payroll expenses occurred—when, in fact, the benefits to the organization actually occurred in other forms. This point is illustrated in a CBA completed by National Institute for Health's Center for Information Technology. This analysis, which does an exceptional job of cost analysis, includes only one source of benefits—employee time saved. In this example, investing in the new system was projected to reduce staff time required by 75%, resulting in a 53% ROI. Admirably, this organization was required to conduct a postimplementation review within 18 months to examine actual versus estimated costs and benefits and to determine whether use of the new system should be continued. The postimplementation analysis revealed that time saved was only 50%, not 75%. As a result, instead of the expected 53% ROI, the revised ROI was only 6%. One can only wonder what might have happened if the amount of time saved had been only 45%, since using their CBA formulas would have resulted in a negative ROI. Would this organization have been forced to abandon this new system? Interestingly, in the postimplementation analysis, the evaluators pointed to other benefits to justify the continued use of the new system. However, since they were not included in the original analysis, bringing them into the postimplementation review may be seen by some as inappropriate. However, an indirect benefit, such as improved employee morale, found in the postimplementation evaluation would be a powerful indication that the HRIS investment was worthwhile. In addition, employee morale has been directly linked to voluntary turnover, for which costs can be measured.

Third, be sure that value estimates assigned to time saved are reasonable. Many HRIS investments purport to save employee time, making it a common component of HR technology CBA. When new HRIS functionality will save enough time to make it feasible to reduce the number of employees or reduce overtime expenses, time saved is a source of direct cost reduction. However, more often HR technology saves time in smaller increments that do not permit direct savings. That is, the amount of time saved does not permit whole positions to be eliminated. In these circumstances, time saved is an indirect benefit. The value of the time saved actually depends on what value-generating activities employees engage in during the time made available to them. For example, if the implementation of self-service functionality reduces workload but does not lead to head count reductions, the new functionality might still have tremendous organizational value if those saved hours are used to improve the effectiveness of recruitment efforts or some other value-generating activity, such as the development of a team-training program.

Time saved, though, may not always have value. Consider a situation in which an individual engages in an activity that requires 5 minutes everyday, but the application of new HRIS functionality is estimated to cut this time from 5 to 1 minute. What is the value of the 4 minutes saved each day? Generally, larger blocks of time are more easily employed in value-enhancing activities. Consider your own use of time during the day. Could you constructively employ an additional minute of time each day? In most cases, we already have several of these minutes in our schedule that, because of the ebb and flow of daily events, are difficult to use productively. Therefore, it is questionable whether most employees can consistently use short periods of time (i.e., blocks of less than 5 minutes, for instance) productively. Thus, it may be very difficult to generate value for HR technology that is expected to save time but does so in many small increments.

Obviously, knowledge of your organization's business, as noted earlier in this chapter, will be important in identifying potential benefits. Use your own knowledge, but enlist other knowledgeable professionals and managers in this process as well. Individuals in your organization who are currently responsible for HR functionality prior to implementation of the HRIS, that is, recruiting, or are downstream customers of these HR products or services are good resources to enlist to identify benefits. They can help fill in the gaps and highlight other sources of benefits that might not be readily apparent to others. Vendors are a second resource. A review of the features and benefits cited by vendors in the relevant HRIS product space can also be used to identify potential sources of benefits. Vendors may also provide case studies that describe the experiences of companies that have implemented their products and the outcomes that were effected in those organizations. Using a combination of these sources can ensure a comprehensive list of the benefits to be gained when new HRIS functionality is developed.

Packaging the Analysis for Decision Makers

When you have completed your analysis, you should have (1) data that identify each benefit and cost component examined; (2) estimates of the dollar magnitude of each, including upper and lower bounds; (3) estimates of when the organization will incur each cost and receive each benefit; and (4) documentation justifying each decision you made in developing these values. The importance of documentation has been emphasized in all previous chapters and will be re-emphasized in Chapters 7 and 8. After Steps 1 to 4 above are completed, the next step is to package the analysis for decision makers in your organization. Obviously, this process involves "selling" the analysis to senior management so that it should not be overlooked or minimized. Managerial decision makers prefer well-organized and clear CBAs to help them make their investment decisions.

Packaging the analysis for consideration by decision makers includes deciding what data to include and how the data should be organized. A table outlining the value and timing of costs and revenues is likely to be the central focus of the analysis. Some experts encourage limiting the number of sources of benefits presented to decision makers to simplify the presentation and the required justifications. This approach is satisfactory for small projects, that is, a stand-alone HRIS application such as applicant tracking, but would be inappropriate for a complex HRIS project.

While being able to make your case on a single page is beneficial, there are several advantages in including all cost and benefit components that influence the likely outcomes of the investment decision. First, this offers the most complete, best estimate of the value of the investment, thereby giving decision makers the best information to make an appropriate investment decision. Second, it provides the decision maker with a fuller understanding of the investment and the impact of the investment on the organization. Particularly with respect to indirect benefits, contingent actions taken by managers are likely to influence the extent to which the estimated benefits will be achieved. Making decision makers aware of these contingencies can help enlist their assistance in ensuring each investment's future success.

The Role of Variance in Estimates

Since the estimates produced for cost-benefit analyses are necessarily based on forecasting future events and may also depend on events outside the control of management, actual outcomes are likely to deviate from those estimated. For example, one may expect an average reduction of 2 hours in transaction processing time. However, the actual amount of reduction will vary depending on the mix of transaction types, operator expertise, and other job requirements. *The primary estimate of interest is the overall average expectation.* However, particularly for indirect benefits, it is useful to develop expectations about the range and potential distribution of possible outcomes. Lower- and upper-bound estimates as well as standard deviations from the average (variance) for magnitude and value estimates are useful auxiliary information that can help convey expectations about potential variability in outcomes.

Variance estimates can be developed by each of the estimation methods described in Table 6.4. For direct estimation, HR and IT professionals could produce estimates of the range and likelihood of various outcome levels. In addition, multiple estimators could be used if two or more equally knowledgeable individuals exist. Each could be instructed to estimate a target value and upper and lower bounds for the estimated expectations, and these could then be averaged to develop overall estimates. Variance estimates for benchmark data from other organizations in the same industry are more difficult to acquire, since most sources only report averages and do not report variance data. In some instances, it may be possible to request the standard deviations associated with each benchmark value from other organizations. However, with internal analysis, variance estimates can be calculated from the archival records of existing HR or IT processes before and after implementation. In all instances, an estimate of the standard deviation of outcomes could then be used to provide a range of the most likely outcomes. However, remember that in the absence of compelling evidence to the contrary, the best estimate is the one you developed, and that should be the focus of your analysis.

Conclusion

Accurately identifying and estimating the value of the benefits and costs of new HRIS functionality will play a critical role in HRIS investment decisions in the foreseeable future. A renewed interest in detailed investment analysis is healthy and should be embraced by analysts and decision makers. In addition to supporting improved investment decisions, detailed CBAs of HRIS investments are also likely to identify implementation contingencies and opportunities that can increase the chances for successful implementations. These analyses also provide the desired organizational targets against which to judge the effectiveness of an investment postimplementation.

Summary

The central focus of this chapter has been estimating and understanding the cost effectiveness dynamics of new investments in HRIS by completing a CBA. The calculation of a CBA has become critical for any new investment by an organization, as CBAs are closely linked with strategic goals such as profitability and survival of an organization. Without a well-done CBA, it is becoming less likely that managerial decision makers will approve expenditures for new HRIS investments. In the past, investments in an HRIS were primarily driven by a risk avoidance strategy or cost reductions made possible by replacing paper-and-pencil or out-of-date systems. Since Y2K, organizations have had to rely on organization enhancement strategies to justify the investment in new HRIS functionality. Organization enhancement strategies highlight how firms' effectiveness will be improved by the addition of a new or improved HRIS, as measured by estimated increases in benefits (e.g., revenues) compared with estimated costs in a formal CBA. This requires that we change our approach of cost justifying HRIS to account for these new types of benefits.

This chapter also addressed the importance of adopting an appropriate mental approach to CBA before any numbers are analyzed. Appropriately framing the analysis as an opportunity to improve organizational effectiveness, with the focus on really understanding the dynamic effect an HRIS investment may have on the organization, is critical to good decision making, and perhaps just as critical to effectively managing implementations and the ongoing use of these systems to provide the greatest opportunity for the estimated benefits to be realized.

An organizational enhancement strategy was shown to be the appropriate approach for conducting a CBA to justify an HRIS investment in today's organizations. Instructions on how to estimate direct and indirect costs and benefits were covered in detail with a focus on creating a palatable CBA report for managerial decision makers. Finally, both AEC and utility analysis were covered as methods to assess the indirect benefits of an HRIS investment. It was argued that, when possible, a utility analysis approach should be used. However, both approaches to estimation of indirect benefits, as well as the other methods for estimating costs and benefits discussed in this chapter, should be used for postimplementation evaluation of the HRIS. Finally, as recommended in the earlier chapters, the CBA should be documented carefully and completely, as it will be useful in both HRIS project management and HRIS implementation.

DISCUSSION QUESTIONS

1. How has the use of HRIS evolved over the past 10 years in organizations, and how might this influence an organization's evaluations of additional or updated investments in HRIS?

2. Why is it important to estimate the benefits to be derived from new HRIS functionality before you estimate the costs? If costs were estimated first, how might this change the analysis?

3. Organizations have traditionally used employee time saved as the primary source of benefits in justification of HRIS and other types of information system investments. Why can this be problematic?

4. What makes indirect benefits so difficult to include in CBA? What techniques might be used?

5. When should benchmarking be preferred to direct estimates of the magnitudes of benefits? When should direct estimates be preferred? Is it appropriate to use both?

6. Why does average employee contribution offer a better estimate of the contribution of individuals to an organization than total compensation (wages, incentives, and benefits)?

7. What are the advantages to an organization's decision makers of distinguishing between conducting a CBA for new investments and the process of selling that investment?

CASE STUDY

Investment Associates, Inc. (IA)[3] started as a small firm in 2001 with four employees plus its owner, Jim Tower. The company specialized in providing financial investment and tax advice to its clients. Jim had brought a substantial number of clients from his private practice, which had become too large for him to handle by himself. His four employees included three colleagues who had some experience in financial investment advice and a secretary/administrative assistant. Jim and his three colleagues were all certified public accountants (CPAs), and a considerable portion of the company's business was in tax consultation and completion of individual and corporate tax returns.

IA was quite successful and by 2007 had added 42 new employees—financial and tax advisors and additional administrative staff, including an office manager, Marian Sweet. In addition to the office manager's supervisory tasks, Marian had to complete federal and state reports on the employees as required by law.[4] However, Marian was not trained in HRM, and she suggested to Jim that the company needed to hire someone with a background in HRM before they "got into trouble" with the government. Marian was particularly concerned about gender and racial discrimination but did not understand how to apply the provisions of the appropriate laws and guidelines.

In November 2007, IA hired Sylvia Wong, who had an undergraduate degree in psychology and four years' experience in HR. In addition, in December 2007, Jim was negotiating to purchase the financial consulting business of an old friend who was retiring. This purchase would mean the addition of 17 new employees in February or March 2008. Sylvia met with Jim in mid-January 2008 to discuss the growing burden of employee reports and payroll processing, all of which were currently being done using a paper-based HR system. She advised Jim that the company needed an HRIS to process employee records and complete the required government reports. As an example, she stated that by searching all employee files, it took her a full week to complete the Equal Employment Opportunity Report (EEO-1)[5] required by the federal government. Furthermore, based on this report, it appeared that the company could have problems in terms of compliance with several federal laws. She suggested that the company purchase an HRIS to assist with company record keeping and required reports.

Since the company had been using computer-based applications for financial analysis and tax reporting, Jim thought that Sylvia's suggestion to computerize employee records was a good one. However, given his financial background, he wanted Sylvia to develop a business case, including a cost-benefit analysis, for the purchase of an HRIS.

Your task is to help Sylvia justify the purchase of an HRIS.

Case Study Questions

1. What approaches to justifying this investment might Sylvia consider?

2. What are some of the ways you can use the HR metrics, that would be available using the HRIS, to justify the purchase of an HRIS?

3. In preparing a CBA for this project, what are some of the costs and benefits involved in this investment in an HRIS?

4. Explain how to estimate costs and benefits, both direct and indirect, in terms that Jim will understand. (Remember, Jim always has his eye on the "bottom line.")

5. Explain how to calculate a CBA to justify the HRIS project. Would you use a cost reduction or organizational enhancement (or both) as a strategy for justifying the purchase?

6. What are the three common problems that could occur in your CBA for an HRIS? How would you avoid them?

7. Finally, and most important, explain how variance estimates that can be generated for a CBA would be useful to Jim in the management of his company.

NOTES

1. The content of this chapter was based in part on two articles published in the *IHRIM Journal* (Carlson, 2004a, 2004b).

2. Dollars will be used as an example of currency throughout this chapter. When used so, it implies that other currencies such as euro, yen, or peso could be substituted for it.

3. The names of the company and employees are fictional to protect their confidentiality.

4. See Chapter 9 for a discussion of some of these reports.

5. See Chapter 9.

REFERENCES

Boudreau, J. (1991). Utility analysis for decisions in human resource management. In M. D. Dunnette & L. M. Hough (Eds.), *Handbook of industrial and organizational psychology* (Vol. 2, pp. 621–752). Palo Alto, CA: Consulting Psychologists Press.

Browne, G. J., & Rogich, M. B. (2001). An empirical investigation of user requirements elicitation: Comparing the effectiveness of prompting techniques. *Journal of Management Information Systems, 17*(4), 223–249.

Bureau of Labor Statistics. (2008). *Employer costs for employee compensation–March 2008.* Retrieved April 21, 2008, from ftp://ftp.bls.gov/pub/special.requests/ocwc/ect/ececrlse.pdf

Carlson, K, D. (2004a). Estimating the value of the indirect benefits of new HR technology. *IHRIM Journal, 8*(4), 22–28.

Carlson, K. D. (2004b). Justifying HRIS investments post Y2K: Identifying sources of value. *IHRIM Journal, 8*(1), 21–27.

Cascio, W. F. (1987). *Costing human resources: The financial impact of behavior in organizations* (2nd ed.). Boston: Kent.

Cascio, W. F. (2000). *Costing human resources: The financial impact of behavior in organizations* (4th ed.). Boston: Kent.

Dooney, J., & Smith, N. (2006). *Human capital benchmarking study: 2006 executive summary.* Washington, DC: Society of Human Resource Management.

Drake, N., & Robb, I. (2002). *Exit interviews.* Alexandria, VA: SHRM White Paper.

Ewusi-Mensah, K. (1997). Critical issues in abandoned information systems projects. *Communications of the ACM, 40*(9), 74–80.

Fitz-Enz, J. (2001). *How to measure human resources management* (3rd ed.). New York: McGraw-Hill.

Galbreath, R. (2002). *Employee turnover hurts small and large company profitability.* Alexandria, VA: SHRM White Paper.

Hollmann, R. W. (2002). *Absenteeism: Analyzing work absences* (SHRM White Paper). Retrieved February 16, 2008, from www.shrm.org/hrresources/whitepapers_published/CMS_000381.asp

Howes, P. (2002, February/March). Calculating the ROI for an HRIS business plan. *IHRIM.link,* 12–15.

Judiesch, M. K., Schmidt, F. L., & Mount, M. K. (1992). Estimates of the dollar value of employee output in utility analyses: An empirical test of two theories. *Journal of Applied Psychology, 77,* 234–250.

Kahneman, D., & Tversky, A. (1979). Prospect theory: An analysis of decisions under risk. *Econometrica, 47,* 313–327.

Kavanagh, M. J., Gueutal, H. G., & Tannenbaum, S. I. (1990). *Human resource information systems.* Boston: PWS-Kent.

Lemon, W. F., Bowitz, J., Burn, J., & Hackney, R. (2002). Information systems project failures: A comparative study of two countries. *Journal of Global Management, 10*(2), 28–39.

Kluttz, L. (2003). *Employment management association cost per hire staffing metrics survey.* Alexandria, VA: SHRM Research Department.

Lilly, F. (2001). *Four steps to computing training ROI.* Alexandria, VA: SHRM White Paper.

Ofsanko, F. J., & Napier, N. K. (1990). *Effective human resource measurement techniques: A handbook for practitioners.* Alexandria, VA: SHRM White Paper.

Schmidt, F. L. & Hunter, J. E. (1983). Individual differences in productivity: An empirical test of estimates derived from studies of selection procedure utility. *Journal of Applied Psychology, 68,* 407–414.

Schmidt, F. L., Hunter, J. E., McKenzie, R. C., & Muldrow, T. W. (1979). Impact of valid selection procedures on work-force productivity. *Journal of Applied Psychology, 64,* 609–626.

SHRM. (2008). *HR Metrics Toolkit.* Retrieved April 12, 2008, from www.shrm.org/hrtools/hrmetrics_published/cms_002620.asp

PART III

HRIS
Implementation

Project Management Development and HRIS Acceptance

Salvatore Belardo

Peter Otto

Michael J. Kavanagh

EDITORS' NOTE

This chapter focuses on the implementation and maintenance of the HRIS, the final two stages of the System Development Life Cycle. Remember that the maintenance stage also involves the evaluation of the HRIS in terms of its original objectives. Project management (PM) involves a planned and organized effort to accomplish a specific (and usually) one-time effort—for example, implement a new HRIS. PM includes the following: (1) a project plan, (2) project goals and objectives, (3) tasks to achieve goals, (4) the resources needed, and (5) developing a budget and timelines for completion. The role of PM in the development of an HRIS is where knowledge from both HRM and IT/IS[1] is combined to ensure successful implementation. IT provides us with PM technical approaches, techniques, and tools, while HRM provides behavioral knowledge, team management advice, and change management techniques. PM is absolutely crucial to the success of the HRIS and begins in the early stages of the HRIS immediately after management approval for the project has been obtained. There is some redundancy with the material in other earlier chapters in this book. However, this redundancy is important to illustrate how effective management of an HRIS project uses and affects both HR and IT professionals. Finally, this chapter examines critical success factors in the management of the HRIS project.

CHAPTER OBJECTIVES

After completing this chapter, you should be able to

♦ Understand how the use of PM approaches, techniques, and tools help throughout the SDLC

♦ Understand the contributions that HRM makes to the management of the HRIS project

♦ Understand how the combination of knowledge from the IT and HRM literature makes the development and implementation of the HRIS successful

♦ Be able to describe what factors are used to develop **program evaluation and review technique (PERT)**, critical path method (CPM), and Gantt charts

♦ Be able to describe how IT factors can affect HRIS project success

♦ Understand how knowledge from HRM literature provides guidance for handling the behavioral problems and issues that arise in HRIS development

♦ Understand the different roles of the steering committee and PM team in the HRIS project

♦ Be able to describe how training and documentation are important to both the development and implementation of an HRIS

♦ Be able to describe how critical success factors affect the success or failure of an HRIS project.

VIGNETTE

In a national organization with 24 plant locations within the United States, a new software package for use in recruiting and selecting new employees, that is, applicant tracking, was being developed and implemented as an add-on to the firm's current HRIS. The software was created by an external vendor; however, the implementation was being done by the internal HR and IT staff. As part of the contract, the vendor agreed to make modifications to the software as needed until the management of the organization felt it was operating properly. (This feature of an external vendor contract is typically required in the Request for Proposal [RFP].)

The project team had used a PM approach (PERT) and technique (**Gantt chart**) described in this chapter. This plan included (1) a project plan, (2) project goals and objectives, (3) tasks to achieve goals, (4) resources needed, and (5) developing a budget and timelines for completion. As will be seen in this chapter, these tools from the IT field are very useful in keeping an HRIS project on time within cost and other constraints. As part of the PM plan, there was a steering committee and a project team at the corporate level; and each company location was to form steering committees and project teams at their location that included IT and HR professionals.

The initial phase of the implementation involved a pilot test of the first version of the new software in two plant locations to make appropriate changes to the software based on this initial review and trial. This first phase took 3 months to complete, and the necessary modifications to the software were made. The next phase, to be accomplished over the next 3 months, was to field test the revised version of the software in all company locations. It was decided to have the corporate-level leader of the HRIS project teams visit each location to meet with the HR and IT staff on the local project team to answer questions and generally assist with any problems during the field test. The feedback from this field test was to be sent to the vendor for any additional modifications of the software.

In 23 of the firm's locations, the meetings with the HR and IT staff went extremely well, and the managers of these locations were pleased with their progress in implementing the software. In one company location, however, no formal meetings on the field test had been held. In this location, the HR and the IT departments have had many difficulties cooperating in the past, and each blamed the other for the problems beginning the field test even though a local project team had been appointed that had both IT and HR professionals as members. The corporate project team leader conducted several interviews to determine the source of this problem.

Even though meetings had been scheduled by the local project leader, there were always key personnel, IT or HR, missing at each meeting. Unfortunately, the key personnel missing changed from meeting to meeting, making the accomplishment of the field test near impossible. After intervention by senior management and 6 months of struggling with this company location, the field test was completed. This set the timetable for the total software implementation back by 3 months longer than anticipated.

Even though the corporate project team had used well-tested IT approaches and techniques from the PM field, the management of the people in the one company location failed miserably. The information in this chapter will focus on both the *necessity* to have well-tested PM techniques and tools as well as *effective management of* the project team and other end users.

Introduction

Statistics measuring the success of systems development efforts are not very encouraging. Browne and Rogich (2001) assert that "despite good faith efforts by organizations, analysts, and users, a majority of systems are either abandoned before completion or fail to meet user requirements." Inordinate delays, excessive budget overruns, postimplementation testing, user dissatisfaction, late deliveries, poor reliability, and maintenance problems are some of the most cited reasons for the failure of IT projects. It has been estimated that this problem costs organizations in the United States alone at least $100 billion a year (Ewusi-Mensah, 1997). Of those systems that are completed, more than 55% will exceed cost and time estimates by a factor of 2. Even more troubling is the fact that only 13% of the IS projects that are completed are considered successful by the executives who sponsor them (Lemon, Bowitz, Burn, & Hackney, 2002).

The failure to deliver successful systems poses risks not only to those whose operations depend on them but also to those responsible for delivery. The inability to employ "quality" systems can prevent the firm from satisfactorily performing critical operations. A classic example is the well-documented failure of Hershey Foods' $112 million computer system (Nelson & Ramstad, 1999). Due to poor design and implementation, Hershey was unable to fill an order for 20,000 lb. of candy placed by a regional distributor in mid-September in anticipation of Halloween demand. The distributor, in turn, could not satisfy 100 of his 700 retail customers. The journal article further quoted a candy buyer for Lowes Foods, a chain of supermarkets, who advised stores to stop reordering Hershey candies and switch to a competitor. While Hershey claimed that it only lost a small percentage point in its market share, others contended that the shelf space that it lost would be difficult to win back.

Internal IS departments as well as those external to the firm that develop any systems, including an HRIS, for their customers risk damage to their reputation as well as their pocketbook when systems that are developed do not provide satisfactory results. In a suit brought against PeopleSoft, Deloitte & Touche LLP, and Deloitte Consulting, the plaintiff W. L. Gore claimed that both the software company and the consultants failed to live up to the terms of the contract. As a result, W. L. Gore sought unspecified punitive damages as well as triple compensatory damages. They asked that Deloitte refund nearly $3 million in fees and PeopleSoft refund more than $600,000 in charges (MacDonald, 1999). These problems could have been avoided if a proper PM methodology was employed. PM methodologies provide the tools and techniques to enable project managers and teams to organize their work so as to ensure that satisfactory systems are developed and implemented.

This need for effective management of an HRIS development project was extensively discussed by Walker (1982) when he identified the 10 most common mistakes in developing an HRIS. One of the major issues that he identified was loose project control, consistent with the problems in the Hershey incident described in the previous paragraph. Likewise, Kavanagh, Gueutal, and Tannenbaum (1990) provided a list of 14 recommendations based on a review of the HRIS literature. Prominent among these recommendations was to "make a detailed plan," "develop a checklist to monitor implementation," "documentation . . . is critical for successful implementing and maintaining of the HRIS," and "audit the new system periodically for maintenance" (p. 191). The use of the approaches and techniques covered in this chapter will focus on meeting these recommendations so as to result in a successfully implemented HRIS.

Project Management

Effective PM for the HRIS depends completely on a positive relationship between the IT and HR departments. Without this *necessary cooperation, the HRIS development and implementation will fail.* In the next several sections of this chapter, the contributions from the fields of IT and HR will be described along with a prescribed approach to combine them to make the HRIS fulfill the needs of all end users.

The IT Perspective

PM Literature

An examination of the PM literature reveals a number of PM methodologies. Information on PM in general and PM techniques and tools can be found at the following Web sites: University of Washington (www.washington.edu/computing/pm), State of Kansas (www.da.ks.gov/kito/ITPMM.htm), MIT (http://web.mit.edu/ist/pmm), and the Project Management Institute (www.pmi.org). There are a number of PM approaches and methods described in these Web sites. Regardless of the methodology employed, each has four general PM process phases in common. These phases are quite similar to the SDLC for an HRIS project and basically parallel the various steps and requirements in the development and implementation of an HRIS covered in Chapters 3 to 5. However, it is important to examine project phases from the perspective of the IT discipline since this examination can uncover additional issues regarding the success of an HRIS project.

The PM methodologies all begin with the project initiation phase. In this phase, a project concept and a **project proposal** are developed. The project concept describes the key stakeholders and seeks to ensure that the right questions are asked so that the right problem is solved. In the initial stages of an HRIS, this is critical information. The project proposal, also called a **project charter**, contains objectives and performance targets (e.g., cost, time, scope). The project concept and proposal must be approved by top management to fulfill the requirements of this phase and begin the development of an HRIS. Without a firm commitment from top management on timelines and budget, the HRIS project will likely fail.

The second phase of project planning identifies the tasks that must be performed. A **Work Breakdown Structure** is created along with **Work Packages** (i.e., what must be done, by whom, using what resources, in what time, and at what cost). During this phase, the order in which activities, tasks, and jobs are to be performed is decided, and specific check or monitoring points are established. These monitoring points could affect the direction, scope, or requirements of the HRIS project.

As discussed in the IT field, the third phase is called project execution. In this phase, the HRIS project is tracked, and periodic progress reports are prepared for management and the project team. During this phase, five key factors are assessed: *schedule, budget, open issues, risks, and communication.* PM approaches such as the PERT and the **CPM** are used at this point in conjunction with visual tools such as Gantt chart and bar chart. A description of the use of these approaches and tools is available on the Internet (http://en.wikipedia.org/wiki/Project_management_software).

The final phase is project close-out, which involves the implementation, evaluation, and maintenance of the HRIS. This phase includes the following goals and activities:

1. Accepting the project's products (indicated by user sign off)

2. Completing the Post Implementation Evaluation Report (PIER)

3. Disbursing resources (staff, facilities, and automated systems)

4. Conducting a "lessons learned" session

5. Completing and archiving project records

6. Recognizing outstanding achievement

7. Celebrating project completion

The celebration of the project completion is as important as the initial proposal since it will help employees feel more committed to making the new HRIS operate properly.

As can be seen, the IT field offers a number of techniques and approaches to PM developed by professionals. Using these techniques, one can develop an *overall work plan* based on the work breakdown structure and work packages described above. This overall work plan is a written time schedule of tasks and responsibilities with deadlines so that the HRIS project will be done in the total time allotted. Note, however, that the orientation is to the management of the project itself not the people who are responsible for the development and implementation of the HRIS. The management of the people involved, the project team and end users, is contained in advice from the HRM and HRIS fields. This distinction between the IT and HR fields is sometimes referred to as the *gap* between the IT capabilities of the organization and the use of these capabilities by HR professionals. Frequently, there is a mismatch—positive or negative—between what the HR department wants and the capabilities available through the IT department. This fact, as seen in the opening vignette, underscores the need for cooperation between these departments in staffing the project team. The next section discusses some of these issues regarding the formation and operation of the project team.

PM Approaches and Tools

The IT field has provided some powerful approaches and tools to be used in managing any project. PERT is a method for analyzing the tasks involved in completing a given project, the time needed to complete each task, and the minimum time needed to complete the total project. It was invented in 1958 by the U.S. Department of Defense's U.S. Navy Special Projects Office and was intended for complex, one-of-a-kind projects such as its first application, the Polaris mobile submarine-launched ballistic missile. One of the most relevant features of the technique is "PERT Networks," that is, charts of intersecting timelines. PERT is capable of incorporating uncertainty and variability because it estimates the time required to complete jobs according to probabilistic distributions.

CPM, meanwhile, is a mathematically based algorithm for scheduling a set of project activities that was developed by DuPont and Remington Rand Corporation for managing plant maintenance projects. CPM is used to construct a project model that includes the following:

1. A list of all activities required to complete the project

2. The time (duration) that each activity will take to complete

3. The dependencies among the activities

Using these values, CPM calculates the starting and ending times for each activity and determines which activities are critical to the completion of a project (called the critical path) and which activities have "float time" (are less critical). In PM, **a critical path** is the sequence or project network with the longest overall duration determining the shortest time possible to complete the project. Any delay in activity on the critical path directly affects the planned project completion date (i.e., there is no float on the critical path). A project can have several, parallel critical paths. An additional parallel path through the network with a total duration shorter than the critical path is called a subcritical or noncritical path.

Finally, one can develop a *Gantt chart,* which is a graphical representation of the duration of tasks against the progression of time in a project. Wikipedia (http://en .wikipedia.org/wiki/Gantt_chart) defines it as follows:

> A Gantt chart is a popular type of bar chart that illustrates a project schedule. Gantt charts illustrate the start and finish dates of the terminal elements and summary elements of a project. Terminal elements and summary elements comprise the work breakdown structure of the project.

For a more detailed and technical explanation of PERT, customer relationship management (CRM), and Gantt charts, there are several good texts available (O'Brien, Crnkovic, & Belardo, 2006; Wiest & Levy, 1969). In addition, Jon Peltier (2008; http://pubs.logicalexpressions.com/Pub0009/LPMArticle.asp?ID=343) has developed a method using EXCEL to build Gantt charts.

There are multiple advantages in using these PM approaches and tools; the major one is a tighter control over the process to ensure successful implementation of the HRIS. This tighter control is attained by the following means:

1. Definition of all activites to be accomplished to complete the project

2. Establishment of a specific schedule for activities that includes an estimate of when each activity will start and end

3. Project milestones that are used to monitor specific activities set by this schedule

4. Assignment of resources in terms of equipment, people, and, thus, costs for all activities

5. Computation of the total budget and allocation of the budget needed to accomplish each activity

6. A graphical picture of the entire project showing all activities, their costs, and their milestones

Extending these IT ideas and providing more detail for the management of an HRIS project, Rampton, Turnbull, and Doran (1999) indicate that every project has resource limits and specifications in the following categories:

- Time—start and end dates
- People—identification, specific skills they bring to project, availability, costs
- Tools—equipment, software
- Money—budget (p. 76)

In addition, they note that PM also brings a critical capability to the HRIS project—namely, *evaluation of the project's performance* by monitoring progress against the planned timetable. This monitoring allows for periodic adjustments as well as ensuring that **project creep** is not occurring.

Software has been developed for all the PM approaches and tools—CPM, PERT, and Gantt charts. The interested reader can consult Wikipedia, the free encyclopedia (http://en.wikipedia.org/wiki/Project_management_software) for a fairly comprehensive listing. Software applications will not be recommended in this book since each organization's situation will vary, and choosing software/hardware for HRIS decisions is a complicated matter. The International Association for Human Resource Information Management (IHRIM) has a buyers' guide for HRIS software that is available to members, and if any outside consultants are used, they usually have information on the most current and effective software for the HRIS project.

General IT Factors Affecting PM Success

Rather than presenting a detailed discussion of the various stages and templates found on the University of Washington and State of Kansas Web sites, there are three general problems that must be addressed that are critical to the success of any of these methodologies. *First* is the importance of solving the right problem. All too often, IT developers create systems that they *think* end users want. The end users are frequently dissatisfied with the results, thus accounting for the dismal statistics cited above. *Second* is having IT system developers who do not understand the HRM domain and its problems and constraints. It is necessary to have systems developers who are sensitive to HR issues and willing to learn about the constraints so that the information requirements phase can be completed within the time frame and budget constraints specified by the project plan. In most organizations, this problem can be solved by having both IT and HR professionals on the project team. Obviously, if the organization has an HRIS professional, this problem will be greatly reduced. *Third*, project managers, from either an IT or an HR department, must understand the dynamic nature of any HRIS project and how the interrelations among various factors might render decisions ineffective or even counterproductive. For example, studies have shown that assigning more people to an overdue project might actually delay project completion.

In addition to these three problems, three general factors that affect successful PM are time, cost, and scope. The cost of project development depends on a number of variables, including labor rates, material, plant (buildings, machines, etc.), equipment, and profit. In addition to the total fixed and variable costs are contingency costs and time to completion;

this can be broken down into the units of time required to complete each task. Scope refers to what the project is supposed to accomplish and what the end result should be (i.e., what the end user wants). Time and cost are process measures of performance and, therefore, measures of efficiency. Scope, on the other hand, is about effectiveness and is measured by whether the right questions have been asked and whether the right problem is being addressed. Staying within the project costs, time, and scope depends highly on the ability of the project team to gather the correct information requirements for the HRIS project during the needs analysis, which was described in Chapter 4.

The HRM Perspective

The techniques of PM from the IT literature will ensure the development of an overall written work plan for the HRIS project. However, there are still a number of organizational requirements involved in the successful completion of the HRIS project. The HRM literature provides guidance on how to handle the behavioral and management issues that arise in fulfilling these requirements during the HRIS project. The organizational requirements include the following:

1. Identification of steering committee and project charter

2. Configuring the PM team

3. Identification of available resources and constraints

4. Controlling project creep

5. Selection of the implementation team

6. Training and documentation

Each of these requirements and their use in PM will be described in the following sections.

Identification of the Steering Committee and Project Charter

During the initial considerations for the development of an HRIS, typically, there are strategic goals set for the project. Often this process is referred to as "making the business case" for the HRIS project, which would include estimating both the costs and the benefits of the new system—that is, estimating its cost-effectiveness. However, the central focus before project initiation would be on strategic goals—for example, (1) reducing the transaction costs in HR processing; (2) improving the quality of HR information for managerial decisions; or (3) improving the HR processes of talent management, which includes the recruiting and selecting of new employees as well as retention of valued ones. Regardless of the specific strategic goals for the new system, the project will still have constraints in terms of resources available.

As such, the composition of the steering committee must include representatives of senior management from HR, finance, systems, marketing, and operations. A crucial player is the senior management member who is selected as the **project sponsor**, since this person typically has overall fiscal responsibility for the project. The primary responsibility of the steering committee is the *oversight of the project* in terms of progress toward meeting strategic goals and staying within the project budget. Thus, the steering committee does not get involved in the day-to-day activities and operations involved in the development of the HRIS. This is the role of the project team, which will be covered later.

One important task for the steering committee is the development of the project charter. The project charter was discussed in Chapter 3, and it included the following items:

- It makes the case for the implementation.
- It shows connection to organizational goals and strategies.
- It has a plan for end users' involvement and participation.
- It provides identification of **project scope**.
- It identifies implementation team members.
- It identifies additional expertise that might be available.
- It provides a training plan.
- It explains the agreed on decision-making process.
- It discusses the process by which customization requests will be reviewed and acted on.
- It covers the PM methods used.
- It defines reporting requirements.
- It identifies deliverables.
- It defines political relationships of importance to project success.

The development of the project charter and the coordination of the members of the steering committee involve a great deal of communication and interpersonal skills on the part of the project sponsor who serves as the chair. As Rampton et al. (1999) note, the communications of project planning and project status in the steering committee and throughout the organization involves an inordinate amount of time. Thus, patience on the part of the project sponsor and the steering committee with an eye on meeting project deadlines is an art. Having well-done PM tools such as CPM, PERT, or Gantt charts is an absolute necessity for the HR project. However, it is people not the existence of the charts that make the project successful. Merely sending a memorandum indicating progress on a Gantt chart will not ensure cooperation from either the steering committee or the project team members. Frequently, steering committees will hire outside "process consultants" to help develop and maintain good working relationships within the steering committee, with the project team, and with the end users in the organization.

Configuring the PM Team

A central idea that has been discussed through the first six chapters of this book is that end-user involvement and participation is crucial if the HRIS project is to be successful. In systems development, getting the end users to tell system developers what they know about their domain, for example, HR programs and processes, and their information/decision requirements, largely depends on the developer's ability to ask the right questions. If the system developer knows how to ask the right questions, knowledge of the users' domain and their unique problems and needs will be easier to obtain. Thus, Belardo, Ballou, and Pazer (2004) contend that it is necessary to teach developers how to ask the right questions and to develop the interpersonal skills necessary to gain the cooperation of the users.

Whereas the steering committee oversees the entire HRIS project, the PM team is involved in the day-to-day activities necessary to develop and implement the new HRIS. It is their job to complete the activities specified by the CPM, PERT, or Gantt chart according to the defined timetable. The team must be capable of estimating the actual resources, both personnel and monetary, needed to complete the project. A major responsibility of the team is to communicate—by way of written reports on a regular (weekly or monthly) basis—with both the steering committee and the important stakeholders, for example, Vice President of HR, the progress on the HRIS project. If the organization has a newsletter or a company bulletin board, these should be used to keep all members of the organization apprised of the progress of the HRIS project.

The PM team should comprise representatives from the functional units affected, most notably the HR and IT departments. There may be other units affected, for example, operations, marketing, or finance, and a judgment must be made whether to include representatives from these functional units or simply supply regular update reports on the project to them. The HR professionals chosen for the team should have significant functional knowledge—for example, manager of employment or compensation—with some technical proficiency, as well as having a positive status within their department and the organization. Likewise, IT professionals could include systems analysts, hardware and software specialists, and HRIS professionals, all of whom should be respected members of the organization.

One of the critical issues faced by the PM team is the selection of the team project manager. This person should have strong communication skills, including the ability to speak, listen, and write effectively. The project manager must ensure that the team members understand the importance of regular communication with their supervisors. To be successful in implementing the new HRIS, all potential users must be made aware of the project progress and how it will affect them. Feedback loops should be developed so that users can provide valuable information to the project team during development and implementation. Kavanagh (2001) used surveys to assess users' attitudes regarding the implementation of a new system. The results of these surveys were then used to guide the development and implementation of the new system as well as for providing feedback to members of the organization.

Identification of Available Resources and Constraints

The steering committee, by way of the project charter, will have established preliminary estimates on available resources and constraints on the project scope. Except in unusual situations, the constraints established by the steering committee cannot be altered. However, sometimes it may be necessary to change the initial identification of needed resources, that is, personnel time and other costs. One of the major tasks of the PM team is to identify the need for more resources in the early phases of the project. As a result, the project manager must be in constant communication with team members regarding any unforeseen difficulties—for example, if a project team member leaves the organization. In these situations, it is the project manager's responsibility to communicate the necessity for a change in resources immediately with the steering committee chair.

Controlling Project Creep

Project creep is defined as the enlargement of the original boundaries of the project as defined in the project charter. Project creep can easily occur as end users see the potential usefulness of computerization. If effective communications have been established within the project team as well as with the entire organization, project creep can be contained by frequent updates on the project's progress that includes a definition of the project charter. In addition, using PM tools such as a Gantt chart ensures that the project is meeting its goals and not being extended into activities not contained on the Gantt chart. Surveys of users, as noted above, are also useful to ascertain if system users' perceptions of the project have started to creep. In other words, continuous and regular communication is the key to avoiding project creep.

Selection of Implementation Team

In some cases, the entire PM team will serve as the implementation team. A more common configuration is that a subset of individuals from the PM team is tasked to be focused on implementation issues such as employee cooperation and training as well as change management techniques. It is not unusual to have an external consultant provide technical assistance on implementation using change management techniques such as survey-guided feedback and focus groups. The implementation team also has primary responsibility for communication with the entire organization and, as noted in Chapter 3, begins this communication with the initial planning for new system development. The implementation team should include professionals from both HR and IT, as well as representatives of all functional departments in the organization. It is also important to have a senior manager serve as the leader of the implementation team. Note that these additional people can be added as the project enters its actual implementation phase; however, these individuals must be in the communication loop throughout the entire project.

Training and Documentation

There are a variety of activities involved in training and for the new system and its documentation. However, without the needed training, the system will either fail to be developed properly or fail during its implementation. Likewise *complete, accurate, and up-to-date documentation* of the system is critical for the implementation of a successful HRIS. Documentation in terms of notes diaries, memorandum, and reports created during the development and implementation of the HRIS will be invaluable when updates to the system are needed.

There are several different training programs that are necessary for the development and use of the new HRIS. As discussed earlier, one of the first considerations when beginning the HRIS project is to develop a project plan using CPM, PERT, and/or Gantt charts. It is desirable to use an employee (IT or HR) who is certified by the Project Management Institute (www.pmi.org/Pages/default.aspx) or who has taken seminars on PM from the American Management Association (www.amanet.org/seminars/category.cfm?cat=209). Obviously, without a carefully developed project plan using PM techniques, no amount of communication or employee involvement will suffice to make the HRIS a success. If there is no one within the organization with PM skills, companies frequently use outside consultants to develop the project plan.

It is also recommended that the PM team receive training in both group processes such as decision making and communication skills. Furthermore, it is necessary that the project team leader and the implementation team members be trained in the use of planned change or "change management" methods. Change management is a structured approach to changing individuals, groups, and organizations to accept new ideas and processes, that is, a new HRIS. Lewin (1951) described change management as involving three phases—unfreezing current attitudes and behaviors, changing to new attitudes and behaviors, and refreezing these new attitudes and behavior. There are other change management approaches in the literature (Kotter, 1996; Luecke, 2003). The important point is that these approaches work and are absolutely critical for the successful implementation and use of the HRIS. These approaches will be covered in detail in Chapter 8.

The final training that needs to be done is training on the new system. Most vendors of new software will provide training on the new system and more extensive training at an additional cost. The additional cost depends on the level of training needed for the users. To determine the amount and type of training needed for users, the organization should complete an analysis of the training and follow the recommended phases for effective training (Wexley & Latham, 2002). In most organizations, the HR department will have training professionals who should be used to complete the training phases. It is important that this training effort be included in the project plan in terms of time needed for the training and the costs. Premature introduction of a new HRIS or introducing it without appropriate training will lead to failure (Kavanagh et al., 1990).

Critical Success Factors

Several authors have discussed "critical success factors" in HRIS development and implementation (Ceriello & Freeman, 1991; Kavanagh et al., 1990; Rampton et al., 1999; Walker, 1982). These lists of success factors and mistakes serve as both cautions and recommendations for a successful HRIS project. Some of these mistakes as well as the success factors have been mentioned in previous chapters as well as earlier in this chapter. However, this compilation will represent a convenient place in this book to which the student can refer. The success factors are as follows:

1. *Top management support*: Simply stated, the project must have top management support at the beginning and throughout implementation and evaluation. The top management, that is, the CEO and department/unit heads, must be willing to provide the necessary resource and authority for project success.

2. *Provision of adequate and timely resources*: These resources include technology, money, time, and personnel. Without a carefully constructed PM plan, organizations will typically have inadequate resources to develop and implement the HRIS. The development of a "business plan" for the HRIS project is an absolute necessity for success. Chapter 6 provides excellent approaches to the development of a business plan for the HRIS.

3. *Ongoing communication:* Everybody involved in and affected by the HRIS project needs to be constantly informed about the goals, progress or lack of it, issues, and challenges throughout the life of the project so that there is less room for organizational politics, rumor mongering, and misapprehensions. Constant monitoring and feedback are an integral part of the communication process.

4. *Conducive organizational culture:* The culture of the organization will be strongly affected by the history of change in the organization and how it was done. Contrast an organization in which change was dictated by management versus one in which there was extensive participation by employees in the change effort.

5. *User involvement:* As indicated in Chapters 3 and 4, user involvement is critical to effective development and implementation of the HRIS. This ensures that the project is designed and implemented in accordance with user requirements and, therefore, will have a better chance of being accepted by them.

6. *Project champions:* The best possible situation would be to have two champions for the HRIS project—the steering committee chair and the project team manager. Obviously, this means that the selection of these individuals must be done carefully, and the persons selected should enjoy a good reputation and status in the organization.

7. *Organizational structure:* Typically, the implementation of a new HRIS will require changes in reporting lines of authority as well as changing responsibilities for HR and IT. If the departments are not used to cooperation and collaboration, they will develop a "silo mentality" and will compete against each other to the detriment of the organization.

8. *Change management methodology:* The assumption that employees will "love" the new system because of its sophisticated features is naive. Communication and user involvement throughout the development and implementation phases of the project, as well as good training on the new HRIS, are critical to success.

9. *Project control and monitoring:* Trying to execute an HRIS project without a written project plan—for example, the Gantt chart—will lead to failure. Likewise, failure to communicate project milestones and progress by the project team will severely damage the project effort. This loose project control could also be the result of a weak project team or steering committee. The necessary communication from both of these groups will ensure strong project control.

10. *Cross integration between business systems:* Poor integration between systems is usually the result of poor communication across functional departments during the development of the HRIS. Without effective communication, the HRIS will be unable to interface with other business systems, for example, the financial, operations, or marketing systems.

Summary

This chapter has been concerned with the overall management of the entire HRIS project. It has discussed the utilization of tools and techniques from both IT and HRM fields for improving the management of HRIS projects. Issues relevant to the use of both PM approaches from the IT literature and behavioral approaches from the HRM field have been explored in terms of their application to the efficient and effective management of the development and implementation of the HRIS. A dynamic perspective has been presented that uses the joint contribution of IT and HRM approaches with the strong argument that the organization cannot rely only on IT approaches such as CPM, PERT, and Gantt charts, thus excluding the behavioral approaches found in the HRM literature. Likewise, using only the behavioral, group, and organizational approaches from the HRM literature without a written plan provided by a bar or Gantt chart will result in either a poorly designed HRIS or the abandonment of the project.

This chapter has focused not only on PM tools from IT and HRM but also on the steps involved in the HRIS PM process and how to deal with the disruptions that occur during project development and implementation. Rather than presenting a host of templates employed in the four stages of PM or a discussion of PM guidelines readily available on the Web, we have introduced techniques that address the challenges faced by all project managers—namely, how to improve project effectiveness and efficiency. Following from this discussion, success (or common error) factors have been identified for the overall HRIS project from both the IT and the HRM literature. Finally, throughout the chapter there has been an emphasis on documentation for the entire HRIS project. This includes not only the project plan (Gantt chart) but all communications from and to the steering committee and the PM team. The importance of this documentation was linked to the implementation processes for the HRIS; however, a complete discussion of implementation processes will be provided in Chapter 8.

DISCUSSION QUESTIONS

1. What are the advantages of using a PM approach from the IT literature for the management of an HRIS project?

2. How does the behavioral advice from the HRM literature complement the formal IT tools, such as a Gantt chart?

3. What is the information needed to construct a CPM, PERT, or Gantt chart?

4. In which phases of the SDLC is documentation important? Why?

5. Do the critical success factors from the IT and HRM literature complement each other? Or is there disagreement between the recommendations from these two fields? Explain your answer.

6. Discuss the organizational factors that might affect the quality of the HRIS being developed. For example, how does a change in organizational structure or in project leadership influence the outcome of a systems development initiative?

CASE STUDY: IMPLEMENTING AN HRIS

ABC Finance provides financial services to customers and employs around 2,500 staff. The organization is currently facing major changes in its environment, both internally and externally. Externally, factors such as increasing globalization, new and innovative technologies, changing demographics and demands of customers, increasing deregulation, and competition in the industry have forced the firm to be more competitive by reducing costs and offering innovative services and to do more with less. Internally, there has been a shift over the past few years to a client focus from a product focus, continued growth in the organization resulting in geographical dispersion across the country, and a move toward delivery of online services. Historically, different functional departments within the firm have rarely collaborated with each other to solve organizational issues. The organization is cautious and consultative in its decision making and could best be described as bureaucratic.

The organization has made a decision to implement a new HRIS along with a new finance system and a new CRM system. The existing systems are all more than 10 years old and do not support the current or future environments in which the organization sees itself operating. The existing HRIS will be unsupported by the current vendor in the next 6 months, and there is an urgent need to implement the new system as soon as possible. The implementation has the support of key senior people in the organization. The HR, finance, and customer relations business units see this as a business project with the software and IT resources as the enabler of better and more effective services.

The organization has two support units—corporate services (HR, finance, operations, CRM) and information services—and three business lines: retail services, commercial services, and investment products. A major organizational restructuring took place only 2 years ago. The introduction of this structure was largely successful, particularly in the corporate services units. However, there was little emphasis on managing the change issues during the restructure, and as a result, some of the areas in the business lines are still coming to terms with the change and have become highly suspicious of new programs and initiatives that emanate from corporate services and information services. There is a perception that the "head office" is too concerned with itself and does not take into account the needs of other areas and locations. There have been complaints in the past about the quality of consultation and inclusion from the different geographic locations.

The organization includes an HR function and a separate payroll function that reports through to the finance function. HR and payroll currently use the same HRIS. The HR function was, until 2 years ago, a decentralized function with many HR services staff reporting through to different business lines. Following the company wide restructuring (CWR), the HR function was predominantly centralized so that the majority of staff now report through to the HR director. Some areas were not centralized and continue reporting to the relevant head of a business unit. After implementation, a new business model may be required to assist with a more complex and integrated system particularly as the HRIS and the CRM will share some aspects of the same database.

A major factor affecting the CWR is that it currently does not have staff who are sufficiently skilled in project managing and implementing a system of this size and complexity. It has looked to external organizations to assist it in implementing the new systems. ABC Finance expects to gain a transfer of skills, knowledge, and methodologies to its own staff for the ongoing maintenance of the production system, so that it may manage future upgrades and implementations.

The existing HRIS was poorly documented when it was implemented, and the vendor provided limited documentation. Because of the decentralized history of HR, data were input with various codes and into various fields; that is, there was no consistency in the way data were recorded. It is a well-known fact that the data in the current IS are neither up-to-date nor correct. The HR data in the current system carry little credibility in the CWR.

Furthermore, the software vendor has advised of an upgrade to their product that is nearing completion. This upgrade will provide for additional functionality that will support the objectives of process efficiency, cost reduction, and the use of Web and work flow at no extra cost. It is known that the software provider has a history of not delivering new versions on time and that these can sometimes be shipped with "bugs."

The project has a fixed budget. While there are some contingency funds, it is expected that this will be for emergency issues only, such as unforeseen costs within the existing scope. While it is still some time off, the CWR needs to make a decision soon on the postproduction support model. Previously, each system had its own support team. The CWR is considering an integrated support model where staff are multiskilled in each of the major areas—HR/payroll, finance, and CRM.

The CWR has undergone significant change in the past few years, and all staff are feeling some change fatigue. However, there is a significant commitment to managing the change process as part of this project. A change management team has been appointed comprising training and communication staff.

Case Study Questions

1. What PM approaches, techniques, and tools that have been discussed in this chapter can be applied to this organization in successfully managing the HRIS project?

2. It is often said that people factors are more important in technical project success than technology. From this perspective, explain the contribution that the HRM department can make to the management of this project.

3. Prepare a list of critical success factors that you think are most important for this project and compare them with the list presented in this chapter.

NOTE

1. For ease of reading, the IT/IS field will be referred to as the IT field in this chapter.

REFERENCES

Belardo, S., Ballou, D. P., & Pazer, H. L. (2004). Analysis and design of information systems: A knowledge quality perspective. In K. V. Anderson & M. T. Vendelo (Eds.), *The past and future of information systems* (pp. 43–60). New York: Elsevier.

Browne, G. J., & Rogich, M. B. (2001). An empirical investigation of user requirements elicitation: Comparing the effectiveness of prompting techniques. *Journal of Management Information Systems, 17*(4), 223–249.

Ceriello, V. R., & Freeman, C. (1991). *Human resource management systems: Strategies, tactics and techniques.* New York: Lexington Books.

Ewusi-Mensah, K. (1997). Critical issues in abandoned information systems projects. *Communications of the ACM, 40*(9), 74–80.

Kavanagh, M. J. (Chair & Presenter). (2001, August). *Planned change of information technology in the NYS probation department.* Professional Development Workshop presented at the annual meetings of the Academy of Management, Washington, DC.

Kavanagh, M. J., Gueutal, H. G., & Tannenbaum, S. I. (1990). *Human resource information systems.* Boston: PWS-Kent.

Kotter, J. P. (1996). *Leading change.* Boston: Harvard Business School Press.

Lemon, W. F., Bowitz, J., Burn, J., & Hackney, R. (2002). Information systems project failures: A comparative study of two countries. *Journal of Global Management, 10*(2), 28.

Lewin, K. (1951). *Field theory in social science.* New York: Harper & Row.

Luecke, R. (2003). *Managing change and transition.* Boston: Harvard Business School Press.

MacDonald, E. (1999, November 2). W. L. Gore alleges Peoplesoft, Deloitte botched a costly software installation. *Wall Street Journal,* p. b.14.

Nelson, E., & Ramstad, E. (1999, October 20). Hershey's biggest dud is its new computer system. *Wall Street Journal,* p. a. 1.

O'Brien, J. A., Crnkovic, J., & Belardo, S. (2006). *Management information systems.* New York: McGraw-Hill.

Peltier, J. (2008). *Gantt charts in Microsoft EXCEL.* Retrieved January 18, 2008, http://pubs .logicalexpressions.com/Pub0009/LPMArticle.asp?ID=343

Rampton, G. M., Turnbull, I. J., & Doran, J. A. (1999). *Human resources management systems: A practical approach.* Scarborough, Ontario, Canada: Carswell.

Walker, A. J. (1982). *HRIS development: A project team guide to building an effective personnel information system.* New York: Van Nostrand Reinhold.

Wexley, K. N., & Latham, G. P. (2002). *Developing and training human resources in organizations* (3rd ed.). Upper Saddle River, NJ: Prentice Hall.

Wiest, D., & Levy, J. (1969). *A management guide to PERT/CPM.* Englewood Cliffs, NJ: Prentice Hall.

8

Change Management

Implementation, Integration, and Maintenance of the HRIS

Romuald A. Stone

Joyce Mason Davis

EDITORS' NOTE

Perhaps one of the major obstacles in the use of an HRIS is its implementation. The IT as well as the HR literature is filled with stories about the failure to implement well-designed and well-developed computer technology. This failure has occurred not only in HRIS implementation but also in operations, marketing, and financial computer-based systems. While technical challenges will always remain in implementing complex HRIS, the major challenge to successful implementation is more behavioral than technical. Lack of employee and user involvement has been one of the central problems with the reported failures. In this chapter, we will examine various theoretical and practical approaches to organizational change and apply them to the problem of implementing a new or reautomated HRIS.

CHAPTER OBJECTIVES

After completing this chapter, you should be able to

♦ Understand what is the management of change

♦ Understand why HRIS implementation can fail

♦ Discuss the elements important to successful implementation

♦ Discuss the importance of integration of the HRIS within the organization

♦ Discuss the importance of continual maintenance of the HRIS

It's not the progress I mind, it's the change I don't like.

—Mark Twain

VIGNETTE

The Arizona Department of Administration, Human Resources Division manages the largest HR system in Arizona.[1] The division has a customer base that includes more than 9,000 retirees and more than 62,000 active employees from 100 state agencies, boards, and commissions, and 3 state universities. The Department administers the State's HR information solution system.

The HR Division initiated a program in 2002 to update its HRIS. The implementation of the new system would proceed in phases. Phase 1 was completed in December 2003, and Phase 2 was to be completed in 2004. According to department estimates, the new system would "produce more than $100 million in cost savings over the next 10 years by automating functions previously performed by administrative staff and [by] reducing turnover due to increased employee satisfaction" (Office of the Auditor General, 2005, p. ii).

The implementation plan failed to meet planned milestones by a wide margin and, in fact, exhausted most of the project budget early into Phase 2. With the loss of funding, the HRIS project staff was reduced from 60 to 18 positions. As a result, some state agencies have had to rely on in-house systems or manual processes to ensure that they have the necessary personnel information-processing capabilities. Compounding this situation was the fact that the implementation team had been slow to address some of the user requests for Phase 1 modifications, some of which are needed to correct programs that do not function properly. The net result of this poor management of the HRIS implementation project was that state agencies had not realized the anticipated efficiency savings from the new system (Office of the Auditor General, 2005).

In 2005, the HR Division was rethinking a new plan to restart the project. Some of the questions the change leadership team was thinking about included the following: Did they have the right change management competencies to manage this project? What were the likely obstacles that they would face during this next phase of the project—and could they prepare for them in advance? Could they deal with the resistance from some agency managers and users? What mistakes made in the earlier effort could they avoid going forward? And finally, would the Division be ready for this new implementation project—what other steps were needed to ensure that the HRIS project was successful?

We hope to answer many of these questions in this chapter.

Introduction to the Management of Change

Most mangers face **change management** issues every day; managing change is now a permanent part of every manager's job. It's clear that HR departments and leaders are in the middle of this climate of seemingly endless change, change that involves not only the functioning of the HR department but also its role within the enterprise and the HR technology used to provide strategic value to the business (Fletcher, 2005).

The evidence is clear that successfully introducing major HRIS into organizations requires an effective blend of good technical and good organizational skills. As Lorenzi and Riley (2000) remind us,

> A "technically best" system can be brought to its knees by people who have low psychological ownership in the system and who vigorously resist its implementation. The leader who knows how to manage the organizational impact of information systems can sharply reduce the behavioral resistance to change, including to new technology, to achieve a more rapid and productive introduction of information technology. (p. 116)

Effective management of change represents a critical core competence that all organizations and HR leaders must master. By better understanding the field of knowledge and competencies related to managing change, HR professionals can better manage change in organizations and reap the rewards that accrue to successful change initiatives. However, as the HRIS literature suggests, the track record of most change initiatives—be they restructuring, introduction of new technology, mergers, **process** improvement, or **reengineering**—is poor. One expert in the field noted that at best only one third of these kinds of initiatives achieve any success at all (Beer & Nohria, 2000). Clearly, learning to effectively manage change is an important managerial competency and competitive advantage.

What Is Change Management?

We define change management as a systematic process of applying the knowledge, tools, and resources needed to effect change in transforming an organization from its current state to some future desired state as defined by its vision (Potts & LaMarsh, 2004, p. 16). And because what happens in an organization is driven by the attitudes and behaviors of the individuals in that organization, change management must also consider altering the behavior patterns of the people within that organization. If the change is planned, the process typically involves the use of a systematic approach that includes both a vision and a plan to ensure that the change activities are on course and on target with respect to cost, time, and expected results. One of the ways in which this process is controlled is by the use of project management as discussed in Chapter 7.

Consider this example. When the catalog retailer Lillian Vernon Corporation undertook a major transformation of their IT infrastructure, the initial results proved dismal. What happened was that the change management team—which included the president and the chief information officer (CIO)—failed to take change management seriously. In particular, they overlooked the importance of assessing and managing readiness for change. "Employees resisted mightily, avoiding training and blaming new applications for their frustration. . . . The employees had already made up their minds that the system was not going to work, and they didn't want any part of it" (Paul, 2004, p. 1). The net result was that the company fell short of its ambitious timeline for implementation and missed an opportunity to leverage the new information system to improve overall performance. The lesson here is that implementing change goes beyond just installing the physical equipment and system. What Lillian Vernon failed to do was help the employees understand how the new IT system will be better than the current system. Effective communication is critical to the change process, as discussed later in this chapter. Successful change requires a "critical mass of people who are committed, are willing to change and will sustain their new behavior to align with the needs of the change" (Miller, 2004, p. 10).

The Change Management Process: Some Terminology

Organizations are in a constant state of change, which enables them to remain competitive in the marketplace. Some of the forces for change are external, such as the appearance of new technology, while others are internal, for example, downsizing the work force. Regardless of the reason, change must be effectively managed or chaos will exist. The person who is in charge of the change is referred to as a **change agent** or a *change leader*. This change agent can be internal to the organization, for example the Director of HR, or external to the organization, for example, a consultant. The process of managing change typically begins with a **gap analysis**. A gap analysis indicates the differences between the current state of affairs in the organization and the desired future state. Sometimes this analysis is done by senior management or the HRIS project team, in terms of strategy forecasts, and sometimes it is done through questionnaires distributed to employees. After the gap analysis has been completed and plans for the change process have been made, the next stage is to begin the implementation of the change. At this point, a major consideration is the **resistance to change** from members of the organization. Overcoming this resistance to change is one of the primary aspects of this chapter.

There is a discipline to managing change. As such, we know that managing change can be applied to any change initiative with a reasonable expectation of success. We begin by discussing several models of change in the following section.

Models of the Change Process

In this section, we introduce and describe a general model of the change process and then four specific models of organizational change that have received considerable attention in the change management literature: **Lewin's change model**, Gleicher's change formula, **Nadler's congruence model**, and Kotter's eight-stage change model. Some of these models are focused at the individual employee or group level, what is referred to as the microlevel, while others are focused at the organizational or macrolevel. These models help draw our attention to the elements important in successful managing of any HRIS implementation project.

Action-Research Model

We begin this section of the chapter with an introduction to a process model of the management of change in organizations. The **action-research model** can best be seen as a general perspective to use in any planned change effort. Examination of the use of any successful change effort will reveal some of, if not all, the components of the action-research model. Thus, although we use the term *model* to describe the prescriptions of action research, it is better viewed as an approach to the management of change. Careful reading of the change management literature reveals that the action-research model appears in, or is part of, most change management projects.

The term *action research* is not new. It can be traced to the work of Collier (1945) and of Lewin (1946) and his student (Lippitt, 1950), while others (Corey, 1953; French & Bell, 1973) have provided excellent descriptions of the action-research model. Frohman, Sashkin, and Kavanagh (1976) provided the following definition:

> Action-research describes a particular process-model whereby behavioral science knowledge is applied to help a client (usually a group or social system) solve real problems and not incidentally learn the processes involved in problem-solving, while generating further knowledge with respect to the field of applied behavioral science. (p. 130)

The basis of the action-research model is the interaction of managerial or organizational action and research that both evaluates the action taken and provides data for future planning of the change effort. Thus, using this model involves the interlocking of the research processes of data collection, analysis, and evaluation and the management action processes of planning, directing, and implementing change. As seen in Figure 8.1, a cycle in the action-research model would include the following: (1) initial data collection and gap analysis, (2) feedback of results to the HRIS project team, (3) action planning for the next phase of the HRIS project, (4) directing and implementing changes during the next phase, (5) data collection and analysis to evaluate the changes, and (6) feedback of results to the project team and action planning for the HRIS project.

Lewin's Change Model

One of the earliest and key contributions to organizational change is Kurt Lewin's three-step change model (see Figure 8.2). Lewin's (1946) framework serves as a general model for understanding planned change. The model has been used to explain how information systems can be implemented more effectively (Benjamin & Levinson, 1993).

The genesis of Lewin's (1946) change model evolved from his interest in resolving social conflict and in improving the human condition through behavioral change. In his study of group behavior, Lewin argued that behavior was a complex interaction

❖ **Figure 8.1** The Action-Research Cycle

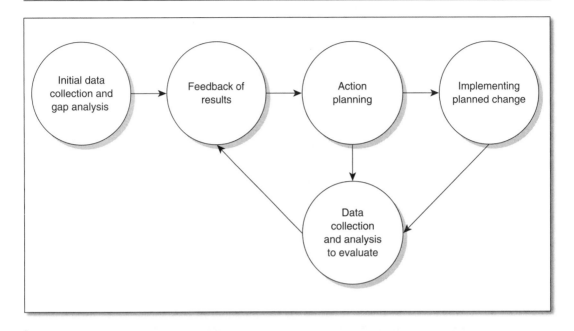

SOURCE: Reprinted with permission from Kavanagh, Gueutal, and Tannenbaum (1990).

❖ **Figure 8.2** Lewin's Three-Step Change Model

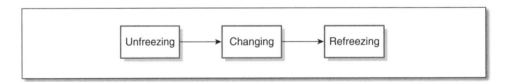

of what the individual brought to the situation and the environment (or **"field"** as he called it). We can express this relationship as $B = f(P, E)$, where behavior is defined as a function of the person and the environment. In the main, Lewin believed that the existing condition (or status quo) was maintained by a set of forces affecting the situation. And only by identifying and plotting the potency of these forces could we bring about change.

Lewin's (1946) change model conceived of change in terms of a modification of the forces that stabilize a system's behavior. In particular, he envisioned a dynamic where there are two sets of opposing forces—those that are focused on maintaining stability and the status quo and those driving change. When we have a balance between these two opposing forces, we have what Lewin called a state of "quasi-stationary equilibrium." To alter that state, it is possible to decrease the forces that oppose the change while simultaneously increasing the forces for change, or some combination of the two.

To better understand these forces, we can use a change tool called **force-field analysis.** To develop a force-field analysis, create two columns on a sheet of paper. In one column list the forces that drive or support a change in an HRIS, for example, and in the other column, list the forces that will inhibit the change. It is helpful to also assign a relative potency or strength to each force listed. By plotting the forces, we can better understand which forces need to be strengthened or diminished to bring about change. Lewin (1946) suggested that the path of least resistance—that is, modifying those forces maintaining the status quo—would produce less tension and resistance than would increasing the forces for change; thus, the former is a more effective change strategy than the latter.

The key to understanding this approach, at the individual level, is to see change as a profound psychological dynamic process (Schein, 1996). This psychological process involves painful unlearning and difficult relearning as one cognitively attempts to restructure one's thoughts, perceptions, feelings, and attitudes. Lewin (1946) viewed these three steps as follows.

Unfreezing

At the outset, every change project requires getting people to change their minds and behavior regarding the old way of doing things and to embrace the new state. This means that people need to "see the purpose of the change, agree with it, be supported by rewards and recognition, have the skills to perform the new activities, and see key people modelling the new behavior" (Warhaftig, 2005). This means that the quasi-stationary equilibrium supported by the complex set of driving and restraining forces needs to be destabilized (unfrozen) before the old way of doing things could be discarded (unlearnt) and the new behavior successfully adopted (Burnes, 2004, p. 985). Unfreezing is sometimes accomplished through a process of "psychological disconfirmation." By introducing information that shows discrepancies between behavior desired by organization members and those behaviors currently exhibited, individuals can be motivated to engage in change activities.

However, the unfreezing process is not that easy to accomplish. Edgar Schein (1996) in his excellent reflection on Lewin's (1946) impact on his own thinking and work argues that three processes are necessary for readiness and motivation to change to occur: (1) disconfirmation of the validity of the status quo, (2) the induction of guilt or survival anxiety, and (3) creating psychological safety (Schein, 1996). Schein suggests that for any change to occur, some form of dissatisfaction or frustration with the status quo must be presented. People need to know what drives the need for change, why they should change, and where they are headed. What is/is not going to change? What is the business case or rationale? The emotional and motivational needs of those affected by the change also need to be addressed. For example, help people understand what's in it for them. What are the rewards or consequences of changing? Not changing?

This is where Schein's "survival anxiety" comes into play. The reason for change is not always enough. We also need to convince people that if we do not change, individual and organizational goals will be frustrated. This is what Kotter (1996) calls creating a sense of urgency. Without a sense of urgency, "people won't give that extra effort . . . they won't make needed sacrifices. Instead they will cling to the status quo and resist initiatives from above" (p. 5).

Psychological safety refers to mitigating the anxiety that people feel whenever they are asked to do something different or new. People are concerned about losing their identity, looking dumb, and losing their effectiveness or self-esteem. As such, this anxiety can be a significant restraining force to change. Without sufficient psychological safety present, change leaders will find the road to change filled with more obstacles than they planned on. We can address psychological safety by addressing employee needs: What must I do differently? What are the new ways I will have to work? How do I learn the new things that I'm going to have to do? Who's going to teach me? Am I capable of making the changes that I will need to make?

Changing/Transition

Where unfreezing creates the motivation to change, the changing or transition stage focuses on helping change the behavior of organization members to the new state of affairs. William Bridges (2003) defines this stage as "psychological; it is a three-phase process that people go through as they internalize and come to terms with the details of the new situation that the change brings about" (p. 3). Without getting everyone through the transition phase, the outcome of the change project may be in jeopardy. The transition phase consists of three key elements: ending → neutral zone → new beginnings (pp. 4–5):

1. *Ending:* Before you can begin something new, you have to end what used to be. You need to identify who is losing what, expect a reaction, and acknowledge the losses openly. Repeat information about what is changing—it will take time to sink in. Mark the endings (Cameron & Green, 2004, p. 108).

2. *Neutral zone:* The step between the old and new way of doing things is a "neutral zone" where people need to make the psychological adjustments necessary to say goodbye to the old and begin to welcome the new. In the neutral zone, people feel disoriented, motivation falls, and anxiety rises. Consensus may break down as attitudes become polarized.

3. *New beginnings:* This final step is about coming out of the transition and making a new beginning. This is when people develop a new identity, experience the new energy, and discover the new sense of purpose that makes the change begin to work.

As Bridges (2003) reminds us, if change agents

don't help people through these three steps in the transition process, even the most wonderful training programs often fall flat. The leaders forget endings and neutral zones (Steps 1 and 2); they try to start with the final stage of the transition. And they can't see what went wrong! (p. 6)

Refreezing

This final step seeks to stabilize the organization at a new state of equilibrium and to ensure that the new behaviors are relatively safe from regression (Burnes, 2004, p. 986). Refreezing often requires changes in the organization's **culture** and norms, policies, and practices. We address culture in a later section.

Change Equation Formula

When initiating an organizational change project, it's important early on to determine how ready people are to accept and implement the change (Burke, 2002, p. 150). Gleicher's formula helps us assess this degree of readiness as follows (Beckhard & Harris, 1987):

$$C = (D \times V \times F) > R,$$

where C is the change, D the dissatisfaction with status quo, V the vision, F the first steps (feasibility), and R the resistance to change (costs).

If we refer to Lewin's (1946) *force-field analysis* discussed earlier, D, V, and F are all "forces for change," while R represents the "forces against change." It provides a simple and straightforward perspective that reveals the possibilities and conditions at work in organizational change. Note that all three forces for change must be active to offset the forces against the change, which is usually manifested as resistance to change from organizational members. The change program must address *dissatisfaction* with the present situation, a clear *vision* of the future and what is possible, and knowledge of the first *steps* necessary to reach the vision. If any one of the three is missing, the product of the equation will tend toward zero and the *resistance to change* will dominate.

In sum, this

> change formula is deceptively simple but extremely useful. It can be brought into play at any point in a change process to analyze how things are going. When the formula is shared with all parties involved in the change, it helps to illuminate what various parties need to do to make progress. (Beckhard & Harris, 1987, p. 104)

Nadler's Congruence Model

According to David Nadler (1998), one of the key steps in understanding and managing change is to first fully understand the dynamics and performance of the organization. For without this understanding of the varied issues affecting performance, successful change may be misdirected by focusing on the symptoms rather than the true causes of a problem issue. A useful tool that helps change leaders understand the interplay of forces that shape the performance of each organization is Nadler's congruence model (p. 41). The model is based on many years of academic research and practical application in a wide range of companies and industries (see Figure 8.3).

There are several benefits in using the congruence model (Mercer Delta Consulting, 2003, pp. 10–12):

1. If we use a computer metaphor, at its core, the model depicts both the "hardware" and the "software" dimensions of an organization. The hardware represents the strategy, work, and formal organization—how the firm is organized to coordinate, communicate, and motivate the workforce in accomplishing its vision and goals. The software side of the model makes up the social dimension of the organization—its people and the informal processes (e.g., shared values) that shape the behavior and performance of an organization's people.

❖ **Figure 8.3**   The Congruence Model: Managing Change

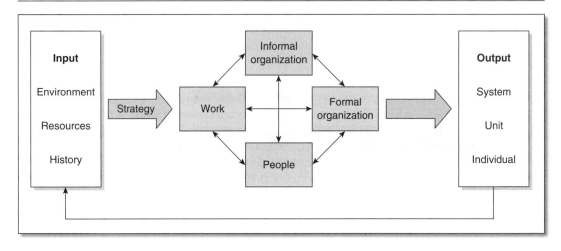

2. The model helps us understand the dynamics of change by allowing us to predict the impact of change throughout the organization system. When leaders conduct a gap analysis to compare results with expectations, it may trigger a review of strategy and a reassessment of what change is needed to achieve stated goals and objectives. This may lead to changes in work and formal organization, where too many change leaders stop, without undertaking the difficult but critical task of reshaping the firm's culture to align it with the new strategy.

3. Finally, the model helps change leaders see organizations not as inflexible, static structures that produce outputs but as an organic, dynamic set of people and processes that are interdependent. It helps us recognize that managing real change is a function of several complex dimensions. It provides a useful "mental model" for understanding organizational problems and for enhancing our ability to pinpoint a solution.

Nadler's congruence model is an organizational performance model that is built on the view that organizations are systems and that only if there is congruence ("fit") between the various organizational subsystems can we expect optimal performance. As reflected in the model, the basic components of any organization system include the following elements (Nadler, 1998):

- The *input* is taken from both internal and external sources. These include the organization's macroenvironment, resources, and history.
- The *strategy* of the firm translates management's vision into a set of decisions about how to deploy its resources given the demands, opportunities, and constraints within its operating environment and moderated by its history.
- The *output* reflects the products and services that the organization creates to fulfill its financial and strategic objectives.
- The *operating organization* is at the core of the congruence model. This is the transformation mechanism that takes the strategy, in the context of history, resources, and environment, to convert input into output.

The transformation process of any organization is composed of four components, or subsystems, which all depend on each other (Nadler, 1998, p. 32):

- *The work:* This is the actual day-to-day activities carried on by the organization, its departments, and its people. Any change effort must consider the characteristics of the work to be performed, the knowledge and skills required, and the stress and uncertainty that it involves.
- *The people:* This reflects the skills and characteristics of the people who work in an organization. It's important to identify their needs and preferences in terms of the rewards (both intrinsic and extrinsic) that they expect to receive from their work.
- *The formal organization:* This refers to the structure, systems, and processes in place to organize and coordinate the work in ways to achieve the strategic objectives.
- *The informal organization:* This consists of all the informal, unwritten guidelines that exert a powerful influence on people's collective and individual behavior. It encompasses the beliefs, values, and norms of the organization (its culture).

This model proposes that effective management of change means paying attention to the alignment of all four components, not just one or two. You can't assume that changing one element will cause the other elements to fall into place (Nadler, 1998, p. 42). Cameron and Green (2004) use an apt metaphor to highlight this important point:

> Imagine tugging only one part of a child's mobile. The whole mobile wobbles and oscillates for a bit, but eventually all the different components settle down to where they were originally. So it is with organizations. They easily revert to the original mode of operation unless you attend to all four components. (p. 104)

If alignment of each of the components—work, people, structure, and culture—with each other is deficient, then performance will suffer. The greater the fit or congruence, the greater will be the organization's ability to manage a change process.

The Nadler model is helpful because it provides a useful framework for understanding the organization as a social and technical system.

> The model is particularly good for pointing out in retrospect why changes did not work, which although psychologically satisfying is not always a productive exercise. It is important to note that this model is problem-focused rather than solution-focused, and lacks any reference to the powerful effects of a guiding vision, or to the need for setting and achieving goals. (Cameron & Green, 2004, p. 104)

Kotter's Process of Leading Change

Kotter's (1996) eight-stage model was developed after studying more than 100 organizations undergoing change The model offers a process to successfully manage change and avoid the common pitfalls that beset failed change programs (see Figure 8.4). We can view his approach as a vision for the change process, one that calls attention to its key phases.

❖ **Figure 8.4**   Kotter's Eight-Stage Change Process

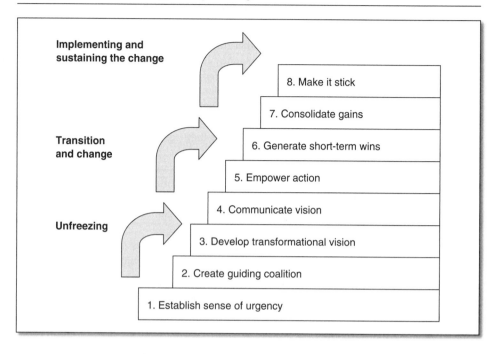

The model provides two key lessons, first that the change process goes through a series of phases, *each lasting a considerable period of time*, and, second, that critical mistakes in any of the phases can have a devastating impact on the momentum of the change process.

The Eight-Stage Change Process (Kotter, 1996)

The first four stages focus on the practices associated with "unfreezing" the organization:

1. Establishing a greater sense of urgency
   a. Getting people to examine seriously the competitive realities
   b. Identifying crises, potential crises, or major opportunities

2. Creating the guiding coalition
   a. Putting together a group with enough power to lead the change
   b. Getting the group to work together like a team

3. Developing a transformational vision and strategy
   a. Creating a vision to help direct the change effort
   b. Developing strategies for achieving that vision

4. Communicating the change vision
   a. Using every vehicle possible to constantly communicate the new vision and strategies
   b. Modeling needed behavior by the guiding coalition

The next three stages introduce many new practices ("change/transition"):

5. Empowering a broad base of people to take action.
   a. Getting rid of blockers
   b. Changing the systems or structures that seriously undermine the change vision
   c. Encouraging risk taking and nontraditional ideas, activities, and actions

6. Generating short-term wins
   a. Planning for some visible performance improvements
   b. Creating those wins
   c. Visibly recognizing and rewarding people who made the wins possible

7. Consolidating gains and producing even more change
   a. Using increased credibility to change all systems, structures, and policies that don't fit together and don't fit the transformation vision
   b. Hiring, promoting, and developing people who can implement the change vision
   c. Reinvigorating the process with new projects, themes, and change agents

Finally, the last stage is required to ground the changes in the corporate culture ("refreezing") and make them stick:

8. Institutionalizing new approaches in the culture
   a. Creating better performance through customer and productivity oriented behavior, more and better leadership, and more effective management
   b. Articulating the connections between new behaviors and firm success
   c. Developing the means to ensure leadership development and succession

The model requires that all the stages must be worked through in order, and completely, to successfully change. Skipping even a single step or getting too far ahead without a solid base almost always creates problems. People under pressure to show results will often skip the unfreezing activities (the first four steps). In this case, you rarely establish a solid enough base on which to proceed. Failure to reinforce earlier stages as you move on results in the urgency dissipating or the guiding coalition breaking up. Without the follow through that takes place in the final step, you may never get to the finish line and make changes stick. It is also important to view the change process as a continuous cycle rather than as a step-by-step progression. More than one step may be activated at any one time.

Next, we turn our attention to the factors that contribute to HRIS implementation failures.

Why Do System Failures Occur?

Increasingly, the failure to successfully implement information systems has less to do with the hardware or software aspects of the new system and more to do with the skills of the change leader and the people and organizational issues related to the change. Research has identified a number of key factors that contribute to IT system implementation failures (see Figure 8.5). While no one single factor is the culprit, Lorenzi and Riley (2000) suggest that "a snowball effect is often seen, with a shortcoming in one area leading to subsequent shortcomings in other areas" (p. 117). We have grouped

❖ **Figure 8.5**   Reasons for IT System Failure

Leadership	• Lack of executive support • Lack of strong leadership and change management skills in project manager • Lack of recognition for team's efforts • Lack of accountability for implementing the change
Planning	• No clear vision for the change • Failure to define a clear and comprehensive project scope • Lack of a comprehensive project plan • Failure to fully define the functionality of the system • Insufficient project staffing; staff turnover and complacency • Insufficient project funding • Roles and responsibilities not clearly defined or understood by everyone • Failure to meet budget and deadlines • The change leadership team doesn't include early adopters, resisters, or informal leader • Inadequate testing of the system
Change management	• Culture and level of readiness for change are not assessed prior to the start of the project • Change leaders fail to respect the power of the culture to kill the change • No strategies to nurture or grow a new culture • The change isn't piloted, so the organization doesn't learn what's needed to support the change • Organizational systems and other initiatives aren't aligned with the change • End users are not involved in the process • Lack of a plan for user resistance/rejection • Processes are not reengineered
Communication	• Lack of a comprehensive communication plan • Ineffective ongoing communication with all affected stakeholders • Failure to customize communications to different audiences • People leading the change think that announcing the change is the same as implementing it
Training	• Inadequate or poor-quality training • Poor timing of training—too early or too late • People are not enabled or encouraged to build new skills • Lack of ongoing training

the key causal factors related to HRIS implementation failures into five main categories: leadership, planning, change management, communication, and training (Lorenzi & Riley, 2000; Kandel, n.d.; Blanchard, 2007, pp. 203–204).

Leadership

Major change is almost impossible without top leadership support. "Leadership must set the direction, pace, and tone and provide a clear consistent rationale that brings everyone together behind a single mission" (U.S. Government Accountability Office, 2003, p. 2).

Lack of executive support is one of the main reasons why HRIS implementations fail. Without this support, organizations lack the funding, approvals, and leadership necessary to properly implement, integrate, and maintain the system.

Project managers lacking in leadership skills have also contributed to project failure. Those individuals given the responsibility to manage the HRIS project are often very knowledgeable in HR or IT. However, they cannot lead a major change project effectively unless they possess strong leadership and communication skills. They must be able to communicate clearly, prioritize projects, make tough decisions, manage people effectively, and navigate the political environment (Kandel, n.d.).

Any successful major change initiative must also be driven by a strong and stable project management team. It would take a superhuman individual to lead a successful change initiative by himself or herself. What is needed for successful change is a team of individuals that includes a mix of key executives, department heads, managers, and front-line employees who are committed to the change and who can work together as a team.

Planning

All successful projects have a clearly identified project scope and strategy that outline key business requirements and project goals. It is important to keep team members on the same page and working toward the same outcome. Additionally, a clearly defined project scope will prevent "scope creep" from occurring—an enlargement of the project as it progresses.

Oftentimes, organizations begin HRIS implementation projects without a clear definition of the scope of the project. The project scope must be defined in advance and should identify the project objectives, priorities, goals, and tasks—these serve as the guiding principles for the team throughout the project's life cycle (Kandel, n.d.).

Inadequate funding and staffing further contribute to project failure. Organizations often consider the initial start-up costs for an HRIS project but fail to fully consider the costs of the change management process, ongoing training, and support and maintenance of new systems. Change leaders must look at the big picture and the resources that will be required to successfully implement and maintain the system.

One key resource relates to adequate staff to manage the project. Change leaders make the mistake of thinking that part-time staff can implement a new system while continuing to perform all their regular duties. The time requirements needed to manage a project are often severely underestimated. While in smaller organizations, individuals may need to continue with their regular duties, all efforts should be made to have at least some team members dedicated full-time to the project. If team members are not fully dedicated, their regular responsibilities will almost always take priority over the project, causing delays and lack of focus.

Change Management

Without question, change management is an ongoing challenge for HR leaders and organizations. Prager and Overholt (1994) argue that a failed effort to implement new technology is always a failure to understand and adequately manage the change process. They indicate that projects often fail not because of technical flaws but because the people in the organization reject them (p. 64). In fact, research shows that the critical factor in achieving rapid and complete adoption of new technology is effective change management (Correll, 2005, p. 12). Unfortunately, too many change initiatives fail to deliver their promised value.

Likewise, a review of the research literature on change suggests that a large percentage of change efforts end in discouraging results. Experts suggest that the figure may be as high as 70% (Mourier & Smith, 2001; Pascale & Millemann, 1997). If only 30% of change efforts are successful, consider then the cost in terms of economic and human resources: "In too many situations the improvements have been disappointing and the carnage has been appalling, with wasted resources and burned-out, scared, or frustrated employees" (Kotter, 1996, p. 4). In a world where the only constant is change, this poor track record is disappointing to say the least and suggests that there is lot of room for improvement in successfully managing change.

Eric Abrahamson offers an excellent suggestion to help mitigate any forgetfulness or perpetuating failures from past change initiatives. He says that we should not ignore the memory of employees who have been involved in change programs in the past. To this end, we can learn about "whether a proposed change was attempted previously and what its outcome was and why" (Abrahamson, 2004b, p. 4).

Margaret Wheatley (1997) offers an equally compelling insight when considering whether a change effort is successful. She suggests that change leaders need to ask the following questions:

1. Are people in the organization more committed to being here now than at the beginning of this effort?

2. Do people feel more prepared for the next wave of change?

3. Did we develop capacity [for change] or just stage an event?

4. Do people feel that their creativity and expertise contributed to the changes? (p. 28)

When we pay attention to these kinds of questions as indicators, Wheatley (1997) argues that

we can create organizations [cultures] that know how to respond continuously" to the driving forces in their operating environment. Why? Because we tap what she calls "the intelligence that lives everywhere" in organizations, and in the process, we succeed in engaging people and their capacity to deal with change. (p. 28)

In a world where the only constant is change, this poor track record is disappointing to say the least and suggests that there is a lot of room for improvement in successfully managing change.

Given the high potential for failure, we next review some of the key change management issues affecting HRIS implementation.

Communication

Effective change communication can make the difference between success and failure of an HRIS implementation project. Employee communication is especially critical when we're "trying to get others to see and do things differently" (Duck, 2001, p. 27).

Armenakis and Harris (2002, p. 169) suggest that change leaders who overlook the importance of communicating a consistent change message and vision fuel some of the negative responses (resistance) encountered in managing change. It is the communication process that starts to unfreeze and predispose people to change (Eccles, 1994, p. 158). As Duck (2001) reminds us,

> If leaders want to change the thinking and actions of others, they must be transparent about their own. If people within the organization don't understand the new thinking or don't agree with it, they will not change their beliefs or make decisions that are aligned with what is desired. (p. 28)

No matter what kind of change initiative an organization's leadership may desire, the change won't be successful without the support and commitment of a majority of its managers and employees. Getting people "unstuck"—that is, getting them to not only embrace the vision but also change their beliefs and thinking to move in the new direction—is a huge communication challenge.

For example, the catalog retailer Lillian Vernon encountered huge problems with their IT transformation project when they failed to effectively communicate to employees why the project was necessary and how it would affect each employee specifically. In discussing the end-user training for the new system, the CIO's comments are particularly poignant:

> Before the classes began, "we should have put everyone in a room and said, Here is how you fit into this new picture." . . . Instead, the project team fell back on blanket statements that everyone's job would be "better." Once rollout began, however, they were angry when their jobs were harder instead. Since most had not taken the training seriously, they did not know how to use the application. And many were uncertain as to how their jobs had changed. "People were blaming the system for everything." (Paul, 2004, para. 21)

We should recognize too that there are many rationalizations for not communicating. Figure 8.6 highlights some common reasons why change leaders do not communicate (Bridges, 1991, pp. 27–28). In the Lillian Vernon example, when the CIO began work on the IT transformation project, he expressed his rationalization for not communicating this way:

> We're bringing in vendors who will bring change management expertise to the table. We have capable, gung-ho teams. Giddyap, let's go. . . . In other words, launch the projects and fix problems later. [The CIO] learned that far from being a frill, basic communication creates the underpinning for a successful implementation. The essence of change management . . . is a few well-placed, well-delivered conversations to the right audience. And then you follow up, again and again. (Paul, 2004, para. 21)

The lesson the CIO learned from this experience is that it is crucial for leaders to develop and widely communicate a compelling case for change. Mercer Delta Consulting (2000) suggests that five key elements (see Figure 8.7) make up a persuasive case for change:

> *Reason for the change:* Answers the question "Why change?" and creates motivation for change. Simply saying that one's job will be better is not sufficient. Employees need to know the business case for the change and how it affects the bottom line.

❖ **Figure 8.6** Common Reasons Why Change Leaders Don't Communicate

1. ***They don't need to know yet. We'll tell them when the time comes. It'll just upset them now.*** For every week of upset that you avoid by hiding the truth, you gain a month of bitterness and mistrust. Besides, the grapevine already has the news, so don't imagine that your information is a secret.

2. ***They already know. We announced it.*** OK, you told them, but it didn't sink in. Threatening information is absorbed remarkably slowly. Say it again. And find different ways to say it and different media (large meetings, one-on-ones, memos, a story in the company paper) to say it.

3. ***I told the supervisors. It's their job to tell the rank and file.*** The supervisors are likely to be in transition themselves, and they may not even sufficiently understand the information to convey it accurately. Maybe they're still in denial. Information is poor, so they may not want to share it yet. Don't assume that information trickles down through the organizational strata reliably or in a timely fashion.

4. ***We don't know the details ourselves, so there's no point in saying anything until everything has been decided.*** In the meantime, people can get more and more frightened and resentful. Much better to say what you do know, say that you don't know more, and tell what kind of schedule exists.

❖ **Figure 8.7** Defining the Case for Change

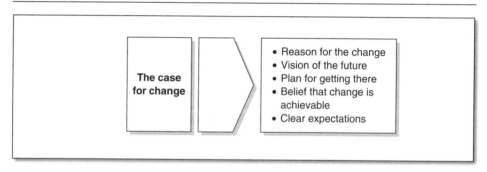

Vision of the future: Serves as a starting point and anchor for what we do. Answers the question "Change to what?" by providing leadership's vision of the new organization; creates energy and excitement about the future. We address this factor more deeply later in the chapter.

Plan for getting there: Answers the question "How are we going to change?" and mobilizes people toward a common direction. Here, we want to provide the big picture—the agenda, key strategies, and implementation plans.

Believe change is achievable: Answers the question "Is this really possible?" and encourages interest, engagement, and optimism.

Clear expectations: Answers the question "What can I expect of you and what is expected of me?" and helps people prepare for the change while reducing their uncertainty.

In sum, communication plays a vital role in the success of change programs. It is difficult to engage everyone based only on communication alone. Ideally, people must participate in the process from beginning to end. If the sentiment is that the change is imposed from the top, then gaining commitment will be tough.

Training

Ongoing, effective **training** is essential in any change management initiative, particularly when new technology and work processes are involved. Successful companies typically offer training in the early stages of the project to reduce uncertainty about the new technology by providing information about its characteristics and to generate user acceptance (Ruta, 2005, p. 38).

The value of training cannot be underestimated:

> At E&P, the budget for training was cut in the midst of an implementation project. One site was able to do more training with their staff because they had some additional resources they could use. Even though it wasn't much more, there was a difference in how much better the users were able to take advantage of the new system than those from other locations. (Jones & Price, 2004, p. 32)

At the beginning of the project, a training plan should be developed. This plan should include a complete assessment of the current skills and future requirements for all who will be affected by the change. The plan must also include the following:

- What training will be provided
- When training will be provided for implementation team members and user groups
- Who will provide the training—vendors, consultants, staff, other
- A plan for training new users and addressing turnover issues
- A plan for ongoing training, including advanced skills and refresher training
- A plan for training users in the event of system upgrades or procedural changes
- The resources needed—financial and human—to provide the training

While some training early in the process is recommended, full training should not be offered until just before the system will be used. One common error is providing too detailed training too early in the learning process. If training is provided too early, users will not retain the material. A person may learn how to perform 10 new tasks on the system. Of those, they may only encounter 5 in a normal work day, 3 over the next year, and 2 in exceptional circumstances, by which time the training will have been forgotten. Additionally, advanced training should be provided in phases, as users become accustomed to performing routine tasks. On-the-job training, coupled with self-paced e-learning and personalized assistance as required, is a more effective way of ensuring that staff get training that is relevant to their jobs (Dawson & Jones, n.d.).

We should not overlook training for employee self-service applications. If training is not provided, employees will be less likely to use and accept the system. Training should also be provided in new employee orientation programs.

> At Chevron, training in self-service is backed up with supplementary material, including online guides and laminated cards to guide employees through the process of scheduling a

vacation or changing their address. Employees can refer to them if they run into problems, and in most cases, they find them useful as memory aids in the first weeks following formal training. (Twentyman, 2006, p. 24)

The use of **"Power Users"** can be an effective training technique. Organizations may use individuals who adapt to the new technology quickly to provide one-on-one on-the-job training to those who do not learn the system as rapidly.

USWhole used a power user concept for changing users. They identified users in each of the business units that were influential in their units and interested in the new technology and trained them extensively to do transaction processing as well as in how processes were changing and being integrated. As power users shared their knowledge with other users, knowledge about how to use the system began to permeate the organization. (Jones & Price, 2004, p. 29)

Organizational and Individual Issues in HRIS Implementation

Cultural Issues

One of the challenges with implementing any new or updated HRIS is getting people to use the technology. Simply introducing the new system does not automatically lead to successful implementation. Successful implementation is more than putting in new technology; it often requires a change in the organization's culture. A wide variety of people and cultural issues play a huge role in any change effort or transformation.

Culture can "not only stop a change effort dead in its tracks, it can also propel it to great heights. Wisdom during organizational change is understanding the power of culture and how to get it to work for you instead of against you" (Senn & Childress, 2000, p. 1). How do you get employees suddenly to change their most basic assumptions about their company? This is the challenge for change leaders—often the need to create a new organizational culture that is congruent with the realities of its changing environment and that supports the implementation of the new system.

We define organizational culture as a complex set of shared beliefs, guiding values, behavioral norms, and basic assumptions acquired over time that shape our thinking and behavior; they are part of the social fabric of the organization—its genetic code. As such, culture drives the organization and guides the behavior of everyone in that organization—how they think, feel, and act. In other words, the culture forms a behavior template.

Not understanding a firm's culture in implementing an HRIS project can be fatal. The change literature is clear: Any change initiative is unlikely to be successful—that is, implemented and sustained—unless there is an appropriate organizational culture in place to support the plan. So it's critical that change leaders fully understand the organization's cultural profile before undertaking the change. How then can we go about getting an accurate picture of an organization's culture so that leaders can transition its current value set to a new value set?

An assessment of a firm's culture (sometimes called a gap analysis) is a useful tool in ensuring that the correct cultural elements are in place to support and align the strategy/vision, resources, and systems required to affect the road map to change. Change leaders must align all four elements with each change initiative to ensure lasting transformation. This alignment is conveyed by the arrows in Figure 8.8. All the arrows should be pointing in the same direction—that is, aligned with one another.

Whenever there is an incongruity between the current culture and the goals of the change initiative, the culture always wins (Conner, 1998, p. 207). For this reason, many change initiatives are ultimately unsuccessful due to lack of the appropriate cultural support needed to get people to embrace and implement the change. So, in effect, what is done to assess the cultural infrastructure is to define the existing organizational culture (i.e., what is the shared mindset of the people within the organization), characterize the target culture needed to support the change, define what gaps exist between the current culture and desired culture, and then devise a way to bridge that gap.

Perhaps Lou Gerstner (2005), former CEO of IBM, puts this all in perspective with his apposite observation:

> Leading cultural change is not just one of the things you do when you change an enterprise—it's a totality of what you have to work on if you are going to do a true, transformational change. At the end of the day, you do not change an institution, fundamentally altering how it thinks and behaves, without a deep understanding of the cultural bearings that exist. (p. 18)

❖ **Figure 8.8** Elements of Change Aligned

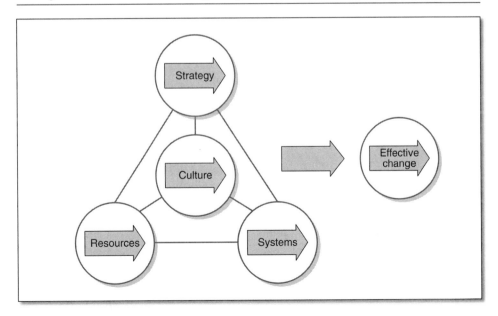

As we discussed previously, many organizational change initiatives often fail to meet planned expectations. When the elements of change are not in alignment, the picture looks more like the one shown in Figure 8.9. This figure portrays an organization with nonaligned elements of change, with its arrows pointing in all sorts of directions. That the arrows are pointing in different directions may reflect the impacts of previous leadership on these dimensions or failure to consider the implication of these factors on executing change. For example, while the strategy for change may reflect the change vision and steps for reaching that vision, the organization's resources remain inadequate, the organization's systems are unchanged, and the organization's behavioral norms remain fixed as they have for years. It's these kinds of misalignments that put an HRIS change effort in jeopardy of not achieving the desired outcome. What is required is alignment, getting all the arrows to all point in the same direction as the strategy for change.

The elements of change can become misaligned for many reasons, but at least two stand out. The change leaders either don't recognize the need to align the four dimensions, or they do so "only perfunctorily because they don't understand the implication of the required alignment" (Higgins, 2005, p. 7). We should note that not all four elements need to be misaligned to reduce the effectiveness of the change. The misalignment of the culture, for example, is enough in itself to lead to difficulties in successfully executing the transformation.

Culture, although difficult to measure precisely, is a real and very powerful force in organizations. Change leaders can use the information gained through the assessment of a firm's culture to help guide each phase of the change process, from the unfreezing phase and determining readiness for change, from implementing the

❖ **Figure 8.9**   Nonaligned Elements of Change

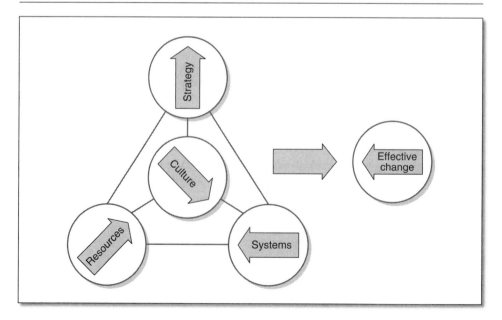

transformation, to consolidating and institutionalizing the new state. Through careful planning and effective change techniques and processes, change leaders can shape and develop organizational cultures that are in alignment with, and supportive of, the desired changes.

Process Reengineering

Implementing the right technology infrastructure and streamlining the business processes that flow through it is an essential ingredient for effective organizational change (Dawson & Jones, n.d.). One of the reasons why organizations do not realize their full **return on investment (ROI)** from new technology is that they simply automate existing processes rather than using the implementation as an opportunity to reengineer them.

Reengineering business processes is often one of the greatest drivers—but also the greatest challenge—involved in new HR software implementations. Every process, from how payroll staff enter data to how employees file their expenses, has to be redesigned in order to obtain the full advantages offered by the new technology (Twentyman, 2006, p. 24).

Resistance to Change

At a basic level, when we ask employees to totally change the way they have been working, it's like asking a basketball team to now switch to playing golf. People are not like play dough, where we can twist and mold them into any shape we want. Unlike play dough, people cannot change their behaviors overnight, "get smarter over the weekend, or 'grow' skills they do not have" (Williams, 2003).

Lou Gerstner (2002), former CEO of IBM, aptly noted why organizational change can be so difficult: "Nobody likes change. Whether you are a senior executive or an entry-level employee, change represents uncertainly and, potentially, pain" (p. 77). It's natural for individuals to resist change because they are comfortable with the status quo. Gerstner's observation suggests that it's much easier to hang onto what made you great than to change, which can be costly.

Both groups and individuals resist change. As Mark Twain said, "Habit is habit, and not to be flung out of the window by any man, but coaxed downstairs a step at a time" (*Directory*, n.d.). Indeed, people's habits are hard to change. Michael Beer (1987) captured the essence of why people resist changing old habits:

> Changes usually mean losses of power as responsibility and accountability are shifted; losses in relationships as new patterns of interaction are demanded by new approaches to management; losses in rewards, particularly status, money, and perquisites as power shifts; and losses in identity as the meaning people make of their work lives is threatened by changes in the firm's strategy and allocation of responsibility. (p. 52)

> In the end, what people resist is the loss of control over their lives that they fought so long and hard to create. This sense of loss of control often leads to a lot of uncertainty about the future. One way to help people regain control of their work lives is effective two-way communication. People need to understand what is happening, that change is essential. It is through change we learn and grow, although not always without pain. (Handy, 1989, p. 28)

Another barrier to organizational change related to maintaining the status quo is the tendency for many organizations to develop a comfort level based on their current performance. John D. Rockefeller (1973) described the conservatism of large organizations:

> An organization is a system, with a logic of its own, and all the weight of tradition and inertia. The deck is stacked in favor of the tried and proven way of doing things and against the taking of risks and striking out in new directions. (p. 72)

What happens is that management become overconfident, complacent, and even a bit arrogant about their success. They develop a myopic view of their company as the center of the competitive universe. They rationalize, Why should we rock the boat or change the formula that has led to our success? And in the process of making better widgets, they fail to notice that the competitive landscape and customer preferences are changing. "That very reluctance to change ultimately turns success into failure" (Handy, 2002).

In addition, Kotter (1996) suggests that change initiatives can encounter challenges because of "inwardly focused cultures, a paralyzing bureaucracy, parochial politics, low levels of trust, lack of teamwork, arrogant attitudes, lack of leadership in middle management, and the general fear of the unknown" (p. 20). To effectively manage change, change agents and managers must learn to address these barriers to change and do it well.

We also know that if an organization accumulates a series of failed change initiatives, big or small, expensive or relatively inexpensive, employees can become burned out and cynical. When this happens, it's hard to create a feeling of enthusiasm and zeal for the next change. People no longer are motivated, nor do they exhibit the level of commitment and buy-in necessary for any change program to be a success.

The same outcome can result with what Eric Abrahamson (2004a) calls "repetitive-change syndrome," whose symptoms include initiative overload, change-related chaos, and employee anxiety, cynicism, and burnout (pp. 2–3). Initiative overload is like huge waves rolling in off the ocean—people are hit with one change initiative after another. Before one change program can be brought to fruition and institutionalized, there comes another wave. Soon people become so overwhelmed that they lose track of which change initiative they are working on and why. To cope with this dilemma, Abrahamson suggests that leaders nurture an organizational culture that is capable of ongoing adaption. This may require what Abrahamson calls "pacing": "alternating periods of change . . . with periods of stability during which a business can recover" (Abrahamson, 2004b, p. 4).

If we go beyond the inertia to change or to preserve the status quo, there are indeed powerful lessons to be taken from understanding why change programs fail. Unfortunately, not many organizations bother to assess why change programs don't succeed. Instead, they try some other change initiative. To paraphrase Samuel Johnson, the new change initiative is like a second marriage, where one looks to the triumph of hope over experience. By recognizing the mistakes to avoid in managing change, we can better focus on the key success factors necessary to increase the probability of success while trying to avoid some of the key pitfalls.

The barriers and pitfalls to change notwithstanding, change leaders need to anticipate and take on these challenges and manage them accordingly. It's important to remain sensitive to the fact that every individual may have concerns that can lead him or her to act in a way that undermines the change effort (Baum, 2000, p. 13).

Despite the fact that the new systems are being implemented to improve the efficiency and effectiveness of the HR function, fear and resistance to the new system from HR staff is common and must be anticipated and addressed. HR staff may be concerned about job loss due to the more efficient processes, or they may fear the new roles, responsibilities, and uncertainty that will result from the change. It should be noted that in general, HR technology doesn't cause the reduction of staff. But it certainly can change the skills that are needed from the people in the HR department (Gunsauley, 1999, p. 23).

When employees outside the HR department are affected by new technology, such as with manager or employee self-service, resistance to the change is also a common source of problems in an implementation. These systems represent a change in the relationship between HR and the rest of the organization. Employees may view this with suspicion—they may feel that HR is eliminating customer service to cut costs. They may feel as though they are being left to fend for themselves. Employees and managers alike may fear the new technology or the responsibility of taking on new roles.

All these issues can be prevented or addressed with proactive, continuous communication and effective, ongoing training.

User Acceptance

Mourier and Smith (2001) remind us that for any change initiative to be successful, the management must cultivate the soil (culture) and provide the nourishment (motivation) needed for the change to grow and develop to fruition. One expert suggests that 20% of employees buy in and tend to support and drive a change from the beginning, another 50% are fence sitters and don't commit, and the remaining 30% tend to take a hard-core stand and oppose the change ("In Times of Change," 1997). One approach to improving the odds of convincing people that the change is necessary is to help them understand that the vision for the change is headed in the right direction.

For example, people's response to change depends on whether they understand the basic purpose of the change. Why is it necessary? What is the big *picture* of how the end result will look and feel; people need to visualize the change project before they can commit to it in their hearts. What is the step-by-step *plan* for carrying out the change? And what *part* do the employees play in the change? What must they do to support the change? (Bridges, 2003, p. 52). It's important that people understand both emotionally and intellectually why they need to change. The emotional component is what Kotter (1996) calls "Creating a Sense of Urgency," where without it "people won't give that extra effort that is often essential. They won't make needed sacrifices. Instead they cling to the status quo and resist initiatives from above" (p. 5). Along with the needs of employees, we also need to mobilize the support of key players—both inside and outside the organization—who will be affected by the change.

❖ **Figure 8.10** Basic HRIS User Acceptance Model

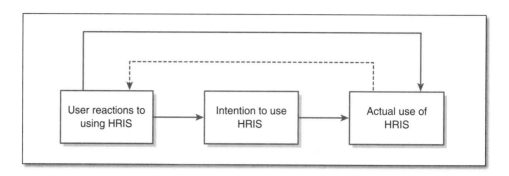

Ultimately, acceptance of the new technology and new processes represents project success. While the technical challenges in implementing any system can be great, it is the people "challenges that cannot be overlooked (although often are) during the implementation phase" of an HRIS (Ruta, 2005, p. 36). Organizations cannot simply rely on the strategy of "if you build it, they will come." Change leaders must use appropriate change management techniques to create **user acceptance** or risk failure.

The research on the user acceptance of IT is well developed. The basic framework that underlies this research is depicted in Figure 8.10.

Venkatesh, Morris, Davis, and Davis (2003, p. 427) reviewed the user acceptance literature and from their study defined a unified theory of acceptance and use of technology. Their model contains four main elements considered the prerequisites of user acceptance: effort expectancy, performance expectancy, social norms, and facilitating conditions.

To aid our efforts to predict success in the acceptance of an HRIS, it is important that we understand how users will develop and experience the information system (Ruta, 2005, p. 40). User perception related to ease of use of the HRIS (effort expectancy) is an important determinant of user acceptance. The extent to which a user perceives that the HRIS will enhance his or her job performance (performance expectancy) is considered the strongest predictor of intention. This is obviously important in the early stages of the implementation of the project. Social influence (subjective norms) is defined as the degree to which users perceive how others in the organization feel that the system is important and how user behavior will be viewed by others. In other words, users are more likely to accept the HRIS because they wish to fit in and conform with the behavior of others (Ruta, 2005). Facilitating conditions relates to the extent users believe that the organization is committed and resources are in place to support implementation and use of the system.

End users must be involved and feel ownership of the new system. When future users participate in the planning, acceptance testing, and conversion to a new HRIS, their commitment to the project increases. The project team can actively engage others who are not directly involved by inviting them to attend occasional meetings, keeping them informed, asking for feedback, and telling them why decisions were made (Keener, Heard, & Morgan, 2000).

Informal ambassadors or change agents can help influence the rest of the organization and can make or break the acceptance of the new system. Implementation teams should identify influential individuals and those who have shown an interest in the project and engage them in becoming informal ambassadors for the change (Prager & Overholt, 1994, p. 67; Ruta, 2005, p. 46).

It may also be a good idea to identify the most resistant users and involve them right from the beginning to gain their buy-in (Keener & Fletcher, 2004). Otherwise, they may influence others negatively toward the change.

Individuals or departments may use the new technology, but not to its full capacity. Research indicates that up to 70% of the functions of new HR systems go untapped, because users make the new system do only what the old system did (Roberts, 1998, p. 40). A strong focus on communication, ongoing training, and process reengineering will help prevent this.

Instituting a phased implementation plan or an initial pilot program can provide a higher comfort level, allowing some users to "try out" the new system and sharing their outcomes (hopefully positive) with the remaining users. In more complex or highly challenging implementations, Morgan (2000) recommends starting with small steps to increase user acceptance. Starting with less critical tasks, such as completing online surveys, viewing HR policies or organizational newsletters, responding to holiday party invitations, or enrolling in United Way campaigns online, can increase the level of comfort before requiring them to perform complex or critical tasks, such as enrolling in benefit plans (p. 22).

One of the major obstacles in gaining user acceptance is getting users to try out the new system. This can be especially challenging when the users are not required to use the system to perform their job.

The use of rewards to encourage user participation of new systems can be very effective. By including the use of new technology and revised procedures in performance goals and linking those goals to compensation, we can reinforce the importance of the change. Of course, this is only applicable to situations where the new technology is required for an individual's job. In cases where the system usage is not required for an individual's job, incentives can still be used. Some examples follow:

- The State of Kentucky offered those who completed an online survey providing feedback on the new system a chance to win a weekend stay at a Kentucky State Park (Anheier & Doherty, 2001).
- One organization awarded gift certificates to the first 50 employees who used the system to update their personal information.
- One organization gave employees a $100 bonus for completing their annual benefits enrollment online.

A small investment in rewards such as these can be returned with increased user comfort and acceptance.

Research clearly shows that acceptance is improved if information is clearly communicated, if users are involved in the process, and if ongoing training is provided. Not everyone will accept the changes at the same time. User acceptance can be influenced by culture and demographics. Younger employees may accept the new technology more quickly, considering their higher comfort level with technology and personal computers (Morgan, 2000, p. 20). Those who have been working in the same capacity with the former system and processes for an extended period of time may take more time to accept the change than someone who has only recently joined the company.

The Importance of HRIS Integration

HRIS should be integrated with other systems within HR and the rest of the organization when appropriate to obtain maximum benefits and efficiencies. Systems should certainly be integrated with payroll and automated time systems. Benefits enrollment systems and other similar vendor software can also be integrated to avoid duplicate entries and prevent errors. Ideally, other corporate functions, such as financial systems, should be integrated for an efficient flow of information.

Practical Approaches to Implementation

Implementation can be completed all at once, or in phases. The advantage in implementing all at once is that everyone is moved at one time. The disadvantage is that there is no test period, and resources are more strained. Phased implementations or pilot programs allow for testing of the system with smaller groups so that unforeseen problems can be fixed and success can be communicated and celebrated.

> Nestle USA, the California based food company, opted for a gradual phased in implementation rather than going live all at once. They started by implementing a new payroll system—first to a small group of 600 employees, then to other business units over time. "By focusing on a small group first, we were able to address many of our interface and reporting needs upfront with a small population of employees," said Mike Benson, Director of HRIS. "Demonstrating successes and celebrating them along the way reinforced senior management's decision to fund the project, and motivated our team to keep going." (Henson, 1996, p. 3)

When new systems are introduced, running the old system in parallel for a period of time allows you to test the capabilities of the new system and compare the results achieved by each system. It also allows for a backup in the event of problems with the new system—which, it is hoped, would not occur at this point. The downside of this tactic is that there will be duplicate work performed during this phase. A potential problem to watch out for in this scenario is user resistance causing users to remain with the old system and resist using the new system as long as the old system remains available.

Postimplementation and Maintenance of the HRIS

The ongoing task of operating and maintaining the new system is often forgotten. Turnbull (2005) reminds us that revised business practices and processes require new organizational structures with new roles and budgets. HR should have a process in place to audit, review, and reconsider business processes (p. 13).

Organizations must determine who will be responsible for the ongoing maintenance of the system. This includes performing system updates and upgrades and adjusting for legislative changes and changes in organizational procedures. While in some smaller organizations, HR professionals take on HRIS responsibilities along with their other tasks, larger organizations will have one or more dedicated HRIS professionals to manage the system. Typically, this function will report to the HR department.

Organizations should establish a help desk to assist end users with system questions, problems, and report-writing issues. A best practice is to have the project team provide support for a period of time, allowing them to track issues, followed by an HR system help desk that coordinates with the IT technical help desk as required. Generally, most issues that arise are functional rather than technical, which are best handled by the HR staff (Anheier & Doherty, 2005; Turnbull, 2005).

Turnbull (2005) reminds us that we need to ensure that the system is being used correctly and validate the integrity of the new data. The issue of data security and privacy must be also addressed, and policies and procedures regarding electronic data should be established and maintained, along with scheduled audits.

User satisfaction and acceptance must be measured to evaluate the effectiveness of the project and identify any areas for correction. While user feedback can help us get a picture of satisfaction levels, actual usage has been shown to be a more precise measure of both satisfaction and acceptance (Ruta, 2005, p. 38). Organizations can use these results to diagnose problem areas and provide additional information or training to users. If there is a trend of light usage in one department compared with other departments, the reasons can be identified and addressed (Anheier & Doherty, 2001).

Finally, ongoing refresher training and advanced user training must be planned to reinforce the new system and processes as well as expand the knowledge of the users. User group meetings can be a good informal way of providing training support and information sharing.

Summary

Perhaps one of the major obstacles in the use of an HRIS is its implementation. While technical challenges will always remain in implementing complex HRIS, the major challenge to successful implementation is more behavioral than technical.

The evidence is clear that successfully introducing major HRIS into organizations requires an effective blend of good technical and good organizational skills. Effective management of change represents a critical core competence that all organizations and HR leaders must master. By better understanding the field of knowledge and competencies related to managing change, HR professionals can better manage change in our organizations and reap the rewards that accrue to successful change initiatives.

Change management is a process by which an organization moves from its current state to some future desired state as defined by its vision.

In this chapter, we introduced and described a general model of the change process and then four specific models of organizational change that have received considerable attention in the change management literature: Lewin's change model, Gleicher's change formula, Nadler's congruence model, and Kotter's eight-stage change model. Some of these models are focused at the individual employee or group level, what is referred to as the microlevel, while others are focused at the organizational or macrolevel. These models help draw our attention to the elements important in successful managing of any HRIS implementation project.

Increasingly, the failure to successfully implement information systems has less to do with the hardware or software aspects of the new system and more to do with the skills of the change leader and the people and organizational issues related to the change. Research has identified a number of key factors that contribute to IT system implementation failures, including leadership, communication, planning, change management, and training.

Process reengineering is a critical component in HRIS implementation. One of the reasons why organizations do not realize their full ROI from new technology is because they simply automate existing processes rather than using the implementation as an opportunity to reengineer them.

Finally, change leaders must prepare for the inevitable resistance to change and plan to gain user acceptance. A plan must also be created for ongoing maintenance of the new system.

Discussion Questions

1. Discuss each of the theoretical change models introduced in this chapter. How can we use them when planning an HRIS implementation to increase our chances of success?

2. Analyze the main reasons for HRIS implementation failure. How can we prevent these from happening to us?

3. Discuss the importance of communication in managing a technology change. What roadblocks might an organization face if they fail to create a good communication plan?

4. If you were asked to develop a training plan for an HRIS implementation, what kinds of things would you include?

5. Discuss the role of culture in HRIS implementation. How might two different organizations with very different cultures approach the same HRIS implementation differently?

6. Create recommendations for an organization that is facing resistance to change from their own HR department. What are some of the likely causes of this resistance? How can they be overcome?

7. Discuss how informal leaders within the organization might be used to increase user acceptance.

Case Study: The Grant Corporation

The Grant Corporation is a financial services firm based out of Chicago, Illinois. Its revenue exceeded $1 billion last year, with a net income of $530 million. It has just over 1,000 employees. While the organization has been in business for almost 10 years, it has experienced rapid growth in the past 2 years due to tremendous business growth and a merger with the Enelrad Group, another local firm. They have had difficulty keeping up with this growth, especially in the HR area, which has been stretched thin to keep up with staffing needs and their other mainly administrative duties.

Six months ago, the CEO, Todd Jackson, recognized the need to expand the size and functionality of the HRD and hired Julia Woodland to be the Director of HR, reporting directly to him. This was a newly created position, replacing the role of the HR Administrator, who had previously reported to the VP of Finance and made the decision to retire when the new HR position was announced.

When Woodland was hired, Jackson told her that she would have "full reign" to create a more strategically focused HR department that would be better equipped to handle the organization's needs. She had had quite a bit of experience at her previous company and was eager to take on the task.

While the organization used advanced technology for their business applications, HR was still using a basic payroll processing software program and Excel spreadsheets to track various categories of employee information, including personal data, benefits enrollments, performance evaluation schedules, and compensation. All payroll and benefit information was manually entered into their respective systems, and much of the information had to be entered into multiple spreadsheets when there was a change. The department could not keep up with the information needs—new hires were getting paid incorrectly, or not at all. Benefits enrollments were delayed or contained mistakes, and performance evaluations and pay raises were late. The printed employee handbook, benefits binder, and orientation materials were in serious need of updating. In addition, they had 16 open positions and stacks of resumes everywhere. It was no wonder that the HR Administrator had decided to retire!

Julia Woodland spent long hours trying to determine what she could do to address the immediate and long-term concerns of her new department. She brought in a temporary employee to help her staff file, process paperwork, and enter data. She focused on hiring two higher-level HR representatives and a payroll clerk. She turned to a staffing agency to help them identify candidates for their open positions, including those in HR. Finally, she proposed the purchase of an integrated payroll/HRIS that was capable of integrating with the Finance department's system as well as their benefit and 401(k) providers' systems. It also offered the option of a Web-based employee portal, which would allow employees to view information online and change their personal data. Jackson responded favorably, and told her to "go ahead and do whatever she needed to do to fix the mess." The next day, Woodland contracted with the HRIS provider.

Woodland spent the next week meeting with her new HRIS vendor representative to discuss the installation and implementation of the system. Because she was so overwhelmed and wanted to get the new system in as quickly as possible, she didn't have time to discuss the project with her staff right away, but she knew that they would be excited about the new system and the opportunities it would open up for them as the burden of administrative tasks eased. She closed her door during the meetings, so they could concentrate. She wanted to be able to implement the system by January 1, so that their year-end payroll data were accurate and they could track other data on an annual basis with a full year of data. Since she had been through the process in the past and was familiar with such systems, she figured that she could manage the implementation with the help of IT and her staff as needed. She would make all key decisions to move the project along and meet her deadline.

The current HR staff consisted of an HR Assistant and two generalists who seemed to function as clerks and recruiters. They had all been hired at the same time more than 5 years ago, when the HR Administrator was the sole member of the department. They were very proud of how they had worked so hard together to build HR and keep up with the increasing demand. They were just getting used to working with Woodland but thought that she was very nice and had high hopes for the improvements and new strategic focus that she would help them implement.

Day by day, the staff watched the vendor representative come and go, along with a parade of candidates for the new HR Representative positions sent over by the agency. They soon began to wonder about all the changes that their new boss was making and what these changes would mean for them. They started making assumptions that had them very concerned.

Woodland contacted the IT Director to tell him about the project. He expressed concern over the ability of their server to handle the new system and how they would address **firewall** issues with the portal. Furthermore, all his staff were tied up with a critical upgrade to their customer service system, which had caused more than its share of problems. He demanded to know why they had not been involved sooner and told her that it would be unlikely that they would be able to participate in the implementation or help her meet her deadline. Upset, she called Todd Jackson, who advised her not to worry about it—he would tell them to get it done.

When she contacted Finance to obtain information that the HRIS vendor needed to link the HRIS to their system, the Finance Manager was more than willing to help— but she did not know where to get the system information from and did not understand how the information would flow from one system to another. She asked why they couldn't just keep the systems separate and enter the necessary data into the finance system from reports provided by HR. "That's the way we've always done it," she said. "It doesn't take long, and it will be much simpler that way."

In the meantime, morale was declining in HR. Whenever Woodland asked them for information about payroll or their Excel spreadsheets, they seemed uneasy and never provided her with exactly what she was looking for. She didn't understand their antiquated forms or their backward processes but decided she could fix those after the new system was in. Also, it felt like the rest of the company was suddenly treating her differently. They had all made her feel so welcome 6 months ago when she came on board. Now, employees approached her with caution, and managers always seemed abrupt.

Julia Woodland began to wonder if this was the right role for her. Why were things so difficult? She thought that everyone would be thrilled about the new system and its efficiencies, and would be eager to help. Was it her problem or theirs?

She thought that perhaps people didn't realize the impact she was making in the organization. She decided to make an announcement about the exciting new system that would help make things more effective and efficient in HR and help the employees simplify their lives as well. She sent out a companywide e-mail announcing the new payroll/HRIS and outlining its ability to interface with other systems and its Web portal capabilities. To her disappointment, no one seemed to understand the significance or even pay attention. A few employees asked her if their paychecks would be delayed as a result.

She wondered how she would ever get through this and what she needed to do to get everyone on board.

Case Study Questions

1. Overall, what did Julia Woodland do right? What could she have done differently?

2. Were the correct people involved in the process? Who would you have included and why?

3. What errors did Woodland make with her own staff? What impact might these errors have had on the success of the implementation? What should have been done?

4. Discuss the cultural issues involved in this case. Are there things Julia Woodland should have taken into consideration prior to starting the implementation? Why are they important?

5. If you were in Julia Woodland's position, what would you include in your communication plan for the implementation?

6. How can training be used in this case to make the implementation more successful?

7. How can The Grant Corporation increase user acceptance of the system?

8. Discuss the potential benefits of process reengineering in this implementation. What impact might it have had?

9. After the implementation, what steps should the HR department take to ensure proper maintenance and support of the system?

NOTE

1. See Arizona Department of Administration, Human Resources Web site, www.hr.state.az.us.

REFERENCES

Abrahamson, E. (2004a). *Change without pain.* Boston: Harvard Business School Press.

Abrahamson, E. (2004b, February). The road to better recombination. *Harvard Management Update, 9*(2), 1–4.

Anheier, N., & Doherty, S. (2001, October). *Employee self-service: Tips to ensure a successful implementation* (SHRM HRTX Forum Library). Retrieved March 3, 2007, from www.shrm.org/hrtx/library_published/IC/CMS_000210.asp

Armenakis, A. A., & Harris, S. G. (2002). Crafting a change message to create transformational readiness. *Journal of Organizational Change Management, 15*(2), 169–183.

Baum, D. (2000). *Lighting in a bottle.* Chicago: Dearborn.

Beckhard, R., & Harris, R. (1987). *Organizational transitions: Managing complex change* (2nd ed.). Reading, CA: Addison-Wesley.

Beer, M. (1987). Revitalizing organizations: Change process and emergent model. *Academy of Management Executive, 1*(1), 51–55.

Beer, M., & Nohria, N. (2000). Resolving the tension between theories E and O of change. In M. Beer & N. Nohria (Eds.), *Breaking the code of change* (pp. 1–33). Boston: Harvard Business School Press.

Benjamin, R., & Levinson, E. (1993, Summer). A framework for managing IT-enabled change. *Sloan Management Review, 34*(4), 23–33.

Blanchard, K. (2007). *Leading at a higher level.* Upper Saddle River, NJ: Prentice Hall.

Bridges, W. (1991). *Managing transitions: Making the most of change.* Reading, CA: Addison-Wesley.

Bridges, W. (2003). *Managing transitions* (2nd ed.). Cambridge, MA: Perseus Books.

Burke, W. W. (2002). *Organizational change.* Thousand Oaks, CA: Sage.

Burnes, B. (2004). Kurt Lewin and the planned approach to change: A re-appraisal. *Journal of Management Studies, 41*(6), 977–1002.

Cameron, E., & Green, M. (2004). *Making sense of change.* London: Kogan Page.

Collier, J. (1945). United States Indian administration as a laboratory of ethnic relations. *Social Research, 12,* 275–276.

Conner, D. R. (1998). *Leading at the edge of chaos: How to create the nimble organization.* New York: Wiley.

Corey, S. M. (1953). *Action research to improve school practices.* New York: Columbia University, Teachers College, Bureau of Publications.

Correll, B. (2005, February/March). Change management: Using the right techniques and technologies to ensure success. *IHRIM.link, 12.*

Dawson, M. J., & Jones, M. L. (n.d.). Human change management: Herding cats. *IHRIM Online.* Retrieved March 5, 2007, from www.ihrim.org/resources/Articles/SystemsSel/change.asp

Directory of Mark Twain's maxims, quotations, and various opinions. (n.d.). Retrieved September 6, 2004, from www.twainquotes.com/Habit.html

Duck, J. D. (2001). *The change monster.* New York: Crown Business.

Eccles, T. (1994). *Succeeding with change.* London: McGraw-Hill.

Fletcher, P. A. K. (2005). Personnel administration to business-driven human capital management. In H. G. Gueutal & D. L. Stone (Eds.), *The brave new world of eHR* (pp. 1–21). San Francisco: Jossey-Bass.

French, W. L., & Bell, C. H., Jr. (1973). *Organization development.* Englewood Cliffs, NJ: Prentice Hall.

Frohman, M. A., Sashkin, M., & Kavanagh, M. J. (1976). Action-research as an organization development approach. *Organization and Administrative Sciences, 7,* 129–161.

Gerstner, L. V. (2002). *Who says elephants can't dance? Inside IBM's Historic Turnaround.* New York: HarperCollins.

Gerstner, L. V. (2005). Lou Gerstner on change. *Leadership Excellence, 22*(6), 18.

Gunsauley, C. (1999). Losing sight of human mission can trigger new systems failure. *Employee Benefit News, 13*(8).

Handy, C. (1989). *The age of unreason.* Boston: Harvard Business School Press.

Handy, C. (2002, Spring). Elephants and fleas: Is your organization prepared for change. *Leader to Leader.* Retrieved November 9, 2004, from www.leadertoleader.org/knowledgecenter/journal.aspx?ArticleID=119

Henson, R. (1996, November). HRIMS for dummies: A practical guide to technology implementation in human resource information management system. *HR Focus, 73*(11), 3–5.

Higgins, J. M. (2005, March). The eight s's of successful strategy execution. *Journal of Change Management, 5*(1), 3–13.

Jones, M., & Price, R. L. (2004). Organizational knowledge sharing in ERP implementation: Lessons from industry. *Journal of Organizational and End User Computing, 16*(1), 21–40.

Kandel, A. (n.d.). *The eight fatal flaws of HR system implementations and how to avoid them* (SHRM HRTX Forum Library). Retrieved March 14, 2007, from www.shrm.org/hrtx/library_published/nonIC/CMS_006586.asp

Kavanagh, M. J., Gueutal, H. G., & Tannenbaum, S. I. (1990). *Human resource information systems.* Boston: PWS-Kent.

Keener, D., & Fletcher, R. (2004, January). *Good planning, realistic scope and executive sponsorship important in HRIS projects* (HRTX Library). Retrieved from www.shrm.org/hrtx/library_published/nonIC/CMS_006631.asp

Keener, D., Heard, D., & Morgan, M. (2000, February). *Implementing human resources system: Lessons learned* (SHRM White Paper). Retrieved March 5, 2007, from www.shrm.org/hrtx/library_published/IC/CMS_000199.asp

Kotter, J. P. (1996). *Leading change.* Boston: Harvard Business School Press.

Lewin, K. (1946). Action research and minority problems. *Journal of Social Issues, 2,* 34–46.

Lippitt, R. (1950, September). *Value-judgment problems of the social scientist participating in action-research.* Paper presented at the annual meeting of the American Psychological Association.

Lorenzi, N. M., & Riley, R. T. (2000). Managing change: An overview. *Journal of the American Medical Informatics Association, 7*(2), 116–124.

Mercer Delta Consulting. (2000). *Transition leadership: A guide to leading change initiatives.* Retrieved October 6, 2005, from www.biasca.com/archivos/for_downloading/management_surveys/Mgmt_Change_and_TransitionLeadership.pdf

Mercer Delta Consulting. (2003). *The congruence model.* Retrieved February 26, 2007, from www.mercerdelta.com/organizational_consulting/help_change_metrics.html

Miller, D. (2004). Building sustainable change capability. *Industrial and Commercial Training, 36*(1), 9–12.

Morgan, L. (2000). Technology changing the role of human resources. *Workspan, 43*(3), 16–22.

Mourier, P., & Smith, M. (2001). *Conquering organizational change.* Atlanta, GA: CEP Press.

Nadler, D. A. (1998.) *Champions of change: How CEOs and their companies are mastering the skills of radical change.* San Francisco: Jossey-Bass.

Office of the Auditor General. (2005). *Performance audit* (Department of Administration, Report No. 05–02). Retrieved February 28, 2007, from www.auditorgen.state.az.us/Reports/State_Agencies/Agencies/Administration_Department_of/Performance/05-02/05-02.pdf

Pascale, R., & Millemann, M. (1997, December). Changing the way we change. *Harvard Business Review, 75*(6), 126–139.

Paul, L. G. (2004, December 1). Time to change. *CIO Magazine.* Retrieved December 16, 2004, from www.cio.com/archive/120104/change.html

Potts, R., & LaMarsh, J. (2004). *Master change, maximize success.* San Francisco: Chronicle Books.

Prager, K. P., & Overholt, M. H. (1994). How to create a changed organization. *Information Systems Management, 11*(3), 64–70.

Roberts, B. (1998, February). The new HRIS: Good deal or $6 million paperweight? *HR Magazine, 43,* 40–48.

Rockefeller, J. D., III. (1973). *The second American revolution.* New York: HarperCollins.

Ruta, C. (2005). The application of change management theory to HR portal implementation in subsidiaries of multinational corporations. *Human Resource Management, 44*(1), 35–53.

Schein, E. H. (1996). Kurt Lewin's change theory in the field and in the classroom: Notes toward a model of managed learning. *Systems Practice, 9*(1), 27–47.

Senn, L. E., & Childress, J. R. (2000). *Why change initiatives fail: It's the culture dummy!* London: Senn-Delaney Leadership Consulting Group.

In times of change, managers should forget noisemakers and focus on fence-sitters. (1997, November 3). *Chemical and Engineering News.* Retrieved October 30, 2004, from http://pubs.acs.org/hotartcl/cenear/971103/change.html

Turnbull, I. (2005). After the implementation: Maintenance of your new HR system. *Canadian HR Reporter, 18*(19), 13..

Twentyman, J. (2006, May 30). Teams before technology. *Personnel Today,* pp. 24–25.

U.S. Government Accountability Office. (2003, July). *Results-oriented cultures: Implementation steps to assist mergers and organizational transformations* (Publication No. GAO-03–669). Retrieved January 16, 2007, from GAO Web site: www.gao.gov/new.items/d03669.pdf

Venkatesh, V., Morris, M. G., Davis, G. B., & Davis, F. D. (2003). User acceptance of information technology: Toward a unified view. *MIS Quarterly, 27*(3), 425–478.

Warhaftig, W. (2005). Flight to the future: managing change in financial services for sustainable growth. *LIMRA International.* Retrieved March 11, 2007, from www.limra.com/abstracts/abstract.aspx?fid=5184

Wheatley, M. (1997, Summer). Goodbye, command and control. *Leader to Leader.* Retrieved February 2, 2007, from www.leadertoleader.org/knowledgecenter/journal.aspx?ArticleID=147

Williams, W. (2003). Why almost all organizational change efforts fail. *CEO Refresher.* Retrieved October 19, 2004, from www.refresher.com/!wwfail.html

PART IV

HRIS Applications

HR Administration and HRIS

Linda C. Isenhour

EDITORS' NOTE

This chapter begins the examination and discussion of the HRM applications enabled by the successful development and implementation of an HRIS. It is appropriate to begin the applications chapters with an introduction to HR Administration. The first eight chapters of this book explained how to build an HRIS, so in a sense the first eight chapters were the building blocks for the HRIS "house." Now the filling of the "house" begins. One of the crucial outcomes of following the advice from the first eight chapters is that the employee database, frequently referred to as the Basic Employee Information Module (BEIM),[1] will be accurate and up-to-date. This characteristic of the *module* allows HR professionals to use the software in the HRIS to develop HR programs such as recruitment and compensation with confidence. The use of HRIS for compliance with government laws and guidelines discussed in this chapter absolutely requires an accurate and timely database. In addition, benchmark data for use in cost-benefit analyses of HR programs demand accuracy in the BEIM or serious and costly mistakes could be made in decisions to continue or expand an HR program such as e-learning. Finally, as explained in this chapter, the accuracy of the BEIM is doubly important because of the use of the data and results to build the HR balanced scorecard, which is used in assessing strategic alignment with organizational goals.

CHAPTER OBJECTIVES

After completing this chapter, you should be able to

♦ Discuss the complexity of HR administration and the advantages of an HRIS over a "paper-and-pencil" HR operation

♦ Discuss the advantages of having a service-oriented architecture (SOA) for the HRIS

♦ Differentiate among the four structural approaches to HR administration for an HRIS within SOA

♦ Discuss the advantages and disadvantages of each of the four structural approaches to HR administration

♦ Understand the importance of having an accurate and timely BEIM

♦ Understand how legal compliance with government mandates is an important part of the HRIS functionality and how it adds to the complexity of an HRIS in both domestic and multinational organizations

♦ Understand the HR principles on which governmental laws are based and applied in a global economy

♦ Discuss the various privacy laws, particularly as they relate to an HRIS

♦ Discuss the elements important to successful measurement of strategic alignment of the HR scorecard and how it is related to the strategic alignment of an organization

VIGNETTE

In 1998, Procter & Gamble (P&G) had more than 98,000 employees in 80 countries. Identifying common measures, improving service, and reducing HR administrative costs were strategic imperatives for this global consumer products company.

The human resource managers at P&G considered a variety of solutions. Should they maintain their decentralized global operation in HRM and use technology such as Internet service portals to improve efficiency, join the burgeoning trend toward *shared-services centers* (SSCs) to centralize their operations, or investigate outsourcing for selected human resource functions? With so many countries and governmental regulations involved, how could P&G achieve sufficient standardization through HRIS to gain increased savings and still meet its varied responsibilities to those multiple entities? Would its internal customers view the move from decentralized to centralized shared services as meeting their needs? How would such changes be measured from an internal customer satisfaction perspective? Which measures for the various administrative approaches would best align the HR functions with the P&G **balanced scorecard** strategic goals and objectives?

These are common problems in HRM today. We hope to help you answer many of these questions in this chapter.

Introduction to HR Administration in an HRIS Environment

Human resource management (HRM) administration deals with the efficient performance of the transactional activities introduced in Chapter 1. Recordkeeping, updating policy and informational materials for a **self-service portal**, generating and disseminating internal reports, complying with governmentally mandated external reporting, and administering labor contracts are all examples of HRM administration associated with managing an organization's workforce. Research has shown that approximately 65% to 75% of all HR activities are transactional (Wright, McMahan, Snell, & Gerhart, 1998). Human resource information systems (HRISs) are vital tools in managing these increasingly complex transactional requirements. For this reason, it is absolutely crucial that the employee database, frequently referred to as the BEIM (Kavanagh, Gueutal, & Tannenbaum, 1990), be carefully constructed so that the information is *accurate and timely* (Kavanagh et al., 1990; Walker, 1982). The BEIM is a record and repository for all relevant employee information and must be created prior to any other modules for programs such as recruiting and applicant tracking. The approaches and technological techniques described in this chapter ensure that the BEIM, once initially built, remains accurate and up-to-date.

HRIS can assist managers charged with improving the efficiency of HR administration by reducing costs, enhancing the reliability of reporting, and improving service to internal customers. Information technology facilitates administration in multiple ways. First, HRIS can help improve data accuracy by reducing the need for multiple inputs, eliminating redundancies in data, and reducing the opportunity for human input errors and associated corrections. In addition, HRIS, through *relational databases* (see Chapter 2), speed the process of building reports with simple query capabilities. Moreover, HRIS, if properly designed for flexibility, can support differences in reporting mandated by global governmental jurisdictions. Finally, a properly designed HRIS permits secure global distribution of data, facilitating consideration of alternative methods of consolidating and improving services to internal customers (Ceriello, 1991; Gueutal & Stone, 2005; Kavanagh et al., 1990; Osle & Cooper, 2003; Walker, 1982, 1993, 2001).

Administrative issues associated with specific HRM functions as part of the development and implementation of an HRIS have been briefly mentioned in earlier chapters (e.g., recruiting, training, compensating) and will be discussed in more detail in later chapters. However, HR managers face a variety of other administrative requirements in the rapidly evolving HRIS era. The HRM administrative issues highlighted in this chapter include organizational approaches for providing HR in a global economy (i.e., self-service portals, SSCs, outsourcing, **offshoring**); compliance mandates for record maintenance and report requirements associated with government laws in both the U.S. (i.e., Equal Employment Opportunity report [EEO-1], **Occupational Safety and Health Act [OSHA]**) and other countries' labor laws; and measurement of HRM contributions to an organization's strategic goals via a balanced scorecard.

HRM Administration and Organizing Approaches

Historically, HR managers operated as adjunct staff to organizations, overseeing the daily transactions associated with hiring, paying, and training employees and reporting on employee issues as required by managers in organizations. As organizations grew more complex, administering these daily transactions also grew more complex. The introduction of mechanization to handle payroll signaled the changing future of HR administration; technology would play an increasingly important role in managing daily employee transactions. Walker (1982, 1993, 2001) detailed chronologically the technological (i.e., transistors, Internet) and social (i.e., employment regulations and laws, rise of multinational corporations) changes that "pushed and pulled" HR administration into the modern era.

Today, computer hardware and the accompanying software packages offer considerable support for daily HR transactions and make it possible to move beyond the limited administrative approaches available to the HR managers of the 1950s (PricewaterhouseCoopers, 2006). HR professionals of that era, whose work involved managing numerous employees charged with collecting, recording, and maintaining thousands of handwritten records, fought annual budget battles to secure more employees to perform the mushrooming functions and more filing cabinets to store the increasing numbers of paper records. In contrast, modern HR professionals engaged in administration actively seek ways to reduce organization costs, while improving data accuracy, employee productivity, and customer service through effective use of technology designed to provide continuously improving HR processes (Bender, 2001; Ulrich, 1997). Indeed, 89% of the companies worldwide included in the 2006 CedarCrestone HR technology survey indicated the use of some type of HR administrative technology. The next section briefly describes the enabling architecture that allows HR administrators to leverage technology.

Service-Oriented Architecture and Extensible Markup Language

Service-oriented architecture (SOA) "is a paradigm for organizing and utilizing distributed [computing] capabilities that may be under the control of different ownership domains . . . providing a uniform means to offer, discover, interact with and use capabilities to produce desired [business] effects" (OASIS, 2006, p. 8). It is focused on providing overall service that is well-defined, self-contained, context- and platform-independent and adds value to the organization's business purpose rather than simply addressing the technology itself. In effect, SOA is a collection of internal and external services that can communicate with each other by point-to-point data exchange or through coordination among different services to achieve a business purpose. Figure 9.1 demonstrates the business-driven SOA process (Marks & Bell, 2006).

For example, an HR administration manager in the United States who needs to generate the mandated, annual, government Equal Employment Opportunity report (EEO-1) cares little about where the information is stored or which applications, servers, communications technologies, or programming languages are used. Rather, the manager wants easy access to the myriad data necessary to complete the report in a

❖ **Figure 9.1**   SOA Business-Modeling Process

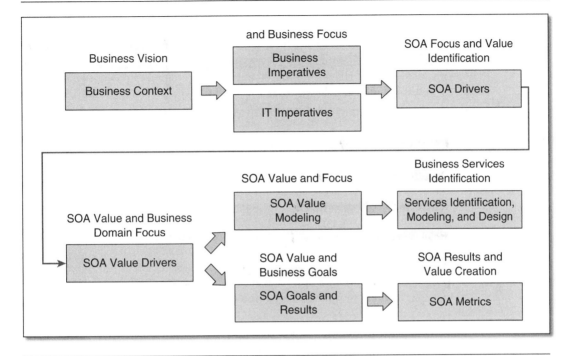

SOURCE: Marks and Bell (2006, chap. 3).

timely manner. SOA focuses on fulfilling that need, moving away from a point-to-point perspective (e.g., HR linked to a single EEO database) to a market perspective of services, reusing data and applications from multiple sources as long as the required service is provided. The principles of SOA include loose coupling, flexibility, autonomy, standards-based computing, reusability, modularity, and services discoverability and optimization. The architectural benefits of SOA include (Campbell & Mohun, 2007)

- IT consolidation opportunities and *standards-based integration,* using a standards-based approach to integration for IT systems that are very complex and heterogeneous to reduce both cost and complexity over time;
- faster implementation and change management through reuse, modeling, and composite development; and
- improved alignment of business processes and IT implementation.

SOA is enhanced by extensible markup language (XML) described in Chapter 3. XML combines text and other information about the text, such as its structure, allowing data sharing across different information systems across the Internet. XML underpins SOA such that SOA is ineffective without it. Specifically, XML improves interface technology through platform-independence and protocols, such as security and transactions, previously unavailable in interfaces (Erl, 2005). Platform independence refers to software that does not rely on any special features of any single platform (e.g., Windows) or, if it does, handles those special features such that it can deal with multiple platforms.

Advantages of XML-Enhanced SOA

Although HR administration managers may not make final decisions about the information technology described above, they need to recognize the benefits associated with having such architecture. For example, Schwartz (2003) reported that Oracle's introduction of HR-XML standards would reduce the requirement to manually input applicant resumes. Therefore, today's use of HR portals for job application receipt and processing, including resume submission, is related directly to this technology. Thus, HRIS capabilities are leveraged dramatically by SOA and XML such that (Lublinsky, 2007; Walker, 2001)

- security is improved—this is especially important because of the privacy protection issues associated with HR data and applications;
- performance is enhanced—this aids in reduced transaction costs and increased customer satisfaction;
- auditing capabilities are added—this supports increased requirements to demonstrate compliance with corporate quality and policy mandates;
- change capabilities are enhanced—this improves reaction time to better meet business-driven change requirements; and
- alternative HR administration structures (e.g., self-service portals, SSCs, outsourcing) are facilitated—this encourages HR managers to consider multiple approaches to meeting the HR administration goals of cost reduction and service improvement.

The remainder of this section will focus on the four structural approaches to HR administration facilitated by technology. Each has opened paths to increased efficiency, effectiveness, improved service, and cost controls unimagined by HR professionals a decade ago. The four HR administrative approaches, self-service portals, SSCs, outsourcing, and offshoring, presented in this chapter are shown in Figure 9.2.

❖ **Figure 9.2** Typical HRM Administration Service Delivery Alternatives

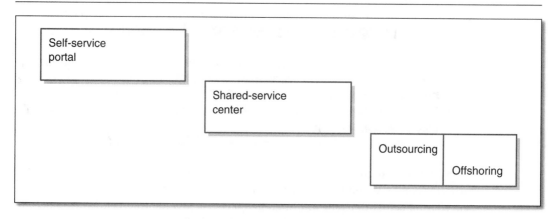

- The self-service portal is an electronic access point to an organization's HRM information, such as company policies, benefits registration, and an individual's payroll data or other records; access may be via the organization's computers and intranet or remotely from other locations via the Internet.

- A **shared-service center (SSC)** is a technology-enabled HRM group focused on value creation by providing excellent service to internal customers while reducing costs through increased efficiency and continuous improvement.
- Outsourcing is the practice of contracting with vendors to perform HR services and activities.
- Offshoring is an extension of outsourcing that involves contracting with vendors outside a nation's boundaries to effect additional cost savings or gain other benefits over domestic outsourcing alone.

Following a discussion of the theories underpinning these approaches to HR administration, the purpose, advantages, and disadvantages of each will be highlighted. Next, differences in how each alternative approach facilitates HR administrative reporting mandated by government entities will be provided. The chapter concludes with a discussion of how each administrative alternative can be measured to demonstrate the value-added nature of efficient, effective HR administrative functioning in support of an organization's strategic goals and balanced scorecard.

Theory and HR Administration

The first theory that explains alternative approaches to HR administration is the resource-based view of the firm (Barney, 1991, 2001). Barney, in delineating the resource-based view of organizations, argued that organizations are bundles of resources, identified as physical capital, organizational capital, and human capital. Physical capital includes an organization's technology, geographic locations, physical assets (e.g., plants, money), and access to raw material. Organizational capital includes its formal reporting structure, its coordinating, planning, and organizing systems, and its internal/external group relationships; human capital includes the experience, capabilities, relationships, and insights of individual employees. Taken together, these resources are combined and managed to determine an organization's *opportunity* to win sustainable competitive advantage in the marketplace.

To achieve sustainable competitive advantage, a firm's resources, when compared with its competitors, must be valuable, rare, difficult to imitate, and invulnerable to substitutes. Based on this theory, then, it is likely that innovative combinations of technology (physical capital), organizing systems (organizational capital), and strategic individual knowledge, skills, and abilities may serve to give an organization a strategic position in its marketplace. Thus, alternative HR administrative approaches seek to combine HR technology (e.g., HRIS and Internet) with organizing systems (e.g., self-service portals) and strategic HR knowledge, skills, and abilities (e.g., compensation expertise) to leverage a specific firm's competitive position. It is important to note that this theory suggests that EACH firm in an industry is likely to acquire resources such as human talent to support its *unique* combinations based on its strategic choices; it is this unique combination that leads to *sustainable* competitive advantage. *Merely benchmarking or following trends is unlikely to lead to sustainable competitive positioning for a firm!*

An example of the application of this theory can be seen in Wal-Mart. In the 1990s, Wal-Mart gained a substantial competitive advantage with its innovative combination of "just-in-time" supply chain management and proprietary technology. This approach linked each Wal-Mart store directly to its suppliers such that when an item was sold the supplier was notified electronically; when a store's predetermined inventory level was reached, the supplier shipped replacement items without any interaction with store managers. This resulted in significant cost savings and improved service with fewer individuals involved. For a time, it appeared that this might lead to a sustainable competitive advantage. However, competitors were able to imitate the management supply chain techniques and even improve on the technology to negate the advantage. Wal-Mart's innovation did lead to an advance for the entire industry, but did not provide a sustainable advantage for the firm because the innovation could be imitated. Thus, organizations looking to achieve sustainable competitive advantage are more likely to reach that goal through strategic and unique combinations of physical, organizational, and human capital rather than reliance on any one resource.

A second theory that explains alternative approaches to HR administration is transaction cost theory (Coase, 1937; Williamson, 1975). Transaction cost theory suggests that organizations can choose to purchase the goods and services they need in the competitive marketplace or make those goods and services internally. Transaction costs are the expenses associated with an economic transaction, whether internal or external. Managers can compare the "transaction costs" required to purchase products/service from external providers, such as contract administration, licenses, and delivery services, with those incurred in providing the same product/service internally by using, for example, additional personnel, retraining employees, and purchasing hardware/software. Thus, they can make optimum economic decisions for their organizations. This is the classic "make or buy" economic choice facing rational economic actors. Behaving rationally, organizations would make such decisions based on total costs, choosing to "buy" from external providers when total costs were lower and products/services were readily available or choosing to "make" the products/services internally when total costs from external sources were higher or products/services were not readily available. Of course, this example assumes that the "make or buy" benefits of either choice are straightforward and equal. Typically, however, such decisions are more complex; thus, a cost-benefit analysis (CBA; described in Chapter 6) should be completed to determine if the organization should "make or buy." For example, a small business might elect to "buy" HR compensation/payroll services from an external provider rather than decide to "make" its own HR compensation program, which would require purchasing hardware and HRIS software and adding compensation specialists.

An example of the application of this theory can be seen in General Motors (GM). In the 1990s, amid market pressure to reduce costs as competitors increased their market share at GM's expense, GM elected to divest itself of its fully integrated parts manufacturing functions. GM managers found that its "transaction costs" would be reduced if it standardized automobile parts and purchased them from multiple external providers rather than continuing to manufacture them internally. Transaction costs associated with internal parts production were increasing rapidly in terms of employees' wages, salaries, benefits, and ongoing maintenance of aging production plants. Thus, GM spun off its Delphi unit as an independent company in 1999. Although Delphi continued to sell to GM, GM no longer relied exclusively on the now independent company for parts, helping reduce its overall corporate costs. Increasing internal transaction costs, coupled with a robust external parts production market, determined GM's strategic "make or buy" choice.

Both resource-based and transaction cost theories can explain the different choices organizations make in their preferences for HR administration approaches. For example, the increasing internal transaction costs of recruiting and hiring employees may lead to the search for an external vendor who specializes in recruitment and selection of new employees. Organizations may then decide to compare those internal transaction costs and benefits with external transaction costs and benefits from the specialized recruitment and selection providers, leading to outsourcing. Alternatively, strategic concerns about the security of having external providers inadvertently "share" crucial talent-positioning information with competitors, coupled with the decreasing costs of technology, might lead organizations to focus on internal innovation involving physical and organizational resources (e.g., self-service portals coupled with SSCs) to reduce transaction costs, while increasing spending on strategic talent management issues (e.g., hiring, development) to achieve a sustainable competitive position in its industry. Keep these theoretical perspectives in mind as we examine each of the HR administration approaches.

Self-Service Portals and HRIS

The first structural approach to HR administration (Figure 9.2), employee self-service (ESS) HR portals, provides an electronic means for a company's employees to access its HR services and information. Such portals provide a single sign-on capability for employees, who can complete transactions based on data previously established in records and/or knowledge bases, without HR assistance. ESS portals can range from simple intranet Web sites that allow employees to access static HR policies such as safety requirements to sophisticated Internet Web sites that allow employees to access and change their individual records. For example, adding a new child to an employee's medical benefits, from any computer location on a 24-hour, 7-day basis, would be possible with ESS portals. A partial list of information and services commonly available via ESS portals is given in Table 9.1.

In addition to providing an interface for current employees, ESS portals are also available to prospective employees. For example, individuals who have applied for jobs online through an employer's Internet Web site have accessed the HR portal to complete the application and forward their resumes (Anheier & Doherty, 2001; Gueutal & Falbe, 2005; Walker, 2001). CedarCrestone (2006) reported that 51% of the responding companies used ESS portals, with 22% planning to add the capability within 36 months. Chapter 11 discusses Web recruiting in more detail.

Manager self-service (MSS) portals are becoming more prevalent in organizations as well. CedarCrestone (2006) reported that 31% of responding companies used MSS portals, with an additional 27% planning to add the capability within 36 months. MSS portals are specialized versions of ESS portals designed to allow managers to view extensive information about their subordinates and perform many of their administrative tasks electronically, including **traditional HR** functions. For example, in typical MSS applications, managers can complete job requisitions and view resumes of prospective applicants. In addition, managers can view **performance appraisals**, subordinate salaries, productivity, training histories, and model annual salary increases. However, MSS is not limited to HR functions and may also include budgeting and tracking, reporting, and staff policy/procedure development (Gueutal & Falbe, 2005; Walker, 2001).

❖ **Table 9.1** Sample Employee Self-Service (ESS) Functionality

Communications	Benefits Services	Personal Data	Development
Review company communications	Research and view plan rules and requirements	Update emergency contact, address, telephone information	Enroll in training courses
Access company policies or procedures	Enroll in cafeteria-style programs (medical, dental, insurance)	Correct errors in personal data (degree, graduation date)	View completed training
Access HR policy manuals and e-mail inquiry/help request	Add and/or delete dependents	Change W-4 withholding forms	Access e-learning internal/external courses
Complete employee surveys or 360° feedback data	Model retirement and/or access 401K savings investment records	View previous/current pay and performance information	View/apply for internal job vacancies
View/respond to personal information requests from HR	Model health plan alternatives' costs (e.g., HMO, PPO)	Enter time reports, vacation/sick days, and travel expense reports	Complete employment tests for new jobs

Advantages of Self-Service Portals for HR Administration

Self-service portals provide several advantages in achieving HR administration goals. First, they improve the speed and quality of service to employees and managers for routine inquiries and changes. Reduced inquiry transactions requiring direct HR staff involvement facilitate keeping information current. For example, changes in the doctors/ hospitals allowed for each medical plan or status of hiring a new employee are more likely to be updated as required. In addition self-service portals enhance employee satisfaction by permitting employees to control when and where such access activities occur. This empowers employees, increases their productivity, especially for those who travel frequently, and offers privacy for those who prefer to handle such matters without the presence of coworkers. In addition, self-service portals facilitate easy, increased access to HR information, helping employees ensure that important personal data such as individual job performance appraisals used by managers in making decisions about employment rewards such as salary increases or promotions are accurate and up-to-date.

Moreover, executives believe that having managers use this more accurate, timely information contributes to improved managerial decision making (Gueutal & Falbe, 2005; Walker, 2001). Finally, self-service portals help reduce the number of transactions for HR employees and, correspondingly, overall HR costs. For example, CedarCrestone's (2006) survey showed that companies with 500 to 10,000+ employees reported that those firms with minimal HR technology served an average of 93 employees per HR staff member. By comparison, organizations with ESS portals served an average of 99 employees per HR staff member, whereas those with MSS portals served an average of 118 employees per HR staff member. Such savings relieve HR specialists of routine

transactional work and allow them to focus more on both traditional and transformational strategic activities described in Chapter 1.

Disadvantages of Self-Service Portals for HR Administration

Although HR administrators can gain advantages from deploying self-service portals, they
are also faced with multiple disadvantages. First, permitting employees to access company
data through Internet self-service portals may increase the possibility of security breaches
and associated negative outcomes for affected employees, including identity theft. For
example, more than 52 million customer and business records were stolen in 2005 because
of poor security, and losses from identity fraud rose to $54.4 billion in 2005 (CMO
Council, 2006). In the United States, CMO Council reported that individuals are increasingly concerned about identity theft (80%), guarding financial information (70%), and
Internet transaction security (65%). Moreover, employees are concerned that even having
their data in company HRIS can lead to misuse of such information by others in the organization. Phillips, Isenhour, and Stone (2008) suggest that employees may feel that their
privacy is being invaded when organizations fail to limit access to an employee's personal data in HRIS. For example, managers may learn negative information, such as employee medical disabilities, through MSS portal access that would have been unavailable in a
paper record system. Even inadvertent use or sharing of such information may preclude
training or promotional opportunities for employees. Misuse of this personal information in this manner can constitute a violation of labor laws such as the Americans With
Disabilities Act (ADA) in the United States. Privacy and security issues will be discussed
in more detail later in this chapter as well as Chapter 15.

In addition to security issues, HR administrators may find that unions and managers resist using the self-service portals. In particular, unions may argue that employees are "doing HR work" when they enter data and make changes online via ESS.
Union members who perform such transactions on their own time may request overtime pay for completing such functions, which are not part of their job duties, or may
choose to do such functions at work, thus reducing productivity. Managers may also
resent having to do work that previously was handled completely by HR staff, particularly when such work previously involved calling the staff rather than completing
forms. For example, managers may have had relationships with HR staff that permitted the managers to bypass established procedures for requesting a new hire. Thus,
using MSS portals would not only require more actual work for the managers, but
would enforce standardized interfaces and might lead managers to perceive a reduction in status and power in the organization. Accordingly, HR managers should recognize and take action to ameliorate such perceptions and concerns as part of the project
management planning and implementation process for an HRIS.

Shared-Service Centers and HRIS

The second structural approach to HR administration (Figure 9.2), SSCs, generally
appeared in response to the increasing globalization of competitive markets by multinational enterprises (MNEs). To compete successfully, organizations were pressured to
reduce costs through consolidation of administrative transactions while still providing
excellent service. Such a challenge involved balancing the constant organizational

❖ **Figure 9.3** Functions in Shared Services

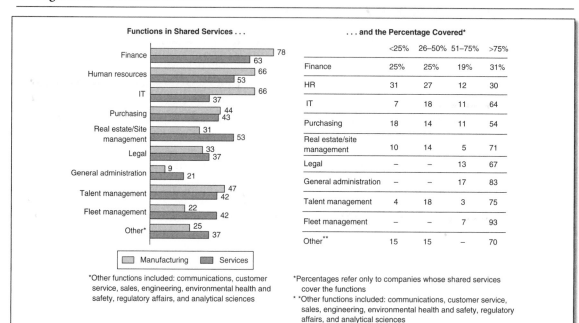

SOURCE: Powell (2004).

conflict associated with the desire for control inherent in administrative centralized structures versus the desire for flexibility inherent in decentralized administrative structures (Lucenko, 1998; Quinn, Cooke, & Kris, 2000; von Simson, 1990). Over time, many organizations have chosen SSCs as the structural solution to that pressure.

> Shared services is a collaborative strategy whereby [one or more] staff functions of a firm are concentrated in a semi-autonomous organization and managed like a business unit . . . to promote greater efficiency, value generation and improved service for internal customers. (Goh, Prakash, & Yeo, 2007, p. 252)

To emphasize this aspect of SSCs, some organizations have described them as "centers of excellence" (Bender, 2001). Figure 9.3 illustrates that SSCs include HR in 66% of manufacturing and 53% of service companies (Powell, 2004).

Powell (2004, p. 6) identified the following common elements of SSCs:

- Centralizing/decentralizing of business processes
- Using economies of scale to reduce unit costs
- Developing customer relationship models (CRM) to better meet the needs of customers
- Concentrating on cost reduction to enhance competitive positioning
- Deploying quality tools to ensure continuous process improvement

To be successful, a SSC involving HR, for example, must view itself as an independent business unit offering products, for example, HR reports, which it must "sell" to its customers at a price (internal transaction cost) they are willing to pay. These internal customers are managers in different business units such as operations and marketing. If the HR function is unsuccessful in reducing costs, providing desirable services, and adding value, it may find itself "outsourced" by business unit managers who perceive that they can get better service and value from an external provider. To demonstrate added value to the organization, SSC should establish measures that demonstrate customer satisfaction levels, productivity, cost controls, and quality. Such measures are necessary to allow internal customers to assess the value of the consolidated unit and to facilitate continuous improvement by SSC managers.

Accenture (2007) outlined several principles to embrace when considering the use of SSCs:

- Establish a "global good" vision for SSC that include its definition and benefits to ensure that business units "losing" functions are willing to make the commitment to transfer its work.
- Identify leaders in all affected groups to sponsor the SSC vision, promote its value to the organization, and serve as responsible change agents.
- Support transparency regarding who (e.g., affected employees), what (e.g., which functions), when (e.g., transition plans), and where (e.g., location of the new center). This is essential to building the trust needed to initiate and maintain the center's effectiveness.
- Conduct initial and ongoing customer "values and requirements" meetings to build trust, establish performance and service expectations, and solve problems. Implementing jointly acceptable measures facilitates SSC success and internal customer satisfaction.
- Focus on viewing the SSC "end-to-end" purpose in all aspects of daily functions to bolster the value-creating goal. This encourages the recognition of interdependencies inherent in the SSC concept.

Advantages of Shared-Service Centers for HR Administration

There are a number of advantages of SSCs for HR administration (Robinson & Robinson, 2005; Ulrich, 1997; Walker, 2001). First, SSCs permit HR administration managers to focus on delivering timely, high-quality transactions necessary to fulfill corporate requirements such as mandated governmental reporting, particularly for MNEs that have to respond to labor laws of multiple countries. For example, Ulrich (1997) suggests that one way SSCs improve transaction delivery is by removing the artificial barriers inherent in the generalist-specialist continuum common in HR organizations, smoothing work and communication processes.

In addition, by combining such transactional responsibilities in a single business unit, organizations can encourage a focus on customer satisfaction for specific user interactions such as responses to employee questions/requests for assistance, freeing specialists to focus on more strategic activities. Moreover, SSCs encourage efficiency and standardization to support strategic cost-control goals by consolidating individuals responsible for transactions, providing motivation for redesigned and more effective procedures. Finally, such centers facilitate development of measures of efficiency, quality, and customer responsiveness necessary to demonstrate appropriate contributions to strategic goals. However, there are several potential pitfalls associated with SSCs.

Disadvantages of Shared-Service Centers for HR Managers

Frequently, organizations combine multiple, unrelated shared services into a combined business unit. Depending on the nature of such functions, synergies to consolidate and improve processes may be less prevalent. For example, combining vehicle fleet management and HR transactions may offer few synergies. Moreover, leaders of such units may be stretched as they seek to unify and manage diverse functions. However, careful development of the mission and appropriate selection of leaders of such units can overcome this problem, providing a shared mindset among those involved (Walker, 2001).

In addition, creating SSCs may lead to unanticipated power shifts in organizations. For example, combining financial and HR transactions in a single center may lead to reduced emphasis on HR transactions since business managers are especially concerned with budget reporting associated with financial transactions. Again, establishing effective mission and goals for the center can forestall such power shifts (Ulrich, 1997).

Finally, SSCs can lead to depersonalization. For example, line managers, accustomed to personal contact with HR professionals, may feel isolated when handling transactions through self-service portals. Similarly, they may feel abandoned when traditional communication patterns are disrupted by consolidating specialists in SSCs. Moreover, because such units are concerned with efficiency and cost controls, individuals working in them can become more involved with the technology with which they work and less involved with other people engaged in the day-to-day aspects of the business (Ulrich, 1997).

Outsourcing and HRIS

The third approach to HR administration (Figure 9.4), outsourcing, is the practice of contracting with vendors to perform HR services and activities. Outsourcing is not new in HR administration. For example, Automatic Data Processing, Inc. (ADP) moved quickly in 1945 to offer its expertise in payroll and tax calculations to businesses facing increasingly complex employee income tax and withholding calculations (Dominguez, 2006). Nonetheless, few would have predicted the explosion in specialized organizations capable of providing a few or all of an organization's HR functions (Hewitt, 2005). Figure 9.4 reflects the percentage of processes outsourced by respondents in the 2007 EquaTerra HRO survey. Apparently, ADP had it right! Even today, payroll and benefits are the most frequently outsourced processes. Esen (2004) reported that 60% of businesses engage in one or more forms of outsourcing.

HR outsourcing firms are hardly uniform. There are many different types of providers, reflecting the diverse needs of organizations.

In 2006, human resource outsourcing (HRO) firms provided HR services for 3.3 million employees in North America (Everest Research Institute, 2007). Moreover, satisfaction with HRO levels increased over time for firms with more than 1,000 employees and revenues of greater than $100 million participating in comprehensive outsourcing defined as

❖ **Figure 9.4**   Percentages of HR Processes Outsourced

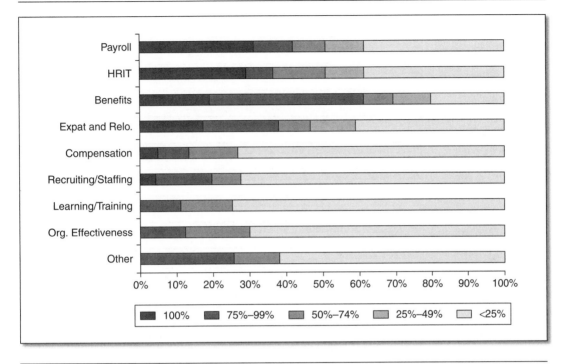

SOURCE: EquaTerra (2007, p. 4).

more than five human resource functions outsourced. Of the 310 firms surveyed, HRO satisfaction on a scale of 1 (*not at all satisfied*) to 5 (*very satisfied*) improved from an average of 2.9 in the first two years to 3.4 after two or more years (EquaTerra, 2007).

Outsourcing contracts should include specific pricing agreements (e.g., flat/fixed fee per process/employee served, unit prices per transaction levels, hourly/overtime rates, revenue sharing, risk-reward sharing, failure penalties), expected performance and associated measures (e.g., transaction quality standards, error rates, systems availability and downtime, customer satisfaction levels, hours of operation), and terms and conditions (e.g., start/end, extensions, termination, dispute resolution procedures, audit procedures). Obviously, HR administration managers would require significant assistance from multiple groups such as the legal, operations, and information systems departments within the organization to establish and monitor the contract, ensuring that the organization is adequately protected from incompetent or unethical outsourcing providers.

Reasons to Pursue HR Outsourcing

HR administration managers elect to pursue HRO for multiple reasons (Keebler, 2001). Weatherly (2005) suggests that managers may pursue discrete, multiprocess, or total process HRO. Figure 9.5 compares discrete, or selective, outsourcing with multiprocess, or comprehensive, outsourcing.

❖ **Figure 9.5** Selective Versus Comprehensive HR Function Outsourcing

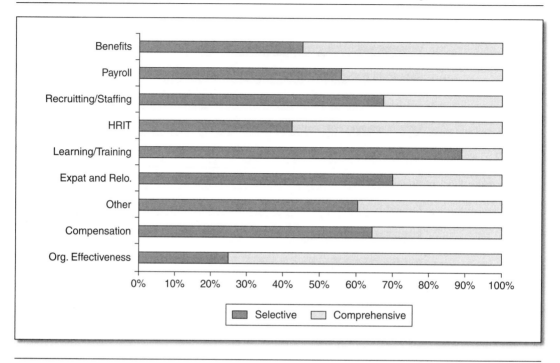

SOURCE: EquaTerra (2007, p. 4).

Some organizations outsource only discrete or selected functions, pursuing *tactical* HRO through niche third-party providers. This involves having specialized external firms deal only with a particular HR function. External HR recruiting firms, for example, fall into this category. Such an approach is common for smaller organizations with limited numbers of HR professionals or larger organizations with few, sporadic recruiting requirements. Also included in this category are outsourcing of parts of HR functions. For example, even organizations with large, effective recruiting staffs may elect to outsource executive or specialty (e.g., multilingual positions) recruitment functions to external search firms which have their unique expertise. Similarly, organizations may outsource only annual benefits enrollment, flexible spending accounts (FSA) administration, or payroll administration.

Generally, such discrete function outsourcing is attractive for two reasons. First, discrete HRO can reduce company needs for the ongoing costs of highly specialized internal HR professionals (e.g., executive recruiters) or HRIS expertise (e.g., FSA administration) associated with infrequent functions. In addition, discrete HRO can reduce HR administration costs associated with frequent, high-volume transactions such as payroll. In both cases, discrete HRO serves to reduce HR administration employee and HRIS expenses while ensuring the desired strategic outcome of hiring the right executive or paying employees correctly on schedule. Although discrete tactical HRO has existed for many years, it still remains a popular HR administration approach for achieving strategic goals (Figure 9.5).

HR administration managers may also pursue multiprocess HRO. This involves outsourcing all of one or more related HR functions (e.g., recruitment and selection, defined and 401K retirement plan administration) to niche third-party providers. Also known as *comprehensive or blended services outsourcing*, this approach has become more popular with the increase in the number of specialized vendors providing such services and the spread of enabling Internet portal capabilities. For example, organizations were less likely to outsource pension administration when employees needing information had to meet with in-house HR experts. With an HR portal and HRIS, however, employees can model pension decisions independently, to determine pension amounts associated with different retirement dates, and then change 401K investment directions by speaking to pension specialists at the third-party vendor when questions arise. This outsourcing of sets of functions reduces the number of specialized HR employees, improves service levels to employees, and reduces HRIS hardware/software upgrades and ongoing maintenance costs. Overall, such an HR administration approach can provide significant cost reductions and simultaneously maintain or enhance service levels.

Total HRO is the third type of outsourcing approach and involves having all, or nearly all, HR functions handled by one or more external vendors. All traditional HR administrative and functional activities would be managed through third-party vendors. Employees would contact the vendor for assistance or inquiries directly, without any company HR employee involvement or knowledge. Certainly, such a plan would reduce internal HR employee expenses, HRIS expenditures, and administration costs dramatically; however, such savings would be offset by costs for vendor contract administration, quality controls, and oversight. In addition, the HR strategic functions, such as long-term force planning and strategic business unit support, should not be outsourced since third-party vendors frequently deal with multiple clients, one or more of whom might be competitors. It is not hard to imagine how even the most sincere vendor efforts to secure strategic HR plans might be inadvertently disclosed, leading to severe strategic disadvantages.

Although this HR administration approach is not as prevalent as either discrete or multiprocess outsourcing, it is gaining in popularity. Organizations might opt for such a total HRO solution to deal with the myriad HR requirements associated with a global workforce of a MNE, to focus on HR strategic issues, or to reduce costs. For example, Convergys Corporation announced that it had entered into outsourcing arrangements with Johnson & Johnson for $1 billion over 10 years for global HR "administrative and transactional services" (Datamonitor Newswire, 2007).

Advantages of HR Outsourcing

The advantages of HR administration outsourcing can be both financial and strategic (Keebler, 2001; Weatherly, 2005). For example, organizations seeking to increase financial profitability and enhance shareowner value might employ HRO to reduce ongoing expenses for employees and software, forestalling capital expenditures for new buildings and equipments. This would entail a careful "make-buy" assessment of the total costs and benefits of continuing internal operations versus contracting for them in the external market. Benefits of such an approach might include redesigned processes, improved quality, centralized or consolidated operations, access to technology, and enhanced employee satisfaction. The CBA approach covered in Chapter 6 would be essential in this situation.

Strategic advantages of HRO might include the ability to focus better on a firm's core business through HR transformation, moving from a historical focus on administrative activities to a strategic business partner perspective. Organizations recognize that, more than ever, effective talent management may be the source of sustainable strategic advantage in a knowledge-based, global economy. However, many HR professionals are mired in day-to-day transactional administrative tasks that preclude the value-added consulting, planning, and visioning activities required from them to achieve strategic goals (Fletcher, 2005; Lawler, 2005). HRO could free HR professionals to focus on strategic issues such as talent management, while providing the firm with skilled transactional and professional services in both the HR functional areas such as compensation and administrative areas such as governmental compliance and regulations, powered by up-to-date technology provided by the external vendor.

Disadvantages of HR Outsourcing

Although there are a number of financial and strategic reasons for considering HR administration outsourcing, there are also serious potential problems for firms that use the approach without fully understanding how to manage it to achieve desired goals. For example, firms that used HRO to achieve HR transformation and cost savings rated their success as an average of 3 on a 5-point (1 = *benefits not at all achieved* and 5 = *benefits fully achieved*) scale (EquaTerra, 2007). Thus, one big disadvantage of HRO is the likelihood that the organization will not achieve its strategic goals. Such a failure could have significant, negative impact on the organization's ability to survive. Steps to minimize such a failure include realistic cost-benefit analyses (see Chapter 6), successful project planning and implementation (see Chapter 7), unambiguous goals and measures of HRO success, rigorous vendor assessment and selection processes, and skilled vendor contract negotiation, management, and auditing (Weatherly, 2005). Indeed, one of the primary responsibilities of HR administration managers in an outsourcing environment is to ensure that the contract terms are fulfilled on a daily basis and that corrective actions are immediately taken when failures occur.

Another disadvantage of HRO includes the loss of institutional expertise in the outsourced functions, making an HRO decision reversal difficult or impossible. Frequently, when outsourcing is undertaken, HR subject matter experts are reassigned or released. This can be a serious strategic error if the vendor is unable to fulfill its contractual obligations. As noted above, an organization would be unwise to outsource core or strategic HR planning functions because of the possibility that competitors may learn its plans from vendors. In addition, loss of internal strategic HR expertise may be devastating to an organization over time. Moreover, HR organizations may lack the contract management expertise to oversee the vendor and hold it accountable for contract terms. Other potential problems include security risks in multivendor outsourcing, internal employee and manager resistance, compliance failures, and cultural clashes between the organization and its vendors.

In summary, HRO is another approach to HR administration that offers potential for cost reduction, process improvement, and employee satisfaction. However, managers of HR administrative functions must be highly skilled at using HRO strategically to achieve organizational goals.

❖ **Figure 9.6**   Company Reasons for Considering Offshoring

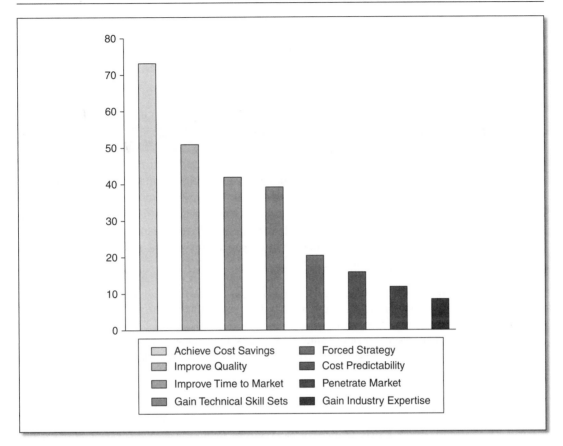

Offshoring and HRIS

The final approach to HR administration (Figure 9.2), offshoring, is an expansion of HR outsourcing that includes sending work outside the United States to vendors located in other countries. Technological capabilities and global competition have combined to make HRO a global business, and offshoring for MNEs is quite complex. For example, if Australian airlines have call centers in India to obtain improved cost performance, why not have its SSC for HR there as well? Based on responses from 5,231 executives in North America and Europe, Hatch (2004) reported that 19% of all companies, and 95% of the *Fortune* 1000 companies, are considering offshore outsourcing. Moreover, there are now more than 10,000 offshore vendors in 175 countries competing for the business. However, only 65 of these vendors can offer full-service HRO worldwide (EquaTerra, 2005). Figure 9.6 shows the various reasons organizations consider offshoring.

Esen's (2004) survey of HR managers reported that organizations consider offshoring primarily for financial reasons, including lower labor costs (76%), increased profits (50%), and reduced health care costs (23%). For example, researchers found that labor costs for a software developer in India were $6 per hour as opposed to the $60 per hour earned for doing the same job in the United States (Chiamsiri, Bulusu, & Agarwal, 2005). In addition, some firms were seeking skilled employees (16%) or productivity (10%) and service improvement (7%). Only 7% considered offshoring for strategic reasons. In fact, 40% of HR managers reported that their organizations would not consider offshoring because it was inconsistent with strategic direction (Esen, 2004).

Types of HR Offshoring

When their organizations pursued offshoring, HR managers reported that manufacturing (43%) functions were most common, followed by IT (29%) and computer programming (22%), customer call centers (29%), and HR functions (16%). Such organizations used both offshore ownership and offshore outsourcing (Esen, 2004). Offshore ownership may include opening a new subsidiary in the foreign country, entering into a joint venture with an existing firm in that country, or purchasing an existing firm. By comparison, offshore outsourcing is a traditional contractual relationship with an existing firm.

Offshore ownership is riskier than simple offshore outsourcing. In addition to appropriate strategic and financial due diligence, organizations considering offshore ownership must pay particular attention to

- ready availability of necessary employee knowledge, skills, and abilities such as language;
- information and communication systems compatibility with HRIS;
- governmental regulations and legal employment requirements such as wage laws;
- political stability of the country for facility and employee security; and
- cultural differences such as expectations about participative versus directive supervision.

Although an offshore outsourcing strategy is less risky than offshore ownership, organizations still face more risk than they would if outsourcing domestically. HR managers should always perform due diligence in assessing the reputation and business capabilities of an outsourcing partner. However, such processes are more complex when dealing with organizations located halfway across the globe. For example, concerns about electrical power availability, which might determine whether HRIS processing can occur as scheduled, are rarely discussed with outsourcing firms in the United States, but might be a significant issue in parts of Indonesia. In addition, worker availability to meet a 24/7 service center requirement is less of a problem in the United States than in countries where overtime is limited to a few hours per month, such as in the European Union (EU). Finally, oversight and audit functions for U.S. companies may be less onerous and expensive when working with offshore outsourcing in nearby countries such as Canada or Mexico than in more distant venues such as India or China.

Summary of HR Administration Approaches

Based on the above discussion, it is clear that HR administration managers have a number of approaches that can contribute to the goals of reducing costs, improving efficiency, and increasing service levels for internal customers. It is also important that such alternatives be pursued consistent with each organization's strategic plan to achieve sustainable competitive advantage in its industry. Moreover, multiple approaches may be appropriate based on those strategic goals. For example, HR portals may be combined with SSCs and selective outsourcing or offshoring to achieve the optimum solution for a particular firm.

In assessing whether one or more approaches is best, HR administration managers must understand the impact of their decisions on specific administrative functions to be accomplished. Therefore, the next section describes two specific U.S. governmental reporting mandates (i.e., EEO and OSHA) that are included among the many HR transactions for which HR administration is responsible. Following a discussion of the governmental mandates, their legal underpinnings, and the actual reports and records maintenance required, we explore how HR administration approaches can facilitate improved accuracy, reduced costs, and increased organizational value in successfully completing such HR transactions.

Legal Compliance and HR Administration

As noted in Chapter 1 (Figure 1.2), the country and its general environment have a major effect on HRM and the development and implementation of HRIS (Beaman, 2002). Whether the organization pursues a "domestic only" (i.e., doing business in only one country) or an MNE strategy, countries' government and labor laws are an important external force in establishing the context for business (Hersch, 1991). In particular, the labor laws provide the foundation of employee protections in the workplace. For example, in the United States, the Constitution and its Amendments establish the rights of citizens in general. In addition, multiple employment laws have been passed by the U.S. Congress to complement those rights. Some of the more important of these U.S. employment laws are identified in the Glossary provided at the end of the book. For a discussion of the employment laws in the United States, see Ledvinka (1982).

It is important to recognize that U.S. employment laws underpin the *general principles* used in the practice of HRM. There are a number of laws in the United States prohibiting unfair discrimination on the basis of employee sex, race, age, and disability. There are similar laws and regulations in other industrialized nations that prohibit unfair discrimination (Brisco & Schuler, 2004). The *general principle* underlying the unfair discrimination laws and regulations is that job performance should be the primary basis for employment decisions that change the employment status of an individual. When hiring new employees, for example, their expected job performance, based on employment tests and interviews, should be the primary basis for hiring. Whether applicants are male or female is irrelevant in all but a few cases (i.e., restroom attendant). Similarly, decisions to award a pay raise, promote, or to terminate an employee should be based on the employee's job performance. As noted above, general principles underlying employment laws in the United States bear significant similarities to employment laws or regulations in other countries, such as those specified in the EU directives (Briscoe & Schuler, 2004; Dowling & Welch, 2005; Paskoff, 2003). Since compliance with employment laws and regulations is a critical part of HR administration, provisions for handling the employment laws of multiple countries need to be considered in the development of an HRIS for MNEs.

What complicates U.S. employment laws for HR professionals is that the 50 states frequently expand on or adopt rules and regulations that differ from or add additional protections not covered by federal law. For example, a partial comparison of the elements of the Family Medical Leave Act (FMLA) among the federal and state laws of California and Oregon demonstrates the variations. Both California and Oregon deviate from the federal FMLA statute, but do so in different ways. The federal law specifies that its provisions apply to private employers with 50 or more employees in at least 20 weeks of the current or preceding year (U.S. Department of Labor, 2007). California law applies the provisions of the FMLA to *all* employers with 50 or more employees. In contrast, Oregon applies the provisions of the FMLA to employers with 25 or more employees in at least 20 weeks of the year. In this case, HR managers operating in both California and Oregon would be required to provide annual reports demonstrating that they have complied with both the federal and the state laws that are applicable. Since country-level and local laws can differ for all nations, administrative expenses to comply with employment laws can mushroom for firms with national and international exposure, even when an HRIS is used to support such compliance requirements. Indeed, this example reinforces the need for flexibility in HRIS software to accommodate such reporting differences.

This is, of course, just one example among many that demonstrates how governments affect HR administration. There are many laws and regulations in the United States that have reporting requirements to government agencies (Ledvinka, 1982). All these reports are tedious, time-consuming, and account for a significant amount of the transactional activities for the HR department. The processing for these activities was affected significantly by the introduction of computer technology and has always been a part of any integrated HR software package. The next sections take an in-depth look at two U.S. governmental mandates associated with EEO and employee safety. Specifically, HR administration and related concerns associated with EEO records and reporting (EEO-1 report) and OSHA recordkeeping and reporting will be highlighted. As you read about the reporting requirements of these laws, just imagine the tremendous amount of time it would take to complete an EEO-1 report manually for a medium-sized company of 1,000 employees; that is a considerable amount of "paper shuffling." Again, it is important to recognize that the following discussion is illustrative of HR administration, employment laws, and the use of an HRIS and, thus, could be applied to any country in the world.

HR Administration and Equal Employment Opportunity

U.S. Civil Rights Act of 1964, Title VII, and the EEO-1 Report

Figure 9.7 displays the broad categories of HRM administration associated with governmental mandates for meeting the requirements of EEO and affirmative action laws and guidelines. That all individuals should be considered for employment based on knowledge, skills, and abilities rather than irrelevant factors (e.g., sex, race, religion) is the *general principle* of EEO. **Title VII of the Civil Rights Act** of 1964 provides the requirements for such EEO. Under Sec. 2000e-2 (Section 703) of the statute, it is illegal for employers with 15 or more employees working 20 or more weeks per year

(1) to fail or refuse to hire or discharge any individual with respect to his compensation, terms, conditions, or privileges of employment because of such individual's race, color, religion, sex, or national origin, or

❖ **Figure 9.7**   EEO/Affirmative Action Plan (AAP) Administrative Functions

EEO recordkeeping and reports	AA planning and program monitoring	EEO/AAP legal support

(2) to limit, segregate, or classify his employees or applicants for employment in any way that would deprive or tend to deprive any individual of employment opportunities or otherwise adversely affect his status as an employee because of such individual's race, color, religion, sex, or national origin. (U.S. EEOC, 1964)

In addition, employers who engage in business with the federal government and have contracts valued at $50,000 or more must comply with additional requirements that include providing a written **Affirmative Action Plan (AAP)** to the Office of Federal Contract Compliance Procedures (OFCCP). This report details how the employer is actively seeking to hire and promote individuals in protected classes. Specifically, the AAP must (1) provide a detailed comparison of the available labor force with the employer's workforce by race, color, religion, national origin, or sex; (2) specify goals and timetables for achieving workforce balance if underutilization exists; and (3) indicate the specific steps to be taken to attain the goals in order to erase underutilization. Congress expanded protection against illegal discrimination in employment in 1967 by including the age criterion (i.e., persons aged 40 or older) with the passage of the **Age Discrimination in Employment Act (ADEA)**, and in 1990 it provided protection to individuals with disabilities with its passage of the **Americans With Disabilities Act (ADA)**. One example of the many-mandated government report is the EEO-1 report.

EEO-1 Report (Standard Form 100)

To monitor and assess employment EEO practices, the Equal Employment Opportunity Commission (EEOC) was charged with gathering data, investigating alleged violations, and bringing legal charges against employers who failed to comply with Title VII requirements. Accordingly, all employers with 15 or more employees must keep records regarding their compliance with the law based on occupational category (i.e., professional, technical, managerial, craft) and sex and race/ethnicity. Although the records historically included six EEO categories (i.e., white, black, Hispanic, Asian or Pacific Islander, Native American), changes in the number and designation of categories were made based on the 2000 U.S. Census, with reporting by the revised categories beginning in 2007.

A sample of the Employment Data section of the EEO-1 report (Standard Form 100) with its revised categories is shown in Figure 9.8. Substantial changes in the report include expanding occupational categories from 4 to 10 and, more important, allowing individuals to specify more than one race/ethnicity category. Previously,

Section D – EMPLOYMENT DATA

Employment at this establishment—Report all permanent full- and part-time employees including apprentices and on-the-job trainees unless specifically excluded as set forth in the instructions. Enter the appropriate figures on all lines and in all columns. Blank spaces will be considered as zeros.

Job Categories		Number of Employees (Report employees in only one category)													
		Race/Ethnicity													
		Hispanic or Latino		Not-Hispanic or Latino												
				Male						Female						Total Col A-N
		Male	Female	White	Black or African American	Native Hawaiian or Other Pacific Islander	Asian	American Indian or Alaska Native	Two or more races	White	Black or African American	Native Hawaiian or Other Pacific Islander	Asian	American Indian or Alaska Native	Two or more races	
		A	B	C	D	E	F	G	H	I	J	K	L	M	N	O
Executive/Senior Level Officials and Managers	1.1															
First/Mid-Level Officials and Managers	1.2															
Professionals	2															
Technicians	3															
Sales Workers	4															
Administrative Support Workers	5															
Craft Workers	6															
Operatives	7															
Laborers and Helpers	8															
Service Workers	9															
TOTAL	10															
PREVIOUS YEAR TOTAL	11															

1. Date(s) of payroll period used: _____ (Omit on the Consolidated Report.)

O.M.B. No. 3046-0007
Revised 00/2006
Approval Expires 1/2009

SOURCE: U.S. EEOC (2006).

individuals were limited to a single designation. The EEO-1 report must be prepared each September 30 by

> all private employers . . . with 100 or more employees . . . showing the name, address and total employment for each establishment employing fewer than 50 persons . . . by race, sex, and job category. . . . Employment data for multi-establishment companies . . . must include employees working at each company establishment or subsidiary establishment. (U.S. EEOC, 2006)

Revised reporting instructions include definitions of the revised designated racial/ethnic categories shown below, columns for reporting individuals who specify more than one race/ethnicity, and strong encouragement to have employees "self-identify" rather than relying on the employer's visual categorization (U.S. EEOC, 2006).

- *Hispanic or Latino*—A person of Cuban, Mexican, Puerto Rican, South or Central American, or other Spanish culture or origin regardless of race.
- *White (not Hispanic or Latino)*—A person having origins in any of the original peoples of Europe, the Middle East, or North Africa.
- *Black or African American (not Hispanic or Latino)*—A person having origins in any of the black racial groups of Africa.
- *Native Hawaiian or Other Pacific Islander (not Hispanic or Latino)*—A person having origins in any of the peoples of Hawaii, Guam, Samoa, or other Pacific Islands.
- *Asian (not Hispanic or Latino)*—A person having origins in any of the original peoples of the Far East, Southeast Asia, or the Indian subcontinent, including, for example, Cambodia, China, India, Japan, Korea, Malaysia, Pakistan, the Philippine Islands, Thailand, and Vietnam.
- *American Indian or Alaska Native (not Hispanic or Latino)*—A person having origins in any of the original peoples of North and South America (including Central America) and who maintain tribal affiliation or community attachment.

EEO-1 and HRIS

Smith (2006) suggests that the recent changes to the EEOC guidelines will be the most sweeping change in the history of the EEOC, as workers reclassify themselves based on the new EEO designations and organizations pore through job descriptions to classify individuals into the new work categories. For example, individuals who classify themselves as white could also classify themselves as Asian under the new plan. Even small firms without HRIS have a large amount of work to do. However, HRIS changes will be significant as well (Jossi, 2004). For example, HRIS and resource planning systems (ERP) have generally used a single field letter or number to represent race/ethnicity categories. Potential system changes required by the updated EEO-1 report include the following:

- Track race separately from ethnicity (e.g., Hispanic or not Hispanic).
- Provide separate codes for Asian and Native Hawaiian or Other Pacific Islander.
- Modify limitations on reporting only one race (e.g., individual may be black and Asian).
- Ensure that queries can identify all individuals in a particular category (e.g., American Indian), even when individuals self-identify as two or more race categories.

Moreover, the EEOC is encouraging electronic HRIS or online reporting of the EEO-1 and, simultaneously, discouraging manual reporting (U.S. EEOC, 2006). Thus, in addition to generating direct costs associated with software changes, employee self-designation, and employer job reclassifications, such government changes also affect, albeit in a more subtle way, firms' HRM administration by reducing costs (i.e., government compliance) through improved productivity in firms that comply with electronic reporting. This description of the details for an EEO-1 report is provided to facilitate understanding of how complex HR administration can be. The point is that the amount of paperwork required for compliance with all federal and local employment laws and regulations would be overwhelming without HRIS. The HRIS applications software helps greatly reduce this complexity. Nevertheless, no matter how sophisticated the HRIS and its reporting software, the employee and organizational data must *be entered accurately* into the system. To understand the complexity of governmental reporting requirements, a second example of government impact on HRM administration is associated with OSHA safety functions.

Occupational Safety and Health Act Recordkeeping

Figure 9.9 displays the broad categories of HRM administration associated with governmental mandates for safety requirements in the OSHA. In 1970, with work-related fatalities reaching 15,000 annually, Congress charged the U.S. Department of Labor with responsibility for establishing, monitoring, and enforcing occupational safety and health standards and practices for firms engaged in interstate commerce. OSHA primarily established, in the general duty clause of the law, that employers must provide a workplace free of known hazards likely to cause death or serious injury. The National Institute for Occupational Safety and Health (NIOSH) researches and publishes safety and health standards under the law. For all businesses with 11 or more employees, OSHA compliance officers are required to arrive unannounced for an OSHA inspection. The inspector then proceeds to (Noe, Hollenbeck, Gerhart, & Wright, 2004)

- review employer records of workplace deaths, injuries, and illnesses;
- conduct on-site inspections of the work premise and note observed violations;
- conduct employee interviews to elicit any safety concerns; and
- discuss findings and violations or issue citations to the employer.

❖ **Figure 9.9** Occupational Health and Safety Administrative Functions

| Accident reporting and recordkeeping | Safety and health training records | Workers' compensation claims |

Penalties for failing to correct violations or maintain required records can result in substantial fines and jail sentences for employers.

❖ **Figure 9.10**   OSHA Form 300

SOURCE: U.S. Department of Labor (2004).

OSHA Form 300 (Log of Work-Related Injuries and Illnesses) and HRIS

All covered employers are required to notify OSHA within 8 hours of any accident involving a fatality or in-patient hospitalization of three or more employees. In addition, all covered employers must complete an annual OSHA Form 300 recording all reportable work-related injuries and illnesses. Form 301 (Injury and Illness Report) is used to record supplementary information about reportable cases. Finally, Form 300A (Summary), displaying total injuries and illnesses for the year, must be posted for all employees to view. A sample of the Form 300 is shown in Figure 9.10.

HR administration managers must be aware daily of any safety problems in order to meet OSHA Form 300 regulations and ensure that up-to-date records are available for OSHA inspections. Generally, details for the report must be obtained from the reporting supervisor involved in the reportable accident/illness investigation and recorded on OSHA Form 301. However, in smaller organizations, HR managers may be directly involved in accident/illness investigations. Reportable incidents are defined as work-related injuries and illnesses resulting in "death, days away from work, restricted work, transfer to another job, medical treatment beyond first aid, loss of consciousness or diagnosis of a significant injury or illness" (U.S. Department of Labor, 2004). Because safety issues differ for different types of businesses, the HRIS may not have a standard safety module. More likely, limited fields are added to permit tracking and facilitate federal and state reporting (Ceriello, 1991). However, including safety modules in HRIS can be beneficial. Desirable functions would include HR portal access at remote locations by supervisors entering accident/illness data, linkages to safety training and equipment records, and interfaces with required workers' compensation claims, in addition to recordkeeping and report generation. Such functionality can be an important part of an overall safety program as well as a means of increasing HRM administrative efficiency (O'Connell, 1995).

HR Administration Approaches and Mandated Governmental Reporting

With such complex legal requirements, what role can technology-enabled HR administration approaches have in increasing efficiency, quality, and cost reduction in fulfilling reporting requirements for these sample HR transaction requirements? Certainly, the increasing use of HRIS is essential for accurate, timely recordkeeping and reporting for both EEO and OSHA mandates. For example, accurate, timely completion of the EEO-1 reports presupposes ready access to employee records, where such information is maintained. For a smaller employer, paper records may suffice. For larger national or international employers with multiple locations, however, paper records are inadequate. Such a paper record arrangement would require that each location search the records of each employee, manually record the appropriate information, and forward it to a centralized location for consolidation into the company report. For organizations with centralized HRM, either operations employees or managers would be required to do the report at each remote location. However, this waste of productive time is substantially reduced by the presence of an HRIS in the following ways:

- HRIS records can be established coincident with the employee application, including optional self-reporting of EEO race/ethnicity and sex data. No separate input functions are required unless corrections are needed. Self-reported data are likely to be more accurate and are preferred for compliance reporting.
- Simple queries of the HRIS database can secure required employee job classification, sex, and race/ethnicity in the EEO-1 format if desired.
- Required information for either EEO or OSHA reporting can be secured in minutes, with minimal HR employee involvement, rather than taking days or weeks to manually review records, compile the information, and forward it to a centralized location for further compilation.
- HR employees can handle the complete reporting function without interrupting productive time in operational units.
- Changes in mandated reporting requirements (e.g., increase in the number of job classifications) can be handled mechanically by HR, without involvement of field employees.
- Electronic reporting (i.e., computer to computer) can ensure timely receipt of reports.

If an ESS portal is available, government-mandated changes can be accomplished more easily, even when individual employees must be involved. For example, HR administration managers can communicate directly with employees, explaining the changes in EEO categories, and request that each employee update his or her information directly via the ESS portal. Moreover, supervisors can be notified via the MSS portal of individual employees who have not updated their information, precluding meetings with all employees for this type of change. Finally, if the employee refuses to update the information, the supervisor can use the MSS portal to enter the updated data directly.

If an SSC is added to the HR portal capabilities, individual employees with questions about the reporting requirements can directly contact the center for assistance. The supervisor need not be involved, and employees will receive rapid responses to allow them to complete the update more quickly and accurately. Thus, an HRIS, augmented by HR portals (i.e., ESS and MSS) and SSCs, can substantially improve accuracy and timeliness of mandated governmental reporting, while reducing productive hours wasted on administrative work.

Similarly, HR portals, SSCs, and even outsourcing can facilitate OSHA recordkeeping and reporting, reducing costs and enhancing timely reporting. For example, HRIS records and MSS portals permit supervisors to complete the required record of a reportable accident electronically, filling out the 300A form immediately after an accident occurs via computer terminal. In addition, updates can be handled with minimal effort. With appropriate linkages, workers' compensation reporting to state agencies can be generated by the system. If an employee files a workers' compensation claim and the company disagrees, HR administration managers can access the data and provide the rationale for disallowing the claim. Moreover, if an organization outsources either workers' compensation reporting or accident investigation to third-party vendors, electronic linkages can notify those groups immediately so that appropriate procedures can be instituted. Finally, HR administration managers can generate the accurate, up-to-date Form 300 whenever required for inspection, posting, or safety performance analysis without involving productive employees.

Privacy and Security in an HRIS

It is important to differentiate between privacy and database security in an HRIS environment. The latter involves the protection of proprietary, company-owned information about human resources. Privacy, however, involves data in an HRIS database that should not be made known universally and is protected by U.S. federal and state laws. Of course, database security and personal privacy are related since a breach of data security may well involve releasing personal information about employees. However, we will focus only on privacy issues in this chapter since data security was covered in Chapter 3. Privacy has become a very important topic with the advent of identity theft and confidentiality of health records (i.e., Health Insurance Portability and Accountability Act of 1966 [HIPAA]) as well as of any medical or disability information that is protected information under the Family and Medical Leave Act of 1993 and the Americans With Disabilities Act of 1990.

The laws regarding personal privacy have added more requirements to the HRIS software, and often updates are needed due to court decisions or modifications to legal requirements. The initial federal privacy law was the Privacy Act of 1974, which allowed employees to review their personnel records, but the law applied only to federal agencies. Most states have extended this law to apply to all public and private organizations. The Fair Credit Reporting Act of 1970 permits applicants and employees to know of the existence and context of any credit files maintained on them. The 1974 Family Education Rights and Privacy Act, also know as the Buckley Amendment, prohibits educational organizations from supplying information about students without their consent and gives students the right to inspect their educational records.

All the aforementioned laws protect records on individuals from disclosure; however, the Electronic Communications Privacy Act of 1986 was enacted to protect private information from being communicated via electronic means. The law specifically prohibits the interception, recording, or disclosure of wire, electronic, and oral communications through any electronic, mechanical, or other device. An interception would take place when an employer monitors a telephone call or e-mail while it is occurring. However, the law permits employer monitoring for legitimate business reasons. The existence of e-mail, the Internet, and voice mail (to include text messages) can lead to very positive uses that enhance both employee and organizational productivity. However, some people may misuse these communication tools provided by their employer in unauthorized and unscrupulous ways, which could lead to legal problems for the organization. As a result, many organizations monitor Internet, e-mail, and phone uses by employees to avoid litigation.

Actually, employers have considerable latitude to monitor the equipment they own. Court cases have supported the right of companies to monitor any information created, received, or sent by electronic means for business-related reasons. Many employees *incorrectly* assume that their right to privacy extends to all electronic media, whether personal or company owned; however, it does not. In fact, employees can be disciplined or terminated for inappropriate use of company e-mail, Internet, or telephones. It is highly recommended that employers create and disseminate policies indicating when employees can be monitored when using the employers' electronic media. It is wise to have employees sign a form indicating that they have read and understand the policy.

All this need for security and privacy directly affects HR administration within the context of an HRIS. It is most important that the employee database be secure, and this means limiting access to individuals through the use of passwords. In an ESS system, each employee needs to have a password, and the type of information the employee is permitted to access must be clearly indicated. Likewise, password security for immediate supervisors, upper-level managers, as well as professionals from HR, IT, Marketing, Finance, and Operations should be provided. The underlying principle for database security and individual employee privacy is the "need to know" rule; only persons with a "need to know" can access specific personnel records and reports. Adding these requirements to the HRIS makes it more complex; however, the gain in operating efficiency for HR administration compensates for the difficulties with building and maintaining the HRIS. Of course, the United States is not the only country that has privacy and data security laws. In fact, these laws may differ significantly from country to country, which would add more complexity to an HRIS for an MNE.

Summary of Government-Mandated Reports and Privacy Requirements

The EEO-1 report and the OSHA Form 300 are only two of the many required administrative transactions for which HR administration managers are responsible. In addition, the privacy laws add more complexity to the administration of the HR function via an HRIS. As noted above, HRIS capabilities can be enhanced by the use of one or more HR administration approaches to improve accurate and timely reporting while reducing costs and increasing productivity. These examples demonstrate how effective HR administration can help organizations comply with government mandates while supporting strategic goals. The final HR administration issue included in this chapter is how HR managers can measure their activities in ways that demonstrate their contribution to an organization's strategic goals using a balanced scorecard approach. Following a brief introduction of the balanced scorecard use in strategic management, we will examine which HR measures that are part of an HR administration can contribute to the balanced scorecard for an organization.

HR Strategic Goal Achievement and the Balanced Scorecard

As should be obvious from the topics covered thus far in this chapter, HR administration is crucial to effective HRM functioning. As discussed in Chapter 1, HR has historically been a "paper-pusher" function in organizations, seen as a costs-only operation. One of the major reasons for this situation was that HR could not easily or accurately generate metrics describing its operations and programs. The paper system existed, but it was exceedingly difficult to extract HR metrics. With the advances in computer technology, particularly as it applied to the HR function and its programs, the calculation of these metrics, described in Chapter 6, became possible. As a result, CBAs could also be calculated to evaluate the effectiveness of the HR department and its programs. The next step for HR was to become a part of the strategic management system in the organization.

The historic sequence and outcome described in the previous paragraph depends on building an accurate, up-to-date database with easy access and manipulation. This is critical for all HR programs, and it all begins with a correctly designed HRIS that supports HR administration. The data from HR administration, particularly HR metrics (Chapter 6), are also used to support strategic goals, and one of the best examples of their use is in the balanced scorecard. Kaplan and Norton (1992, 1996, 2006) recognized that an organization could no longer rely solely on a simple financial measure to assess its ability to achieve sustainable competitive advantage. They devised the balanced scorecard to facilitate the organization's efforts to measure its success in achieving the strategic goals required to meet the needs of its stakeholder groups. A *balanced scorecard* is both a management and a measurement system that "enables organizations to clarify their vision and strategy and translate them into action, . . . [providing] feedback around both the internal business processes and external outcomes to continuously improve strategic performance and results" (Arveson, 1998).

Kaplan and Norton (1996) defined the four components of the balanced scorecard as financial, customer, internal business processes, and learning and growth. Inclusion of these components reflects an organization's commitment to balance its strategic goals, reflecting the expectations of its multiple stakeholders. An overview of all four components can be seen in Figure 9.11 along with the key question associated with each of the four.

❖ **Figure 9.11**   Balanced Scorecard Components

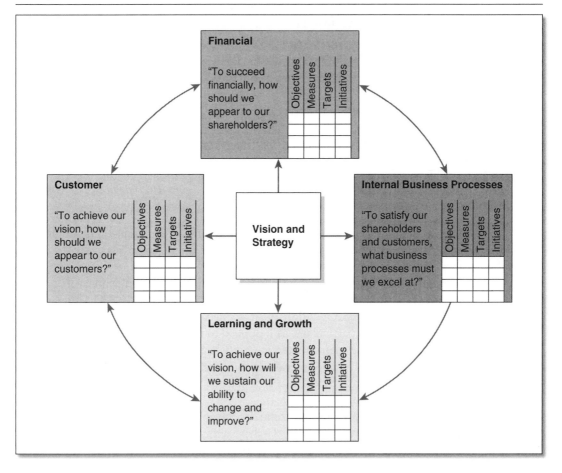

SOURCE: Arveson (1998).

HRM and the Balanced Scorecard

HRM is often not viewed as a strategic function in organizations primarily because its managers fail to develop measures demonstrating its strategic business value (Lawler, 2005; Ulrich, 1997). For example, successful HR administration efforts that ensure compliance with governmental mandates (e.g., EEO, OSHA) are often viewed as simple administrative transactions rather than measures of strategic imperatives. However, failing to hire and retain the diverse workforce reflected in EEO compliance reports can result in expensive lawsuits and reduced stock prices (Hersch, 1991), as well as diminished firm credibility (Pomerenke, 1998) and decreased long-term innovation (Florida, 2002, 2005; Page, 2007). Each of these items is directly related to the balanced scorecard categories. Specifically, lawsuits and stock price are associated with financial success, reputation is associated with the customer category, and innovation is part of the learning and growth category. Certainly, HR professionals understand the impact effective human capital management has on an organization. However, unless measures

❖ **Figure 9.12**   Sample HR-Balanced Scorecard Linkage

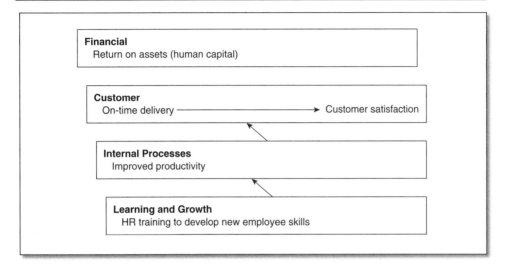

to reflect the value-added nature of HRM in leveraging human capital are developed and linked to the strategic goals reflected in a firm's balanced scorecard, it is unlikely that organizations will view such HRM-linked activities as strategic.

Figure 9.12 provides a simple example of the linkage between HR functions and an organization's balanced scorecard. The next section will highlight the development of an HR scorecard.

HR Scorecard, Its Measures, and Its Alignment With the Organization's Balanced Scorecard

Suppose that the company is losing some customers, and analysis indicates that on-time product delivery, customer complaints, and new orders declined just before these losses. HR professionals want to identify the processes and measures to support the strategic goal of customer retention. The steps that they might take are as follows:

1. Specify the business strategy to be supported (e.g., customer retention).
2. Identify leading (e.g., on-time order delivery) and lagging (e.g., customer satisfaction levels) indicators.
3. Identify associated internal processes (e.g., worker productivity, product quality).
4. Identify HR linkages (e.g., training, rewards).
5. Specify the HR strategy (e.g., offer enhanced productivity training for workers to reduce product time-to-market and ensure on-time order delivery).
6. Measure worker productivity increase, on-time deliveries, and reduction in customer complaints to demonstrate the strategic value of HR training in the Customer and Learning and Growth balanced scorecard categories.

A leading indicator is a predictor of future outcomes (e.g., on-time order delivery), whereas a lagging indicator shows what has already occurred (e.g., customer satisfaction level). Thus, to ensure on-time order delivery required to retain customers, HR

❖ **Figure 9.13**   Sample HR Scorecard Measures Linked to Firm Balanced Scorecard

HR Functions to support Learning and Growth Category (e.g., employee development)	• Backup talent ratio—Value Creation • Competency development expense per employee—Cost Control • No. of "special projects" for employee development—Value Creation • No. of employees with development plans—Cost Control
HR Internal Efficiency Measures to support Financial Category	• HR departmental expense/$ of sales revenue—Cost Control • HR sales training expense/$ of sales revenue—Value Creation • HR recruitment expense/R&D hires—Cost Control • No. of patents per R&D hires—Value Creation

professionals must understand the internal business process and identify the HR functions (e.g., training) that can be employed to improve the process (e.g., increased productivity) and increase the probability of the desired strategic outcomes (customer retention).

HR Scorecard and Balanced Scorecard Alignment

Researchers have long recognized the need to ensure goal alignment in organizations (Beatty, Huselid, & Schneider, 2003; Becker & Gerhart, 1996; Becker, Huselid, & Ulrich, 2001; Lawler, 2005). For example, Boswell (2006) reported that employees who did not have "line of sight" between their work and strategic goals of the organization were more likely to have poor work attitudes and consider leaving the organization. In addition, Decoene and Bruggerman (2006) reported that failure to properly implement the business scorecard (i.e., cascading strategic goals to all levels in the organization) reduced middle managers' motivation to support strategic goals such that the organization failed to achieve its strategic financial objectives.

In recognition of the importance of alignment between the organization's balanced scorecard and HRM strategic initiatives, researchers (Becker et al., 2001) have suggested that HR professionals develop an HR scorecard as a means of establishing measures for HR that reflect such alignment. HR measures should reflect a balance of cost controls (e.g., improved productivity) and value creation (e.g., increased innovation) consistent with the business balanced scorecard and strategic goals.

Figure 9.13 identifies sample HR measures that might be included in an HR scorecard (Becker et al., 2001).

From the discussion above, we can see multiple opportunities for HR administration managers to align with the strategic goals covered by the balanced scorecard. For example, deploying HR portals (i.e., ESS, MSS) can provide simultaneous support for financial goals (e.g., cost control through reduced employee expense) and learning and growth (e.g., e-learning courses). Similarly, strategic use of outsourcing can support financial (e.g., cost reductions) and internal processes (e.g., improved time from vacancy request to hiring). Thus, HR administration managers can make decisions that support the strategic goals contained in the balanced scorecard.

DISCUSSION QUESTIONS

1. Discuss the theoretical bases for the four HR administrative approaches introduced in this chapter. Are such theories useful to HR professionals in their efforts to improve transactional performance? Why or why not?

2. Why is SOA/XML important to HR administration? Choose two HR administrative approaches and discuss how each is facilitated by this architecture.

3. What are the primary advantages of HR portals and shared-services centers? Give examples of how HR professionals might use each to better achieve cost controls and service enhancement.

4. What are the primary purposes of ESS and MSS? What are the advantages and disadvantages of each?

5. Define outsourcing and offshoring. Compare and contrast the two as HR administrative tools. Give examples of the decision factors to consider when choosing one over the other.

6. Using the EEO-1 report as an example, discuss the purpose of government mandates. Give examples of penalties that organizations incur when they fail to comply with government mandates such as EEO and OSHA.

7. Based on information in this chapter, suggest the most effective HR administrative approach(es) for the owner of a small business with less than 50 employees and infrequent staffing needs. Would that same approach work for a business with 5,000 employees and high turnover? Why or why not? Defend your position with information from the chapter.

8. Identify and explain the purpose of each of the four perspectives included in the balanced scorecard. Give two examples of HR measures for each of the four areas that would demonstrate the value of HR in achieving the strategic goals of organizations.

9. Return to the vignette that opened this chapter and answer the questions posed in the situation.

CASE STUDY: THE CALLEETA CORPORATION

Jan Samson, CEO at CalleetaCO, sat staring at the now empty boardroom. Her Board of Directors had reacted negatively to Jan's growth proposals for expanding CalleetaCO globally, leaving Jan with a big problem. Shareholders, who had bought its stock as the Radio Frequency Identification (RFID) manufacturer led the boom in new uses for its products, were restless as financial returns slowed. In addition, Board members expressed concern that CalleetaCO plants in Mexico and Vietnam were becoming targets of activists who advocated that organizations ensure the humane working conditions common in the United States in its offshore facilities. Finally, Board members demanded that Jan move immediately to rein in the employee costs in the U.S. operation. Those costs were growing at a rate of 12% annually, compared with an industry average of 4%. HR Vice-President John Nosmas defended his practice of hiring the best, paying them well, and providing them with expensive benefit programs to keep developing the innovative products the market demanded. However, Board members were adamant and demanded a plan at the next meeting, only 6 weeks away.

CalleetaCO, with its current 1,900 employees spread across three countries (i.e., the United States—1,000, Mexico—200, Vietnam—700), had grown rapidly over its 8-year existence. Starting as a small entrepreneurial company, CalleetaCO was challenging the top providers in its industry as it pursued its goal to become the global leader in RFID products. RFID use exploded after introduction of memory for passive radio transponders, which led to production of RFID tags, microchip field radios embedded in products, for electronic inventory, replacing traditional bar codes and manual scanning.

Electronic product coding associated with RFID has been embraced by retailers and consumers alike. Retailers such as Gillette, Hewlett-Packard, and Wal-Mart benefit through more rapid restocking, less likelihood of out-of-stock items, and electronic identification of product expiration dates. In addition, consumers can more easily return purchases. Applications seem unending. Members of Congress have introduced legislation to track sales of tobacco products, for example. New U.S. passports contain RFID tags. "Swipe-less" checkouts, RFID medical alert bracelets, or security identification wristbands are on the horizon. However, some groups are concerned that RFID proliferation could lead to surreptitious tracking of an individual's purchases and other privacy violations, especially since individuals may be unaware that their purchases include RFID devices. In addition, hackers may be able to steal identity information by remotely scanning an individual's passport, credit card, or driver's licenses. For example, California is likely to use RFID to comply with the 2005 Real ID Act mandated by Congress (Billingsley, 2007).

Jan's company had grown rapidly by perfecting several of these products. To keep the innovations coming, Jan and John Nosmas devised a human capital talent acquisition and retention plan to attract the most highly skilled individuals in the industry. The company had 25 HR recruiters focused solely on identifying potential employees, 17 selection specialists to test and interview them, and above-market compensation and benefits at its U.S. location to retain them (e.g., health/dental/life insurance at no cost to the employee, 6 weeks of paid vacation annually, elder care, child care, onsite pet boarding, liberal performance bonuses, 401K matching at 10%, stock options, onsite spa/exercise facility). The programs had been incredibly successful in finding the right people to fuel the company's innovative products.

With the company's success had come an even larger HR department. For example, employees regularly stopped by the HR office to chat with their designated HR support representatives (i.e., 1 HR support representative for every 10 employees). The employees were thrilled with the personal service and responsiveness to inquiries on everything from health questions to veterinary referrals. Managers had access to their own HR support specialists, who handled everything from performance appraisals and salary increases to filing vacancy requests and overseeing employee discipline. When the company had formed a SSC for information technology and financial services, HR had balked at participating because employees were so satisfied with service levels, even though departmental costs were 20% higher than its counterparts at competitor firms. The firm's HRIS remained under the control of HR information technology specialists in the department, and there seemed few reasons to pursue portals. However, employees who traveled to Mexico and Vietnam had begun to complain about their inability to access HR support specialists for needed information because of time differences. U.S. expatriate managers from CalleetaCO controlled employees from Mexico and Vietnam at the offshore locations. HRO firms had recently approached John about the possibility of purchasing or managing those locations, but John had not yet explored such a possibility.

Jan picked up the telephone to call John. She explained the problem and asked him to prepare a list of ideas that could help them demonstrate how successful CalleetaCO's talent programs had been and help them meet the Board's requirements for cost controls. Jan knew that she would need to get John to work miracles to help meet the Board demands. She didn't want to stop talent searches or above-average total compensation, but the Board members were unyielding. Unless Jan could develop a successful plan to slow employee expense growth, control the activist stakeholder groups, and ultimately improve earnings, she could easily become the ex-CEO.

Case Study Questions

1. What are the key business issues facing Jan?

2. In what ways are CalleetaCO's HR operations contributing to the company's success? How do these contributions support the company's strategic goals? What changes can John make in his HR operations to meet the Board's demands?

3. Describe whether each will hinder or help CalleetaCO achieve sustainable competitive advantage? Which ones would you choose if you were in John's position? Defend your choices.

4. How would a balanced scorecard help Jan explain the value of her HR talent approach? Provide sample measures for each of the four categories that would support Jan in her presentation to the Board.

NOTE

1. This electronic record has also been called the Master File for compensation or, simply, the Employee Master File in general use.

REFERENCES

Accenture. (2007). *Managing shared services change: Beyond communications and training.* Retrieved June 22, 2007, from www.accenture.com/Global/Services/By_Subject/Finance _Mgmt/R_and_I/ManagingTraining.htm

Anheier, N., & Doherty, S. (2001, October). Employee self-service: Tips to ensure a successful implementation. *SHRM HRTX Forum Library.* Retrieved March 3, 2007, from www.shrm.org/hrtx/ library_published/IC/CMS_000210. asp

Arveson, P. (1998). *What is the balanced scorecard?* Retrieved January 7, 2007, from www .balancedscorecard.org/basics/bsc1.html

Barney, J. (1991). Firm resources and sustained competitive advantage. *Journal of Management, 17,* 99–120.

Barney, J. (2001). Resource-based theories of competitive advantage: A 10-year retrospective on the resource based view. *Journal of Management, 27,* 643–650.

Beaman, K. (Ed.). (2002). *Boundaryless HR: Human capital management in the global economy.* Austin, TX: IHRIM Press Book.

Beatty, R., Huselid, M., & Schneider, C. (2003). New HR metrics: Scoring on the business scorecard. *Organizational Dynamics, 32,* 107–121.

Becker, B., & Gerhart, B. (1996). The impact of human resource management on organizational performance: Progress and prospects. *Academy of Management Journal, 39,* 779–801.

Becker, B., Huselid, M., & Ulrich, D. (2001). *The HR Scorecard: Linking people, strategy, and performance.* Boston: Harvard Business School Press.

Bender, J. (2001). HR service centers: The human element behind the technology. In Walker (Ed.), *Web-based human resources* (pp. 212–225). New York: McGraw-Hill.

Billingsley, K. (2007). *Playing tag: An RFID primer.* Retrieved August 21, 2007, from liberty.pacificresearch.org/docLib/20070706_RFID.pdf

Boswell, W. (2006). Aligning employees with the organization's strategic objective: Out of "line of sight," out of mind. *International Journal of Human Resource Management, 17,* 1489–1511.

Brisco, D. R., & Schuler, R. S. (2004). *International human resource management* (2nd ed.). New York: Routledge.

Campbell, S., & Mohun, V. (2007). *Mastering enterprise SOA with SAP Netweaver and my SAP.* Indianapolis, IN: Wiley & Sons.

CedarCrestone. (2006). *Workforce technologies and service delivery approaches.* Retrieved April 14, 2007, from www.cedarcrestone.com/whitepapers/CedarCrestone_2006_HCM_Survey.pdf

Ceriello, V. (1991). *Human resource management systems.* San Francisco: Jossey-Bass.

Chiamsiri, S., Bulusu, S., & Agarwal, M. (2005). Information technology offshore outsourcing in India: A human resource management perspective. *Research and Practice in Human Resource Management, 13,* 105–114.

CMO Council. (2006). *Secure the trust of your brand.* Retrieved April 14, 2007, from http://wp.bitpipe.com/resource/org_1087482373_918/10139_CMO_TTsyndication.pdf

Coase, R. (1937). The nature of the firm. *Economica, 4,* 386–405.

Datamonitor Newswire. (2007, May 30). *Convergys wins $1bn Johnson & Johnson HR deal.* Retrieved June 7, 2007, from http://web.lexis-nexis.com.ezproxy.emich.edu/universe/document?_m=6fa57a9a773a7c9e891678b666544800&_docnum=6&wchp=dGLzVlz-zSkVA&_md5=ff41de535198d7dfe7c8e968fd24b9c1

Decoene, V., & Bruggerman, W. (2006). Strategic alignment and middle-level managers' motivation in a balanced scorecard setting. *International Journal of Operations & Production Management, 26,* 429–449.

Dominguez, L. (2006). *The manager's step-by-step guide to outsourcing.* New York: McGraw-Hill.

Dowling, P. J., & Welch, D. E. (2005). *International human resource management: managing people in a multinational context* (4th ed.). Mason, OH: Thomson/South-Western.

EquaTerra. (2005). *EquaTerra research brief: Human resources outsourcing.* Retrieved October 14, 2006, from www.equaterra.com/KR/research/eq-research-brief-all.aspx

EquaTerra. (2007). *Taking the pulse of today's human resources outsourcing market.* Retrieved May 18, 2007, from www.equaterra.com/KR/download.aspx?fn=EquaTerra-HRO-Buyer-Pulse-Results-April-2007.pdf

Erl, T. (2005). *Service-oriented architecture (SOA): Concepts, technology, and design.* New York: Prentice Hall PTR.

Esen, E. (2004). *SHRM human resource management outsourcing survey report.* Alexandria, VA: Society for Human Resource Management.

Everest Research Institute. (2007). *Human resources outsourcing (HRO) market update: May 2007.* Retrieved May 28, 2007, from www.outsourcing-requests.com/common/sponsors/60629/Human_Resources_Outsourcing_HRO_Market_Update .pdf

Fletcher, P. (2005). Personnel administration to business-driven human capital management. In H. Gueutal & D. Stone (Eds.), *The brave new world of eHR* (pp. 1–21). San Francisco: Jossey-Bass.

Florida, R. (2002). *The rise of the creative class: And how it's transforming work, leisure, community and everyday life.* New York: Basic Books.

Florida, R. (2005). *The flight of the creative class: The new global competition for talent.* New York: HarperCollins.

Goh, M., Prakash, S., & Yeo, R. (2007). Resource-based approach to IT in a shared services manufacturing firm. *Industrial Management & Data Systems, 107,* 251–270.

Gueutal, H., & Falbe, C. (2005). eHR trends in delivery methods. In H. Gueutal & D. Stone (Eds.), *The brave new world of eHR* (pp. 190–225). San Francisco: Jossey-Bass.

Gueutal, H., & Stone, D. (Eds.). (2005). *The brave new world of eHR.* San Francisco: Jossey-Bass.

Hatch, P. (2004). *Offshore outsourcing 2005 research: Preliminary findings and conclusions* (Ventoro [January 22, 2005 version] Report). Retrieved February 7, 2007, from www.ventoro.com/Offshore2005ResearchFindings.pdf

Hersch, J. (1991). Equal employment opportunity law and firm profitability. *Journal of Human Resources, 26,* 139–153.

Hewitt. (2005). *A fresh look at the logic of HR outsourcing.* Retrieved February 8, 2007, from www.outsourcing-requests.com/common/ sponsors/54934/A_Fresh_ Look_at_the_Logic_of_HR_Outsourcing.pdf

Jossi, F. (2004). *Reporting race.* Retrieved January 7, 2007, from www.shrm.org/hrtx/library_published/nonIC/CMS_006477.asp

Kaplan, R., & Norton, D. (1992). The balanced scorecard: Measures that drive performance. *Harvard Business Review, 70,* 71–80.

Kaplan, R., & Norton, D. (1996). *The balanced scorecard: Translating strategy into action.* Boston: Harvard Business School Press.

Kaplan, R., & Norton, D. (2006). *Alignment: Using the balanced scorecard to create corporate synergies.* Boston: Harvard Business School Press.

Kavanagh, M., Gueutal, H., & Tannenbaum, S. (1990). *Human resource information systems: Development and application.* Boston: PWS.

Keebler, T. (2001). HR outsourcing in the Internet era. In A. Walker (Ed.), *Web-based human resources* (pp. 259–276). New York: McGraw-Hill.

Lawler, E. (2005). Making strategic partnership a reality. *Strategic HR Review, 4,* 3.

Ledvinka, J. (1982). *Federal regulation of personnel and human resource management.* Boston: Kent.

Lublinsky, B. (2007, May). Versioning in SOA. *Architecture Journal,* 11. Retrieved May 18, 2007, from http://msdn2.microsoft.com/en-us/arcjournal/bb491124.aspx

Lucenko, K. (1998, March). *Shared services: Achieving higher levels of performance* (The Conference Board Report R-1210–98-CH). Retrieved February 7, 2007, from http://www.conference-board.org/publications/describe.cfm?id=396

Marks, E., & Bell, M. (2006). *Service-oriented architecture: A business planning and implementation guide for business and technology.* Indianapolis, IN: Wiley.

Noe, R., Hollenbeck, J., Gerhart, B., & Wright, P. (2004). *Fundamentals of human resource management.* New York: McGraw-Hill.

O'Connell, S. (1995, June). Safety first: computers to the rescue. *HR Magazine.* Retrieved February 22, 2007, from http://findarticles.com/p/articles/mi_m3495/is_n6_v40/ai_ 17191250

Organization for the Advancement of Structured Information Systems. (2006). *OASIS reference model for service oriented architecture 1.0.* Retrieved April 7, 2007, from www .oasis-open.org/committees/download.php/18486/ pr-2changes .pdf

Osle, H., & Cooper, J. (2003). *Structuring HR for maximum value.* Retrieved January 7, 2007, from www.ihrim.org/resources/Articles/HRapps/HRmaxvalue.pdf

Page, S. (2007). *The difference: How the power of diversity creates better groups, firms, schools, and societies.* Princeton, NJ: Princeton University Press.

Paskoff, S. M. (2003, September). *Around the world without the daze: Communicating international codes of conduct.* Paper presented at the fourth annual program on International Labor and Employment Law, Dallas, TX.

Phillips, T., Isenhour, L., & Stone, D. (2008). The potential for privacy violations in electronic human resource practices. In G. Martin, M. Reddington, & H. Alexander (Eds.), *Technology, outsourcing, and transforming HR* (pp. 193–230). Oxford: Butterworth Heinemann.

Pomerenke, P. (1998). Class action sexual harassment lawsuit: A study in crisis communication. *Human Resource Management, 37,* 207–219.

Powell, A. (2004). *Shared services and CRM.* Technical Report E-0005–004RR. The Conference Board. Retrieved February 3, 2007, from www.conference-board.org/cgi-bin/MsmGo .exe?grab_id=81&EXTRA_ARG=&SCOPE=Public&host_id=42&page_id=8849920 &query=E000504RR&hiword= E000504RR+

PricewaterhouseCoopers. (2006). *Key trends in human capital: A global perspective—2006.* Retrieved February 17, 2007, from www.ihrim.org/resources/Articles/Strategy/pwc_ keytrends_mar06.pdf

Quinn, B., Cooke, R., & Kris, A. (2000). *Shared services: Mining for corporate gold.* London: Pearson Education.

Robinson, D., & Robinson, J. (2005). *Strategic business partner: Aligning people strategies with business goals.* New York: Berrett-Hoehler.

Schwartz, E. (2003, December 8). Oracle launches HR-XML product; Will Microsoft WORD follow? *InfoWorld.com.* Retrieved January 21, 2007, from www.infoworld.com/ article/03/12/08/HNoracle_1.html

Smith, A. (2006). *New EEO-1 report kicks in for 2007 survey.* Retrieved June 1, 2007, from www.shrm.org/hrnews_published/archives/CMS_ 015698.asp

Ulrich, D. (1997). *Human resource champions.* Boston: Harvard Business School Press.

U.S. Department of Labor. (2004). *OSHA instructions.* Retrieved April 7, 2007, from www. osha.gov/pls/oshaweb/ owadisp.show_document?p_table=DIRECTIVES&p_id=3205

U.S. Department of Labor. (2007). *Federal vs. State Family and Medical Leave Laws.* Retrieved June 12, 2007, from www.dol.gov/esa/programs/whd/state/fmla/index.htm

U.S. Equal Employment Opportunity Commission. (1964). *Title VII of the Civil Rights Act of 1964.* Retrieved April 7, 2008, from www.eeoc.gov/policy/vii.html

U.S. Equal Employment Opportunity Commission. (2006). *EEOC instruction booklet.* Retrieved April 7, 2007, from www.eeoc.gov/ee01/instruction_rev_2006.pdf

von Simson, E. (1990). The "centrally" decentralized IS organization. *Harvard Business Review, 68*(4), 158–162.

Walker, A. (1982). *HRIS development: A project team approach to building an effective personnel information system.* New York: Van Nostrand Reinhold.

Walker, A. (1993). *Handbook of human resource information systems.* New York: McGraw-Hill.

Walker, A. (Ed.). (2001). *Web-based human resources.* New York: McGraw-Hill.

Weatherly, L. (2005). HR outsourcing: Reaping strategic value for your organization. *SHRM Research Quarterly.* Retrieved January 4, 2007, from www.shrm.org/research/quarterly/ 2005/0805RQuart_essay.asp

Williamson, O. (1975). *Markets and hierarchies.* New York: Free Press.

Wright, P., McMahan, G., Snell, S., & Gerhart, B. (1998). *Strategic HRM: Building human capital and organizational capability* (Technical report). Ithaca, NY: Cornell University.

10

Job Analysis and HR Planning

Hazel Williams

EDITORS' NOTE

This chapter is the first of four on topics that are related to **talent management**.[1] Talent management has become an extremely important strategic goal for organizations, both domestic and global. Talent management has multiple meanings; however, all these definitions recognize that to gain competitive advantage in the marketplace, an organization's talent (i.e., its people) must be managed. This management of people includes attracting, selecting, training, compensating, and retaining employees. However, the underlying requirement for talent management is forecasting the need for talented employees in terms of both numbers and skills. To forecast these needs, the organization must have accurate information about the **knowledge, skills, and abilities (KSAs)** necessary for job performance, and these are identified through job analysis. Thus, this chapter is focused on (1) using job analysis to obtain accurate job descriptions, (2) forecasting the demand for and supply of employees through HR planning (HRP), and (3) understanding how an HRIS can assist both job analysis and HRP. Chapter 11 will focus on recruiting and selecting of employees with the desired talent; Chapter 12 is concerned with improving talent by training and developing employees; and Chapter 13 deals with managing employees' talent through performance management practices, as well as compensating employees based on their exhibited job performance.

CHAPTER OBJECTIVES

After completing this chapter, you should be able to

♦ Explain how accurate job descriptions are developed in a company through job analysis

♦ Discuss how KSAs are derived from job descriptions and form the basis for HR programs in organizations

♦ Explain how the HRIS can assist in the process of developing and maintaining accurate and up-to-date job descriptions

♦ Explain the importance of HRP in the talent management process and its impact on strategic management in a company

♦ Discuss the steps in the development and use of an HRP program

♦ Explain and demonstrate the use of HRP in forecasting supply of and demand for new employees

♦ Identify and discuss the important HR metrics for both job descriptions and the HRP program of a company

♦ Discuss the legal considerations in both the development of job descriptions and the use of an HRP program

VIGNETTE

Rudiger is sitting at his desk on the seventh floor, a corner office, in the city of London reflecting on life. At 43, he is at the top of his game. He has everything he could wish for—a lovely partner, a four-year-old in a private nursery, a new executive house in the suburbs, a holiday home in southern Italy, and a remuneration package that is the envy of his peers and beyond anything his German immigrant parents could have imagined. But it hasn't been easy, oh no! Hard work, long hours, geographical moves every 2 or 3 years, and sacrifices in terms of his personal life.

But now he has a problem. Rudiger has just been appointed Global Head of People and Talent, responsible for the future of 35,000 people worldwide, the bulk of whom are based in the United States, the United Kingdom, and Southern Europe, with manufacturing likely to relocate to China in the next 2 years. In his previous role, his responsibilities covered the United Kingdom and Northern Europe, with operational oversight for 11,000 people. An initial consideration of his remit has identified a number of people issues for the next 5 years: recruiting and retaining particular specialist and skilled personnel; some of the brightest and most experienced midlevel management leaving; an aging senior directorship looking toward early retirement. But the main problem is that although he knows he has a problem, he doesn't have enough detailed information to know the scale of the problem.

Talent Management

Recently, there has been a newly developed literature around the notion of talent management. The Chartered Institute of Personnel and Development (CIPD, 2007) in the United Kingdom defines talent as consisting of "those individuals who can make a difference to organizational performance, either through their immediate contribution or in the longer term by demonstrating the highest levels of potential." In a previous report, the CIPD (2006b) defined the process of talent management as "the systematic attraction, identification, development, engagement/retention and deployment of those individuals with high potential who are of particular value to an organization." A report for The Chartered Management Institute developed this definition further, emphasizing that "talent management is the *additional* management processes and opportunities that are made available to people in the organisation who are considered to be 'talent'" (Blass, 2007, p. 3 [italics added]).

Organizations are beginning to develop their own descriptions for talent management. For example, the HR Director for South America at Foodcom[2] notes the "leadership and talent definitions for the corporation that are applicable on a global level no matter what geography or Foodcom business you are in." At Google, the dynamic and creative environment is one where innovation and radical thinking are expected as a norm (CIPD, 2007). Employees need to create new realities and experiences and, thus, new knowledge. Those regarded as talented are referred to as being a "Googler"—persons with a particular mindset regardless of their role: Specifically, this is related to characteristics such as being confident, an "ideas person," a "challenger," and thinking outside the box.[3]

An Inclusive or Exclusive Approach?

A central concern within any talent management initiative is the strategic perspective taken: an inclusive or exclusive approach, that is, one for all or all for one. This perspective shapes the way in which talent and talent management are defined within the organization. In addition, there are various contextual influences that have an impact on an organizational definition. Some see that an "inclusive talent management strategy is a competitive necessity" (Bones cited in Warren, 2006, p. 25), where the development of talent at all levels of the organization is included. In addition, organizations must consider how they will address diversity matters for particular groups, such as women, the disabled, ethnic minorities, older workers, part-time workers, and temporary workers. An inclusive approach to talent management presents some challenges, such as getting beyond a "them and us" mentality. Research in the public sector from the Society of Chief Personnel Officers (SOCPO, 2005) reported that "all senior HR respondents rated their processes as diversity friendly but a minority across all respondents believed they did not actively pursue diversity in practice" (p. 5).

Generally, however, organizations have chosen an exclusive talent management strategy, focusing on specific groups of employees, such as college graduates, particular professional or skilled groups, and primarily on the future leadership of the organization. A key challenge is the need to be absolutely clear about what characterizes the talent exemplar in a specific level or cohort—what are the components of "an exceptional manager . . . one who makes a difference" (Delbridge, Gratton, & Johnson, 2006, p. 141). An exclusivity approach does present problems though: e.g., what about those who are not considered talented?; or where it is only the chosen few, the elite who are considered to have high potential, who are counted. The academic and practitioner debates and discussions are still heated in this area.

High Performers and High Potentials

Organizations that have started to develop talent pools have developed typologies to help structure their thinking so that policy develops within a rational and defendable framework. Most typologies include *high performers* (HIPERs)—those who are considered to be performing well in their current role—and *high potentials* (HIPOs)—those who have the potential to develop further and wish to do so. The aim is to develop several talent pools addressing different future needs: In 2006, Ethical Bank, a large international banking organization,[4] provided a useful example (see Figure 10.1).

❖ Figure 10.1   Examples of Talent Pools at Ethical Bank

- Business leaders who are likely to be future country chief executives
- A pool of midcareer hires from nonfinancial services disciplines or careers to provide a source of new talent, thinking, and perspectives
- A pool of 40 MBA recruits from key business schools globally (the plan is to double this pool)
- A talent pool for high-potential women
- An international graduate pool of over 250 graduates with high potential recruited for an international assignment as a precursor to a fast-track career under a very rigorous selection route

Talent Diversity

It is potentially dangerous for organizations to take the view that because they are successful now, all that is necessary in terms of a future talent pool is to clone the skills, knowledge, and competencies of current employees. Although there will be a need to retain the best current people, it is also important to recognize that the global environment is dynamic and fast moving. Future business leaders and core contributing employees will come from several sources, and this is to be welcomed. The HR Director, Foodcom, United Kingdom and The Netherlands, noted,

> I think . . . from a business performance perspective, diversity of thought and how people operate is probably the most important talent in the sense that that will drive the business forward. Whether that diversity of thought comes from a male or female, or someone who is a Christian or a Muslim or what have you, to me it doesn't really matter.[3]

A generally aging, ethnically mixed, global working population that is living longer with diverse personal ambitions offers a platform for innovative HRM strategies.

Summary

This introduction to talent management provides contextual comments on some of the influences and constraints affecting the use of an HRIS focused on HRP activities. Alongside the difficulties of organizationally defining what is meant by talent and talent management, a key concern is to establish who is to benefit from such strategies. This is an evolving field of academic study and practice.

Job Analysis: Keystone of HR Planning

Introduction

Although the first part of this chapter has discussed employees as leaders, high performers, and high potentials, HRP encompasses all the employees of an organization. The aim of an effective HRP program is to have the best available people working in the proper jobs at the appropriate time, so that the organization is maximizing its productive capacity. Fulfilling this goal means that future employee needs are forecasted accurately, based on annual employee turnover and expected strategic directions. For example, if a strategic goal for a company is to increase market share by 3% over the next 2 years, this will affect the number of new employees needed in multiple job categories. With accurate estimates of employee turnover in those job categories added to the forecasted employee needs based on the strategic goal, the company can begin planning to recruit new employees as well as train current ones. To make these forecasts accurate, however, it is crucial that the KSAs required in the forecasted jobs be known. Job analysis provides this information by producing job descriptions. Job analysis is the process of systematically obtaining information about jobs by determining the duties, tasks, or activities of jobs, from which KSAs can be estimated.

Before examining the process of job analysis and how it is used in HRP, it is important to recognize the importance of job analysis and job descriptions in organizations. Job descriptions, the product of job analyses, define the working contract between the employee and the organization. In the United States and other industrialized countries, job descriptions are always entered into evidence for any litigation involving unfair discrimination in hiring, promoting, or terminating employees. Job descriptions are also used for the development of all the HRM programs in organizations; for example, recruitment, selection, training, and performance appraisal programs. Job descriptions are also used in developing compensation structures as well as in employee disciplinary programs and union grievances. In fact, job descriptions are often termed the "heart" of the HRM system. Given the importance of job descriptions, it is *critically important that they be accurate and timely.*

Job Analysis Approaches and Techniques

There are a variety of approaches to job analysis that are covered in detail in other sources (Ghorpade,1988); thus, only a general approach to conducting job analyses will be discussed in this chapter. As emphasized previously, the most important characteristics of job descriptions is that they are accurate and up-to-date (timely). Job analysis involves the following phases or considerations:

1. The sources of information about the job must be identified. The best sources are usually job incumbents and their supervisors; however, job analysts can be used for newly created or complex jobs. Company records and the Internet, specifically the **U.S. Department of Labor's O*Net database** (http://online.onetcenter.org/), are also good sources for information about jobs.

2. The type of job information or data must be identified. This information can include tasks, duties, responsibilities, the knowledge required, **performance standards**, job context, and the equipment used. A determination of what specific information will be used for the analysis of all jobs must be made to maintain consistency across the final job descriptions.

3. The methods of collecting the job data must be determined. Again, there are several techniques to include interviews, questionnaires, observation, and focus groups. The choice of technique or combination of techniques depends on the number of jobs to be analyzed and the funding available.

4. Finally, there are standardized techniques to do job analysis, such as Functional Job Analysis, the **Position Analysis Questionnaire** System, the Task Inventory Analysis, and the Critical Incident Method (see Ghorpade,1988).

Regardless of the approach or technique used to analyze the jobs in an organization, it should be emphasized that the outcome must be to obtain accurate and timely job descriptions. As discussed previously, the outcome of job analysis is job descriptions and KSAs for all jobs in the organizations. In Table 10.1 is presented information from the O*Net on the job of professor (http://online.onetcenter.org/link/summary/25–1011.00). As can be seen from Table 10.1, the KSAs for the job of professor are identified; however, note that this is a generic description of the job of a professor. To make sure that this description and the KSAs are accurate and timely for a specific college or university, additional information and reviews of this initial job description would need to be done. In all likelihood, the job description for a professor would differ for small 4-year colleges versus large graduate research universities.

It is important to remember that this example of a job description for a college professor means that one job out of the many jobs in a college or university now has been described and the KSAs identified. There are numerous other jobs to be analyzed and described for these educational organizations, and they must also be done accurately. How can an HRIS assist in establishing and maintaining the accuracy of job descriptions?

Establishing and Maintaining Accurate Job Descriptions: HRIS Applications

Completing job analysis and deriving job descriptions can be accomplished through online survey techniques. Job analysis questionnaires can be administered online to job incumbents and supervisors, and the resulting job descriptions can be obtained through statistical analyses. This online questionnaire capability can be part of an integrated HRM software package, that is, a package that contains HRM software for a large number of HR programs, or it can be stand-alone software. The Position Analysis

❖ **Table 10.1** Summary Report for Business Teachers, Postsecondary

Teach courses in business administration and management, such as accounting, finance, HR, labor relations, marketing, and operations research.

Sample of reported job titles: Professor, Instructor, Business Professor, Business Instructor, Business Administration Professor, Management Professor, Faculty Member, Business Office Technology Instructor, Marketing Instructor, Marketing Professor

Tasks

- Prepare and deliver lectures to undergraduate and/or graduate students on topics such as financial accounting, principles of marketing, and operations management.
- Evaluate and grade students' classwork, assignments, and papers.
- Compile, administer, and grade examinations, or assign this work to others.
- Prepare course materials, such as syllabi, homework assignments, and handouts.
- Maintain student attendance records, grades, and other required records.
- Initiate, facilitate, and moderate classroom discussions.
- Plan, evaluate, and revise curricula, course content, and course materials and methods of instruction.
- Maintain regularly scheduled office hours to advise and assist students.
- Keep abreast of developments in your field by reading current literature, talking with colleagues, and participating in professional organizations and conferences.
- Advise students on academic and vocational curricula and on career issues.

Knowledge

Education and training: Knowledge of principles and methods for curriculum and training design, for teaching, and for individuals and groups, and the measurement of training effects

English language: Knowledge of the structure and content of the English language, including the meaning and spelling of words, rules of composition, and grammar

Computers and electronics: Knowledge of circuit boards, processors, chips, electronic equipment, and computer hardware and software, including applications and programming

Economics and accounting: Knowledge of economic and accounting principles and practices, the financial markets, banking, and the analysis and reporting of financial data

Customer and personal service: Knowledge of principles and processes for providing customer and personal services, including customer needs assessment, meeting quality standards for services, and evaluation of customer satisfaction

Administration and management: Knowledge of business and management principles involved in strategic planning, resource allocation, human resources modeling, leadership technique, production methods, and coordination of people and resources

Mathematics: Knowledge of arithmetic, algebra, geometry, calculus, statistics, and their applications

Psychology: Knowledge of human behavior and performance; individual differences in ability, personality, and interests; learning and motivation; psychological research methods; and the assessment and treatment of behavioral and affective disorders

Clerical: Knowledge of administrative and clerical procedures and systems, such as word processing, managing files and records, stenography and transcription, designing forms, and other office procedures and terminology

(Continued)

❖ Table 10.1 (Continued)

Communications and media: Knowledge of media production, communication, and dissemination techniques and methods, including alternative ways to inform and entertain via written, oral, and visual media

Skills

Instructing: Teaching others how to do something

Reading comprehension: Understanding written sentences and paragraphs in work-related documents

Speaking: Talking to others to convey information effectively

Critical thinking: Using logic and reasoning to identify the strengths and weaknesses of alternative solutions, conclusions, or approaches to problems

Active learning: Understanding the implications of new information for both current and future problem solving and decision making

Active listening: Giving full attention to what other people are saying, taking time to understand the points being made, asking questions as appropriate, and not interrupting at inappropriate times

Learning strategies: Selecting and using training/instructional methods and procedures appropriate for the situation when learning or teaching new things

Writing: Communicating effectively in writing as appropriate for the needs of the audience

Time management: Managing one's own time and the time of others

Monitoring: Monitoring/assessing performance of self, other individuals, or organizations to make improvements or take corrective action

Abilities

Oral expression: The ability to communicate information and ideas in speaking so others will understand

Written comprehension: The ability to read and understand information and ideas presented in writing

Oral comprehension: The ability to listen to and understand information and ideas presented through spoken words and sentences

Written expression: The ability to communicate information and ideas in writing so others will understand

Speech clarity: The ability to speak clearly so others can understand you

Deductive reasoning: The ability to apply general rules to specific problems to produce answers that make sense

Inductive reasoning: The ability to combine pieces of information to form general rules or conclusions (includes finding a relationship among seemingly unrelated events)

Near vision: The ability to see details at close range (within a few feet of the observer)

Problem sensitivity: The ability to tell when something is wrong or is likely to go wrong (does not involve solving the problem, only recognizing there is a problem)

Information ordering: The ability to arrange things or actions in a certain order or pattern according to a specific rule or set of rules (e.g., patterns of numbers, letters, words, pictures, mathematical operations)

Work activities

Training and teaching others: Identifying the educational needs of others, developing formal educational or training programs or classes, and teaching or instructing others

Updating and using relevant knowledge: Keeping up-to-date technically and applying new knowledge to your job

Interpreting the meaning of information for others: Translating or explaining what information means and how it can be used

Interacting with computers: Using computers and computer systems (including hardware and software) to program, write software, set up functions, enter data, or process information

Getting information: Observing, receiving, and otherwise obtaining information from all relevant sources

Thinking creatively: Developing, designing, or creating new applications, ideas, relationships, systems, or products, including artistic contributions

Coaching and developing others: Identifying the developmental needs of others and coaching, mentoring, or otherwise helping others improve their knowledge or skills

Analyzing data or information: Identifying the underlying principles, reasons, or facts of information by breaking down information or data into separate parts

Establishing and maintaining interpersonal relationships: Developing constructive and cooperative working relationships with others and maintaining them over time

Communicating with supervisors, peers, or subordinates: Providing information to supervisors, coworkers, and subordinates by telephone, in writing, through e-mail, or in person

Questionnaire, for example, has its own software package (see www.paq.com/ ?FuseAction=home.main), and the Economic Research Institute (ERI) has **Occupational Assessor Software** (www.erieri.com/index.cfm?fuseaction=EDOT.Main) to aid in completing job analysis.

Maintaining accurate job descriptions can also be aided by an HRIS. In Chapter 9, service-oriented architecture (SOA) with self-service portals for employees (ESS) and managers (MSS) was discussed. These portals can be used to make sure that job descriptions remain accurate and timely. For example, if a new work procedure or equipment is introduced, it would be easy to request that the persons affected by the change, both employees and supervisors, access the current job descriptions via portals to make any necessary changes to the job descriptions. In addition, it is a good idea to establish an annual review of all job descriptions to maintain their timeliness. If a company requires annual reviews of employee performance and these forms are generated by the HRIS, it would be quite easy to generate a copy of the current job description to accompany each request for a job performance evaluation. The employees and the supervisors could then review the accuracy of the job descriptions and submit any changes necessary through portals. With accurate and timely job descriptions, HRP is now possible.

A Framework for Strategic HR Planning

HRP[5] is well documented within the academic literature. The term is derived from the manpower planning literature of the 1960s, where the focus is on management and control practices with short-term objectives. A resurgence of interest during the 1990s saw HRP emerge as a focal HR activity, as an essential and prominent **boundary-spanning function** (Richards-Carpenter, 1989; Walker, 1989). Originally viewed as a linear process (Hercus, 1992), a more current perspective is one of a continuous cycle (Hendry, 1995), without a particular start point.

Planning by its very nature is characterized as strategic—something that takes place in advance of action and is described as a top-down process. However, in practice, it is more likely to be multidirectional (top-down, bottom-up, and horizontal across hierarchal layers). Although the intent is a top-down strategic offering of the corporate goals and objectives, the practice is likely to be influenced by many who are closer to ground. The reality is often a combination, and taking this a step further, the final strategy is likely to emerge over time. For HR professionals, it is expected that the HR strategy combines explicit and emergent elements.

HRP is the action component of an HR function's strategy. HR plans are intertwined with other functional strategies: They do not occur in a vacuum as the day-to-day management of people is not controlled exclusively by concerns of the HR function. However, it is suggested here that an HR professional should be part of the planning team for all other management functions so that the people implications of operational management plans can always be considered; this rarely happens in practice.

The view taken here is that HRP is a dynamic and strategic process, acknowledging the elements of Guest's (1987) four policy goals: (1) plan for vertical and horizontal strategic integration; (2) be able to elicit employee commitment behaviors; (3) provide a flexible workforce for a changing external and internal context; and (4) be able to drive through quality people management and development that will have an impact on the products or services provided. The achievement of these policy goals will encourage a supportive environment to enable competitive advantage.

To provide a structure for shaping our discussion of HRIS in the context of HRP, we will use Bramham's (1994) (see Figure 10.2) notion of human resource planning as a sense-making framework for this chapter. A detailed critique of this framework is discussed in Williams (2002); however, we offer a descriptive overview here. We employ the Bramham framework here using a talent management lens, paying particular attention to how HRIS can be used to go beyond automation and enable the HR specialist to analyze data and make them usable for decision making (Zuboff, 1988) within the context of talent management and HRP.

Analysis and Investigation

External Labor Market

The past two decades have seen a major change in the way in which organizations understand their external labor market. The rise and increasing use of technology in the workplace have revolutionized the supply and geographical base of the external labor force. Organizations do not just think in terms of their local or national population but increasingly in terms of a global perspective. Indeed, the key challenges are summarized by the CIPD (2006b, p. 4) as

> an increasingly global labor market [with the recent erosion of long-term employment as a norm], an increasingly virtual workplace, a vastly diverse workforce, in terms of age, race and culture, and a workforce with independent views about their own lifestyles and access to information about career opportunities.

❖ **Figure 10.2** HR Planning

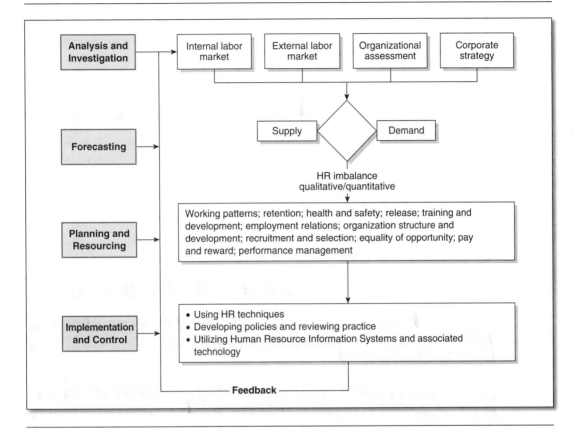

SOURCE: Adapted from Bramham (1994).

Overall, there is an increasing propensity for firms to acquire their staff and skill capacity through the external labor market (McCann, 2006). For example, the focus for the next 5 years for the U.S.-based processing firm Foodcom is on identifying and retaining talented leaders and managers in an increasingly competitive marketplace across different economies and geographies. For many organizations, this means acquiring new human resources, performance management, or human resource development. For Foodcom, it is about taking a more integrated approach and drawing on all three to achieve results.

Talent acquisition, retention, and management are becoming such critical success factors that this is no longer solely the purview of the HR specialist. A recent report from the U.K.-based Economist Intelligence Unit (2006) suggests that chief executive officers (CEOs) in 10 countries (19 organizations across the United States, the United Kingdom, Australia, China, India, Singapore, Japan, and Sweden) are typically spending more than 20% of their time on talent management and related issues. The report states that "chief executive officers (CEOs) are increasingly responsible for, and involved in, talent management. The heads of human resources departments play an important, supporting role in executing talent strategy" (p. 3). There is an acknowledgment here that "talent management has become more important because of a growing recognition that it helps to drive corporate performance, even *though the exact impact is hard to quantify*"(italics added, p. 3).

Internal Labor Market

Doeringer and Piore (1971) define the internal labor market (ILM) as "an administrative unit, such as a manufacturing plant, within which the pricing and allocation of labor is governed by a set of administrative rules and procedures" (pp. 1–2). In the U.S.-style or "Anglo-Saxon" model, also observed in the United Kingdom, labor markets are flexible, with light, voluntary regulation for the most part and relatively weak employment protection compared with other European economies, such as Germany and France (Hofstede, 1991). In the United Kingdom, recent qualitative research offers evidence of changed working practices in jobs where many of the historical traditions of ILMs, in which people are not hindered by divisional boundaries and have long-term employment security, have been eroded (Marchington, Grimshaw, Rubery, & Wilmott, 2004).

For HRP purposes, a review of the ILM consists of an inventory exercise, taking account of seasonal averages and the different parts of the organization. It includes, for example, the number of employees; labor turnover; a skills audit; a demographic profile; performance/productivity levels; absenteeism; and personal, technical, and management competencies.

Sparrow and Hiltrop (1994) suggest that organizations are proposing two contrasting strategies: reliance on the external labor market or the development of an internally mobile, multiple, and highly skilled workforce. This *make or buy* approach is very visible in, for example, the construction industry. Coase (1952) and Williamson (1975, 1981, 1994) suggest that recruitment strategies are historical and the result of the company's initial decision about which activities to carry out internally (*make* strategy) and which activities to purchase from the market (*buy* strategy). In the construction industry, this results in a highly skilled and highly paid core workforce, retained on permanent contracts, and a more transient, semi- or unskilled workforce used for particular projects and generally located geographically close to the project. The decision as to the right blend of "make or buy" within a talent management HRP strategy is fundamental.

Another perspective is that an ILM can be determined as a comparison of internal promotions vis-à-vis external hires for key positions. An early example of the outcome of this approach is seen in the work of Doeringer and Piore (1971). They studied executives of large and traditional Japanese firms recruited just after their graduation from university and promoted from within through ILMs. Sels (2002, p. 1291) suggests that the closed nature of an ILM can be measured by the extent to which preference is given to internal transfers. He goes on to note, "Companies which systematically give preference to internal candidates when vacancies arise therefore pay significantly more attention to needs detection" (p. 1294). Green (1993) observes that ILMs in large firms facilitate employee retention and increase the chance of returns on training investments. Cappelli (1995) goes further by stating that "the return on the investment in training is higher in companies with an internal labour market."

The financial and banking sector in the United Kingdom provides a useful illustration of the development of an ILM. Organizations such as Standard Chartered Bank (CIPD, 2007), Abbey National (Storey, Cressey, Morris, & Wilkinson, 1997), and Barclays Bank have refocused their efforts in recent years toward internal promotion and development, with external hiring of specialist or midcareer positions being more widespread. Ethical Bank recruits graduates at the beginning of their professional career and develops them vertically via professional and leadership programs. In addition, they hire "experts" as midcareer experiences hires, inculcating them into their leadership program alongside internal candidates. In the past few years, the approaches described here have been reconceptualized and introduced again as talent management initiatives within an HRP framework.

This focus on internal development is particularly important with respect to exclusive talent management initiatives, as there are significant elements concerning strategic succession planning and the career development of identified individuals. It is noted that the investment needs to be targeted and focused around the *quality* of training and development rather than the *quantity* of investment. Historically, organizations have required HRIS to report, for example, the number of training days, the number of employees who have participated in different training and development programs, and how individuals perceive that the training initiative met individual expectations. Although useful and aligned with the first level of evaluation, the mainly qualitative levels of role, unit, and organizational evaluation provide a more focused opportunity for strategic impact (Kirkpatrick, 1998). Clearly, these latter areas are more challenging, but not impossible, to measure. It is such data, strategically aligned to corporate goals, that can provide organizations with useful information to enable better decision making and focused talent management programs and initiatives.

A further consideration is the suggestion that ILMs have more complex remuneration systems (profit sharing, pay for skill, etc.). This implies the need for sophisticated information that will generate a link between individual performance and revenue and/or profit, depending on the chosen approach. **Personnel economics**, defined as "the use of economics to understand the internal workings of firms" (Lazear, 1999, 2000), is a relatively new field of study in the past 25 years. Personnel economics provides a useful lens to examine more complex remuneration systems and other elements of HRP, such as recruitment and selection practices, career and succession planning, performance management, job design and analysis, and talent identification. Personnel economics gives the HR specialist a rigorous methodological framework to generate appropriate econometric models that can be customized to the specific requirements of an organization or a part of that organization. Thus, individual remuneration packages can be developed that more closely mirror the contributions of a particular individual or team of employees and the cost-benefit analysis generated by this remuneration program.

Perhaps the most obvious and widespread use of an HRIS is to automate standard HR reporting. Various authors have noted that there is a tendency for HR software vendors to provide a built-in facility to report on many elements of the employee **data**

warehouse. These reports tend to be descriptive, offering a snapshot of a particular aspect of the employee population, and they are quite useful for a broad-brush overview. They also provide a good starting point for deeper examination. Often, HR specialists do not have enough information prior to purchasing or upgrading a system to establish which reports are essential and which are desirable. Thus, it is often the case that many of these reports remain unused by the organization but are part of the basic HRIS. Therefore, as with many aspects of information systems, there is an approach of *buy and be dammed* rather than *buyer beware*.

Information elicited from more recent versions of sophisticated HR software permits the HR specialist to move beyond the production of one-time reporting (e.g., the average revenue per employee) and historical trend analyses (e.g., absences over the past 5 years). Even simple systems based on spreadsheets and use of straightforward descriptive statistics can be further developed to produce projective forecasting prediction of future human capital. An illustration of this type of predictive modeling is a demographic analysis that accounts for retirement projections and historical employee turnover for a particular employee age cohort (e.g., employees over 60 years of age). An employee turnover analysis provides useful information to identify trends and patterns. However, it must be possible to analyze free-text input via content analysis in order to fully understand the data captured. This is more challenging, but it is possible through forms of nominal coding. This provides the opportunity to "informate" (Zuboff, 1988).

Organizational Assessment

This element of HRP provides the opportunity to consider wider organizational issues. This may include areas such as the underpinning philosophy and culture, values, and belief sets held within and throughout the organization. One key perspective is the organizational view of the employee: Are employees viewed as a cost or as an investment for the business? Clues here will include how information about employees is captured and discussed. Other factors assessed will include the effectiveness of HR policies and practices and the place of the HR department in the organizational structure.

An HRIS can support this analysis by providing trend analysis for the next 1, 5, or 10 years based on previous comparable periods. Exception reports, for example, employee attitude surveys and an employee demographic breakdown, can be automated (Zuboff, 1988). When information regarding organizational talent is the focus, reports can be structured around the aggregate number of employees within particular talent pools, as well as knowledge and job performance levels. The outcome of this review is likely to provide a narrative report that gives the reader a feel for "how we do it here."

Corporate Strategy

The literature on corporate strategy is vast and beyond the scope of this discussion. However, an organization's strategic direction does have a significant impact on HRP and talent management strategy making. Recent research from the United Kingdom reveals that "talent management is most effective when directly linked to corporate strategy . . . and other HR processes" and is overwhelmingly seen as a "future-focused activity" (CIPD, 2007, p. 11). HRP is usually considered as a proactive, strategic activity. However, for many organizations, the development of a talent management strategy is still an organic and emergent process. There are potential difficulties for HRIS specialists, who need to develop strategic systems that are fairly static and considered a long-term investment alongside emergent dynamic talent management processes and practices that may require significant annual updating.

The increasing use of the term **human capital management (HCM)** in the past 5 years has implications for HRP vis-à-vis corporate strategy. However, according to Jason Averbook, Chief Executive of the consulting firm Knowledge Infusion and a former PeopleSoft executive, "HCM is a business strategy. It's not necessarily a [human resource information] system." Jim Kizielewicz, Vice President of Corporate Strategy at the HR software firm Kronos, suggests that "much of the talk about talent management tools in recent years has been overheated" (Frauenheim, 2007a, p39). Therefore, we need to be careful when promoting such links.

Clearly, there is a willingness among many stakeholders to engage in tripartite linkages between corporate strategy, HRP, and talent management, but there is limited evidence at this stage to suggest that this is happening in practice. Although predating the current interest in talent management, Fombrun, Tichy, and Devanna's (1984) observation that "the quality of the strategic decisions made in organisations is linked to the quality of the human resource data that feeds into the decision-making process" still holds true.

Forecasting

Traditionally perceived as the "hard" element of HRP, forecasting is concerned with the identification of strategic options and the creation of HR scenarios. Essentially, this means providing a calculated expert guess of the shape of the organization in the near future. The notion of an expert guess is almost contradictory until one looks to the data and information that are being drawn on. Fundamental to the success of forecasting is the assumption that the data contained in the HR data warehouse are clean, accurate, and current. Often this is problematic, with few HR functions being able to claim 100% accuracy and currency.

Various statistical formulas, such as **regression analysis,** are employed to provide trend analyses for a rolling 5-year period. In this way, for example, employee turnover is tracked and reported in regular, perhaps quarterly, reports. Historically, this has been the limit for many HRIS. However, recent developments, and particularly the advent of third-party reporting software (e.g., Crystal Reporting), have made it possible for HR specialists to request more sophisticated reporting on data held in disparate databases. We can now expect an HRIS to be able to provide a breakdown of employee turnover by business unit, department, or employee cohort, not just as a traditionally aggregated figure. This allows forecasting decisions to be made based on the value and impact each business unit, department, or employee cohort has on strategic performance indicators. Systems that are more sophisticated may also offer analysis of possible drivers or causes of employee turnover and potential recommendations for future action. This

❖ **Table 10.2**   Techniques for Forecasting the Demand and Supply of Labor (Williams, 2002)

	Quantitative Analysis	Qualitative Analysis
Demand	Ratio-trend analysis Econometric modeling Work-study	Experienced managerial judgment Delphi-group techniques Nominal-group techniques
Supply	Stocks and flows analysis Staff profiles Labor turnover analysis Stability index Half-life analysis Cohort analysis Retention profile Census technique	Succession planning Career planning

development is particularly important for focused talent management strategies as information can provide focused guidance for short- and long-term action plans.

Demand

The aim of demand forecasting is to gain a view of the shape of people needs in the future by identifying the influential elements of the external industry sector environment and matching this with the future organizational strategic vision, cultural style, and organizational structures. One way is to look to the past to attempt to analyze past trends in order to predict future trends. Indeed, this is the fundamental *raison d'etre* of HRP, to identify the skills, knowledge, and capabilities—the human capital—necessary to achieve this vision. Analyses of unit costs, productivity ratios, and past trends are its basic components. Two main types of analysis take place: Quantitative analysis acts on embedded facilities; qualitative analysis captures processes and decisions (Williams, 2002; see Table 10.2).

Supply

Particularly important for talent management strategies is the ability to track future corporate and HR objectives and project how they will affect **high-performance employees (HIPERs)** and **high-potential employees (HIPOs)**. There is a need here to be able to align key performance indicators (KPIs) and the movement of HIPERs and HIPOs within the organization. Organizations such as Ethical Bank and Foodcom begin by establishing the number of employees and then identifying specific cohorts that they wish to track. For example, Ethical Bank is interested in developing the careers of women as they have identified low female representation at senior levels. Ethical Bank is not alone in this observation, but their HRIS is able to provide them with detailed and focused data that support their initiative. This means that in a relatively short time frame, they have adjusted several HR policies and procedures that may be perceived as potential barriers for career development for women.

For other organizations, the problems are more fundamental. Just knowing how many people are employed at any one time can be a problem for large, global organizations or one that has high variation in the seasonal workforce. Given that the number of employees is part of the base equation for many calculations, it is important that this figure is as accurate as possible and includes as many categories of employees as possible. If certain categories are not included, there should be a rationale for their exclusion.

Central to forecasting the internal supply for labor is the need to analyze the workforce in different ways. Demographics, length of service, skills, knowledge and future capability, leaver trends, and employee satisfaction survey analysis are all core data. Most HR information applications include these in the 20 or so "standard" reporting sets supplied on purchase. For talent management purposes, these core data must be available for deeper analysis—for "informating" (Zuboff, 1988). A number of quantitative and qualitative techniques are available (Williams, 2002; see Table 10.2).

HRIS are ideal for solutions requiring quantitative analysis. It is possible to develop formulas for qualitative analysis, but care needs to be taken to determine what data need to be collected and how they will be stored. Although applications are improving, information systems do not like too much of "fuzzy" data. Sometimes, therefore, there is a disconnect between what the HR specialist wants to know and what the system can provide.

Planning and Resourcing

This element of the Bramham model focuses on the horizontal integration of HR tactical and operational work areas. *Resourcing* is a term used to describe the establishment of the entire HRM function within an organization. Thus, the emphasis is on how an HRIS can ensure "fit" without overlap and duplication. Figure 1.2, in Chapter 1, exhibits the location and interrelationships of the HRIS with the HR programs, the strategic management systems, and the external environment of the organization. The policy areas discussed here are not intended to provide an exhaustive list, as many will be organizationally specific; however, they do cover the main work packages available currently.

HRIS Utilization for Talent Management and HR Planning: The Current Status

"The market for HCM applications is forecast to expand 11 percent annually between 2006 and 2011, to $10.6 billion, according to analysis firm AMR Research" (Frauenheim, 2007a, p. 40). However, there is considerable evidence to suggest that many organizations are not using their HRIS with particular reference to talent management and HRP in the early part of the 21st century. The majority of systems in use have the capacity to automate administrative activity and offer some **transactional capabilities**; however, this is somewhat limited (Broderick & Boudreau, 1992; Hall & Torrington, 1989).

As can be seen from Figure 10.3, taken from a recent report from the CIPD (2005), more than 80% of organizations use HRIS as an "electronic filing cabinet" to

❖ **Figure 10.3**   Reasons for Introducing HRIS

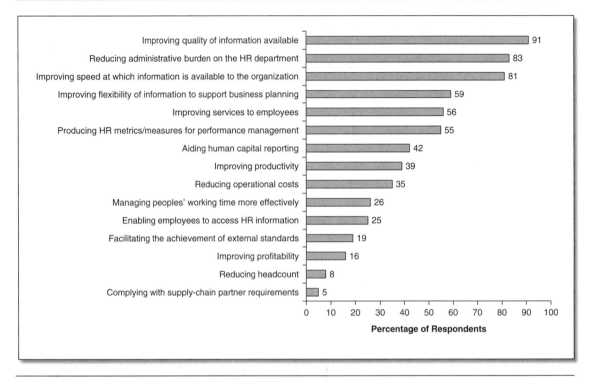

SOURCE: CIPD (2005, p. 6).

hold employee records, produce standard reports, automate administration, and improve transactional functionality. Some organizations (55%) are beginning to use HRIS to produce human capital metrics to manage performance, and fewer (42%) are using HRIS to report on human capital either internally or externally. Interestingly, of the 300-plus organizations surveyed, none are using HRIS to specifically report or track talent.

However, software vendors recognize that this is an emerging and potentially lucrative area, and some applications are currently being marketed that purport to offer this facility. Perhaps one of the best-known suppliers is SAP, which is promoting "mySAP ERP HCM," which "enables a singular view of available talent worldwide while at the same time allowing all talent related practices to speak a common language" (SAP, 2006, p. 6). The aim is to provide dynamic, real-time analysis in an ever-changing context. For most organizations, this is not yet a reality, but it is certainly on the "wish list" for many senior HR directors and specialists. Key to this strategic intent is an integrated employee data warehouse.

The challenge for most HR organizations is the many legacy systems in place that had been developed in an ad hoc manner. It is only relatively recently that strategic thinking has become part of the HR mindset; this is reflected in the academic literature of the past few years (Legge, 1995; Lengnick-Hall & Lengnick-Hall, 1988; Manzini &

Gridley 1986; Pfeffer, 1994; Schuler & Jackson, 1996; Sparrow & Marchington, 1998; Storey, 1992; Ulrich, 1997). Although HR directors and specialists have strategic know-how, they are often constrained by their lack of knowledge regarding strategic information systems. This is recognized within professional qualification schemes but still does not have the prominence needed for HR specialists to eloquently promote HRIS and gain business and financial backing for HRIS projects.

The advent of HR shared services, supported by large technological systems, has changed the role of information systems at the society level (with e-government systems) as well as inside organizations with enterprise-wide systems (often also incorporating strategic systems such as the balanced scorecard; Marr & Neely, 2003; also, see Chapter 9, this volume). Such systems are having a major impact on structures, job roles, and tasks within organizations.

Utilization of HRIS for Talent Management, Tracking, and HR Planning

> *We have a systems challenge, linking those that run Performance Management to those for Talent Management. . . . In addition there is a challenge caused by the speed of our growth. As we grow, tracking movement across the organisation globally is one of the things we're trying to deal with.*

—HR Director, Search Engine Organisation (2006)

The increase in self-service applications and shared-service centers and the growing burden of employment legislation indicate that employers are looking for the next-generation HR applications (CIPD, 2006a). These applications need to take account of metrics for the whole talent management pipeline and elements such as workforce management, of which workforce optimization and talent management are critical areas. There also appears to be a desire to create innovative information databases on talent pools. This raises questions such as the following: Are the applications used for tracking "fit for purpose"? Will they provide good access for all who need it? Who will be tracked, how closely, and how frequently?

Researchers in the investment sector in the United Kingdom considered metrics appropriate for external reporting (Scott-Jackson, Cook, & Tajer, 2006). They determined that it is essential to capture five key measures: leadership, employee motivation, training and development, performance improvement, and pay and reward structures. These HR practice areas are essential elements of the talent pipeline and provide a good starting point for talent-oriented metrics. While there are a number of methods, equations, and systems available for determining the makeup of particular metrics, it is vital that they are specific to the organizational context (see Tansley, Newell & Williams, 2001, for examples of key metrics; see Table 10.3). The SOCPO (2005) survey in the public sector found that

> little attempt is made to develop a "talent data-base" where information is systematically collected over time about aspiring future leaders—only 40% of people in the organisations surveyed are one-to-one career discussions held and just over 30% of staff get quarterly/half-yearly appraisals. (p. 4)

❖ Table 10.3   Examples of Metrics (Tansley, Newell, & Williams, 2001)

Individual HR Data	Collective HR Data
Application form, interview and tests records, job history (transfers, promotions, etc.), current and historical pay details, inventory of skills and competencies, education and training records, performance assessment details, absence, lateness, accident, medical and disciplinary records, warning and suspensions, holiday entitlements, pensions data, termination record/exit interview/reengaging, etc.	Numbers, grades, and occupations of employees; skills audit data—analysis of the skills available; absenteeism, labor turnover, and lateness statistics; accident rates; age and length of service distributions; wage rates and salary levels; employee costs; overtime statistics; records of grievances and disputes and training records, etc.

Although it is drawn from SAP marketing material, Table 10.4 does illustrate the potential of a fully integrated HRIS, orientated to talent management and HRP. Implicit here are skills sets and know-how that cross a number of areas—for example, HR management (HRM), financial management, information and systems management, business acumen, and strategic thinking. Individuals with these competencies are rare; many have a blend of these or focus on one area or another.

A number of approaches are made possible using sophisticated techniques within an HRIS that may facilitate a transformatory approach to HRP. Three key approaches include job forecasting, scenario planning, and future-oriented competency modeling.

Traditional **job forecasting** techniques can be enhanced that look at the future of particular jobs and roles in line with the strategic plan. This may uncover the need for different elements of human capital (e.g., skills, knowledge sets, and attitudes) for these roles and show how they can contribute to the future success of the organization.

Scenario planning identifies possible alternative futures and can be undertaken alongside strategic scenario planning. Once the drivers for change are established, scenarios can be developed using a small number of criteria or boundaries. Strategic scenario planning has been used by various organizations (the best-known example is Royal Dutch Shell) and in traditional HRP forums using Nominal or Delphi groups: The use of an HRIS improves the speed of response. Examples of the outcomes of this

❖ Table 10.4   Metric Management Within SAP (2006)

- Consolidating analytics needed to plan, monitor, and measure
- Integrating end-to-end business processes to speed decision making, drive effectiveness, and reduce costs
- Tying investments in recruiting, training, and compensation to business results
- Maximizing reuse of HR data to drive HCM processes
- Providing direct visibility into workforce performance
- Enabling agility in workforce deployment so that organizations can readily respond and adapt to change

type of exercise may include different versions of job descriptions and person specifications for the same role, depending on the strategic direction taken.

The aim of **future-oriented competency modeling** is to consider the future needs of a particular department or role type. The emphasis here is a focus on the "ideal" competencies and behaviors observed in those with the highest performance appraisal evaluations. This technique identifies aspects that describe the difference between the very good HIPO and the excellent HIPO.

Human Capital Metrics and Analytics

Some innovative organizations are now beginning to achieve competitive advantage using analytics (Davenport, Cohen, & Jacobson, 2005). At an enterprise level, organizations are being more innovative, vertically integrating across functions developing integrated predictive modeling to forecast the need for critical skills, data, and other resources so that multiple business functions can be correlated. This requires a sophisticated set of knowledge and skills across levels and functional areas. For an HRIS, the challenge is to develop new and broader capabilities for extracting and cleaning data, loading and maintaining data warehouses, **data mining**, and query and reporting. Historically, most of these techniques were embedded in specialist third-party software that did not necessarily integrate easily with on-going management and contractual problems. The past 5 years have seen vendors of HRIS software beginning to develop their own analytics packages (e.g., SAP-HR Analytics) to market at the enterprise level. In addition, there is an emergence of joint ventures between specialist software companies to combine traditional "best-of-breed" packages (e.g., SAP-HR and Microsoft producing "Duet"). What is certain is that many (large) organizations are making great efforts to track HIPOs and HIPERs in a timely manner (Deliotte, 2007). It is suggested by some industry observers that 35% of companies with 2,500 employees or more are in the process of implementing analytics software (Frauenheim, 2007b, p. 25) that brings a scientific and rational precision to what may have been considered an art until very recently. What is less certain is how to develop the most effective "bundles" of metrics, particularly for talent management purposes.

Summary

There is growing evidence that HRIS are being used to support strategic tasks (Lawler & Mohrman, 2003). A small study (Hussain, Wallace, & Cornelius, 2007) shows that organizations are becoming more reliant on HRIS regardless of their size and the HR software applications marketplace is growing at a phenomenal rate (Frauenheim, 2007a).

Technology continues to challenge talent management and HRP boundaries and practices. There is a need to develop fully integrated, fully implemented HRIS, providing focused talent-orientated data and information that meet the needs of senior decision makers and HR professionals. Historical, piecemeal approaches will not enable an organization to achieve competitive advantage. There is an opportunity for HRM to demonstrate that it is strategic and can add value—channeled via talent management initiatives.

DISCUSSION QUESTIONS

1. Why is it important to establish the meaning of talent and talent management in a particular organizational setting?

2. Why are job descriptions critical to the effective management of an organization? What role(s) does job analysis play in an HRP and talent management program?

3. How can an HRIS assist in establishing and maintaining accuracy and timeliness in job descriptions?

4. How does the strategic direction of the organization influence HRP activities?

5. What specific analytical tools would be helpful to assist each of the four steps of the HRP processes?

6. Given the different needs of the HRP process discussed in this chapter, what types of data would you expect the HRIS data warehouse to contain?

7. What would be the most effective "bundles" of metrics for talent management?

8. How would one justify the purchase of software for an HRP program?

CASE STUDY: RETURN TO OPENING VIGNETTE

18 months later . . .

Once again, Rudiger is sitting at his desk on the seventh floor of his offices in central London reflecting on life. The move from Barcelona to England went smoothly, with the last crate arriving only 2 months later than the rest. He is still working hard, but the hours are slightly better since the introduction of the work-life balance policy last year, and his family has settled down well in the idyllic English countryside.

As Global Head of People and Talent, he still has problems though—just different ones. The talent strategy "Our People—Our Talent—Our Future," presented to the board in his third month, identified the need for robust HRP information and analyses that required a new version of HRP software. It is in its early stages, but the intensive data cleansing and updating activity have been straightforward so far. More of a concern are the metrics responsible for producing the information needed to develop far-reaching HRP policies and practices for the future. The metrics are relatively easy to construct, but it is proving tricky to find the right "bundles" of predictive metrics—this is holding up progress with the analysis application package. In addition, there have been cost overruns in the implementation of the HRP software, and some senior managers are wondering if the new software should be abandoned.

At least 3 of the 12 board members will retire in the next 2 years, and they are looking to groom their successors. At least one will have to be hired from outside the organization, and Rudiger is not sure what the CEO wants for this position. In addition, employee turnover and an aggressive growth strategy mean hiring new employees as well as training and transferring current employees. The work that is involved in defining competencies (KSAs) at skill levels within jobs is progressing well, with hard-won support from the unions. However, job descriptions that can be found are at least 3 to 5 years old, and some jobs have no descriptions. The new apprenticeship scheme is about to be launched, and the international graduate student package and development program have been completely revised. Overall, things are progressing reasonably well, but there is still much to be done.

Case Study Questions

1. How would you recommend that Rudiger begin to develop an HRP program? What are the steps that he needs to take?

2. How should the problem with the job descriptions be handled? Should the union be involved?

3. What are some of the problems in the past that have led to this current situation?

4. Why do you think there are cost overruns? How could this have been avoided?

5. Why are there problems with implementation of the new software?

6. How should job descriptions be developed for the jobs of board member and international student intern?

Notes

1. The sections on job analysis were written by Michael J. Kavanagh.

2. Foodcom (a pseudonym), based in the United States of America, with annual sales of $60 billion and approximately 150,000 employees in over 60 countries, is a provider of food and agricultural products and services worldwide.

3. Here, the definitions are taken from Hazel Williams's interview research notes with participants for the CIPD (2007) report *Talent: Strategy, Management, Measurement.*

4. Ethical Bank (a pseudonym) has an extensive global network of over 1,400 branches (including subsidiaries, associates, and joint ventures) employing approximately 55,000 employees in over 50 countries in the Asia Pacific Region, South Asia, the Middle East, Africa, the United Kingdom, and the Americas.

5. HRP is frequently referred to as workforce planning (WFP), particularly in the European Union (EU) countries.

References

Blass, E. (2007, November). *Talent management: Maximising talent for business performance.* London: Chartered Management Institute.

Bramham, J. (1994). *Human resource planning* (2nd ed.). London: Institute of Personnel and Development.

Broderick, R., & Boudreau, J. W. (1992). Human resource management, information technology, and the competitive edge. *Academy of Management Executive, 6*(2), 7–17.

Cappelli, P. (1995). Rethinking employment. *British Journal of Industrial Relations, 33,* 563–602.

Chartered Institute of Personnel and Development. (2005). *People management and technology: Progress and potential.* London: Author.

Chartered Institute of Personnel and Development. (2006a, June). *HR and technology: Beyond delivery.* London: Author.

Chartered Institute of Personnel and Development. (2006b). *Talent management: Understanding the dimensions.* London: Author.

Chartered Institute of Personnel and Development. (2007, August). *Talent: Strategy, management, measurement.* London: Author.

Coase, R. H. (1952). The nature of the firm. In G. J. Stigler & K. E. Boulding (Eds), *Readings in price theory* (pp. 386–405). Homewood, IL: Irwin. (Original work published 1937)

Davenport, T. H., Cohen, D., & Jacobson, A. (2005). *Competing on analytics.* Babson Park, MA: Babson Executive Education.

Delbridge, R., Gratton, L., & Johnson, G. (Eds). (2006). *The exceptional manager.* Oxford, UK: Oxford University Press.

Deliotte. (2007, June). *Aligned at the top: How business and HR executives view today's most significant people challenges—and what they're doing about it.* New York: Economist Intelligent Unit.

Doeringer, P. B., & Piore, M. J. (1971). *Internal labor market and manpower analysis.* Lexington, MA: Heath Lexington.

Economist Intelligence Unit. (2006, May). *The CEO's role in talent management. How top executives from ten countries are nurturing the leaders of tomorrow.* London: The Economist, in collaboration with Development Dimensions International.

Fombrun, C. J., Tichy, N., & Devanna, M. (1984). *Strategic human resource management.* New York: Wiley.

Frauenheim, E. (2007a). HCM software: Does not meet expectations . . . yet. *Workforce Management, 86*(17), 39–47.

Frauenheim, E. (2007b). *Keeping score with analytics software* [online] *workforce.com.* Retrieved June 12, 2007, from www.workforce.com/tools/reports/070521_specialreport_hrtech_talentmgmt.pdf

Ghorpade, J. V. (1988). *Job analysis.* Englewood Cliffs, NJ: Prentice-Hall.

Green, F. (1993). The impact of trade union membership on training in Britain. *Applied Economics, 25*(8), 1033–1043.

Guest, D. (1987). Human resource management and industrial relations. *Journal of Management Studies, 24*(5), 503–521.

Hall, L., & Torrington, D. (1989). How personnel managers come to terms with the computer. *Personnel Review, 18*(6), 26–31.

Hendry, C. (1995). *Human resource management: A strategic approach to employment.* Oxford, UK: Butterworth Heinemann.

Hercus, T. (1992). Human resource planning in eight British organisations: A Canadian perspective. In B. Towers (Ed.), *The handbook of human resource management.* Oxford, UK: Blackwell.

Hofstede, G. (1991). *Cultures and organisations.* London: McGraw-Hill.

Hussain, Z., Wallace, J., & Cornelius, N. E. (2007, January). The use and impact of human resource information systems on human resource management professionals. *Information and Management, 44*(1), 74–89.

Kirkpatrick, D. L. (1998). *Evaluating training programs: The four levels.* San Francisco: Berrett-Koehler.

Lawler, E. E., & Mohrman, S. A. (2003). HR as a strategic partner: What does it take to make it happen? *Human Resource Planning, 26*(3), 15–29.

Lazear, E. P. (1999). Personnel economics: Past lessons and future directions. *Journal of Labor Economics, 17*(2), 199–236.

Lazear, E. P. (2000). Future of personnel economics. *Economic Journal, 110*, 611–639.

Legge, K. (1995). *Human resource management: Rhetorics and realities.* London: Macmillan.

Lengnick-Hall, C. A., & Lengnick-Hall, M. L. (1988). Strategic human resource management: A review of the literature and a proposed typology. *Academy of Management Review, 13*(3), 454–470.

Manzini, A. O., & Gridley, J. D. (1986). Integrating human resources and strategic business planning. New York: AMACOM.

Marchington, M., Grimshaw, D., Rubery, J., & Wilmott, H. (2004). *Fragmenting work: Blurring organisational boundaries and disordering hierarchies.* Oxford, UK: Oxford University Press.

Marr, B., & Neely, A. D. (2003). *Balanced scorecard software report.* Stamford, CT: Garner.

McCann, L. (2006). The case of the UK: Emulating the US model. In C. Kohler, K. Junge, T. Schroder, & O. Struck (Eds), *Trends in employment stability and labour market segmentation: Current debates and findings in Eastern and Western Europe.* Jena, Germany: Sonderforschungbereich 580.

Pfeffer, J. (1994). *Competitive advantage through people: Unleashing the power of the workforce.* Boston: HBS Press.

Richards-Carpenter, C. (1989). Manpower planning makes a comeback. *Personnel Management, 21*(7), 55–65.

SAP. (2006). *mySAP™ ERP Human capital management: Solution overview.* Retrieved June 29, 2007, from www.sap.com/community/pub/showdetail.epx?itemID=6627

Schuler, R. S., & Jackson, S. E. (1996). *Human resource management: Positioning for the 21st century* (6th ed.). Minneapolis, MN: West.

Scott-Jackson, W., Cook, P., & Tajer, R. (2006, July). Measures of workforce capability for future performance: Vol. 1. Identifying the measures that matter most. London: Chartered Management Institute.

Sels, L. (2002, December). "More is not necessarily better": The relationship between the quantity and quality of training efforts. *International Journal of Human Resource Management, 13*(8), 1279–1298.

Society of Chief Personnel Officers. (2005). *Talent management: The capacity to make a difference.* London: Veredus.

Sparrow, P., & Hiltrop, J. (1994). *European human resource management in transition.* London: Prentice Hall.

Sparrow, P., & Marchington, M. (1998). *Human resource management: The new agenda.* London: Pitman.

Storey, J. (1992). *Developments in the management of human resources.* Oxford, UK: Blackwell.

Storey, J., Cressey, P., Morris, T., & Wilkinson, A. (1997). Changing employment practices in UK banking: Case studies. *Personnel Review, 26*(1/2), 24–42.

Tansley, C., Newell, S., & Williams, H. (2001). Effecting HRM-style practices through an integrated human resource information system: An e greenfield site? In Managing the employment relationship in Greenfield sites [Special issue]. *Personnel Review, 30*(3), 351–370.

Ulrich, D. (1997). *Human resource champions: The next agenda for adding value and delivering results.* Boston: Harvard Business School Press.

Walker, J. W. (1989). Human resource roles for the '90s. *Human Resource Planning, 12*(1), 55–61.

Warren, C. (2006). Talent management curtain call. *People Management, 12,* 24–29.

Williams, H. (2002). Strategic planning for human resources. In J. Leopold (Ed.), *Human resources in organisations.* Harlow, Essex, UK: Pearson Education.

Williamson, O. E. (1975). *Markets and hierarchies: Analysis and antitrust implications.* New York: Free Press.

Williamson, O. E. (1981). The economics of organization: The transaction cost approach. *American Journal of Sociology, 87*(3), 548–577.

Williamson, O. E. (1994). Transaction cost economics and organisation theory. In N. Smelser & R. Swedberg, (Eds.), *The handbook of economic sociology* (pp. 77–107). Princeton, NJ: Princeton University Press.

Zuboff, S. (1988). *In the age of the smart machine.* New York: Basic Books.

11

Recruitment and Selection in an Internet Context

Kimberly M. Lukaszewski

David N. Dickter

Brian D. Lyons

Jerard F. Kehoe

EDITORS' NOTE

This chapter is the second one that is concerned with talent management of employees. As noted in previous chapters, talent management is an extremely important strategic goal for organizations, both domestic and global, and relates directly to the HR scorecard discussed in Chapter 9. After the need for external hiring of new employees has been identified via HR planning (HRP) (Chapter 10), the next step is to design recruitment and selection programs that will result in the successful hiring of needed talent. Successful recruiting and hiring of new talent is the first step in the talent management process, which concludes with the retention of high-performance and committed employees. This chapter will cover the concepts of recruitment and selection and the use of the Internet and an HRIS to improve the operation of these HR programs.

CHAPTER OBJECTIVES

After completing this chapter, you should be able to

♦ Understand the relationship between the Internet and organizational recruiting objectives

♦ Discuss the potential advantages and disadvantages of online recruitment in the framework of recruiting objectives

♦ Understand the relationship between selection and assessment with HRIS

♦ Discuss the technological issues that influence selection and the solutions that have been reached

♦ Understand the value of HRIS selection applications through the use of utility analysis

VIGNETTE

A company looked for a computer-based solution for their problem of merging selection tests with their applicant-tracking software application and found that this could be done (SHRM, 2004). Bank of America wanted to improve the quality of the applicant pool they obtained through Internet recruiting by adding selection tests to the process. By adding valid selections tests, the company wanted to improve the quality of candidates such that those assessed by tests could be much more likely to be successful on the job than those candidates who simply applied through the Internet. Also, the company, by increasing applicant quality through testing, could reduce applicant-processing time.

Bank of America contracted with Development Dimensions International (DDI) to improve its selection system first. DDI created competency profiles for jobs by interviewing about 50 current job incumbents and managers to ascertain that the competency profile for each job had the correct skills listed for the job. A "set of inventories was then identified to map onto the confirmed competencies and serve to identify the candidates who had the greatest potential for success in the job and would be the right candidates scheduled for final interviews" (SHRM, 2004, p. 1). The next aspect of the project was to change the interface on the Web page for Bank of America, so that recruiters could get the applicant information they needed to manage applicant information for 100 hiring sites for Bank of America.

Next, the promising applicants were asked to visit a Bank of America staffing facility, where they completed three tests and inventories on a computer terminal. Once there, candidates watched a job preview video and then were directed to a computer terminal to key in basic contact information and complete three more tests. Candidates who were not comfortable with computers were able to access a built-in tutorial. After completing this procedure on the computer, the site administrator had just-in-time access to the test results. This enabled the administrator to conduct on-the-spot interviews with the candidates or schedule just-in-time interviews for a later time. Thus, Bank of America was able to introduce technology in one area of the selection process rather than trying to automate the entire process. In addition, this procedure allowed human contact with the candidates and maintained system security, particularly for the selection tests.

By combining online testing with its applicant tracking system, Bank of America netted some significant results. DDI's Kevin Cook reports the following:

Improved ability to identify successful performers. Of those who passed the test phase and were hired, 84 percent were rated as successful performers by their supervisors. In fact, passing candidates are five times more likely to be successful on the job.

Significant return on investment. The estimated annual return on investment from using the system in selecting for the Operations job family was more than 2,000 percent.

Favorable reactions from candidates. Ninety-seven percent of respondents expressed overall satisfaction with the selection process and agreed that the answers they were asked to provide represented their abilities.

Valid and fair assessment of candidates. The inventories included in the system were able to distinguish between high and low performers and increase the probability of selecting the best candidates. In addition, analyses broken out by race, gender, and age showed that the inventories treat all groups fairly. (SHRM, 2004, p. 2)

Introduction

To remain competitive in today's global environment, organizations are searching for more efficient and effective means of acquiring and maintaining a highly qualified workforce. One popular and highly productive strategy for meeting this goal has been the use of technology, especially the Internet. Thus, the focus of this chapter is to consider the impact of technology on the recruitment and selection processes in organizations. In the paragraphs that follow, we will discuss the effects of technology on these two key processes. In the recruitment section, we address the objectives of the recruitment process and whether or not online recruitment is helping to achieve these objectives. The recruitment objectives, which are based on the model of Breaugh and Starke (2000), include cost of filling a job opening, speed of filling a job opening, psychological contract fulfillment, employee satisfaction, retention rates, quality of applicants, quantity of applicants, and diversity of applicants. In addition, the impact of the attributes of the organizational Web site on applications is discussed. In the selection section, we address the importance of assessment and its role in HRIS. Technology issues surrounding selection, such as validity, computerized assessment, security, and proctoring, are also discussed. We then present the ways in which HRIS has been integrated with the function of selection and assessment to address the issues mentioned previously. Finally, we demonstrate the value of selection with HRIS selection applications through the use of utility analysis.

Recruitment and Technology

The goal of the recruitment function is to identify, attract, and hire the most qualified people (Cascio, 2006). However, this task has become quite challenging because there is a growing competition for talent in the labor market. Companies are increasingly being required to expand their search for applicants beyond local and domestic borders in order to find qualified talent. As a result, they have begun using the Internet as a means of attracting job applicants. In the United States, over 90% of large companies use the Internet to recruit applicants for job openings (Cappelli, 2001). In addition, over 95% of the Fortune 500 organizations currently have an online job page or career section on their corporate Web site (Taleo, 2006). With more than 46 million people looking for job openings online (PewInternet, 2006), it is no surprise that many organizations, both large and small, are jumping onto the online recruitment bandwagon. Although there are certainly a number of benefits associated with using online recruitment, there are also several issues that need to be considered before organizations adopt this strategy. For instance, is online recruitment a win-win situation for both job applicants and organizations? A good way to answer this question is to step back and examine the degree to which online recruitment (a) enables organizations to meet their recruiting objectives and (b) provides applicants with the means of obtaining jobs. Given these questions, we discuss these issues in the sections below.

The Impact of Online Recruitment on Recruitment Objectives

Research by Breaugh and Starke (2000) has identified a number of objectives for the recruitment process, including (a) cost, (b) speed of filling job vacancies, (c) psychological contract fulfillment, (d) satisfaction and retention rates, (e) quality and quantity of applicants, and (f) diversity of applicants. In the paragraphs below, we will consider the extent to which online recruitment helps organizations meet each of these objectives.

Recruitment Objective: Cost of Filling the Job Opening

One important recruitment objective that organizations constantly strive for is to minimize the cost of filling job openings (Breaugh & Starke, 2000). Research has consistently shown that online recruitment does reduce costs (Cappelli, 2001; Chapman & Webster, 2003; Galanaki, 2002). For example, one study showed that organizations saved 95% of recruitment costs when they used online recruitment as opposed to more traditional methods (e.g., newspaper ads). Other estimates revealed that the cost of traditional systems of recruitment was $8,000 to $10,000 compared with $900 for online recruitment (Cober, Brown, Blumental, Doverspike, & Levy, 2000). This cost difference has prompted many organizations to replace more traditional systems with online recruitment. So it appears that online recruitment can save companies money when compared with traditional methods, but does this cost savings apply to all organizations? The answer is, not necessarily.

The evidence presented above is quite enticing and would probably persuade most organizations to jump into the online recruitment arena: however, before doing so organizations should not assume that online recruitment will save money for all organizations. First, organizations need to consider whether or not online recruitment is appropriate for their company. More specifically, organizations need to plan how to process resumes and screen out those applicants who do not possess the qualifications needed. Failure to think through the entire process may generate greater administrative burdens for the HR department or departmental managers. This would definitely cut into any cost savings produced by online recruiting. A good example is found in an article written by Seminerio (2001), which profiled the **online recruiting** efforts of Sutter Health, a nonprofit health care network. Sutter Health decided to post jobs online to facilitate their recruitment process. The use of online recruitment generated an enormous number of resumes—more than 300,000—for the less than 10,000 open positions. In most situations, this is something an organization would desire; however, Sutter Health failed to think past the generation of applicants. They had not planned how they would accommodate such a large volume of resumes in terms of processing and screening of applicants. Although in this case resumes were received quickly, they often sat for weeks on end before processing and selection occurred. Sutter Health quickly realized their error in planning and realized that they needed to revamp the use of online recruitment to serve their needs better.

In addition, organizations also need to track the effectiveness of the online recruitment method through the assessment of yield ratios and placements made. When dealing with a Web site for recruiting, it may be useful to monitor the numbers of hits your company's Web sites are receiving on career pages. However, the number of hits on a Web site is only one small component in measuring effectiveness (Cober et al., 2000). In one study conducted in the United Kingdom, large organizations with 5,000 employees or more were surveyed about the effectiveness of online recruitment (Reed Company, 2003). The results of the study found that about 40% of the organizations felt that online recruitment is a more effective means than any other traditional method of recruitment. These results imply that organizations need to track the outcomes (e.g., successful placements) of using online recruitment and compare this method with other recruiting methods before adopting new systems.

Thus, although some research shows that online recruiting may result in cost savings, other research shows that the use of online recruiting may generate a large number of applications, which may result in quite an administrative burden for organizations. As a result, organizations need to consider the overall costs associated with the entire recruitment process before implementing these new systems.

Recruitment Objective: Speed of Filling Job Vacancies

Another recruitment objective for assessing the effectiveness of recruitment is the speed of filling the job vacancy (Breaugh & Starke, 2000). Research has shown that online recruitment can decrease cycle time and increase the efficiency of the process by allowing organizations to spend less time gathering and sorting data (Cardy & Miller, 2003; Chapman & Webster, 2003; Cober, Brown, Levy, Keeping, & Cober, 2003; Web Recruiting Advantages, 2001, as cited in Braddy, Thompson, Wuensch, & Grossnickle, 2003). One estimate indicated that online recruitment can decrease hiring cycle time by 25% (Cober et al., 2000). Another study using data from 50 Fortune 500 companies showed that the use of online recruitment reduced their average hiring cycle time of 43 days by 6 days and allowed them to cut 4 days off the application process (Recruitsoft/iLogos, cited in Cappelli, 2001). Another study at Cisco Systems found that online recruitment allowed the company to fill job openings quickly. When Cisco Systems adopted online recruitment, they attracted more than 500,000 individuals in 1 month, and this enabled them to hire 1,200 people in just 3 months' time (Cober et al., 2000).

It is evident from the review above that online recruiting can decrease the cycle time and enhance the speed with which vacancies are filled, but this leads to other questions that need to be answered. Does this speediness enable organizations to hire the most qualified employees? Do these hires remain with the organizations? What is the diversity of these new hires? These questions and others may offset the benefits of the shortened hiring cycle and need to be examined further.

Recruitment Objective: Psychological Contract Fulfillment, Employee Satisfaction, and Retention Rates

Psychological contract fulfillment, employee satisfaction, and retention rates are three other important goals of the recruitment process. These three goals have a close relationship. The psychological contract is the employees' beliefs about the reciprocal obligations and promises between them and their organizations (Morrison & Robinson, 1997). Not surprisingly, when employees believe that their psychological contracts with the organization have been breached, they are more dissatisfied and more likely to leave the organization (Rousseau, 1990). Thus, it is important to explore the extent to which online recruitment can help ensure that employees' psychological contracts are fulfilled.

The information gathered and disseminated during the recruitment process shapes the expectations that lead to psychological contract fulfillment, which directly affects employee satisfaction and retention rates (Breaugh & Starke, 2000). There are numerous types of expectations that shape the psychological contract. These expectations include the work role (skills use, job performance), social relations (coworker and customer interactions), economic rewards (raises, monetary incentives), and company culture (Baker, 1985). It is critical during the recruitment phase that both the potential employee and the employer communicate what these expectations are and recognize whether this employment relationship will be able to meet the expectations of both parties (Baker, 1985).

Information that is provided by the applicant and by the recruiting company is a crucial part of the recruitment process. Oftentimes the recruitment process is rushed by the recruiters to complete the task of filling job openings. When a process is rushed, job seekers may find incomplete or vague information regarding job openings and company expectations. Furthermore, when job seekers receive sugar-coated information from recruiters that exaggerates the opportunities and provides unrealistic expectations about the company, then the expectations of employees are incongruent with those of the organization. Inaccurate, overly optimistic, or vague information is something organizations need to minimize or avoid. The use of such information can often lead to unrealistic expectations about the psychological contract between the organization and the individual. This is problematic for organizations because the new hires may begin to see the inconsistencies in their expectations that were formed throughout the recruitment process and feel that their psychological contract has been breached by their employer. Violations of the psychological contract can often result in negative attitudes and behaviors and higher levels of employee dissatisfaction and, eventually, will lead to greater turnover (Morrison & Robinson, 1997). Therefore, organizations really need to monitor and distribute accurate and timely information to potential job seekers to avoid such problems in the workplace.

Given that numerous companies now have their own Web sites, which contain a job page and endless space to provide information, more realistic information can be offered to job seekers. In addition, since the information is posted in real time—changes in content can be made at a moment's notice so that information is up-to-date and accurate. Therefore, it is no surprise that applicants rely more on posted information to form their expectations about the job and the company. Thus, companies can use Web sites to help provide realistic expectations about the companies and form psychological contracts. Companies really need to make sure that the message being conveyed on their Web sites is producing the psychological contract that can be fulfilled for both the employees and the employer. Once again, considering that fulfillment of the psychological contract should affect satisfaction levels and turnover levels, it is worthwhile for companies to determine the types of messages that can help increase the satisfaction and retention levels of employees. The use of a realistic recruitment message and the employment brand message will be the focus.

Realistic Recruitment Message

A realistic recruitment message is one that describes the organization and the job as they truly are without sugar coating (Heneman & Judge, 2006). One important tool many organizations use is the realistic job preview. A realistic job preview is when applicants are given the positive and negative attributes of a job they are applying for to see if this job is truly what they desire or thought it was (Wanous, 1992). Realistic job previews can be communicated through written information that is posted on the employers' Web sites, but more and more companies are using video clips or webcams that allow candidates to view what it is like to work for the organization in real time. One example is found at Monsanto, an agricultural firm, which posts video clips on its Web site so you can see what working there is like (www.monsanto.com/monsanto/layout/careers/default.asp). Some companies are taking this a step further by allowing some kind of interaction with current employees to gain realistic information about what it is like to work for the company. One example of a company that uses this feature is Cisco Systems, which offers online applicants a chance to "Make a Friend at Cisco." This allows the applicant to communicate with someone inside Cisco, who can describe what it is like to work for the organization (Cascio, 1998).

In addition to realistic job previews, organizations are also using the unlimited space on their company Web sites to provide a realistic culture preview (Cober et al., 2003; McCourt-Mooney, 2000). A realistic culture preview allows an organization to expand beyond the traditional job information and provide information about the company philosophy, value systems, history, diversity, salary structure, and benefits. This information could be vital for constructing realistic expectations in forming the psychological contract.

Research has shown that the availability of particular information (i.e., advancement opportunities, salary) can have a positive impact on applicants' attraction to an organization (Cober et al., 2003; Mohamed, Orife, & Wibowo, 2002). The use of a realistic culture preview is also helpful since often applicants seek out jobs and organizations that best fit their own personal values and beliefs (Dineen, Ash, & Noe, 2002). This could help develop a better relationship between the organization and the applicant and could lead to the building of trust between the applicant and the organization, which is key in the psychological contract. In addition, if the company fits the applicants' values and beliefs, they may experience higher satisfaction and stay with the company longer. Since research has shown that applicants feel that they have a better chance of collecting realistic information from Web sites than from traditional sources (Rozelle & Landis, 2002), online recruitment is a critical recruitment tool.

Overall, the use of realistic recruitment messages in online recruitment should enable organizations to increase the degree to which employees' perceive that their psychological contracts are fulfilled and should also enhance satisfaction and retention levels. Realistic recruitment messages should not only help organizations attract applicants who possess the skills and values that are aligned with those of the company but should also communicate what they look for in candidates applying for job openings. This could potentially help applicants construct realistic expectations, which could lead to a well-developed psychological contract that could be fulfilled in the future on the job if they are selected for the job. The fulfillment of the psychological contract could lead to a long and productive relationship for both the employee and the employer, where satisfaction and retention rates could be increased.

Employment Brand Messages

A company's employment brand can be a powerful tool to attract applicants to their Web sites. A company's employment brand is often based on the organization's well-known values or distinctive image and culture (i.e., Southwest Airlines, Microsoft). Companies often set themselves apart from their competitors by means of their employment brand (Ulrich, 2001; Stone, Stone-Romero, & Lukaszewski, 2003), or it can help create a particular image in the hope of attracting job applicants (Galanaki, 2002). For example, Cisco Systems uses its image of being technologically advanced and, therefore, relies only on recruitment through the Internet to fill openings (Cascio, 1998).

Research shows that the use of online recruitment can help some organizations create a specific brand identity in the labor market (Chapman & Webster, 2003; Ulrich, 2001). One unique example is found on the Johnson & Johnson Web site (www.jnj .com/careers/global.htm); they brand themselves "the small company environment: big company impact" to attract individuals who are familiar with their brand but don't want to get lost among the number of employees. In addition, the current brand or reputation is another way that companies can lure applicants to their job pages, by simply linking employment opportunities to their products and services. This is quite helpful in attracting applicants who are familiar with the company's products but possibly never thought about the company's employment opportunities.

Overall, the employment brand may be an important determinant of applicants' attraction to organizations and subsequent satisfaction and retention rates. If a person believes and identifies with a particular company, he or she may find fulfillment and satisfaction and stay there if extended a job opportunity. However, more research is needed in this area to examine the direct impact of this type of message.

Quantity, Quality, and Diversity of Applicants

The quantity, quality, and diversity of applicants are three other important recruitment objectives (Breaugh & Stark, 2000). Each topic will be discussed in greater detail.

Quantity of Applicants

Online recruitment is extremely convenient for applicants and is available to them 24 hours per day and 7 days a week. It also allows them to fill out an online application or upload a resume for various positions in a matter of seconds. Although this convenience can be very beneficial, it may encourage applicants to apply for jobs without assessing their own qualifications for the job. This results in a large number of applicants for every job opening. To offset this volume, organizations need to put into place methods to screen out applicants who are not qualified for the job. Many organizations are using resume management systems that allow for keyword searches (i.e., degrees, skills) to scale down the large volume of applications. However, some caution needs to be taken when using keyword searches. Applicants may tailor the content of their resumes to words in the job descriptions to enhance their chances of passing through the resume-screening systems (Mohamed et al., 2002), which may result in selection of those who use the right words but are not necessarily the most qualified for the job. Therefore, organizations need to be concerned with the quality of the numerous applications received.

Quality and Diversity of Applicants

Two other important goals of the recruitment process are to generate highly qualified applicants with diverse backgrounds. The quality and diversity of the applicant pool are determined by the users of online recruitment. Some research indicates that online recruitment systems place artificial limits on the applicant pool. Most applicants who typically use online recruitment are computer-literate, well-educated, driven individuals with a high need for achievement, seeking relatively high-level jobs (McManus & Ferguson, 2003). However, research also shows that these applicants are more likely to be job hoppers than those who do not use online recruitment (McManus & Ferguson, 2003). In addition, online recruitment users often have low levels of computer anxiety or high levels of computer self-efficacy (Marakas, Yi, & Johnson, 1998). Research has also found that college students preferred to use online recruitment as compared with other sources (Zusman & Landis, 2002).

Although online recruitment appeals to fairly well-educated applicants, research shows that there are also ethnic differences in the use of online recruiting (Kuhn & Skuterud, 2000). The breakdown for usage rate for online recruitment is 7% of Hispanics, 9% of blacks, and 16% of whites. However, the research findings on ethnic differences in the use of online recruitment have been somewhat contradictory. For example, one study found that African Americans often react quite favorably to online recruiting and use it to self-select themselves out of the application process (McManus & Ferguson, 2003). Some possible explanations for low Internet usage is attributed to lack of access to computers, lack of computer skills, and poverty (Kuhn & Skuterud, 2000). Others have argued that cultural differences in relationship orientation may affect Hispanics' use of online recruiting systems (Stone, Lukaszewski, & Isenhour, 2005).

There are also gender and age differences in the use of online recruitment. Employed men are more likely to search for jobs on the Internet than employed women (Kuhn & Skuterud, 2000). The reason for this may be that females generally have more computer anxiety and lower computer self-efficacy than males (Jackson, Ervin, Gardner, & Schmitt, 2001). Research has also shown that older individuals (55 or above) tend to have lower computer self-efficacy (Reed, Doty, & May, 2005) than younger adults, which may inhibit older applicants' ability and perceived ability to use online recruiting. Given these findings, it is clear that the use of online recruitment may limit the extent to which an organization attracts qualified women, Hispanic Americans, and older workers.

Thus, if an organization relies only on Web-based recruitment, the system will indirectly influence the overall composition of the workforce and decrease the level of diversity within the organization (Stone et al., 2005). Therefore, online recruiting may facilitate workforce homogeneity and, as a result, hinder innovative and creative decision making (Schneider, Goldstein, & Smith, 1995). Organizations must be aware of the potential biases created by their recruiting practices and align their recruiting strategy with the overall business strategy to create competitive advantage (Becker & Gerhart, 1996; Wright & Snell, 1998). For example, if an organization wants to hire an individual for an HRIS-related job, the organization may find Web recruiting to be a cost-efficient and effective source of recruitment, because the applicant pool is technologically proficient and would most likely use the Web in their job search. Conversely, if the organization is looking for a person in a nontechnical position (e.g., staff writer, creative consultant), then the use of traditional recruitment sources may be more effective than the use of online recruitment alone.

Overall, it is apparent that online recruitment may help organizations meet the objective of increasing the number of job applicants (Chapman & Webster, 2003; Galanaki, 2002). However, it is not clear whether the use of online recruitment will help organizations attract high-quality applicants. If an organization is looking for job applicants with particular skills (e.g., computer skills), then they may be able to find and attract such applicants with online recruitment. However, the use of online recruitment may also result in some dysfunctional consequences. For instance, online recruiting may attract job hoppers and may be less likely to attract those with low levels of computer self-efficacy. Furthermore, online recruitment may have a negative impact on the extent to which organizations are able to attract women, older workers, and some minorities (e.g., Hispanic Americans). However, research is not clear about the extent to which online recruitment helps organizations attract African Americans. Further research is needed on this topic.

Organizations need to be very cautious about using online recruitment as their only source of recruitment, especially since online recruitment may not help organizations meet their diversity-related goals. There is clearly potential for an adverse impact on women, minorities, and older applicants, which may pose potential legal problems for organizations (Hogler, Henle, & Beamus, 2001). Therefore, it is important that organizations consider the potential legal issues associated with the use of online recruitment and ensure that all applicants are given the opportunity to apply for jobs (Stone et al., 2003). Furthermore, organizations may want to use online recruitment in conjunction with other recruitment sources (e.g., newspaper ads, job fairs) to ensure that their recruitment processes are fair.

Attributes of the Recruiting Web Site

Another factor that may affect the acceptance and effectiveness of online recruiting is the attributes of the Web site. In general, the best Web site design is user-friendly in that users can easily navigate and browse through multiple Web pages to find information. The extent to which the Web site is usable or not has been referred to as **"Web site usability"** in the empirical literature (Cober et al., 2003; Karat, 1997; Nielsen, 2000). The construct of Web site usability has been conceptualized as encompassing a number of dimensions, including **navigability**, **content information**, and **aesthetic features**. Each dimension and its use in recruitment are further discussed below.

First, navigability can be defined as the overall ease with which a user can browse through multiple Web pages to locate topics of interest. Hosting a Web site that displays current information and includes active hyperlinks to retrieve information is essential in maintaining user interest within the site. To achieve this goal, organizations should follow the "three-click" rule for users to locate information of interest. For instance, users who wish to browse job opportunities on the organization's Web site should be able to reach the desired Web page by the third hyperlink from the home Web page.

Next, content information refers to the degree to which the Web site hosts relevant information that the user deems valuable and informative in nature. Providing information that the user desires is another mechanism by which organizations can maintain user interest and satisfaction with the Web site. In terms of recruitment, an organization would be advised to host a Web site that includes information about the organization and its products, available job opportunities, developmental opportunities, compensation, and culture (Barber & Roehling, 1993; Cable, Aiman-Smith, Mulvey, & Edwards, 2000; Cable & Graham, 2000; Judge & Cable, 1997). Consequently, hosting information that applicants value will most likely facilitate "fit"-related decisions. Specifically, when applicants perceive similarity between their qualifications and personality and the job and organization, it is more likely that they will pursue employment with the organization (e.g., Cable & Judge, 1996; Carless, 2005; Kristof-Brown, Zimmerman, & Johnson, 2005). Conversely, those applicants who perceive a mismatch between their qualifications and personality and the job and organization are more likely to self-select themselves out of the position and not apply. Overall, these applicant-evaluative processes cannot be formed if the organization did not include useful information on its Web site. For example, on Texas Instruments' employment Web page, a personality "fit check" is provided that enables applicants to answer and receive feedback about how well they match the organization's culture. The efficacy of this "fit check" function was empirically tested on a fictitious Web site, where applicants were found to be more attracted to the organization when **positive feedback** was provided about their fit with the firm's culture (Dineen, Ash, & Noe, 2002).

Finally, aesthetic features represent the overall stylistic or innovative aspects of a Web site, such as contrasting colors, pictures, animation, and playfulness, which keep the user engaged while navigating through multiple Web pages (Cober, Brown,

Keeping, & Levy, 2004). When a user is engaged, it is more likely that he or she will maintain interest in the organization and browse for more information about the organization (Cober et al., 2003). Similarly, the aesthetic features of a Web site may affect applicant perceptions and behavior. For example, if the Web site has attractive stylistic features, such as streaming video, it may exude perceptions of innovation or creativity that the applicant may attribute to the organization's culture. In turn, if the applicant values such innovation or creativity, it may stimulate higher perceptions of fit and attraction toward the organization. Thus, the aesthetic features of a Web site may serve as a signal for applicants to make favorable or adverse attributions about the organization.

Integrating these attributes together, a Web site's usability has been found to affect applicant perceptions and attitudes toward the organization. In a study by Cober et al. (2003), applicant perceptions of Web site content and style were found to be positively related to organizational attraction. More specifically, those Web sites that contained valuable information about the organization and engaged the user when browsing such information resulted in a higher degree of attraction toward the organization as a potential employer. Similarly, another study found that organizations with more navigable Web sites engendered higher ratings of intentions to apply for a position than those that were less navigable (Braddy et al., 2003). Similarly, Williamson, Lepak, and King (2003) found that higher perceptions of Web site usability produced higher perceptions of organizational attraction. All these studies converge on the finding that Web site usability perceptions influence applicant attitudes toward an organization. As a result, organizations should be attuned to how their Web sites influence applicant perceptions and be prepared to update their Web design to embody high navigability, content fidelity, and engaging aesthetic features. HR and IT employees should monitor the usability of their Web site by surveying applicant perceptions of and reactions to the Web recruiting process, especially in situations where the Web recruiting function entails gathering applicant data and preliminary online ability testing.

The decision to host job openings and having the capability of screening job applicants for positions on organizational Web sites should be based on the firm's resources and strategy. With this statement in mind, the purpose of an organization's recruitment Web site can be classified as either recruiting and screening oriented, or just recruitment oriented (Williamson et al., 2003). A recruiting and screening oriented Web site has the capability to list job openings and accept applications through a secure server. Conversely, a Web site that is only recruiting focused just hosts a list of job openings with the option of submitting an application via mail, e-mail, or fax to an organizational representative. Williamson et al. (2003) articulated that both recruitment orientations can be effective in attracting applicants; however, it could be contended that applicants may prefer submitting personal information through Web sites that they perceive to be secure and trustworthy (Stone et al., 2003). Therefore, if an organization does not have the financial resources to invest in building a secure server to accept applications, an alternative would be to still offer information about the organization and its culture on the Web site's employment Web page and then have a hyperlink that connects interested applicants to jobs that are hosted by a third-party vendor, such as *Monster.com*. A more logical alternative would be to host an organization's job opportunities on a third-party vendor's Web site (e.g., Monster.com, Careerbuilder.com) and include a hyperlink on each announcement that connects the applicant to the organization's home Web page. These alternatives would allow the organization to achieve the benefits associated with Web recruiting and provide the applicant an opportunity to learn more about the organization by browsing their home Web page. Also, from the applicant's perspective, these options would reduce any anxiety or adverse perceptions about privacy and Web-security-related issues concerning those organizations that the applicant is not familiar with or does not entirely trust.

Summary of Online Recruitment

In summary, organizations should consider the extent to which online recruitment enables them to meet their recruitment objectives. Our discussion above provides evidence that online recruitment can help organizations reduce the costs of recruiting, decrease the cycle time of filling job vacancies, and generate large quantities of applicants. However, organizations must remember that these are not the only recruitment objectives and must focus on finding the impact of online recruitment on the other recruitment objectives (quality and diversity of applicants, psychological contract fulfillment, employee satisfaction, retention rates). In addition, the attribute of the Web site can affect the acceptance and effectiveness of online recruiting. The best Web site design is user-friendly in that users can easily navigate and browse through multiple Web pages to find information that is valuable and conveys whether or not the applicants fit not only the job requirements but the organization's value system as well. Last, the aesthetic features of a Web site, combined with the thought content presented, may shape the attributions of job seekers toward the organization in a positive manner. However, the attraction of applicants to job openings is only the beginning—organizations now have to focus on assessing the applicants who constitute their applicant pools. Therefore, we now need to switch our focus to a discussion of selection.

Selection and Technology

This section focuses on **tests and assessments** of individual employees and candidates, which are at the heart of the evaluation processes that enable organizations to manage their talent. These tools are used for selecting employees, placing them in positions in the organization, training and developing them, promoting them, and evaluating them. Tests and assessments are important for HRIS, because they provide data that are used for making organizational decisions. To explore the databased decision-making process in further detail, we focus our discussion on the use of tests and assessments to make a critical decision—whether or not to hire a particular candidate.

What Are Selection Tests and Assessments, and Why Are They Used?

Most organizations that seek HRIS expertise on selection will likely consider the term *test* to refer to traditional multiple-choice examinations that can be used to measure ability, personality, or knowledge and to **skills tests**, such as typing tests. Organizations seeking assessments may be referring to these same tests, or, alternatively, they may be

❖ **Figure 11.1**   Specific Examples of Tests and Assessments

Knowledge test: A multiple-choice training posttest of knowledge of the tools, machines, and equipment used in a factory and designed to measure how well the new hire has learned essential job information taught in classroom training.

Skill test: A practical exercise or simulation that tests the candidate's effectiveness in using Microsoft Word software.

Ability test: The Watson-Gleser Critical Thinking Appraisal, a multiple-choice reasoning test, in which the examinee reads a short or medium-length passage and draws logical conclusions about the statements, choosing the answer that makes the best logical sense. Many other ability tests are similar in appearance and format to educational tests that are familiar to students (e.g., the Scholastic Aptitude Test [SAT], the Miller Analogies Test [MAT], and the Graduate Record Examination [GRE]).

Personal attributes test: A multiple-choice personality assessment, in which the examinee reads statements, such as "I enjoy making presentations in front of large groups of people," and indicates the extent to which she or he agrees or disagrees with the statement. Results are scored on several scales or dimensions.

Work simulation: An in-basket exercise in which the examinee must examine the variety of types of information (correspondence, reports, and other information) and also interact with simulated coworkers, employees, or other business associates (whether computer simulated or role played by actors over the telephone or in person). The examinee is evaluated on a variety of dimensions, from accuracy and the quality of decisions to work-related competencies, interpersonal skills, and other personal attributes.

thinking of different types of selection procedures and tools, such as reference checks or work samples. Whatever the label, tests and assessments are job-related decision-making tools that provide information about candidates that organizations can use in selection. Figure 11.1 contains examples of the major tests and assessment instruments. For this section of the chapter, we use the terms *test, assessment, selection tool,* and *selection procedure* interchangeably to refer to any measurement tool designed to measure attributes of individuals for the purpose of selecting employees.

Here is a more comprehensive list of assessments, as provided by the Society for Industrial and Organizational Psychology (SIOP, 2003; our notes are added in brackets). Selection procedures refer to any procedure used singly or in combination to make a personnel decision, including, but not limited to, paper-and-pencil tests, computer-administered tests, performance tests, work samples, inventories (e.g., personality, interest), projective techniques [ambiguous stimuli such as inkblots or pictures, often used for personality assessment], polygraph [lie detector] examinations, individual assessments, assessment center evaluations [summaries of multiple assessments, as evaluated by multiple raters], biographical data forms or scored application blanks, interviews, educational requirements, experience requirements, reference checks, background investigations, physical requirements (e.g., height or weight), physical ability tests, appraisals of job performance, computer-based test interpretations, and estimates of advancement potential (SIOP, 2003, p. 3). While this chapter will address a variety of important concepts about selection and assessment for personnel decision making, a full discussion is beyond the chapter's scope. Interested readers are encouraged to consult additional sources, including the document cited above. We also recommend the text by Guion (1998), one of the essential references on the topic. The U.S. Department of Labor (1999) offers a less technical summary white paper. And the SIOP Web site (www.siop.org) provides links to many useful Web sites and papers.

Why Is Assessment Important for HRIS?

When used for employee selection, assessments have value because they assist organizations in identifying those individuals who are more likely to succeed on the job and prevent the hire of those who are less likely to succeed. The following paragraphs provide several reasons why it is important for HR managers to understand the purpose and use of assessments.

All Organizations Use Assessments

Resumes are assessment tools, and so are interviews. Every company that has ever had more than one candidate for a job opening has assessed, in some form, whether or not it uses structured, professionally developed assessments to make hiring decisions. Increasingly, HRIS is supporting organizations' selection processes: how they identify the most qualified candidates and determine whom to choose for internal positions and promotions. The reason is that many organizations are using some type of selection instrument or tool in addition to the employment interview and, in most cases, the tools involve HRIS. In 40% of the Fortune 100 companies, for example, there is some form of individual assessment of job candidates (Shaffer & Schmidt, 2006). In 2005, *Newsweek* estimated that the business of testing and assessing job candidates, including both development and administration of the tests, was a $400 million industry, growing at 8% per year.

Organization Leaders Know That Employees' Abilities, Skills, and Personal Attributes Are Critical for Success

To see the evidence, pick up a book by a business leader, such as former General Electric CEO Jack Welch, or a popular-press book on successful businesses, such as *Good to Great* (Collins, 2001). If, as leaders often say, an organization's greatest asset is its people, then selection determines the value of the company's most important advantage.

Some Selection Systems Work Better Than Others

Better designed selection systems are more likely than poorly designed systems to select successful employees. In fact, many company-grown and commercially available assessments are of little value. The most frequent problems that occur include the following: (a) they assess attributes that are not relevant to job performance, (b) they are not used consistently or as intended, and (c) they are unreliable indicators of job-relevant attributes. HR departments must learn how to distinguish between effective and ineffective selection systems and how to choose or improve selection systems.

To be effective, assessments must be valid, they must provide information that is clearly related to the intended use, and the information must be related to the job's requirements in a manner that can be demonstrated by research. For instance, the research might show that the assessment mirrors the content of the job, such as a typing test or work sample that duplicates or simulates the actual job duties that are essential for employees to perform. Another aspect of validity involves the ability to predict important criteria: measures of work performance or behavior such as productivity, accident rate, absenteeism, tenure, reject rate, training score, and supervisory ratings of job-relevant behaviors, tasks, or activities (SIOP, 2003). For instance, an **ability test** can be shown to be valid if scores on the test are statistically correlated with scores on a posthire training evaluation that measures the knowledge individuals have acquired that is critical for successful job performance. Unfortunately, many commercially available assessments are poorly designed and researched, and their creators make unjustifiable claims about their effectiveness. When deciding whether to purchase assessment tools and systems from vendors, the organization should always obtain validation documentation that follows professional and legal guidelines, including the federal government's *Uniform Guidelines on Employee Selection Procedures* (U.S. Equal Employment Opportunity Commission, 1978; see also www.uniformguidelines.com) and the SIOP *Principles* publication (2003).

Importantly, validity involves not only research but also proper use. It would be irresponsible to use a test for a purpose other than that for which it was validated, such as installing a typing test to predict training success if there is no reason to believe the two would be related. Thus, the selection system, and the methods, procedures, and policies concerning the use of selection tools, matters as much as the tools themselves.

Employee Selection Is Regulated by Antidiscrimination Laws

Many laws, such as the Civil Rights Act of 1991 and the Americans with Disabilities Act, regulate companies' employee selection decisions. HRIS experts can contribute to their organizations by being aware of these laws. The primary intent of these laws is to prohibit employment practices that unfairly discriminate against people in various protected groups, such as racial/ethnic minorities, women, and older candidates. In general, these federal, state, and local laws require that selection decisions must be valid and fair, if they differentially affect protected group members. Selection decisions that differentially affect protected group members must provide equal treatment and be equally predictive of success for minorities and other protected groups in order to be fair and legal. The most commonly used term, but only part of the story, in an evaluation of fairness is adverse impact, when candidates from a protected group, A (e.g., women and minorities) are proportionately less likely to be hired than candidates in the group, B, with the highest selection rate (for good discussions on the topic, see Guion, 1998; SIOP, 2003). Often, but not always, the group with the highest selection rate is the nonminority group. A rule of thumb that federal and state enforcement agencies and courts use is the 80% rule. By this rule of thumb, adverse impact may be judged to exist if protected Group A's selection rate is less than .80 of Group B's selection rate. Importantly, having adverse impact does not, by itself, make a selection system illegal. A selection system that causes adverse impact may be legal if it can be shown to be job relevant (i.e., valid) and consistent with business necessity (i.e., important for business success). Interested readers should consult U.S. Equal Employment Opportunity Commission (1978) and SIOP (2003) for more details.

The Value of Selection Is Quantifiable

HR departments and HRIS experts, in particular, should understand how to use selection-related data in order to (a) provide strategic information to the company and (b) demonstrate the return on the company's investment in assessments.

Being able to provide important strategic information about the company, such as the expected skill levels of new employees who have been tested and the implications of these skills for business unit performance, can help transform the HRIS manager's role from a supporting, transactional contribution to that of a valued partner with key insight into the company's strategic directions. And, of course, being able to show a return on investment is essential for the survival of HRIS projects. A good system improves the quality of hires in a way that can be measured and verified. While no selection system is perfect, not all individuals who are selected can be guaranteed to succeed, and not necessarily all who are rejected would have been unsuccessful on the job, HRIS can measure the dollar value of selection to prove its value as a company investment. This topic is discussed in more detail later in this chapter.

Technology Issues in Selection

The most common use of technology for selection systems is the use of computers to administer and score tests. HRIS experts need to be aware of several general concerns about the computer administration of selection procedures. First, where traditional paper-and-pencil assessments are computerized, does the computer version have different measurement properties? Second, as the capabilities of microprocessors increase, it is possible to make assessments that more closely simulate the job, that is, closely approximate the work that would be done once the candidate is hired. What are the benefits and risks of high fidelity **work simulations**? Third, how does online testing affect the validity of selection systems? Does the technological ability to take a test anywhere, and organizations' increasing interest in using that ability, compromise the test security that is present in traditional settings with proctored examinations?

Equivalence Between Conventional and Computerized Assessments

Most of the first computerized employment tests were meant to look like their paper-and-pencil, low-tech counterparts, except that they were delivered on a computer to answer the questions (generally multiple choice) via a keyboard or a mouse or to administer a skill test (e.g., a typing test). Interestingly, although today there are also simulations that mirror the job, traditional multiple-choice tests still abound, in part because the format is easy to administer and score and in part because there are many good multiple-choice tests in use that predate the availability of inexpensive stand-alone computers and online testing.

Organizations tend to assume that paper-and-pencil and computerized forms (versions) of a test are interchangeable, assuming that the test items and instructions are the same. (Often, particularly in large organizations, both types are used, depending on the availability of computer facilities at different offices and whether or not large test sessions are conducted at recruiting events and in other locations where there are not enough computers available at once.) However, the assumption of equivalence may not be justified, and the HRIS expert must know when the assumption is warranted. The primary concern is that the mode of administration (paper or computer) will affect the measurement properties of the test. For assessments that do not include ability, such as personality tests and career interest inventories, most researchers have little concern that giving the test on paper will result in a different measure from a computerized test. However, there is clear evidence that the mode of administration matters for ability tests that are speeded, those for which there is time pressure and where many candidates do not finish all the items in the allotted time (e.g., see Mead & Drasgow, 1993; Potosky & Bobko, 2004). For such tests, the physical or virtual materials and test administration methods affect the time (in seconds) it takes to complete a test item and, thus, the results. For instance, think of a paper test form that the candidate writes on and matches to an answer sheet versus a computer screen where the examinee sees one item at a time and uses a mouse to click on the answers. Total scores, average scores, and performance on individual test items are affected. The more speeded a test is, the more likely that there will be differences between the paper and computer results. In contrast, power tests, tests in which there is no designated time limit to create time pressure or in which the time limit is set such that most candidates will complete the test without working hastily, typically do not show differences between paper and computerized testing modes. To understand the differences, an industrial/organizational psychologist or some other expert in tests and measurements will conduct a study of the equivalence between the two. The study entails administering both types of tests, ideally to the same individuals, with the order of administration counterbalanced across participants, and examining and comparing the overall results and the statistical results for each item. Then, when necessary, a formula equating the two can be developed to adjust for differences. The result is a method of ensuring that irrespective of whether the candidate takes the paper test or the computerized test, he or she will have the same opportunity to perform well.

Bandwidth Versus Fidelity: How Closely Should We Simulate the Job?

Technology has enabled organizations to create work sample simulations that represent the job with high fidelity. Company leaders may want this because they believe that no assessment could be nearly as good as a simulation that closely matches the work that will be performed on the job. However, as Figure 11.2 illustrates, an analysis of decades of assessment research has found that general cognitive ability tests can, on average, predict success virtually as well as simulations, and when combined with other types of assessments, they can exceed the predictive ability of simulations. The bar chart in Figure 11.2 displays statistical correlations between assessment scores and job performance data. Schmidt and Hunter (1998) provided these data in a comprehensive meta-analysis, research that quantitatively summarizes the data from many studies on a particular topic—in this case, the personnel selection research literature. The research is most supportive of work simulations, ability tests, structured interviews, and personality testing. Higher scores on these types of assessments are predictive of higher job performance. For comparison, less valid assessments are also shown, such as education and training ratings, and graphology (handwriting analysis), which has been shown to have little or no validity.

It is also important to be aware of the trade-off between fidelity and bandwidth, the range of settings to which the simulation might apply. For example, suppose that a

❖ **Figure 11.2** Correlations Between Assessment Scores and Job Performance

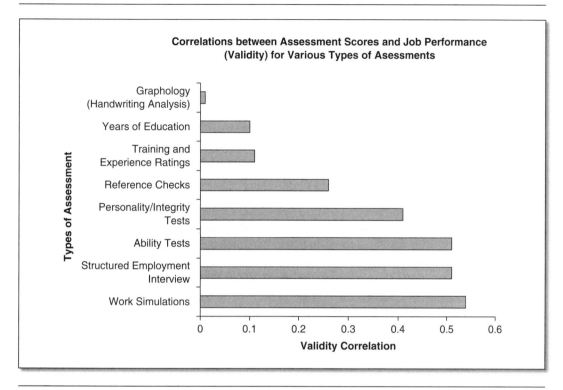

SOURCE: Schmidt and Hunter (1998).

management simulation is designed to closely represent a particular line of business in the actual organization chart and reporting structure, as well as the unique subject matter that is addressed in the management job from day to day. If the company then wants to use the simulation for a different business unit or job, the details that made the simulation highly appropriate in the first setting may interfere with its use in the other setting. The same problem applies to jobs and settings that change over time, as most do. Therefore, although as the HRIS expert you may be adept at creating an assessment that looks just like the job, such a tool might have a narrow range of uses. Also, simulations generally require that the job candidate already know how to do the job, at least at some basic level or that the job is simple enough that so that the candidate can learn the job tasks quickly to perform the simulation. In general, HRIS managers should keep in mind that, depending on the effort and expense one is willing to expend on assessment development and installation, lower-fidelity simulations and/or combinations of other types of assessments might be preferable. Schmidt and Hunter (1998) argued the following about ability tests, for example: Of all procedures that can be used for all jobs, whether entry level or advanced, it has the highest validity and lowest application cost. Work sample measures are slightly more valid, but they are much more costly and can be used only with applicants who already know the job or have been trained for the occupation or job (p. 264).

Validity and Security Issues Created by Unproctored Online Testing

Numerous consulting companies offer online tests. These tests may be administered in the same way as paper-and-pencil or stand-alone computer tests, conducted in an office by a proctor who gives instructions, checks identification, and monitors the test session. Online testing also allows for the possibility of unproctored (unsupervised) administration, with tests taken anywhere, at any time. (Note that this could also be said for other types of technology-enabled tests that are available, such as those administered by telephone keypad or telephone-based interactive voice response systems. Others that involve fixed facilities in particular, in-store kiosks in particular, are similarly unproctored and convenient.) Such testing can be attractive to organizations because of the convenience for both the candidate and the hiring organization.

However, this convenience may come at a cost. A panel of industrial/organizational psychologists convened at the annual SIOP conference in 2006 and published an article that summarizes the issues well and describes the opinions of the various members of the panel, who are employed by a range of different types of organizations: a university, several test-publishing firms, the U.S. government, and a publicly held company in the finance industry (Tippins et al., 2006). The issues included candidate identity, test security and cheating, and fair access to testing for minorities.

Candidate identity is a straightforward issue, currently without a straightforward method to verify it. In contrast to in-office testing requiring identification, when testing is unproctored, anyone might be taking the test in the candidate's place. Perhaps a live video feed and/or biometric method of verifying the candidate's identity would provide more assurance. Alternatively, the organization might choose to retest all the candidates who qualify, using a proctored setting. However, there are technical problems with evaluating and acting on score differences, and retesting diminishes the convenience and cost savings that were the original reasons for unproctored testing (Tippins et al., 2006).

A related issue is test security. One facet of this is keeping the test content under lock and key for future use. The HRIS manager must take precautions to prevent the test content from being copied and compromised. Another facet is preventing cheating. In addition to having someone else take the test or assist the candidate, the candidate might use resources that are not permitted (e.g., Internet search engines or offline dictionaries, calculators, etc.). Cheating is of particular concern when the tests have right answers (e.g., ability tests) and/or require skills that the candidate can have others perform (e.g., typing tests). Common sense tells us that the higher the stakes in a testing situation, the higher the likelihood of cheating.

HRIS experts also must be aware of a third issue, equal and fair access. In particular, tests must be fair to legally protected groups, yet unproctored testing and, indeed, Internet recruitment and candidate processing in general run the risk of having a chilling effect on minorities, who, because of the so-called "digital divide," might have greater difficulty accessing the Internet to apply for jobs. Organizations must provide for multiple ways to gain entry.

The above issues do not have easy solutions for organizations that wish to rely on unproctored Internet testing. Tippins et al. (2006) discussed the pros and cons of unproctored Internet testing but did not come to a consensus about the ethics of administering unproctored tests and keeping the process fair.

Applying HRIS to Selection and Assessment

Selection systems are information management systems for organizational decision making and administration. Therefore, HRIS plays an important part in their development and use. One uniquely HRIS-centered role is database design. Selection systems require the careful design of systems to store and keep track of individuals' selection data prehire and posthire and the ability to link information in interrelated systems, such as candidate test data and demographics, employment data for those who are hired, and job movement and position histories within the company. Increasingly, HRIS experts will be called on to assist in integrating the organization's various HR systems. At a minimum, integration involves linking data in two or more systems, such as the candidate/employee identification, so that one may conduct database queries and follow individuals as their information passes through the different systems. Integration often also involves linking transactional operations in a system, such that after the first system has conducted a transaction that requires follow-up in the next system, the first system contacts the next system to launch the required transaction. For instance, once a candidate has completed an online application, he or she may be automatically sent to another Web-based application to complete an assessment. The HRIS manager must have a conceptual understanding of what it means to link a test delivery system with other systems, such as applicant-tracking systems. In addition, organizations frequently wish to integrate a homegrown system with a vendor system or to integrate multiple systems, many or most of which are Internet based. Therefore, HRIS must have technical knowledge of protocols and programming languages for sharing data between Web-based systems, such as eXtensible Markup Language (XML).

Another general HRIS role in selection systems is the development of scoring and decision rules, and the administrative functions of the system. Whether the output of the completed assessment is simple to interpret (e.g., pass/fail) or complicated (e.g., multiple sources of information, levels of performance, and the screening events that could follow), the HRIS expert who participates in the scoring/decision rules must be sure that they are easy for HR and the business to understand and apply consistently throughout the organization. Another key HRIS role is helping to design and apply the administrative functions the system features permitting access to assessments results and assigning the right to distribute candidate information. Below are some more specific considerations for designing a computerized or Web-based selection system (Kehoe, Dickter, Russell, & Sacco, 2005):

- *Test access and security:* HR must decide how candidates will gain access to the test (By permission? Will there be prescreening? Is testing open to anyone?) and how the test content will be kept secure.
- *Test inventory and administrative privileges:* The HRIS expert must consider how the computerized tests will be purchased and inventoried (if accessed from a vendor) and who should be assigned the right to work with particular types of test data. Will there be multiple levels of access? Will individuals be able to delegate record-viewing rights to others?
- *Options for scoring:* Will there be multiple ways to score an assessment, with a variety of possible scoring rules? How might examinees' scores be compared with reference groups to make them more meaningful?

- *Accessing results:* In what data format and by what methods will test results be stored, transmitted, and interpreted?
- *Applying test policies:* What organizational requirements will affect the testing methods (e.g., systems that allow accommodations for disabilities) and the data that are kept and used (e.g., mandatory waiting periods before retests)?

For additional discussion on psychological testing on the Internet, the interested reader may wish to consult an article published by the American Psychological Association (Naglieri et al., 2004).

Demonstrating the HR's Value With HRIS Selection Applications

As mentioned earlier in the chapter, the HRIS manager plays a key role in proving the value of a selection system, through knowledge of how to obtain and use the right data on individual and organizational outcomes that will demonstrate a return on investment in the system. This expertise is also critical for defending the selection system, which is generally a high-stakes event: The use of the selection information determines individual careers and the company's ultimate success.

Demonstrating the value of selection requires that we know how well the employees who were assessed eventually perform on the job. For instance, if we measure their productivity (e.g., more products assembled or repaired, customers served, or products sold), we may find that people who score higher on the tests also are more productive. As another example, suppose the assessed individuals are supervisors. Among this group, we may find that the higher the supervisors' assessment scores, the better they supervise their subordinates, who have higher skill levels (perhaps as measured with a **knowledge test**) and lower turnover than the subordinates of people whose assessment results were not as high. Testing experts refer to this value or return on investment as utility, the extent to which a selection system results in selection of better candidates than would have been possible if the system had not been used (Blum & Naylor, 1968). The quality of the candidates may be defined in terms of one or more of the following (Cascio, 1991):

1. The proportion of candidates who are successful on the job

2. The average numeric value of an outcome of interest (such as number of products sold or customers served)

3. The dollar amount of benefit resulting to the organization (such as the annual increase in revenue)

If a selection system produces a higher proportion of successful candidates (e.g., a 10% increase in the number of new financial advisors who, once hired, can pass a government-mandated licensure exam), then that system has clear value to the company. The same can be said of a selection system that results in an increase in some **performance criterion** (e.g., cable service technicians who are able to complete an average of 20% more installations per day as a result of testing). And the same can be said for a benefit that can be measured in dollars (e.g., for every 10 points higher a salesperson scored on a sales skill assessment, annual sales increased by $1,000).

There are many approaches to estimate utility. Apart from an anecdotal approach (Does it seem like more people are successful on the job now?), perhaps one of the simplest approaches is to conduct pre- or postcomparisons of measurable performance to see if the selection system has coincided with a change in performance. As a more precise alternative, industrial/organizational psychologists frequently use a utility formula that takes several factors into account: the **selection ratio**; the **validity coefficient**, expressed as the correlation between assessment scores and criteria (outcomes); and information about the dollar value of performance. The utility formula and related concepts are described here in some detail.

The selection ratio is the number of candidates who, based on the assessment, are chosen for the job, divided by the number of candidates who are assessed. The validity coefficient is a statistical correlation that indicates the correspondence between test scores and job performance or some other important work outcomes. When validity is high, there is a close correspondence between assessment performance and work results. In general, a high-validity, low-selection-ratio system produces the greatest benefit of selection but also incurs the highest cost of selection, all else being the same. When the selection ratio is low, the bar is set high on the assessment, and more rarified, higher-performing candidates will be chosen. (This generalization works as long as the selection ratio is not so high or so low that nearly everyone is hired or no one is hired, respectively; in those cases, the assessment has little value as a decision-making tool.) Information about the dollar value of job performance that is used is described below. The value can be obtained from job experts at the organization. Alternatively, published research may be used to estimate this value, and in many cases, the published value is used for utility estimates.

The result of the utility calculation is the dollar value of the selection system per individual, or group of individuals, hired. (Note that here utility refers to the dollar benefit of selection, without consideration of the cost. Certainly, it is important to compare this benefit with its corresponding cost to make good business decisions about selection systems.) The formula for utility is $?U = r_{xy} * SD_y * N * ?/?$, and the elements of the calculation are as follows:

1. $?U$ is the utility or annual change in the dollar value of productivity. Items 2 through 5 will be multiplied to calculate this number.

2. r_{xy} is the validity coefficient of the assessment, quantified as a correlation that falls between −1 and +1 and notated as a correlation between x (the assessment score) and y (the performance criterion score). Positive values indicate that the assessment (also called the predictor) and the criterion (work outcome) increase together; for instance, looking at the range of candidate data, as ability test scores increase, so might evaluations of ability to learn on the job. Negative values indicate that as one increases, the other decreases. For instance, as scores on an assessment of conscientiousness and work ethic increase, the frequency of absence and tardiness might decrease.

3. SD_y is the standard deviation (SD) of performance (y), that is, the difference, in dollar terms, between an average and a superior performer, which on a normal curve would be estimated as a 1 standard deviation difference. Estimated at 40% of salary based on

published research across the spectrum of jobs in the U.S. economy, this value has consistently been shown to approximate the difference in the value of productivity between average and above-average employees (Hunter & Schmidt, 1982).

4. N is the number of employees hired.

5. $?/?$ refers to the test score of employees who are selected and is expressed in a statistically standardized form (the standard deviation units in this value and the standard deviation of performance in Item 3 cancel out, leaving a dollar value for the utility estimate).

For example, suppose an employer tests 2,500 clerical job candidates on an assessment with a validity of 0.43 and hires the top 1,000 scorers at an annual salary of $20,000. Therefore, $r_{xy} = 0.43$. The standard deviation of job performance (SD_y; 40% of salary) is estimated to be $8,000. One thousand employees are hired ($N = 1,000$). The selection ratio is 40% (4 out of 10 qualify); for this ratio, $?/?$ can be determined from statistical tables of the normal curve; this value is 0.64. Therefore, $?U = (0.43)$ * (8000) * (1000) * $(0.64) = \$2,201,600$, meaning that the average increase in utility per person hired is $2,202 per year. If all 1,000 employees were to stay 3 years, we would estimate the utility over that period at approximately $6.6 million. Supposing that the testing program expenses were $300,000 per year, the return on investment for a 3-year period would still be about $5.7 million. This example serves to illustrate a method of estimating utility and also shows that when many people are hired, the total value of the assessment quickly yields high numbers. While organizational stakeholders occasionally are skeptical because of the extremely high utility values that are possible, the principles behind the numbers are sound.

After reading this section, it is reasonable to conclude that there are a variety of technical concepts related to selection and assessment with which HRIS experts should familiarize themselves. Our intent has been to provide an overview of these topics and the trends that are currently taking place in organizations, in the testing industry, and in research programs. By familiarizing oneself with this work, the HRIS student will become aware of the major issues he or she is likely to face when implementing database decision-making systems.

Summary of Selection

In summary, this section explained the intersection between the use of technology in the selection process and the use of HRIS in organizations. This highlighted the need for HRIS experts to understand how to use selection-related data in order to provide strategic information to the company and demonstrate the return on the company's investment in assessments. In addition, technology issues surrounding the selection process were addressed. Measurement properties of paper-and-pencil assessments and their computer version were discussed. Assessments that do not include ability are of little concern for researchers since giving the test on paper will not result in a different measure from a computerized test. However, there is clear evidence that the mode of administration (paper vs. computerized) matters for ability tests that are speeded. The more speeded a test is, the more likely that there will be differences between the paper and computer test results. A second issue focused on is the trade-off between fidelity and bandwidth. Technology has enabled organizations to create work sample simulations that represent the job with high fidelity. However, if the company then wants to use the simulation for a different business unit or job, the details that made the simulation highly appropriate in the first setting may interfere with its use in the other setting. In general, HRIS managers should keep in mind that, depending on the effort and expense one is willing to expend on assessment development and installation, lower-fidelity simulations and/or combinations of other types of assessments might be preferable. The final issues dealt with unproctored testing, which can be convenient to both the applicant and the organization, but this gives way to a floodgate of concerns such as candidate identity, test security and cheating, and fair access to testing for minorities. The chapter further examined the role that HRIS experts have to play in combating these issues through the use of technology and the decision to develop and use an HRIS.

DISCUSSION QUESTIONS

1. What recruiting objectives are being met through the use of online recruitment?

2. What are some of the advantages and disadvantages of using online recruitment?

3. Should organizations rely solely on recruiting through the Internet? Why or why not?

4. What are some of the technological issues that arise through the use of technology in the function of selection?

5. Describe how the use of technology in the selection process is adding value to organizations.

CASE STUDY

The case from Chapter 10 will be used here, since recruitment and selection are the next step in the operationalization of a talent management strategy. The background for this chapter case is the case material from Chapter 10; at the end of this background material, more details relevant to the recruitment and selection of new employees will be presented.

Rudiger is sitting at his desk on the seventh floor corner office in The City, London, reflecting on life. At 43, he is at the top of his game. He has everything he could wish for—a lovely partner, a 4-year-old in a private nursery, a new executive house in the suburbs, a holiday home in southern Italy, and a remuneration package that is the envy of his peers and beyond anything his German immigrant parents could have imagined. But it hasn't been easy, oh no! Hard work, long hours, geographical moves every 2 or 3 years, and sacrifices in terms of his personal life.

But now he has a problem. Rudiger has just been appointed Global Head of People and Talent, responsible for the future of 35,000 people worldwide, the bulk of whom are based in the United States of America, the United Kingdom, and Southern Europe, with manufacturing likely to relocate to China in the next 2 years In his previous role, his responsibilities covered the United Kingdom and Northern Europe, with operational oversight for 11,000 people. An initial consideration of his remit has identified a number of people issues for the next 5 years: recruiting and retaining particular specialist and skilled personnel; some of the brightest and most experienced midlevel management leaving; an aging senior directorship looking toward early retirement. But the main problem is that although he knows he has a problem, he doesn't have enough detailed information to know the scale of the problem.

18 months later . . .

Once again, Rudiger is sitting at his desk on the seventh floor of his offices in central London reflecting on life. The move from Barcelona to England had gone smoothly, with the last crate arriving only 2 months later than the rest. He is still working hard, but the hours are slightly better since the introduction of the work-life balance policy last year, and his family has settled down well in the idyllic English countryside.

As the Global Head of People and Talent, he still has problems though—just different ones. The talent strategy "Our People—Our Talent—Our Future," presented to the board in his third month as the Talent Management Project, identified the need for robust HRP information and analyses that required a new version of HRP software. It is in its early stages, but the intensive data cleansing and updating activity have been straightforward so far. More of a concern are the metrics responsible for producing the information needed to develop far-reaching HRP policies and practices for the future. The metrics are relatively easy to construct, but it is proving tricky to find the right "bundles" of predictive metrics—this is holding up progress with the analysis application package. In addition, there have been cost overruns in the implementation of the HRP software, and some senior managers are wondering if the new software should be abandoned.

At least 3 of the 12 board members will retire in the next 2 years, and they are looking to groom their successors. At least one will have to be hired from outside the organization, and HR is not sure what the CEO wants for this position. In addition, employee turnover and an aggressive growth strategy mean hiring new employees as well as training and transferring current employees. The work that is involved in defining competencies skills, knowledge, and abilities (SKAs) at skill levels within jobs is progressing well, with hard-won support from the unions. However, job descriptions that can be found are at least 3 to 5 years old, and some jobs have no descriptions. The new apprenticeship scheme is about to be launched, and the international graduate student package and development program have been completely revised. Overall, things are progressing reasonably well, but there is still much to be done.

Case Supplemental Material

On the basis of your analyses and answers completed in Chapter 10, assume that Rudiger has completed an acceptable HRP program and his staff have completed current and accurate job descriptions for all positions in the Talent Management Project. These job descriptions all contain the specific duties, tasks, and responsibilities as well as the SKAs needed for each job.

Rudiger's next task is to recruit and select individuals for jobs. He wants to use the new HRIS software applications that the company has purchased and implemented for recruiting and selecting new employees. Fortunately, he can get assistance on this task from the IT department, which has built and maintains the company's Web site. In addition, he has several staff members with doctorates in industrial/organizational psychology who can work with the IT professionals to develop recruitment and selection materials. However, Rudiger must provide the guidelines for the selection and recruitment of individuals who can fit into the Talent Management Project.

Case Study Questions

1. What guidelines would you establish as part of Rudiger's plan that emphasized the use of the Internet via a company's Web site to communicate the recruiting objectives of the talent management project?
   a. What are the potential advantages and disadvantages of online recruitment to communicate recruiting objectives?

2. What guidelines would you establish for the use of an HRIS for selection and assessment of potential employees?
   a. What selection and assessment tools could be used on the Internet, and which ones would need to be done on a face-to-face basis?
   b. What are the technological issues that affect selection via the Internet and the solutions that have been suggested?
   c. What guidelines would you develop to make sure that a utility analysis was done for all HRIS selection applications?

REFERENCES

Baker, H. G. (1985). The unwritten contract: Job perceptions. *Personnel Journal, 64,* 36–41.

Barber, A. E., & Roehling, M. V. (1993). Job postings and the decision to interview: A verbal protocol analysis. *Journal of Applied Psychology, 78,* 845–856.

Becker, B., & Gerhart, B. (1996). The impact of human resource management on organizational performance: Progress and prospects. *Academy of Management Journal, 39,* 779–801.

Blum, M. L., & Naylor, J. C. (1968). *Industrial psychology: Its theoretical and social foundations* (Rev. ed.). New York: Harper & Row.

Braddy, P. W., Thompson, L. F., Wuensch, K. L., & Grossnickle, W. F. (2003). Internet recruiting: The effects of Web page design features. *Social Science Computer Review, 21,* 374–385.

Breaugh, J. A., & Starke, M. (2000). Research on employee recruitment: So many studies, so many remaining questions. *Journal of Management, 26,* 405–434.

Cable, D. M., Aiman-Smith, L., Mulvey, P. W., & Edwards, J. R. (2000). The sources of accuracy and job applicants' beliefs about organizational culture. *Academy of Management Journal, 43,* 1076–1085.

Cable, D. M., & Graham, M. E. (2000). The determinants of job seekers' reputation perceptions. *Journal of Organizational Behavior, 21,* 929–947.

Cable, D. M., & Judge, T. A. (1996). Person-organization fit, job choice decisions, and organizational entry. *Organizational Behavior and Human Decision Processes, 67,* 294–311.

Cappelli, P. (2001). Making the most of on-line recruiting. *Harvard Business Review, 79,* 139–146.

Cardy, R. L., & Miller, J. S. (2003). Technology: Implications for HRM. In D. Stone (Ed.), *Advances in human performance and cognitive engineering research* (pp. 99–118). Greenwich, CT: JAI Press.

Carless, S. A. (2005). Person-job fit versus person-organization fit as predictors of organizational attraction and job acceptance intentions: A longitudinal study. *Journal of Occupational and Organizational Psychology, 78,* 411–429.

Cascio, W. F. (1991). *Applied psychology in personnel management* (4th ed.). Englewood Cliffs, NJ: Prentice Hall.

Cascio, W. F. (1998). *Managing human resources: Productivity, quality of work life, and profits* (5th ed.). New York: Irwin/McGraw-Hill.

Cascio, W. F. (2006). *Managing human resources: Productivity, quality of work life, and profits* (7th ed.). New York: Irwin/McGraw-Hill.

Chapman, D. S., & Webster, J. (2003). The use of technologies in the recruiting, screening, and selection processes for job candidates. *International Journal of Selection and Assessment, 11,* 113–120.

Cober, R. T., Brown, D. J., Blumental, A. J., Doverspike, D., & Levy, P. (2000). The quest for the qualified job surfer: It's time the public sector catches the wave. *Public Personnel Management, 29*(4), 479–494.

Cober, R. T., Brown, D. J., Keeping, L. M., & Levy, P. E. (2004). Recruitment on the Net: How do organizational Web site characteristics influence applicant attraction? *Journal of Management, 30,* 623–646.

Cober, R. T., Brown, D. J., Levy, P. E., Keeping, L. M., & Cober, A. B. (2003). Organizational Websites: Website content and style as determinants of organizational attraction. *International Journal of Selection and Assessment, 11,* 158–169.

Collins, J. C. (2001). *Good to great: Why some companies make the leap... and others don't.* New York: HarperCollins.

Dineen, B. R., Ash, S. R., & Noe, R. A. (2002). A web of applicant attraction: Person-organization fit in the context of Web-based recruitment. *Journal of Applied Psychology, 87,* 723–734.

Galanaki, E. (2002). The decision to recruit online: A descriptive study. *Career Development International, 7,* 243–251.

Guion, R. M. (1998). *Assessment, measurement, and prediction for personnel decisions.* Mahway, NJ: Lawrence Erlbaum.

Heneman, H. G., & Judge, T. A. (2006). *Staffing organizations* (5th ed.). Boston: McGraw-Hill.

Hogler, R., Henle, C., & Beamus, C. (2001). *Internet recruiting and employment discrimination: A legal perspective.* Retrieved February 25, 2001, from www.biz.colostate.edu/ faculty/rayh/ netantrev.html

Hunter, J. E., & Schmidt, F. L. (1982). *Personnel selection programs based on cumulative knowledge.* Presentation at the PTC fall conference on validity generalization, Newport Beach, CA.

Jackson, L. A., Ervin, K. S., Gardner, P. D., & Schmitt, N. (2001). Gender and the Internet: Women communicating and men searching. *Sex Roles, 44,* 363–379.

Judge, T. A., & Cable, D. M. (1997). Applicant personality, organizational culture, and organizational attraction. *Personnel Psychology, 50,* 359–394.

Karat, J. (1997). Evolving the scope of user-centered design. *Communications of the ACM, 40,* 33–38.

Kehoe, J. F., Dickter, D. N., Russell, D. P., & Sacco, J. M. (2005). e-Selection. In H. G. Guental & D. L. Stone (Eds.), *The brave new world of eHR* (pp. 54–103). San Francisco: Jossey-Bass.

Kristof-Brown, A. L., Zimmerman, R. D., & Johnson, E. C. (2005). Consequences of individuals' fit at work: A meta-analysis of person-job, person-organization, person-group, and person-supervisor fit. *Personnel Psychology, 58,* 281–342.

Kuhn, P., & Skuterud, M. (2000). Job search methods: Internet versus traditional. *Monthly Labor Review, 123,* 3–11.

Marakas, G., Yi, M., & Johnson, R. (1998). The multilevel and multifaceted character of computer self-efficacy: Toward clarification of the construct and an integrative framework for research. *Information Systems Research, 9,* 126–163.

McCourt-Mooney, M. (2000). Internet briefing: Recruitment and selection—R&D using the Internet—Part III. *Journal of Managerial Psychology, 15,* 737–740.

McManus, M. A., & Ferguson, M. W. (2003). Biodata, personality, and demographic differences of recruits from three sources. *International Journal of Selection and Assessment, 11,* 175–183.

Mead, A., & Drasgow, F. (1993). Equivalence of computerized and paper-and-pencil cognitive ability tests: A meta-analysis. *Psychological Bulletin, 114,* 449–458.

Mohamed, A. A., Orife, J. N., & Wibowo, K. (2002). The legality of key word search as a personnel selection tool. *Employee Relations, 24,* 516–522.

Morrison, E. W., & Robinson, S. L. (1997). When employees feel betrayed: A model of how psychological contract violation develops. *Academy of Management Review, 22,* 226–256.

Naglieri, J. A., Drasgow, F., Schmit, M., Handler, L., Prifitera, A., Margolis, A., et al. (2004). Psychological testing on the Internet. *American Psychologist, 59,* 150–162.

Nielsen, J. (2000). *Designing Web usability.* Indianapolis, IN: New Riders.

PewInternet. (2006). *Internet activities.* Retrieved February 4, 2007, from www.pewinternet.org/trends/Internet_Activities_1.11.07.htm

Potosky, D., & Bobko, P. (2004). Selection testing via the Internet: Practical considerations and exploratory empirical findings. *Personnel Psychology, 57,* 1003–1004.

Reed, K., Doty, H. D., & May, D. R. (2005). The impact of aging on self-efficacy and computer skill acquisition. *Journal of Managerial Issues, 17,* 212–228.

Reed Company. (2003). *The Reed Recruitment Index report.* Retrieved June 1, 2007, from www.onrec.com/content2/news.asp?ID=1981

Rousseau, D. M. (1990). New hire perceptions of their own and their employer's obligations: A study of psychological contracts. *Journal of Organizational Behavior, 11,* 389–400.

Rozelle, A. L., & Landis, R. S. (2002). An examination of the relationship between use of the Internet as a recruitment source and student attitudes. *Computers in Human Behavior, 18,* 593–604.

Schmidt, F. L., & Hunter, J. E. (1998). The validity and utility of selection methods in personnel psychology: Practical and theoretical implications of 85 years of research findings. *Psychological Bulletin, 124,* 262–274.

Schneider, B., Goldstein, H. W., & Smith, D. B. (1995). The ASA framework: An update. *Personnel Psychology, 48,* 747–773.

Seminerio, M. (2001). E-recruiting takes next step. *eWeek, 18,*16, 51–54.

Shaffer, D. J., & Schmidt, R. A. (2006). Personality testing in employment. In *Society of Human Resources Management legal report.* Retrieved February 21, 2007, from www.shrm.org/hrresources/lrpt_published/CMS_000991.asp

SHRM. (2004). *Merging tests with applicant tracking systems.* Retrieved June 12, 2008, from www.shrm.org/ema/library_published/nonIC/CMS_006199.asp

Society for Industrial and Organizational Psychology. (2003). *Principles for the validation and use of personnel selection procedures* (4th ed.). Bowling Green, OH: Author.

Stone, D. L., Lukaszewski, K. M., & Isenhour, L. C. (2005). e-Recruiting: Online strategies for attracting talent. In H. G. Gueutal & D. L. Stone (Eds.), *The brave new world of eHR* (pp. 22–53). San Francisco: Jossey-Bass.

Stone, D. L., Stone-Romero, E. F., & Lukaszewski, K. (2003). The functional and dysfunctional consequences of human resource information technology for organizations and their employees. In D. L. Stone (Ed.), *Advances in human performance and cognitive engineering research* (pp. 37–68). Greenwich, CT: JAI Press.

Taleo. (2006). *Career site recruiting in the FTSE 100 companies: A missed opportunity.* Retrieved February 4, 2007, from www.taleo.com/whitepapers38

Tippins, N. T., Beaty, J., Drasgow, F., Gibson, W. M., Pearlman, K., Segall, D. O., et al. (2006). Unproctored Internet testing in employment settings. *Personnel Psychology, 59,* 189–225.

Ulrich, D. (2001). From e-business to e-HR. *International Human Resources Information Management Journal, 5*, 90–97.

U.S. Department of Labor. (1999). *Testing and assessment: An employer's guide to good practices.* Washington, DC: Author.

U.S. Equal Employment Opportunity Commission, U.S. Civil Service Commission, U.S. Department of Labor, & U.S. Department of Justice. (1978). Uniform guidelines on employee selection procedures. *Federal Register, 43*(166), 38295–38309.

Wanous, J. P. (1992). *Organizational entry.* Reading, MA: Addison-Wesley.

Williamson, I. O., Lepak, D. P., & King, J. (2003). The effect of company recruitment Web site orientation on individuals' perceptions of organizational attractiveness. *Journal of Vocational Behavior, 63,* 242–263.

Wright, P. M., & Snell, S. A. (1998). Toward a unifying framework for exploring fit and flexibility in strategic human resource management. *Academy of Management Review, 23,* 756–772.

Zusman, R. R., & Landis, R. S. (2002). Applicant preferences for Web-based versus traditional job postings. *Computers in Human Behavior, 18,* 285–296.

12

Training and Development

Issues and HRIS Applications

Ralf Burbach

EDITORS' NOTE

Training is one of the major programs offered by HR departments and is an important aspect of the organizations' talent management program. Organizations use training not only for both skill and knowledge learning but also to develop employees for future positions. In addition, training plays an important role in the motivation of employees. It shows that the organization is concerned about the development of the employees and would like to retain them. However, training generally captures the largest portion of the HR department budget. Due to the heavy costs, the application of an HRIS to save money is very important. In the applications section of this chapter, you will learn how training can be made to be cost-effective through an HRIS that serves both as a more efficient transaction processor and as an aid to managerial decision making.

CHAPTER OBJECTIVES

After completing this chapter, you should be able to

- ♦ Discuss how training can be used as a source of competitive advantage
- ♦ Differentiate between training and development (T&D)

- ◆ Understand how T&D affects both learning and motivation
- ◆ Explain the steps in a systems model of training
- ◆ Understand the essential features of the culture of a learning organization
- ◆ Explain the factors that influence transfer of training
- ◆ Understand both the costs and the benefits metrics associated with training
- ◆ Discuss the critical importance of the evaluation of training
- ◆ Understand MIS, HRMS, and DSS (see Chapter 1) training applications
- ◆ Explain the advantages and disadvantages of Web-based learning
- ◆ Develop a practical application, using EXCEL, in the evaluation of training

VIGNETTE

Mid-Western Mighty Markets (Triple M)[1] is one of the largest supermarket chains in five states with 275 store locations. The corporate director of training, June Grady, was hired externally and has been on the job for 2 months. Thus, she has inherited the job with little information about what had been happening in the past relative to training and the use of any computer-based technology to manage the training activities and programs. She has begun a careful examination of the training activities, particularly supervisory training since that is where the next higher-level managers will be identified. The annual budget for train-ing has been $2.2 million, of which $1.1 million is devoted to supervisory training.

Supervisory training is 1 week in length and occurs on a monthly basis in each state at a central location. It is focused on training assistant department managers (e.g., pro-duce, meat, and grocery) in the supervisory skills needed to be a department manager. Based on department managers' recommendations, assistant managers are sent to train-ing at a central location in their state. However, all assistant managers across the states have the same training content and training activities. At the conclusion of the training, all trainees complete an evaluation of the training program based on their experiences.

The company has an HRIS software application developed by PeopleSoft and imple-mented 3 years ago. It is used for the management of all the training in the company. There are a number of reports that can be generated from the software, including atten-dance by states, stores, and departments within the stores. This information is useful for the Director, June, to make sure that training is occurring evenly across departments, stores, and states. Other reports are also available that can be sent to department and store managers as well as regional managers of Triple M.

June has been examining all these reports available from the HRIS software to deter-mine if anything is missing. During her examination, she notices that no one has been accessing the reports summarizing the trainees' evaluations of the training programs. On further examination, she finds that some store managers receive these summary reports but rarely use them. In addition, she discovers that there is an additional report that has been designed to be generated by the software. This report is based on evaluation data that are to be collected from department managers 3 months after the trainees have returned to their jobs. This report appears quite important since it asks the department managers to rate the trainees' job performance after they have completed training to determine any effects of the training.

June sees a serious problem with this lack of training evaluation data since the trainees' posttraining evaluations are not being analyzed by the available software and, more important, the department managers' ratings of job performance are not being completed. Therefore, even though the company owns sophisticated (and costly) software, it is not being used to evaluate the supervisory training programs. More seriously, June has no idea if the $1.1 million being spent on supervisory training has had any effect on the job performance of the trainees.

Introduction

The nature of work and the structure of organizations are rapidly changing. Internationalization, globalization, and changing customer expectations of service and quality standards require firms to perpetually improve and transform themselves to remain competitive. Emerging concepts such as the global marketplace, knowledge economy, knowledge worker, information age, and digital revolution underscore that an organization's ability to survive in a constantly changing business environment is founded on its capacity to generate new knowledge, to share knowledge, and to continuously innovate (Nonaka & Takeuchi, 1995; Porter, 1990; Senge, 1990). In the new global economy, knowledge is now the new lever for success, since knowledge potentially adds more value than the traditional factors of production—capital, raw material, and labor (Harrison, 2005). This new knowledge-based economy is

> directly based on production, distribution and use of knowledge and information. Knowledge is now recognised as the driver of productivity and economic growth, leading to a new focus on the role of information, technology, and learning in economic performance. . . . Employment in the knowledge-based economy is characterized by increasing demand for more highly skilled workers. . . . The knowledge-based economy is characterized by the need for continuous learning of both codified information and the competencies to use this information. (Organisation for Economic Co-operation and Development [OECD], 1996, pp. 3, 7, 13)

Knowledge is created by a firm's knowledge assets. That is, its **human capital**[2] (see OECD, 2001, p. 18), which has long been recognized as one of the key sources of competitive advantage (Grant, 1996; Prahalad & Hamel, 1990; Wright, Dunford, & Snell, 2001). Hence, the learning, training, and development (LT&D) of employees has now taken center stage in today's organizations to ensure long-term competitiveness, excellence, quality, flexibility, and adaptability. Changing work practices and new services and products necessitate new knowledge, competences, and skills. However, a range of other reasons exist as to why organizations train and develop their workforce—for instance, to enable employees to cope with their daily workload. T&D also alleviates possible future skill shortages. High-commitment organizations train and develop their employees to foster employee motivation and satisfaction (Pfeffer, 1996, 1998). In a time where job security is diminishing and employability is of increasing value, employees place much greater emphasis on career prospects and career development in their choice of employer. This is of particular relevance for specialist knowledge workers who are in short supply in a tight labor market. The strategic importance of individual and organizational learning and development is mirrored in the continued interest in the concepts of the learning organization and organizational learning. These terms are often used interchangeably. However, the learning organization is the ultimate state of organizational learning at which the organization is able to facilitate the learning of all its members and can continuously transform itself (Argyris & Schon, 1978; Pedler, Burgoyne, & Boydell, 1991). "It is the potential of organizational learning to enable organizations to reinvent themselves in order to compete in the changing and increasingly uncertain and competitive environment that is making it such an attractive proposition for many managers" (Burnes, 2004, p. 129). Yet it has been argued that few firms, if any, have actually achieved this aim. Nonetheless, the notion of the learning organization illustrates that organizational learning is inextricably linked to individual LT&D. It is also closely linked to the notion of lifelong learning and continuous professional development. Employees at all levels of the organization will have to demonstrate their commitment to these, especially when they seek a new employer, pay increases, or promotions. T&D is thus closely allied with the **performance management** and talent management process. The majority of large organizations use human resource information systems (HRIS) to collect, store, and analyze T&D information. This information is generally contained in specialist talent management modules, T&D modules, and/or **learning management systems (LMS)** to reflect the strategic importance of LT&D in the organization. This chapter examines the strategic implications of T&D, before it expounds the systems model of T&D. This section will look in detail at the four stages of the systems model—identifying T&D needs, designing T&D solutions, implementing T&D, and evaluating T&D. Then, training metrics and benefit analysis will be discussed. The next section develops some HRIS applications in training followed by some implementation issues. The chapter concludes with a summary of the key issues.

Training and Development: Strategic Implications and Learning Organizations

The introduction to this chapter has already alluded to a number of key terms associated with T&D. Some of the terms, such as *learning, training, development,* and *education,* are frequently used in combination and sometimes even, incorrectly, as substitutes. To comprehend the processes involved in LT&D, the key concepts ought to be differentiated. *Education* is aimed at developing, usually as part of a formal program of study, general knowledge, understanding, and moral values. *Training* refers to the planned acquisition of knowledge, skills, and abilities (KSA) to carry out a specific task or job in a vocational setting. The purpose of training interventions is to attain a positive change in performance. *Development* is a continuous process of systematic advancement, of "becoming increasingly more complex, more elaborate and differentiated, by virtue of learning and maturation" (Collin, 2007, p. 266). Development in an organizational context ensures that employees possess the KSA required to fulfill future roles in the organization. Hence, development may be conceived as a lever for career development, succession planning, performance management, and talent management (Gunnigle, Heraty, & Morley, 2002). Training focuses on immediate job performance, whereas development centers on long-term continuous changes of an individual's potential. Learning is defined as the process of assimilating new knowledge and skills in consequence of experience or practice that will bring about relatively permanent changes in behavior. Effective learning necessitates a capacity to integrate new knowledge with existing knowledge (Learning, 2007). Learning at an individual or organizational level is ineluctably linked to the creation and management of knowledge. Learning is the basis for any T&D activity. The outcomes of learning include skills, competencies, know-how or tacit knowledge, and higher-level cognitive and other skills (Collin, 2007). *Skills* are directly related to performance and the ability to carry out a task. It has been argued that new organizational realities require higher levels of cognitive skills. Bloom's taxonomy of learning, for example, identifies six increasingly higher levels of thinking—knowledge, comprehension, application, analysis, synthesis, and evaluation (Bloom, Engelhart, Furst, Hill, & Krathwohl, 1956). *Competencies* consist of KSA and the underlying characteristics of a person that allow the jobholder to perform a task effectively. The *knowledge* of employees is a tacit commodity, an intangible asset. It is associated with an understanding of and a constructive application of information (Grant, 1996). In a knowledge-based economy, organizations must become knowledge-productive organizations and its employees, knowledge workers and knowledge assets. Knowledge-intensive organizations are those organizations that heavily depend on knowledge creation and knowledge sharing, such as firms with a significant research and development focus or consultancy firms. *Knowledge management* (KM) essentially consists of five separate activities, which are the acquisition, documentation, transfer, creation, and application of knowledge (Yahya & Goh, 2002). Whereas knowledge is generated by individuals, organizational knowledge and learning are the result of the combined learning of everybody in the organization and the acquisition of knowledgeable individuals (Grant, 1996). Hence, a firm environment and organizational culture that encourage and reward learning are beneficial to effective KM and to the transformation into a knowledge organization (Mayo, 1998; Soliman & Spooner, 2000). Sharing, codifying, storing, and replicating of knowledge within the organization is greatly facilitated by information and communication technology (ICT). Consequently, KM focuses on the interaction of human beings and ICT and the subsequent creation of knowledge and, in addition, on the alignment of technology with people systems within a firm. The HR department plays a vital role in determining where, among employees, tacit knowledge exists, what type of knowledge is present, and whether and to what degree this knowledge is conducive to attaining present and future organizational goals (Soliman & Spooner, 2000). Should the HR function detect a gap between existing knowledge and the knowledge necessary to pursue strategic objectives, it can initiate procedures to remedy this shortfall through recruitment, socialization, and T&D initiatives. It is evident that the concepts of KM and organizational learning are closely related. Organizational learning is by no means a new concept. Argyris and Schon (1978) suggested a three-level model of organizational learning, consisting of single-loop, double-loop, and triple-loop learning. Single-loop learning is adaptive and focuses on the detection of deviations in performance from established organizational norms, practices, policies, and procedures. Double-loop learning questions the suitability of norms, practices, policies, and procedures that define performance standards. Triple-loop learning challenges the rationale of the organization with the aim of completely transforming it (Burnes, 2004). One of the most influential proponents of the learning organization is Peter Senge. In his book *The Fifth Discipline*, he puts forward five interrelated disciplines that an organization should cultivate among its employees to engender learning and success (Senge, 1990):

1. *Personal mastery:* individual growth and learning

2. *Mental models:* deep-rooted assumptions that affect the way in which employees perceive people, situations, and organizations

3. *Shared visions:* a shared view of the organization's future

4. *Team learning:* a shift from individual learning to collective learning

5. *Systems thinking:* or the Fifth Discipline, which connects the previous disciplines (Burnes, 2004)

Other writers promote generic organizational characteristics that stimulate organizational learning. Cummings and Worley (2001), for instance, advocate a flat teamwork-based organizational structure to facilitate networking; the use of information systems to collect, process, and share information; human resource practices such as appraisals and rewards that reinforce learning; effective leadership that is supportive of organizational learning; and an organizational culture that encourages openness, creativity, and experimentation among members of the firm. A learning culture is one of the key levers for organizational learning, training, and development. Transfer of training is far more likely to occur in an environment where the basic assumptions, shared values, norms, and artifacts of an organization espouse successful LT&D, where employees are encouraged to create, process, and share information and knowledge (Cummings & Worley, 2001). A T&D intervention can only be considered successful if transfer of training has occurred and a permanent change in behavior has taken place.

Systems Model of Training and Development

The approaches to T&D adopted by organizations are quite possibly as diverse as the organizations that employ them. The literature is teeming with different, sometimes competing, models, which mirror the approaches to T&D found in practice. One of the most frequently cited models is the systems or systematic approach. This formal or planned approach to workforce T&D consists of four interrelated and connected steps, which are illustrated in Figure 12.1. The steps are arranged as a cycle to highlight the cyclical and continuous nature of the process in much the same way as employee development is an ongoing activity. Thus, the model is applicable to both training and development. Its simplicity and clear structure make it ideally suited in the context of HRIS applications in this area. In addition, the model provides a rational foundation for the allocation of resources throughout the T&D process. However, the systematic

❖ **Figure 12.1**   The Systems Model of Training and Development

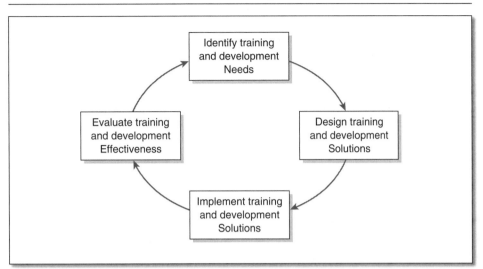

model has also received some criticism *because* of its simplicity, because of the fact that it is a closed system, and because it does not take account of individual differences among the learners. Notwithstanding these criticisms, the model continues to find broad application, for instance, in the development of national training standards and indeed in many IT-based T&D applications that are designed based on the four steps (Stewart, 1999).

Identifying T&D Needs

The first step of the systems model is concerned with the identification of the learning and development needs of organizational members. The training needs analysis (TNA) is the key activity of the systematic approach and essentially serves to identify any discrepancies, the T&D "gap," between existing KSA and those required in the present and in the future. Thus, it ensures the integration of employee T&D activities with the business needs of the firm. Hence, the TNA must assess the validity of initiatives, it ought to assist in prioritizing T&D objectives and initiatives, and it has to be able to determine the actual training needs. Training needs may arise at three distinct levels:

- At an organizational level (current and future employee T&D requirements that an organization has to fulfill in order to attain its strategic long-term objectives)
- At a job level (relevant KSA that are part of specific jobs)
- At a personal level (the competences required) (Boydell, 1983)

Because of the crucial importance and comprehensive nature of the TNA, many organizations employ an HRIS to collect, store, and analyze training needs data, thus ensuring that the resulting information is both timely and accurate. Data sources range from business objectives and statistics, at the organizational level, to job descriptions and output levels, at the job level, to staff appraisals, biographical data, and individual training records, at the personal level. Most HRIS can be configured to gather data from these and other sources. However, a host of specialist T&D software (discussed further on in this chapter) exists that will aid a firm in accomplishing its T&D activities. In the event, however, that the TNA highlights a considerable gap between existing and desired KSA, an organization may decide to recruit staff external to the organization that already possesses the required competencies. In that case, it will be of vital importance that the organization has access to skilled personnel and demographic data, which might provide some indication regarding the skill levels of the wider population and the environment in which the firm operates.

Developing T&D Initiatives

The second stage of the cycle focuses on the development of T&D initiatives, objectives, and methods that should be capable of meeting the three levels of needs identified during the first phase, the TNA. Organizations have a wide array of T&D methods at their disposal, and advances in and access to ICT and mobile technologies will further increase the number of methods and ways of content delivery available. Faced with an apparent overabundance of methods, how should organizations choose the ones most appropriate for their needs? A number of criteria will guide the decision-making process.

The effectiveness of individual learning plans and events ultimately hinges on the design of these T&D interventions. A learning activity can be considered successful if it leads to transfer of learning as well as a noticeable and permanent change in behavior in the trainees. The aim of the HRIS in this context is to compare employee training data with subsequent performance data. Successful learning events must achieve a "best fit" between

- the content of what is to be learnt,
- the media through which content is delivered, and
- the method used to facilitate learning (see Figure 12.2).

With regard to individual learning, it is important to note that every individual has his or her preferred learning style and that these learning styles must be taken into consideration when designing a training event to encourage learning transfer (explained below). Based on Kolb's (1984) learning cycle, which involves a concrete experience, reflective observation, abstract conceptualization, and active experimentation, Honey and Mumford (1992) developed four preferred learning styles—activists, reflectors, theorists, and pragmatists.

In today's highly regulated working environments, it is also essential to attain internal and external consistency. Internal consistency is achieved if learning interventions are mutually supportive of one another and of the business objectives. External consistency is attained if T&D activities are aligned with external regulations (e.g., health and safety legislation), best practice in the industry, and the stipulations and standards of external training award bodies. The conditions for a successful learning event are illustrated in the best-fit learning event model in Figure 12.2.

❖ **Figure 12.2** Best-Fit Learning Event Model

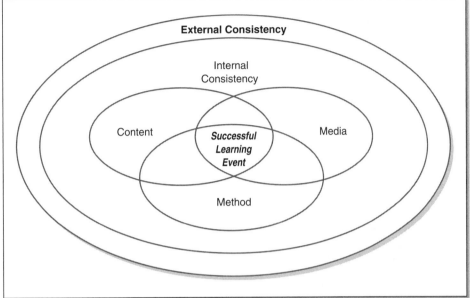

T&D methods essentially fall into two broad categories—on the job and off the job, albeit the emergence of e-learning has somewhat diluted this distinction, as it can be either. On-the-job training usually involves peer observation and can be informal, structured, or unstructured, although successful learning outcomes are more likely to occur in a structured rather than an unstructured environment. Compared with off-the-job training, on-the-job training is relatively inexpensive. While off-the-job methods may provide greater exposure to expert knowledge, they may also be more time-consuming and may not encourage knowledge transfer. Table 12.1 lists a number of examples of T&D methods in each category.

e-Learning

e-Learning (also elearning, Elearning, or eLearning) is an umbrella term and broadly refers to any learning facilitated using electronic means. e-Learning can capitalize on a variety of delivery media depending on the approach taken:

- Printed media (including textbooks but also online text and online magazines and journals)
- Audio (e.g., traditional audiotapes, CDs, MP3s, WAV, and other electronic file formats)
- Video (e.g., traditional videotapes, CD-ROMs, interactive videos, DVDs, video streaming, satellite or cable transmissions)
- Other combined media, including hypermedia, collaborative software, or social networking technology (e.g., Web sites, discussion forums, e-mails, blogs, wikis, myspace, YouTube, Second Life)

❖ Table 12.1   Training Methods

On-the-Job Training Methods	Off-the-Job Training Methods
Observation	Simulation
Mentoring	Role play
Coaching	Case study
Job rotation	Business games
Apprenticeship	External course/workshop
Self-directed learning	Behavior modeling
	Placement

Other technologies used in e-learning encompass computer-aided assessments, animations, simulations, games, and electronic performance support systems (EPSSs). EPSSs are not learning technologies per se. However, they provide an electronic support infrastructure that allows employees to carry out their work. An EPSS would typically include assistants (e.g., Microsoft Office Assistant), wizards, knowledge bases, help, and advice functions.

Some of the media employed in e-learning may be interactive; that is, the learner interacts with the media. A number of e-learning methods to address different training needs are identified in Table 12.2. However, rapid developments in ICT also imply that many methods and approaches have a relatively short shelf life; that is, they quickly become obsolete (e.g., computer-based training). In addition, the distinction between some of these e-learning methods has become blurred, and the terminology can be confusing as terms are often used interchangeably.

The e-learning methods explained in Table 12.2 are arranged according to the extent to which they use the Internet, the degree to which they facilitate interaction between peer learners and instructors, and the degree to which computers are networked or not networked. Therefore, Web-based training shows the highest level of interaction and networking. However, this does not imply that methods that rely on greater student interaction or that allow greater access to external resources are necessarily the better option—the choice of e-learning method will depend on the best fit with the training needs that ought to be addressed (see Figure 12.2).

An emerging issue in online learning is that of digital collaboration. The term *digital collaboration* denotes networking and communication via the Internet. While digital collaboration is of vital importance in the effectiveness of virtual teams in the business world, online collaboration between learners also tends to increase learning and learning transfer. Intranet-based collaborative technologies, such as Groupware (electronic meeting software), provide a company forum for tracking, sharing, and organizing information. Groupware combines e-mail, document management, and electronic bulletin boards and allows users to collaborate on projects and documents simultaneously. The most common Groupware is Lotus Notes (Noe, 2002).

❖ **Table 12.2** e-Learning Methods

e-Learning Methods	Explanation
Computer-based training (CBT) or technology-based training, computer-managed instruction (CMI), computer-aided (assisted) instruction (CAI), computer-based learning (CBL)	Interactive training experience using a stand-alone computer, when no collaboration and access to external resources is necessary; media used include CD-ROM, DVDs, interactive video
Multimedia-based training (MBT)	Training experience that combines text, colors, graphics, audio, and video to engage the learner; MBT can range from a simple graphical presentation of text to a complex flight simulation
Distance learning (or education)	Learner and tutor are in different locations; the approach uses both synchronous and asynchronous communication; the course provider usually provides online support and supplies students with a course pack, including printed and audio visual materials; courses follow a predetermined curriculum and schedule
Open learning (or education)	Learner has complete control over how, what, when, where, and at what pace learning occurs; any type and combination of media may be used
Open distance learning (ODL)	Umbrella term that covers both open and distance learning
Virtual learning environment (VLE) or virtual classroom	Online environment in which learning takes place
Web-based training (WBT) or online learning (or education), Internet-based training (IBT)	Any training and learning that takes place online, that is, via the World Wide Web
Mobile learning	Any T&D that involves mobile technologies. Mobile technologies include personal digital assistants (PDA), cell/mobile phones, MP3 players

Internet-based collaborative technology, or social networking technology (e.g., blogs, wikis, or podcasts), plays an increasingly important role in informal peer-to-peer learning, which is much faster, more flexible, and more responsive than formal modes of training (Frauenheim, 2007). Collaboration and communication in this context may be synchronous or asynchronous. The former refers to "real-time" or live communication using tools such as messenger services or video conferencing. These virtual classrooms operate in much the same way as traditional classrooms would.

However, not all collaboration can occur in real time, especially if learners are geographically dispersed across different time zones. While asynchronous communication

❖ Table 12.3   e-Learning Communication Typology

Synchronous	• Virtual learning environments (VLEs)
	• Instant messaging services
	• Audio and video conferencing
	• Digital chat rooms
	• Shared whiteboard applications
	• Application sharing
Asynchronous	• E-mail
	• Discussion forums/Weblogs
	• Threaded discussions
	• Self-paced learning

still makes use of the Internet, communication is delayed, and learners access the learning spaces at their own convenience. Table 12.3 provides some examples of synchronous and asynchronous methods.

Although it is important to make a distinction between different forms of collaboration, most e-learning combines various types of communication, collaboration, e-learning methods, and, in some cases, more traditional approaches to maximize learning transfer. Testing and assessment of e-learning may rely on traditional paper-based methods, electronic submission of files, and/or interactive assignments (including online discussions). The combination of e-learning methods with traditional face-to-face methods is referred to as **blended learning**. According to industry reports, the use of blended learning in workplace training is rapidly increasing (Rossett & Frazee, 2006; Shaw & Igneri, 2006; Sparrow, 2004). This hybrid approach promises to combine the advantages of both traditional and e-learning approaches to training. For instance, one of the key issues in workplace training is the ability to apply new skills to the actual job. However, most online training does not provide for the application of new knowledge and skills, which is one of the key elements of Kolb's learning cycle. Blended learning, thus, allows the learner to apply new skills in a real-life situation, either in a classroom or on the job.

The development of e-learning programs and resources requires significant investments in time and money. However, the volatile nature of the global marketplace and the rapidly changing information needs of firms necessitate a different approach to e-learning. While standard e-learning solutions can take months to develop, **rapid e-learning (REL)** solutions may be developed in weeks, days, or even hours depending on the complexity of materials to be created. Essentially, REL allows companies to produce a large amount of content, using limited resources, in a short time interval, which can be delivered in real time to a large number of people. Therefore, it is not surprising that industry observers predict significant increases in the REL market in the years to come (Archibald, 2005; van Dam, 2002). REL has a number of key characteristics:

- It has a short development time.
- Subject matter experts (SMEs) act as the key source of content development.
- It can be created using standard presentation software.
- It allows for easy assessment and tracking of training.
- Auxiliary multimedia tools (including flash applications) can be used to enhance training experience.
- Training units can be undertaken in minutes rather than hours.
- It can be synchronous as well as asynchronous (Bersin, 2005).

REL should be ideally used to deal with

- urgent and training needs,
- short shelf life of training,
- critical information needs and standard information broadcasts,
- training that is purely informational in nature,
- training that does not require mastery,
- prerequisite and introductory training, and
- training updates

but finds limited application for training in new skills and competencies (Bersin, 2005).

Although e-learning methods diverge on a number of levels, for instance, the level of interaction between learners, a range of advantages and disadvantages of e-learning in general to the learner and to the organization can be identified. These are shown in Table 12.4. The key advantage of e-learning is flexibility; that is, it affords learners with the choice over what, when, where, and how much is learnt. The key disadvantages center on the lack of human contact and technological issues.

Implementing T&D

The third stage of the systems model of T&D involves the implementation of training. Although this stage is depicted as a separate phase of the training process, it is closely linked with the preceding stage, the design stage. Indeed, many book chapters on T&D consider both stages in unison. The reason for this is that the design of a training solution ultimately determines its implementation, as any issues and factors that could arise during the implementation phase should be anticipated at the design stage (Stewart, 1999). For instance, if an organization wanted to roll out e-learning to its entire workforce via the company intranet, the firm would have to ensure that every employee had access to the intranet. To ensure that the implementation phase runs smoothly, organizations ought to formulate an implementation plan that should specify

- the resources required,
- how the training should be carried out,
- who should facilitate the training, and
- the period within which the training should occur.

❖ Table 12.4 Advantages and Disadvantages of e-Learning

Advantages	Disadvantages
• Cost advantages compared with traditional methods • Improves computer skills • Self-paced • High degree of learner control • Choice over learning environment • Interactive • Tracking of learner progress and engagement is easy • Real time feedback • Consistent delivery method • Variety of formats and methods available • Consistent content • Unlimited access in terms of time and locale • Better support/help functions/knowledge base than other methods • Appeals to several senses simultaneously • Increased benefits through the combination with traditional training methods • Can be both synchronous and asynchronous • Accommodates different learning styles	• Basic computer skills necessary • Use of computers might cause apprehension • Not suitable for certain content • Privacy concerns if based online • Requires self-motivation to learn • Learners may feel isolated from instructors and peers • Lack of human contact in general • Technical difficulties impede access

The requisite resources vary with the training method chosen. While traditional face-to-face training necessitates physical training rooms and equipment, e-learning requires initial investments in ICT. Available resources are normally set out in predetermined annual training budgets. The training design will provide answers to the questions of how, by whom, and by when training should be implemented. The implementation of a T&D can only be considered successful if transfer of learning has occurred.

Training Transfer

Positive and long-lasting changes in employee behavior and, ultimately, increased shareholder value can only be attained if training (or learning) transfer occurs. Training transfer is the continuous application of KSA acquired during the training exercise. Various classifications of transfer of training exist depending on the context:

- Near versus far (how close the training task is to the actual job task)
- Specific versus general (transfer of skills vs. transfer of principles)
- Positive versus negative (linked to the perception of the training experience)
- Lateral versus vertical (Hayashi, Chen, & Terase, 2005)

Lateral transfer is about the application of training to similar tasks at the same level of complexity, while vertical transfer implies analysis and synthesis, that is, the ability to apply training to more complex tasks (Gagné, 1985). Training transfer depends on a number of variables, which can be summarized under five headings:

1. Trainee characteristics (the trainee's predisposition to training)

2. Training design (the organization of the learning environment)

3. Work environment (the immediate factors at work that affect transfer)

4. Learning and retention

5. Generalization and maintenance (ensuring that the trainee is given the opportunity to continuously use the acquired KSA) (Baldwin & Ford, 1988)

Only if the trainee possesses the necessary characteristics, if training design and workplace environment foster learning transfer, and when the trainee is given ample opportunity to apply the training will learning and retention take place. In addition, it has been demonstrated that transfer of training is *critically* dependent on the organizational climate that supports the training transfer (Lance, Kavanagh, & Brink, 2002; Rouiller & Goldstein, 1993; Tracey, Tannenbaum, & Kavanagh, 1995; Velada, Caetano, Michel, Lyons, & Kavanagh, 2007).

Evaluating T&D

To assess whether a particular training initiative, method, or solution has met the training needs and objectives of the firm and whether transfer of learning has taken place, organizations must evaluate their T&D efforts. Training evaluation is not an isolated activity. It is part of the T&D cycle and must be considered alongside and aligned with **needs analysis**, design, and implementation to provide a holistic picture of the entire T&D process. Similar to the T&D cycle, the evaluation process should be viewed as a cyclical process. The steps in the evaluation process are illustrated in Figure 12.3.

The evaluation process commences with the needs analysis. Training needs must then be translated into measurable learning outcomes. Appropriate metrics must be identified against which outcomes can be measured. The next step involves the selection of an appropriate evaluation strategy. Not all training can be assessed in the same manner considering the diversity in training methods. Once an evaluation has been carried out, the results must be analyzed and fed back into the training process. The final step is omitted in many evaluation models, even though it is crucially important to use evaluation data to make decisions on future training initiatives. An HRIS can be invaluable in supporting this process as it contains a vast amount of data related to training and performance that can form the basis of any T&D decision making.

However, many organizations pay lip service to evaluation without having a clear concept of what evaluation means and what purpose it serves.

> People often confuse the process of monitoring, validation and evaluation. The purpose of monitoring is to take the temperature of a learning event from time to time, picking up any problems or emerging needs. Validation measures the achievement of a set of learning objectives of a learning initiative or process. Evaluation looks at the total value of that event or process, thereby placing it into its organizational context and aiding future planning.

❖ **Figure 12.3** Evaluation Process

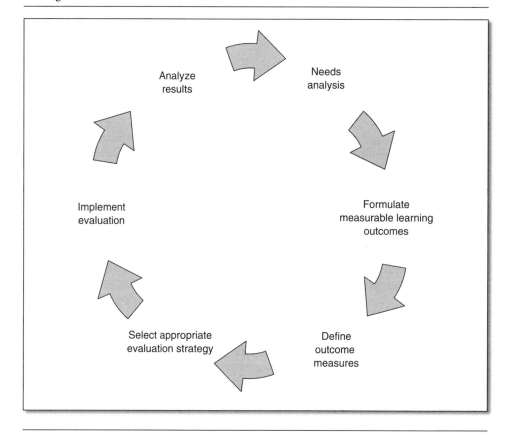

SOURCE: Developed from Noe (2002).

Faced with an evaluation task, there are four crucial questions to answer: why, who, when and how? (Harrison, 2005, p. 143)

Hence, the purpose of evaluation is manifold. Figure 12.2 shows that training initiatives must attain internal and external consistency to be effective. Thus, training is frequently validated under these aspects. Internal and external validations assess the degree to which stipulated T&D objectives are attained (Stewart, 1999). Easterby-Smith (1986) proposes three primary purposes of evaluation, which are outlined in Table 12.5.

Training outcomes fall into a number of distinct categories. The number of training evaluation models in the literature seems almost infinite. Kirkpatrick (1960) suggests four levels of outcomes comprising reaction, learning, behavior, and results. Warr, Bird, and Rackham's (1970) CIRO framework entails context, inputs, reactions, and outcomes (immediate, intermediate, and ultimate). Easterby-Smith (1986) suggests a CAPIO framework comprising context, administration, process, inputs, and

❖ **Table 12.5**   Purposes of Evaluation

Summative	Quantitative in nature; establishes whether T&D was effective, efficient, has added value, and has met its objectives
Formative	Qualitative in nature; assesses how training, learning, and development can be improved, that is, how could it be made more efficient and effective
Learning	Quantitative and qualitative assessment of learner's post-training performance to evaluate whether learning transfer has occurred

outputs. A comparison of these and other frameworks reveals a significant overlap between these evaluation models and a number of key learning outcomes contained therein. Table 12.6 provides a summary of these outcomes. The individual outcomes in this table are based on Bloom's taxonomy of learning domains (cognitive, psychomotor, and affective), which is one of the most widely used models to describe learning outcomes (Bloom et al., 1956; Bloom, Masia, & Krathwohl, 1964).

❖ **Table 12.6**   Categories of Training Outcomes

Outcomes	Details	Examples
Individual outcomes	Cognitive (knowledge based)	Awareness of health and safety regulations or company policies and procedures
	Psychomotor (skills based)	Ability to use a new piece of machinery or software
	Affective (attitudinal)	Satisfaction, motivation
Organizational outcomes	Any measurable impact on measures of organizational performance	Quantity (e.g., sales) Quality (e.g., customer satisfaction) Business processes (e.g., machine downtime) Resources (e.g., wastage rates) Stakeholder perception (e.g., employee relations) HR (e.g., skills level of workforce) (Sadler-Smith, 2006)
Return on investment (ROI)	Profits derived from training compared with costs	

SOURCE: Based on Easterby-Smith (1986).

The key objective of any evaluation process will be to assess the broad range of individual outcomes and organizational outcomes as well as return on investment (ROI). Hence, one of the key considerations will be whether T&D has had any measurable impact on the firm's bottom line to justify training expenditure and training budgets. The following section will consider some of the complexities involved in establishing the costs and the actual benefits of T&D initiatives.

Training Metrics and Cost-Benefit Analysis

The costs involved in training can be established relatively easily. These overheads can be substantial and involve direct costs and indirect costs (see Chapter 6 for cost-benefit analysis) (Noe, 2002). A considerable direct cost is the loss of production sustained through the absence of trainees from work for the duration of the training. e-Learning significantly reduces the element of direct costs, as trainees generally do not have to leave their place of work to participate in online training (provided they have access to a computer). Online courses may also be taken outside of work. In many cases, employees can avail of online training through an intranet, which can be accessed from work and from home, thus allowing for greater flexibility at a reduced cost.

However, the actual benefits to the firm may be much more difficult to ascertain, as many of the benefits take a long time to materialize or can often be of an intangible nature. Moreover, it may prove almost impossible to isolate the effects of training on performance completely from other organizational variables. The preoccupation with the quantification of the business benefits of training has frequently been described as the search for the "Holy Grail," and those organizations that evaluate training employ a number of different models and approaches to do so, including the balanced scorecard (Kaplan & Norton, 1992, 1993) or ROI (Phillips, 1996b). Russ-Eft and Preskill (2005) highlight three critical factors in HR development evaluation that complicate the assessment of training outcomes:

1. Evaluation occurs within a complex, dynamic, and variable environment.

2. Evaluation is essentially a political activity.

3. Evaluation ought to be purposeful, planned, and systematic.

Notwithstanding these factors, Phillips (1996a) advocates that any available post-training data should be analyzed and converted into monetary values to establish ROI. Phillips's (1996c, 2005) ROI methodology (or ROI process) produces six types of data, which are based on Kirkpatrick's (1960) evaluation taxonomy:

1. Reaction, satisfaction, and planned action

2. Learning and application

3. Implementation

4. Business impact (see organizational outcomes, Table 12.7)

5. ROI

6. Intangibles

The ROI method advocates five useful steps for converting hard (tangible) data and soft (intangible) data into monetary values:

1. Focus on a single unit of improvement in output, quality, or time.

2. Determine a value for each data unit.

3. Calculate the change in output performance directly attributable to training.

4. Obtain the annual amount of the monetary value of the change in performance.

5. Determine the annual value (the annual performance change times the unit value).

Having identified relevant data sources and applying these best practices, firms can use a number of approaches to quantify the relationship between training costs and benefits. These approaches are shown in Table 12.7. Organizations may use one or more of these ratios to determine the costs and benefits of planned and existing learning technology projects.

It is possible to enter basic values into a spreadsheet application to calculate the ratios listed in Table 12.7. However, the variety of possible outcomes from training, the variety of factors that affect these outcomes, and the variety of data to be collected to produce any meaningful results appear to make the evaluation process a rather tedious task that would be next to impossible to complete efficiently and effectively without the help of a computerized system. Most commercial HRIS can

❖ **Table 12.7**   Cost-Benefit Approaches

Approach	Explanation
Benefit-cost ratio (BCR)	Monetary benefits of T&D projects Costs of T&D projects
Cost-benefit ratio (CBR)	Costs of T&D projects Monetary benefits of T&D projects
Payback period	Costs of T&D projects Annual savings
Return on investment (ROI)	Monetary benefits of T&D projects Costs of T&D projects

SOURCE: Sadler-Smith (2006).

be customized to record, analyze, and report on the training metrics that have been identified by a firm. For instance, the system could be configured to collect information on the monetary benefits of T&D projects, such as increased production output or a reduced number of complaints, and compare this information with data collected on the costs of T&D projects. T&D data will usually be stored in the T&D module of the HRIS. In addition, a broad range of dedicated T&D systems is commercially available. The following section will discuss the data elements and various HRIS applications used in the training function.

HRIS Applications in Training

Traditionally, training software applications have been employed to record information associated purely with training administration purposes (Noe, 2002). Today, firms place much greater demands on training applications in terms of compatibility with existing systems, analytical functionality, and accessibility to meet business needs. The primary demand on any system, however, must be that it furnishes usable information to key decision makers to achieve both administrative and strategic advantages (Kovach, Hughes, Fagan, & Maggitti, 2002).

Hence, useful HRIS information should possess three key characteristics:

1. It must be presented in a user-friendly manner.

2. It must be meaningful and appropriate (Keebler & Rhodes, 2002).

3. It must be used effectively in the decision-making process to support an organization's overall business strategy (Kovach & Cathcart, 1999).

However, Kovach and Cathcart (1999) argue that HRIS do not need to be intricate or even computerized to serve the information needs of a business. Elementary HRIS training databases are easily set up using commercial or open-source desktop software (see Figures 12.4 and 12.5). These databases may then be used to collect, store, and analyze training-related HR information. The amount of data that can be stored, the manner in which it is collected, and the level of analysis possible will depend on the application used. Table 12.8 shows the basic data elements an electronic T&D database should contain. The first column, Data Elements, shows the main categories of data elements, while Subcategory 1 and Subcategory 2 provide examples of the type of information these data elements could include.

Using these essential data elements, a spreadsheet may be created (see Figure 12.4). This basic database contains relevant training information and possesses limited search and reporting capabilities. Should a firm decide to upgrade to commercial training software, data stored in a spreadsheet can be imported into most training applications.

Clearly, the amount of information that can be collected and the level of analysis that a spreadsheet application permits are limited. Therefore, many organizations create bespoke databases, which offer greater possibilities regarding the collection and

❖ **Figure 12.4** Example of an HRIS T&D Database in Spreadsheet Format

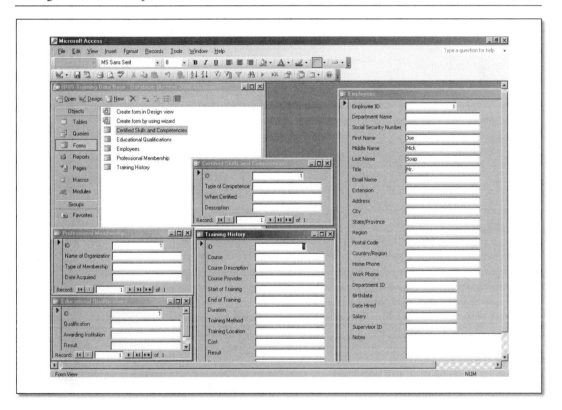

❖ **Figure 12.5** Example of a Database

presentation of training data. These database applications allow users to run queries using customizable search criteria; they provide greater reporting options; and information on different screens can be linked to avoid multiple entry of data. An example of such a database including the data elements and subcategories of Table 12.8 is shown in Figure 12.5.

❖ **Table 12.8** Basic Data Elements for an HRIS Training Database

Data Element	Subcategory 1	Subcategory 2
Employee information	Employee ID	
	Employee name	Title
		First name
		Middle name
		Second name
	Social security number	
	Department	List of departments
	Position	List of positions
	Reporting to	
Training history (training course completed)	Date of training (start and end)	
	Training methods	(see above)
	Course (including description)	List of common courses
	Course provider	List of common providers
	Training location	In-house
		Out-of-house
		Online
	Result	
	Duration	
	Cost	
	Notes on performance	
Certified skills and competencies		
Professional memberships		List of professional organizations
Educational qualifications		

As firms grow in size, their need to manage training activities and training data more effectively and efficiently increases accordingly. A host of commercial systems service the broad spectrum of T&D, ranging from stand-alone training administration software to fully integrated expert systems. T&D software is available in many guises. The most common applications are discussed here.

HRIS/Learning Applications: LMS

The vast majority of large organizations rely on fully integrated enterprise-wide systems, called enterprise resource planning (ERP) systems, to satisfy their information needs. An ERP system amalgamates the management information systems (MIS) from all functional areas in a business, for example, finance, production, marketing, and HRM, into a single system. The ERP system component, or MIS, which supports the HR function, is commonly referred to as an HRIS or human resource management system (HRMS), although these are also available as stand-alone systems. These data repositories for HR-related information typically comprise a number of modules, which in turn can support every area of HR, including T&D. Traditionally, firms used HRIS T&D applications and modules for administrative purposes only. The capabilities of today's HRIS T&D applications, also called learning management software (LMS), range from training administration to training management, to talent management. The uses and capabilities of LMS are shown in the LMS classification in Table 12.9.

The use of administrative systems is restricted to transaction processing, including the calculation of training costs. Training management systems can facilitate the entire T&D process (see Systems Model of T&D above) from TNA to training evaluation. *Learning content management software* (LCMS), as the name implies, can be used to store

❖ **Table 12.9** Learning Management System Classification

Classification	Uses and Capabilities
Administration system	• Basic employee and T&D records • Calculation of training costs • Administrative permissions (who has data access, who can enter data)
Training management system (including learning content management system)	• Scheduling and access to training courses • Set up of training courses and initiatives • Assignment of training based on skills and certification requirements • Authoring of training courses and initiatives • Online access to courses • Training evaluation • Tracking of training attendance and results • ROI measurement
Talent management system	• KSA assessment • Performance reviews and appraisals • Recruiting • Succession planning • Career planning • Management development

SOURCE: Adapted from e-Learning Consulting (2007).

and develop T&D content, such as multimedia files, templates for training courses, or assignments. It may also be employed to track training attendance and completion records or for quality assurance purposes. LCMS is frequently used in combination with REL. *Talent management systems/software* (TMS), sometimes referred to as human capital management systems, are integrated software suites that can comprise a range of applications such as applicant tracking, succession and career planning, performance management, compensation and benefits management, and learning management. TMS allow employees to create personal electronic *talent profiles,* which can be updated and usually reflect their KSA and goals. Organizations can use these data to generate information on the talent profile of the organization and to develop macro- and microlevel employee development plans. A large number of commercial LMS exist (see list of vendor Web sites in the Appendix). These range from off-the-shelf products to server and Web-based enterprise solutions. The choice of system will be determined principally by an organization's LT&D needs, LT&D budget, and ICT capabilities. The reporting, analytical, and strategic potential of these systems will diverge accordingly. The degree to which LMS can assist strategic decision making may be assessed using Beckers and Bsat's (2002) decision support system (DSS) classification. Their model consists of five levels:

1. Management information systems (MIS)

2. Decision support systems (DSS)

3. Group decision support systems (GDSS)

4. Expert systems (ES)

5. Artificial intelligence (AI)

Each consecutive category offers the users more extensive reporting and analytical capabilities that can support strategic T&D decision making. MIS can be used to support T&D decision making at the operational, functional level of the organization. DSS and GDSS are designed to facilitate senior management decision making in the long term and relate to the overall mission and objectives of an organization. They are based on "what if" scenarios. Expert systems consist of a knowledge base, a decision-making function, and an interface. They replicate the decision-making capabilities of human experts. An example of a system that uses AI is an intelligent tutoring system (ITS). ITS can be employed to tutor, coach, or empower employees. The advantages of ITS are that instruction can be aligned with learner needs, that the system responds to learner actions, and that learner progress can be modeled (Noe, 2002). ES and AI aid strategic T&D decision making at the board level of the organization. However, capital investments in sophisticated HRIS T&D applications alone will not necessarily improve LT&D in the organization, nor will they lead to knowledge creation or organizational learning. Any HRIS project requires careful planning and ample resources (time, money, and expertise).

HRIS T&D Applications: Implementation Issues

Many HRIS T&D projects fail to meet the expectations of key decision makers. The reasons for this are manifold. Some firms introduce a new TMS only because competitors have done likewise, without having the necessary expertise to operate the system. Frequently, decision makers have false expectations of ROI or apply training metrics that merely focus on cost savings and fail to take note of intangible gains derived from T&D (see the section Training Metrics and Cost-Benefit Analysis). In other cases, the HRIS T&D application strategy is not aligned with training needs and the overall T&D, HR, and business strategies. Few organizations involve employees during the implementation stage of the HRIS, which can lead to underutilization and dissatisfaction with the system (Burbach & Dundon, 2005). For a variety of reasons (see Disadvantages in Table 12.4), many employees never actually complete the e-learning programs they are enrolled on. Sometimes, disenchantment is simply the result of poor planning and the resulting incompatibility of various disjointed HR systems, albeit an increasing number of organizations purchase one or more items of TMS from a single vendor to prevent these problems (Frauenheim, 2006). A number of authors have suggested success factors for the introduction of HRIS T&D applications (Gascó, Llopis, & González, 2004; Noe, 2002; Sadler-Smith, 2006) and for increasing e-learning completion rates (Frankola, 2001):

- Align e-learning strategy with T&D strategy, HR strategy, and overall business strategy.
- Create a corporate learning culture that fosters e-learning and the use of HRIS T&D applications.
- Assess HRIS T&D projects by their suitability to meet the T&D strategy of the organization rather than the technical sophistication and elegant features of the system.
- Carefully plan HRIS T&D projects to guarantee compatibility with **legacy system**s and with sufficient budget allocation and expertise to use the system.
- Involve line managers and employees in HRIS T&D projects to ensure greater buy-in.
- Match HRIS T&D applications and e-learning initiatives with their ability to meet training needs to encourage learning transfer.
- Establish a suitable evaluation strategy to assess the extent to which training technology meets training needs and evaluate regularly.
- Identify suitable T&D metrics that take account of all direct and indirect training outcomes.
- Promote the use of HRIS T&D applications and e-learning.
- Make managers accountable for uptake of e-learning and HRIS T&D utilization.
- Reward employees for use of e-learning.
- Ensure that T&D systems and e-learning are user-friendly and provide quality information.
- Develop a data security policy for the T&D system and applications.
- Do not focus on financial gains from HRIS T&D projects alone.
- Train managers and employees in the use of T&D technologies.

Summary

This chapter highlighted the strategic importance of LT&D in an increasingly knowledge-intensive global economy. The discussion showed that it is important to distinguish between learning, training, and development to understand the processes that lead to the acquisition of KSA. Other key concepts such as KM and the learning organization were also explained. Knowledge creation, innovation, and organizational learning are inextricably linked to an organization's capacity to remain competitive. This chapter identified and explained a range of e-learning methods, their role in knowledge acquisition, and their advantages and disadvantages. Nonetheless, traditional face-to-face methods still carry considerable credence, which is reflected in the increasing use of blended learning, which combines both traditional and online methods of learning. A careful analysis of training needs, various LT&D methods, and individual learning styles is necessary to ensure that transfer of learning occurs and that, ultimately, the strategic objectives of the organization can be attained. HRIS T&D applications are vitally important tools in pursuing a systematic approach to LT&D, that is, to identify training needs, to design LT&D solutions and methods, to implement these initiatives, and to evaluate the effectiveness of training including the assessment of ROI on training. As many LT&D outcomes are of an intangible nature and/or take a long time to materialize (note the definition of development in this context), it is inherently intricate to determine appropriate training metrics that may be employed to perform any meaningful CBA. The key is to analyze any available data. Notwithstanding these difficulties, a number of approaches to ascertain ROI using HRIS T&D applications were offered. This chapter also expounded on how an elementary T&D system can be created using a spreadsheet or database desktop application. A variety of HRIS T&D applications exist. LMS may be embedded in an HRIS or ERP. LMS vary considerably in their capacity to manage the training process, to generate reports, or to assist strategic decision making. Talent management suites integrate a range of applications, including succession planning and learning management. LMS with DSS and ES capabilities offer the greatest strategic value. However, the choice of system is contingent on the T&D needs of an organization, its budget, and its ICT capabilities. This chapter concluded with a discussion of surrounding the implementation of HRIS T&D applications.

Discussion Questions

1. What is the systems model of T&D? Discuss how HRIS T&D applications can assist in carrying out the steps in the systems model.

2. Explain synchronous and asynchronous communication in relation to e-learning.

3. What are the advantages and disadvantages of e-learning?

4. How can HRIS T&D applications help firms foster organizational learning?

5. Explain how organizations should choose appropriate T&D methods.

6. What is transfer of training? What role does transfer of learning play in e-learning?

7. Explain the issues involved in establishing ROI for T&D initiatives. What role do HRIS T&D applications play in establishing ROI?

8. Outline how standard desktop applications such as a spreadsheet or database can be used to set up a basic T&D system.

9. Discuss the different types of HRIS T&D applications and their reporting and decision-support capabilities.

10. What issues might arise during and as a result of the implementation of HRIS T&D applications?

CASE STUDY

Meddevco (name changed) is a large multinational corporation that operates in the medical devices sector. The firm employs around 33,000 people in five divisions and has operations in 120 countries. A total of 66% of the multinational's revenue is generated from products that are less than 2 years old, and 80% of employees are working on products that are less than 2 years old. These figures illustrate the highly competitive and fast-paced nature of the medical devices sector. This sector is also characterized by high levels of regulatory control and a need to comply with industry norms. Meddevco is headquartered in the United States and Switzerland. The information needs of a firm of this size are substantial, and it would be next to impossible to collect, store, and analyze HR-related information without the use of a fully integrated global HRIS. Moreover, the diversity of the workforce, the multiplicity of skills required in the different divisions and product lines, and the pressure of compliance necessitate a perfectly orchestrated T&D effort. Needless to say, HRIS T&D applications play a major role in managing the T&D function. Meddevco uses an HRIS by PeopleSoft (now Oracle) to manage the majority of its global HR processes, including e-recruitment and performance appraisals. With regard to data entry into the system, the corporation operates a strict "no customization unless legally required" policy to ensure data compatibility across the system. In the United States, most HR services are centralized in an HR shared services center. The corporation has a dedicated HRIS center in Europe, and negotiations are ongoing to implement a European HR shared services model. The company uses a number of different payroll systems in Europe for compliance reasons. All employees in the corporation have access to a company intranet called My Meddevco, which also includes a learning portal that provides access to online training programs, which employees can use at work and at home. The intranet also includes a knowledge base and detailed company information, including a full listing of all employees and their job titles and location. Employee transfers and promotions are also listed. A number of years ago, the corporation made the decision not to use the training module included in PeopleSoft and opted for a training management system called SABA to coordinate and manage training initiatives; for example, the recent rollout and training for the use of SAP (an ERP system) for production facilities was managed through SABA. In addition, Meddevco has recently commenced using the talent management module included in PeopleSoft to identify and track high-performing employees for promotion. Every employee is required to complete an online talent profile, which is similar to an online CV and which can be updated by the employee. The combination of systems and applications and the careful analysis of HR information contained therein allow the organization to develop and implement a global T&D strategy. However, the firm also faces some challenges arising from the use of these systems. As the organization largely grew through acquisition, a number of legacy systems still coexist with the global HRIS among some of its subsidiaries. Data compatibility issues also derive from the use of SABA, which is not part of PeopleSoft. In addition, the firm is also using SAP, and it is questionable whether Oracle (the owner of PeopleSoft) will support data exchanges with a system supplied by its chief competitor. Furthermore, because Meddevco did not involve the workforce in the implementation process of the TMS, employees are reluctant to complete their talent profiles. Moreover, the need to customize the HRIS locally to comply with national legislation in its subsidiaries further complicates the collection and transfer of data within the global HRIS.

The example of Meddevco illustrates how large organizations employ HRIS to manage their workforce and how they leverage HR development through the use of HRIS T&D applications, learning portals, and specialized LMS. However, it is also apparent that careful planning is essential to avoid compatibility issues and to ensure a consistent global flow of HR- and T&D-related information.

Case Study Questions

1. What should Meddevco have done to avoid some of their problems?

2. How could Meddevco now solve the problems created by not involving employees during the implementation of the HRIS?

3. What else should Meddevco do now to improve the operation of their system?

NOTES

1. The company's name must remain confidential.

2. The bold terms in this chapter are included in the Glossary. These terms cannot and do not purport to provide an exhaustive list of HRIS T&D applications. However, they furnish explanations of the key concepts discussed in this chapter. More extensive e-learning glossaries are available on the World Wide Web, for instance, the ASTD (www.learningcircuits.org/glossary) and WorldWideLearn (www.worldwidelearn.com/elearning-essentials/elearning-glossary.htm) glossaries.

REFERENCES

Archibald, D. (2005). *Rapid e-learning: A growing trend.* Retrieved May 10, 2007, from www.learningcircuits.org/2005/jan2005/archibald.htm

Argyris, C., & Schon, D. A. (1978). *Organization learning II: Theory, method and practice.* Reading, MA: Addison-Wesley.

Baldwin, T. T., & Ford, J. K. (1988). Transfer of training: A review and directions for future research. *Personnel Psychology, 41*(1), 63–105.

Beckers, A. M., & Bsat, M. Z. (2002). A DSS classification model for research in HRIS. *Information Systems Management, 19*(3), 41–50.

Bersin, J. (2005). Making rapid e-learning work. *Chief Learning Officer, 4*(7), 20–24.

Bloom, B. S., Engelhart, M., Furst, E. J., Hill, W., & Krathwohl, D. (1956). *Taxonomy of educational objectives: Vol. 1. The cognitive domain.* New York: McKay.

Bloom, B. S., Masia, B. B., & Krathwohl, D. (1964). *Taxonomy of educational objectives. Vol. 2: The affective domain.* New York: McKay.

Boydell, T. H. (1983). *A guide to the identification of training needs.* London: British Association for Commercial and Industrial Education.

Burbach, R., & Dundon, T. (2005). The strategic potential of human resource information systems: Evidence from the Republic of Ireland. *International Employment Relations Review, 11*(1/2), 97–118.

Burnes, B. (2004). *Managing change: A strategic approach to organisational dynamics.* Harrow, UK: Prentice Hall/Financial Times.

Collin, A. (2007). Learning and development. In J. Beardwell & T. Claydon (Eds.), *Human resource management: A contemporary approach* (5th ed.). Harlow, UK: Prentice Hall, Financial Times.

Cummings, T. G., & Worley, C. G. (2001). *Organization development and change* (7th ed.). Cincinnati, OH: South-Western College Publishing.

Easterby-Smith, M. (1986). *Evaluation of management, training and development.* Aldershot, UK: Gower.

e-Learning Consulting. (2007). *Learning management systems.* Retrieved February 10, 2007, from www.e-learningconsulting.com/consulting/what/learning-management.html

Frankola, K. (2001). Tips for increasing e-learning completion rates. *Workforce, 80*(10), 56.

Frauenheim, E. (2006). Talent management software is bundling up. *Workforce Management, 85*(19), 35.

Frauenheim, E. (2007). Your co-worker, your teacher: Collaborative technology speeds peer-peer learning. *Workforce Management, 86*(2), 19–23.

Gagné, R. M. (1985). *The conditions of learning and theory of instruction* (4th ed.). New York: Holt, Rinehart & Winston.

Gascó, J. L., Llopis, J., & González, M. R. (2004). The use of information technology in training human resources: An e-learning case study. *Journal of European Industrial Training, 28*(5), 370–382.

Grant, R. M. (1996). Toward a knowledge-based theory of the firm. *Strategic Management Journal, 17*(10), 109–122.

Gunnigle, P., Heraty, N., & Morley, M. (2002). *Human resource management in Ireland* (2nd ed.). Dublin, Ireland: Gill & Macmillan.

Harrison, R. (2005). *Learning and development.* London: Chartered Institute of Personnel and Development.

Hayashi, A., Chen, C. C., & Terase, H. (2005). Aligning it skills training with online asynchronous learning multimedia technologies [Electronic version]. *Information Systems Education Journal, 3*(26). Retrieved June 10, 2007 from http://isedj.org/isecon/2004/2434/ISECON.2004.Hayashi.pdf

Honey, P., & Mumford, A. (1992). *Manual of learning styles* (3rd ed.). London: Peter Honey.

Kaplan, R. S., & Norton, D. P. (1992). The balanced scorecard: Measures that drive performance. *Harvard Business Review, 70*(1), 71–79.

Kaplan, R. S., & Norton, D. P. (1993). Putting the balanced scorecard to work. *Harvard Business Review, 71*(5), 134–140.

Keebler, T. J., & Rhodes, D. W. (2002). e-HR: Becoming the "Path of least resistance." *Employment Relations Today (Wiley), 29*(2), 57–66.

Kirkpatrick, D. L. (1960). Techniques for evaluating training programmes. *Journal of the American Society for Training and Development, 14,* 13–18, 25–32.

Kolb, D. A. (1984). *Experiential learning: Experience as a source of learning and development.* Englewood Cliffs, NJ: Prentice Hall.

Kovach, K. A., & Cathcart, C. E. (1999). Human resources information systems (HRIS): Providing business with rapid data access. *Public Personnel Management, 28*(2), 274–282.

Kovach, K. A., Hughes, A. A., Fagan, P., & Maggitti, P. G. (2002). Administrative and strategic advantages of HRIS. *Employment Relations Today, 29*(2), 43–48.

Lance, C. E., Kavanagh, M. J., & Brink, K. E. (2002). Retraining climate as a predictor of retraining success and as a moderator of the relationship between cross-job retraining time estimates and time to proficiency in the new job. *Group and Organization Management, 27,* 294–317.

"Learning." (2007). In *Encyclopædia Britannica.* Retrieved March 14, 2007, from www.britannica.com/eb/article-9369902

Mayo, A. (1998). Memory bankers. *People Management, 4*(2), 34–38.

Noe, R. A. (2002). *Employee training and development* (2nd ed.). New York: McGraw-Hill.

Nonaka, I., & Takeuchi, H. (1995). *The knowledge-creating company.* New York: Oxford University Press.

Organisation for Economic Co-operation and Development. (1996). *The knowledge based economy.* Paris: Author.

Organisation for Economic Co-operation and Development. (2001). *The well-being of nations: The role of human and social capital.* Paris: Author.

Pedler, M., Burgoyne, J., & Boydell, T. (1991). *The learning company: A strategy for sustainable development.* Maidenhead, UK: McGraw-Hill.

Pfeffer, J. (1996). *Competitive advantage through people: Unleashing the power of the work force.* Boston: Harvard Business School Press.

Pfeffer, J. (1998). *The human equation: Building profits by putting people first.* Boston: Harvard Business School Press.

Phillips, J. J. (1996a). How much is the training worth? (Cover story). *Training & Development, 50*(4), 20.

Phillips, J. J. (1996b). ROI: The search for best practices. *Training & Development, 50*(2), 42.

Phillips, J. J. (1996c). Was it the training? *Training & Development, 50*(3), 28.

Phillips, J. J. (2005). The value of human capital: Macro-level research. *Chief Learning Officer, 4*(10), 60–62.

Porter, M. (1990). *The competitive advantage of nations.* New York: Free Press.

Prahalad, C. K., & Hamel, G. (1990). The core competencies of the corporation. *Harvard Business Review,* 79–91.

Rossett, A., & Frazee, V. (2006). *Blended learning opportunities.* New York: American Management Association. Retrieved June 10, 2007, from www.amanet.org/blended/pdf/WhitePaper_BlendLearn.pdf

Rouiller, J. Z., & Goldstein, I. L. (1993). The relationship between organizational transfer climate and positive transfer of training. *Human Resource Development Quarterly, 4,* 377–390.

Russ-Eft, D., & Preskill, H. (2005). In search of the Holy Grail: Return on investment evaluation in human resource development. *Advances in Developing Human Resources, 7*(1), 71–85.

Sadler-Smith, E. (2006). *Learning and development for managers: Perspectives from research and practice.* Oxford, UK: Blackwell.

Senge, P. (1990). *The fifth discipline.* New York: Doubleday.

Shaw, S., & Igneri, N. (2006). *Effectively implementing a blended learning approach. Unpublished Whitepaper.* Eedo Knowledgeware, American Management Association.

Soliman, F., & Spooner, K. (2000). Strategies for implementing knowledge management: Role of human resources management. *Journal of Knowledge Management, 4*(4), 337–345.

Sparrow, S. (2004). Blended is better. *Training & Development, 58*(11), 52–55.

Stewart, J. (1999). *Employee development practice.* London: Financial Times/Pitman.

Tracey, J. B., Tannenbaum, S. I., & Kavanagh, M. J. (1995). Applying trained skills on the job: The importance of the work environment. *Journal of Applied Psychology, 80,* 239–252.

van Dam, N. (2002). *e-Learning development at the speed of business.* Retrieved 10 May 2007, from www.clomedia.com/content/anmviewer.asp?a=850&print=yes

Velada, R., Caetano, A., Michel, J. W., Lyons, B. D., & Kavanagh, M. J. (2007). The effects of training design, individual characteristics, and work environment on transfer of training. *International Journal of Training and Development, 11*(4), December, 282–294.

Warr, P., Bird, M., & Rackham, N. (1970). *Evaluation of management training.* Aldershot, UK: Gower.

Wright, P. M., Dunford, B. B., & Snell, S. A. (2001). Human resources and the resource based view of the firm. *Journal of Management, 27*(6), 701–720.

Yahya, S., & Goh, W.-K. (2002). Managing human resources toward achieving knowledge management. *Journal of Knowledge Management, 6*(5), 457–468.

❖

Performance Management, Compensation, Benefits, Payroll, and the HRIS

Charles H. Fay

Ren Nardoni

EDITORS' NOTE

This chapter is the fourth one involving an organization's talent management program and its utilization as aided by an HRIS. This chapter completes all the activities involved in talent management—planning and forecasting the need for talent (Chapter 10); recruitment and selection of talent (Chapter 11); and training for talent management (Chapter 12). Ultimately, the purpose of talent management is to achieve an organization's strategic goal to remain competitive in its market through the effective management of its HR. The focus of this chapter is on management of employee performance in a systematic manner. This performance management (PM) system involves evaluation of both individual job performance and the reward system of the organization that supports the evaluation. The reward system of the organization involves the design, decision making, and administration of both compensation and benefits practices. The uniqueness of this chapter is its description of the design and operation of typical HRIS applications in the PM, compensation, and benefits programs of the HRM function.

CHAPTER OBJECTIVES

After completing this chapter, you should be able to do the following

♦ Understand the PM cycle and the role of the HRIS in PM design, decision making, and administration

♦ Understand typical compensation practice and the role of the HRIS in compensation design, decision making, and administration

♦ Understand typical benefits practice and the role of the HRIS in benefits design, decision making, and administration

♦ Understand payroll systems

♦ Understand how performance and rewards are integrated through the HRIS

♦ Discuss the special needs placed on the HRIS by performance, rewards, and payroll

VIGNETTE

As Mark walked into his work area, he was fuming. "Those idiots in HR and Payroll are really the gang that couldn't shoot straight," he announced to everyone in the vicinity. "What did they do now?" asked Marsha. "Don't tell me they got it wrong again!"

"They sure did," said Mark. "After I complained last month you'd think they would at least check to make sure they corrected their mistake. If I treated a customer this way I'd get fired!"

Mark's paycheck is wrong once again, and the story is a complicated one. It started with the performance review Mark had received from his boss the previous month. The review was good and Mark had earned an "Exceeds standards" summary rating. Somehow, when an HR data entry clerk entered the approved rating into the system an error was made and "Does not meet standards" went into the compensation review system. The error snowballed, and Mark received no merit increase or bonus for the year. In fact, because of increased deductions for health coverage, his check was actually smaller than the one he had received 2 weeks earlier. Apart from the financial costs, Mark was psychologically shattered because his boss had discussed in their performance review meeting how good his performance was.

After his boss intervened, HR and payroll corrected the error and noted that Mark would receive the expected increase and a one-time adjustment for back pay. On the strength of that,

Mark made additional financial commitments. When the latest check was direct deposited into Mark's bank account, the mistake had not been corrected, and a check Mark had written was returned for insufficient funds. Payroll's excuse? HR had not gotten the approved changes to them within the 1 week prior to payroll deadline for changes.

How can errors like this be avoided? They are not uncommon. A large state university in the Northeast makes salary adjustments to faculty who receive performance increases in two stages: The adjustment becomes part of the biweekly paycheck in late spring, and the adjustment for January 1 through late spring is paid out as a lump sum in summer. Last summer, the back pay adjustment was considerably higher than it should have been because of a data entry error in the adjustment formula. No one caught the error until this year, when the University had to notify all faculty members that the back pay adjustment for this year would be reduced by the excess adjustment received the previous year.

PM, compensation, benefits, and payroll are sensitive areas for most employees. Most employees "keep score" on their relationship with their employer through these systems. It is critical that IT systems in these areas be flawlessly executed from the employee's perspective because getting the wrong (or no) paycheck sends a very bad message to the employee. Given the amounts of money involved, it is critical that IT systems in these areas be flawlessly executed from the employer's perspective as well.

In this chapter, we will provide an overview of PM, compensation, benefits, and payroll, so that you have an idea of the complexity that must be captured if the HRIS is to work well.

Introduction to Performance, Rewards, and Payroll

Performance, rewards, and payroll systems are the basic exchange between employees and employers: Employees provide performance, and in exchange employers provide rewards, which are distributed via payroll systems. These systems also serve as good examples of several IT issues in HRM. PM systems are usually entirely internal to the organization, but data must be linked to several other systems, including rewards, staffing, training and development, and career development. PM systems are used as working tools by managers and must, therefore, be inherently self-explanatory. Much of the data are specific to the individual, although various summary measures must be comparable across subsets of employees or all employees.

In contrast, reward systems have both internal and external ties to multiple other information systems. Both pay and benefits must be linked (or linkable) to external survey data, legal requirement data, and internal systems such as budgeting and planning systems. Parts of reward systems usage are restricted to HR professionals, while other parts must be widely available to employees for self-queries. Most organizations consider rewards data to be highly confidential, so system security is critical. Reward systems data focus on the individual, small-group, unit, and organization levels for different purposes, and the same variable (e.g., value of a specific benefit, seniority, option value) may have to be defined, calculated, stored, and reported in multiple ways depending on the need.

In the case of payroll systems, flawless data integrity and even more flawless execution are critical. Anyone who has ever received an inaccurate paycheck will understand the frustration and anger that occur; a payroll system that is not flawless is an administrator's nightmare. Payroll systems must be linked to external data (e.g., federal and state requirements for minimum wage) and internal data (e.g., general ledger, benefit choices) and must be capable of incorporating constant change. The payroll system is generally used only by payroll specialists, but every employee "audits" his or her own results. One final aspect of payroll is that some summaries of payroll data are not likely to match summaries of the same variables used in compensation or other HR systems. Even in as seemingly simple a question as number of employees, the compensation system is likely to contain only currently active employees; benefits might also include employees on leave, retired employees, and those ex-employees who have elected continuation of benefits under the Consolidated Omnibus Budget Reduction Act of 1986 (COBRA), while payroll files contain everyone for whom a check is cut.

This chapter focuses on the data inputs, typical reports that are generated, data outflows to other systems, and ways that the IT system can provide decision support to organizations and managers in the areas of PM, rewards, and payroll. Before that discussion can be meaningful, however, a brief overview of each of the areas is necessary.

Performance Management

Overview

Until recently, most discussion in organizations focused on the performance appraisal process. The emphasis was on getting the "best" appraisal format and training managers to "rate" employees using the format. Most research, whether by scholars or professionals, was on rating formats, rater error, and the training of raters. The assumption was that if the correct format could be developed and managers were trained, the resulting ratings would be accurate.

During the 1980s, professionals and some scholars became interested in a different goal: improving performance (Banks & May, 1999; Bernardin, Hagan, Kane, & Villanova, 1998). This led to a reconsideration of the whole performance process, and attention shifted to PM. The PM process consists of three parts: performance planning, observing performance and providing positive and **corrective feedback**, and developing periodic performance summaries to serve as a basis for performance planning for the next period while providing data for a variety of HR decisions, including rewards, staffing, training, and other decisions affecting the employee's relationship with the organization.

PM is now considered within the framework of "talent management," which encompasses all areas of HR that have to do with onboarding, developing, evaluating, and managing the workforce through all the normal cycles. PM is just one of the areas connected to others such as

- Recruiting (external)
- Staffing (internal)

❖ **Figure 13.1**   Model of Contemporary Talent Management

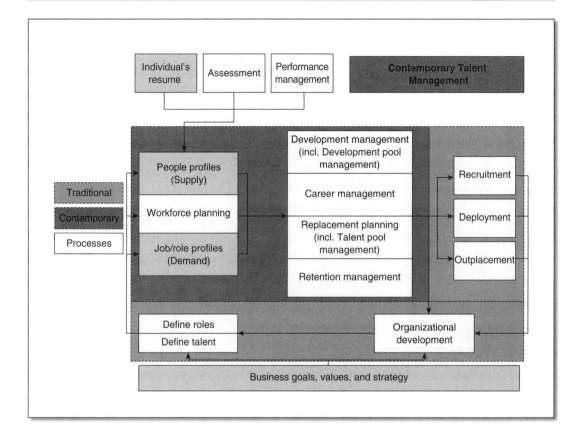

- Career management
- 360° assessment
- Development management
- Retention management
- Workforce planning

The model of contemporary talent management is shown in Figure 13.1.

Note that many organizations today, although having installed expensive and expansive enterprise resource planning (ERP) systems, which were supposed to provide a single platform for all these integrated applications, found that it was necessary to add specialized talent management solutions from third-party vendors to achieve the necessary functionality.

The link from the resulting performance and compensation processes to the core payroll systems, however, still remains as an integral link between the ERP systems and the specialized talent management solutions. In the example given in the opening vignette, if there were an integrated talent management system linking the performance module and compensation, there would be no need for anyone to enter the performance rating into the compensation system since the performance rating would have already been there as a result of the approved employee review.

Performance Planning

Performance planning, like most management processes, must be constructed in such a way that any manager can do it, regardless of management style or skills. Better managers involve the employee collaboratively in all phases of the PM process, but the system is designed so that even directive managers can follow the process. This discussion assumes that the manager is more directive than collaborative.

The manager must first define what performance means in the case of a specific **direct report**. At the broadest level, this refers to what the manager would have to do if the direct report was terminated and a replacement could not be hired. Ideally, this definition is based on a cascade of goals beginning with the organizational strategy and operating plan, with the immediate source being what the manager is expected to accomplish during the period and ending with the direct report's expected part of that accomplishment (Evans, 2001). The manager must then move from the general to the specific, usually expressed in terms of desired outcomes. This constitutes the performance dimensions for the direct report.

Where outcomes are difficult to observe or measure, behaviors that are expected to lead to desired outcomes are added. For each performance dimension, the manager must develop specific outcomes and behaviors that will be used to measure the direct report's performance. For a performance dimension of budget management, an outcome might be "Stays close to budget for each budget category." A behavior on the same dimension might be "Checks expenditures against budget." After the measures are determined, the manager must set appropriate standards for each measure. The standard for "Checks expenditures against budget" might be "Checks expenditures against budget weekly." After defining standard performance, "Exceeds standards" and "Fails to meet standards" would be defined. The exceeds standards level for "Checks expenditures against budget" might be "Checks expenditures against budget weekly; where discrepancies exceed 2%, checks those categories daily until discrepancies disappear." The "Fails to meet standards level" might be "Misses weekly check of expenditures of expenditures against budget; allows discrepancies to continue without any follow-up." It should be noted that performance dimensions, measures, and standards are unique to each position, although attempts should be made to develop common standards for employees with identical job titles.

When performance dimensions, measures, and standards have been developed, the manager must communicate them to the direct report. The manager must make certain that the direct report understands measures and standards. The manager then gets the direct report to set goals for performance for the coming year. Note that goals and standards are not the same thing. The standard is what is expected of a fully job-knowledgeable employee who exerts normal effort. One purpose of PM is to get employees to set stretch goals, to be better than the standard. At the end of the goal-setting discussion, the direct report has agreed on some performance level as a goal. The set of performance measures, with standards and goals, becomes the performance "contract" for the period.

Formats

Most organizations define the performance instrument differently depending on the type or level of the employee. For example, a nonmanagement or clerical position may have a relatively standard set of criteria that requires little or no change year over year. On the other hand, management employees tend to use a format that combines both goals and objectives together with a competency evaluation. A well-designed performance application can automatically map the correct "format" based on the employee who has logged into the performance Web site.

For the management format, the goal portion and the competency components might be weighted (i.e., 60% of the overall rating will be based on the goals results, while 40% will reflect the competency ratings). Also, within each section, each goal or competency might be rated. Therefore, the overall result could be pure weighted calculation of each goal, competency, and section result. Web-based performance systems can easily perform these calculations for the user. Even if the organization prefers that the employee and/or the manager actually determine the overall rating, the system can provide "advice" as to the reasonableness of the entered rating versus the underlying ratings.

Performance Period

During the performance period, the manager uses the performance contract as a benchmark for observing the direct report. When performance above standard is observed, the standard becomes the basis of positive feedback. When performance is below standard or below the goal set by the direct report, corrective feedback is used, again relying on the standard and on the goal set as the benchmarks for the performance observed. When discussion about performance is couched in terms of known measures, standards, and goals performance, feedback can be much more objective, and it is less likely to be seen as criticism of character. The direct report is not bad per se, but it is simply not performing at the agreed on level on one or more measures.

Periodic Performance Summary

At some point, a summary of performance during the period is provided to the direct report. In most organizations, this is an annual event, but some organizations have quarterly or semiannual performance summaries. At this point, the manager provides a summary of how the direct report has done on each performance measure and whether standards and goals have been met. Consequences of achieving various performance levels are communicated, and planning for the next period's performance begins. If PM has been done correctly, the summary appraisal should have no surprises for the direct report. As shown in Figure 13.1, development is a critical component. One of the more important outputs of the performance process is an individual development plan (IDP) that is used to document any steps necessary to improve employee performance. Each employee should have an IDP.

The process described above applies to PM at the individual level. Yet most employees today work as an integrated part of one or more teams. The PM process does not change significantly for a team. It is usually easier to get outcome performance measures for a team than for an individual, and it is more difficult to get individual performance measures for a team member (Bing, 2004). Some organizations have elected to use team output as the primary outcome measure of performance for all team members and then develop a "team citizenship measure" for each team member.

Typical Data Inputs

Data inputs for PM systems include organizational-, job-, and individual-level data. Organizational-level data consist of links to organizational and unit goals and strategies and business plans. Performance plans should be able to tie back to unit and organizational plans; ideally, it should be possible to consolidate individual performance plans to the unit level and consolidate unit plans to the organizational level.

Job-level data is a significant part of the PM system. Key tasks, responsibilities, and outcomes should flow from job data sets to individual performance plans. Performance exists only within the context of the job.

Since performance begins at the individual level, most of the data in the PM system are individual-level data. Data include all the performance criteria developed by the manager for the individual, the particular measures that will be used to rate the individual's performance on each criterion, and the performance standards for each measure. If rating information is to be provided by more than the manager, the names of other raters and the criteria for which they will provide rating information need to be in the system. Usually, the entire performance contract will be a part of the system. Most systems will include space for the supervisor (and other raters) to enter observed performance and performance incidents. Contemporary systems allow both employees and managers to enter comments and observations at any time during the review period with the option to have the system automatically sweep all those comments into the final review in a concatenated area for editing by the user. There should also be space for documentation of positive and corrective feedback. While creating an IDP, many systems can recommend and provide a library of development activities that can be used to correct specific problems.

Typical Reports

The most important standardized reports produced by the HRIS are the performance contract for each employee and the annual summary appraisal for each employee. Other reports include aggregate performance data by unit and reports comparing aggregated unit performance with unit output (Cohen & Hall, 2005, p. 64). The HRIS needs to have the capability of archiving data, so that long-term performance trends for individuals and groups can be tracked. If competency assessments are used as a part of the review, HR can monitor systemic developmental requirements based on the aggregated (business unit, location, level, etc.) competency results.

Data Outflows

Performance data are used in many HRM decisions and will flow automatically into some processes or be available for others as needed. One automatic flow will be into compensation. Organizations with merit pay need performance distributions to construct a merit matrix. (Note that many performance applications also have the capability for the compensation functionality to be built in.) The performance measure used is the summary performance level for each employee. Performance data on various performance dimensions are used in decisions relating to promotion, lay-offs, assignment to training programs, and developmental assignments. Performance data are also central to HR planning.

Decision Support

The basic decision support system in the area of PM is the entire system. Having performance criteria, performance measures, performance standards, and recent performance documentation in a single place allows managers to keep track of how each direct report is doing and what interventions need to be made to improve performance (Evans, 2001). Similarly, the direct report can view the same data and use them as a basis for deciding on areas where improvement is needed. Indeed, PM software can be categorized as either preformatted appraisal systems—systems that allow the development of customized appraisals—or systems that diagnose performance problems (Forrer & Leibowitz, 1991, pp. 104–106).

Flowers, Tudor, and Trumble (1997) note that such systems should allow managers to update information, serve as a support in conducting the appraisal interview, allow the creation of effective appraisal forms, and support all legal mandates relevant to performance appraisals. A system supporting **360° appraisals** is described by Meyer (1998).

Group performance can also be tracked and the data used for performance improvement; since most employees work as part of teams, there has been increased interest in measuring and managing team performance (e.g., Jones & Schilling, 2000). Stegner and Kofahl (2004) provide a case study in a process for group performance improvement that could not exist without heavy input from the HRIS. In some cases, systems tie closely with marketing and management information systems; Charles, Kurlander, and Savage (2000) describe a sales performance tracking system that keeps home office and sales personnel aware of results against quotas and suggests where efforts need to be made to enhance sales performance.

Finally, automated PM systems allow managers and HR managers to track the administrative aspects of PM: Have all managers completed performance contracts with their direct reports? Are summary appraisals done on time? Do ratings by a manager and the performance of the manager's unit jibe? These are questions that can be answered by the system. Additionally, performance ratings can be checked for possible bias against protected groups. This includes not only the ratings themselves but also their use in HR decisions. Under the Uniform Guidelines (1978), performance appraisals are considered "tests" when used for HR decisions, such as promotions, and are subject to the same validity and reliability requirements as other tests when they are found to have an adverse impact on protected groups.

Web-based systems can also provide a calibration tool for employee performance ratings that allows for a visual inspection of the distribution of ratings for a population. This is often essential as a tie-in to the compensation process since performance ratings often dictate how much employees may receive for their annual merit review. The example (Figure 13.2) being used by a large utility organization allows managers to view the distribution and even drag-and-drop employees within the ratings to adjust for any discrepancies.

❖ **Figure 13.2**   Example of Relating Performance to Compensation

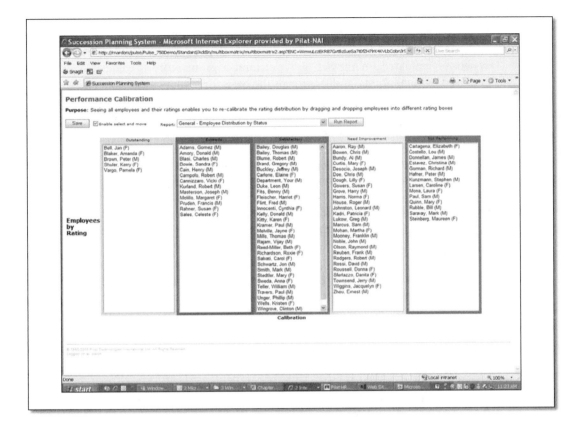

Compensation

Overview

Compensation is one of the most complex topics in HRM, and attempting to present an overview is ambitious. Organizations faced with the complexities of creating and administering compensation systems are increasingly turning to technology for help. Wright (2003, p. 55) estimates that a 12,000-person firm can save as much as $850,000 per year in administrative costs by automating compensation planning alone. Brink and McDonnell (2003) point out that nearly all processes used to design, communicate, and manage pay are moving toward Web applications.

The basic compensation system includes **base pay**, merit pay, short-term and long-term incentives, **perquisites**, **recognition awards**, and attraction/retention awards. There are many processes associated with each of these, all of which must be coordinated. If that were not enough, there are also special populations that have unique pay processes: executives, sales personnel, scientists and engineers, expatriates, unionized workers, and the whole panoply of temporary/contract/part-time workers.

Base pay is built around two processes: **job evaluation** and **market benchmarking**. Job evaluation creates an internal hierarchy of value. In the most common form of job evaluation, a set of factors is developed that reflects characteristics that add value to work in the specific organization (e.g., the education required). Each factor is weighted by importance, and scales are developed. Every job that will be in the base pay system is evaluated on the set of scales, and a point score is calculated. Jobs are arranged by total points, and this forms the basis for a salary structure.

Market benchmarking is used to price the structure (or individual jobs). Market data are collected for as many jobs as possible. In most organizations, one or more surveys may be developed in-house to collect market benchmarks; but the bulk of benchmark data come from commercial and association surveys. Many of these surveys are now available electronically (either on disk or through a Web site) and can be integrated into the compensation information system. Entering data can be done through a Web site with a format maximizing ease of data entry (Tobin, 2002). However, Web sites with salary data are not without problems; employees frequently access Web sites that may have unrepresentative data and argue that they are underpaid based on bad data (Menefee, 2000).

Employees are placed in the salary grade appropriate for their job. Each grade has a midpoint that serves as a proxy for all the jobs in that grade, and a range (minimum and maximum salary for jobs in that grade, usually ±20% from the midpoint) is built around the midpoint; exact placement in the range is usually a function of performance and individual characteristics (quality of degree, experience).

The structure is adjusted each year based on market movements. If the market were to increase by 3%, for example, the midpoints would increase by 3% as well. However, not all employees receive a 3% increase if the organization uses a merit pay system. In a merit pay system, the size of the increase is a function of performance level and where the employee is in the range. The higher the performance, the larger is the increase. Generally, the lower the place in range, the higher the increase will be. A merit matrix is developed to provide guidelines based on performance and place in the range that ensure that the total amount spent by the organization is no more than the specified percentage of payroll.

There are many forms of short-term **incentive pay**. Unlike merit pay, short-term incentive pay is rarely added to base pay and must be re-earned every year. Typical short-term incentive programs include bonuses, gain sharing, goal sharing, small-group incentives, and profit sharing. With the exception of profit sharing, short-term incentive programs usually have specific measures that will drive payout set up prior to the beginning of the program. Gain sharing, for example, bases payouts on reductions in production costs due to more efficient use of labor. Specific preplanned formulas based on past production costs drive payouts. Bonus systems can be driven by preplanned criteria related to manufacturing, customer service, safety, or anything else that the company wishes to motivate employees to achieve. Profit sharing is usually retrospective; the board decides after the books have closed for the fiscal year that some percentage of profits will be shared with employees. In all cases, the measures driving short-term incentive payouts must be collected, either through existing measurement systems or through special systems designed for the purpose.

Long-term incentives are primarily based on organization stock, options to buy organization stock, or phantom (make-believe) stock. The goal of long-term incentives is twofold: to align the interests of employees with those of shareholders and to incent aligned performance over periods of more than 1 year.

Perquisites are rewards that are a function of organizational status. Executive dining rooms, first-class or corporate jet air travel, and club memberships are examples. Perquisites frequently have tax consequences to the employee receiving them and, thus, must be included as part of the pay system. In the past several years, some organizations have transformed perquisites into incentive rewards based on performance; go to any Disney property, and you will see parking spaces near the employee entrance that are reserved for high performers.

Recognition awards are low cost/no cost awards that are retrospective: When an employee does something of note, he or she receives an award that may have little financial value but is psychologically rewarding. The use of Web sites in recognition programs, so that every employee can go online and find where he or she stands in comparison with other eligible employees, can greatly enhance the motivational impact of such programs (Perlmutter, 2002). Attraction/retention awards are one-time awards that are used to attract prospective employees to the organization or persuade them to remain with the organization. These awards may take the form of cash, stock options, benefits, or adjustments to benefits rules. The goal is to incur a one-time cost that does not drive up base pay.

While the types of compensation mentioned above are made up of multiple programs, it is critical that all compensation programs be integrated, so that employees receive a single message about what adds value in the organization and the type of behavior and culture that is desired.

Compensation programs must meet federal and state statutory and regulatory requirements. The **Fair Labor Standards Act (FLSA)** differentiates **exempt and nonexempt workers**; the organization must pay nonexempt workers at least the minimum wage, must pay time worked in excess of 40 hours a week overtime at a rate of 1.5 times the normal pay, and must provide records to the federal government on hours worked and regular and overtime pay for all nonexempt workers. OFCCP (Office of Federal Contract Compliance Programs) requires annual evidence of nonbias with respect to race and gender for SSEGs (similarly situated employee groups) and requires multiple linear regression analyses as evidence.

Typical Data Inputs

Compensation data inputs include internal, external, and generated data. Internal data include information about jobs (descriptions, specifications), people (performance, salary history), and organizational units (salary budget, job evaluation system). External data would include market survey data and information on rewards practices. Internal and external data would be combined and used to generate job evaluation results, salary structures, merit matrices, and a variety of reward guidelines. Incentive programs will require input data on whatever behavior or outcome is being incented; such data might include customer survey results, accident data, time-to-market data, or product quality data.

Compensation for special employee groups usually requires data specific to that group. Executive compensation is likely to require organization-wide sales, productivity, profit, share price, market share, and other financial, market, and production data indicative of organizational success. Sales compensation systems may require data on quotas, sales, bonus or commission rates, and competitive market data. Gain-sharing programs require historical averaged data on labor costs as a proportion of value of production. Bargaining unit employee pay systems require data on contract specifics. For nonexempt employees, hourly rates and hours worked per week are required.

In short, there are very few data within the organization that might not be required by some part of the compensation system. As an example, a company that market-prices jobs will collect as much market data on wages as possible. Even so, it is unlikely that market data can be found for all jobs. The "market rate" for these jobs must be estimated. It is common to use multiple linear regression for this purpose. As much information about all jobs is collected as possible, either using job specification data or aggregate information from job incumbents. Some specific information that might be collected from the HRIS includes the average education level of job incumbents in each job, the average amount of training incumbents in each job have had, the average number of direct reports each incumbent in a job has, and so forth. While logic may guide the choice of independent variables to use in the regression equation to predict market rates, the goal is to get the best prediction, and whatever variables end up providing the best prediction are the ones that will be used. Similarly, incentive programs may make use of any financial, market, or production data to determine whether bonuses should be paid and, if so, how much and to whom.

Typical Reports

There are a number of standard reports in the compensation arena, although because of the sensitive nature of compensation information, they are not widely circulated. The most common reports include budget reports to managers showing how their actual compensation costs compare with the projected costs. Most organizations provide each employee with an "Annual Compensation Report" showing the total amount of money spent by the organization on the employee, including money spent on wage or salary, incentive pay, and the cost of benefits paid for by the organization. Similar reports, such as incentive reports that tell people how they are doing with respect to earning a specific incentive award, become much more effective when a Web site is used for communication (Stiffler, 2001).

Companies participating in wage surveys produce reports for use by surveying organizations. In some cases, a compensation analyst draws the data from the HRIS and enters them into the survey, but in other cases, an automated application gathers data from the HRIS and enters them into the survey program.

A new report on the analysis of possible "systemic compensation bias" among "similarly situated employee groups" is now required by the OFCCP of the U.S. Government. This report will be due annually, along with the organization's Affirmative Action Report.

Data Outflows

The primary data outflow from compensation modules is to payroll. Compensation analysts draw on the data for additional analyses. Managers preparing budgets draw on compensation as they project costs over the next budget period. Benefits analysts draw on compensation data as they analyze probable future costs of wage-based benefits (pensions are usually a function of salary level, while health benefits are largely independent of salary level).

Data are sent to federal, state, and local agencies, including taxing agencies, labor departments, and other units tracking wage data. Many organizations provide data to reward survey firms.

Decision Support

The major rewards decision that has to be made about every employee is how much should he or she be paid? Decision support systems in compensation are all aimed at that decision. Because of the complexity of compensation, a series of decisions must be made. Thus, there are decision support systems dealing with job evaluation, the use of market data, market pricing, building a salary structure, developing a merit matrix, and running incentive programs. Koski (2003) describes a project that automated a worldwide employee bonus system; executives and managers got a self-service system, and compensation executives could keep track real time of award amounts and payouts. Computer and Web products now support these processes and generally offer advantages to the organizations using them (Zingheim & Schuster, 2005). Indeed, Zingheim and Schuster (2004) argue that Web management of pay and rewards is one of two great innovations in the rewards field.

There can be difficulties with Web management of pay. Van De Voort and McDonnell (2003) point out that working "live" can create problems when numbers change during the process. As an example, if a manager is calculating merit pay and is working off a specific budget number, changes to that number by a senior manager can create confusion and bad decisions. The use of a frozen, or static, database ensures that everyone is working with the same assumptions and figures.

Other decision support systems deal with sales compensation. Cocks and Gould (2001) note that compensation software is critical in defining commission levels, designing compensation plans, and managing compensation, since all three areas require on-the-fly complex calculations on a repeated basis. Weeks (2000) notes that virtual sales teams in widely separated areas can be much more effective in maintaining customer satisfaction; only the Web allows the coordination between team members required to pull off this strategy, and it also allows sales compensation experts to audit and fine-tune the sales compensation system to maintain high motivation levels.

A whole set of applications relate to executive pay. Since the Enron scandal and the subsequent passage of the Sarbanes-Oxley Act (SOX), compliance reports, including those dealing with executive pay, are required. SOX compliance is greatly supported by data from the HRIS ("How HRIS Can Help With SOX Compliance," 2005; Sherman, 2005).

Benefits

Overview

A full discussion of benefits programs is beyond the scope of this chapter. There are five broad types of benefits programs in most U.S. organizations. Because some company-provided benefits in this country are government provided in other countries, a different typology would be required for organizations abroad.

The first set of benefits programs that is common in U.S. companies includes pension plans (both defined benefit and defined contribution), individual savings plans (such as Keoghs, SEPs, and IRAs), and Social Security. While few Americans think of Social Security as a benefit, the organization must fund contributions to Social Security just as an employee does. The goal of all these benefits programs is to ensure that the employee will have continued income after retirement. The second set of benefits programs includes workers' compensation, unemployment insurance, long- and short-term disability insurance, and life insurance. The goal of these programs is to ensure that employees who cannot work (through no fault of their own) have some income until they can work again and to provide income protection to employees' families.

The third set of benefits programs includes medical and other health benefits such as hospitalization and medical care insurance; surgical and major medical care insurance; long-term care; dental, vision, and hearing care insurance; and prescription drug coverage insurance. These benefits are designed to make sure that employees and their families are not bankrupted by illness or accident and can obtain preventative and curative care. The fourth area of benefits is paid time off and includes vacation, holidays, personal days, special purpose days (such as jury duty, bereavement, and military service), and family leave. The goal of paid time off is to recognize that employees need to recharge their batteries and spend time with their families for celebrations or other significant life events.

Benefits programs differ from compensation in two major ways. First, in the majority of organizations, employees pay part (or all) of the costs for most benefits. (Even when benefit costs are borne entirely by employees, group purchasing reduces the cost that the employee would pay for an equivalent self-purchased benefit.) Second, most organizations have some flexibility in the benefits program. All employees receive a core benefits package but then choose additional coverage or additional benefits, or both, up to the level of the total benefits package. (**Flexplans** also allow the employee to purchase additional coverage or benefits or both at cost.) These two characteristics of benefits programs make them relatively complex to administer; each employee in the organization may have a slightly different benefit package with a unique salary deduction profile. Things even get complicated with paid time off. Not only may different employee groups (e.g., bargaining units, executives) get different paid time off configurations, but these configurations may also differ within groups based on seniority. In addition, many organizations have what is called a paid time off bank, through which employees can trade paid time off for cash or other benefits, can buy additional paid time off, or can donate paid time off to other employees (e.g., in cases of long-term illness). All this makes benefits programs extremely complex and difficult to administer.

Legal requirements for benefits programs are also more stringent than those for compensation programs. Most benefits programs are influenced by the Employee Retirement Income Security Act (ERISA), which grants benefits a tax-favored status. However, to be qualified (for favorable tax treatment), the benefit must meet stringent requirements. These requirements include reports to benefits recipients and to the federal government, demonstrating that requirements for qualified status are met. In addition, many organizations offer nonqualified benefits to some employee groups, particularly to executives.

Typical Data Inputs

There are HRIS benefits modules with different purposes, and each requires a different type of data input. One set of functions focuses on the organization relationship with current and prospective vendors. Data input in this case will focus on aggregate data about the people to be covered and the relevant demographics for the covered group, along with program coverage desired and cost limitations.

A second set of functions focuses on internal management of benefits programs and will be used to track usage, employee choices (in the case of flexplans), and costs. Experience, usage, and costs will be fed into this program.

A third, and most common, set of programs focuses on employee input about enrollment and other coverage choices, changes in coverage desired, and changes in employee status (e.g., addition of a dependent, change in marital status) that may affect coverage and employee costs. These programs may also allow employees to file claims with the organization. In these programs, many of which are Web based, employees feed in personal data, coverage choices, and other data relevant to their use of the benefit.

The fourth set of data placed into the system consists of the myriad federal, state, and local laws and regulations governing benefits practice. These laws and regulations provide decision support system "rules" for managers using the system.

Typical Reports

The most common report is the annual benefits report to employees required for tax-qualified plans under ERISA. This report requires organizations to report to employees annually about certain benefit facts, such as vested pension levels. Most organizations have gone beyond the ERISA requirements and provide a report to each employee showing the total value of all compensation and benefits received by the employee during the year. This Annual Compensation Report is the "rewards scorecard" for the employee. Ceccon (2004) estimates that putting this annual report online rather than distributing printed copies can save a company with 30,000 employees $678,000 actual costs over 5 years and that productivity savings from reducing the amount of time employees use to find benefit account balances, pay information, and other rewards information on multiple sites or via phone calls to HR can save $625,000 per year. HR productivity increases net an annual savings of $30,000, and increased employee retention would reduce costs by $150,000 per year. With 5-year savings of $678,000 and annual productivity savings totaling $805,000, Web reporting is clearly advantageous.

There are dozens of reports required by federal and state government units, including the IRS, units of the Department of Labor, and other federal agencies, and similar units at the state level.

Data Outflows

Data generated by benefits programs have to be transferred to payroll and accounting internally. Data are sent externally to benefits providers, outsourced benefits administrators, and a variety of federal, state, and local agencies. Aggregate data are provided to benefits survey firms.

The real-time transfer of data can result in large cost savings. Moynihan (2000) notes that AT&T saved $15 million when it switched to providing updated enrollment information to all its various health plans. Previously, tardy data transfer resulted in health plans denying coverage to employees who were in fact eligible and paid out on claims of people who no longer worked for AT&T.

Decision Support

Decision support tools overlap to some extent with reports in the benefits arena, since it is frequently the report that triggers a need to make changes to comply with federal, state, or local requirements. As an example, McCormack (2004) notes that the Family Medical Leave Act (FMLA) has complicated administering employee leave. Many states have more stringent leave requirements than FMLA or the 40 other federal leave laws. A system that tracks these laws and can tell the HR manager exactly what the leave requirements are in a specific locality ensures compliance and minimizes risks of lawsuits and fines.

Similarly, tax-qualified benefit plans are subject to federal bias regulations. In this case, "bias" refers to income level rather than protected group status. Federal policy is that tax laws should not underwrite benefits that are available only to highly paid employees. If an organization is to have a qualified 401(k) retirement plan, for example, it must be available to both low- and high-paid employees and, in addition, must be used by both. Tracking enrollments against those eligible for participation can trigger efforts to get more low-paid employees to participate in the plan.

When organizations offer flexible benefit plans, it is common to track the choices made by employees to guide plan development. A few organizations have looked at benefits choices made by high performers to see if they differ from the choices made by low performers. Others look at the choices made by protected groups. Recruitment literature can then be tailored to specific groups to ensure a better yield of desirable applicants.

Web-based services also offer decision support to employees deciding what levels of coverage to sign up for (Dawson, 1997). Employees can readily compare the cost of various levels of benefits service and more readily understand the cost/benefit trade-off that they are going to make. Similarly, transferring the enrollment process to the employees themselves can save the organization money (Teer, 1997). However, such savings are not likely to occur unless the system is easy to use for all employees, not just the technologically savvy (Ashley, 2006).

Payroll

Overview

Payroll is the transactional process through which compensation is transferred to employees and federal, state, and local income and payroll taxes are withheld from employees' checks. It is also through payroll that any benefits costs borne by employees are withheld. While some employees receive actual checks for net pay, it is more common, especially among large organizations, for direct deposits to be made to employees' bank accounts. For companies that outsource, there is a need to make sure that the compensation and benefits modules of the HRIS interface flawlessly with the provider's payroll input. Even for companies who do payroll in-house, the payroll module is usually part of the accounting system rather than the HRIS, and it is critical that the interface between the HRIS and the payroll software works flawlessly (Walker, 1987, pp. 118–119).

In the majority of organizations, payroll is a function administered by finance or accounting rather than an HR department function. HR departments feed compensation data and benefits coverage (and employees' coverage choices) to payroll, which makes sure that all appropriate federal, state, and local income and payroll taxes are withheld at the correct rate and that any deductions for benefits are also withheld at the correct rate. Payroll usually has the responsibility for keeping track of income and payroll tax rates and applicable salary levels. Payroll results are fed back into the general accounting system by payroll. Because labor costs are the largest variable cost for most organizations, it is critical for the organizations' financial well-being that payroll records are accurate and timely. Because the paycheck is a signal of the employment relationship and because many employees rely on their paycheck to meet bills that are due, it is critical that the payroll system delivers accurate and timely paychecks or bank transfers. Little will anger or demoralize an employee more than a missing or inaccurate paycheck or transfer. In short, payroll is a transactional task that must be flawless.

Payroll is the most heavily outsourced HRM function. Great economies of scale can be achieved by a payroll processor with respect to keeping up with the intricacies of income and payroll tax deductibles requirements and maintaining (and upgrading) software that ensures that payroll is accurate and completed in a timely manner. However, outsourcing companies do not work in a vacuum, and compensation and benefits functions must deliver data to the outsourcer, and the accounting and finance functions must receive data back from the outsourcer. And some companies argue that integrating HR and payroll makes sense and saves data entry and labor costs while providing greater accuracy and timeliness (Gale, 2002).

Typical Data Inputs

Data entered into the payroll system from inside the organization include compensation data, benefits data, and other payroll addition (e.g., special awards) and deductions data (e.g., union dues, wage garnishment for child support, credit union repayment installment). Time and attendance data are usually handled in a special module, and data from this module are also fed into payroll (Robb, 2004). Data external to the organization include federal, state, and local income and payroll tax rules that allow the organization to withhold appropriate amounts from each employee's paycheck. There may be payments made to individuals who are not active employees. Although it is usually taken care of in a separate COBRA module, there may even be payments from ex-employees for continuation of benefits. The most frequent data input are change data. Every time a new employee goes on the payroll, an employee changes status, an employee makes benefits elections changes, governments change tax or withholding rates, or the organization makes changes such as pay increases, data reflecting all changes have to go into the payroll system.

In addition to internal and external data, the system generates data that it stores and uses over time. For example, FICA (Social Security) taxes (in 2008) are withheld on the first $102,000; the maximum tax withheld is $6,324. Payroll must keep a running total of FICA paid so that it does not deduct too much from the employee's paycheck.

Typical Reports

There are a number of standard payroll reports. These show for the organization as a whole (or for subunits) the actual amount paid to employees for a period (and cumulatively) and the amounts deducted for various purposes. Reports go to federal, state, and local agencies, including taxing authorities. Reports go to benefits providers. Employees receive reports with their paychecks or notices of deposit; the report shows gross pay and all deductions. Usually year-to-date accumulations are also provided.

Data Outflows

Payroll data go to accounting, federal, state, and local agencies and to benefits providers. These payroll data are the input for a variety of processes in those units.

Decision Support

Payroll data are not usually used for decision-making purposes. They are used extensively for audit purposes.

Summary

The combined PM, compensation, benefits, and payroll systems constitute the most important parts of the HRIS. Money may not be at the forefront of how people talk about the organization and their linkages to it, but let ratings result in lower than expected increases, bonuses be miscalculated, benefits elections not be implemented, or a paycheck be miscalculated or (worse still) not delivered, and employees become vocal. Because pay and benefits constitute the largest variable cost to any organization, and the largest cost to many organizations, it is critical that managers plan, track, and audit outlays on a real-time basis. A significant proportion of data and reports owed to federal, state, and local agencies come from the compensation, benefits, and payroll modules. The consequences of inaccurate, misleading, or unsubmitted data and reports include embarrassment, fines, and even jail time. And this is just the transactional part of these modules.

A key part of strategic HR is aligning employee behaviors with the strategic intent of the organization. It is important to hire the best people and provide them with the training and development needed. Without PM, the success of hiring strategies is unknown, and similarly, the need for training and development interventions is unknown. PM systems support the translation of corporate strategy into individual performance plans. Compensation and benefits systems can be used to hire the right people, retain the high performers, and motivate all employees to perform at a higher level. Compensation can also be used to motivate poor performers out of the organization. As systems technology has progressed, managers have increasing ability to enhance the performance of their direct reports and to tailor compensation and benefits programs that will attract, retain, and motivate the best.

DISCUSSION QUESTIONS

1. Discuss how a manager might make sure that the performance plan for each of her direct reports was driven by organizational strategy and the business plan. How can information systems support this goal?

2. Merit increases require a single "performance" number, while most incentive plans have multiple and varying performance measures. How can the PM system meet both needs?

3. Compensation strategy includes how competitive the organization wants to be, the number of different compensation systems the organization wants to have, the mix of various reward and benefit components, and the basis of increases. Discuss the data inflows that an organization that wanted to automate the compensation design and administration processes would have to do.

4. Both PM and benefits information systems make provision for employee access and input. What access would you provide in each of these systems, and what leeway would you provide employees in reading, entering, and changing data?

5. A lot of compensation information is available to employees today on the Web (e.g., Salary.com), and much of it is inaccurate. How can an organization assure employees that they are fairly compensated (assume they are) when public data suggest otherwise?

6. Flexible benefit plans are common today. Discuss ways in which employers can ensure that employees make good choices about the benefits and benefit levels that they choose within the benefits information system itself.

7. Payroll and benefits are commonly outsourced. Discuss which parts of PM, compensation, benefits, and payroll you would consider outsourcing, justifying your views.

CASE STUDY: GRANDVIEW GLOBAL FINANCIAL SERVICES, INC.

Grandview Global Financial Services is an international corporation providing multiple financial services. Although they are one of the smaller players in the field, they have about 20,000 employees worldwide. Their strategy has focused on serving a niche market (high net worth individuals) with all the wealth management services they require. These services include investments, insurance, banking, real estate, financial planning, and related services.

The lynchpin making all these services work well is the quality of the employees and the degree to which they are motivated to provide "over the top" attention to clients' needs. Clients have come to expect this level of service regardless of where they might happen to be and regardless of the time. With high expectations by clients, every employee is expected to provide flawless service.

As it has expanded globally, Grandview has hired employees from all the countries in which they do business. While all employees are expected to speak English, business is conducted in nine different languages in 45 locations. Grandview has invested heavily in developing a uniform corporate culture but has not succeeded in doing so in all locations.

One difficulty has been the PM and reward systems. Each geographic area developed its own PM tools reflecting local culture and the past experiences of local national employees. There are a variety of systems using different performance criteria. Most of the PM materials are in Microsoft Word. Some of the systems seem to work all right, while others do not. None of the systems are coordinated, except to the extent that final performance ratings are sent to Grandview corporate HR. There has been enormous push back and noncompliance with PM policies from the employees because of the difficulty of the paper performance process as well as the nine different languages being used worldwide.

Rewards systems are similarly localized. Base pay, incentive systems, and benefits have grown up in each geographic location in accord with local market practice, local laws, and customs. The complexity and number of Excel spreadsheets needed to manage the financial targets and the resulting compensation plans for that many employees have created perceived and actual inequities. It is difficult to transfer employees across geographic areas because of the different systems in place, and awareness that employees in different locations have very different terms and conditions has created morale problems.

Corporate HR has PM and rewards modules in its HRIS covering U.S. employees, but this covers only about 60% of Grandview's employee population. An executive rewards module does cover about 2,000 senior executives worldwide, but all foreign data are sent from different locations and entered into the module at headquarters. Part of the historic reason for this is legal requirements in the EU and some other locales covering **information privacy**; it is easier to get executives to grant permission for transmission of specific data when those data are used to calculate stock option awards and other executive incentive payments granted by the corporate.

Corporate HR would like to move away from local systems and institute a corporate-wide system that does not rely on Word documents for performance reviews and Excel spreadsheets for the resulting compensation plans that result from the overall performance rating. It was thought that common systems for PM and rewards would support a more unified culture and help translate Grandview's corporate strategy into individual performance plans worldwide.

The ideal system would be a Web-based, multilingual, integrated PM and compensation system. The PM system would be accessible by managers and their direct reports and would be tied to corporate strategy and the current business plan. Managers and their direct reports could access the system at any time to see performance criteria, measures, and standards and look at current progress against standards. The rewards and benefits modules, while based on local law and custom, would be standardized with respect to process, fostering a more uniform rewards culture. It is critical to HR managers that the technology selected would be flexible enough so that yearly changes to the application could be made efficiently and legal requirements in different locations could be accommodated, as well as changes in those requirements.

Since the performance goals are based on financial targets and employees' merit, and incentive payments are directly related to their performance as well as Grandview's overall results, all necessary functionality for the compensation process should be built into the performance system. At year end, results should be able to be imported directly from corporate financial systems and used to generate performance reviews and compensation plans for the employees. The resultant pay increases and bonus payments would be fed directly into the payroll system already in use by

Grandview in the United States and abroad. The system administrators could ensure worldwide compliance with the performance process directly from the system through a variety of reports.

Case Study Questions

1. What is the role of PM in establishing and maintaining corporate culture?

2. What is the role of compensation and benefits in establishing and maintaining corporate culture?

3. Since laws, labor markets, and customs relevant to PM, compensation, and benefits differ from country to country, does it make sense to try and maintain a common global process for managing each of these areas?

4. Given all the cross-country differences, why would a global organization want to have a common HRIS?

5. How should Grandview go about implementing a global PM system?

6. How should Grandview go about implementing a global rewards system?

7. How should Grandview go about implementing a global benefits system?

8. How should Grandview go about implementing a global HRIS to manage these functions?

REFERENCES

Ashley, D. (2006). Intuitive technologies increase employee adoption of human resource solutions. *Compensation & Benefits Review, 38*(1), 62–68.

Banks, C. G., & May, K. E. (1999). Performance management: The real glue in organizations. In A. I. Kraut & A. K. Korman (Eds.), *Evolving practices in human resource management: Responses to a changing world of work* (pp. 118–145). San Francisco: Jossey-Bass.

Bernardin, H. J., Hagan, C. M., Kane, J. S., & Villanova, P. (1998). Effective performance management: A focus on precision, customers, and situational constraints. In J. W. Smither (Ed.), *Performance appraisal: State of the art in practice* (pp. 3–48). San Francisco: Jossey-Bass.

Bing, J. W. (2004). Metrics for assessing human process on work teams. *IHRIM Journal, 8*(6), 26–31.

Brink, S., & McDonnell, S. (2003). e-Compensation. In *The e-merging technologies series* (pp. 4.1–4.18). Burlington, MA: IHRIM Press.

Ceccon, A. (2004). The real value statement. Aggregating pay and benefits on the Internet. *Compensation & Benefits Review, 36*(6), 53–58.

Charles, E. W., Kurlander, P., & Savage, B. (2000). Tracking sales performance. *ACA News, 43*(3), 38–41.

Cocks, D. J., & Gould, D. (2001). Sales compensation: A new technology-enabled strategy. *Compensation & Benefits Review, 33*(1), 27–31.

Cohen, A. J., & Hall, M. E. (2005). Automating your performance and competency evaluation process. *WorldatWork Journal, 14*(3), 64–70.

Dawson, S. (1997). Leveraging an Intranet for employee self-service: A Q & A with Unisys corporation. *IHRIM.link, 2*(3), 54–65.

Evans, E. M. (2001). Internet-age performance management: Lessons from high-performing organizations. In A. J. Walker (Ed.), *Web-based human resources: The technologies and trends that are transforming HR* (pp. 65–82). New York: McGraw-Hill.

Flowers, L. A., Tudor, T. R., & Trumble, R. R. (1997). Computer assisted performance appraisal systems. *Journal of Compensation and Benefits, 12*(6), 34–35.

Forrer, S. E., & Leibowitz, Z. B. (1991). *Using computers in human resources: How to select and make the best use of automated HR systems.* San Francisco: Jossey-Bass.

Gale, S. F. (2002). How three companies merged HR and payroll. *Workforce, 81*(1), 64–67.

How HRIS can help with SOX compliance. (2005). *HR Focus, 82*(10), 7, 10.

Jones, S. D., & Schilling, D. J. (2000). *Measuring team performance: A step-by-step, customizable approach for managers, facilitators, and team leaders.* San Francisco: Jossey-Bass.

Koski, L. (2003). Executive/manager self-service: Stat Street Corporation's annual incentive program. *Compensation & Benefits Review, 35*(2), 21–25.

McCormack, J. (2004). Compliance tools: Technology can help HR stay on the right side of the law. *HR Magazine, 49*(3), 95–98.

Menefee, J. A. (2000). The value of pay data on the Web: Nominal or real? *Workspan, 43*(9), 25–28.

Meyer, G. (1998). *360 on the net:* A computer toolkit for multirater performance feedback. *HR Magazine, 43*(11), 46–50.

Moynihan, J. J. (2000). HIPPA compliance offers human resource department savings. *Healthcare Financial Management, 54*(3), 82–83.

Perlmutter, A. L. (2002). Taking motivation and recognition online. *Compensation & Benefits Review, 34*(2), 70–74.

Robb, D. (2004). Marking time. *HR Magazine, 49*(7), 111–115.

Sherman, E. (2005). Use technology to stay in SOX compliance. *HR Magazine, 50*(5), 95–99.

Stegner, R., & Kofahl, B. (2004). Case study: Human performance improvement model at work. *IHRIM Journal, 8*(6), 18–20.

Stiffler, M. A. (2001). Incentive compensation and the Web. *Compensation & Benefits Review, 33*(1), 15–19.

Teer, M. S. (1997). Surfing for benefits. *IHRIM.link, 2*(3), 66–74.

Tobin, N. (2002). Can technology ease the pain of salary surveys? *Public Personnel Management, 31*(1), 65–77.

Uniform guidelines on employee selection procedures. (1978). *Federal Register, 43*(166), 38290–39309.

Van De Voort, D. M., & McDonnell, S. W. (2003). Computers in compensation. In W. A. Caldwell (Ed.), *Compensation guide* (pp. 21–1–21–32). Minneapolis, MN: Thomson/West.

Walker, A. J. (1987). *HRIS development: A project team guide to building an effective personnel information system.* New York: Van Nostrand Reinhold.

Weeks, B. (2000). Setting sales force compensation in the Internet age. *Compensation & Benefits Review, 32*(2), 25–42.

Wright, A. (2003). Tools for automating complex compensation programs. *Compensation & Benefits Review, 35*(6), 53–61.

Zingheim, P. K., & Schuster, J. R. (2004). What's the next great pay and reward innovation? Business value, paying for skill, and the Internet! *IHRIM Journal, 8*(5), 47–50.

Zingheim, P. K., & Schuster, J. R. (2005). Evaluating human resource pay and reward computer and Web products. *Compensation & Benefits Review, 37*(5), 42–45.

14

International Human Resource Management

Michael J. Kavanagh

John W. Michel

EDITORS' NOTE

In Chapter 1, emergence of the global marketplace as one of the most important trends in the field of HRM was emphasized. In this chapter, some of the significant differences between domestic HRM and international human resource management (IHRM) are covered, and some of the HRM issues involved in an international organization are also described. The contrast between the operation of an HR department in a "domestic-only" firm versus its operation in a multinational enterprise (MNE) is also covered. To understand the operation of companies in the global marketplace, different organizational forms that can exist are identified. The importance of the influence of national culture on the external environment in which the firm competes for market share is highlighted. The external environment also has a major impact on the IHRM department's activities and program—that is, the management of the human capital of a firm. This impact in terms of its effects on IHRM programs is discussed. Naturally, these added international issues and additional complexities pose significant challenges for the design, development, implementation, and use of an HRIS, which are covered at the end of this chapter.

CHAPTER OBJECTIVES

After completing this chapter, you should be able to

♦ Understand the differences between domestic and international HRM

♦ Identify the types of organizational forms used for competing internationally

♦ Understand the different types of employees who work in MNEs

♦ Discuss the staffing process for individuals working in MNEs

♦ Understand the problems that handling expatriates poses for the IHRM department

♦ Describe the training needs of and programs for international assignees

♦ Reconcile the difficulties of home-country and host-country performance appraisals

♦ Identify the characteristics of a good international compensation plan

♦ Understand the modifications necessary for using HRIS applications in IHRM

VIGNETTE

Skylor Electronics,[1] an MNE with headquarters in Seattle, Washington, was having considerable difficulty with **expatriate failure** in its overseas subsidiaries. Although there were a number of failures in the European Union (EU) countries, the largest failure rate was in its subsidiary in China. The vice president for HR, Marvin Russell, was deeply concerned since the costs of expatriate failure were very high, from $145,000 in the EU to over $400,000 in China. These comprised the direct costs, that is, dollars lost. The indirect costs of having the expatriate return early from the assignment were also quite heavy in terms of the negative image it created for the company in the local economy. In fact, the plant manager for one of the subsidiaries in China refused to accept any more American expatriates until they "could function in the Chinese culture."

The HR Vice President was looking for answers to this problem, and called a meeting with the Director of Overseas Operations, Elaine Peterson, and his Director of Career Development, Bill Seamon. Elaine was also quite upset with this expatriate failure, since it was very disruptive in terms of meeting production deadlines and maintaining quality in the production of their electronic products. Bill did not understand why there was a problem since he, along with the Director of Training, Dawn Fisher, had each expatriate attend a 3-hour orientation meeting that provided information on their destination country. As Bill noted, there was a 45-minute film, followed by a question-and-answer period. Then, the **expatriate** was given written material on the country.

Marvin indicated that he had spoken directly to several expatriates who returned early to determine the problem for the high failure rate. In general, each former expatriate had mentioned "not being prepared" for the new country and its culture. This experience of "**culture shock**" was most severe for the failed expatriates from China. After some discussion, it was clear that no one really knew what all the problems were with the expatriate failure problem and that no systematic data existed to help understand the problem. Marvin directed Bill and Dawn to investigate this problem and to provide a report in 2 weeks. Elaine indicated that she would provide a member of her staff to help this investigation.

Two weeks later, Bill and Dawn presented their report to Marvin and Elaine. The gist of the report was that the predeparture training for the expatriates and their families was totally inadequate. In fact, there was no training for expatriates' families, and one of the most common problems that led to the premature return of the expatriate was that the spouse was extremely unhappy. Bill and Dawn proposed a predeparture, 2-week training program for potential expatriates and their families as well as a trip, paid by the company, to the country where the expatriate was to be assigned. When Marvin objected to the costs of this program, Bill and Dawn were able to show that the costs savings by reducing expatriate failure exceeded the costs of the predeparture training program.

Introduction: Increasing Importance of International Human Resource Management

As noted in Chapter 1, globalization of business is one of the major changes in the world of work. Tsui (2007) notes that a "crude measure of economic globalization is that the aggregate world exports as a percentage of world gross domestic products (GDP) increased from 11.6 percent in 1970 to 30.7 percent in 2006" (p. 1353). Further illustrating this change, the competitive environment for businesses is the topic of a recent executive action report from The Conference Board (Iyer, 2005) that raised the question: "Globalization: Will Your Company Be Left Standing?"

Perhaps one of the major changes in the world's business economy has been the formation of regional free-trade zones. The passage of the North American Free Trade Agreement (NAFTA) in 1994 established the world's largest free market, increasing trade between Mexico, the United States, and Canada. Subsequently, the EU was formed and includes over 25 member countries (a membership that's still growing) engaged in free trade. Other trade agreements, such as the Association of Southeastern Nations (ASEAN), the East Asia Economic Group, the Asia-Pacific Economic Cooperation (APEC), and the South Asia Association for Regional Cooperation (SAARC), have improved trading relationships in Asia. One can only expect that there may be an African, and perhaps a Middle Eastern, free-trade zone in the future.

As illustrated in the diagram in Chapter 1 (see Figure 1.2), organizational functioning is contained *within* a national culture envelope. There is little doubt that the external environment for global business is significantly affected by the country in which it occurs, that is, the host country. The host country and its culture will affect all the factors in the *external environment:* government regulations, labor market, societal concerns, technology, HRM research, and competition. As noted by Bartlett (2002),

> The most important corporate transformation in 75 years is taking place right now. It will radically change human resource management and its role in the organization. . . . Behind this transformation are numerous forces, such as privatisation, deregulation, the information revolution, and above all, globalization. (p. xi)

Many of the issues raised by globalization of business and, in turn, changes in the IHRM function are clearly caused by factors in the external environment. However, there are still *internal issues* to consider in the effective globalization of an MNE. As noted by Beaman (2002), "The heritage of the industrial age prevents many organizations from creating the organizational structures, operational infra-structures, HR policies, and company cultures required to effectively function in the global economy" (p. v). As will be covered in this chapter, there has been considerable progress in handling these internal issues, and much of it has come from implementation of an HRIS in these MNEs.

There are a variety of factors that have led to the increased globalization of business and increased the importance of the IHRM function. These factors include the following:

1. Imported products have increased competition in every nation. Global competition has increased dramatically.

2. Deregulation in the United States, Germany, and other industrialized countries has changed the domestic business environment in those countries. There has been increased market accessibility.

3. There has been an increase in international mergers and acquisitions.

4. There is an increased awareness of the existence of talented human capital in all countries of the world. This availability of talented individuals has helped the globalization process. Globalization means managing human resources around the world.

One cannot overlook the fact that one of the major factors, in fact maybe the most important one, that has led to the increasing number of firms that have become international is the availability and cost effectiveness of computer technology. Computer technology has had a major influence on the acquisition and use of physical and financial resources, as well as greatly enhancing the marketing capabilities of MNEs. However, the most important impact of computer technology has been in HRM. Improved communications, worldwide recruiting and selecting, and better talent and performance management programs tied to career planning are only a few of the HR programs in MNEs that have been improved by the use of computer technology. In this chapter, we will examine the characteristics of MNEs and the management of people within these MNEs. In addition, we will be covering the various ways in which computer technology and a well-developed HRIS have affected the field of IHRM.

Finally, a caveat is that this chapter cannot cover the immense literature and issues in IHRM. However, for the interested reader there are excellent and comprehensive textbooks available on IHRM (Adler, 2002; Briscoe & Schuler, 2004; Dowling & Welch, 2005; Evans, Pucik & Barsoux, 2002).

Types of International Business Operations

In today's global economy, organizations tend to compete based on different levels of participation in international markets (Noe, Hollenbeck, Gerhart, & Wright, 2006). International business operations differ primarily by their level of global participation on a continuum from a domestic organization to a global organization. While many organizations only have limited global scope, a growing number, such as Dell and Microsoft, have a large number of personnel and facilities throughout the world (Bohlander & Snell, 2007). The following section provides a brief description of the general types of international business operations described by their level of global participation.

Domestic Corporation

A domestic corporation is characterized by an organization whose headquarters and operations are in the parent country. Most organizations start out as a domestic corporation (Noe et al., 2006). Because the organization only operates in one labor market, managing its human resources is much easier than that of organizations operating in multiple countries.

The focus of the HR function in a domestic organization is recruiting, hiring, training, and compensating the workforce composed of individuals from the local labor market (Noe et al., 2006). While domestic organizations do not experience the same issues as their global counterparts, they do face cultural differences with respect to demographic differences based on the region of the United States in which they reside. For example, even within the United States educational systems are better in some parts of the country than in others. As a result, the quality of human resources differs by region. In addition, the workforce in the United States is becoming more diverse as more females and minorities are entering the workplace. Therefore, managing diversity is a major issue even for domestic organizations.

International Corporation

An international corporation uses its existing core competencies to expand operations into foreign markets (Bohlander & Snell, 2007). These organizations compete in the global marketplace by exporting existing products and eventually opening facilities in other countries. While their corporate headquarters reside in the parent country, international corporations have foreign operations in one or more host countries. Companies operating as international corporations include Honda, General Electric, and Proctor & Gamble (see Bohlander & Snell, 2007).

This type of international business operation presents various unique challenges for the HRM function of the organization. Two issues particularly relevant to international corporations are the host country's legal system and the host country's national culture. An example of a legal issue is related to minimum wage. In some countries, the minimum wage is relatively high, driving up labor costs (Noe et al., 2006). Examples of cultural differences affecting international corporations are communications and morale problems.

Multinational Corporation

A multinational corporation is a more complex international business operation. Multinational corporations operate as fully autonomous units in multiple countries in an attempt to capitalize on lower production and distribution costs (Bohlander & Snell, 2007; Noe et al., 2006). An example of a multinational corporation is General Motors (GM). While GM's headquarters and some of its operations are located in the United States, many of their manufacturing facilities have been relocated to places such as Mexico and China with the goal of reducing production costs by paying lower employee wages. Locating facilities to China has allowed GM to sell to the Asian markets with reduced distribution costs. The HRM issues experienced by multinational corporations are similar to those encountered by international corporations, only exacerbated.

One approach taken by multinational corporations has been to hire expatriates from countries other than the parent country to help with staffing and management issues (Noe et al., 2006). As noted by Noe et al. (2006) while hiring expatriates from other countries has its advantages, it often requires greater cross-training of cultural and managerial skills.

Global Corporation

Global corporations are similar to multinational corporations; however, global corporations integrate their operations worldwide through a centralized home office (Bohlander & Snell, 2007). Multinational corporations produce and distribute identical products and services worldwide. Global corporations on the other hand emphasize flexibility and mass customization to meet the needs of differing customer needs worldwide (Noe et al., 2006). Ford represents an example of a global corporation. Ford offers a different line of automobiles from its American consumers compared with its European consumers. For example, to meet the needs of European consumers, that is, smaller more fuel efficient cars, Ford offers the Ka—a car similar to the Smart Car.

Because of this integrative international focus, global corporations must manage their human resources through a transnational HRM system. This type of system is characterized by three attributes: (1) it is essential that HR decisions are made from a global rather than a national perspective, (2) it is important that the company's management is composed of people from all over the world, and (3) it is imperative that decision-making and planning processes include people from a variety of cultures and backgrounds (Noe et al., 2006).

The type of international business operation chosen by the corporation will inevitably influence the way in which the organization manages its human resources. It is feasible to conceptualize organizations on a continuum based on their level of global participation, from the domestic corporation representing the lowest level of global participation to the global corporation representing the highest level of global participation.

With this in mind, the following sections of this chapter provide a discussion of issues surrounding the management of human resources internationally. Although these distinctions among MNEs are important, the actual structure of the MNE determines its effectiveness. There is no "best structure" that fits the distribution and marketing needs of all MNEs. Perhaps having a flexible approach to structure is the best way to manage an MNE.

Differences in HRM in MNEs

Even though there were a number of different types of international business operations described in the previous section, for convenience, these types will all be referred to as MNEs. As one might expect, there are differences in HRM programs and practices between a domestic enterprise and an MNE. One immediate and obvious difference is that there are the three different types of employees in a typical MNE as opposed to one type in a domestic firm. These MNE employees include **parent-country nationals** (PCNs), **host-country nationals** (HCNs), and **third-country nationals** (TCNs). Parent country refers to the country in which the corporate headquarters of the MNE is located, while host country refers to the location of subsidiaries. Obviously, TCNs are employees from countries other than the parent or host countries. In spite of these differences in the types of employees between a domestic enterprise and an MNE, the major programs of HRM, for example, talent management and compensation, exist in both domestic and international organizations. However, the fact that an MNE competes in multiple countries versus the single company orientation of a domestic contributes to the complexity of IHRM. In addition, there are also other factors that affect the complexity of IHRM; Dowling and Welch (2005) argue

that the complexity of international HR can be attributed to six factors:

- more HR activities
- the need for a broader perspective
- more involvement in employees' personal lives
- changes in emphasis as the workforce mix of expatriates and locals varies
- risk exposure
- broader external influences. (p. 7)

Each of these factors will be discussed briefly to provide an understanding of how the complexity of HR practices increases as one goes from a domestic to an international firm.

More HR Activities

An HR department in an international firm must be concerned with activities that would not be part of an HR department in a domestic firm. One of the first and most important activities is relations with host governments where work permits and visas may be required for expatriates and their families. The IHRM department must also be aware of the labor laws and guidelines in the host country and determine to which type of employee (i.e., PCN, HCN, or TCN) they apply. This can be especially tricky when a practice that is illegal in the home country is legal in the host country. For example, the United States has stringent laws on unfair discrimination against females and minorities in personnel decisions (e.g., hiring), whereas these laws do not exist in other countries. In addition, the IHRM department has to be responsible for administrative details of the employees, such as international taxation, international relocation, and orientation, as well as for special administrative activities of expatriates. Finally, there are typically activities that could involve language translation or training, housing for expatriates, and, on occasion, education for families of expatriates.

The Need for a Broader Perspective

The HR professionals and managers in MNEs need to develop a broader worldview in dealing with different groups of employees, that is, PCNs, HCNs, and TCNs. Recognition of cultural differences among employees as well as differences in work ethic and practices in the employees' home countries is crucial to managing this diverse workforce. One specific issue that could cause management problems, as noted by Dowling and Welch (2005), is the fact that some countries pay their expatriates a premium for accepting overseas assignments. This could lead to feelings of inequity by the host country and third-country employees since they would not be receiving this premium compensation. Unfortunately, paying a premium on top of the compensation for an expatriate is frequently the only way a firm can get the person to accept the international assignment.

More Involvement in Employees' Personal Lives

As would be expected, there is a major difference in HR activities in the personal lives of employees and their families in a multinational versus a domestic firm. Involvement in the personal lives of employees in a domestic environment is fairly limited except where prescribed by law. For example, many countries have some form of pregnancy and/or family leave requirements. However, in an international setting, the IHRM department has to get much more involved in the personal lives of employees in the areas of taxation, education, and even banking services. In the case of expatriates, there will usually be provisions for the expatriate and his or her family to return to their homeland for visits, and often these arrangements fall on the IHRM department. Finally, the whole issue of visas and housing arrangements for PCNs (expatriates), TCNs, and their families is something that the IHRM department must handle.

Changes in Emphasis as the Workforce Mix of Expatriates and Locals Varies

In an MNE, there are likely to be employees from a number of countries. As mentioned in the introduction, there has been a new awareness among the industrialized countries that there is an immense pool of untapped talent that has been largely ignored in the past. One of the problems that this mix can create is that there are multiple languages being spoken. English has been used extensively in most MNEs because in a large number of countries, English is learned as a second language. However, with the mix of PCNs, HCNs, and TCNs, this may not be the case; and thus, language training in a common language would be required. Another example of this new awareness of the immense labor pool available can be found in the experience of a manager of a large building maintenance corporation in the United States. This person was responsible for the building maintenance contracts in New York City, and these contracts included approximately 75% of the buildings on Manhattan Island. This manager observed that the new immigrants to America had a much stronger work ethic than citizens born in America, and he preferred managing them in spite of language difficulties.

Risk Exposure

The obvious concern that an MNE has is the risk to the well-being of its employees. The level of risk depends on the political climate and the threat of terrorism in the country. The IHRM department must be aware of the risks to its employees and keep them appraised of any significant problems. In addition, the IHRM department typically must be prepared for, and be involved in, any necessary evacuation of employees from a country in times of danger. Another type of risk is the financial one that occurs when expatriates fail in their assignments, which will be discussed in more detail later in this chapter.

Broader External Influences

As discussed earlier, the external environment has many factors that influence the functioning of the MNE and the operation and activities of IHRM. In reference to Figure 1.2 from Chapter 1, it would appear that government regulations and relations, the labor market, societal concerns, and technology would have the *most impact* on the programs and activities of the IHRM department. Government regulations could define working hours and conditions as well as the requirements for specific hiring practices, for example, a quota of HCNs. The labor market will have a direct impact on the level of wages but will also influence the number of expatriates (PCNs) and TCNs who need to be hired to supplement the available labor pool and skills of the HCN population. Societal concerns would be driven by the culture of the country, which would include the values, religious beliefs, communication, and social structure in the country. These considerations would have a direct impact on the training activities of the IHRM department, particularly for PCNs and TCNs, but could also result in cross-cultural training for all employees. Finally, the level of evolution of technology in the country would have a serious impact on the availability and operation of the HRIS as well as other information systems, for example, production and marketing.

Managing Different Types of Employees in MNEs

Managing in the global business environment creates unique complexities for managers—especially expatriate managers. To understand these complexities, it is important to distinguish between the three groups typically employed by MNEs—PCNs, HCNs, and TCNs. Over the past 25 years of globalization, organizations based in the United States have relied on expatriates as a major source of staffing their overseas operations (Schuler & Tarique, 2007). However, because of the rising costs of employing expatriates, MNEs from the United States are turning toward HCNs and TCNs for staffing both managerial and nonmanagerial positions (Schuler & Jackson, 2005;

Tarique, Schuler, & Gong, 2006). While the diversity of the workforce will depend on the type of international business operation adopted by the MNE, more and more MNEs are shifting from an expatriate-focused workforce to a global workforce. Subsequently, it is important to understand a number of cultural differences between expatriates and the host- and third-country workforce. Understanding these cultural differences can make it easier for expatriate managers to relate to and manage their global workforce. Some of the most important cultural factors include education, politics and law, and economics (see Bohlander & Snell, 2007).

Education

The first of these factors includes the educational level and the resultant human capital of the workforce. It is important for expatriate managers to understand that *human capital*, that is, the productive capabilities of people, within the host country will be different from that in the United States (Noe et al., 2006). This is especially true in Third World countries where human capital is lower because of a lack of investment in formal education. This problem is further exacerbated when TCNs are hired to work within the organization. It is important for expatriate managers to understand and deal with the human capital needs of a highly diverse workforce made up of individuals (1) coming from different cultural backgrounds, (2) possibly speaking different languages, and (3) having different educational experiences.

Therefore, it is important for expatriate managers to provide a supportive work environment for their diverse workforce. One important aspect of support, especially within the realm of IHRM, is training. Because of the diversity of employees, it is important for expatriate managers through the IHRM department to provide training to ensure that the workforce can work well together and competently perform their required tasks. As a result, IHRM departments could provide training on (1) cultural differences, (2) verbal and nonverbal communication, and (3) specific skill sets particular to the employee's role.

Political/Legal System

A second factor is the political/legal system within the host country. The type of HRM practices adopted and how these practices are used will be determined by the political and legal system of the host country (Noe et al., 2006). The laws and regulations of the host country are determined in part by the societal norms of that country. For example, the United States has created laws governing issues such as equal employment opportunities and fair pay standards (Noe et al., 2006). Many of these laws are specific to the United States and evolved from racial and gender issues particular to its history, but they do not exist in other countries.

Similarly, in the United States, free speech is a right provided to everyone. The United States is a democratic society, and free speech is a **cultural norm**. It is acceptable for organizations and individuals to speak out against the government if they do not like certain government regulations or taxes or feel that they are being unfairly treated. However, in other parts of the world, it may be highly inappropriate, and possibly dangerous, for organizations to speak out against the government. As a result, it is important for expatriate managers to be knowledgeable of and sensitive to the laws and political norms of the host country. This will require that the IHRM department prepare expatriate managers to be acculturated to the host country and provide training with respect to the laws of the host country.

Economic System

A third factor is the economic system of the host country. From an IHRM perspective, the economic system is one determinant of the extent to which the host country provides incentives toward the development of human capital (Noe et al., 2006). The economic system of the host country affects human capital through its compensation system (Noe et al., 2006). Countries such as Germany, Switzerland, and Japan have strong educational systems and provide employees with good wages. In comparison, Third World countries such as Sri Lanka, Afghanistan, and Haiti have poorer educational systems and provide substantially lower compensation to their workforce.

It is apparent that, because of lower wages, it would be less costly to operate an MNE in a Third World country. However, from an IHRM perspective, this provides a number of potential disadvantages. One disadvantage is poorer human capital. From a managerial perspective, this would likely require expatriate managers to spend time training and developing the workforce on basic skills to perform their tasks. Another potential disadvantage is equity in the compensation structure, which will be discussed later in this chapter.

A study by the U.S. Department of Labor (2002) indicates that the average compensation for employees in the manufacturing sector in Sri Lanka was $0.42 per hour, compared with $21.33 per hour for manufacturing employees in the United States. As an example, if the workforce of an MNE in Sri Lanka was composed of employees from both Sri Lanka and the United States an equity issue may arise once the Sri Lankan workforce learned of the pay differential.

This discussion points to some of the important cultural differences among countries. These cultural differences directly affect the type of HR practices implemented by the MNE. One of the primary focuses of IHRM is on relocation, orientation, and translation services for helping expatriate employees adapt to the host **country's culture** (Bohlander & Snell, 2007). A second focus is to help HCNs and TCNs adapt to the corporate culture of the home country organization. In other words, IHRM is concerned not only with the typical HR functions, for example, staffing, training, and performance management, but also with the management of cultural differences.

HR Programs in Global Organizations

International Staffing

The complexities inherent in managing a global organization make staffing an especially important part of the IHRM system. As noted previously, in the past, MNEs were staffed heavily with expatriates, particularly during the start-up of a new subsidiary. However, the numerous costs associated with sending expatriates overseas, providing language training, offering family support, and repatriating these employees have prompted MNEs to rely more heavily on HCNs and TCNs to staff their organizations (Schuler, Budhwar, & Florkowski, 2002). However, because of cultural differences, HCNs and TCNs are often hired based on their social status, family ties, language, and common national origin, even if otherwise unqualified (Bohlander & Snell, 2007). With this in mind, how can MNEs ensure that their organizations are properly staffed with qualified HCNs and TCNs?

When staffing managerial and nonmanagerial employees, the MNE needs to determine if these personnel will be selected from the home-country (expatriates), host-country, or third-country talent pool. As described by Bohlander and Snell (2007) each of these employee groups provides a different advantage for the MNE. The following provides a discussion of the advantages of staffing an MNE with different types of employees.

Home-Country Nationals

Staffing the organization with expatriates (PCNs) is advantageous because the organization can rely on the talent currently available. These employees typically have experience with the company and are therefore knowledgeable about the corporate culture, policies, and procedures. This also gives the organization greater control over and mobility with these employees, since there is an already established psychological contract between the organization and the employee. However, because of the costs associated with expatriates, organizations are relying less on these employees for their day-to-day operations. Expatriates are most often employed as managers or consultants to ensure that overseas operations are consistent with the goals of the parent organization.

Host-Country Nationals

Staffing positions with HCNs provides a number of advantages for the MNE. First, on the whole, HCNs are less costly, in terms of both time and money (Bohlander & Snell, 2007). While it may take some time to socialize these employees into the company culture and provide them the necessary training to perform their role consistent with company expectations, the organization saves in other areas. For example, these employees do not have to be relocated to a new country. Furthermore, HCNs do not need language training or time to adjust to the environment and national culture. Second, it is likely that the organization can retain these employees for a longer period of time. Expatriates work in the host country for an average of 2 to 3 years (Dowling & Welch, 2005); however, eventually these employees go back to their home country. Since host-national employees do not need to move from their country of origin, they are likely to stay with the organization for a longer period of time. Third, these employees are often preferred by the government of the host country (Bohlander & Snell, 2007). Employing HCNs provides an incentive to the host country—less expensive labor and more jobs for its citizens. As a result, HCNs are appropriate for some managerial and most nonmanagerial positions.

Third-Country Nationals

TCNs provide an interesting employment advantage. Since they are not part of the parent or host country, they bring a different and often broad experience to the organization. In particular, TCNs add an international outlook to the workforce (Bohlander & Snell, 2007). Furthermore, oftentimes some of these employees are multilinguistic. However, it is likely that these employees would require extensive training, for example, in a common language, and socialization to adapt to the country and the organization. There is also the possibility that employing certain TCNs could negatively affect the relationship with the host country government if these employees come from a country with a strained relationship with the host country.

The processes of staffing HCNs and TCNs in an MNE is not much different from staffing U.S. citizens for a domestic organization. However, there is considerable complexity in the required information for selection as well as the selection techniques used when multiple countries are involved in the MNE. For example, the United States, Canada, and the United Kingdom rely heavily on standardized tests for selection, whereas many of the EU countries rely on interview data. Therefore, we will not provide a specific discussion about the selection process for these groups of employees but rather refer the reader to Chapter 11 of this book for a discussion on various recruitment and selection strategies that are part of applications of an HRIS. It should be emphasized, however, that different approaches by different countries will cause considerable complexity in the selection process; and having an HRIS designed for the IHRM department with this country-by-country information would be very helpful in all selection programs of the MNE.

Selecting Global Managers: Managing Expatriates

One of the most difficult responsibilities of IHRM is the selection of managers from the parent country, commonly referred to as expatriates, for assignments in the host countries. In addition to the issues and concerns with international staffing discussed in the previous section, the selection of expatriate managers involves more difficulties. Why do MNEs use expatriates? As a rule, the expatriate is being used in a job for which there are no HCNs available. In the early stages of the establishment and development of a new subsidiary in a different country, it is difficult to staff it entirely with HCNs. In fact, PCNs are used for many of the professional, technical, and managerial jobs during the start-up of the subsidiary. As discussed above, however, it is desirable to increase the number of HCNs in these jobs and decrease the number of PCNs over time. This does not mean that there will be a complete absence of PCNs in the subsidiary, since expatriate assignments serve the dual purpose of bringing expertise to the subsidiary and providing career development experience for the expatriate manager.

Most of the literature on this topic is focused on the selection of expatriates, whether they be PCNs, HCNs, or TCNs. The reason for grouping these three types is that, at the managerial level in an MNE, these individuals will move from country to country to gain international experience for their career development regardless of their home country. Thus, the term *expatriate* will be used to designate global managers, regardless of the home country. It should be kept in mind that not all expatriates are managers. They can be technical specialists, and many of the comments in this section will also refer to them. However, technical specialists usually have short-term assignments (1–3 months), and thus, the MNE does not face the same set of IHRM issues that are created by longer-term managerial expatriates. To fully understand the difficulty in being successful in selecting expatriates, we will discuss in this section (1) the cultural environment of countries, (2) expatriate failure and its causes, and (3) selection criteria and procedures for expatriates.

The Cultural Environment of Countries

One of the most important aspects of an expatriate's job that will significantly affect his or her performance is the interaction with the local government and people of a country. Because of this interaction, most expatriates will experience *culture shock* as they move from country to country within an MNE. Culture shock is the adjustment that occurs in a relatively short time when moving from one country to another. Culture shock can be mild, for example, for a German manager who relocates to a subsidiary plant in France, or quite severe, for example for an Australian manager who moves to a subsidiary in Egypt. Thus, one of the most important tasks of the IHRM department is to gather information about the culture of countries where the MNE does business. This is one of the main areas where an HRIS can be very useful in that it can be used as a repository of this information, and thus, cultural profiles of countries can be quickly generated. This information is quite useful in both the selection and the predeparture training of expatriates.

Further emphasizing the importance of a country's culture, Briscoe and Schuler (2004) stated,

> Knowledge about and competency in working with country and company cultures is the most important issue impacting the success of international business activity. And possibly the area of business that is most impacted by cultural differences is the human resource function. (p. 114)

Culture, as defined by Hofstede (1991), "is the collective programming of the mind which distinguishes the members of one group or category of people from another" (p. 6). There have been numerous studies of the effect of country culture on management practices; however, Hofstede's research was the first systematic study done. In it, he identified five dimensions on which the cultures of countries differ:

1. *Power distance*—the degree to which the values of a country indicate the amount of perceived social inequality between employees and managers. A low amount would indicate that people in that culture do not perceive wide differences in status between employees and managers, whereas a high amount would mean the opposite.

2. *Collectivism versus individualism*—the degree to which the values of a country support individual versus collective effort. For example, people in Great Britain are high on the value of individual effort, whereas people in Taiwan are high on the value of collectivism.

3. *Masculinity versus femininity*—the degree to which the values of a country support personal traits traditionally defined as feminine, for example, compassion, or as masculine, for example, aggressiveness.

4. *Uncertainty avoidance*—the degree to which the values of a country define the tolerance of ambiguity. A high amount would indicate that risk taking is valued, whereas a low amount would indicate a more conservative approach to life.

5. *Long-term versus short-term orientation*—the degree to which the values of a country are oriented toward long- versus short-term goals. For example, people in Russia value short-term goals, whereas people in China value long-term goals.

In addition to Hofstede's work, there have been other studies of the differences in national culture (GLOBE Research Team, 2002; Trompenaars, 1992). Trompenaars, like Hofstede, found five distinct cultural factors that differentiated country cultures, while the Global Leadership and Organizational Behavior Effectiveness (GLOBE) research project categorized countries on nine cultural dimensions. Regardless of the study examined, all authors agree that the cultural environment of a country has a strong effect on the management of employees and should be considered when selecting expatriates. To define the culture of a country, Bohlander and Snell (2007) list the following elements that will differentiate countries in terms of their cultural environment for international business: (1) education/human capital, (2) values/ideologies, (3) social structure, (4) religious beliefs, and (5) communication. Information gathered in these five categories could be used to create a profile of the cultural environment of countries in which the MNE does business. It is most important to emphasize that this information could be stored electronically in the HRIS and maintained by the IHRM department. Both of the major IT platforms, Oracle PeopleSoft (www.peoplesoft.com/corp/en/public_index.jsp) and SAP (www.sap.com/usa/index.epx), have this capability, or it can be customized by the MNE.

As a final note on country culture, it will have an *effect on all the activities and programs* of the IHRM function to include selection, training compensation, and performance management.

Expatriate Failure and Causes

Expatriate failure is defined as the return of an expatriate to the home country before the period of the assignment has been completed. Thus, expatriate failure represents an error in a selection decision. The reason there is such an emphasis on expatriate failure is because of its costs to the MNE. There are two categories of costs— direct and indirect. Direct costs include the actual money spent on selecting and training, relocation costs for the expatriate (and family), and salary. These costs can be quite substantial. However, indirect costs can frequently be higher than direct costs. Indirect costs are harder to quantify, but they could include loss of market share in the country, negative reactions from the host country government, and possible negative effects on local employee morale. For example, the negative effect felt by the local host government could lead it to insist that, in the future, only an HCN fill the position. Finally, there will be the indirect costs experienced by the returning expatriate in terms of personal failure, loss of respect by peers, and possibly negative influences on future promotions.

What are the causes of expatriate failure? Although there has been considerable research on this topic, the answer is not completely clear. It is safe to say that one cannot generalize from the research results to every expatriate situation; however, the results do provide a guide to the information that should be collected during the selection of expatriates. In general, one could state that the major factor affecting expatriate failure is the *inability to adjust to the new situation and culture* by the expatriate and her or his family.

In terms of specific reasons for expatriate failure, Dowling and Welch (2005) cite the Organizational Research Counselors Worldwide (2002) and the GMAC Global Relocation Services (2002) global surveys. The problems reported by expatriates and companies in these surveys were

- spouse/partner dissatisfaction,
- inability to adapt,
- difficulties with family adjustment in the new location,
- difficulties associated with different management styles,
- culture and language difficulties, and
- issues associated with the accompanying partner's career development.

Similarly, Briscoe and Schuler (2004) indicate that "a number of surveys and studies have found that the most important factors in the early return of expatriates . . . lie in the inability of their families (and/or themselves) to adjust to the foreign environment" (p. 242). The clear implication of these findings is that the expatriate's family and/or partner must be considered in the selection decision process.

Selection Criteria and Procedures for Expatriates

In selecting expatriates, it is especially important to remember that the selection process is an exchange process between the organization and the employee. Furthermore, the prospective expatriate's family must be involved in the exchange. In terms of the utility of selection, that is its cost effectiveness, covered in Chapter 10 and earlier in this chapter, making a mistake is extremely costly. IHRM professionals must be cognizant of the causes of expatriate failure when developing the selection procedures, for example, tests, interviews, and also have an understanding of the cross-cultural issues in the evaluation and recommendation of employees for an expatriate assignment.

The factors involved in the selection of expatriates can be divided into two general categories—individual and situational (Dowling & Welch, 2005). In the individual category are technical ability, cross-cultural suitability, and family requirements. Technical ability is quite clear and would include both managerial and technical skills. The person selected must be technically proficient in his or her field (e.g., electrical engineering) and also must have a good performance record as a manager. Technical ability is very important to the selection process, as indicated by the results of the Organizational Research Counselors (ORC) Worldwide survey (2002), in that 72% of responding firms used it as the first screening criterion in their selection procedure. In selection terms, technical ability would be the *absolute minimum* requirement for the first screening of prospective employees for the assignment. Note that technical incompetence or poor performance is not mentioned as a cause for expatriate failure; however, job-related factors could possibly cause premature departure—for example, the nature of the job not being as described or the expatriate being unable to transfer technical or managerial skills to the new assignment.

The second individual factor, cross-cultural suitability, has several aspects. It could include language ability, cultural empathy, adaptability, and a positive attitude toward the assignment in the specific country being considered. Although technical ability is very important for success in the assignment, cross-cultural suitability is equally important since a number of the causes of expatriate failure are directly related to this factor.

The third individual factor, family requirements, has a great deal to do with the success of the expatriate's assignment. In all the research and surveys on causes for expatriate failure, the adjustment of the accompanying spouse/partner and children has been well documented as one of the major causes of expatriate failure. Although it is appropriate to use standard testing and interview techniques to assess the technical ability and cross-cultural suitability of potential expatriates, evaluation of these factors means the involvement of the family. Interviewing the spouse/partner and children regarding the assignment is frequently done. In addition, most MNEs have learned to build a pre-assignment visit for the expatriate candidate and his or her family as part of the selection process. This involvement of the entire family in the selection process has become a common practice for MNEs. In fact, if there are two possible locations for the assignment, companies may encourage a pre-assignment visit to both countries.

With regard to the general factors that affect the assignment situation, Dowling and Welch (2005) list country/cultural, language, and MNE requirements. Country/cultural requirements could include work permits and visas. Generally, the work permit is given to the expatriate, and the accompanying spouse/partner may not be permitted to work. As for the children, there may not be schools that would be acceptable, particularly if the children do not speak the language of the host country. In some expatriate assignments, either the children receive language training or there is a school in which their native language is spoken. The opportunity for the spouse/partner and the children to learn another language is sometimes seen as a benefit of the international assignment. Of course, this relates to the second factor of language. Difficulties in language are a major barrier to cross-cultural communication; thus, this is a very important factor for the expatriate and the family. Fortunately, many companies offer language training to the entire family prior to departure for the assignment. The final factor, MNE requirements, could involve getting permission from the host country for the selection of any expatriate. This is common in joint international ventures. Other factors could be the duration and type of assignment. When the duration of the assignment is only for 2 to 3 months and/or the assignment is in a "high-risk" country, the family members would usually not accompany the expatriate.

Selection of expatriates is a critical function of IHRM, particularly in MNEs where expatriate assignments are used to "groom" managers for higher levels of management. Many of the factors to consider in selecting expatriates and the factors causing expatriate failure are handled by training. However, many of the software applications available can greatly reduce the time required to make this process work. The next section focuses on training in the MNE, primarily the training of expatriates.

Training and Development of Expatriates

This section will focus primarily on training and career development for expatriates. As was done in the previous section, all managers in an MNE will be considered as expatriates since their career assignments and development typically mean that they will move from country to country. Training and development activities and programs in MNEs also include nonmanagerial employees of all types—PCNs, HCNs, and TCNs. Since traditional training and development was covered in detail in Chapter 12, most kinds of typical organizational training (e.g., orientation or technical training) will not be discussed. However, the use of an HRIS and its applications covered in Chapter 12 will still be discussed. In fact, the use of the training applications that are a part of the HRIS will be very useful for training of expatriates. Not only will the expatriates' personal information, work experience, and skills stored on the HRIS be easily accessible, but also the results of the training in terms of expatriate success or failure can be recorded. This information should be useful for future expatriate selection.

The corporate IHRM department has responsibility for all training; however, this responsibility is usually decentralized by delegating it to the MNE's subsidiaries. There may be training programs developed at the headquarters of the MNE, but it is unusual for these IHRM professionals at headquarters to deliver programs to the subsidiaries when it can be done more economically by the local IHRM professionals. Most of this local training for nonmanagerial employees will vary by different geographic locations of the MNE. As such, this means that some cross-cultural training for nonmanagerial employees who are not HCNs will be necessary, for example, language training; but again, Chapter 12 covers the approach and design of these training programs.

This section will cover expatriate training in detail. The section will be divided into the following subsections: (1) Purpose of Expatriate Training, (2) Predeparture Training to include repatriation of expatriates, and (3) Transfer of Training.

Purpose of Expatriate Training

The dual purpose of *any* training program is to inform and motivate employees. Even training that is focused on learning a manual skill, for example, keyboarding, has both knowledge and motivational aspects. Clearly the employee is learning a new skill, but with the proper training method, the employee can be encouraged to be more productive; and with the improved skill, the employee may be happier in the job. In addition to these two purposes of training, the first specific purpose of expatriate training is to supplement the selection process and assist the expatriate and her or his spouse/partner/family in adjusting to the new situation. It must be emphasized that selection of expatriates is never perfect. Why else would there be expatriate failure? Thus, the training program content for expatriates is based on both the selection criteria identified above and the causes of expatriate failure.

The second specific purpose of expatriate training is economic. Recall that the expatriate brings both technical and managerial expertise to the subsidiary when there are no HCNs ready to fill the positions. In addition, the expatriate assignment is used by MNEs as a career development process for managers. Thus, there are significant economic reasons for using expatriates for the MNE. When one calculates the potential **direct and indirect costs of expatriate failure**, the amount of the investment increases. The MNE makes a major investment in selecting employees for placement in its subsidiaries, and training programs are another IHRM element used to protect that investment.

Predeparture Training

It should be noted that predeparture training programs do not focus on the technical ability of the expatriate, unless there are new technical or managerial skills necessary for the assignment, for example, the introduction of new technology. Since one of the major causes of expatriate failure is the dissatisfaction or lack of adjustment by the spouse/partner/family, the inclusion of these people in predeparture training is very important. To assist the adjustment of the expatriate and his or her family to a new culture, predeparture training typically includes training in cultural awareness, language, and practical matters regarding daily living in the new culture. Most MNEs will also include preliminary visits as a part of predeparture training.

Another element in predeparture training that is highly recommended is repatriation training. Repatriation is the process that occurs as the expatriate and family return to their homeland. It is critically important that repatriation programs be established since there is a readjustment (reverse culture shock) to the home culture on return for both the family and the expatriate. Furthermore, the expatriate may find on return that the situation that was expected in the home country (e.g., a promotion to a new position) is not available; and thus, the expatriate will seek other employment. This problem of losing expatriates during the repatriation process has been well documented in the literature (Black, 2000; Feldman & Tompson, 1993; Poe, 2000; Solomon, 1995). There is considerable discussion in the available literature on the design and implementation of repatriation programs to be commenced on the return of the expatriate (Briscoe & Schuler, 2004; Dowling & Welch, 2005; Evans, Pucik & Barsoux, 2002), and most companies consider repatriation as part of the career development program of the MNE. It must be emphasized, however, that the above-cited literature strongly suggests that the repatriation process should begin in the predeparture training program.

Training in cultural awareness, language, and practical matters regarding daily living in the new culture constitutes the predeparture training that the expatriate and family will attend. It is important to recall that expatriate selection is a two-way street. The expatriate still has the right to decline the assignment. Thus, the predeparture training both informs and attracts, which are the two purposes of training. There are a large number of topics that can be included in predeparture training. The topics listed in Table 14.1 make up a possible content for the predeparture program. Note that this list could change depending on the host and parent countries involved.

Transfer of Training

The idea that the predeparture training program could change as a function of the two countries involved has been recognized by scholars, and several models have been proposed to provide guidelines on predeparture training programs (Mendenhall, Dunbar & Oddou, 1987; Tung, 1981, 1998). These researchers argue that predeparture

❖ **Table 14.1**   Topics for Predeparture Training

1.	Cultural values and religions
2.	Web sites for country information
3.	Country history, recommended readings, videos,[a] and achievements in the country
4.	Classical literature describing the country's history, its folkways, and heroes and heroines
5.	Information about other HCN expatriates in the country
6.	Descriptions of the educational facilities and opportunities for families
7.	Current news about the country, particularly its relationship to the parent country
8.	Traditional family roles of father, mother, and children
9.	Locations for shopping and shopping hours
10.	Dominant language of country; extent of bilingualism in country
11.	Nonverbal gestures and their meanings
12.	Political structure, particularly as it affects the operation of the MNE
13.	Descriptions of currency, temperature variations, transportation, hours of business
14.	Sightseeing, including historic, artistic, and important cultural locations that would appeal to all the family

NOTE: This is a very general list, which will vary from country to country.

a. Videos should be made available to expatriates and their families, either to review or to keep.

training should not be viewed as a "one size fits all" but rather that the training design and program should be contingent on other factors in the expatriate assignment. According to Tung (1981, 1998), the two factors that most affect predeparture training design are (1) the dissimilarity between the expatriate's native country and the host culture—low to high—and (2) the expected amount of interaction between the expatriate and members of the host country—low to high. Based on an analysis of these two factors, Black and Mendenhall (1989) argue that the design of the training program can then vary on three dimensions: (1) the training methods used, (2) the level of training rigor, and (3) the duration of the training program. For example, if both the dissimilarity between the expatriate's native country and the host culture and the expected amount of interaction between the expatriate and members of the host country are quite high, then the predeparture training should be rigorous and the length of training should be 1 to 2 months. In this situation, the training methods would attempt to immerse the expatriate in the host country's culture through assessment centers, simulations, sensitivity training, and extensive language training. As mentioned earlier, the use of the HRIS to analyze the success or failure of these training programs will enable the MNE to make more effective decisions about expatriates and their training in the future.

Performance Appraisal in MNEs

Performance appraisal is an important process for documenting the performance of employees, determining areas for development, deciding on pay increases and promotional opportunities, and giving employees the opportunity to express their views (Von Glinow, Drost, & Teagarden, 2002). The type and content of performance appraisal conducted depend on the specific job requirements and personal attributes of the person being appraised (Schuler et al., 2002). This is particularly true when comparing the appraisal of expatriates with that of HCN and TCN employees. The section in Chapter 13 on performance evaluation and performance planning covers a number of HRIS applications that could be used for performance appraisal in an MNE. Naturally, the inclusion of plants with a diverse employee population in multiple countries creates considerable complexity, particularly when the results of the appraisals are being used to move managers from country to country. However, most vendors of HRIS products have packaged available software applications that can be modified for local conditions in each specific country. Readers are referred to the Web sites for Oracle PeopleSoft or SAP for information on these applications for international companies. There are also stand-alone application software packages available, but they are usually not as comprehensive as those available from SAP or Oracle PeopleSoft.

Appraising Expatriate Performance

When appraising the performance of expatriate employees, it is important to consider who should appraise their performance and what performance criteria are specific to the expatriate's situation (Bohlander & Snell, 2007). The first question is *who* should complete the performance appraisal. Typically, the performance of employees is appraised by their supervisor. Expatriate managers are geographically distanced from their parent country supervisors, and as a result, supervisors who are located in the parent country cannot observe the day-to-day activities of these employees (Dowling & Welch, 2005). Therefore, managers of expatriates tend to base their evaluations of the person on the objective criteria used for other employees in similar positions located in the parent country. A potential problem with this type of assessment is that the parent-country manager does not have direct information or observational data about the more subjective performance criteria, such as the expatriate manager's leadership skills and performance within the context of the subsidiary (Borman & Motowidlo, 1993). Moreover, the supervisor located in the parent country may not be aware of culturally bound biases that constrain the job performance of the expatriate manager.

Because of these complexities, it may be most appropriate to obtain multiple ratings of the expatriate's performance through the use of a 360° feedback system (Dowling & Welch, 2005). Ratings of the expatriate manager's performance could be garnered from his or her superior, peers, and subordinates in the expatriate assignment, as well as the expatriate himself (herself). This would provide a clearer picture of the expatriate's total job performance. In fact, in a study of 58 U.S. multinational firms, Gregersen, Hite, and Black (1996) found that 81% of the companies used more than one rater when assessing the job performance of expatriate employees.

What Performance Criteria Should Be Appraised?

As with managers in domestic assignments, it is important to evaluate the specific job-related competencies of the expatriate manager. However, the role of an expatriate is somewhat more complex in that there are non-job-related qualities they need to possess to perform their role effectively (Schuler et al., 2002). First, it is important that the expatriate manager possess cross-cultural interpersonal skills. In other words, it is important for expatriate managers to get along and build relationships with people in the culture of the country in which they are working. Second, it is important for expatriate managers to understand and have sensitivity to differences in norms, laws, and cultures relative to her or his home country. Third, it is important that expatriate managers are capable of adapting to uncertain and unpredictable circumstances. Since expatriates are working in a new culture, they will face new experiences that may be vastly different from their experiences in the United States. As a result, it is important that the HR department of the parent country recognize the impact of these aspects of the expatriate's experience in their performance appraisal.

Appraising Host- and Third-Country Nationals' Performance

Appraising the performance of HCNs and TCNs is somewhat different from appraising the performance of domestic employees in the United States. It is important for PCNs to be sensitive to cultural differences in appraising performance. For example, in Japan, discussing the negative aspects of an employee's performance may be taken as an insult (Dowling & Welch, 2005). Because "saving face" is so important in Japan, discussing the negative attributes of an employee may cause them to distrust the manager. To deal with these cultural differences, organizations should employ HCNs to assist in the development and administration of performance appraisals (Dowling & Welch, 2005). HCNs know what type of information is culturally sensitive. Unlike expatriates, they are less likely to be perceived as outsiders. This is important since performance evaluations are used to determine pay increases and promotional decisions, training opportunities, and dismissal decisions.

Finally, these appraisals can help identify individual performance problems that can be solved by training.

Managing International Compensation

The management of compensation[2] in an MNE is one of the most complex but critically important functions of the IHRM department. Its complexity comes from having a mix of PCNs, HCNs, and TCNs within one company and, thus, having to handle wage, salary, and benefits information that differs across countries. As a result, the IHRM compensation manager must be aware of differences in taxation, labor laws affecting compensation and benefits, currency fluctuations, and cost-of-living differences within and between countries where the MNE has a presence. The criticality of compensation and benefits management by the IHRM rests in part on the effects that salary and benefits have on employee motivation. In spite of differences across countries regarding the motivational factors in the workplace, money seems to be consistently at the top of the list.

The other reason for the critical importance of compensation management in subsidiaries is its link to the strategy of the MNE. To help us understand some of the important elements and dynamics of compensation in an MNE, this section will cover (1) the objectives of international compensation, (2) the components of international compensation, and (3) two approaches to international compensation.

The Objectives of International Compensation Policy

Actually, the objectives of a compensation policy in an MNE are similar to those in a domestic company. It has been fairly well established in the management research literature that compensation administration has a very close relationship with the strategy of the firm. For example, if the company has forecasted increased sales in the next year and thus has determined a need for new employees with specialized skills, it may be necessary to pay above the labor market's "*going salary rate*" in order to get the best available individuals. This would be especially true when the information from the labor market indicates that there is a shortage of people in a particular country having the skills necessary for the target job—for example, computer programmers. Similarly, when the labor market statistics indicate that there is an abundance of people with the skills needed for a specific job, it would be recommended that the compensation level match the labor market values.

Similar to a domestic firm, the *first objective* for an MNE is to align its compensation administration with the strategy of the firm. Of course, compared with the domestic firm, this alignment is much more complex for the MNE. It requires the MNE to have accurate and up-to-date labor market compensation information for all the countries in which the MNE has a presence. This requirement is one of the most powerful advantages of having an HRIS with labor market information for the IHRM department. Labor market statistics, such as average compensation as well as forecasted shortages and surpluses for jobs, are available for most countries and can be stored in the HRIS. The applications in the computer software that produces analyses of these data would be quite similar to those described in Chapter 13. However, it is clear that the reports generated from the HRIS would be much more complex in an MNE since multiple countries would be involved. As with a domestic firm, compensation administration can serve several motivational purposes. It must motivate employees to (1) join the firm, (2) be productive while members of the firm, and (3) stay with the firm.

The MNE's *second objective* is identical, but more complicated since multiple cultures are involved. Although most cultures see monetary rewards as motivational, there are clear differences across world cultures in terms of the other factors that motivate employee behaviors. For example, the meaningfulness of the work may be very important in some cultures, whereas the opportunity for promotion would be most important in other cultures.

The *final objective* of compensation policy for an MNE is that it must be perceived as fair by the employees. This notion of fairness or equity has been shown to be a powerful motivator of human behavior (Adams, 1965), and it may be the most important objective of an international compensation policy. With the mix of employees from different companies (PCNs, HCNs, TCNs), *perceived or real* differences in wages or benefits between groups of employees could lead to considerable dissatisfaction among the less privileged groups and consequently affect retention of employees.

The Components of International Compensation

The components of an international compensation system are very similar to those of a domestic program. The major components are a base salary and a set of benefits. However, extra pay premiums would be much more complex for an MNE. For example, there may be a foreign service or hardship premium for expatriates, whether they be from the parent or a third country. Other premiums could be based on the "riskiness" of the assignment in the country. Although most domestic companies give cost-of-living allowances (COLAs) based on where one works (e.g., rural vs. urban locations), MNEs must also use between- and within-country COLAs to have an equitable compensation system. These considerations, along with the other compensation issues discussed, make managing the compensation system a "nightmare" for the IHRM department. The existence of the employee, country, and compensation/benefits data in an HRIS means that IHRM professionals have the ability to quickly access important information for making both policy and operational decisions about compensation in an MNE.

Two Approaches to International Compensation

The IHRM textbooks mentioned earlier in this chapter (Briscoe & Schuler, 2004; Dowling & Welch, 2005; Evans, Pucik, & Barsoux, 2002) all discuss two approaches to international compensation—the "going rate" and the "balance sheet" approaches. In the going rate or "host-country" approach (Bohlander & Snell, 2007), the base salary for international employees is tied to the salary levels in the host country. For example, an expatriate would earn pay that is comparable with the salaries of employees in the host country. Thus, the compensation levels for employees would depend on wage surveys of (1) local nationals (HCNs), (2) expatriates of the same nationality, and (3) expatriates of all nationalities (Dowling & Welch, 2004). For low-pay countries, the base pay and benefits could be supplemented with additional payments. It should be obvious that HRIS applications for compensation based on the going rate would be useful for establishing initial compensation levels, particularly for expatriates. Having this database would also be quite useful for handling complaints by any MNE employee regarding the equity of his or her compensation. Computer-based compensation applications are available from the major providers of software platforms such as Oracle PeopleSoft or SAP.

The second approach to compensation policy, the balance sheet approach, has as its goal the maintenance of a home-country living standard plus a financial inducement for accepting an international assignment. As Dowling and Welch (2004) noted, "The home-country pay and benefits are the foundation of this approach, adjustments to home package to balance additional expenditure in the host country, and financial incentives (expatriate/hardship premium) are added to make the package attractive" (p. 146). Although this approach would appear to be more attractive to the expatriate, it has the disadvantage for the IHRM department that it can be very complex to administer. Although the use of software applications and reports from an HRIS can assist in untangling these objective, and probably perceived, inequalities, it still requires the IHRM professional along with line managers to explain these programs to employees.

In sum, compensation is probably the most difficult and complex of the HR programs to implement and administer in an MNE. However, it is critically important to the equity exchange (or psychological contract) between the company and its employees. Ergo, it can affect employee motivation. Interactions between employees and their immediate supervisors in a domestic enterprise or an MNE regarding compensation have the greatest impact on motivation of the employees. Having an HRIS produce the needed data and information on the equity of compensation among employees is a tremendous boon to employee relations.

HRIS Applications in IHRM

Introduction

It should be apparent from the previous sections of this chapter that management, and HRM in particular, in an MNE is exceedingly more complex than in a domestic firm. As business becomes more global, ignoring its international aspects would be foolish. International companies functioning in the 1970s through the 1990s were hampered by the lack of information sources and transmission of important HR information for effective management decisions. However, with the powerful computer technology available today, difficulties in executing the basic HR functions of planning, recruiting, selecting, training, and managing performance in MNEs have been reduced.

Specific HRIS applications for MNEs have been noted previously, mostly in concert with two software platforms, Oracle PeopleSoft and SAP. Not only are these the only software providers available for software applications in the IHRM field, but they are also good starting points for the interested student. Thus, this last section of this chapter will focus on broader issues in the application and use of an HRIS in IHRM. These issues and potential answers will be briefly examined[3] and discussed in terms of three topics: (1) organizational structure for effectiveness, (2) IHRM-HRIS administrative issues, and (3) HRIS applications in MNEs.

Organizational Structure for Effectiveness

The issue of the *most effective* structure for the operation of an HRIS in an MNE has been a "moving target." The most common advice regarding the management of an MNE has been to "think global, act local." This advice applies to the total management process of an MNE—its strategy, operations, finance, marketing, and HR—and has been followed religiously for many years in international management. However, Beaman (2007) has provided arguments for a different approach, at least in terms of the development and use of an HRIS in international organizations. As she stated,

I maintain that we have been going about globalization the wrong way. The slogan, "Think Global, Act Local," . . . is completely the inverse of what we should be doing with our HRIT (synonym for HRIS) organizations. Rather, it is only by first "thinking locally" to truly understand the needs of our local business communities, and then "acting globally" to seamlessly knit together diverse business functions and systems into a holistic, global approach that we can built an effective, efficient and competitive organization. (p. 6)

A well-established piece of advice in the management literature has been that "structure does not drive success—people do." In building an organizational structure for an HRIS in an MNE, it would seem very reasonable to consider Beaman's suggestion.

IHRM-HRIS Administrative Issues

Service Oriented Architecture (SOA)

It may be repetitive, but it is important to reexamine some of the HRIS approaches covered in Chapter 9 in terms of HRIS applications in an MNE. These applications can be much more useful in an international firm than in a domestic one. One of the most important approaches for handling administrative issues in an MNE is the use of a service-oriented architecture (SOA). As discussed in Chapter 9, an SOA "is a paradigm for organizing and utilizing distributed [computing] capabilities that may be under the control of different ownership domains . . . providing a uniform means to offer, discover, interact with and use capabilities to produce desired [business] effects" (OASIS, 2006, p. 8). The SOA is focused on providing a service for a function that is well-defined, self-contained, and context and platform independent that adds value to the organization's business purpose rather than simply focused on the technology itself. In effect, SOA is a collection of internal and external services that can communicate with each other by point-to-point data exchange or through coordination among different services to achieve a business purpose. As a result, an SOA can combine multiple business functions from different organizational departments, for example, production, marketing, and HR, that have similar electronic transactions (such as change of address or salary level) into a central procession unit. SOAs were created when it was discovered that the various departments of organizations (marketing, finance, operations, R&D, and HR) were storing the same basic information on employees. Creating an SOA was a way to use the IT capabilities of an organization more efficiently.

Outsourcing, Offshoring, and Insourcing

MNEs were the first organizations to outsource many of their jobs that required low levels of skills (e.g., call centers). Outsourcing in HR had been done for years, for example, using Automatic Data Processing (www.adp.com/corporateLanding) for payroll administration, but the HR departments in the 1990s were looking to outsource other programs (recruiting and selection) to supposedly save money for their operations. Thus, using the Internet for outsourcing HR programs became a reality (Gueutal & Stone, 2005; Walker, 2001). Most of these approaches failed for a variety of reasons; the major one had to do with the privacy and confidentiality of employees' personal data. There were tremendous financial benefits if the MNE could use outsourcing or *offshoring*, and many companies jumped to outsource many of their production and HR activities. However, there were problems. Perhaps the major problem with HR programs was that many companies outsourced (offshored) functions that were a critical part of the primary business of the organization, for example, talent management. Thus, many companies began *insourcing* certain business processes, particularly those in the HR department.

Data Privacy and Security

The cautions and guidelines for maintaining data privacy and security given in Chapters 3 and 10 also apply to MNEs. In addition to the normal safeguards used in a domestic company, the MNE has to create additional ones to be in compliance with security and privacy laws and regulations in different countries. As noted by Harris (2002), 36 countries in the world have legislation governing the manner in which personal information can be collected and handled. The Safe Harbor program, negotiated by the European Commission and the U.S. Department of Commerce, is an attempt to create a single set of privacy regulations regarding the use and transfer of personal information. These regulations represent a compromise between the American and European approaches to privacy issues with personal data. To go further in terms of privacy and security in an MNE, Harris (2002) suggested,

> Adopting a global approach to employee privacy issues, and building an internal culture of respect for privacy, is the best course of action open to a multinational corporation that wants to act as a global employer in the current regulatory environment surrounding the collection and use of personal information. (p. 198)

HRIS Applications in MNEs

As discussed in this chapter, most of the HRIS applications for a domestic company can be used for MNEs. However, some modifications are necessary due to the complexity of the database in an MNE. For example, rather than having a compensation database for a domestic corporation operating in a single labor market, it is necessary to have a database that includes labor market data for all countries in which the MNE has a presence. A great number of the modifications to an HRIS in MNEs would be driven by the different labor laws and regulations of the country. As noted, there is software available for IHRM, but the use of this software demands that the database be accurate and timely. Being able to create and access reports based on employee data, and do it quickly, requires that the data be accurate and up-to-date—an axiom that has been emphasized throughout this book.

Summary

Globalization is a reality. Twenty-five years ago it referred primarily to major corporations such as GE and IBM. Now it has become increasingly important for midsized firms— the fastest-growing group in all countries. This chapter has examined the implications of this globalization on the HRM function in MNEs and has documented the explosion of the HRM function into a separate field, IHRM. The complexity of the expansion on the traditional HR functions of selection, training, and compensation was also covered. The complexity of having diversity of employees (PCNs, HCNs, TCNs), along with the varying laws and practices of the countries, dictated that MNEs abandon the paper-and-pencil system for computer technology.

The advantages of having employee information stored, manipulated, and reported using computer technology were discussed relative to the use of these capabilities in multiple IHRM programs. However, some of the more critical information that an HRIS can store, analyze, and produce reports on is the cultural and legal profile of countries. This information is valuable in all the activities and programs of the IHRM department and significantly influences the management of the many parts of an MNE.

DISCUSSION QUESTIONS

1. Describe the differences between domestic and international HRM.

2. What are the different types of organizational forms corporations use for international operations?

3. What are the three types of employees who work in MNEs? Explain how an HCN could change to become a TCN in an MNE.

4. Describe the staffing process in an MNE. How does it differ from a domestic-only corporation?

5. What are the causes of expatriate failure?

6. Describe the training program for expatriates. Why is it recommended that the family of the expatriate also receive training?

7. What is the best method for completing performance appraisals for the three different types of employees in an MNE?

8. What are the objectives of an international compensation plan?

9. What are the modifications necessary for using HRIS software applications that are designed for domestic companies in an MNE?

CASE STUDY

A large MNE in the cookware industry was having difficulties maintaining its market share due to a number of mergers among other competing firms in the industry. The MNE, with corporate headquarters in Canada, had production plants in 15 countries and a company presence[4] in a total of 29 countries. Although the firm had a number of competitors, their product was considered as having the highest quality—the Mercedes of cookware. The firm was family owned and founded in 1937. The most pressing problem was how the firm could stay competitive in the market place and stop decreases in sales. Naturally, it was highly desirable to increase the sales beyond their average annual sales, but first, the firm had to change something to stabilize their place in the market.

The CEO and the corporate board, consisting of all the corporate vice presidents as well as the CEOs of all the international locations, examining the problem, concluded that it was necessary to reduce operating costs by 5% to 6% to remain competitive. Thus, it was decided to determine if these cost savings could be achieved in operations, raw materials, finances, or HR.

The MNE managers examined the latest production technology in their industry. The firm discovered that their technology was fairly up-to-date and the few technological changes available would only help decrease costs by less than 1%. However, these modifications to their current technology were very expensive and did not appear to have a favorable return on investment (ROI).

Trying to obtain better financing was nearly impossible since the MNE had very favorable financing currently. The same was true for raw materials, since a decision to use cheaper materials would greatly reduce the quality of their products.

As a result, the management of the MNE asked the IHRM department for some suggestions as to how personnel costs could be trimmed. However, there was one constraint established by tradition in the company. The MNE had never had a lay-off of employees in its history, and the CEO refused to use this option to reduce personnel costs. One of the complicating factors was the different labor laws as well as the very different cultures in the 29 countries in which the MNE did business.

Case Study Questions

1. How would you approach a solution to this problem for the MNE?

2. Assuming that reducing personnel costs is the best, and probably only, way to reduce overall corporate costs, what specific programs would you suggest to help reduce costs? And why?

3. How would an HRIS for the MNE aid in finding HR programs to help solve this problem? What would be the important data to access in the HRIS for all the units and divisions of the MNE to determine feasible HR programs?

4. Are the problems of reducing personnel costs for an MNE different from those for a domestic-only company? Explain.

NOTES

1. To maintain confidentiality, the company and individual names used are fictitious.

2. In this chapter, compensation will refer to the entire wages, salaries, benefits, and extra allowances available in a MNE.

3. It is difficult to target exactly where the IT, HR, or HRIS fields are in terms of their development at any specific time. Thus, this section will only provide a snapshot of the field when this chapter was written.

4. A company presence for an MNE means that the firm has at least a sales office in the country.

REFERENCES

Adler, N. J. (2002). *International dimensions of organizational behavior.* Cincinnati, OH: South-Western.

Bartlett, C. (2002). Foreword. In K. Beaman (Ed.), *Boundaryless HR: Human capital management in the global economy.* Austin, TX: IHRIM Press.

Beaman, K. (Ed.). (2002). *Boundary less HR: human capital management in the global environment.* Austin, TX: Rector Duncan & Associates.

Bohlander, G., & Snell, S. (2007). *Managing human resources* (14th ed.). Mason, OH: Thomson South-Western.

Borman, W. C., & Motowidlo, S. J. (1993). Expanding the criterion domain to include elements of contextual performance. In N. Schmitt & W. C. Borman (Eds.), *Personnel selection in organizations* (pp. 71–98). San Francisco: Jossey-Bass.

Black, J. S. (2000, January/February). Coming home. *HR World,* 30–32.

Black, J. S., & Mendenhall, M. (1989). A practical but theory-based framework for selecting cross-cultural training methods. *Human Resource Management, 28*(4), 511–539.

Briscoe, D. R., & Schuler, R. S. (2004). *International human resource management* (2nd ed.). London: Routledge.

Dowling, P. J., & Welch, D. E. (2005). *International human resource management: Managing people in a multinational context* (4th. ed.). Mason, OH: Thomson South-Western.

Evans, P., Pucik, V., & Barsoux, J. (2002). *The global challenge: Frameworks for international human resource management.* New York: McGraw-Hill.

Feldman, D. C., & Tompson, H. B. (1993). Expatriation, repatriation, and domestic relocation: An empirical investigation of adjustment to new job assignments. *Journal of International Business,* 507–529.

GLOBE Research Team. (2002). *Culture, leadership, and organizational practices: The GLOBE findings.* Thousand Oaks, CA: Sage.

GMAC Global Relocation Services/Windham International. (2002, October). *Global relocation trends 2002 survey report.* New York: Author.

Gregersen, H. B., Hite, J. M., & Black, J. S. (1996). Expatriate performance appraisal in U.S. multinational firms. *Journal of International Business Studies, 27,* 711–738.

Gueutal, H. G., & Stone, D. L. (Eds.). (2005). *The brave new world of e-HR.* San Francisco: Jossey-Bass.

Harris, D. (2002). Managing data privacy in global systems. In K. Beaman (Ed.), *Boundaryless HR: Human capital management in the global environment* (pp. 173–199). Austin, TX: Rector Duncan & Associates.

Hofstede, G. (1991). *Cultures and organizations.* New York: McGraw-Hill.

Iyer, R. (2005, December). *Globalization: Will your company be left standing?* (No. 101). New York: Conference Board.

Mendenhall, M., Dunbar, E., & Oddou, G. (1987). Expatriate selection, training and career-pathing: A review and critique. *Human Resource Management, 26,* 331–345.

Noe, R. A., Hollenbeck, J. R., Gerhart, B., & Wright, P. M. (2006). *Human resource management: Gaining a competitive advantage* (5th ed.). New York: McGraw-Hill Irwin.

Organizational Research Counselors. (2002, September). *Dual careers and international assignments survey.* Retrieved February 21, 2008, from www.orcinc.com (Name changed to ORC Worldwide in 2003)

Organization for the Advancement of Structured Information Systems (OASIS). (2006). *OASIS reference model for service oriented architecture 1.0.* Retrieved April 7, 2007, from www.oasis-open.org/committees/download.php/18486/pr-2changes.pdf

Poe, A. C. (2000, March). Focus on international HR: Welcome back. *HR Magazine,* 94–105.

Schuler, R., Budhwar, P. S., & Florkowski, G. W. (2002). International human resource management: Review and critique. *International School of Management Review, 4*(1), 41–70.

Schuler, R., & Jackson, S. (2005). A quarter-century review of human resource management in the U.S.: The growth in importance of the international perspective. *Management Revue, 16,* 11–35.

Schuler, R., & Tarique, I. (2007). International human resource management: A North American perspective, a thematic update and suggestions for future research. *International Journal of Human Resource Management, 18,* 717–744.

Solomon, C. M. (1995, January). Repatriation: Up, down, or out. *Personnel Journal,* 21–26.

Tarique, I., Schuler, R., & Gong, Y. (2006). A model of multinational enterprise subsidiary staffing composition. *International Journal of Human Resource Management, 17,* 207–224.

Trompenaars, F. (1992). *The seven cultures of capitalism.* New York: Currency Doubleday.

Tsui, A. S. (2007). From homogenization to pluralism: International management research in the academy and beyond. *Academy of Management Journal, 50,* 1353–1364.

Tung, R. (1981). Selecting and training of personnel for overseas assignments. *Columbia Journal of World Business, 16,* 68–78.

Tung, R. (1998). A contingency framework of selection and training of expatriates revisited. *Human Resource Management Review, 8*(1), 23–37.

U.S. Department of Labor. (2002). *International comparisons of hourly compensation costs for production workers in manufacturing.* Retrieved March 21, 2008, from www.bls.gov/fls

Von Glinow, M. A., Drost, E. A., & Teagarden, M. B. (2002). Converging on IHRM best practices: Lessons learned from a globally distributed consortium on theory and practice. *Human Resource Management, 41,* 123–140.

Walker, A. J. (Ed.). (2001). *Web-based human resources.* New York: McGraw-Hill.

PART V

Special Topics in HRIS

15

Information Security and Privacy in HRIS

Yuk Kuen Wong

Mohan Thite

EDITORS' NOTE

This chapter further expands on the information security and privacy issues in HRIS described in Chapters 3 (system development) and 9 (HR administration). Many organizations mistakenly believe that the biggest threat to information security is from outside. This chapter explains how present and past employees can pose a greater threat in the light of the emergence of collaborative and convergent technologies and what HR managers can do to safeguard information security and privacy in collaboration with IT departments. It describes the importance, legal aspects, and best practices in maintaining and promoting safe information-handling procedures.

CHAPTER OBJECTIVES

After completing this chapter, you should be able to describe

♦ The importance of information security and privacy in today's technology-intensive and information-driven economy

♦ The legal requirements pertaining to information security and privacy

♦ Best practices in safe information-handling procedures

VIGNETTE

A recent survey suggested that **information security** is one of the critical issues in technology management and highlighted the following issues and implications (Ernst & Young, 2003):

- Companies are increasingly recognizing the significance of internal threats, such as employee misconduct involving information systems.
- However, managers are hard pressed to formulate and present a good business case because of their inability to explain the relevance of information security to the broad, overall business or information security strategies.
- Only one third of the companies address some of the information security problems and would consider adopting new information security solutions.
- Most companies take a one-dimensional, reactive, and risk-averse approach rather than a proactive and holistic approach to address information security.

Another report estimates that 70% of the security breaches that involve losses of more than $100,000 are perpetrated internally, often by disgruntled employees, and inside attacks are potentially more costly (Ernst & Young, 2003). This bolsters the argument that security is to a large extent a people management issue, and HR managers play a critical role in addressing security issues.

Introduction

For the past two decades, it has been argued that an information revolution is taking place that is having a significant impact on all aspects of company life (Neuberger, Andrew, & Levetown, 2004). If applied effectively as strategic HR, information can result in the realization of significant corporate benefits; indeed, it has been contended that "information is the lifeblood of the company" (Confederation of British Industry, 1992, p. 2). It can be argued that information is vital to the success of the business, as it contributes directly to the employee's performance and the company's operational performance and financial health (Kotulic & Clark, 2004; Wong, 2006a). However, information will only be recognized as a vital organizational resource if employees can readily gain access to the information they require. Many employees are desperate to gain access to the information they need. Unfortunately, as a consequence of the high incidence of security breaches, many companies are failing to consistently provide the information resources that their employees require (Von Solms & Von Solms, 2004).

Many organizations, including governments, financial institutions, hospitals, and private businesses, amass a great deal of **confidential information** about their employees, customers, and suppliers (Dhillon, 2004; Wong, 2006a). Human resource managers must make every effort to ensure that their information resources achieve data integrity, confidentiality, and availability. However, the increasing integration of HRIS both within and among companies, coupled with the growing value of corporate information resources, has made information security management a complex and challenging undertaking (Gerber, Von Solms, & Overbeek, 2001). Indeed, it is estimated that "security breaches (internal and external) affect 90% of all businesses every year, and cost some $17 billion" (Austin & Darby, 2003, p. 121). Moreover, protective measures can be very expensive: "The average company can easily spend 5% to 10% of business budget on security" (Austin & Darby, 2003). One increasingly important mechanism for protecting corporate and employee information, in an attempt to prevent security breaches, is the formulation and application of an information security policy in HRIS (Gordon & Loeb, 2004; Hone & Eloff, 2002). **Information security in HRIS** means protecting information in the HRIS from unauthorized access, use, disclosure, disruption, modification, or destruction. The objectives of information security are to ensure confidentiality, integrity, and **availability of information** (Pfleeger, 2006; Wong, 2006a).

The history of information security can be traced back to World War II (Kizza, 2007, pp. 101–116), when physical protection of information, with barricades and armed guards controlling access to information, was introduced in the military. Today, with the rapid growth of and advancements in information and communication technologies, most organizations can afford to deploy powerful computers in their workplaces to conduct their business (Pfleeger, 2006). The Internet and mobile technologies have enhanced the interconnectivity of many computers and information systems. With the widespread use of electronic data processing, online processing, and data exchange through Internet, mobile technology, wireless access points, and home computers, there is an urgent need for better control mechanisms to protect company information (Dhillon, 2004; Freeman, 2007).

Threats to Information Security

When confidential information about employees, businesses partners, or customers falls into the hands of competitors, such a breach of security could lead to business losses, law suits, or even bankruptcy (Townsend & Bennett, 2003). Protecting organizational information is an essential element of a company's security policy (International Organization for Standardization [ISO], 2000), and in many countries it is also a legal requirement and part of corporate social responsibility (Ball, 2001).

The following are the common security threats:

• *Human error:* Where an HRIS is not well designed, developed, and maintained and employees are not adequately trained, there is a high potential threat of security breaches (Wong, 2006b, pp. 198–200). A survey suggested that human errors, such as incorrectly entered data or accidental destruction of existing data, constitute security threats to the availability, accessibility, and **integrity of information** (Wong, 2006b).

• *Damage by employees:* One of the concerns overlooked by HR managers is that information may be damaged by disgruntled employees. A recent survey suggested that a third of companies felt that their information security was at risk from disgruntled employees (Ernst & Young , 2003).

• *Misuse of computer systems:* One of the predominant internal security threats is employees' unauthorized access to or use of information, particularly when it is confidential and sensitive.

- *Theft:* The value of information can be much higher than the price of hardware and/or software. With the advances in technological developments, a relatively small computer chip (e.g., a USB device) can easily store up to 120 GB of data.

- *Computer-based fraud:* There is growing evidence that computer-based fraud is widespread. Over 90% of companies have been affected by computer-based fraud, such as data processing or data entry routines that are modified (Garg, Curtis, & Halper, 2003).

- *Viruses, worms, and Trojans:* These are common external security threats from outside the organization and often come with e-mail attachments (De Campeaux, 2002). They have the capability to automatically replicate themselves across systems and networks, as well as typically delivering mischievous functionality or damaging the information.

- *Hackers:* Another significant threat is the penetration of organizational computer systems by hackers. A hacker is defined as someone who accesses a computer or computer network unlawfully. Such attacks, often termed "intrusions" (Austin & Darby, 2003, p. 122), can be particularly dangerous, as once the hacker has successfully bypassed the network security, he or she is free to damage, manipulate, or simply steal data at will. Related to this aspect of security threat is cyber-terrorism, incorporating, for example, unlawful attacks designed to intimidate (Austin & Darby, 2003). Cyber-terrorists usually send a threatening e-mail stating that they will release some confidential information, exploit a security leak, or launch an attack that could harm a company's systems or networks. Cyber-terrorism—leveraging of an information system, particularly via the Internet—is intended to cause physical, real-world harm or severe disruption of a system's infrastructure (Hinde, 2003). A spy has high computer and network skills and is hired to break into a specific computer or computer network to steal or delete data and information.

- *Natural disasters:* Most typical forms of natural disasters are floods, earthquakes, fires, or lightning strikes, which destroy or disrupt computing facilities and information flow.

To manage these security threats, risks, and vulnerabilities, proactive management of information security is required (Lippert & Swiercz, 2005; Wong, 2006b). Organizations must address the blurring of the security perimeter and seek to develop a security-conscious culture in employees with leadership from senior executives, including HR.

Components of Information Security

Three main goals of information security are to achieve confidentiality, integrity, and availability (see Figure 15.1) within an HRIS. The HRIS is composed of three components: hardware, software, and communications as mechanisms of protection in a **client-server** architecture design at physical, personal, and organizational levels (Freeman, 2007; ISO, 2000; Lippert & Swiercz, 2005). Security procedures and policies are essential as they provide guidelines to employees on how to use the HRIS to ensure security of information within the organization (Doherty & Fulford, 2003).

❖ **Figure 15.1**   Components of Information Security

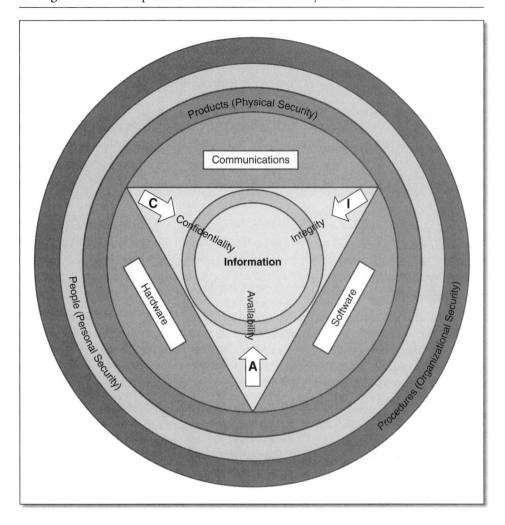

SOURCE: Wikipedia (2007).

Confidentiality

Confidential information must only be accessed, used, or disclosed by authorized users (Lippert, & Swiercz, 2005; Townsend & Bennett, 2003). Confidentially is important for maintaining the privacy of the employees' personal details.

Integrity

Integrity means that data must be created, modified, or deleted only by authorized users. Employees' personal information that is stored in an HRIS must be accurate and current (Sadri & Chatterjee, 2003).

Availability

Information availability means that authorized users must be able to process and access the information when required (Ashbaugh & Miranda, 2002). Employees need to fulfill their obligations to the contract for using the HRIS. Common techniques such as digital signature and password are used to establish authenticity and nonrepudiation in HRIS (Townsend & Bennet, 2003).

Legal Requirements for Information Security

Governments, at various levels, in most of the developed countries have enacted several laws and regulations to safeguard information security and data protection. Some of these legal requirements from Europe and North America are listed below (Kizza, 2007; Townsend & Bennett, 2003; Wikipedia, 2007):

- *Personal Information Protection and Electronics Document Act:* The act was enacted in Canada to support and promote electronic business by protecting personal information that is collected, used, or disclosed in certain circumstances.
- *Security Breach Notification Law:* This law in the state of California requires organizations to notify customers or employees when unencrypted personal information may be compromised, stolen, or lost.
- *Computer Misuse Act, 1990:* The act was proposed to make computer crime (e.g., hacking or cyber-terrorism) a type of criminal offence in the United Kingdom.
- *The European Union Data Protection Directive (EUDPD):* This requires that all EU members must adopt national regulations to standardize the protection of data privacy for citizens throughout the European Union.
- *Health Insurance Portability and Accountability Act:* This act requires health care providers, insurance companies, and employers to safeguard the security of health information of individuals. This sets national standards for electronic health care transactions.

Role of HR in Information Security

Information security issues are no longer solely the domain of the IT Department and IT managers. To have effective information security in place, HR managers need to align information security with their HR objectives. To do this, they must eliminate the hierarchical layers between the functional managers, who have historically viewed information security as a technology issue and not an HR issue. Having the active involvement of senior management in security-related decisions is crucial in establishing this alignment. Companies need to back up their talk about the importance of protecting their valuable organization and employee information (digital assets) by investing in information security. Too often, it requires a security breach, a competitor being attacked, or a regulatory mandate for the HR department to take action. Even then, core HR objectives are ignored, and a temporary fix is applied to the problem. Measured, proactive spending is less costly in the long run than reactive spending, which is often overspending in response to an incident.

Many HR managers still tend to think that security threats refer to external security breaches (e.g., virus outbreaks or malicious hackers). However, HR managers should focus more on the less obvious threats, such as disgruntled employees and ex-employees, network links to business partners who don't have proven trustworthy systems, misuse of computers by employees, and insecure network access points set up by employees. These may not only cause serious damage but also destroy a company's reputation and increase its long-term costs. The growing complexity of employees' profiles (part-time, casual, and full time employees; contractors; ex-employees; and employees of business partners) makes the problem even worse.

The best practices for handling information in HRM/HRIS include (Canavan, 2003; David, 2002; Tansley & Watson, 2000) the following:

- Adopt a comprehensive information security and privacy policy.
- Store sensitive personal data in secure HRIS and provide appropriate encryption.
- Dispose of documents properly or restore computer drives and CD-ROMs.
- Build document destruction capabilities into the office infrastructure.
- Conduct regular information security practice training for all employees.
- Conduct privacy "walk-throughs," and make spot checks on proper information handling.

Kovach, Hughes, Fagan, and Maggitti (2002) and Grundy, Collier, and Spaul (1994) suggest the following additional measures:

- The careful selection of staff with due regard to their honesty and integrity
- The raising of information security awareness among staff and ensuring that employees are aware of the company's security policies
- Measures to address the personal problems of staff, such as gambling and drug addiction, which might lead them to indulge in computer abuse for financial gains
- Access to effective grievance procedures, since the motivation for much computer abuse is retaliation against management

Information Security Management for HRIS

A well-known information security management practice is ISO/IEC 27002 (ISO, 2000), as stipulated by the ISO (Dresner & Wood, 2007; Freeman, 2007). The security management process consists of administrative/procedural, logical/technical, and physical controls (see Table 15.1) (Department of Broadband, Communications and the Digital Economy [DBCDE], 2007; Freeman, 2007).

Information Privacy

Privacy is a human value consisting of four elements (Kovach & Tansey, 2000):

- *Solitude:* The right to be alone without disturbances
- *Anonymity:* The right to have no public personal identity
- *Intimacy:* The right not to be monitored
- *Reserve:* The right to control one's personal information, including the methods of dissemination of that information

For the individual, information security has a significant effect on privacy, which is viewed very differently in different cultures.

❖ **Table 15.1**   Information Security Program for HRIS

Information Security	Descriptions
Control types	*To mitigate a risk, it is recommended that the following control strategies be used in designing an HRIS:*
Administrative	• Administrative control (also known as procedural control) consists of policies, procedures, standards, and guidelines. An administrative control is developed from the information security framework for managing people and organizational operations. Some of these policies, procedures and guidelines are regulated by laws. Examples of administrative controls include the corporate security policy, password policy, hiring policies, and disciplinary policies.
Logical	• Logical control (also referred to as technical control) regulates access to information in HRIS. For example, passwords, network- and host-based firewalls, network intrusion detection systems, access control lists, and data encryption are logical controls. The common problem of logical controls is access privileges when an employee's job duties change or he or she is transferred to another department. The access privilege required by the new role is frequently added onto his or her already existing access privilege, which may no longer be necessary or appropriate.
Physical	• Physical controls refer to the physical environment, such as computer facilities in the workplace. Separation of duties ensures that an individual cannot complete a critical task by himself or herself. For example, an employee who submits a reimbursement request should not also be able to authorize payment. An HR manager who manages the employees' database should not manage the finance database—these roles and responsibilities must be separated from one another.
Security classification for information	• An important aspect of information security and risk management is recognizing the value of information and defining appropriate procedures and protection requirements for it.

Information Security	Descriptions
	Classification of information to be assigned should take into account how much value that information has to the organization. All employees in the organization must be trained in the classification schema and should understand the required security controls and handling procedures for each classification. The HR department plays a significant role in the process.
Access control	• Access to protected information must be restricted to people who are authorized to access the information. Control techniques such as identification and authentication are important for the HRIS. The most common access control technique is user name and password. HR managers need to ensure the obligations of employees using the HRIS.
Cryptography	• Cryptography is a computer technique to ensure that sensitive information is only read and used by authorized employees. There have been significant academic research and technological developments in cryptography.
Defense in depth	• To fully protect the information during its lifetime, each component of the information processing system must have its own protection mechanisms. The building up, layering on, and overlapping of security measures is called "defense in depth." The strength of any system is no greater than its weakest link. When using a defense-in-depth strategy, should one defensive measure fail, there are other defensive measures in place that continue to provide protection.

SOURCE: Department of Broadband, Communications and the Digital Economy (DBCDE)(2007).

There is a tenuous relationship between employee privacy concerns and organizational needs (Ball, 2001; Kovach & Tansey, 2000). Fair information policies suggest that employees have the right to know how their personal information is used, to prevent the use of personal information by other parties (e.g., government, insurance companies), and to take reasonable precautions to prevent misuse of their personal information (Camardella, 2003; Kovach & Tansey, 2000). The human resource literature mainly focuses on invasion of privacy perceptions and procedures of handling information about the hiring process (from job application to hiring decisions) (Kovach et al., 2002). An important element in the success of managing this personal information is the HRIS, a database of personal information about each employee and job applicant. Because of the authority given to them to access and use HRIS information, HR managers must be aware of the ethical and legal issues associated with both creation and use of personal information in the HRIS (Kovach & Tansey, 2000; Sadri & Chatterjee, 2003). The information privacy concerns related to HRIS include (1) what types of employee information can be collected and stored in the system and (2) who can access and update the information (Noe, Hollenbeck, Gerhart, & Wright, 1994; Sadri & Chatterjee, 2003). It is recommended that organizations should only collect and store information based on sound and valid business reasons (Hubbard, Forcht, & Thomas, 1998).

Because the organizations are accountable and liable for their information practices and procedures, it is prudent to ensure that the collection, maintenance, use, and dissemination of personal information is *necessary, lawful, current, and accurate* (Camardella, 2003). By focusing on the purpose for and amount of data collected, HR managers can minimize privacy-based litigation in their organizations while maintaining high ethical standards. There are a number of common privacy violations, including violation of Internet usage, intentional misuse of information, interception of information, and information matching. As the HRIS is integrated with many other information systems, Web sites, and databases, employees can use the information-matching technique to generate the specific information they want. The difficulty with information matching is that no one may know what the profiles built from the matched information will be used for and by whom.

In recent times, governments have moved to enact legislation to protect an individual's right to privacy. You may recall that Chapter 11 provides a detailed description of U.S. federal and state laws on privacy, with particular reference to HRIS.

The major privacy concerns include determination of what types of employee information should be stored on the system and who can access and modify information in the HRIS databases (Camardella, 2003). Below are given some of the best practices that HR managers should consider to secure information security and privacy (Noe et al., 1994; Pfleeger, 2006):

- Train users on how to securely use and handle the equipment, data, and software.
- Train employees to "log off" personal computers after they are through using them.
- Do not allow passwords to be shared. Change passwords frequently.
- Run software through a virus detection program before using it on the system.
- Ensure that backup copies, data files, software, and printouts are used only by authorized users.
- Make backup copies of data files and programs.
- Ensure that all software and mainframe applications include an audit trail (a record of the changes and transactions that occur in a system, including when and who performed the changes).
- Use edit controls (such as passwords) to limit employees' access to data files and data fields.
- Employees should take responsibility for updating their employee records themselves via the self-service system.

DISCUSSION QUESTIONS

1. Why are information security and privacy important considerations in the design, development, and maintenance of HRIS?

2. List and discuss the major information security and privacy threats to organizations.

3. What are the important goals/considerations of information security?

4. Identify the important legal provisions governing information security and privacy in your country.

5. What is the role of HR professionals in information security and privacy management?

6. What are some of the best practices to manage information security and privacy in terms of procedural, technical, and physical controls?

CASE STUDY: PRACTICAL APPLICATIONS OF INFORMATION PRIVACY PLAN

XYZ University is a medium-size tertiary education provider in the state of Queensland, Australia. In undertaking its normal business of teaching, learning, and research, the university collects, stores, and uses "personal information," that is, anything that identifies a person's identity.

With respect to students, it may include, among other things, records relating to admission, enrollment, course attendance, assessment, and grade; medical records; details of student fees, fines, levies, and payments, including bank details; tax file numbers and declaration forms; student personal history files; qualifications information; completed questionnaire and survey forms; records relating to personal welfare, health, equity, counseling, student and graduate employment, or other support matters; records relating to academic references; and records relating to discipline matters.

The bulk of this information is retained in the student management information systems and in the file registry. Academic and administrative staff, at various levels, have access to these records only as required to carry out their duties. Portions of the information held in university student records are disclosed outside the university to various agencies, such as the Australian Taxation Office; Department of Education, Science and Training; other universities; consultant student services providers; Department of Immigration and Multicultural Affairs; and overseas sponsorship agencies.

The university has a well-documented information privacy policy in accordance with the community standard for the collection, storage, use, and disclosure of personal information by public agencies in Queensland. The policy relies on the 11 principles developed in the Commonwealth Privacy Act of 1988. These principles broadly state the following:

- Personal information is collected and used only for a lawful purpose that is directly related to the collector's function.
- Before the information is collected, the individual concerned should be made aware of the purpose, whether it is required by law, and to whom the information will be passed on.

- Files containing personal information should be held securely and protected against loss; unauthorized access, use, modification, or disclosure; or any other misuse.
- Personal information can only be disclosed to another person or agency if the person concerned is aware of it and has consented and the disclosure is authorized or required by law.
- Personal information should not be used without taking reasonable steps to ensure that it is accurate, up-to-date, and complete.

Presented below are three scenarios where you need to decide how to apply the privacy policy and principles. A complete statement of the relevant privacy principles can be found at www.dva.gov.au/health/ethics/ipps.pdf

Scenario 1

Roger, a photocopier technician, has been asked to repair a photocopier at the office that just broke down while copying a grievance matter against an employee of the agency. The officer who was copying the file takes the opportunity to grab a cup of coffee and leaves Roger in the photocopy room while the photocopier cools down. While waiting, Roger flicks through the file and realizes that the person against whom the grievance was made lives in the same street as him.

Scenario 2

Tom telephones a student at home about attending a misconduct hearing. The student is not at home; however, the student's partner, Christine, answers the phone. She states that she knows all about the misconduct hearing but asks for clarification of the allegations. When pressed, Tom provides further details. Tom feels comfortable about providing this information to Christine because she is the student's partner and she has already told Tom that she knows all about her partner's misconduct hearing.

Scenario 3

Brad works in a student administration center, and Janet is a student. They know each other as they used to attend the same high school. Occasionally, they get together at the University to have a coffee and a chat about mutual friends. Brad knows that Janet's birthday is coming up because Janet happened to mention that she'll be another year older in the near future. Brad decides to access the student information system to find out Janet's date of birth and home address. A few weeks later, Janet receives a birthday card from Brad sent to her home address.

Case Study Questions

With regard to the above scenarios, you need to decide

1. what information privacy principles (IPPs) have been breached,

2. how, and

3. what would you do to address the situation?

SOURCE: This case study has been prepared using the information provided by Griffith University on its Privacy Plan at www.griffith.edu.au/ua/aa/vc/pp (accessed June 20, 2008).

REFERENCES

Ashbaugh, S., & Miranda, R. (2002). Technology for human resources management: Seven questions and answers. *Public Personnel Management, 31,* 7–20.

Austin, R. D., & Darby, C. A. (2003, June). The myth of secure computing. *Harvard Business Review, 81*(6), 121–126.

Ball, K. S. (2001). The use of human resource information systems: A survey. *Personnel Review, 30*(6), 677—693.

Camardella, M. J. (2003). Electronic monitoring in the workplace. *Employment Relations Today, 30*(3), 91.

Canavan, S. (2003). *An information security policy development guide for large companies.* Bethesda, MD: SANS Institute. Retrieved February 23, 2008, from http://www.sans.org/reading_room/whitepapers/policyissues/1331.php

Confederation of British Industry. (1992). *IT: The catalyst for change.* London: Author.

David, J. (2002). Policy enforcement in the workplace. *Computers and Security, 27*(6), 506–513.

De Campeaux, D. (2002). Taking responsibility for worms and viruses. *Communications of the ACM, 45*(4), 15–16.

Department of Broadband, Communications and the Digital Economy. (2007). *Secure your information: Information security principles for enterprise architecture.* Retrieved February 23, 2008, from www.dbcde.gov.au

Dhillon, G. (2004). The challenge of managing information security. *International Journal of Information Management, 24,* 3–4.

Doherty, N. F., & Fulford, H. (2003, May 18–21). Information security policies in large organisations: Developing a conceptual framework to explore their impact. In M. Khosrow-Pour (Ed.), *Information technology and organizations: Trends, issues, challenges and solutions* (pp. 1052–1053). Information Resources Management Association International Conference, Philadelphia. Hershey, PA: Idea Group.

Dresner D. G., & Wood, J. (2007). Operational risk: Acceptability criteria. In *Proceedings of the Third International Symposium on Information Assurance and Security* (pp. 301–306), Manchester, UK.

Ernst & Young Security Survey. (2003). *Global Information Security Survey 2003.* Retrieved February 12, 2008, from www.ey.com/global/download.nsf/Germany/Global_IT-Security_Studie_2003/$file/Global%20IT-Security%202003.pdf

Freeman, E. H. (2007). Holistic information security: ISO 27001 and due care. *Information Systems Security, 16*(5), 291–294.

Garg, A., Curtis, J., & Halper, H. (2003). Quantifying the financial impact of information security breaches. *Information Management and Computer Security, 77*(2), 74–83.

Gerber, M., Von Solms, R., & Overbeek, P. (2001). Formalizing information security requirements. *Information Management and Computer Security, 9*(1), 32–37.

Gordon, L. A., & Loeb, M. P. (2004). *Economics of information security.* New York: Springer.

Grundy, E., Collier, P., & Spaul, B. (1994). Auditing personnel: A human resource approach to information systems control. *Managerial Auditing Journal, Bradford, 9*(6), 10–16.

Hinde, S. (2003). Cyber-terrorism in context. *Computers and Security, 22*(3), 188–192.

Hone, K., & Eloff, J. H. P. (2002). Information security policy, international security standards say? *Computers and Security, 21*(5), 402–409.

Hubbard, J. C., Forcht, K. A., & Thomas, D. A. (1998). Human resource information systems: An overview of current ethical and legal issues. *Journal of Business Ethics, 17,* 1319–1323.

International Organization for Standardization. (2000). *Information technology. Code of practice for information security management, ISO 17799.* Geneva, Switzerland: Author.

Kizza, J. M. (2007). *Ethical and social issues in the information age.* London: Springer-Verlag.

Kotulic, A. G., & Clark, J. G. (2004). Why there aren't more information security research studies. *Information & Management, 41,* 597–607.

Kovach, D. K. A., & Tansey, K. (2000). The balance between employee privacy and employer interests. *Business and Society Review, 105*(2), 289–298.

Kovach, K. A., Hughes, A. A., Fagan, P., & Maggitti, P. G. (2002). Administrative and strategic advantages of HRIS. *Employment Relations Today, 29*(2), 43–48.

Lippert, S. K., & Swiercz, P. M. (2005). Human resource information systems (HRIS) and technology trust. *Journal of Information Science, 31*(5), 340–353.

Neuberger, M. J., Andrew, S., & Levetown, A. S. (2004). Special employment considerations to ensure the security of your IT department. *Employment Relations Today, 31*(1), 35.

Noe, R. A., Hollenbeck, J. R., Gerhart, B., & Wright, P. M. (1994). *Human resource management: Gaining a competitive advantage.* Burr Ridge, IL: Irwin.

Pfleeger, C. P. (2006). *Security in computing.* Englewood Cliffs, NJ: Prentice Hall.

Sadri, J., & Chatterjee, V. (2003). Building organisational character through HRIS. *International Journal of Human Resources Development and Management, 3*(1), 84–98.

Tansley, C., & Watson, T. (2000). Strategic exchange in the development of human resource information systems (HRIS). *New Technology Work and Employment, 15*(2), 108–122.

Townsend, A. M., & Bennett, J. T. (2003). Human resources and information technology. *Journal of Labor Research, 24*(3), 361–363.

Von Solms, B., & Von Solms, R. (2004). The ten deadly sins of information security management. *Computers and Security, 25,* 371–376.

Wikipedia. (2007). *Information security.* Retrieved February 17, 2008, from www.wikipedia.org

Wong, Y. K. (2006a). Issues of software quality and management in practice. *International Journal of Internet and Enterprise Management, 4*(1), 37–53.

Wong, Y. K. (2006b). *Modern software review: Techniques and technologies.* Hershey, PA: IRM Press.

The Future of HRIS

Emerging Trends in HRM and IT

Michael J. Kavanagh

Mohan Thite

EDITORS' NOTE

In Chapter 1, the history of HRM was discussed along with its eventual merging with the field of IT, thus creating a new field of study and managerial practice—human resource information systems (HRIS). This book provides information on the development and implementation of an HRIS. Most of the HRIS development and sophistication began in the United States, but HRIS have spread rapidly throughout the industrialized countries of the world. The question to be answered here is where the field of HRIS is going in the future. Forecasting the future is always difficult. One can expect evolutionary, rather than revolutionary, changes in the HRIS field. This chapter will discuss some of these trends in the field of HRIS.

CHAPTER OBJECTIVES

After completing this chapter, you should understand

- The future trends in HR
- The future trends in IT/IS and workforce technologies
- How HR and IT/IS are combining for future business applications

Future Trends in HRM

Today, HRM is seen in a strategic context and not merely as an administrative or support service. HR's contribution to competitive advantage lies in its adding value to strategic capabilities and business processes (Becker & Huselid, 2006), as covered in Chapters 9 and 10. This can be accomplished by effective talent management, helping with change management, influencing strategy, and a host of other value-added activities that affect effectiveness (Lawler, 2005). One implication of strategic HRM (SHRM) is that it needs to be viewed from a holistic or systems perspective; that is, the HR functions and processes have a bundle effect on organizational performance rather than any one HR function acting alone (Figure 1.2). This has an important implication for HRIS, as the very purpose of a computer-based system is to integrate diverse processes into a coherent whole. A note of caution here is that while routine, highly programmed technologies and tightly regulated operations auger well for any technology implementation, they can also inhibit knowledge generation and transfer owing to their inherent rigidity, inertia, and resistance to change (Lengnick-Hall & Lengnick-Hall, 2006).

SHRM also recognizes the importance of environmental contingencies; that is, what is best for an organization in terms of the use of HRM concepts and practices relates to the context in which it is applied. To achieve best fit, HRM needs to be both data driven and evidence based. HRIS applications can be very useful in drilling down data and deriving appropriate reports to help managerial decision making. For example, workforce strategy needs to be embedded in proper workforce planning from a long-term perspective. It also means that in measuring the effectiveness of HRM functions and practices, appropriate HR metrics and analytics need to be developed, expanded, and improved on (Lawler, 2005; see also Chapter 6). To measure an organization's return on HRM programs and practices, one needs to move beyond traditional financial metrics and create conditions that increase intangible value by building a compelling vision and fostering employee trust and commitment (Ulrich & Smallwood, 2005). Creating value for HRM practices and programs requires that HR professionals recognize that value is defined by the receiver more than the provider. As such, HR professionals must start by identifying which stakeholders (e.g., employees, managers, stockholders) are the targets for establishing value for HRM products and programs (Martin, 2008). Most important, as Martin (2008) states, "They (HR professionals) should make a clear connection between the HR contributions and the company's end results" (p. 23). As we have seen in the previous chapters, technology can be a great enabler in designing and delivering many of the SHRM concepts, such as e-recruitment, e-training, total rewards package, and self-service portals, by relating them to the company's business model.

To examine future trends in the HR field, one must look within countries, since labor laws differ from country to country and, thus, could have a significant impact on any new developments in HRM for that country. However, in examining the international HRM literature, there are some similarities in terms of HR trends across other countries (e.g., a focus on the cost effectiveness of HR programs). The future trends in the United States will be discussed here with the understanding that other countries may differ somewhat in terms of other future trends. A special expertise panel created by the Society of Human Resource Management examined the results of a 2006 survey by the Society on future trends in HRM to determine if these trends were still viable in 2007–2008. In the report on the panel's findings, Schramm (2007) identified 12 future trends important for HR in the United States for 2007–2008. The remainder of this section will cover these important future trends.

Examining the trends from the 2006 SHRM survey, the expert panel also developed a rank ordering of the trends in terms of importance for 2007–2008. The panel judged 13 trends in HR in terms of importance, which will be discussed in this section.[1]

1. The trend ranked first was the increased emphasis on corporate social responsibility (CSR). The panel felt that there is a need for leaders of business to get involved and support CSR in their companies, as well as integrating CSR into the strategy of the business. In addition, there was an emphasis on expanding the awareness of gaps within and between countries among the "haves" and "have nots." Finally, the issue of differences in priorities among generations, that is, aging workers versus new entrants, is growing in importance.

2. The second trend in importance was an increased focus on employee health, safety, and security. This trend is most apparent in the United States, with rising health costs as well as an awareness of specific legislation in terms of the American Disabilities Act (ADA) and the **Family and Medical Leave Act** (**FMLA**), covered in Chapter 9. There is also increased monitoring of possible fraud by employees using this and other legislation for workers' compensation. There also appears to be issues with e-mail in terms of its monitoring and storage. Again, there are generational differences in terms of a variety of topics, such as values, retention, drug testing, and environmental concerns.

3. There is more attention to employee relations as it relates to talent management. The panel noted that employee retention, particularly in terms of talented and highly skilled ones, is growing in importance. It was felt that HR will have an increasingly important function, establishing a closer link between employees' performance and the accomplishment of business objectives. Companies also need to address the problems and challenges of managing a multigenerational workforce relative to recruitment of new employees and retention of valued ones. Finally, it was noted that the increase in domestic and global changes due to outsourcing, mergers, and acquisitions is leading to more focus on tying HR strategy and operations to the overall business strategy.

4. The interpretation and application of ethical issues in the workplace are growing in terms of differences in perception and understanding across generations. As discussed in Chapter 15, ethics involves a variety of topics, such as the use of new technology, compliance with ethical standards, employee use of communication techniques (blogs), the management of ethics in a global corporation, and the need for ethics training of all employees.

5. The effects of globalization and the necessity to understand multiculturalism are of increasing importance to both domestic and international companies. Talent management in international companies (MNEs) across different countries is critical to achieve strategic objectives. The existence of multiculturalism in both domestic and international companies needs to be managed so as to develop respect for the different cultural backgrounds of the employees. There is a growing need to develop leadership in global companies, and an awareness of the generational differences in work styles as well as the changing needs of talent as the baby boomers retire.

6. The role of the HR professional in consulting and outsourcing has changed and has become more important relative to allowing HR professionals to focus on strategic objectives. HR professionals are discovering the need to manage outside vendors and outsourcing relationships, particularly in terms of HR metrics, to evaluate the cost effectiveness of these relationships. Finally, HR is expanding the scope of outsourcing as more companies are becoming global operations.

7. There is an increased emphasis in HR on accountability by using human capital measurement and HR metrics. For every HR activity from recruiting through retention programs, there is more emphasis on accountability in terms of the impact of the programs on company profitability. This increased emphasis was discussed in Chapter 6 relative to a new or updated HRIS.

8. Labor relations have been growing in importance due to increased union consolidation and attempts to unionize workers in new sectors of the economy. In addition, the impact of traditional U.S. labor relationships in the global market has become quite important as it collides with cultural norms and labor laws. There is an increasing impact of the increased costs of health care and other benefits on contract negotiations.

9. There is an increased awareness of organizational development and the effect of better working relationships on the bottom line. This awareness is focused on both individual as well as team development and functioning, and it includes recognition of the importance of company culture in working relationships. The impact of changing demographics of the workplace, for example, the aging workforce and retirement of baby boomers, needs to be recognized, and specific organizational development programs need to be focused on the generational issues in working relationships.

10. There is a major emphasis on staffing management, as firms will need to focus on talent management in general. This means acquiring, training, and motivating new talent. There is an increasing awareness of the effect of both shifting demographics (generational differences) and globalization on staffing management. The use of technology in recruiting (Internet recruiting) and a focus on the use of HR metrics is increasing. Finally, HR planning through forecasting labor needs and supply, particularly due to the retirement of baby boomers, is becoming important in staffing management.

11. There is a continued focus on technology and HR management due to the rapid growth of technology and the pervasiveness of social networking (e.g., MySpace and blogs). This trend is the basis for this book, as covered in all the previous chapters.

12. The analysis of total rewards/compensation and benefits as they influence employee retention is growing in importance. This trend is affected by more focus on the transparency of executive compensation, the impact of an aging workforce on compensation and benefits (e.g., retirement funding), and new talent acquisition. Finally, the effect of reward systems on performance is becoming increasingly important.

13. There is an increasing emphasis on improving workforce diversity and linking it to corporate strategy. This emphasis is being felt in both domestic and international companies by linking diversity to the overall business strategy. All the previous 12 trends relate to this trend since increasing diversity will affect them all.

As seen by these trends, the field and practice of HR are changing in many ways, all of them creating more complexity in the management of organizations. The argument in this book is that a well-developed and implemented cost-effective HRIS can be a great aid in handling this complexity in the future.

Future Trends in the Fields of IT/IS and HRIS

When examining future trends in HRIS, it is impossible to separate the future trends in IT/IS without relating them to the field of HRM. The knowledge economy is being profoundly influenced not only by the intensity but also by the speed of technological evolution. Information technologies have been steadily evolving and improving from mainframes to client servers and now to Internet/Web interfaces (Roberts, 2006). While robotics and nanotechnology are some of the broader technological trends, network communication technologies (broadband and wireless), convergence technologies (e.g., cell phones and PDAs), collaborative tools (e.g., Web 2.0, portals), service-oriented architecture (SOA), and business intelligent systems are some of the notable developments that have affected the field of HRIS and its related technologies. Apart from achieving better coordination and integration of different systems within an enterprise, these technologies are empowering both employers and employees to deploy, share, and use their knowledge for the common benefit of their company.

Software as a Service (SAAS)

Traditionally, IT systems, such as ERPs, have been large, time-consuming, and expensive undertakings. Typically, ERPs are developed in-house by large firms, but more often, they are purchased from vendors—that is, a third-party provider. Traditional software development models are being replaced by "on demand" software in which the company/customer pays only for the HR parts and programs of the software that are needed. By selecting only the HR parts/programs needed, the company can save money over purchasing entire integrated systems. The customer/company pays to use and not to own the software. With significant drops in the price of computer processing power and with innovative delivery options, such as Software as a Service (SAAS) (Zeidner, 2007) or Application Service Provider's (ASP's) model, HRIS technologies are now within the reach of small to medium enterprises (SMEs), which are the largest customers for new HRIS packages.

Service-Oriented Architecture

One of the major problems during this technological evolution has been the frustration associated with frequent system upgrade cycles. SOA may be a solution, as it converts monolithic and static systems into modular and flexible components. According to Roberts (2006), "The big change in enterprise software that will impact everything from financials to HR is standards-based, service-oriented software (SOA)" (p. 104). The self-contained services in an SOA are loosely coupled, like a set of Lego pieces, and can be reconfigured to suit a particular business process and end-user applications, rather than hard-coded together as they were in the past.

SOA is about "efficient modular design and deployment, and reusable software is at the heart of the architecture" (Macy, 2007). The key feature of SOA is that "functionality is decomposed into distinct units (services), which can be distributed over a network and can be combined together and reused to create new business applications" (http://en .wikipedia.org/wiki/Service_oriented_architecture). SOA offers several advantages to end users, who can change the business process when needed and purchase or develop only those applications that are involved in the new processes. This approach is much better than working around the existing system or purchasing a package from a vendor based on predetermined processes and applications. Thus, under SOA, the business process dictates the IT system to be used and not the other way round. In the long run, this will reduce technology costs and should improve productivity.

In Chapter 9, XML-enhanced SOA was discussed. Whether SOA delivers what it promises depends on how the major companies in the ERP market respond. For example, having acquired PeopleSoft and JD Edwards, Oracle may need to integrate its own systems before harnessing the potential of SOA. Oracle Fusion and SAP NetWeaver, the two strategies adopted by Oracle and SAP around SOA, will play an important role in how HRIS technology evolves in the future. In addition, Workday, a new firm in the IT/IS/HRIS field, is developing a product built around a document-centric data structure, like Google (Roberts, 2006).

Web 2.0

This term refers to a second generation of Web-related communities and services focusing on creativity, collaboration, and sharing, in contrast to traditional isolated information silos. Web 2.0 users not only access information but also generate, share, and distribute new content. According to Dario de Judicibus, "Web 2.0 is a knowledge-oriented environment where human interactions generate content that is published, managed and used through network applications in a service-oriented architecture" (http://en.wikipedia.org/wiki/Web_2.0).

Examples of Web 2.0 include the following:

- Social networking sites (e.g., chat rooms, MySpace, Facebook)
- Wikis (publicly available collaborative Web dictionaries enabling users to contribute to online documents or discussion)
- Blogs (short for Web logs, i.e., online journals or diaries hosted on a Web site, both personal and corporate)
- Mash-ups (software composed of two or more composite applications—e.g., pulling up a rental car booking site within an airline booking site)
- Podcasts (audio or video recordings)
- RSS (rich site summary) feeds (e.g., news items)
- Personal Web sites
- Peer-to-peer networking (P2P; sharing files, e.g., text, music, and videos)
- Collective intelligence (sharing knowledge to tap the expertise of a group)
- Web services (Web enabled instant communication between users to update information or conduct transactions—e.g., a supplier and a retailer updating each other's inventory systems) (McKinsey, 2007)

Web 2.0 has also encouraged businesses to promote user collaboration to share knowledge and to communicate with business partners, such as suppliers and outsourcing providers. With an emphasis on sharing, Web 2.0 can dramatically change the way in which employees communicate with each other and with customers. Using Web 2.0 will require the HR department to pay greater attention to the legal, ethical, and security implications of information exchange.

Enterprise Portals

Enterprise portal is the general term used to refer to the ways in which individuals can interact with each other. They can be information portals, collaboration portals, expertise and knowledge portals, operation portals, or a combination of all these. Within an HRIS, employee and manager self-service portals are powerful examples of the potential use of such portals (see Chapter 9). In the context of portals, two of the most commonly used standards are WSRP (Web Services for Remote Portlets) and JSR (Java Specification Request). One very important implication regarding the establishment and use of enterprise portals is their effect on the family-work conflicts that dual wage earners face. Being able to respond to, and it is hoped, solve work problems from one's home will be increasingly important in the future.

Future Trends in Workforce Technologies

In terms of future workforce technologies, Henson (2005), predicted that

- the technology of the future will be both collaborative and connected;
- there will be increased and more widespread use of intelligent self-service via employee portals;
- there will be increased use of HR scorecards coupled with workforce analytics and decision trees;
- there will be increases in process automation and the use of online analytical processing (OLAP) for processing raw data;
- faster and cheaper access to accurate real-time HR information will be possible due to advancements in communication tools; and
- the worker of the future will be able to work anywhere, any time, and on any device, which would not only help work-life balance but also turn the workplace into a 24/7 cycle.

It would be appropriate to conclude this chapter by discussing the latest CedarCrestone (2006) survey on human capital management (HCM) workforce technologies and service delivery approaches. The survey data for this report were collected between June and September 2006, and the 324 respondents represent organizations with approximately 7 million employees. The organizations were split about even between domestic and international, and 84% were from North America, with the remainder from Australia and Europe. Based on this survey of future trends, the results indicated the following trends:[2]

1. Organizations using more HRIS software applications experienced more operating income growth than organizations with fewer applications. In addition, the following five software applications were most closely associated with this growth in operating income: (a) manager self-service, (b) career planning, (c) workforce measurement, (d) talent acquisition, and (e) performance management.

2. One of the key objectives of HRIS software applications is to help the organization in meeting its strategic objectives. About 75% of the respondents indicated that workforce technologies enabled the HR department to serve the organization more strategically, for example, gathering and providing HR metrics for budgeting and forecasting.

3. One of the survey questions the respondents were asked was what they wanted in terms of HR technologies that they currently were not receiving. The results indicated that they were least satisfied with analytics (reporting and decision tools), employee development, and recruiting services.

4. In terms of quantitative benefits from HR technologies, the respondents reported that the benefits were realized in reduced time to hire (recruiting), headcount reductions, and lower transactional and compliance costs—mainly through the use of self-service portals.

5. In terms of employees served by HR professionals, organizations with service centers had the largest number of employees served per HR staff. However, the number of employees served by HR staff varied in terms of the size of the organization, with larger organizations having more employees served by HR staff than medium and small ones.

6. The market for different HRIS software applications varies as a function of the type of application. The market for applications for administrative and self-service transactions is developed, while the market for strategic HCM and measure/plan software applications is in an early adopter stage.

7. As noted in Chapters 6 and 9, there is an increasing use of HR metrics in terms of cost justification for HR activities and programs. This survey found that specific analytics applications are not widely used; however, respondents are clearly moving toward metrics-based management.

8. Examining the frequency of use of Web self-service, it was found that organizations are moving away from solutions, away from third-party vendors, and toward Web self-service.

9. In terms of the major providers of HCM technology, Oracle's PeopleSoft Enterprise Capital Management Applications are the most frequently used solutions for all HRIS applications. The one exception is that Kronos is currently the leader in the time and attendance software application.

10. Organizations that have in-house HRIS solutions use employee productivity and ease of integrating new services as their key drivers or reasons to stay with in-house solutions. The key drivers for outsourced HRIS solutions are avoidance of new IT/capital expenditures and reduction in software implementation times.

11. In terms of in-house versus outsourced choices for automating HR processes, selective outsourcing is growing. Technology infrastructure outsourcing (hosting) is expected to show the strongest growth in the next 12 months.

12. In general, the results of the survey indicated that respondents are spending more for outsourced solutions than for in-house HRIS solutions.

13. Consistent with the ideas presented in Chapter 10 regarding talent management, it has been receiving significantly increased attention in terms of software applications. However, business process improvement continues as the number one initiative for organizations.

14. Chapter 8 deals with the issues involved in implementing an HRIS as part of a change management approach. The survey results indicate that change management is the *most important and continuing success factor for the adoption of workforce technologies.*

Summary

As noted early in this chapter, forecasting the future is very difficult. Many of us look to nanotechnology for the major breakthroughs in computer technology. However, the student of HRIS must never forget the human issues in developing and implementing an HRIS. It is interesting to note that one of the findings from the CedarCrest survey was an emphasis on change management—for which an entire chapter of this book was devoted (see Chapter 8). At the end of the day, technology cannot substitute for managerial competence and employee discretionary behavior (Armstrong, 2005). It can only be a messenger, not a message. It is also impractical to expect information systems to supplant the soft functions of HR, such as an online character replacing a good executive coach (Stanton & Coovert, 2004). In sum, technology is extremely important in the field of HRIS, but people are simply more important.

NOTES

1. The 13 trends will be discussed briefly. The interested reader may want to examine the original full report.

2. Some findings were excluded since they were not relevant to the central purpose of this book. The interested reader can find more information on this CedarCrest survey at www.cedarcrestone.com/company.php. The findings for the CedarCrest Human Capital Application Blueprint™ are not covered due to their proprietary nature.

REFERENCES

Armstrong, G. (2005). Differentiation through people: How can HR move beyond business partner? *Human Resource Management, 44*(2), 195–199.

Becker, B. E., & Hueselid, M. A. (2006). Strategic human resources management: Where do we go from here? *Journal of Management, 32*(6), 898–925.

CedarCrestone. (2006). *Workforce technologies and service delivery approaches.* Alpharetta, GA: Author.

Henson, R. (2005). The next decade of HR: Trends, technologies and recommendations. In H. G. Gueutal & D. L. Stone (Eds.), *The brave new world of eHR* (pp. 255–292). San Francisco: Jossey Bass.

Lawler, E. E. (2005). From human resource management to organizational effectiveness. *Human Resource Management, 44*(2), 165–169.

Lengnick-Hall, C. A., & Lengnick-Hall, M. L. (2006). HR, ERP and knowledge for competitive advantage. *Human Resource Management, 45*(2), 179–194.

Macy, J. (2007). Welcome to the Web 2.0 age. *HR Monthly, March,* pp. 36–37.

Martin, E. (2008, February/March). Creating the HR value proposition. *IHIM.link, 13*(1), 22–23.

McKinsey. (2007). How businesses are using Web 2.0: A McKinsey global survey [Electronic version]. *McKinsey Quarterly.* Retrieved April 28, 2008, from www.mckinseyquarterly.com/How_businesses_are_using_Web_20_A_McKinsey_Global_Survey_1913_abstract

Roberts, B. (2006). New HR systems on the horizon. *HR Magazine, 51*(5), 103–107.

Schramm, J. (2007). *The 2007–2008 workplace trends list.* Alexandria, VA: Society for Human Resource Management, SHRM Research Department.

Stanton, J. M., & Coovert, M. D. (2004). Guest editors' note: Turbulent waters: The intersection of information technology and human resources. *Human Resource Management, 43*(2/3), 121–125.

Ulrich, D., & Smallwood, N. (2005). HR's new ROI: Return on intangibles. *Human Resource Management, 44*(2), 137–142.

Zeidner, R. (2007). *SAAS identified as leading trend in HR tech* (SHRM White Paper). Alexandria, VA: Society of Human Resource Management.

Appendix

Additional Resources

Internet Resources

A collection of change theory sites: www.nursing-informatics.com/kwantlen/wwwsites3.html

Abbott, Langer & Associates: www.abbott-langer.com

Advantiv (Decision Director Software): www.advantiv.com

Being First—a change leadership development and transformational change consulting firm with lots of free resources for change leaders and consultants: www.being-first.com/changeresources

Change Management Association: www.cmassociation.org

Change Management Directory: www.change-management-directory.com

Change Management Learning Center: www.change-management.com

Economic Research Institute: www.erieri.com/index.cfm?fuseaction=Home.Main

Employee Benefits Research Institute (EBRI): www.ebri.org

Expert Choice: www.expertchoice.com

Gartner Group: www.gartner.com

Hackett Benchmarking: www.thehackettgroup.com/portal/site/approgrserv/menuitem.af2c6166ff71ba964026079466f069a0

Hay Group: www.haygroup.com

Human Resources—HR Gopher: www.hrgopher.com

Human Resources Software Page: www.hr-software.net

International Association for Human Resource Information Management: www.ihrim.com

International Association for Human Resource Information Systems: www.ihrim.org

International Foundation of Employee Benefits Plans: www.ifebp.org

Kaiser Associates: www.kaiserassociates.com/home.html

Maritz: www.maritz.com

ORC: www.orcinc.com

Salarydotcom: www.salary.com

SalaryExpertdotCom: www.salaryexpert.com

Saratoga Institute: www.valuebasedmanagement.net/organizations_saratoga.html

Six Sigma/Change Management: www.isixsigma.com/ce/change_management

Society of Human Resource Management: www.shrm.org

Structured Analysis Wiki: http://yourdon.com/strucanalysis/wiki/index.php?title=Introduction

Themanager.org provides an excellent collection of topics on change management: www.themanager.org/Knowledgebase/Management/Change.htm

Towers Perrin: www.towers.com/towers/default.asp

U.S. Department of Labor: www.dol.gov

U.S. Department of Labor, Bureau of Labor Statistics: www.bls.gov

WageWeb: www.wageweb.com

Watson Wyatt Worldwide: www.watsonwyatt.com

William M. Mercer: www.mercer.com

WorldatWork (was ACA): www.worldatwork.org

www.cornerstoneondemand.com

www.oracle.com

www.outstart.com

www.plateau.com

www.saba.com

www.sap.com

www.softscape.com

www.sumtotalsystems.com

Additional Readings

2007 survey of employee benefits. (2007). Old Saybrook, CT: Business & Legal Reports.

Abrahamson, E. (2004). *Change without pain.* Boston: Harvard Business School Press.

Adler, S. (1987). Toward the more efficient use of assessment center technology in personnel selection. *Journal of Business and Psychology, 2,* 74–93.

Aguinis, H., Henle, C. A., & Beaty, J. C. (2001). Virtual reality technology: A new tool for personnel selection. *International Journal of Selection and Assessment, 9,* 70–83.

Alavi, M., & Leidner, D. E. (2001). Research commentary: Technology-mediated learning—A call for greater depth and breadth of research. *Information Systems Research, 12*(1), 1.

Allen, E. T., Melone, J. J., Rosenbloom, J. S., & Mahoney, D. F. (2007). *Retirement plans: 401(k)s, IRAs and other deferred compensation approaches.* New York: McGraw-Hill.

Anderson, N. (2003). Applicant and recruiter reactions to new technology in selection: A critical review and agenda for future research. *International Journal of Selection and Assessment, 11,* 121–136.

Armstrong, M. (2006). *Performance management: Key strategies and practical guidelines* (3rd ed.). London: Kogan Page.

Armstrong, M., & Stephens, T. (2005). *A handbook of employee reward management and practice.* London: Kogan Page.

Bartram, D. (2006). Testing on the Internet: Issues, challenges, and opportunities in the field of occupational assessment. In D. Bartram & R. K. Hambleton (Eds.), *Computer-based testing and the Internet: Issues and advances* (pp. 13–37). San Francisco: Wiley.

Bauer, T. N., Truxillo, D. M., & Paronto, M. E. (2004). Applicant reactions to different selection technology: Face-to-face, interactive voice response, and computer-assisted telephone screening interviews. *International Journal of Selection and Assessment, 12,* 135–148.

Bauer, T. N., Truxillo, D. M., Tucker, J. S., Weathers, V., Bertolino, M., Erdogan, B., et al. (2006). Selection in the information age: The impact of privacy concerns and computer experience on applicant reactions. *Journal of Management, 32,* 601–621.

Bebchuck, L., & Fried, J. (2004). *Pay without performance: The unfulfilled promise of executive compensation.* Cambridge, MA: Harvard University Press.

Beer, M., & Nohria, N. (2000). *Breaking the code of change.* Boston: Harvard Business School Press.

Bieg, B. J. (2007). *Payroll accounting 2007.* Mason, OH: Thomson/South-Western.

Braddy, P. W., Meade, A. W., & Kroustalis, C. M. (2006). Organizational recruitment website effects on viewers' perceptions of organizational culture. *Journal of Business and Psychology, 20,* 525–543.

Bridges, W. (2003). *Managing transitions: Making the most of change.* Cambridge, MA: Da Capo Press.

Buckley, P., Minette, K., Joy, D., & Michaels, J. (2004). The use of an automated employment recruiting and screening system for temporary professional employees: A case study. *Human Resource Management, 43,* 233–241.

Burke, W. W. (2007). *Organization change: theory and practice.* Thousand Oaks, CA: Sage.

Carr, D. K., Hard, K. J., & Trahant, W. J. (1996). *Managing the change process.* New York: McGraw-Hill.

Chan, D., & Schmitt, N. (2004). An agenda for future research on applicant reactions to selection procedures: A construct-oriented approach. *International Journal of Selection and Assessment, 12,* 9–23.

Cohen, D. S., & Kotter, J. P. (2005). *The heart of change field guide.* Boston: Harvard Business School Press.

Conner, D. R. (1992). *Managing at the speed of change.* New York: Villard Books.

Conner, M. L. (2002). How do I measure return on investment (ROI) for my learning program? In *Learning and training FAQs.* Retrieved April 5, 2008, from www.learnativity.com

D'Aprix, R. (1996). *Communicating for change.* San Francisco: Jossey-Bass.

Dennis, A. R., Wixom, B. H., & Roth, R. M. (2006). *Systems analysis and design* (3rd ed.). Hoboken, NJ: Wiley.

Duck, J. D. (2001). *The change monster: The human forces that fuel or foil corporate transformation and change.* New York: Crown Business.

Ellig, B. R. (2002). *The complete guide to executive compensation.* New York: McGraw-Hill.

Ensher, E. A., Nielson, T. R., & Grant-Vallone, E. (2002). Tales from the hiring line: Effects of the internet and technology on HR processes. *Organizational Dynamics, 31,* 224–244.

Epstein, J., & Klinkenberg, W. D. (2001). From Eliza to Internet: A brief history of computerized assessment. *Computers in Human Behavior, 17,* 295–314.

Epstein, J., Klinkenberg, W. D., Wiley, D., & McKinley, L. (2001). Insuring sample equivalence across internet and paper-and-pencil assessments. *Computers in Human Behavior, 17,* 339–346.

Feldman, D. C., & Klaas, B. S. (2002). Internet job hunting: A field study of applicant experiences with on-line recruiting. *Human Resource Management, 41,* 175–192.

Flannery, T. P., Hofrichter, D. A., & Platten, P. E. (1996). *People, performance, and pay.* New York: Free Press.

Galpin, T. J. (1996). *The human side of change.* San Francisco: Jossey-Bass.

Gane, C., & Sarson, T. (1979). *Structured systems analysis.* Englewood Cliffs, NJ: Prentice Hall.

Gerhart, B., & Rynes, S. L. (2003). *Compensation: Theory, evidence, and strategic implications.* Thousand Oaks, CA: Sage.

Gilley, J. W., Quatro, S. A., Hoekstra, E., Whittle, D. D., & Maycunich, A. (2001). *The manager as change agent.* Cambridge, MA: Perseus.

Gueutal, H., Stone, D. L., & Salas, E. (2005). *The brave new world of eHR: Human resources in the digital age.* San Francisco: Jossey-Bass.

Harris, M. M. (2006). Internet testing: The examinee perspective. In D. Bartram & R. K. Hambleton (Eds.), *Computer-based testing and the internet: Issues and advances* (pp. 115–133). San Francisco: Wiley.

Hiatt, J. M. (2006). *ADKAR: A model for change in business, government, and our community.* Loveland, CO: Prosci Learning Center Publications.

Hornke, L. F., & Kersting, M. (2006). Optimizing quality in the use of web-based and computer-based testing for personnel selection. In D. Bartram & R. K. Hambleton (Eds.), *Computer-based testing and the internet: Issues and advances* (pp. 115–133). San Francisco: Wiley.

Jellison, J. M. (2006). *Managing the dynamics of change.* New York: McGraw-Hill.

Jones, J. W., & Dages, K. D. (2003). Technology trends in staffing and assessment: A practice note. *International Journal of Selection and Assessment, 11,* 247–252.

Jones, S. D., & Schilling, D. J. (2000). *A step-by-step, customizable approach for managers, facilitators, and team leaders.* San Francisco: Jossey-Bass.

Kotter, J. P. (1996). *Leading change.* Boston: Harvard Business School Press.

Kotter, J. P., & Cohen, D. S. (2002). *The heart of change.* Boston: Harvard Business School Press.

Marshak, R. J. (2006). *Covert processes at work.* San Francisco: Berrett-Koehler.

Meade, J. G. (2003). *The human resources software handbook: Evaluating technology solutions for your organization.* San Francisco: Jossey-Bass.

Milkovich, G., & Newman, J. (2007). *Compensation.* New York: McGraw-Hill.

Nadler, D. A. (1998). *Champions of change.* San Francisco: Jossey-Bass.

Piskurich, G. M. (2003). *The AMA handbook of e-learning.* New York: AMACOM.

Potosky, D., & Bobko, P. (2004). Selection testing via the internet: Practical considerations and exploratory empirical findings. *Personnel Psychology, 57,* 1003–1034.

Risher, H., & Fay, C. H. (Eds.). (1995). *The performance imperative: Strategies for enhancing workforce effectiveness.* San Francisco: Jossey-Bass.

Rynes, S. L., & Gerhart, B. (Eds.). (2000). *Compensation in organizations: Current research and practice.* Thousand Oaks, CA: Sage.

Salgado, J. F., & Moscoso, S. (2003). Internet-based personality testing: Equivalence of measures and assesses' perceptions and reactions. *International Journal of Selection and Assessment, 11,* 194–205.

Searle, R. H. (2006). New technology: The potential impact of surveillance techniques in recruitment practices. *Personnel Review, 35,* 336–351.

Smith, M., & Smith P. (2005). E-selection: Computer-based assessment and interpretation. In M. Smith & P. Smith (Eds.), *Testing people at work* (pp. 220–237). Malden, MA: Blackwell.

Smither, J. W. (Ed.). (1998). *Performance appraisal: State of the art in practice.* San Francisco: Jossey-Bass.

The WorldatWork Handbook of Compensation, Benefits & Total Rewards. (2007). New York: Wiley.

Van Rooy, D. L., Alonso, A., & Fairchild, Z. (2003). In with the new, out with the old: Has the technological revolution eliminated the traditional job search process? *International Journal of Selection and Assessment, 11,* 170–174.

Wallace, J. C, Tye, M. G., & Vodanovich, S. J. (2000). Applying for jobs online: Examining the legality of Internet-based application forms. *Public Personnel Management, 29,* 497–503.

Zingheim, P. K., & Schuster, J. R. (2000). *Pay people right!* San Francisco: Jossey-Bass.

Glossary

2-Tier architecture   The most basic type of computer hardware infrastructure in which a computer server provides information to a client computer.

360° appraisal   Any system where employee performance is rated by managers, peers, subordinates, and (possibly) by outsiders and self.

3-Tier architecture   A type of computer architecture where a client computer interacts with two (or more) servers. One server usually maintains the database and data, while the other server manages the processing logic.

75% rule   If a package can meet approximately 75% of your needs, that is quite good.

Ability test   The Watson-Gleser Critical Thinking Appraisal, a multiple-choice reasoning test, in which the examinee reads a short- or medium-length passage and draws logical conclusions about the statements, choosing the answer that makes the best logical sense. Many other ability tests are similar in appearance and format to educational tests that are familiar to students (e.g., the Scholastic Aptitude Test [SAT], the Miller Analogies Test [MAT], and the Graduate Record Examination [GRE]).

Action-research model   A process model of the management of change in organizations. The basis of this model is the interaction of managerial or organizational action and research that both evaluates the action taken and provides data for future planning of the change effort.

Aesthetic features of Web site   The overall stylistic or innovative features of a Web site, such as contrasting colors, pictures, animation, and playfulness, that keep the user engaged while navigating through multiple Web pages.

Affirmative Action Plan (AAP)   A written report detailing how an employer actively seeks to hire and promote individuals in protected classes. For employers with government contracts totaling $50,000 or more, the Office of Federal Contract Compliance Procedures (OFCCP) requires that an AAP be completed.

Age Discrimination in Employment Act (ADEA)   The 1967 federal legislation prohibiting illegal discrimination in employment against individuals 40 years of age and older.

Americans With Disabilities Act (ADA)   The 1990 federal legislation prohibiting illegal discrimination in employment against individuals with disabilities. A disability is defined as a physical or mental impairment that substantially limits one or more major life activities.

Application server   Software that delivers specific applications, such as a recruiting plan, to computers in the HR department, typically through the Internet and using the HTTP.

Application service provider (ASP)   A third-party firm that hosts and provides access to a bundle of one or more software application services from a central location to multiple clients via the Internet. Clients pay a subscription fee, which generally entails data management and software upgrades. ASPs are often considered a cost-effective way for organizations to manage their information requirements. Many learning management systems are ASP based; that is, access to applications is available through ASPs.

Attributes   Characteristics of the entity in a relational database. For example, an employee has a name, address, phone number, education, and so on.

Availability of information   This means that the authorized users must be able to process and access the information when required.

Balanced scorecard   A means of measuring strategic organizational performance that gives managers a chance to look at their company from the perspectives of stakeholders, including external customers, employees, and shareholders.

"Balance sheet" compensation   An approach for expatriate compensation that has as its goal the maintenance of a home-country living standard plus a financial inducement for accepting an international assignment.

Bandwidth   This term refers to the rate of data transfer, measured in bits per second.

Base pay   The pay received by an employee as the reward for being employed. The employee will make at least this much unless fired. Base pay for some workers is stated in terms of pay per hour; for others, it is stated in terms of annual pay.

Benchmarking (also known as "best-practice benchmarking" or "process benchmarking")   A process used in management, and particularly in human resources strategic management, to evaluate various aspects of their HR function, both activities and programs, usually within their own market sector.

Best of breed (BOB)   An architecture that combines products from multiple vendors.

The Big 3   The Big 3 questions for any HRIS-related project are Where are we at? Where are we going? How are we going to get there?

Blended learning As the term implies, it "blends" various approaches to learning and could incorporate, for instance, face-to-face, formal, informal, and online learning methods.

Boundary-spanning function Any HR management activity or program that must directly interface with the external environment of the organization to be effective.

Business application This consists of a set of one or more computer programs that serve as an intermediary between the user and the DBMS (database management system) while providing the "functions" or "tasks" that the user wants performed.

Business intelligence (BI) A broad category of business applications and technologies for creating data warehouses and for analyzing and providing access to these specialized data to help enterprise users make better business decisions. BI applications include the activities of decision support systems, query and reporting, statistical analysis, forecasting, and data mining.

Business requirements definition The process that occurs when analyzing an HR system, whereby an organization determines and documents its current and future needs. These needs become the targets or goals that the new system will attempt to satisfy. This term is similar to a **needs analysis,** but has financial information as well as cost-benefit analysis (CBA).

Change agent (also known as "change leader") A person who is responsible for leading an organizational change or someone who is influential and can communicate and motivate others to accept a change by informal means.

Change management A structured approach to changing the mindset and perceptions of individuals, groups, and organizations to accept and implement new ideas and processes in an organization.

Civil Rights Act Title VII The 1964 federal legislation prohibiting illegal discrimination in employment based on individuals' race, sex, religion, or national origin. The act also defines and prohibits sexual harassment.

Client-server A term to describe the software and hardware configuration that divides a business application into two tiers, typically with the user interface and some business logic on the user's computer, such as a PC (the client), and the database and mainstream parts of the application stored on a server.

Column-level security This type of security in an HR database would restrict specific information on employees, for example, age or gender, that makes up a column of information in employees' records.

Commercial off-the-shelf (COTS) software   Prewritten or developed software or hardware products that already exist for purchase.

Competency   A combination of some set of knowledge, skills, and abilities. Many industrial psychologists equate competencies with traits.

Confidential information   Confidential information must only be accessed, used, or disclosed by authorized users.

Configuration (also **Fit-gap**)   This process consists of systematically working through every HR process and matching each of those to each of the integral HRIS processes. The result is an understanding of where organizational processes and the software processes mesh (fit) and where they do not (gap). Any gaps that are identified need to be closed either through modification of organizational processes or by software customization.

Content information   The degree to which the Web site hosts relevant information that the user deems valuable and informative in nature.

Context level diagram   The highest-level data flow diagramming that contains the least amount of detail. It is used to represent the system, its boundary, and the external entities that interact with the system.

Corrective feedback   In performance management, information fed back to an employee pointing out the discrepancy between observed performance and performance standard. The purpose is to solve any performance problem and increase performance level.

Country's culture   This refers to the history, myths, traditions, values, religious beliefs, communications, and social structure of a country.

CPM chart   A method for analyzing a project that calculates the starting and ending times for each activity and determines which activities are critical to the completion of a project (called the *critical path*) and which activities have "float time" (are less critical).

Critical path   It is the sequence or project network with the longest overall duration determining the shortest time possible to complete the project.

Cross-cultural suitability   This term refers to an attribute of an expatriate. It could include language ability, cultural empathy, adaptability, and a positive attitude toward the assignment in the specific country being considered.

Cross-tab query   This query performs calculations on the values in a field and displays the results in a datasheet.

Cultural norm A specific belief, attitude, or behavior that is defined as right or wrong, correct or incorrect, within a given culture in a country.

Culture An organization's collective values, beliefs, experiences, and norms that shape the behavior of the group and the individuals within it.

Culture shock The feeling of uneasiness and discomfort when going from one culture to another as well as the adjustment that occurs in a relatively short time when moving from one country to another.

Current analysis The process of analyzing the current state of existing HR processes, technologies, and capabilities. Addresses the Big 3 question, Where are we at?

Customization The modification of a software product to match specific unchangeable organizational processes or needs.

Database A set of data. Importantly, it is a permanent, self-descriptive store of interrelated data items that can be processed by one or more business applications.

Database management systems A set of software applications combined with a database. The main functions of a DBMS are to create the database; insert, read, update, and delete database data; maintain data integrity and security; and prevent data from being lost by providing backup and recovery capabilities.

Data flow DFD component that represents the flow of data within the system. An arrow indicates the direction of flow, and the name of the flow indicates the type of data.

Data flow diagram (DFD) Graphical tool that represents the flow of data through a system and the various processes that manipulate or change the data.

Data migration The process of transferring employee data between storage types and computer systems or software applications.

Data mining It involves statistically analyzing large data sets to identify recurring relationships. For example, data mining an employee database might reveal that most employees reside within a group of particular zip codes.

Data store DFD component that represents the temporary or permanent storage of data within the system. A data store is represented with an open-ended rectangle on the DFD.

Data warehouse A repository of a company's electronically stored data. Data warehouses are designed to facilitate reporting and analysis for decision making.

Decision support systems Software applications that use databases, primarily data warehouses, to assist managers and business professionals in making business decisions by providing the opportunity to ask "what if" questions. This capability allows decision makers the opportunity to assess the benefits of one problem solution against other solutions.

Direct costs of expatriate failure   These costs include the actual money spent on selecting and training, relocation costs for expatriate (and family), and the salary of the expatriate.

Direct report   The employee whose job performance is being evaluated.

Economic feasibility   System feasibility assessment tool that focuses on the financial and economic benefits and costs that a new system would bring to the organization.

Electronic data processing (EDP)   EDP refers to automation of business processes to perform routine, standardized sets of transactional activities.

Enterprise application integration (EAI)   This term refers to the use of software and computer systems architectural principles to integrate a set of enterprise computer applications, for example, employee selection and employee compensation.

Enterprise resource planning   A set of integrated database applications, or modules, that carry out the most common business functions, including human resources, general ledger, accounts payable, accounts receivable, order management, inventory control, and customer relationship management. ERP modules are integrated primarily through a common set of definitions and a common database.

Entity   An external person, department, or agent that interacts with the system through receiving or sending data. An entity is represented as a square on the DFD (data flow diagram).

Equal Employment Opportunity (EEO)   The condition in which all individuals have an equal chance for employment, regardless of their race, color, religion, sex, age, disability, or national origin, as established in federal legislation and the U.S. Constitution and its Amendments (13 and 14).

Exempt   Not subject to the provisions of the Fair Labor Standards Act. See **Nonexempt**.

Expatriate   A parent-country national (PCN) employee assigned to a subsidiary of the MNE in another country.

Expatriate failure   The return of expatriates prior to the completion of their overseas assignment.

eXtensible Markup Language (XML)   The software "Plug and Play" standard is called XML. XML is a tagged language very similar to HTML.

Fair Labor Standards Act (FLSA)   The 1938 federal legislation that established a minimum wage for hourly workers, set the rate of pay for overtime work beyond the defined work-week of 37.5 hours, prohibited oppressive child labor by restricting hours of work for children below 16 years, and listed hazardous occupations too dangerous for children.

Family and Medical Leave Act (FMLA)   The federal legislation that requires organizations with 50 or more employees to provide up to 12 weeks of unpaid leave after childbirth or adoption, to care for a seriously ill family member, or for an employee's own serious illness.

Field   An attribute of an entity that is stored in a table. It appears as a column.

File-oriented data structures   These were simply data-processing systems that performed recordkeeping functions that mimicked the existing manual procedures. Thus, electronic data were stored in computers much the same way they were stored in paper-filing systems.

Firewall   This term refers to a device or set of devices that will permit or deny all computer traffic between computers with different security requirements based on a set of rules.

Fit-gap   See **Configuration**.

Flexplan (also known as "**cafeteria plans**")   A benefits plan in which an employee is provided with some core set of benefits and can then add on some dollar amount of additional benefits paid for by the providing organization.

Force-field analysis   A useful technique for looking at all the advantages and disadvantages of a proposed change.

Foreign key   It represents the primary key from another table that is stored as an attribute in another table. It represents a common key between two tables that is used to form a relationship between the two tables.

Form   An object in a database that you can use to maintain, view, and print records in a database in a more "structured" manner.

Functional experts   These experts are most often the power users, and they bring to the implementation team their extensive knowledge about HR processes as well as some technological skills.

Future-oriented competency modeling   It is to consider the future needs of a particular department or role type.

Gantt chart   A popular type of bar chart that illustrates a project schedule. It provides a graphical representation of the duration of tasks against the progression of time in a project.

Gap analysis   This indicates the differences between the current state of affairs in the organization and the desired future state.

"Going rate" or "host-country" compensation   This is the approach to expatriate compensation that ties the base salary for international employees to the salary levels in the host country. For example, an expatriate would earn pay that is comparable with employees in the host country.

"Go Live"   The first day the new software is used to manage the organization.

Hierarchical access   A set of access rules that provide differential security for employees at different levels or roles in the organization.

High-performance employees (HIPERs)   In a talent management approach, these are the employees who are considered to be performing well in their current role.

High-potential employees (HIPOs)   In a talent management approach, these are the employees who have the potential to develop further and wish to do so.

Host-country nationals (HCNs)   Employees of the MNE who are citizens of a country, other than the parent country, in which a subsidiary is located.

HR functional expert   Their role is to provide expertise about what HR data are needed, how the HR process maps should be interpreted, and what data are required for decision making.

HRIS   The system used to acquire, store, manipulate, analyze, retrieve, and distribute information regarding an organization's human resources.

HRM   Human resource management is an integral part of the organization system and deals with strategies, policies, and practices that aim to attract, develop, and retain high-quality intellectual capital.

Human capital   This encompasses "the knowledge, skills, competencies and attributes embodied in individuals that facilitate the creation of personal, social and economic well-being" (OECD, 2001, p. 18, cited in Chapter 12, this volume).

Human resource management decision system (HRMDS)   HRMDS focuses on generating reports of different types, levels, and frequencies to assist people managers in their decision making.

Hypertext markup language (HTML)   It is the predominant markup language for Web pages. It provides a means to describe the structure of text-based information in a document—by denoting certain text as links, headings, paragraphs, lists, and so on—and to supplement that text with *interactive forms*, embedded *images*, and other objects.

Implementation   The selection, installation, and population of an information technology system.

Implementation team   This team works with the project manager to complete the actual software implementation

Incentive pay   Pay provided for some performance achievement. Unlike merit pay, it is not added to base pay but is a one-off reward that must be re-earned to be received again.

Indirect costs of expatriate failure   Indirect costs are harder to quantify than direct costs, but they could include loss of market share in the country, negative reactions from the host-country government, and possible negative effects on local employee morale.

Information   According to *Oxford English Dictionary*, information is the act of informing, or giving form or shape to the mind. Information provides "structure" and "meaning" to abstract data and is of potential value to organizations.

Information privacy   Privacy is a human value consisting of four elements that refer to human rights, namely, solitude, anonymity, intimacy, and reserve. Information privacy concerns come to play wherever personally identifiable information is collected, stored, and used.

Information security   Information security ensures confidentiality, integrity, and availability of information.

Information security in HRIS   Information security in HRIS pertains to protecting information in the HRIS from unauthorized access, use, disclosure, disruption, modification, or destruction.

Integrity of information   Integrity means data must be created, modified, or deleted by the authorized users.

Internal rate of return (IRR)   A capital budgeting metric that is the annualized effective compounded return rate that can be earned on an investment; it is an indicator of the efficiency of an investment.

The International Association for Human Resource Information Management (IHRIM)   The professional organization for specialists in both human resources and human resources technology.

Internet service portals A Web portal that functions as a point of access to information on the World Wide Web.

IT architecture The basic hardware, software, and networking infrastructure of the organization.

Job analysis The process of systematically obtaining information about jobs by determining the duties, tasks, or activities of jobs from which KSAs (knowledge, skills, and abilities) can be estimated.

Job description The product of a job analysis. It contains the complete decryption of a job to include the necessary duties, tasks, and activities and define the working contract between the employee and the organization.

Job evaluation A rating or ranking system designed to create an internal hierarchy of job value. In many organizations, job evaluation results form the basis of the salary structure.

Job forecasting Planning for future work requirements to determine the number and range of specific jobs required.

Knowledge, skills, and abilities (KSAs) The requirements for each job in the organization. KSAs provide the basis for HR planning and recruitment/selection of new employees.

Knowledge test A multiple-choice training posttest of knowledge of the tools, machines, and equipment used at a factory, designed to measure how well the new hire has learned essential job information taught in classroom training.

Kotter's process of leading change This model provides two key lessons: first that the change process goes through a series of phases, each lasting a considerable period of time, and, second that critical mistakes in any of the phases can have a devastating impact on the momentum of the change process.

Learning management system (LMS) A software application or Web-based technology that allows the creation, delivery, and management of learning resources and content. An LMS can perform a variety of functions, including training administration, performance management, competency management, skills-gap analysis, or resource allocation.

Legacy system A large, outdated computer system or application that is still being used, often because the cost of replacing such a system is high. The cost of maintaining such systems, which increases over time, is often a key driver for a new system investigation.

Legal and political feasibility System feasibility assessment tool that focuses on the legal issues associated with the implementation of a new system and/or any political impacts that would emerge from its use.

Level 0 diagram   The first-level DFD (data flow diagram) that outlines the major processes (functions) of the system, the basic sequence of these processes, the basic data stores, and the external entities that interact with the system.

Lewin's change model   One of the earliest and key contributions to organizational change, Lewin's framework serves as a general model for understanding planned change.

Load balancing   This refers to a technique in computer networking to spread work between computers, network links, or CPUs, in order to get optimal resource utilization from the network.

Logical design   A phase in the SDLC (system development life cycle) in which a new system is designed without regard to the technology (e.g., hardware, software, networking) in which it will be implemented.

Logical model   A model of the system that graphically illustrates what the system does, independent of any technological architecture (e.g., hardware, software, networking).

Long-range planning   It examines an organization's information needs in light of its long-range strategy. Typically, it looks beyond the present, usually focusing on information needs in the future—that is, 1, 5, and 10 years from now.

Magnetic Ink Character Recognition (MICR)   As defined by the American National Standards Institute (ANSI), it is the common machine language specification for the paper-based payment transfer system. It consists of magnetic-ink-printed characters of a special design that can be recognized by high-speed magnetic recognition equipment (www.whatismicr.com).

Maintenance   The ongoing task of operating and maintaining a new system after the initial implementation, including auditing, updating, and upgrading.

Management information systems (MIS)   This refers to structured information flows of business functions to aid managers in performing traditional activities.

Management reporting systems   Software that (1) focuses on information aimed at middle managers; (2) integrates transaction processing data by business function such as manufacturing, marketing, and human resources; and (3) provides reporting of summarized data.

Management sponsor   The senior manager who is ultimately responsible for the successful completion of the project.

Market benchmarking   A compensation practice designed to provide labor market rates for jobs in an organization. The labor markets may be local, regional, national, or global. The underlying rationale is that an organization should pay for a job roughly what other employers in the relevant market pay to attract and retain employees.

Merit pay   A system providing increases to base pay based on merit or performance. Once merit pay is awarded, the employee receives it until he or she leaves the organization.

Middleware   Middleware is a general term for any computer programming that serves to "glue together" or mediate between two separate and often already existing programs.

Nadler's congruence model   An organizational performance model that is built on the view that organizations are systems and that only if there is congruence ("fit") between the various organizational subsystems can we expect optimal performance.

Navigability (of a Web site)   The overall ease with which a user can browse through multiple Web pages to locate topics of interest.

Needs analysis   The process when analyzing an HR system where an organization determines and documents its current and future needs. These needs become the targets or goals that the new system will attempt to satisfy. This is synonymous with **Business requirements definition**.

Nonexempt   Subject to the requirements of the Fair Labor Standards Act. Employers of nonexempt employees must pay them at least minimum wage, pay overtime of one and one-half base pay rate for every hour worked in 1 week in excess of 40 hours, keep track of hours worked, and file reports with the U.S. Labor Department demonstrating compliance.

N-tier architectures   These represent the software and hardware configuration in which databases and applications are distributed among many different computers around the world.

Occupational assessor software   This software is the property of the Economic Research Institute (ERI). It is an automated approach to job analysis.

Occupational Safety and Health Act (OSHA)   The 1970 law that authorizes the federal government to establish and enforce occupational safety and health standards for all places of employment affecting interstate commerce.

Offshoring   An organization's use of groups outside the United States (e.g., India, China) to provide services (e.g., HR call centers) to achieve strategic organizational goals.

Online recruiting (also known as "Web-based recruiting," "Internet-based recruiting," "cyber recruiting," "e-cruiting," and "e-recruiting")   The use of the Internet in attracting job seekers to a company's job openings.

Operational feasibility   System feasibility assessment tool that focuses on how well the new system will fit within the organization, including issues such as development schedule, extent of organizational change, and user responses to the system.

Optical Character Recognition (OCR)   This term refers to the translation of images of handwritten or printed text into computer-editable text, usually by a scanner.

Outsourcing   An organization's use of an outside group to provide from a few (e.g., recruiting, compensation processing) to a broad set of services (e.g., all HR functions) to achieve strategic organizational goals.

Parent-country nationals (PCNs)   Employees of the MNE who are citizens of the country in which the parent, or headquarters, of the MNE is located.

Payback period   A capital budgeting metric that calculates the number of years required for the flow of benefits returned by an investment to equal the cost of the investment.

Performance appraisal   A retrospective system noting how an employee has performed during a previous period. Performance appraisal data usually form the basis for merit pay.

Performance criterion   An outcome, behavior, or competency used in the performance management (or appraisal) process. Performance criteria are the factors on which an employee's performance is rated.

Performance management   A prospective system designed to improve performance. Performance appraisal is a minor subset of performance management, which focuses more on planning for performance and positive and corrective feedback to help an employee continue good performance and improve poor performance.

Performance standard   The level of a performance criterion a fully job-knowledgeable employee who makes a reasonable effort should achieve.

Perquisite   A reward based on job status. Usually reserved for executives (corporate jet, executive dining room, special parking) but now frequently used as performance rewards for other workers.

Personnel economics   This has been used to better understand the internal workings of a firm via economic analysis. For example, personnel economics provides a useful lens to examine more complex remuneration systems and other elements of HR planning such as recruitment and selection practices.

Phase containment   The process of identifying and fixing problems early in the system development life cycle so as to avoid costly rework later. The Y2K bug is an example of phase containment failure.

Physical design   A phase in the SDLC (System Development Life Cycle) in which a new system is designed with particular focus on how the hardware, software, networking, activities, and so on will be implemented.

Position Analysis Questionnaire   A specific technique for completing a job analysis. There is a software package that automates this approach to job analysis.

Positive feedback   Remarks made by a manager to a direct report concerning observed performance and designed to reinforce efforts leading to high performance.

Power user   The most demanding user of HRIS.

Primary key   An attribute that has unique values for each record in a table. For example, each employee has a social security number that is unique (i.e., only one person has a particular number).

Process   The mechanism through which the data are transformed, manipulated, and created into output such as a report, a decision, and so on.

Process mapping   The systematic documentation of organizational processes that directly relate to the ongoing project.

Process reengineering   The analysis and redesign of work flow to improve an organization's efficiency and effectiveness.

Program (or project) evaluation and review technique (PERT)   A method for analyzing the tasks involved in completing a given project, the time needed to complete each task, and the minimum time needed to complete the total project. Once the PERT analysis is completed, a Gantt chart can be constructed to guide the project.

Project charter   A planning document that defines the scope of, and provides a basic "rule book" to facilitate completion of, a software implementation project.

Project concept   It describes the key stakeholders and seeks to ensure that the right questions are asked so that the right problem is solved.

Project creep   This occurs when decisions are made to implement additional functionality beyond what was defined in the project scope.

Project manager   The person chosen by an organization to be responsible for the planning, execution, and evaluation of an HRIS implementation project.

Project proposal (also called a "project charter")   This contains objectives and performance targets (e.g., cost, time, scope) for the HRIS project.

Project scope   The portions of the information system that need to be completely operational to satisfy the needs of the various customers, employees, and senior management.

Project sponsor   This is usually a member of the steering committee who has provided the fiscal resources for the development and implementation of the HRIS.

Psychological contract   Employees' beliefs about the reciprocal obligations and promises between them and their organizations.

Qualified   The status of a benefits plan with respect to favorable tax treatment. A qualified plan cannot discriminate in favor of the highly paid by design or in practice.

Query   A question you ask about the data stored in a database. For example, you may want to know which employees live within a specific zip code.

Rapid e-learning (REL) (just-in-time learning/training/on-demand learning)   The essence of REL is the ability to develop and deliver tailor-made e-learning content swiftly (within weeks, days, or hours) and inexpensively to a large number of learners and to track their learning progress in order to stay abreast of rapidly changing knowledge and information needs. The responsibility for content creation lies with the subject matter experts themselves. REL tools only require limited audiovisual expertise, as they use easy-to-use presentation software. REL solutions may be either synchronous (real time) or asynchronous (on demand). As REL modules can be very short (30 minutes or less), they are convenient and are easily "digested" by the learners.

Recognition award   Any reward (whether cash or noncash) with the primary purpose of celebrating specific performance achievements of individuals or groups. A group implementing a new HRIS, for example, might be treated to a party on successful completion of an important segment of the project. The cash value of the award is less important than the psychological value, even if the award has significant cash value.

Record   A row in a table that represents an "instance" of the entity. For example, in an employee table, each row contains data about a particular employee, and each column contains data that represent an attribute of that employee, such as Name, Phone, and E-Mail Address.

Reengineering   The process of implementing the right technology infrastructure and streamlining the business processes.

Regression analysis   A statistical procedure that provides predictions of future states of the firm based on the history of the firm. For example, changes in market share for a company's product can be linked with the number of employees. Thus, future expected changes in market share (an increase) could be used to estimate the number of new employees needed.

Relational database   Data are stored in tables where each table represents one "entity" in the real world, and the information associated with that entity is stored only in that table. Tables are related to each other through a common attribute or key.

Relationships   These are created by having the same attribute in each table with the value of the attribute being the same in each table. Most often, this is done by taking the "primary key" of one table and including it in the related table.

Reports   These are formatted presentations of data from a table, multiple tables, or queries that are created as a printout or to be viewed on screen. Data displayed in a report are dynamic, reflecting the latest data from the tables on which the report is based.

Request for proposal (RFP)   A document that solicits potential consultants or vendors to submit proposals and bids for proposed work.

Resistance to change   A common response to any major change initiative, where individuals fail to accept the change and strive to maintain the status quo.

Return on investment (ROI)   A capital budgeting metric in which the flow of benefits that results from an investment is compared with the cost of the investment, usually in the form of a ratio, using the cost of the investment as the denominator. ROI is generally expressed as a percentage of the total benefits less total costs over the total costs, and it is usually determined by the following formula:

$$\frac{\text{Total benefit} - \text{Total costs}}{\text{Total costs}} \times 100 = \text{ROI}$$

Return on investment on training   A financial measure of the total benefits (anything that adds directly or indirectly to the bottom line of the organization as a result of training) compared with the total costs of training, including direct and indirect costs. Direct costs involve any costs directly related with training, for example, trainer's/instructor's fees, equipment and facility rental, production and purchase of training materials. Indirect costs are not directly associated with the delivery of training, for example, administrative support or office supplies.

Row-level security   This is similar to column-level security. It refers to a set of rules that define who can access (or is prohibited) information on specific employees; for example, a supervisor can access information on the employees in his group but not on employees under a different supervisor.

Scenario planning   It identifies possible alternative futures. For example, how different roles may develop in terms of a career structure, possible routes to senior management or senior specialist, etc.

Select query   This query allows you to ask a question based on one or more tables in a database.

Selection ratio   The number of candidates who, based on the assessment, are chosen for the job divided by the number of candidates who are assessed.

Self-service portal   An electronic access point to an organization's information.

Shared-service center (SSC)   A technology-enabled centralized group designed to provide excellent service to internal customers at reduced costs.

Short-range planning   Typically, involves planning for the next year—that is, what systems and projects fall within the immediate window for action.

Single data truth   All enterprise data can be accessed by all users wherever and whenever needed.

Skills test   A practical exercise or simulation that tests the candidate's effectiveness in using Microsoft Word software.

Sourcing partner   They are partner organizations to HR functions that require certain information to complete their tasks. They provide information about vacant positions including position description, job specifications, desired candidate competencies, potential salary range, and contact information. The information provided is limited to specific searches for open jobs and is updated as needed.

Steering committee   This committee is usually composed of the project manager, the senior-management member who is the project sponsor, and the lead employee from each involved area (e.g., lead systems analyst, lead database administrator). Also on the steering committee are HR functional experts, whose role is to provide expertise about what HR data are needed, how the HR process maps should be interpreted, and what data are required for decision making.

Strategic HRM (SHRM)   SHRM refers to the strategic alignment of the HR management function with organizational goals and aims to harness the potential of people as a key competitive advantage through the use of their creativity and innovation.

Structured query language (SQL)   A standard programming language used for modifying and managing relational database systems.

System development life cycle (SDLC)   This refers to a set of steps in the formal design of any information processing system. They include analysis, design, development, implementation, maintenance, evaluation, and improvement of the system.

System investigation   The early planning and diagnosis to examine the feasibility of a new system. A business case for change is developed and, if favorable (e.g., return on investment is compelling), leads to the initiation of an HRIS project.

Tables These are used to store information about entities. One table is created for each entity. Attributes are stored as the columns (also called fields) in the table. For example, a table of employee data would have the following characteristics: first name, last name, street address, city, state, social security number, and so on. Each of these characteristics represents an attribute or field of the table.

Talent diversity The selection and development of employees who will provide diversity of thinking about increasing the performance of the organization.

Talent management (Human capital management) This describes a strategic approach to the recruitment, selection, training, development, and management of performance and promotion of employees to meet the strategic objectives of a firm and thus, improve the organization's competitiveness in the marketplace.

Technical feasibility System feasibility assessment tool that focuses on the technical capability of the organization and the availability of the technology necessary to implement a new system.

Tests and assessments Job-related decision-making tools that provide information about candidates that organizations use to make choices about their people. The terms *test, assessment, selection tool,* and *selection procedure* can be used interchangeably. Examples may include polygraphs, work samples, and inventories.

Third-country nationals (TCNs) Employees of the MNE who are citizens of a country other than the parent or host country.

Traditional HR Traditional functions of an HR department, such as recruitment and training. They can add strategic value to the organization depending on how they are conducted.

Transactional capabilities This term refers to the capability and capacity of the HRIS to process routine activities, for example, change of addresses for employees. (See Chapter 9 for more details.)

Transactional HR Routine, day-to-day activities of the HR department, such as recordkeeping, that are important but add little value to the competitive position of the organization.

Transaction processing systems Business applications that focus on processing operational data and whose main functions are (1) data storage, processing, and flows at the daily operational level and (2) efficiency, accuracy, and speed.

Transformational HR High-value-added functions in the HR department, such as cultural change, which can significantly affect the long-term viability of the organization.

Trend analysis   The process of collecting information and analyzing it to identify a pattern, or *trend*, in the information. For example, in HR planning it could be used to determine if there was higher turnover between age or gender groups of employees.

U.S. Department of Labor's O*Net database   (http://online.onetcenter.org)   This database contains job descriptions for a large number of jobs in a variety of industries. It is a good starting point for a job analysis project.

User acceptance   The willingness of a user of a system to employ the new technology for all its intended purposes.

User interface   It defines the communication boundary between two entities, such as a piece of software, a hardware device, or a user.

Validity coefficient   A statistical correlation that indicates the correspondence between test scores and job performance or some other important work outcomes.

"Vanilla"   The version of the software to be implemented without customization is referred to as the "vanilla" version.

Vendor   A company that specializes in making or selling commercial software for purchase by other companies. In the HR context, they are the firms that sell prepackaged software to support the various functional areas of HR.

Virtual private network (VPN)   This term refers to a computer network in which some of the links between nodes are carried by open or virtual circuits in some larger network (e.g., the Internet) instead of by physical wires.

Web site usability   The extent to which the Web site is usable or not. The construct of Web site usability has been conceptualized as encompassing a number of dimensions, including navigability, content information, and aesthetics.

Work breakdown structure   This is created to define the order in which activities, tasks, and jobs are to be performed and specific check or monitoring points are established.

Work packages   They define what must be done, by whom, using what resources, in what time, and at what cost to complete the HRIS project.

Work simulation   An in-basket exercise in which the examinee must examine a variety of types of information (correspondence, reports, and other information) and also interact with simulated coworkers, employees, or other business associates (whether computer simulated or role played by actors over the telephone or in person). The examinee is evaluated on a variety of dimensions, from accuracy and the quality of decisions to work-related competencies, interpersonal skills, and other personal attributes.

Name Index

Subject Index

About the Editors

Michael J. Kavanagh is currently Professor Emeritus of Management at the State University of New York at Albany. He also serves on the faculty of the Universitat des Saarlandes in the Europa-Institut and the Graduate School of Business Administration, Zurich, Switzerland. He is past editor of *Group & Organization Management* and a fellow of the American Psychological Association, the American Psychological Society, the Society for Industrial and Organizational Psychology, and the Eastern Academy of Management. He has been involved in the HRIS field since 1982. He established the HRIS MBA program at the University at Albany in 1984 and has taught numerous courses in the field of HRIS. In 2006, he received the Award for Career Excellence from the International Association for Human Resource Information Management (IHRIM). He received his PhD in I/O psychology from Iowa State University in 1969.

Mohan Thite is a senior lecturer at Griffith Business School, Griffith University, Brisbane, Australia. He has more than 20 years' experience as an HR professional, both in industry and in academia. He is a fellow of the Australian Human Resource Institute. He has been teaching HRIS for several years. His research interests include strategic HRM in the knowledge economy, HRIS and HRM in multinational corporations from emerging economies. His publications include a book on *Managing People in the New Economy* (Sage, India), a forthcoming coedited book on HRM in call centers and the business process outsourcing industry in India, book chapters, and articles in international journals such as *Work, Employment, and Society, International Journal of HRM*, and *International Journal of Project Management*.

About the Contributors

Bradley J. Alge is Associate Professor of Management at the Krannert School of Management at Purdue University. Currently, he teaches courses in organizational behavior, technology, and human capital management and has spent the past 9 years teaching HRIS in Krannert's graduate programs. He has received distinguished teaching recognition at both the graduate and the undergraduate levels. He is also an accomplished researcher. Winner of the Jay Ross Young Faculty Scholar Award, he conducts research on leadership, motivation, team dynamics, prosocial and antisocial work behaviors, creativity, and technology. His research has been published in top-tier outlets, including the *Journal of Applied Psychology, Personnel Psychology, Organizational Behavior and Human Decision Processes*, and *Research in Personnel and Human Resource Management*. He serves on the editorial boards of *Organizational Behavior and Human Decision Processes* and the *Journal of Management*. He received his PhD in organizational behavior and HRM from The Ohio State University.

Michael Bedell is an associate professor of management, MBA Program Director, and a past Bautzer University Advancement faculty member at California State University, Bakersfield. He has previously worked in the banking industry as a TQM expert focused on improving service quality. He has worked for a Fortune 500 retailer in their corporate organizational development group, where his responsibilities included developing/validating selection methods, implementing a PeopleSoft HRIS, and training merchandising teams. His research and consulting interests are centered on HRIS, HR metrics, and HR strategy with a focus on small/family businesses. He is a member of numerous professional and academic organizations. He received his PhD in human resource management with a minor in P/OM from Indiana University in 1996.

Salvatore Belardo is Professor Emeritus of information technology management at the University at Albany. He has been a visiting professor at the Copenhagen School of Business, the Graduate School of Business Administration in Zurich, Switzerland, and the University of Maryland. He has worked with a number of firms, including General Electric, Unilever, Novartis, and Orell Fussli, and has developed information systems for a number of public agencies, including the U.S. Coast Guard, the New York State Department of Transportation, and the U.S. Department of State. He has published widely in a number of top journals, including *Management Science, Decision Sciences*,

IEEE Transactions on Systems Man and Cybernetics, and *Journal of Management Information Systems.* He has been recognized for his contributions to the field of decision support systems. He has written and edited several books, including *Simulation in Business and Management* and *Innovation Through Learning.* He received his PhD in management information systems from RPI in 1981.

Ralf Burbach is a lecturer at the Institute of Technology, Carlow, Ireland. He has also lectured at National University of Ireland, Galway, and Galway-Mayo Institute of Technology, Ireland. He has been teaching HRIS for a number of years. He is a chartered member of the Chartered Institute of Personnel and Development, the United Kingdom's and Ireland's leading professional body for HR professionals. He has been carrying out research into HRIS since 2001, including a government-funded project on HRIS use in small enterprises. His current research interests include global HRIS, e-HRM, and international and comparative HRM.

Mike Canniff has worked in the IT field for more than 15 years, beginning with IBM as a software engineer and, most recently, as Vice President, Development for Acuitrek. This includes several years of developing leading-edge Internet-based products and solutions as Director of Development for PeopleSoft. Currently, he is the acting chief technology officer with the San Joaquin Regional Transit and provides strategic research for software companies such as SAP. He has specialized his career research in the areas of enterprise application integration and electronic commerce systems. He implemented cross-product XML integration standards while at PeopleSoft. He has published several papers on electronic commerce and business process management best practices.

Kevin D. Carlson is Associate Professor and Director of Graduate Studies in the Department of Management at Virginia Tech. He has published research on a wide variety of topics related to the measurement and evaluation of individual, process, and organizational effectiveness. His work has been published in the *Journal of Applied Psychology, Personnel Psychology, Journal of Management, IHRIM Journal,* and *Personnel Review,* and he has presented papers to the Academy of Management, Society for Industrial and Organizational Psychology, and the International Association for Human Resource Information Management (IHRIM). He is an associate editor for *Human Resource Management,* a member of the editorial board for the *Academy of Management Learning and Education,* and a member of the board of directors of IHRIM. His current research addresses how to use HR metrics and workforce analytics to enhance organizational performance.

Joyce Mason Davis is a human resource consultant with 17 years of experience in strategic human resource management. She is also a senior faculty member of Keller Graduate School of Management of DeVry University. She is a member of the Society of Human Resource Management (SHRM) and the International Association for Human Resources Information Management (IHRIM). She has implemented a variety of HR technology in her professional career. She developed the graduate and undergraduate HRIS courses for DeVry University in 2003 and has presented on the topic of HR technology to professional organizations. She received her MBA from Keller Graduate School of Management and her BA from the University of Illinois at Chicago.

David N. Dickter is Senior Manager, Talent Assessment at PSI. He is a consultant to Fortune 500 companies for the selection, assessment, and development of individuals at all levels. Previously, he was in the corporate organization effectiveness group at AT&T. His experience also includes personnel selection and research roles at Educational Testing Service and the United States Air Force. He has published and presented research and practical papers on selection and technology, turnover, decision making, and various other human resources topics. He received his PhD in industrial/organizational psychology from Ohio State University.

James H. Dulebohn is an associate professor of human resource management and organizational behavior at Michigan State University and teaches in the School of Labor and Industrial Relations and the Eli Broad Graduate School of Management. His research interests include decision making, HRIS, compensation and benefits, performance management, and social influence in organizations. His articles have appeared in journals including *Academy of Management Journal, Personnel Psychology, Journal of Management, Journal of Risk and Insurance,* and *Research in Higher Education.* He has consulted for a variety of organizations, including Dow Chemical, Monsanto, Raytheon, TIAA-CREF, State of Illinois, State of Texas, and Marriott. He earned his PhD and masters degrees from the University of Illinois at Urbana-Champaign.

Charles H. Fay is currently a professor of human resource management at the School of Management and Labor Relations, Rutgers University. He has taught undergraduate and graduate courses in rewards management, performance appraisal, HRIS, statistics, and labor economics. He has also taught rewards management, performance management, and HRIS in several executive and management education programs in the United States, Singapore, Malaysia, and Indonesia. His research focuses on rewards and performance management. He is coauthor of several books, including *The Performance Imperative, New Strategies for Public Pay,* and *The Executive Handbook on Compensation.* He was a presidential appointee to the Federal Salary Commission and served as a consultant to the Bureau of Labor Statistics on the National Compensation Survey. He has earned certified compensation professional status from WorldatWork (formerly the American Compensation Association). He has served as an expert witness on compensation issues before the Presidential Emergency Board numerous times and testified before Congress on compensation and performance management issues. He has a PhD in management and organization behavior from the University of Washington.

Barry D. Floyd is currently Professor of Information Systems at California Polytechnic State University. He has designed and developed enterprise application software as well as consulted on ERP implementation projects. He has presented at conferences and published articles on incorporating ERP systems into the business curriculum. His teaching efforts include courses on database design, systems analysis and design, e-commerce, enterprise resource planning, and HRIS. He received his PhD in computer and information systems from the University of Michigan.

Linda C. Isenhour is currently Assistant Professor of Management at Eastern Michigan University, where she develops and teaches courses in HR and technology. Her research interests include recruitment, cultural values, human resource management (HRM) strategy, and human resource information systems. She has published book chapters on HRM and technology, recruitment, HRM and cultural values, and HRM and privacy. In addition, she has presented scholarly papers to the Academy of Management, Society of Industrial and Organizational Psychology, Southern Management Association, and Western Business and Management Association. A member of the Academy of Management, Southern Management Association, and Society for Human Resource Management, she has also earned certification as a Global Professional in Human Resources (GPHR) from the Society of Human Resource Management.

Richard D. Johnson is an assistant professor of management at the State University of New York at Albany. His research interests are human resource information systems, the psychological and sociological impacts of computing, computer self-efficacy, e-learning, and issues surrounding the digital divide. His research has appeared in several journals such as *Information Systems Research, Journal of Applied Social Psychology, Journal of the Association for Information Systems*, and the *International Journal of Human Computer Studies*. He received his PhD from the University of Maryland, College Park.

Jerard F. Kehoe is the President of Selection and Assessment Counseling. He received his PhD from the University of Southern California in 1975.

Kimberly M. Lukaszewski is an associate professor of management at the State University of New York at New Paltz. Her research is focused on electronic human resources, privacy, and diversity issues. Her research has been published in journals such as *Human Resource Management Review, Journal of Business and Psychology, Journal of Business Issues, Journal of the Academy of Business Education, Business Journal of Hispanic Research*, and *International Association for Human Resources Information Management Journal*. She has written various book chapters published in the *Handbook of Workplace Diversity, The Brave New World of eHR: Human Resources Management in the Digital Age, The Influence of Culture on Human Resource Management Processes and Practices, The Handbook of Human Resource Management Education*, and *Advances in Human Performance and Cognitive Engineering Research*. She received her MBA in HRIS and her PhD in organizational studies from the University at Albany.

Brian D. Lyons is an assistant professor of management in the Craig School of Business at California State University, Fresno. His primary research interests center on determining the role Web usability plays in the Web recruitment process and investigating the validity of traditional selection tools in nontraditional employment contexts (professional athletics). He is also interested in the aging workforce, particularly how attitudes toward older workers affect the effectiveness of retention and retraining programs. He received his PhD in management from the University at Albany, State University of New York in 2007.

Janet H. Marler is Associate Professor of Management at the State University of New York at Albany, and in 2007–2008 was Visiting Associate Professor of Management at the

Wharton School, University of Pennsylvania. Prior to earning a PhD from Cornell University's School of Industrial and Labor Relations, she held several senior executive positions in the financial services industry. Her research centers on the strategic use of HRIS, alternative and flexible work arrangements, and compensation strategy and has been published in leading scholarly journals and books. A leader in the use of ERP systems technology in the classroom, she serves on the Oracle Academic Initiative Advisory Board and teaches executive MBA programs in HRIS, HR, and compensation strategy.

John W. Michel is an assistant professor of management at Towson University. His research interests include customer service behavior, social exchange relationships, leadership and influence processes, performance management, training, employee turnover, and the utilization of HRIS in HRM. He received his PhD in Organizational Studies at the State University of New York at Albany. He also holds an MS in Industrial and Organizational Psychology from the University of Baltimore.

Ren Nardoni is President of Nardoni Associates, Inc.—now known as Pilat NAI, the internationally known succession planning and 360 assessment software company. He has consulted with clients such as Merrill Lynch, The World Bank, ConocoPhillips, Nike, Ericsson, RIM, Marriott, IBM, Exelon, WellPoint Health, Philip Morris, Johnson & Johnson, Chase Manhattan, and AT&T. He has served on the board of directors of the New York IHRIM chapter and was the editor of its newsletter. He has been contributing editor to personnel magazines and computers in personnel. He spent more than 17 years with AT&T in a variety of IT, financial, and human resource positions. In 1982, as a founder of Human Resource Technologies, he designed and developed one of the first commercially available PC-based HRIS products.

Peter Otto is Associate Professor for Management Information Systems at Union Graduate College, School of Management. He also has a visiting teaching position at the Graduate School of Business Administration (GSBA) Zurich, Switzerland, and a visiting fellowship at Cornell University, Department of Applied Economics and Management. His present research focuses on group decision making and IT systems implementation and alignment. He has extensive consultancy experience in business strategy and holds an MBA and a PhD in information science, with primary specialization in decision support systems from the University at Albany.

Romuald A. Stone is currently Associate Dean for Business & Management Programs at DeVry University and Program Director, Masters in HRM Program. He is also a senior faculty member in the Keller Graduate School of Management. He has held previous professional appointments at James Madison University and George Mason University. His research and writings include numerous strategy case studies and practitioner-oriented articles. He is the coauthor of *Managing Organizational Change*, a change management textbook. His work has appeared in the *Academy of Management Executive*, *Psychological Reports*, the *Journal of Management Education*, *Computers in Human Behavior*, *Educational and Psychological Measurement*, *Business Horizons*, *Employment Relations Today*, *SAM Advanced Management Journal*, and the *Journal of*

Applied Management and Entrepreneurship. As a practitioner, he has more than 20 years of experience as a trainer and consultant in the areas of organizational management and leadership. He received his DBA from Nova Southeastern University in 1990.

Karen Bruner Upright is currently Systems Manager, Procter & Gamble–Chemicals in Cincinnati, Ohio. She holds several professional designations from the International Foundation of Employee Benefit Plans, including Certified Employee Benefits Specialist (CEBS). She has been involved in HRIS for the past 8 years, focusing on defined benefit pension plans. She spoke on the topic of *Information Security: Protecting a Firm's Most Valuable Assets* at the 2006 symposium of the International Society of Certified Employee Benefits Specialists in Toronto, Ontario, Canada. She earned an MBA from Purdue University and holds a BS in Computer Science from Florida State University.

Hazel Williams is a senior lecturer in human resource management at Nottingham Business School, The Nottingham Trent University, England. She has 15 years' experience as a human resource professional in academia and a range of industry sectors. She has been teaching and researching HRIS and strategic HR since 1997. She leads on this subject for postgraduate and corporate programs based in the United Kingdom, Russia, and Azerbaijan. Her research interests also include strategic human resourcing, talent management, E-HR, and human capital, with a particular interest in the engineering and construction sectors. In 2007, she, along with her colleagues, published the findings of research, commissioned by the CIPD, on talent management, titled *Talent: Strategy, Management, Measurement*. She has also presented conference papers and contributed to international journals and book chapters.

Yuk Kuen Wong is currently working at Griffith University, Australia. Her research work (information management and quality control) is internationally recognized by leading organizations, such as the ICSE (International Conference on Software Engineering). Her recently published research book on quality controls has been listed across disciplines in a number of institutions. She has previously worked at the University of New South Wales and the University of Technology, Sydney. Her teaching areas include data communications, information management and controls, information and computer security, information technology management, system auditing, global data network, data management, and project management. Before her academic appointments, she worked in the areas of enterprise resources planning systems implementation, systems and business processes reengineering and e-business solutions. She is a founding member of the Association of Information System Special Interest Group on IT/IS in Asia Pacific and member of the Association for Information Systems, the Association for Computing Machinery, the Institute of Electrical and Electronics Engineers, and IEEE Communications Society.

Cheryl Wyrick is Professor and Chair of the Management and Human Resources Department at California State Polytechnic University, Pomona, where she has taught HR information systems, benefits, and training and development and other HR courses. She served on the University's project team that implemented PeopleSoft and, in addition, conducted training that introduced the HR staff to strategic metric analyses. She has designed HRIS instructional materials for use in undergraduate courses. She has presented and written on the topic of metrics and technology. An active volunteer, Cheryl has held various leadership positions in HR professional associations, including Society of Human Resource Management, where she served on the HR technology management expertise panel. She is currently a member of the HRCI Board of Directors.